Like many another statesman, John Adams entered the political arena by way of the legal profession. Here, gathered together in three volumes, is an inclusive presentation of the important legal cases in which he was involved. Student notes and Commonplace Book, which show the influences on the young law student in 1758 and 1759, are followed by Adams' Pleadings Book, a collection of forms providing a cross-section of the law in eighteenth-century Massachusetts and showing his work as teacher as well as student.

The sixty-four cases documented are divided into sixteen legal categories such as Torts, Property, Domestic Relations, Town Government, Conservation, Religion, Slavery, and Admiralty. They are preceded by editorial headnotes which discuss the background, significance, and importance of each category and case. Careful and thorough footnotes explain textual and legal problems; a register of John Adams' contemporaries furnishes sketches of his colleagues on the bench and bar; and an exhaustive chronology records his growing practice. But the bulk of the material consists of Adams' own notes and minutes, supplemented by court records, letters, depositions of witnesses, and the minutes of other lawyers, as well as extracts from Adams' correspondence and diary to make the record of each case as full as possible. Many of the cases concern events, personalities, and legal struggles directly related to the American Revolution.

The entire third volume of this imposing collection is devoted to the so-called "Boston Massacre." Confronted by a fascinating mass of conflicting evidence, charges and countercharges, and confused and confusing witnesses, many Americans will be surprised to discover that they must revise their notions about what actually happened on that March evening in 1770, why it did, and what ensued.

The Adams Papers

L. H. BUTTERFIELD, EDITOR IN CHIEF

SERIES III

GENERAL CORRESPONDENCE
AND OTHER PAPERS
OF THE ADAMS STATESMEN

Legal Papers of John Adams

Legal Papers of John Adams

L. KINVIN WROTH and HILLER B. ZOBEL

EDITORS

————————— ☆ —————————

Volume 2 · *Cases* 31–62

THE BELKNAP PRESS
OF HARVARD UNIVERSITY PRESS
CAMBRIDGE, MASSACHUSETTS

1965

Distributed in Great Britain by Oxford University Press · London

Funds for editing *The Adams Papers* have been provided by Time, Inc.,
on behalf of *Life*, and by the Ford Foundation, to the Massachusetts Historical Society, under whose supervision the editorial work is being done.

The William Nelson Cromwell Foundation has made possible the editing
of the *Legal Papers* by means of a grant to the Harvard Law School.

Library of Congress Catalog Card Number 65–13855 · Printed in the United States of America

Contents

Contents

Contents

Contents

Q.   ADMIRALTY—PRIZE JURISDICTION

R.   CRIMINAL LAW

Descriptive List of Illustrations

VOLUME 2

Legal Papers

Cases 31–62

Legal Papers of John Adams

I. Town Government

31. Pingry v. Thurston

1768–1771

EDITORIAL NOTE

On 25 July 1768 the legally qualified voters of Rowley's West Parish met to determine how the parish would dispose of its old meetinghouse and erect a new one on a different plot.[1] Following the procedure prescribed for town meetings, they first chose a moderator, Deacon Richard Thurston.[2] Before the meeting could proceed further, however, someone questioned the qualifications for voting of one Abel Plummer. By statute in such cases, the moderator was required to rule on Plummer's qualifications, basing his decision on the current assessors' valuation.[3] That docu-

[1] See the warning, 15 July 1768, and minutes of the meeting, 25 July 1768, in SF 132134. The West Parish was the Second Parish. A. E. and E. M. A. Jewett, *Rowley, Massachusetts* 101 (Rowley, 1946). According to one historian, "In 1769, a new meeting-house, fifty-five feet by forty, was raised, with a steeple and porch, *all in one day*. This house was dedicated, September, 1770, and the dedication sermon preached, by the eminent Rev. George Whitefield, of England." Thomas Gage, *History of Rowley* 32 (Boston, 1840).

[2] Minutes of the meeting, SF 132134. The procedure was established under Act of 22 Dec. 1716, 2 A&R 30: "[A]t every such meeting a moderator shall be first chosen by a majority of votes, who shall be thereby impowered to manage and regulate the business of that meeting. And when it shall so happen that any matter remains doubtfull after a vote, the moderator is hereby directed and required that the same be decided by the poll, if seven or more desire it, presently after the vote is called in question." Thurston had been a deacon since the founding of the church in 1732. Gage, *Rowley* 95. JA described him as "a venerable old Man, with his snowy, hoary Locks," when they met on the evening of 4 Nov. 1771, possibly to discuss this case. 3 JA, *Diary and Autobiography* 50.

[3] Act of 15 Jan. 1743, 3 A&R 47–48: "[N]o person shall be deemed duly qualified or be admitted to vote in the choice of officers, or in the other affairs to be transacted at any meeting of the town, precinct or parish where he dwells, but such only who are personally present at such meeting, and have a rateable estate in such town or district, besides the poll, amounting to the value of twenty pounds, by the following method of estimation; viz., real estate to be set at so much only as the rents or income thereof for the space of six years would amount to were it let at a reasonable rate; and personal estate and faculty to be estimated according to the rule of valuation prescribed in the act from time to time made for apportioning and assessing publick taxes. . . . [W]hen any dispute shall arise respecting the qualifications of any person offering his vote in any such publick meeting, the same shall be

I

ment listed Plummer's estate at only £18 16s.,[4] which was less than the statutory minimum of £20. Thurston apparently allowed Plummer to vote anyway, at least in an initial show of hands on one of the five questions before the meeting. Unable to determine the result in the question, Thurston called for a "poll," which Adams' minutes, set out below, suggest was conducted like a modern parliamentary "division": all the voters left the meeting house, re-entering it by one of two doors, according to their votes.

Plummer apparently participated in the poll, but it is not clear whether or not Thurston counted him. In any event, according to witnesses, Plummer's vote had not been necessary to a result on the question before the meeting. This was apparently the basis of Thurston's defense in a *qui tam* action of debt brought by Asa Pingry of Rowley on the statute levying a penalty against a moderator who permitted an unqualified voter "to give his voice" in the meeting.[5] If the vote was not necessary, Thurston contended, the moderator could not be said to have permitted the voter to participate within the meaning of the statute. Whatever the weakness of this contention as an exercise in statutory construction, it appears to have had jury appeal. Pingry did take a verdict in the Salem Inferior Court in December 1768, but Thurston, with Adams of counsel, won both the appeal at the Ipswich Superior Court in June 1769 and the action of review at Salem in November 1771.[6] Adams' minutes seem to date from the latter action, in which Daniel Farnham was of counsel with him. John Lowell represented Pingry.

---

determined by the moderator of such meeting according to the list and valuation of estates and faculties of persons, in such town or district, last made by assessors under oath; and if it thereby appear that such person is not qualified as by this act is provided, his vote shall not be received: *provided*, that the value of lands leased shall not be reckoned to qualify the ter-tenant, but to qualify the lessor if he be an inhabitant in such town, precinct or parish. . . . [I]f the moderator of any such meeting shall countenance and permit any person not qualified as aforesaid, whose qualification for voting has been called in question, to give his voice in any such meeting, he shall forfeit and pay the sum of five pounds; and whosoever shall presume to put in more than one vote at a time shall forfeit and pay the sum of five pounds; one moiety of the said forfeitures to be for the use of the poor of the town where the offence shall be committed, and the other moiety to him or them that shall inform or sue for the same in any of his majesty's courts of record."

[4] SF 132134.

[5] For the Act, see note 3 above. *"Qui tam"* is the Latin for the form of the writ in a penal action, in this case, "who sues as well in behalf of the poor of said Town of Rowley as for himself." SF 132134. Compare the practice in Admiralty proceedings under the Acts of Trade. No. 46, notes 28, 80.

[6] For the judgment of the Inferior Court, see SF 132134. For the Superior Court actions, see Min. Bk. 85, SCJ Ipswich, June 1769, N–9; SCJ Rec. 1769, fols. 62–63. Min. Bk. 93, SCJ Salem, Nov. 1771, N–4; SCJ Rec. 1771, fols. 196–197.

ADAMS' MINUTES OF THE TRIAL[7]

Essex Superior Court, Salem, November 1771

Pingry vs. Thurston

Lowell.

Prov. Law, page 29. If any Dispute shall arise, it shall be determined. A Penalty for permitt[ing] a Person to give his Voice who is not a qualified Voter.[8]

Benja. Adams. Parliamentary Abilities. Knew all his Party.

Jona. Herriman. Abel Plummer voted in the Choice of the Moderator. Deacon Thurston said He could, did, and would count him as a Voter. It never was disputed at that Time among the whole People that he was counted. Chaplain said I cant count Abel Plummer. Deacon Thurston said I can, and I do count him. He is as good a Voter as any at [of] the People. Heard the Deacon say since, that he was sorry, he had counted him.

Benj. Adams. They want [*i.e.* weren't] satisfyed at first, and went out of the two Doors, and as they came in, he could and did count him.

Holmes. Deacon said it was pitty, that Pingry should be at the Expence of proving that he allowed Plummer to vote for he did and would allow it, and pleaded Conscience for so doing. He *counted and allowed* him a Voter. He mentioned a Mistake of the Assessors, and said that P[lummer] had more than Estate eno.

Mr. Farnham.

Jeremiah Searl. Clerk of the Meeting, and by the Moderator the whole Time. Many Thought Plummer was a Voter, many Thought otherwise. Much said upon it. Mod[erato]r said he was not acquainted with the Law. A Vote was called by Hand. The Moderator was not satisfyd. A Poll was called for. I heard him declare he should not count Abel Plummer. Anabaptists were all among the opposite side to Plummer. The Moderator condescended to Poll the People, and desired the Constable and one Mr. Chaplain to assist him. Moderator and Constable, and Chap[lain] went to one Door, and Moderator[9] and Constable to the other. Moderator got up and told em to attend to a Vote, there was no need of the Noise, there was a Vote without Plummer. 1/2 a doz. times said he should not reckon him and declared

---

[7] In JA's hand. Adams Papers, Microfilms, Reel No. 185.

[8] See note 3 above. Lowell's citation is to *Temporary Acts and Laws Of His Majesty's Province of the Massachusetts Bay in New-England* (Boston, 1763), where the Act appears at p. 28–30.

[9] Thus in MS.

3

it when he ordered me to record it—a Vote without reckoning Plummer—allowing the Baptists and rejecting Plumer a Vote.[10]

Mr. Spoffard. Moderator commanded silence, and said there was no need of the Clammr. There is a Vote without Plummer, and I declare it a Vote without him. Clerk record it.

Moses Dole. Moderator declared at the Door, *there was a Vote without Abel Plummer.* They need not make such a Clamr.

John Tinney, Constable. An Objection vs. A. Plummer. Moderator tryd by Hand Vote. 48. 58. 68. A Mistake in the Valuation. Moderator tryd 3 Ways. I counted with him, and there was a Dispute about 3 Baptists.[11] I made one Odds for the Vote. Moderator said leaving out Ab. Plummer and counting the Baptists there was one Odds. No need of the dispute. There is a Vote without Plummer. Such a Noise that half could not hear. We dont want[12] him, I declare it a Vote. Afterwards he said he determined to set him aside if there had been a Tye.

Wm. Chandler. 3 Ways. I dont want him to vote, there is a vote without him. I declare it to be a Vote. Clerk record it.

32. Patch v. Herrick

1771–1772

EDITORIAL NOTE

Two leading natural resources of the North Shore, clams and salt-marsh hay, provided the stakes in this unusual trespass action. The land in question lay largely under water in what was then Chebacco Parish, Ipswich, and is now a part of the town of Essex, apparently in the area known today as Cross Island, near the mouth of the Essex River.[1]

Ipswich people, and those from neighboring Gloucester (sometimes called "Cape Ann"), had disputed the common boundary since at least

[10] Thus in MS. JA's notes are slightly garbled, but the sense is clear.

[11] The dispute may have arisen because the Baptists in question were exempt from taxation to support the ministry. See No. 37. If such were the case, it may have been argued that they could not vote on a question involving church affairs. That this argument was invalid in 1768 is suggested by the fact that the ministerial tax exemption act of 30 June 1740, c. 6, §4, 2 A&R 1022, expressly barring persons exempt from tax for religious reasons from voting on questions pertaining to the settlement of ministers and the construction of meetinghouses, expired in 1757. Its successor, the Act of 25 Jan. 1758, c. 20, 4 A&R 67, contained no such bar, and a restriction was not enacted again until the Act of 20 Nov. 1770, c. 10, §5, 5 A&R 113.

[12] That is, "need."

[1] The file includes rough maps. SF 132186. See also U.S. Corps of Engineers charts N4233.75–W7037.5/8 × 7.5 (1944) and N4237.5–W7045/7.5 (1945).

1642, and had apparently resolved the issue by a joint "perambulation" in 1767. Meanwhile, the Proprietors of the Common Lands of Ipswich, otherwise known as the Commoners, had annually let the thatch banks to the highest bidder, only Commoners having the right to bid.[2] They had also attempted to regulate the clam trade, by appointment of a committee and promulgation of a kind of bag limit.[3]

Enter now in canoes, digging, Adams' clients, Israel and John Herrick, Gloucestermen both, and an anonymous crowd of their fellow townsmen. They "trod down, trampled upon, dug, tore up, and consumed the soil and Thatch Banks . . . and thereout dug, took and converted to their own Use one hundred Bushels of Clams of the said Proprietors there being and growing." [4] The Commoners responded by voting John Patch III, Isaac Smith, and Isaac Dodge, a committee to "Persue the Trespassers to finall Judgment and Execution." [5] This the committee tried to do, commencing an action in the Ipswich Inferior Court in March 1771, and after a jury verdict for the Herricks,[6] appealing to the Superior Court.[7] There, on the

[2] T. F. Waters, "The Development of Our Town Government," 8 Ipswich Hist. Soc., *Pubns.* 2, 14 (1900); the file contains copies of records of several annual meetings at which the flats were let. SF 132186.

[3] "Voted, that the Committe take care of all the Flats and Clams therein belonging to the Proprietors of the Common Lands In Ipswich and that no Person or Persons be allow'd to Digg Any more Clams than for their own use and to be Expended in the Town, And that all Owners of Fishing Vessels and Boats shall apply to one of said Committe for Liberty to Digg Clams for their Vessels Use, Fare by Fare [that is, journey or trip], and no Owner of Vessel, or Vessels, Boat or Boats, shall digg more Clams than shall be Allow'd by one or more of said Committe on Penalty of Prosecution; Said Committe are to Allow one Barrel of Clams to Each Man of Every Vessel going to the Banks Every Fare, and so Also in proportion to Boats Fishing in the Bay, And a Majority of said Committe are Impowered to prosecute all Offenders (To this Vote) To finall Judgment and Execution in the Name and Behalf of said Proprietors." SF 132186. Waters, "Development of Our Town Government," says that this vote (4 July 1763) was the first regulation of which he was aware.

[4] Writ, SF 132186.

[5] 13 Feb. 1771. SF 132186.

[6] The Wetmore Notes contain a report of this phase of the case:

"Ipswich Commoners v. Herrick trespass for digging by Glocester men upon Ipswich flats for clams. See the Charter enabling any Subjects (of K. of Eng.) whatever to fish on the Coasts in the seas or arms of the Seas or Salt water Rivers as they have been wont, to *cut and take such Trees and other materials there growing or being* upon any parts or places lying waste and *not in the possession of particular proprietors* for wharves Stages &c. and *for all other necessary helps and advantages* concerning the trade of fishing there in such manner and form as they have been accustomed to do, without wilful waste or spoil.

"Waste is taken for lands in no mans occupation but lying common. So called because the lord cant make such profit of them as of other lands, by reason of others using and passing to and fro on them.

"The plea is not guilty. Plaintiffs' evidence was of leasing *the Bull Island knobs,* the *Thatch grounds* (and once the *Island*) from 1745 to 1768, and of improvement since. The defendants' evidence was of divers peoples improvement by digging clams for several years of the term aforesaid but that Some times they (especially Glocester men) having notice that the Plaintiffs claim'd and let the banks would retire without getting the clams.

testimony summarized in Adams' minute set out below, the jury brought in a special verdict: the land was on salt-water flats on an arm of the sea about two miles up Chebacco River, the Commoners held title to it, the defendants had entered upon it and dug fifty bushels of clams, and damages totaled four shillings. To the judges the jury left the decision whether or not plaintiffs' action was well founded.[8]

Although the file papers and Adams' minutes afford slim evidence of the question the court faced, Adams and John Lowell, his co-counsel, seem to have argued that trespass could not lie here (at least for the clams), because the Province Charter guaranteed free fishing. They also apparently attempted to introduce evidence of a custom of clamming, which plaintiffs opposed on the technical ground that such evidence was inadmissible when the defendants, as here, had merely pleaded "not guilty," and had not raised any legal justification in their plea. On the basis of the materials Adams himself set out, his legal position seems weak. The Court shared this view, and in June 1772 entered up judgment for the plaintiffs for the four shillings plus costs of £16 9s. 8 1/2d.[9]

ADAMS' MINUTES OF THE TRIAL[10]

Essex Superior Court, Salem, November 1771

Patch vs. Herrick. Clams.

Pynchon.[11] Grant of Ipswich or rather Jurisdiction between the Towns from Glocester Town Book. 1642.[12] And from the Province Sec[reta]ry.[13]

"See L. Raym. 1535. Dutch East India Company sue and on non assumpsit must shew the proper instrument by Law of Holland creating the corporation."

The cited case is Jacob Lopes Henriques et al. v. The General Privileged Dutch Company Trading to the West Indies, 2 Ld. Raym. 1532, 1535, 92 Eng. Rep. 494, 496 (H.L. 1730), which seems to hold that when a corporation brings an action, it need not prove its incorporation unless the defendant pleads the general issue.

[7] Under an agreement between counsel that "the appearance of one of the Committee be admitted for all." SF 132186.

[8] SF 132186. Apparently a special verdict of this sort was the product of negotiation between counsel. In the file are three versions of the verdict, the first of which contains no mention of the land's tidewater location. On the verso of this version JA wrote: "and the Flatts where the Clams were dug are upon the Coasts of New England, upon an arm of the Sea, or Salt Water River, Where the King's Subjects had been wont to fish, when the Charter of this Province was made." An unidentified hand added: "Note not the least Evidence hath been offered of this." The second version, and the third, which is a fair copy of it, contain an interpolation to the effect that the lands in question were "salt water flatts lying on an arm of the sea and about two miles up Chebaco River."

[9] Min. Bk. 93, SCJ Ipswich, June 1772, C–9; SJC Rec. 1772, fol. 90.

[10] In JA's hand. Adams Papers, Microfilms, Reel No. 185.

[11] William Pynchon, counsel for Patch et al.

[12] SF 132186: "Bounds between Ipswich and Cape Ann. The grant of our Bounds

1767. Perambulation, from Gloucester between there and Ipswich.[14]

Jacob Story.[15] Perambulated for 20 Years. We did not go to the Marsh.

Wm. Butler.

Wm. Choate. The Line a Mile in the nearest Place I should think. People freely dug.

Lufkin.[16] Freely dug. People on there, when the Commoners and their Assigns, have been ⟨dig⟩ mowing. Talk about 3 Years, about digging. Never forbid till within 3 Years, and never knew of People's asking Leave.

Wm. Choate. 1770. 27 July. 17 Persons. 5 Canoes—75 Bushells. Dont know who they are. Israel Herrick and Jno. Herrick it was then said were there. I went to 'em once, and told em they were trespassing 7 Years ago. 1761 give 20s a Barrell for digging—so that the Custom about 2s a Bll.[17]

Lufkin. 5 Canoes. 15 Persons. Cape Ann People. Know Jno. and Israel Herrick. We said nothing. Nor they to Us. 4 Barells of Meat. 100 Bushells in shells.[18] 4 dollars a Barrell. Never knew prohibited.

Jacob Davis. Went from C[ape] Ann 5 Years ago, and forbid, and we went off. They threatned to prosecute.

---

drawn out of the Country Records the 3 of 3d month 1642. . . . That all the Land lying between Ipswich and Cape Ann Meeting Houses, shall be divided Six Miles to Ipswich & four to Cape Ann, where there are Ten miles, and so by Proportion where Less that is of fifths, three parts to Ipswich and two to Cape Ann, where there Is more than ten miles, the Remainder to Lye to Jeffries-Creek. And this to be measured before the Next General Court."

[13] This refers to a fragmentary copy of an agreement of "3d: 3d Month 1642" concerning the Ipswich-Capetown (Gloucester) boundary, an apparent duplicate of the material set out in note 12 above. Dated 4 Nov. 1771, it bears the following certificate: "I certify that the above (which appears imperfect) is a true Copy from a Duplicate of the General Court Book. The original cannot be found in my office, and may have been consumed with the Town house in the year 1747. Thos. Flucker Secretary." SF 132186.

[14] SF 132186. "Gloucester June 28th 1767. We the Subscribers Being Appointed a Committe by the Select Men of Ipswich, and the Select men of Gloucester to Perambulate the Line between said Towns of Ipswich and Glocester And have been on said Line and Renew'd the Bounds as beforementioned between said Towns in Former Perambulation. . . . We being a Committe Appointed to Perambulate the Line between the Towns of Ipswich and Glocester mett at the Heap of Rocks, the Bounds between Ipswich, Manchester and Gloucester And Renew'd the bounds between the Two Towns as Usual. Gloucester and Ipswich December 29, 1767."

[15] One of the perambulators for Ipswich.

[16] Thomas and Nathaniel Lufkin owned land abutting the flat in question. SF 132186.

[17] This may represent either a bushel or a barrel.

[18] This suggests that clam diggers separated the meat from the shells on the flats, but carried the shells away, or perhaps that the clams in their shells came to one hundred bushels.

July 19. 1744 to 1760. Thatch[19] banks, and all the Knobs, at Bull Island. Leases.[20] 20s., &c. and 21s.

Story.[21] Hired the Knobs. I looked upon it, I hired to low Water Mark as much as the Grass. Rem[embe]r when there was no Grass on the flatts. Now there is, and it increases, and Clams under the Thatch. Digging has a Tendency to prevent the Grass from getting in.

Lufkin. Our Thatch grows poorer. They have dug away most of the Clams where there is no Thatch.

Lowell. Charter last Page.[22]
Mem. † Old Colony Laws. page 90. Tit. Liberties Common.[23]
Gilbert, Tryals Per Pais about pleading Custom.[24]
2. [*Ld*.] Ray. 860. Replevin of a Brass Pan.[25]
† Old Colony Laws.[26] 90. Tit. Liberties. "2. Every Inhabitant who is an Householder, shall have free Fishing and Fowling in any great Ponds, Bays, Coves and Rivers, so far as the Sea Ebbes and Flowes, within the Precincts of the Town where they dwell unless the Freemen of the same Town or the General Court have otherwise appropriated them. Provided that no Town shall appropriate to any particular Person or Persons, any great Pond, containing more than 10 Acres of Land and that no Man shall come upon anothers Propriety without their Leave otherwise then as hereafter expressed.

[19] Saltmarsh grass, the source of saltmarsh hay.
[20] These were leases of the knobs and flats by the Commoners. Some of the leases are in the file of this case. SF 132186.
[21] A Jeremy Storey let the Bull Island Knobs in 1747 for one year at £1 1s. od. Bull Island was a part of what is now called Cross Island. SF 132186.
[22] 1 A&R 19–20: "*And further* Our expresse Will and Pleasure is And Wee doe by these presents for Vs Our Heires and Successors Ordaine and appoint that these Our Letters Patents shall not in any manner Enure or be taken to abridge bar or hinder any of Our loveing Subjects whatsoever to vse and exercise the Trade of Fishing vpon the Coasts of New England but that they and every of them shall have full and free power and Libertie to continue and vse their said Trade of Fishing vpon the said Coasts in any of the seas therevnto adjoyning or any Arms of the said Seas or Salt Water Rivers where they have been wont to fish."
[23] *Laws and Liberties* 90. JA sets out the text of part of the title "Liberties Common" below.
[24] This appears to be a telescoped reference to Gilbert, *Evidence* 253–254 and 2 Duncombe, *Trials Per Pais* 533–535, both dealing with the admissibility of evidence of custom under a plea of not guilty.
[25] Tonkin v. Croker, 2 Ld. Raym. 860, 92 Eng. Rep. 74 (K.B. 1703): Replevin brought to test whether a tenure was by suit-service or by rent, raising the question whether a manor court was customary or not. Holt, C.J., gave it as his dictum that a declaration at common law could not be made good by a replication based on custom; hence a special verdict finding that the plaintiff was supported by custom when he had declared on the common law would not support a verdict for plaintiff. *Id*. at 862–863.
[26] See note 23. Quotation marks supplied.

8

"The which clearly to determine;

"It is declared, that in all Creeks, Coves and other Places about and upon Salt Water, where the sea Ebbes and flowes, the Proprietor, or the Land adjoining shall have Propriety to the Low Water Mark where the Sea doth not Ebbe above an 100 Rods, and not more wheresoever it ebbes further, Provided that such Proprietors, shall not by this Liberty have Power to stop or hinder the Passage of Boats or other Vessells, in or thro any Sea, Creacks or Coves, to other Mens Houses or Lands. And for great Ponds lying in Common, though within the Bounds of some Town, it shall be free for any Man to fish and fowle there and may pass and repass on Foot through any Mans Propriety for that End, so they trespass not upon any Mans Corn or Meadow 1641, 47."

33. Emmons v. Brewer

1772

EDITORIAL NOTE

Redevelopment of Boston's North End is not a wholly modern phenomenon or problem. In the case which follows, Adams represented two housewrights and two bricklayers in an action of trespass brought by Jacob Emmons, alleging that on 30 April 1767 they "with force and arms . . . broke and entered the plaintiff's Close" and "did then and there break down and erase to the foundation the brick walls and chimnies of the plaintiff's dwelling house there standing and did then and there with force as aforesaid fill up the cellars of the plaintiff's said house with dirt, bricks and other rubbage." [1]

The matter was tried at the Suffolk Inferior Court on 7 January 1772, where, upon a sham demurrer to Adams' plea of not guilty, judgment was rendered for the defendants.[2] The matter was appealed to the Suffolk Superior Court, where, at the August 1772 sitting, the pleadings were reopened and Adams put forth his real defense, a plea in confession and avoidance (Document I). After a formal traverse of the force and arms alleged as a necessary part of the declaration in trespass, the plea admitted the acts complained of, but asserted that the defendants had been au-

[1] SF 102174. The defendants were Giles Brewer, William Crafts, Benjamin Richardson, and Asa Stodder.

[2] See the Inferior Court judgment in SF 102174. At the July 1771 term with Samuel Quincy for the plaintiff and Otis for the defendant, the case had been "Continued for Special Pleadings." Min. Bk., Inf. Ct. Suffolk, July 1771, No. 147. Since the pleadings actually filed in the Superior Court are headed, "Common Pleas. Boston January term 1772," (Doc. I) it seems probable that they were originally drawn up for the latter court, but that at the last minute counsel agreed to defer the issue which they presented to the appeal.

9

thorized by law.[3] The house in question had stood in the area desolated by the great fire of 3 February 1767, and the defendants had acted pursuant to statute in clearing a newly widened street which encroached upon the plaintiff's property and in removing the remains of the buildings thereon as a common nuisance and hazard to passersby. Jonathan Sewall for the plaintiff thereupon demurred to the plea. At the hearing on the demurrer, however, as Adams' minutes (Document II) show, Samuel Quincy argued in plaintiff's behalf. The court overruled the demurrer and awarded the defendants their costs, taxed at £4 11s. 2d.[4]

I. NEW PLEADINGS[5]

Suffolk Superior Court, Boston, August 1772

Suffolk Ss. Common Pleas. Boston January Term 1772.

Jacob Emmons Ptf. vs. William Crafts and others Defts.

And the Said William Crafts, Giles Brewer, Benjamin Richardson and Asa Stodder, come and defend &c. and as to the Force and Arms, and any Thing that is against the Peace, and also the whole Trespass aforesaid excepting the Breaking and entering the Dwelling House aforesaid, breaking and entering the Close aforesaid, and breaking down and erasing to the Foundation the brick Walls and Chimnies of the Dwelling House aforesaid, and filling up the Cellars aforesaid with Dirt, Bricks and other Rubbish, the said William, Giles, and Benjamin and Asa say they are not guilty thereof and of this they put themselves on the Country. John Adams

And the Plantiff likewise. Jon. Sewall[6]

And as to the breaking and entering the Close aforesaid and breaking down and erasing to the Foundation the brick Walls and Chimnies of the Dwelling House aforesaid, and filling up the Cellars aforesaid with Dirt, Bricks and other Rubbish the said William, Giles, Benjamin, and Asa Say, the said Jacob, his Action aforesaid thereof against them ought not to have or maintain, because they say, ⟨*that the Close aforesaid, and the Dwelling House aforesaid, and the brick Walls*

[3] As to the traverse of the force and arms (once necessary to avoid a fine to the King, but by this time purely formal) and the plea in confession and avoidance generally, see Sutton, *Personal Actions* 77–78, 83–84, 184–189.

[4] SCJ Rec. 1772, fol. 111. Sewall was also of counsel in the Superior Court. Min. Bk. 95, SCJ Suffolk, Aug. 1772, C–51.

[5] In JA's hand to the point indicated by note 12; most of the remainder is in Jonathan Sewall's hand. SF 102174. As to the heading "Common Pleas Boston January Term 1772," see note 2 above.

[6] The signature is in Sewall's hand.

and Chimnies aforesaid, and the Cellars aforesaid are and at the Time when the supposed Trespass aforesaid is alledged to have been committed were all in a public street or high Way in the Town of Boston aforesaid, and were all then and there common Nusances to the subjects of our Lord the King. And the said Defendants further say⟩ that by an Act or Law of this Province made and passed in the Fourth Year of the Reign of the late King William and Queen Mary, intituled "an Act for building with Stone or Brick in the Town of Boston, and preventing Fire" it is among other Things enacted "That in all void and unbuilt Places, which shall hereafter be improved for building, or when at any Time any total Consumption or Desolation shall happen in any Street or Lane within the said Town, it shall be in the Power of the ⟨said⟩ Justices of the Peace of said Town then in being, together with the Select Men, or the Major Part of both, to State and lay out Such Streets, Ways and Passages, as may be most for the Conveniency and Accomodation of the Place: As also where any Desolation has happened, to regulate and enlarge other narrow and crooked Lanes or Passages." [7]

And the said Defendants further say that the greatest Part of the Lands from Middle Street to Ann Street in said Boston, were by the Fire which happened in said Boston on the third Day of February Anno Domini 1767 [8] become desolate and vacant, that Paddy's Alley So called, which run through those Lands, though very narrow, was from its Situation extremely beneficial and usefull to the Inhabitants of said Town [9] and that it was on the sixteenth Day of April Anno Domini 1767, had been long before and has been ever since absolutely necessary that there should be a commodious public Street or high Way there.

And Samuel Wells, Joshua Winslow, Richard Dana, Foster Hutchinson, John Ruddock, Nathaniel Balstone, John Hill, Edmund Quincy, John Avery and John Tudor Esquires being the Major Part of His Majesty's Justices of the Peace for the County aforesaid, dwelling in

---

[7] Act of 25 Oct. 1692, c. 13, §2, 1 A&R 42.

[8] Middle Street is today part of Hanover Street and Ann Street is North Street. Walter M. Whitehill, *Boston: A Topographical History* 45, 113, 130 (Cambridge, Mass., 1959). As to the fire, see Rowe, *Letters and Diary* 121–122: "February 4 [1767]. After breakfast set out for home and upon the road heard of a great fire in Boston which broke out in Bray the baker's warehouse and spread round about the neighborhood, that it consumed more than twenty houses ... it begun at ten of clock and continued until three in the morning."

[9] "William Paddy, a skinner and merchant, came to Plymouth in 1635, and was in Boston about 1650." Paddy's Alley, known today as North Centre Street, "was laid out through original land of John Jepson. After a fire in 1767 the passage was made wider." Thwing, *Crooked and Narrow Streets* 58.

the Town of Boston aforesaid, and Joseph Jackson, Samuel Sewall, John Hancock, William Phillips, Timothy Newhall and John Rowe being the major Part of the select Men of the same Town, having met together and taken the Premisses into their Consideration, carefully viewed the said Alley and the Lands so made desolate on each side of it, and duely considered the premisses, for the Conveniency and Accommodation of that Place and of the Inhabitants aforesaid, pursuant to the Power given them by a law of this Province, made in the fourth Year of King William and Queen Mary intituled "an Act for building with Stone or Brick in the Town of Boston and preventing Fire," did at said Boston on the Said Sixteenth day of April Anno Domini 1767, State, lay out, and establish, a Street thro the vacant and desolate Lands aforesaid, including the aforesaid alley or Part of it, in manner and Form following, that is to say beginning at the North easterly corner of the yard behind the brick Dwelling House belonging to the Heirs of Mr. Andrew Tyler deceased and running South a little westerly along by the back of the said House and across the said alley including it, nineteen Feet and Eleven Inches, which Line is at the Eastern End of the same new Street, then turning and running West more northerly making a Small bend one hundred and fifty feet and nine Inches, then running West more northerly to the House of Thomas Emmons, ninety and four Feet and Six Inches, then turning north a little Eastwardly, crossing the said Alley, Strait along by the End of Mr. Gidneys House, then occupied by William Crombay, thirty feet, which Line is at the Westerly End of the same Street then returning East, a little southerly, on the northerly Side of the same Street, ninety one Feet, then running East less southerly, Sixty five Feet, where it measures across to the south Side or Line, thirty five feet, then running East again, Something more southerly hence to the said Brick house, Eighty four feet and Six Inches then turning South a little Westerly, along by the same House to the Corner thereof, nine feet and Seven Inches, then turning the said Corner and running along by the same House to the aforesaid Corner of the Yard aforesaid Twenty Eight Feet and about Eleven Inches, where the said new Street ends. And the said Justices and select Men then and there, laid and sett off all the Lands of every Person Whomsoever included and falling within the Lines and Boundaries aforesaid into the same new Street, to remain and continue a Part and Parcell thereof forever.[10]

[10] "April 8 [1767]. Spent the afternoon with the Justices and Selectmen about laying out a new street in Paddy's Alley." "April 16 [1767]. Met the Justices and Selectmen at the Hall and finished the affair of the street." Rowe, *Letters and Diary* 128.

And the Defendants further say, that all that Part of the Plantiffs Close aforesaid described in his Declaration aforesaid, wherein the Brick Walls, Chimnies, aforesaid and the Cellars aforesaid mentioned in said Declaration were at the Time when the supposed Trespass was committed, was included and Fell within the Lines and Boundaries of the aforesaid new street so laid out and established as aforesaid.

And the said Defendants further say, that at said Boston on the said Thirtyeth day of April Anno Domini 1767 the Brick walls and chiminies as in the plaintiff's declaration aforesaid mentioned being part of the [....] occasioned by the Fire aforesaid and in a weak and tottering condition and the Cellar aforesaid in said Declaration mentioned being left by the fire aforesaid open and uncovered, were dangerous to the Lives and Limbs of the Inhabitants of said Town, and of his Majesty Subjects in general who had right and occasion to pass and repass with their Horses and Carriages, in the new Street aforesaid and were common Nusances to his Majestys Subjects in general.

And the Said Defendants on the Day and Time mentioned in the Plantiffs Declaration aforesaid, in order to remove the said Common Nusances, and that they and their fellow subjects might pass and repass in said new street, on foot and with their Horses and Carriages, as they had right and occasion to do broke and entered the said Close, in said Declaration mentioned, and then and there broke down and erased to the Foundation the Brick Walls and Chimnies of the Plantiffs Dwelling House there standing, and did then and there, fill up the Cellars aforesaid of the Plantiffs said House, with Dirt, Bricks and other Rubbish and thereby wholly Spoil and destroy the same, as well and lawfully they might.[11] Which is the Same breaking and entering, the Plantiffs House, and breaking down and erasing to the Foundation the Brick Walls and Chimnies of his Dwelling House and filling up the Cellars of his said House with Dirt, Bricks and other Rubbish and wholly Spoiling and destroying the same, whereof he complains.

[11] No statute gave the precise power claimed here. The Act of 6 Dec. 1693, c. 6, §5, 1 A&R 137 provided that "any gates, rayles or fence upon or across any highway," might be removed by any person, but by the Act of 4 July 1734, c. 2, §1, 2 A&R 711, any incumbrance upon a highway or street could be demolished at the owner's expense by order of the General Sessions upon complaint made out before them. An Act of 20 June 1760, c. 9, §2, 4 A&R 378, provided for the demolition at the owner's expense of buildings encroaching upon streets newly laid out after the fire of that year, upon order of two justices, but there seems to have been no comparable provision for the 1767 fire. At common law, however, "Any one may justify pulling down, or otherwise destroying a common Nusance," presumably at his own expense. 3 Bacon, *Abridgment* 57.

And all this the said William, Giles, Benjamin and Asa are ready to verify wherefore they pray Judgment if the said Jacob his Action aforesaid thereof against them ought to have or maintain.

John Adams[12]

And the said Jacob says that the same plea of the said William, Giles, Benjamin and Asa, last above in Manner and Form aforesaid pleaded, and the Matter therein contained are not sufficient in Law to bar the said Jacob from having and maintaining his Action aforesaid against them, nor is he the said Jacob under Necessity or bound by the Law of the Land to make any Answer to that same plea in Manner and Form aforesaid pleaded; and this he is ready to verify; wherefore for want of a sufficient plea in this behalf, the said Jacob prays Judgment and his Damage by Reason of the Trespass aforesaid to be adjudged him, with Costs.

Jon. Sewall

And the Said William, Giles, Benjamin[13] and Asa say their plea aforesaid in manner aforesaid and the matter therein contained are sufficient in Law to preclude and bar the said Jacob from having and maintaining his Action aforesaid thereof against them which same Matter in the same plea in Bar aforesaid pleaded they the said William Giles Benjamin and Asa are ready to verify and prove when and where &c. Wherefore because the said Jacob has not answered to the same plea in Bar, or in any manner denied the same the said William Giles Benjamin and Asa pray Judgment and that the said Jacob may be barr'd from maintaining his Action aforesaid for their Costs.   John Adams

II. ADAMS' MINUTES OF THE TRIAL[14]

Suffolk Superior Court, Boston, August 1772

Emmons vs. Brewer.

S[amuel] Q[uincy]. Prov. Law. 1st in the Book. Obsolete.[15]
Against common right. Not to be done by Legislature.
Must be strictly pursued.

---

[12] Except for a few words in the last paragraph, here ends the portion of the text in JA's hand. The following paragraph is in Sewall's hand and is signed by him.

[13] Preceding six words in JA's hand; remainder in unknown hand, but signature is JA's.

[14] In JA's hand. Adams Papers, Microfilms, Reel No. 185.

[15] Act of 25 Oct. 1692, note 7 above. It is in fact the first statute in *Acts and Laws, of His Majesty's Province of the Massachusetts Bay in New England* 1–2 (Boston, 1759).

Not a total desolation. The Bricks Wall and Chimney standing.

Dont appear that the Justices and Select Men were notified. The Law says the Major Part of both. It must have been preceded by a Notification of all the Justices and select Men.

Not mentioned any Recompence to the Party.[16]

1. Black. 139.[17] Regard to private Property.

[16] Quincy apparently refers here to the plea, and not to the statute, which provides (in the sentence following the language quoted by JA at note 7 above): "And where any particular persons shall have their land taken away or lessened thereby, a jury of twelve men shall be appointed by two justices of the peace, and sworn to ascertain the value thereof, to be paid by the person to whose land the same shall be added, or by the neighborhood town in proportion to the benefit or convenience any shall have thereby."

[17] 1 Blackstone, *Commentaries* *139: "So great moreover is the regard of the law for private property, that it will not authorize the least violation of it; no, not even for the general good of the whole community. If a new road, for instance, were to be made through the grounds of a private person, it might perhaps be extensively beneficial to the public; but the law permits no man, or set of men, to do this without consent of the owner of the land. . . . [T]he legislature alone can, and indeed frequently does, interpose, and compel the individual to acquiesce . . . by giving him a full indemnification and equivalent for the injury thereby sustained."

J. *Conservation*

34. Wadsworth v. Loring
1766–1768

35. Winslow v. Clark
1767

EDITORIAL NOTE

In these cases the defendants stood accused of violating province laws forbidding interference with the upstream spawning run of alewives. Under the statutes, an action was to be brought in the name of a private citizen on a *qui tam* basis; that is, upon conviction, the penalty sued for would be divided between the informer-plaintiff and the poor of the town where the offense had been committed. Clark's case (Document II) was apparently straightforward, and Adams won "Verdict for Def't Costs" as well as a 48s. fee.[1]

The Loring case was more complicated. From the files [2] it appears that Loring and three others owned a sawmill at the mouth of Island Creek Pond, Duxbury, and that Wadsworth, Adams' client, the town officer responsible for assuring compliance with the law, had commenced an action against them under the statute. Prior to the writ's return day, however, Loring and the others gave Wadsworth a penal bond for £100 conditioned on the town's agreeing to give up its share of the statutory fine. Perhaps behind this arrangement lay an offer of settlement: Wadsworth, who would ordinarily be entitled to half the statutory fine, may have agreed for some reason to accept less than this and to nonsuit himself; [3] but, because Wadsworth could not legally control the town's rights in the litigation, it would be necessary for the defendants to obtain the town's relinquishment of those rights. The bond, therefore, merely protected Wadsworth's interests.

The March 1765 Duxbury town meeting voted "No" to the proposition, but a special meeting on 13 May 1765 voted "Yes." Meanwhile, the bond had fallen due. Wadsworth's action on the bond commenced at the Plymouth Inferior Court, October 1765, and was continued [4] to the Plym-

[1] JA, Docket, Barnstable Inf. Ct., Dec. 1767, Adams Papers.

[2] SF 142238.

[3] Paine's minutes, however, suggest that the settlement may have involved an over-all payment by defendants of £30, to be split between Wadsworth and the Town. Paine Law Notes, Plymouth Inf. Ct., April 1766.

[4] Paine Law Notes, Plymouth Inf. Ct., Oct. 1765.

outh Inferior Court, April 1766,[5] from which Adams' minutes (Document I) date.[6]

The plea raised as defenses not only the May 1765 vote, but also Wadsworth's acts between the execution of the bond and the March meeting. Wadsworth was alleged to have "set himself to invite and perswade the inhabitants . . . to vote against" the proposition and to have succeeded, "by means whereof said condition was rendered impossible to be performed by the plaintiff's own doings." [7]

This plea, something in the nature of a defense in confession and avoidance, threw the burden of going forward upon the defendants. It was therefore they, as Adams' minutes show, whose evidence opened the trial; [8] and it was they for whom the jury returned a verdict.[9]

I. ADAMS' MINUTES OF THE WADSWORTH TRIAL [10]

Plymouth Inferior Court, Plymouth, April 1766

Wadsworth vs. Loring et als.

Paine.[11] Wadsworth, a Commissioner of Duxborough to take Care of the Herring Way.

Q. Whether Wadsworth did any Thing to defeat the Condition? [12]

Levi Loring. Deposition. Making Interest.[13] Told Town, nothing was done.

Thomas Adams.

Pirez Loring. Would make Interest, but Lor[in]g said it was not fair.

---

[5] Paine Law Notes, Plymouth Inf. Ct., April 1766.

[6] JA's minutes almost exactly parallel Paine's; moreover, the cause was not tried in the Superior Court during JA's connection with it. See notes 9 and 10, below. Min. Bk. 82, SCJ Plymouth, May 1766, May 1767, May 1768.

[7] Plea. SF 142238.

[8] "[I]f the only issue was raised by a plea in confession and avoidance the defendant would begin." Sutton, *Personal Actions* 123. It seems, however, that in England, at least, the question of the defendant's right to open was not settled until the early part of the 19th century. See Cotton v. James, M. & M. 273, 278, 173 Eng. Rep. 1157, 1159 (N.P. 1829).

[9] SF 142238. On appeal to the Superior Court new pleadings were allowed and the judgment was reversed. Min. Bk. 82, SCJ Plymouth, May 1766, N–8; *id.*, May 1768, C–5. SCJ Rec. 1767–1768, fol. 186. JA dropped out before final judgment, but his dockets show that he received fees totaling 6s. for the Inferior Court, and £6 7s. 4d. in the Superior Court. JA, Docket, Plymouth Inf. Ct., April 1766; SCJ, May 1766; SCJ, May 1767.

[10] In JA's hand. Adams Papers, Microfilms, Reel No. 185. Facing page is docketed "Supr. Ct. Wadsworth v. Loring & als.," without more. See notes 5, 6, and 9, above.

[11] Robert Treat Paine, counsel for Loring et al.

[12] It is not clear from the MS whether this is JA's query or Paine's.

[13] That is, using influence in order to obtain votes.

Jno. McGlathly. Judah Sampson came and wantd him to see how [many?] would vote for Wadsworth.

Abner Louden. Askd to go to Meeting but not to vote. Voted against it.

Job Brewster. General talk unfair to make Int[erest].
434. 435. 436. Our Act.[14]
Confession—whose case.

Hovey.[15]
Coll. Bradford. Fair Vote.
D[eaco]n Wadsworth. Defendants said make what Interest you can and so will I. Aggrievd the People.
Prior. Enemy.
P. Sampson. Petition not to give up the Priviledge.

II. ADAMS' MINUTES OF THE WINSLOW TRIAL [16]

Barnstable Inferior Court, Barnstable, December 1767

Winslow qui tam vs. *Clark*

Hovey. 239. Page. Nusances in Rivers. Natural, usual or common Passage.[17]

---

[14] "[W]hosoever shall hereafter erect or build any dam across any such river or stream where the salmon, shad, alewives or other fish usually pass up into the natural ponds, to cast their spawn, shall make a sufficient passage-way for the fish to pass up such river or stream, through or round such dam, and shall keep it open, for the free passage of the fish, from the first day of April to the last day of May, annually; and all the owners or occupants of any mill-dam, or other dams heretofore erected and made across any such river or stream where the fish can't conveniently pass over, shall make a sufficient way, either round or through such dam, for the passage of such fish, at or before the first day of September next, and after that to keep such passage-way open from the first day of April to the last day of May, annually, on pain that every person offending, in any of the particulars aforesaid, shall forfeit and pay the sum of fifty pounds for each offence. . . . [T]he owners or occupants of such dam or dams shall allow sufficient water-passage round, through or over such dams, for the passage of such fish or their young spawn, in the season of their going down such rivers or streams, on penalty of forfeiting the sum of fifty pounds for every offence. . . . [T]he several fines and penalties arising by virtue of this act, shall be sued for and recovered in any court of record proper to try the same, by any person that shall prosecute and sue for the same; one half of such sum to be to and for the use of the prosecutor, and the other half to be to and for the use of the poor of the town where the offence shall be committed." Act of 15 Jan. 1742, 2 A&R 1087–1088. The numbers "434. 435. 436" in the text are unexplained. They do not refer to *Acts and Laws, Of His Majesty's Province of the Massachusetts Bay in New-England* (Boston, 1759), where the Act appears at p. 297.

[15] James Hovey, with JA, counsel for Wadsworth.

[16] In JA's hand. Adams Papers, Microfilms, Reel No. 185. Dated from JA,

J. Conservation

Wm. Robbins. Knows the Brook. Saw Clark make a Ware[18] with sticks and stones and Boards. Saw James Clark cat[c]h Fish.
Thos. Snow.

Our Witnesses.

Lt. Freeman. No Water in the guzzell[19] when Winslow Gates are down in Herring Time.
Tupper.
Clark.

Docket, Adams Papers. See note 1 above. Winslow was a justice of the quorum. Whitmore, *Mass. Civil List* 146.

[17] James Hovey, counsel for Winslow, most probably refers to an Act of 1727: "[W]hosoever . . . shall sett up, erect or make any wears . . . or other incumbrances whatsoever, on or across any river for straitning, obstructing or stopping the natural, usual or common passage of fish, in the spring or other proper seasons of the year, without the approbation of the court of general sessions of the peace, shall, for every such offence, forfeit and pay the sum of ten pounds, to be sued for and recovered by plaint, bill or information in any of his majestie's courts of record within the county where the offence is committed; one half thereof to be to him that shall inform and sue for the same, and the other half to the poor of the town or towns where such incumbrances have been made or set up." Act of 3 July 1727, 2 A&R 426. The Act appears at p. 239–240 of *Acts and Laws of the Province of Massachusetts Bay.*

[18] That is, a weir, or dam.
[19] "Guzzle": "a gutter, drain." *OED.*

K. Religion

36. Pierce v. Wright

1768–1769

EDITORIAL NOTE

Colonial Massachusetts is often charged with having supported a religious establishment. As *Green v. Washburn*, No. 37, indicates, there is a sense in which this charge is all too well-merited. The "establishment" which existed in the 18th century, however, was far from being the state-controlled church administering a rigid dogma which the term suggests. Indeed, local autonomy was the very essence of the Congregational faith of the Massachusetts Puritans. The "establishment," whatever support it may have received from the state, was only the sum of several hundred self-sufficient congregations which subscribed to certain common principles but were jealously independent in defining their faith within the limits of those principles and in governing their own temporal affairs. Fundamental to this spirit of independence was the jurisdiction of each church over the conditions of its membership. Deacon Thomas Pierce's suit for defamation against Samuel Wright arose from the latter's invocation of this jurisdiction in the Church of Christ in Wilmington, to which they both belonged.[1]

In September 1767 Pierce and Wright had, with Philemon Chandler, served as arbitrators in a dispute between Jeremiah Bowen and Zacheus Hibberd over the division of certain timber which they had jointly ar-

[1] For an example of the establishment charge, see Jacob C. Meyer, *Church and State in Massachusetts from 1740 to 1833* 1–31 (Cleveland, 1930). As to the force and effect of Congregational autonomy, see Edmund S. Morgan, *The Puritan Dilemma* 76–82 (Boston, 1958). For the doctrinal problems, see Perry Miller, *The New England Mind: From Colony to Province* (Cambridge, Mass., 1952). The diversity of Congregationalism has most recently been expounded by Clifford K. Shipton in his paper, "The Locus of Authority in Colonial Massachusetts," delivered at the Conference on Colonial History, April 1964, published in George A. Billias, ed., *Law and Authority in Colonial America: Selected Essays* (Barre, Mass., in press). Mr. Shipton goes somewhat further in exculpating Massachusetts than would the present editors. See No. 37. Autonomy was recognized in the first statute creating an "establishment." See *id.*, note 2. The Act of 4 Nov. 1692, c. 26, §3, 1 A&R 62, provided "That the respective churches in the several towns within this province, shall at all times hereafter, use, exercise and enjoy all their privileges and freedoms respecting divine worship, church order and discipline, and shall be encouraged in the peaceable and regular profession and practice thereof." For a list of Deacons and members of the Wilmington church, see *Articles of Faith and Covenant, Ecclesiastical Principles, Standing Rules, and List of Members, of the Orthodox Congregational Church, Wilmington, Mass.* 16–20 (Woburn, Mass., 1857). See also Daniel P. Noyes, *Historical Addresses Delivered in the Meeting-House of the Church of Christ in Wilmington, Mass., Sept. 25, 1880* (Boston, 1881).

ranged to have cut and sawed. The award of the arbitrators had provided, among other things, that Bowen should receive "all the Ship Timber and half the Boards they got Sawed," as well as certain "Coals," presumably charcoal. According to later witnesses, after the award was read to the parties, Wright further said that Bowen was to understand that he was not thereby entitled to take any of the "plank" cut, which had been reserved for the floor of Hibberd's barn. Pierce and Chandler did not object to this statement and indicated by later comments that it represented their understanding as well.[2] The next stage in the proceedings occurred two or three weeks later before Justice of the Peace Josiah Johnson, where Hibberd was suing Bowen. It is not clear whether the original arbitration had been conducted as part of this suit, or whether the suit was newly brought on some phase of the award. In any event, the issue seems to have been the right to the "plank." Thomas Pierce was called as a witness and apparently testified that the arbitrators had intended that all of this commodity should go to Bowen.[3]

After an unsuccessful effort to change Pierce's position, Wright submitted a formal complaint against him to Isaac Merrill, pastor of the Wilmington church. The complaint charged that Pierce when under oath had solemnly declared "Things contrary to Truth and contrary to his holy Profession. And . . . dishonorary to God and Religion." [4] After the service on 11 October, the complaint was read to the assembled members, and Wright stated that he had meant to charge Pierce with perjury. Ten days later Pierce demanded in writing that Wright give him "Christian satisfaction" (that is, a retraction and apology before the congregation), threatening otherwise "to seek after it in a Legal Way." [5]

[2] See copies of the award and various depositions in SF 147706. As an instance of the other arbitrators' understanding, the deposition of John Richardson, sworn in the Charlestown Inferior Court, 16 March 1768, records that after the award was read, "Mr. Chandler the other Arbitrator went into the Kitchin and gave Mrs. Hebberd the Wife of the abovesaid Zacheus a slap on her Knee and said are you affronted Mrs. Hebberd. She answered, no I am not affronted at you, but Bowin has run away with all my Husband's Winter's Work and his own too, he has got all the Ship Timber and most of the Coal. Said Chandler answered and said your Husband has got the Plank and the Crop clear and she answered and said what are the Plank, them are but a Trifle." *Ibid.*

[3] No detailed account of the proceedings before Justice Johnson has survived. The nature of Pierce's testimony has been deduced from the declaration (Doc. I) and from conflicting statements in the depositions of witnesses favorable to one or the other of the litigants. SF 147706.

[4] The complaint is set out in full in the declaration (Doc. I). A copy of the original document appears in SF 147706. See also deposition of Mary Tucker, Wilmington, 29 Feb. 1768. *Ibid.*

[5] As to the church meeting, see the declaration (Doc. I), and the testimony of various witnesses, text at notes 20–23 below. Pierce's demand is in SF 147706. The church ultimately postponed consideration of the matter until after the resolution of the civil suit. See note 20 below. As to the jurisdiction of the church in such matters, see Emil Oberholzer, *Delinquent Saints* 172–185 (N.Y., 1956). See also Haskins, "Ecclesiastical Antecedents of Criminal Punishment in Early Massachusetts," 72 MHS, *Procs.* 21 (1957–1960).

No retraction seems to have been forthcoming, because Pierce brought an action of the case against Wright at the November 1767 term of the Middlesex Inferior Court, with separate counts in libel and slander, alleging £500 damages. The declaration (Document I), probably drawn by Jonathan Sewall, counsel for Pierce at the trial, is a classic example of the common-law form in such matters, complete with inducement, colloquium, innuendo, and all.[6] On a plea of the general issue the suit went to the jury at the March 1768 session. Although Benjamin Kent was counsel of record for Wright, Adams argued his case, unfortunately without success. Pierce won a verdict of £3 and both parties appealed to the Superior Court. There at the October 1768 term, with James Putnam joining Sewall, and Adams again appearing for Wright, Pierce obtained a second verdict. On a motion in arrest of judgment the case was continued, but at the April 1769 term judgment for £9 damages and £28 13s. 1d. costs was entered for Pierce on the verdict.[7]

Adams' undated minutes (Document II) have been assigned to the March 1768 Inferior Court trial.[8] They are chiefly of interest because they record an argument in which Adams presented the defense of privilege. He first demonstrated that the Cambridge Platform of 1648, the traditional governing ordinance of the Congregational churches, gave to members the right to accuse before the congregation brothers whom they felt had strayed from the ways of righteousness.[9] This procedure, Adams argued, was necessary to the principal end of the church, the mutual encouragement and preservation of godliness. No action for defamation should lie against one who sought to exercise the right. The possibility of liability would discourage members from coming forward, and the church could not protect itself against the unrighteous. There would be no abuse in the absence of a civil remedy, however. One who sought deliberately to injure another with false charges would be discovered and punished in the

[6] The formal parts of a declaration in libel or slander were the inducement, a prefatory allegation of the plaintiff's reputation and surrounding circumstances; the colloquium, an allegation that the defamation was "of and concerning the plaintiff"; the statement of the defamatory matter and its publication; the innuendoes, allegations which pointed out expressly the defamatory meaning of the remarks; and the damages resulting from the defamation. See 1 Chitty, *Pleading* 381–383, 385; 2 *id.* at at 304–313.

[7] See the pleadings and Inferior Court judgment in SF 147706. JA's Dockets for the Middlesex Inferior Court, Nov. 1767 and March 1768, show that he was retained by Wright. Adams Papers, Microfilms, Reel No. 182. See also note 17 below. For the Superior Court proceedings, see Min. Bk. 88, SCJ Cambridge, Oct. 1768, C–7, C–11; Charlestown, April 1769, C–7, C–8. SCJ Rec. 1769, fols. 42–44. Pierce was awarded further costs in Wright's appeal of £2 3s. 0d. As to the motion in arrest of judgment, see No. 3, note 10.

[8] See note 17 below.

[9] The Platform, although not formally binding, remained the primary instrument of church government until well into the 19th century. See Edward Buck, *Massachusetts Ecclesiastical Law* 76–78 (Boston, 1866); Williston Walker, *The Creeds and Platforms of Congregationalism* 157–188 (N.Y., 1893); Avery v. Inhabitants of Tyringham, 3 Mass. 160, 165, 170, 182–183 (1807). JA's citations appear at notes 26–32 below.

course of the trial of his own accusations. As a separate point Adams also contended that Wright's written complaint was not actionable, drawing an analogy to English authority which held that documents in legislative and judicial proceedings, including those in spiritual courts, were privileged.[10]

Modern theory recognizes two branches of privilege—the absolute privilege to defame regardless of motive that is accorded to participants in judicial and legislative proceedings as a matter of public necessity, and the qualified privilege which exists in certain other circumstances and may be defeated on a showing that the defamer acted with "malice"—that is, abused the privilege by publishing defamation to serve an interest other than that meant to be protected. In the modern view members of religious and other groups have a qualified privilege to defame other members in the course of their proceedings.[11]

At the time of *Pierce v. Wright*, as Adams' authorities show, the common law had long known the absolute judicial and legislative privilege. But the concept of a qualified privilege in other matters was barely in its infancy. It first appeared in something like its modern form in a dictum of Lord Mansfield's in 1769 to the effect that a master was qualifiedly privileged in describing a former servant to a prospective employer.[12] In several early 19th-century American decisions the courts extended a qualified privilege to church deliberations, but the reasons given are confusing. The servant cases were usually cited, as well as a very brief opinion in an English criminal libel proceeding which seemed to give the privilege to church members on the grounds that the affair was "merely a piece of discipline." Courts and counsel relied heavily upon the older judicial-privilege authorities, however, and the opinions are really framed on the analogy of church to court proceedings.[13]

[10] See note 34 below.

[11] See Fowler V. Harper and Fleming James Jr, *The Law of Torts*, 1:419–430, 442, 450–456 (Boston, 1956); Annotation, 63 A.L.R. 649 (1929); Oberholzer, *Delinquent Saints* 244–245.

[12] See Fifoot, *History and Sources* 134–136. For Lord Mansfield's formulation, see Hargrave v. LeBreton, 4 Burr. 2422, 2425, 98 Eng. Rep. 269, 271 (K.B. 1769). Dictum became holding in Mansfield's decision in Weatherston v. Hawkins, 1 Term Rep. 110, 99 Eng. Rep. 1001 (K.B. 1786).

[13] See M'Millian v. Birch, 1 Binn. (Pa.) 178 (1806); Jarvis v. Hatheway, 3 Johns. (N.Y.) 180 (1808); Remington v. Congdon, 2 Pick. (Mass.) 310 (1824). The criminal libel case relied upon in these opinions was King v. Hart, 1 W. Bl. 386, 96 Eng. Rep. 218 (K.B. 1762). This decision may have been available to JA in 1768, although Sir William Blackstone's *Reports* were not published until 1781. 1 Sweet and Maxwell, *Legal Bibliography* 293. The case was reported in slightly different form in Richard Burn, *Ecclesiastical Law*, 2:175–178 (London, 2d edn., 1767). The "quasi-judicial" character of church disciplinary proceedings was relied upon to support the privilege in John Townshend, *A Treatise on the Wrongs Called Slander and Libel* 376–378 (N.Y., 2d edn., 1872). An earlier English treatise equated the privilege granted to church proceedings with that for "confidential communications of friendship," and all "charges as necessarily exclude the suspicion of malice." The only case cited was King v. Hart, above. See Francis L. Holt, *The Law of Libel* 226–228 (London, 2d edn., 1816).

This last analogy runs throughout Adams' argument and is express in his reference to the judicial-privilege cases. His suggestion that abuse of privilege was to be remedied by action within the church shows that he did not envision the modern concept of qualified privilege. Nevertheless, his argument contains a principle that goes far beyond the unrealistic church-court analogy drawn by later cases. In emphasizing the constitution and aims of the church he anticipated the basis of the modern grant of privilege to church members. It is not the judicial nature of the deliberations, but the right of the members to protect or advance the common interests for which they have banded together that requires their proceedings to be privileged.[14] If Adams did not fully articulate the modern theory, he at least saw the significance of the relationship which underlies it more clearly than did the 19th-century judges.

Although a general verdict and the lack of any record of the court's charge make it impossible to know the precise legal bases of the decision in *Pierce v. Wright*, the result would indicate that Adams' arguments were not accepted.[15] With the notion of privilege based on common interests still undeveloped in England, it is not surprising that a Massachusetts court should reject a defense based upon it. That the analogy to judicial and legislative privilege also failed suggests that, to the 18th-century judges and jury at least, the "established" church was not so much a creature of the state that its deliberations had the character of public proceedings.

I. THOMAS PIERCE'S WRIT AND DECLARATION[16]

Middlesex Inferior Court, Charlestown, November 1767

To the Sheriff of Our County of Middlesex, his Under-Sheriff or Deputy, Greeting.

WE Command you that you summon Samuel Wright of Wilmington in our said County Yeoman (if he may be found in your Precinct) to appear before Our Justices of Our Inferior Court of Common Pleas

---

[14] 1 Harper and James, *Torts* 442.

[15] It is possible that the court accepted the privilege argument but found that privilege here was defeated by malice. The facts do not support such a finding, however, and there is no indication that the question was argued. Moreover, JA's suggestion that the remedy for abuse lay in the hands of the church indicates that this aspect of qualified privilege was not recognized. For a much earlier Massachusetts case in which there was a verdict for the plaintiff in a suit for slander in church proceedings, the defense of privilege apparently not having been raised, see Mansfield v. Hathorne and Longley v. Hathorne, 3 *Essex Quarterly Court Records* 24, 30 (Essex Co. Ct. 1663), in Mark DeWolfe Howe, *Readings in American Legal History* 133–137 (Cambridge, Mass., 1952).

[16] Copy on a printed form in the hand of Thaddeus Mason, Clerk of the Inferior Court. SF 147706. The caption, return, subsequent pleadings, and attestations are omitted.

to be holden at Charlestown within and for Our said County of Middlesex on the last Tuesday of November next, Then and there in Our said Court to answer to Thomas Peirce of Wilmington aforesaid Gentleman in a Plea of Trespass on the Case for that whereas the Said Thomas is and from his Nativity has been a Person of good Name, Fame and Reputation and free from the atrocious Crimes of false Swearing and Perjury, and by his pious and virtuous Behaviour had so far obtained the Esteem and good opinion of the Church of Christ in Wilmington aforesaid as to have been received and to have continued for the Space of fifteen years last past a Member in full Communion with the said Church and also had so far obtained their Esteem and good Opinion as that in the month of February A. Dom. 1766 he was elected and appointed one of the Deacons of the Same Church in which office he has ever since continued; Nevertheless the said Samuel, not ignorant of the Premises, but *maliciously minding* and contriving to injure the said Thomas in his good Name, Fame and Reputation and to deprive him of the Esteem and good opinion of the Members of the same Church and of all the other Churches of Christ throughout this and the neighbouring Provinces and thereby to deprive him of the Benefits and Comforts of the holy ordinance of the Lords Supper and also to expose the said Thomas to the Pains and Penalties by Law appointed for those who are guilty of wilfull and corrupt Perjury, did on the tenth Day of October instant at Wilmington aforesaid make and publish the following false defamatory scandalous and malicious Libel of and concerning the said Thomas, Vizt.,

"To the Reverend Mr. Isaac Merrill Pastor of the Church of Christ in Wilmington, please to communicate the following Complaint of me the Subscriber against our Brother Deacon Thomas Peirce a Member of the Church in this Place, Vizt: For that I heard the said Thomas Peirce when under the Solemn Oath of God administered by Mr. Justice Johnson about the middle of September last, say and solemnly declare Things contrary to Truth and contrary to his holy Profession, and as I apprehend dishonorary to God and Religion, as I understand the Matter. I also say that I have proceeded with him according to the Gospel Rule; but can obtain no Satisfaction; Wherefore I remain uneasy and dissatisfyed with our Said Brother; Therefore [I] desire that the Church of Christ in this Place may have an opportunity to hear and inquire further into the matter as the Gospel requires as soon as conveniently may be. Samuel Wright. Wilmington October 10th, 1767."

Meaning that he the said Samuel had heard the said Thomas commit wilfull and corrupt Perjury in a Tryal of a Cause wherein one Zacheus Hibberd was Plaintiff and one Jeremiah Bowen was Defendant at a Court held about the middle of September last before Josiah Johnson Esq. a Justice of the Peace for the County aforesaid, being a Court of Record, and that he the Said Thomas had refused to make Christian Satisfaction therefor when thereto required by the said Samuel, and that therefore he the said Samuel was dissatisfied and uneasy and desired the said Church would deal with the said Thomas according to the Rules prescribed in the Gospel with all convenient Speed.

And the said Samuel afterwards, to wit, on the eleventh Day of October instant at Wilmington aforesaid of his further *Malice* had against the Plaintiff and still further intending and maliciously contriving to injure that Plaintiff did, in the Presence and hearing of diverse of our leige Subjects being members of the Church of Christ aforesaid with a loud Voice speak and publish the following Words, Vizt: "I" (meaning the said Samuel) "meant thereby" (Speaking of and meaning the Libel aforesaid) "to charge him," (meaning the *said Thomas*) "*with Perjury.*"

By means of which Libel so made and published by the said Samuel as aforesaid, and by the Means of the Words spoken and published by the said Samuel as aforesaid the said Thomas has sustained great Injury in his good name, Fame and Reputation and has been and yet is exposed and in Danger of being deprived of the Blessings, Benefits and Comforts of Church Communion and the holy ordinance of the Lords Supper and has been and yet is exposed to the Infamy and Disgrace of being degraded from his said Office of Deacon of the Church aforesaid and of being excommunicated or Suspended from Communion with all and every of the Churches of Christ thro' the Land and has been and still is exposed to the Pains and Penalties of the Law for Perjury, from all which he has suffered grievous Pain and Anxiety of Mind and has been compelled to expend divers Sums of Money to manifest and make known his Innocence in the Premisses.

All which is To the Damage of the said Thomas as he saith the Sum of five hundred *Pounds*, which shall then and there be made to appear, with other due Damages; And have you there this Writ, with your Doings therein. Witness Samuel Danforth Esq; at Cambridge the twenty sixth Day of October In the eighth Year of Our Reign, Annoque Domini, 1767.

II. ADAMS' MINUTES OF THE TRIAL AND NOTES FOR HIS ARGUMENT[17]

Middlesex Inferior Court, Charlestown, March 1768

Pierce vs. Wright.

Sewall.[18]

Action of slander. Not directly charging Perjury.

Things contrary to *Truth* and contrary to his *holy Profession*. Dishonorary to *God*, and *Religion*. I mean to charge him with *Perjury*.[19]
Witnesses.

Buck. Charge in Writing. Mr. Morrill said the Charge was Perjury. Gave a Jogg. Let it go. I meant it so, and am able to prove it with several Aggravations. Ch[urc]h could not finish the Matter. Church did not refuse.[20] Have done nothing. I took it he spoke to Mr. Merrill.

Captn. Walker. Wright said Charge must be read. If I understand Grammar you have charged Pierce with Perjury. I meant it so, and can prove it with several Aggravations.

Benja. Jaquith. Deposition. Vide.[21]

Joseph Lewis. Do you mean to charge him with Perjury or false swearing, or any thing of that sort. Answer, Yes, and I told them so yesterday.

[17] In JA's hand. Adams Papers, Microfilms, Reel No. 185. The MS is undated, but appears in a leaflet with other cases from the court and term to which it has been assigned. The dating is supported by JA's docket entry which shows that he was retained by Wright for the Inferior Court trial and by the fact that the minutes record no argument by James Putnam, who was of counsel with Sewall in the Superior Court. See note 7 above. "Wright v. P[ierce]," the title of the companion action in the Superior Court (note 7 above) is written very faintly in JA's hand at the top of the first page, partly superimposed on "Pierce v. Wright," the title printed here. This suggests the possibility that JA may have used the minute for reference in the Superior Court trial.

[18] Jonathan Sewall, counsel for Pierce.

[19] These three statements convey the sense of the defamatory words alleged in the declaration (Doc. I).

[20] Presumably a reference to a decision of the church on 27 June 1768 to postpone consideration of Wright's charges "Till it be settled by the Court or between themselves." SF 147706. In a much earlier Massachusetts case church and civil court arrived at contrary decisions that could not be reconciled. See Mansfield v. Hathorne and Longley v. Hathorne (Essex Co. Ct. 1663), cited in note 15 above.

[21] See deposition of Benjamin Jaquith, sworn in the Inferior Court, Charlestown, 16 March 1768: "Benjamin Jaquith of lawful Age testifies and says that being *in the Meeting House* in Wilmington some time in October last, after the publick Services were ended, Samuel Wright exhibited a Complaint against Deacon Thomas Peirce, and that after said Complaint was read, the Revd. Mr. Merrill *said, if it meant any Thing it was Perjury,* the abovesaid Samuel stood up and said *let it go, so I meant to have it so and can prove it with several Aggrevations.*" SF 147706.

Moses Baron. Idem. Dont know but what Boin [Bowen] feed them.[22]
They did take a false oath.

Revd. Mr. Morrill. Delivered Copy to Pierce. Wright had been
according to Gospell Rule.

Rich and Tucker. Satisfaction in a Christian Way.[23]

Sewall. Identicall Words unnecessary.

Words of same import as those in the Declaration. Same Reason,
as Declaration on a Promise.

Q. Whether there is any such Thing as slandering a Man in the
Church. Absurd Doctrine. Dangerous. The Worst Men may ruin the
Characters of the best. And establishing Slander by a Law. Wreak
Malice and Vengeance. Without are slanderers Lyars and Backbiters,
not within. Should have been heard in the Church. What Right had
the Church to try Perjury. Platform. All goes upon the supposition
that the Charge is true, Q. about Writs, Petitions.

Sewall. Definition of Libells. Bacon. Written Scandal, held in greatest Detestation.[24]

Eg[o].[25] The Question that is made is Whether there is any such
Thing as slander in the Church?

Platform, Page 12, §2. Church Power is in the People.[26]

[22] Thus in MS. The word is probably "fee'd," *i.e.* paid a fee to. Bowen was
one of the litigants out of whose dispute the problem arose. See text at notes
2, 3, above.

[23] This is a reference to a communication from Pierce to Wright, dated 21 Oct.
1767, and witnessed by Thomas Rich and William Tucker: "To Mr. Samuel Wright
a Member of the Church of Christ in Wilmington, as you have laid a Sad Complaint
against me the Subscriber, before this Church of which I also am a Member, and
have charged me with a high Crime, as I apprehend without Foundation, upon
which I am greatly dissatisfyed with you, I think I have a Right to Christian Satisfaction, and desire you would give it me before next Saturday night, otherwise
you may expect I shall Seek after it in a Legal Way." SF 147706.

[24] See 3 Bacon, *Abridgment* 490 note: "[A libel] is termed *libellus famosus
seu infamatoria scriptura*, and from its pernicious Tendency has been held a public
Offense at the Common Law; for Men not being able to bear having their Errors
exposed to public View, were found by Experience to revenge themselves on those
who made Sport with their Reputations; from whence arose Duels and Breaches
of the Peace; and hence written Scandal has been held in the greatest Detestation,
and has received the utmost Discouragement in the Courts of Justice." The query
raised in the preceding paragraph may be JA's.

[25] That is, the Latin "I," signifying that what follows is JA's own argument.

[26] This and the citations following through note 32 below are references to the
Cambridge Platform of 1648. See note 9 above. The edition of the Platform cited
by JA has not been found. Quotations in this and the following notes are from
Williston Walker's reproduction (N.Y., 1893) of the first edition, Cambridge,
1649. The passage here referred to is apparently ch. 5, §2: "*Ordinary* Church powr,

Page 24, §3. This Government is a mixed one.[27]

Page 25, §5. The Prerogative or Priviledge of the Church, in Choosing officers, in Admission of Members. Case of offence, any Brother hath Power to convince and admonish, and to take one or two, and to tell the Church. Admonition or Excommunication.[28]

Page 27, §9. It belongs to Elders to receive Accusations brought to the Church and to prepare them for the Churches Hearing, and to pronounce sentence with the Consent of the Church.[29]

Page 39. Of Excommunication and other Censures.[30]

Page 40, §3. Offence public, of an heinous and criminal Nature.[31]

---

is either the power of office, that is such as is proper to the eldership: or, power of priviledge, such as belongs unto the brotherhood. The latter is in the brethren formally, and immediately from Christ, that is, so as it may according to order be acted or exercised immediately by themselves: the former, is not in them formally or immediately, and therfore cannot be acted or exercised immediately by them, but is said to be in them, in that they design the persons into office, who only are to act, or to exercise this power." Walker, *Creeds and Platforms* 210.

[27] Cambridge Platform, ch. 10, §3: "This *Government* of the church, is a mixt Government (and so hath been acknowledged long before the term of Independency was heard of). In respect of *Christ*, the head and King of the church, and the Soveraigne power residing in him, and exercised by him, it is a *Monarchy*. In respect of the body, or *Brotherhood* of the church, and powr from Christ graunted unto them, it resembles a *Democracy*, In respect of the *Presbytery* and powr comitted to them, it is an *Aristocracy*." Walker, *Creeds and Platforms* 217–218.

[28] Cambridge Platform, ch. 10, §5: "The power graunted by Christ unto the body of the church and *Brotherhood*, is a prerogative or priviledge which the church doth exercise: I, In *Choosing* their own officers, whether Elders or Deacons. II, In *admission* of their own members and therfore, there is great reason they should have power to *Remove* any from their fellowship again. Hence in case of offence any one brother hath power to convince and Admonish an offending brother; and in case of not hearing him, to take one or two more to sett on the Admonition, and in case of not hearing them, to proceed to tell the church; and as his offence may require the whole church hath powr to proceed to the publick Censure of him, whether by *Admonition* or *Excommunication*; and upon his repentance to restore him again unto his former communion." Walker, *Creeds and Platforms* 218.

[29] Cambridge Platform, ch. 10, §9: "It belongs also unto the Elders . . . to receive the accusations brought to the Church, and to prepare them for the churches hearing. In handling of offences and other matters before the Church they have power to declare and publish the Counsell and will of God touching the same, and to pronounce sentence with the consent of the Church." Walker, *Creeds and Platforms* 219.

[30] The title of Cambridge Platform, ch. 14, in which the sections quoted in notes 31 and 32 below appear. Walker, *Creeds and Platforms* 227.

[31] Cambridge Platform, ch. 14, §3: "But if the offence be more *publick* at first, and of a more *heinous* and *criminall* nature, to wit, such as are condemned by the light of nature; then the church without such graduall proceeding, is to cast out the offender, from their holy communion, for the further mortifying of his sinn and the healing of his soule, in the day of the Lord Jesus." Walker, *Creeds and Platforms* 227–228. The preceding section dealt with private offenses, providing essentially the procedure for dealing with them which was set out in ch. 10, §5 (note 28 above). *Id.* at 227.

Page 42, §8. Toleration of Profane and scandalous Livers, a great sin.[32]

In order to determine the Question, let us consider and enquire what a Church is? A Church is a voluntary society of Christians.[33] Voluntary, because no Man is compellable to join with the Church. A society, a Body politick, framed for certain Ends. What are those Ends? Why their mutual Advancement in Knowledge, and their Growth in Piety and Virtue. Their Connexion is therefore spiritual, merely. No Concern with the Lives, Liberties, Estates or Reputations, of the Members any further than these have Relation to another, a future state. J[esus] Christ is the great Head and Law giver of his Church. And Kings, Princes Parliaments and Judicatories, have no Concern with them as Church Members. One End of Church society, and Government is mutual Watch and Jealousy over each other, mutual Advice, Admonitions Censures, and that all evil Examples may be suppressed. And the only Punishment they have in their Power is Admonition or Excission. Thus the fundamental Principle of Ecclesiastical Polity is that as every Member is a Volunteer, if he will not submit to their Rules he shall be cut off. Come into our Company if you are qualified and will continue to be qualified i.e. continue in the Faith and order of the Gospell, but We will have the Right to examine your Qualifications before we admit you, and We will also hold the Right of observing your Life and Conversation, and if that should become sinfull and scandalous, we will expell you, and if you are not willing to submit to this, dont join Us. The Candidate agrees to this, and takes the Covenant.

But when the Church assembles to admit and receive him, I say that every Church Member has a Right to object to him. And to give his Reasons. Now suppose a vicious Man should ⟨assert⟩ propound his Desires to come into full Communion. Would not the Church Members have a Right to go to the Minister and object, and to tell the Minister his objections. When the Church assemble would he not have a Right to tell the Church, that at such a Time he heard him tell a Lie, at such a Time he saw him drunk. At such a Time he heard him swear, and perjure himself. According to Mr. Sewall he would be liable to an Action of slander, if he did. If he is liable to an

[32] Cambridge Platform, ch. 14, §8: "The suffring of prophane or scandalous livers to continue in fellowship, and partake in the sacraments, is doubtless a great sinn in those that have power in their hands to redress it; and doe it not." Walker, *Creeds and Platforms* 229.

[33] This and the following sentences are a paraphrase of the famous passage from Locke's *Essay on Toleration*, part of which is quoted in No. 37, note 31.

Action will not this forever cutt off the Priviledge of Church Members to object to the Admission of new ones. It is the same after Admission. Every Member may complain again[st] every other. But says the Gentleman it will put it in the Power of the worst Men, to wreak their Malice and Revenge on the best? To this I answer, is it common for the worst Men to be Church Members! By no Means. Church Members are generally much more virtuous, and benevolent than others. It is not to be supposed that Churches will admit such malicious and revengefull Men to their fellowship. But if such an Instance should happen, that a wicked, malicious Man should deceive the Church, and be admitted, and should bring a [malicious?] and false accusation against his Brother, He must do it publickly. He cant propagate his malicious Whispers in secresy. It must come before the Church, and be examined, and the Complainant must prove his accusation, and if he cannot, but appears to have done it from a factious malicious Spirit, he will himself fall under the Censure of the Church. The accused will be honourably acquitted, and the Accuser will be censured. And is not a Church a Competent Judge? Is not the Vote of a Church, concerning a fact, as good, after Examining Proofs as the Verdict of a Jury? Juries try Perjuries, Forgeries, Murders, Treasons, Blasphemies, and why should not the Churches try the same?

Every Writing that contains a false Charge and Accusation vs. a Person is not a Libell. Writs and Declarations, Petitions to the General Court. Libel in the Spiritual Court.[34]

[34] This paragraph seems to be based on 4 Bacon, *Abridgment* 499–500, a section which sets out various cases holding that no action lies for defamatory words contained in pleadings or other proceedings in court or in petitions to Parliament. The section includes this abstract of Westover v. Dabbinet, 1 Rolle, *Abridgment* 33: "A. libels [i.e. commences an action] in the Spiritual Court against B for Defamation, and produces C. as a Witness. Hereupon B. makes an Allegation in Writing, as the Course of that Court is, that C. who was perjured in a Cause between E. and F. at the Assizes at G. ought not to be received as a Witness. Although this Allegation is false, yet, as the Court had Jurisdiction in the original Matter, C shall not have an Action against B. for, if he might, it would prevent the Detection of bad Witnesses." The case is also reported as Weston v. Dobniet, Cro. Jac. 432, 79 Eng. Rep. 369 (K.B. 1618).

37. Green v. Washburn

1769

EDITORIAL NOTE

The Province Charter of 1691 provided that there should be "a liberty of Conscience allowed in the Worshipp of God to all Christians (Except Papists)" who inhabited Massachusetts. Despite these bold if less than all-embracing words, the faith of the founding Puritans constituted the "establishment" of the province. It continued as such beyond the time of independence and well into the 19th century.[1] As the discussion in *Pierce v. Wright*, No. 36, suggests, however, the term "establishment" is here used in a rather special sense. Local autonomy meant that Massachusetts had neither an established religion nor quite an established church.

Nevertheless, there were established churches. Within each town in the Province at least one church or congregation—generally Calvinist in doctrine and congregational in polity—was entitled under the existing laws to receive special favors from the government. Statutes provided financial and other support for the church with which a majority in each "town or place" was affiliated. That majority in almost every case subscribed to doctrines which, however variant, had enough in common to occupy the broad theological center which was Congregationalism. Dissenters to the left and right might worship as they chose, but they were rarely in a position to receive the kind of state sanction and assistance accorded to the Congregational churches. Moreover, despite exemption acts, they had to battle constantly to avoid contributing to support the established order.

The principal dissenting denominations in 18th-century Massachusetts were the Episcopalians, the Quakers, and the Baptists. All three fought establishment actively, but after about 1750, the Baptists were its chief

[1] For the 1691 Charter provision, see 1 A&R 14. As to its construction, see Susan M. Reed, *Church and State in Massachusetts, 1691-1740* 21-23 (Urbana, Ill., 1914). The nature of the problem was altered after independence by the terms of the Declaration of Rights in the Massachusetts Constitution of 1780, which, in requiring the legislature to make the towns provide "for the public worship of GOD," allowed taxes paid by an individual who so requested to "be uniformly applied to the support of the public teacher or teachers of his own religious sect or denomination, provided there be any on whose instructions he attends." Declaration of Rights, Art. III, in Robert J. Taylor, ed., *Massachusetts, Colony to Commonwealth* 128-129 (Chapel Hill, N.C., 1961). For cases and other materials on the gradual decline of the establishment under this provision and its abolition by constitutional amendment in 1833, see Mark DeWolfe Howe, *Cases on Church and State in the United States* 27-54 (Cambridge, Mass., 1952). See also Edward Buck, *Massachusetts Ecclesiastical Law* 39-65 (Boston, 1866); Jacob C. Meyer, *Church and State in Massachusetts from 1740 to 1833* 90-200 (Cleveland, Ohio, 1930); Butterfield, "Elder John Leland, Jeffersonian Itinerant," 62 Amer. Antiq. Soc., *Procs.* 155, 207-215 (1952); Leonard Levy, *The Law of the Commonwealth and Chief Justice Shaw* 29-42 (Cambridge, Mass., 1957).

opponents. *Green v. Washburn* is an example of the varied litigation which their struggle produced.

Barely a year after the promulgation of the Charter, the basic principle of establishment was laid down by statute. "Able, learned, orthodox" ministers "of good conversation," approved by a majority of the church-going voters in a "town or place" were to be supported by taxes levied upon all of the inhabitants. If a town was delinquent in providing itself with such a minister, the Court of General Sessions for the county could "take effectual care to procure and settle a minister qualified as aforesaid, and order the charge thereof and of such minister's maintenance to be levied on the inhabitants of such town." [2] A dissenter was free to support his own church as well, but if he did so he paid twice.

In 1724 the Privy Council ordered the remission of part of the province tax intended to support Congregational ministers in two towns in which a majority of the inhabitants were Quakers. This decision was itself of narrow effect, but the dissenters pressed the attack, perhaps inspired by the Board of Trade's position that the tax in question was contrary to the Charter.[3] At length, in 1728, having previously granted

[2] Act of 4 Nov. 1692, c. 26, 1 A&R 62, as amended by Act of 17 Feb. 1693, c. 46, §§8–11, 1 A&R 102–103. The latter act was made expressly inapplicable to Boston, where ministers had always been supported by voluntary contributions. *Id.*, §9; see Reed, *Church and State in Mass.* 38. Parts of both acts are set out in notes 25 and 26, below. The Act of 13 June 1695, c. 8, 1 A&R 216, provided that a council of ministers called by the church might overrule a town's rejection of the church's choice. Later acts permitted ministerial taxes to be raised in precincts set off for church purposes from existing towns. Act of 9 Nov. 1702, c. 10, §2, 1 A&R 506; Act of 24 Dec. 1732, c. 14, 2 A&R 306. The Act of 19 June 1718, c. 1, 2 A&R 99, permitted taxes to be levied for the construction and repair of meeting houses in precincts. Presumably such taxes were levied in towns under their general power to levy taxes "for the defraying of other necessary charges." Act of 16 Nov. 1692, c. 28, §6, 1 A&R 66. Another provision strengthened the power of the Court of Sessions by authorizing it to appoint assessors in delinquent towns or districts and to direct the grand jury to investigate conditions in such communities. Act of 9 Nov. 1702, c. 10, §1, 1 A&R 505. If the towns remained recalcitrant, the General Court was empowered to settle a suitable minister and provide for his maintenance. Act of 14 Nov. 1706, c. 9, 1 A&R 597; Act of 20 Dec. 1715, c. 17, 2 A&R 26, extended to May 1730 by Act of 5 July 1722, c. 4, 2 A&R 244. As to all of this legislation and its enforcement, see Reed, *Church and State in Mass.* 24–34, 50–85. Despite these provisions, in a few instances where dissenters were in the majority in a town, they were permitted to treat their church as the established one, thus gaining the benefit of the tax collection process. See *id.* at 70–73; Shipton, "The Locus of Authority in Colonial Massachusetts," in George A. Billias, ed., *Law and Authority in Colonial America* (Barre, Mass., in press). After 1760 the requirement that ministers have the equivalent of a college education provided a further basis for opposing this practice. See notes 15, 16, 27, below. Although the Privy Council held certain applications of the establishment acts invalid (notes 3 and 14 below), the basic principle of establishment embodied in the acts of 1692 and 1693 was upheld by the Crown law officers against an attack based on the charter clause in 1732. See 2 A&R 477–484; Reed, *Church and State in Mass.* 183–184.

[3] On the 1724 decision, see Reed, *Church and State in Mass.* 75–78, 119–127. The General Court had acted under the Act of 20 Dec. 1715, note 2 above. The

Episcopalians the right to have their taxes paid to their own pastors in certain cases, the General Court passed legislation relieving Quakers and Baptists (or "Anabaptists" as they were called) from taxes "assessed for the support of the minister or ministers of the churches established by the laws of this province." Eligibility for exemption was first determined on the basis of attested lists of those who attended meeting and professed themselves Baptists or Quakers, which were to be furnished by principal members of the denominations in each town. A re-enactment in 1734 provided that lists of exempt Baptists were to be prepared by the town assessors, but omissions could be supplied on the certificate of "two principal members of that perswasion" that they believed omitted persons "to be conscientiously of their perswasion, and that they do frequently and usually attend their meetings for the worship of God, on the Lord's Day." [4]

---

tax act in question, the Act of 3 July 1722, c. 8, §1, 2 A&R 251, 254–255, had not provided on its face that the assessments were intended to support ministers, although the Quakers presented evidence that this was its effect. The Board of Trade in its report of 20 Dec. 1723 to the Privy Council thus did not recommend disallowance, but pointed out that taxing the majority to support the minority's minister was not consistent with the Massachusetts Charter's grant of an "absolute and free liberty of conscience for all Christian Inhabitants there, except Papists." 2 A&R 276. The tax act for the next year, Act of 29 June 1723, c. 8, §1, 2 A&R 293, 296, contained an express statement of the purpose of the assessment. The Board of Trade, on 6 May 1724, recommended disallowance of this act, urging both the Charter clause and an inconsistency with the establishment statutes, in which it was "laid down as a just and equitable rule that the majority of each Town or Congregation shou'd have the choice of their own Teacher." 2 A&R 277. The Privy Council, in its Order of 2 June 1724, granted relief only under the 1722 act and did not disallow it. *Ibid.*; see 3 *Acts, Privy Council (Col.)* 58–59. Other materials concerning the case, which pertained to Dartmouth and Tiverton, are collected in 2 A&R 269–277.

⁴ The Episcopalian relief measure was the Act of 19 Dec. 1727, c. 7, 2 A&R 459, which provided that members of the Church of England should be taxed at the same rate as members "of the churches established by the laws of this province," but that if there were a minister of the Church of England within a town, taxes assessed against inhabitants who worshipped with him and lived within five miles of the church were to be paid over to him by the town treasurer. They were also exempt from meetinghouse taxes. For the problems of Episcopalians generally, and subsequent legislation concerning them, see Reed, *Church and State in Mass.* 141–143, 148–189; Meyer, *Church and State in Mass.* 14, 27–30, 69–89. The Act of 20 June 1728, c. 4, §1, 2 A&R 495, exempted from tax the polls of Baptists and Quakers "enrolled or entred in their respective societies as members thereof, and who alledge a scruple of conscience as the reason of their refusal to pay any part or proportion of such taxes as are from time to time assessed for the support of the minister or ministers of the churches established by the laws of this province in the town or place where they dwell," with the proviso that they attend "meetings of their respective societies" regularly and live within five miles of the meetinghouse. The provision for determining eligibility for exemption was in *id.*, §3. Persons so exempted were barred from voting on church questions in town meeting. *Id.*, §5. See note 7 below. By Act of 20 Dec. 1729, c. 6, 2 A&R 543, the estates of Baptists and Quakers were exempted under the same conditions. For the passage of this legislation, see Reed, *Church and State in Mass.* 128–135. After the expiration of these acts, separate measures were passed for Quakers until 1758. See *id.* at 135–144; Meyer, *Church and State in Mass.* 15–17. The exemption for

After the Great Awakening of the 1740's had left an irremediable split within Congregationalism, problems in the administration of these laws increased. The "New Lights," who had supported the revivalist movement, in many cases formed Separate churches and sought the same tax relief that had been given earlier to the dissenting sects; but the "Old Lights," and those New Lights who continued to support the established order, resisted, apparently finding outright dissent easier to tolerate than Separatism. The inspiration of the Great Awakening had also produced a division in the Baptist ranks between the old General Baptists with their Arminian beliefs and New Light Baptists, who adhered to the strict Calvinism of the revival. With doctrinal differences few, many Congregational Separates became Baptists, forming for themselves, or joining New Light Baptists in, what came to be called Separate Baptist churches. This development brought forth from the Standing Order and from unconverted Separates alike the charge that the converted ones had had themselves "dipped to wash away their taxes." [5] The criteria for determining who was a Baptist took on a new importance as this sudden growth in what had theretofore been a static and relatively innocuous minority began to threaten both the doctrinal and the financial stability of the established churches.

To meet the situation the General Court tightened the exemption laws, requiring in an Act of 1753 that a Baptist's certificate of faith and attendance was to be given by the minister of his church, as well as by two principal members, all of whom had to be vouched for in turn by three other Baptist churches. [6] The latter requirement, which had proved most

Baptists "who alledge a scruple of conscience" was continued and extended to taxes for the construction of meetinghouses, by Act of 4 July 1734, c. 6, §1, 2 A&R 714. The certificate provision for determining exemption was in *id.*, §2. It was superseded in 1753. See note 6 below. The 1734 act omitted the five-mile requirement, but provided that the exemption did not apply in "new towns." See text at note 9 below. This statute was re-enacted in virtually identical form by Act of 30 June 1740, c. 6, 2 A&R 1021, renewed until 1757 by Act of 29 June 1747, c. 6, 3 A&R 362. For the Baptists' account of the passage and implementation of all of this legislation, see Petition of a Committee of Baptists to the General Court, 29 May 1754, 4 A&R 122–126. See also Reed, *Church and State in Mass.* 132–135, 141–143.

[5] Quoted in Meyer, *Church and State in Mass.* 36. See also *id.* at 18; C. C. Goen, *Revivalism and Separatism in New England, 1740–1800* 213 (New Haven, 1962). Mr. Goen argues convincingly that this charge was largely unfounded, since in some communities even unquestioned Baptists were not able to take advantage of the exemption acts, and where this was not the case many Separates hesitated to become Baptists precisely because of the material advantage. Even the sources which he quotes, however, show that adoption of Baptist principles was urged by some "as the way God had opened to escape such sufferings [*i.e.* ministerial taxes]." *Id.* at 213–215. It is clear, however, that there were many other factors—doctrinal as well as practical—which influenced conversion. *Id.* at 208–257. As to the Great Awakening and its effect generally, see *id.* at 34–67, 206–207, 272–275, 285–287 and throughout; see also Meyer, *Church and State in Mass.* 20–47. For an example of a typical transition from Standing Church to Separate to Separate Baptist, see note 32 below.

[6] Act of 5 Jan. 1753, c. 15, §§1, 3, 3 A&R 644, quoted in part in note 28 below.

obnoxious to the Baptists, was eliminated in 1758 when a statute was enacted to replace all previous exemption acts for Baptists and Quakers, which had by then expired. The new measure carried forward the exemption in terms similar to those of previous acts, but provided that no person was to be "esteemed or accounted an Annabaptist" unless his name appeared on a list given to the assessors over the certificate of the minister and three principal members of his church to the effect that all those on the list were "really belonging thereto, that they verily believe them to be conscientiously of their perswasion, and that they do frequently and usually attend the publick worship in such church on the Lord's day." The first-quoted clause apparently added actual church membership to the requirements under earlier law.[7]

Since the assessors were often hostile toward those seeking exemption, these provisions produced much dispute and consequent litigation. A detailed study of this litigation based upon court records has yet to be made and cannot be undertaken here. Secondary sources and the documents in a few cases in which John Adams was involved indicate that the usual suit was one brought by the dissenting taxpayer against the town officials who had either collected the tax from him or had had his goods or body taken by way of distress. These suits seem to have turned principally on the questions whether the plaintiff's eligibility for exemption was made out by his certificate, and whether the certificate itself was executed in proper form. And procedural points, common to all litigation in Massachusetts, were often present to cloud the issue.[8]

[7] Act of 25 Jan. 1758, c. 20, §§1, 3, 4 A&R 67–68, renewed to 30 Jan. 1771 by Act of 31 Jan. 1761, c. 21, 4 A&R 420. As to the construction of this act, see note 8 below. The 1758 act did not contain the provisions of earlier measures (note 4 above) that those exempted should be deprived of the vote on church matters and that the exemption should not apply in new towns. As to the former, see No. 31, note 11. As to the latter, see text at note 10 below. Subsequent legislation carried forward the exemption and certificate provisions, with the major variation that a town could vote to exempt Baptists and Quakers without regard to certificates. See Act of 20 Nov. 1770, c. 10, 5 A&R 111; Act of 16 June 1774, c. 6, 5 A&R 392. For Baptist objections to the 1753 act, see Petition of 29 May 1754, 4 A&R 122–126, discussed in Goen, *Revivalism and Separatism* 270–271. Although the 1753 act's requirement of certification by other churches (text at note 6 above) was not carried forward by statute after 1758, the practice seems to have been continued. The Baptists of Haverhill in John White's case (note 8 below) submitted to the assessors not only the requisite certificate of their pastor and elders, but certificates of the First and Second Baptist churches of Boston and James Manning's Warren, R.I., church that the Haverhill church had been received as "Breathern and Sisters of the same Denomination," and that the pastor, Hezekiah Smith, was duly ordained and qualified. SF 131793.

[8] For a discussion of many of the cases from the viewpoint of an active Baptist participant in the struggle, see Isaac Backus, *A Church History of New England,* 2:239–265, 277–282 (Providence, R.I., 1784), a continuation of Backus' *A History of New England, With particular Reference to the Denomination of Christians called Baptists* (Boston, 1777). Volume 3 of this work, also entitled *A Church History of New England,* was published at Boston in 1796. See also Meyer, *Church and State in Mass.* 51–68. JA was a participant in one of the best known of these suits, White v. Bartlett. John White, "shopkeeper" of Haverhill, sued Enoch

No. 37. Green v. Washburn

Although larger questions of fundamental rights may have been raised in argument, these cases can hardly be said to have adjudicated any such

---

Bartlett and Jonathan Webster, the town assessors, in trespass for £30 damages, alleging that they had taken from him goods and chattels valued at £16 12s. 8d. White won on demurrer in the Inferior Court, Ipswich, in March 1767, and on appeal to the Superior Court under an agreement stipulating "The trial of this appeal to be final," won a verdict of £30 and costs at the Salem Nov. 1767 term. Min. Bk. 85, SCJ Essex, June 1767, N–11; Nov. 1767, C–19. White remitted £12 to the defendants, but they moved for a new trial on the grounds that the verdict was against law and the damages excessive. The new trial was granted, although the court, apparently paraphrasing English authority, noted that there were "Few new Tryals after a Tryal at Bar. Not to be taken out of the course of the Law." SF 131793. Min. Bk. 85, SCJ Essex, Nov. 1767, C–19; Nov. 1768, C–7. See No. 12. On the new trial at Ipswich in June 1769 it was stipulated by the parties that the issues were limited to the legality of the town's actions, "The sufficiency and legallity of the appellees Certificate in the case (it being agreed that the Certificate was given in to the assessors before the first assessment was voted) and whether the appellee was Conscientiously of the Anabaptist persuasion." SF 131793. With JA now appearing for White, the jury reversed the former judgment, awarding costs to the assessors. Min. Bk. 85, SCJ Essex, June 1769, C–3. Backus was incensed by this result, both on account of the technicality which was used to avoid the agreement that the first appeal would be final and by the fact that Baptists were not allowed to testify on grounds of interest. He reported that the ground for the decision was a ruling by the court that the law exempted only "a steady worshipper," not "a baptized church member," and that White's certificate did not state that he was the former. 2 Backus, *Church History* 241–242. Ezra Stiles, in a diary entry of 11 Jan. 1773, reported that in conversation Justice Peter Oliver of the Superior Court gave a slightly different reason: "By the old Law [*i.e.* pre-1770] the Baptists were to certifie themselves as to three things—that they were conscientiously Baptists—usual Attendants—and Members i.e. baptized by immersion and Communicants. Mr. Whites Certificate showed the two first, not the last; and for this Defect Judgment was given against him." 1 Stiles, *Literary Diary* 333. Oliver's version is borne out by the certificate of the pastor and elders of the Haverhill church that White and fourteen others "are conscientiously of our Persuasion and that they do frequently and usually attend the Publick Worship with us on the Lord's Day." SF 131793. That the content of the certificate was the issue, rather than the actual facts as to White's persuasion, is also suggested by the statutory language (text at note 7 above), which would seem to make the certificate conclusive. If the court found that it could look only to the certificate, despite the stipulation of the parties, then its ruling excluding the Baptists as witnesses may have been based merely on a finding that their evidence as to White's beliefs was immaterial. JA was of counsel in at least one other similar case. See Taft v. Cragin, Min. Bk. 101, SCJ Worcester, April 1774, C–3. SF 152818. He appeared for the assessors also in Follansbee v. Pearson, a case in which a Newburyport Presbyterian was successful in claiming an exemption under an order of the General Court dating from 1752 which expressly exempted members of his society from tax, there being no general statute covering Presbyterians. Min. Bk. 85, SCJ Essex, Nov. 1767, N–11; June 1768, C–12; June 1769, N–8; Nov. 1769, C–11. SF 131661, 131867. In at least two cases involving the tax on members of the Church of England (note 4 above), JA appeared for the church. Richmond v. Walker, Min. Bk. 84, SCJ Taunton, Oct. 1770, N–4. SF 145564 (plaintiff discontinued after jury impaneled); Bass v. Knight, Min. Bk. 93, SCJ Essex, June 1773, N–9; Min. Bk. 102, SCJ Essex, June 1774, C–21; Min. Bk. 108, SCJ Essex, June 1780, C–3. SF 92148, 132321, 132714 (verdict for assessors; on review continued after special verdict until neither party appears).

37

issues. The famous controversy concerning the Baptists of the town of Ashfield did seem to resolve more basic questions, but resolution took place on a level higher than that of the courts of the province. The earlier exemption acts had provided that the exemption should not "extend to new towns, granted upon condition of settling an orthodox minister and erecting a house for the public worship of God, till such time as those things are accomplished." [9] This provision was omitted from the 1758 exemption act, but since that statute applied to taxes levied in a "town, district, precinct, or parish," [10] the practice under the former act of denying exemption in unincorporated "plantations" was apparently continued. After the plantation of Huntstown was "erected into a town by the name of Ashfield" in 1765, indeed, the proprietors continued to assess ministerial taxes against all, regardless of religion.[11] When the Baptists sought legislative relief, they were met with a special act which only strengthened the proprietors' position, providing that the taxes should be levied against every part of each proprietor's right, "in whose hands soever the same may be," and that the lands of delinquents might be sold to pay the tax.[12]

[9] Act of 4 July 1734, c. 6, §5, 2 A&R 715. The provision was carried forward in re-enactments and renewals of this act cited in note 4 above.

[10] Act of 25 Jan. 1758, c. 20, §1, 4 A&R 67. See note 7 above. The Act of 4 July 1734, note 9 above, and its successors prior to the 1758 act applied to taxes levied on Baptists "in the town or place where they dwell."

[11] Act of 21 June 1765, c. 13, 4 A&R 815. §3 of this act provided "That all taxes already raised for settling a minister, or that may be raised for his support, for building a meeting house, clearing and repairing roads, be levied on the several proprietors of said plantation, according to their interests, until the further order of this [*i.e.* the General] court; and that said inhabitants and proprietors of said town proceed by the same rules, in levying and collecting said taxes, as proprietors in new plantations are obliged, by law, to observe." The last clause presumably refers to the Act of 19 June 1753, c. 1, §2, 3 A&R 670, which provided machinery for the proprietors of undivided lands to assess proportionally their individual shares for the purpose of raising funds "for bringing forward and compleating the settlement of such common lands . . . and for carrying on and managing any other affairs for the common good of such proprieties." That the proprietors considered this legislation a sufficient basis for taxing the Baptists and proceeded to do so appears in the complaints of the latter to the General Court in 1768 and 1769 set out in 4 A&R 1036–1037. A provision similar to that involved in the Ashfield controversy is found in other acts of incorporation passed at the same time. See Act of 21 June 1765, c. 14, 4 A&R 815 (Lanesborough); Act of 21 June 1765, c. 15, 4 A&R 816 (Charlmont).

[12] Act of 24 June 1768, c. 5, 4 A&R 1015. Although the proprietors had proceeded to levy taxes under the 1765 act of incorporation, note 11 above, they had been aware of its ambiguities, since in March 1767 they had petitioned the General Court, reciting that the provision for levying taxes was "a clause of great uncertainty" and praying for an act to remedy the consequent difficulties. These appear to have been at least three: (1) the lack of any express authority to tax the Baptists; (2) the fact that many provisions of the statute governing meetings of proprietors of undivided lands (note 11 above) did not apply to lands that were actually within a township and had been laid out; (3) the fact that the Act of 6 March 1762, c. 44, 4 A&R 532, detailing the machinery for levying against unimproved lands, had expired on 1 April 1765. The first problem was met by the statutory language quoted in the text. To resolve the second it was provided that

Despite more petitions, the Baptists' lands were sold in 1769 for non-payment of the tax. The conflict which then arose brought forth a full range of the kind of argument on religious toleration and human rights with which today such controversies are customarily clothed.[13] The General Court remained unmoved, but in 1771 the Ashfield Act came before the Privy Council and was disallowed. While the exact grounds of this decision are unknown, it in effect adopted a Board of Trade recommendation based on a broadly worded finding that "This Clause, whereby all persons of whatever sect or persuasion in religion, occupying Lands in this Township are equally and indiscriminately taxed for the support of the Independent Church therein established, is in our opinion equally unusual and unreasonable particularly in the case of the Sect commonly called the Antipedobaptists." [14]

Perhaps as important to the Baptist churches as the right of their membership to freedom from ministerial taxes was the right of their ministers to the privileges and immunities of the established clergy. An act of 1760 provided that no assessments could be levied for the support of a minister who did not have either a suitable formal education, or the testimony of a majority of the clergy in his county that his learning was sufficient.[15] Baptist ministers apparently both lacked the requisite learning and experienced great difficulty in obtaining the necessary support among

---

meetings were to be called in accordance with the Act of 25 March 1713, c. 9, 1 A&R 704, covering meetings of proprietors of common lands within a town, and that the provisions for levying and collecting taxes were applicable to lands "already laid out or agreed to be laid out." Finally, the machinery of the 1762 act was expressly adopted.

[13] See the various petitions and complaints of the Baptists in 1770 and 1771 in 4 A&R 1038–1045.

[14] The Representation of the Lords of Trade, 31 May 1771, is set out in 4 A&R 1016, and in slightly different form in 5 Acts, Privy Council (Col.) 323–324. For the decision itself, see ibid.; 4 A&R 1045. The memorial on which the Board of Trade acted asserted only that the Ashfield Act was contrary to the general exemption law, but the Board seems to have taken a broader position. It was not until 1774 that the complicated financial questions arising out of the Act's disallowance were resolved. See Act of 6 March 1773, c. 30, 5 A&R 228; Act of 9 March 1774, c. 24, 5 A&R 331. See also notes, 5 A&R 278–279, 371–375. On the controversy generally, see 2 Backus, Church History 246–261; Meyer, Church and State in Mass. 54–66. JA does not seem to have been directly involved in the dispute, but in 1774 as a member of the Continental Congress he felt the effects of the organized Baptist campaign for religious liberty of which the Ashfield matter was a part. Isaac Backus, James Manning, and other Baptist leaders, through the offices of Philadelphia Quakers, procured a meeting with the Massachusetts delegation at which the Ashfield case and other complaints were aired and the intolerance of the Massachusetts establishment was urged as an obstacle to colonial union. JA and his colleagues promised to have action taken on the matter at home, and the Massachusetts Provincial Congress accordingly resolved in favor of the Baptists. A committee of the General Court was appointed to bring in a bill, but the onset of revolution brought a postponement of such problems until after the end of hostilities. See 2 JA, Diary and Autobiography 152–154 and sources there cited; 3 id. at 311–313; Meyer, Church and State in Mass. 92–95.

[15] Act of 13 Feb. 1760, c. 24, 4 A&R 288, set out in part in note 27 below.

their Congregational counterparts. As a result, in one well-known case, even though the majority in the town of South Brimfield were Baptists, they were not allowed to apply their taxes to the support of a minister of their own persuasion.[16]

A further problem was the status of the ministers themselves as tax-payers. The annual acts which authorized the towns to assess and levy province, county, and town taxes exempted a long list of persons, including "settled ministers." In 1762, early in the Ashfield controversy, the town assessors, themselves Baptists, had applied this exemption to their minister, Ebenezer Smith. According to a later report by Smith and one of the assessors, a taxpayer complained to the Hampshire County Court of General Sessions that he had been "overrated." The assessors were summoned and on the trial in May 1762, the court "would not suffer [them] to bring any Proof of the said Ministers Settlement neither by Certificate nor by living Evidence and said that if they should prove his Ordination yet he should not be free paying Taxes. And in the Conclusion cast 4 pounds lawful Money Charges on the two Assessors," denying them an appeal to the Superior Court on the grounds that no appeal lay in such a case.[17]

These problems of ministerial status were at least partially resolved by *Green v. Washburn.* Nathaniel Green, pastor of what was known as the Second Baptist Church in Leicester, had been ordained a minister in October 1763, at which time he took charge of his congregation, which had gathered only the year before. Green's church first met in Spencer, but soon moved to the western part of Leicester. Perhaps because of its pastor's experiences, to be related, the church joined the newly formed Warren Association in 1768 and thus became part of the organized Separate Baptist movement for the attainment of religious liberty.[18]

[16] See 2 Backus, *Church History* 242–243. Compare 4 A&R 876. The minister involved was apparently James Mellen. 3 Backus, *Church History* 185.

[17] Memorial of Ebenezer Smith and Reuben Ellis [1768], 4 A&R 1037. See also 2 Backus, *Church History* 246–247; note 23 below. The statute affording relief for an "overrated" taxpayer provided that he might complain to the General Sessions and be reimbursed whatever amount he was entitled to, "with the charges" (presumably costs of court) to be paid "out of the town or parish treasury." The court had power "to require the assessors to produce the lists of their assessment." Act of 3 Oct. 1730, c. 1, §7, 2 A&R 551. It is not clear whether the "charges" adjudged against the assessors here were merely costs of court, or were a reimbursement of the tax, perhaps assessed against them by analogy to §6 of the Act, which provided that assessors "failing of their duty" should themselves pay the sums which they were to have assessed.

[18] As to the formation of Green's church, see note 32 below. Green (1721–1791) and his congregation moved again in 1772, this time to Charlton, where he remained pastor until his death. See generally 3 Backus, *Church History* 176; Estes, "Historical Discourse," in *The Greenville Baptist Church in Leicester, Massachusetts* 56–57 (Worcester, Mass., 1889); Emory Washburn, *Historical Sketches of the Town of Leicester* 114–115 (Boston, 1860). As to the Warren Association, see David Benedict, *A General History of the Baptist Denomination in America and Other Parts of the World* 469–470 (N.Y., 1848); Henry S. Burrage, *A History of the Baptists in New England* 80–85 (Phila., 1894); Goen, *Revivalism and Separatism* 272, 277–282.

No. 37. *Green v. Washburn*

In December 1767 when Seth Washburn and others, the assessors of Leicester, had levied the province, county, and town taxes upon Green, he had refused to pay. Accordingly, in February 1769, his body was taken in distress by the constable, and he was held in custody for several hours until he paid the tax. At the May 1769 Worcester Inferior Court, with John Worthington as his attorney, Green brought suit against Washburn and the other assessors in an action of the case, alleging that, knowing of his status as a settled minister, they had illegally assessed him, and had ultimately procured his arrest. Adams, for the assessors, entered a plea of not guilty, and the case went to trial.[19]

Adams' minutes of the trial (printed below) suggest that he relied largely on the language of Province statutes dealing with the ministry to define the term "settled minister" in the tax act. The earliest statutes could be read to mean that only those "able, learned and orthodox" ministers who had been approved by a majority of the voters in a town and were to be supported by all of the town's taxpayers were "settled." The act of 1760, already referred to, seemed to add the further requirement of education, or at least ministerial approval. In contrast, the only Act which dealt with the qualifications of a Baptist minister required that for him to certify members of his church to the tax assessors he need have only certificates attesting to his faith from three other Baptist churches.[20] James Putnam, who joined Adams, elaborated upon this theme in a brief but notable address which seemed to sum up all the contempt of the Harvard-bred establishment for the rude and argumentative religion of the Baptists.

Worthington, citing Locke, argued for a broader construction of the tax act, urging that it covered any man chosen by his flock as a minister. Witnesses testified as to Green's ordination and the size and continuing existence of his church. Despite other testimony apparently intended to show that, even among Baptists, Green's was merely a splinter group not entitled to recognition as a church, the jury brought in a verdict for the plaintiff of £2 and costs.[21] On appeal to the Superior Court in September 1769, with Adams no longer involved in the case, Green won again, although his recovery was reduced to £1 13s. 6 1/2d., the amount of the tax, and costs.[22]

[19] See the various warrants in the tax proceedings, the writ, and the pleadings in SF 152427.
[20] The statutes cited by JA appear in notes 25–28 below.
[21] The Inferior Court judgment is in SF 152427.
[22] Min. Bk. 90, SCJ Worcester, Sept. 1769, N–10. SCJ Rec. 1769, fol. 115. According to this source "Sewall" joined Putnam as counsel for the assessors in the Superior Court. While this might not be conclusive as to JA's participation in the argument, an examination of the rest of the cases heard at this term does not reveal his name as counsel in any of them, strongly suggesting that he did not even attend this session of court. An MS account of Baptist sufferings by John Davis states that on appeal to the Superior Court "it went in Greens favor there also and they allowed him Costs, all that it had cost him; that is, what Mony he had expend in the Law, and lawful Cost. The Jury did not go out—because the Judges advise Green to settle it. Green says it cost him 20 Dollars more than what he was allowed—beside all his Travelling for Witnesses—to prove himself a Minister." Isaac Backus Papers,

If no great constitutional pronouncement came out of this case, the principle which it announced was nevertheless considered an important one. In his *Church History of New England*, Isaac Backus, a leading figure in the Warren Association and a participant in many such battles, capped his account of the storms of the 1760's by reporting that "one thing that gave check to oppression was a determination of authority, that the ministers of the Baptist Churches were lawful ministers, so as to have a right to marry people, and to be exempted from civil taxes." This "determination" took place in two Superior Court decisions, one of which was *Green v. Washburn.*[23]

ADAMS' MINUTES OF THE TRIAL[24]

Worcester Inferior Court, Worcester, May 1769

Prov. Law. 16.[25] 33.[26] 386.[27] Temp[orary] Laws. About Certificates for Anabaptist Ministers and People,[28] to be used in the Case following of

Andover Newton Theological School, Newton Center, Mass., on temporary loan to RPB. As to Davis, an important figure in the Warren Association and a member of the American Philosophical Society, see 2 Backus, *Church History* 275–276.

The Warren Association (note 18 above) on 12 Sept. 1769 "Voted to give a Certificate acknowledging that he is regular, and in Fellowship to Rev. Nathaniel Green, to be made use of at the Superior Court at Worcester." MS Minutes, p. 3, Backus Papers. No such document appears in the Superior Court file of the case. SF 152427. The editors are indebted to Prof. William G. McLoughlin of Brown University for these and subsequent references to the Backus Papers, as well as for his invaluable aid in plumbing various ecclesiastical mysteries.

[28] 2 Backus, *Church History* 263. Backus did not positively identify the cases in his printed history, but in a draft of the work, discussing the case of Ebenezer Smith of Ashfield (note 17 above), he said "And though they assert that Mr. Smith is not a minister in law, yet the honorable justices of our Superior court, by their decisions in two parallel cases, have made them know that therein they did not speak the truth: and consequently that it was a violation of law and equity, to punish the baptists assessors in 1762, for allowing him the privileges of such an one." Backus subjoined a footnote identifying the "two parallel cases" as "The case of elder Green of Charlton, and of elder Clark of Wilbaham, the last of which was decided in the court of Northampton near the close of this year [1771]." 2 Backus, Church History (MS—preliminary draft) 248, Backus Papers.

[24] In JA's hand. Adams Papers, Microfilms, Reel No. 185. For the dating, see note 22 above.

[25] The Act of 4 Nov. 1692, *Acts and Laws, Of His Majesty's Province of the Massachusetts Bay in New-England* 16 (Boston, 1759); c. 26, §1, 1 A&R 62, provided "That the inhabitants of each town within this province, shall take due care, from time to time, to be constantly provided of an able, learned orthodox minister or ministers, of good conversation, to dispense the Word of God to them; which minister or ministers shall be suitably encouraged and sufficiently supported and maintained by the inhabitants of such town." The remainder of this section dealt with contracts for the "settlement or maintenance" of ministers and schoolmasters, giving the court of quarter sessions power to oversee such contracts. Under §2, if "any town shall be destitute of a minister qualified as aforesaid, and shall so con-

No. 37. Green v. Washburn

Green vs. Washburn et als.

Worth[ington].[29] All wise States have seen the Necessity of some Religion for the Support of Society.

---

tinue by the space of six months, not having taken due care for the procuring, setling and encouragement of such minister," the Court of Sessions was to order the town to take the necessary steps, or in default, the court was to "take effectual care to procure and settle a minister qualified as aforesaid." §4 provided "That every minister, being a person of good conversation, able, learned and orthodox, that shall be chosen by the major part of the inhabitants in any town, at a town meeting duly warned for that purpose . . . shall be the minister of such town; and the whole town shall be obliged to pay towards his settlement and maintenance, each man his several proportion thereof." §5 required the "settlement and maintenance" of schoolmasters. See, generally, text at note 2 above.

[26] The Act of 17 Feb. 1693, *Acts and Laws* 33 (1759); c. 46, §8, 1 A&R 102–103, repealed §4 of the Act of 1692, note 2 above, providing instead [§9], "that each respective gathered church in any town or place within this province, that at any time shall be in want of a minister, such church shall have power, according to the directions given in the word of God, to choose their own minister. And the major part of such inhabitants [*i.e.* of the town or place] as do there usually attend on the publick worship of God, and are by law duly qualified for voting in town affairs, concurring with the churche's act, the person thus elected and approved, accepting thereof and settling with them, shall be the minister; toward whose settlement and maintenance all the inhabitants, and rateable estates lying within such town, or part of a town, or place limited by law for upholding the publick worship of God, shall be obliged to pay in proportion." Under §10 the inhabitants of a place where there was no church might by majority vote at a town meeting, "with the advice of three neighbouring ordained ministers . . . choose and call an orthodox, learned and pious person to dispense the word of God unto them, to the settlement and maintenance of which minister all rateable estates and inhabitants within such town or place shall be assessed and pay proportionably." See, generally, text at note 2 above.

[27] Act of 13 Feb. 1760, *Acts and Laws* 386 (1759); c. 24, 4 A&R 288: "[I]t shall not be lawful for any town, district, precinct or parish to assess the inhabitants thereof for or towards the support or maintenance of any person who shall be hereafter called to or settled in the work of the gospel ministry in such town, district, precinct or parish, unless such person shall have been educated at some university, college, or publick academy for the instruction of youth in the learned languages, and in the arts and sciences; or shall have received a degree from some university, college, or such publick academy; or shall have obtained testimonials under the hands of the major part of the settled ministers of the gospel in the county where such town, district, precinct or parish shall lie, that they apprehend him, the said person being a candidate for the gospel ministry, to be of sufficient learning to qualify him for the work of such ministry." See, generally, text at note 15 above.

[28] JA probably cites the Act of 5 Jan. 1753, c. 15, § 1, 3 A&R 644, relieving such Anabaptists of taxes for the support of the ministry as should be either upon the assessors' lists, "or such as shall produce a certificate, under the hands of the minister and of two principal members of such church, setting forth that they conscienciously believe such person or persons to be of their perwasion and that he or they usually and frequently attend the publick worship in such church on Lord's days." In §2 it was provided "That no minister, nor the members of any Annabaptist church as aforesaid, shall be esteemed qualified to give such certificate as aforesaid other than such as shall have obtained from three other churches commonly called Annabaptists, in this or the neighbouring provinces, a certificate from each respectively, that they esteem such church to be one of their denomination, and that they conscientiously

The Happiness of Brit[ish] dominions that an order of Men. *The Romans and Grecians would have thought themselves happy if they had had such an order of Men.*

All Ministers are exempted. By the annual Tax Act.[30]

Mr. Locks Defin[ition] of a Ch[urc]h. Ecclesia. A Number of Persons met to worship God.[31] And that Man they choose for their Head shall be their Minister. He thinks him self as orthodox as any.

A Number of People, whether they disliked their former Ministers. About 50 Men and Women agreed to meet. An Anabaptist Church and an Anabaptist Minister.

Witnesses.

Mr. Streeter. About 50 when called. 100 now. 7 male members. About as many females. In Octr. the ordination 1763. The Church unanimous. Not certain whether the Congregation voted. They belonged to Leicester, Spencer and Charlton.[32] Green was a Mason by Trade.

---

believe them to be Annabaptists." This act expired of its own force in 1758 (*id.* §3), and was not renewed, although its provisions were apparently still observed. See text and notes 6 and 7 above.

[29] John Worthington, counsel for Green.

[30] The statute under which the tax in suit was levied was the Act of 23 June 1767, c. 8, §2, 4 A&R 971, which provided that the Province Treasurer should require the selectmen and assessors of each town "To assess all rateable polls above the age of sixteen years ... (excepting the governor, lieutenant-governor and their families, the president, fellows, professors, Hebrew instructor and students of Harvard College, settled ministers and grammar-school masters, who are hereby exempted as well from being taxed for their polls, as their estates being in their own hands, and under their actual management and improvement; as also the estate pertaining to Harvard College)."

[31] Probably a reference to this well-known passage in John Locke's first "Letter Concerning Toleration" (1689): "Let us now consider what a church is. 'A church then, I take to be a voluntary society of men, joining themselves together of their own accord, in order to the publick worshipping of God, in such a manner as they judge acceptable to him, and effectual to the salvation of their souls. . . . A church, then, is a society of members, voluntarily uniting.'" John Locke, *Works,* 2:253–254 (London, 4th edn., 1740). See Anson Phelps Stokes, *Church and State in the United States,* 1:143 (N.Y., 1950).

[32] See the account of the church's founding given by John Davis in his Journal: "Their Constitut[ion] was in [the] year 1762. 13th of July: when a Number of persons, having upon Conversat[ion], found they were of the same opinion in matters of Religion: and agreed to incorporate into a Church.

"In the year 1749 a Number of persons separated from the Standing Church, for 3 Reasons: 1. a Dislike to the Church Constitution. 2. The Manner of Supporting the gospel. 3 Manner of preaching. After they separated they continued in what is called the Separate Order for sometime, but in the same year gathered into a Church, upon what they Call Large Communion: that is mixt Communion.

"In 1762 Nathl. Green, and others separated from the Separates, having been baptized some time before; Green was baptized in Sturbridge by Blunt. Blunt re-

Mr. Alden.[33] Mr. Green came to a general Meeting of the united Churches of the Anabaptist order. Mr. Stillman's Church was not then one. Mr. Mannings of Prov[idence] was not then.[34] We examined him, found him Sound in Principle, and of regular Conduct. We went and read certain Rules.

We were sent to afterwards, and after being formed into a Council, and Enquiry after their Covenant &c., We ordaind him.[35]

---

canted his own Baptism. And the same year, 1762, Mr. Green and others, from Leicester, Spencer, and Charlton became a baptist Church as aforesaid.

"Their Number in Ch[ristiani]ty was 6: who were Joined in a short time by 8 or 10 more. The names of the 6 were, Nathl. Green, Jno. Hill, and Jno. Hill Junr., Dorothy Shaw, Mary Hill, the wife of John Hill Junr. and Dorothy Shaw, Daughter of Dorothy Shaw. In Decem. 10th 1762 the Church called Nathl. Green to the Exercise of his ministerial gifts. He accepted the call, and continued the preacher alone in this Church—on tryal, till 13 of July 1763, when He gave the answer to the call—And was ordain'd their Pastor on the 12 of October 1763.

"Mr. Green had great Difficulties in the Separate Church, [in?] endeavouring to suppress the Strange Spirit of the Separates: and this determined his Leaving the Separates." Journal of John Davis, 27 April 1771, Backus Papers.

See also 3 Backus, *Church History* 176. Rev. John Blunt, pastor at Sturbridge from 1749 to 1752, renounced his Baptism and became a Separate in the latter year. See Goen, *Revivalism and Separatism* 103, 224–225. It has been said that Nathaniel Green's church was formed "by the dismission of several members" from Thomas Green's Leicester church (note 37 below). See Estes, "Historical Discourse" 55–56. There is no evidence of this, but it is possible that some members of Thomas Green's congregation did join Nathaniel at some point, since there seem to have been doctrinal differences between the two churches. See note 39 below.

[33] The witness was probably Rev. Noah Alden, pastor of the Separate Baptist Church at Stafford, Conn., from 1754 until 1766, when he was called to the First Baptist Church of Bellingham, Mass. In 1767 Alden's Bellingham church became one of the initial members of the Warren Association. See Benedict, *General History* 416–417, 469; Goen, *Revivalism and Separatism* 228, 308; George F. Partridge, *History of the Town of Bellingham, Massachusetts, 1719–1919* 107–113, 132–136 (Bellingham, 1919). According to a contemporary record, Alden and Nathaniel Green were both pallbearers at the funeral of Rev. Thomas Green of the First Baptist Church of Leicester (note 37 below) in 1773. Estes, "Historical Discourse" 37 note.

[34] Samuel Stillman (1738–1807) accepted the pastorate of the First Baptist Church of Boston in Nov. 1764. James Manning (1738–1791), first president of Rhode Island College (now Brown University) and a leader in the Baptists' struggles, took a church at Warren, R.I., in the same year, moving to Providence only in 1770. DAB; Burrage, *History of the Baptists* 75–76, 98. Probably the witness' placing Manning in Providence in 1769 is a mere slip. For JA's contact with Manning, see note 14 above. The organization to which Stillman and Manning are characterized as not belonging is presumably an association of about eight Baptist churches, formed in 1763, which included Alden's Stafford, Conn., church (note 33 above) and Wightman Jacobs' Thompson, Conn., church (note 36 below). See 3 Backus, *Church History* 261; Elder Charles Train, Sermon, 31 Dec. 1826, in 7 *American Baptist Magazine* (n.s.) 153–154 (1827), a reference supplied by Professor McLoughlin. This group seems to have expired in 1767 with the founding of the Warren Association, in which Manning was instrumental, and which Stillman's church had joined in 1768. See note 18 above; note 39 below.

[35] Ordinarily when a church wished to have a minister ordained, it called a council of ministers to carry out the task. The ministers would first examine the candidate

Mr. Jacob. Of Killingsley. The Elder 18 Years.[36]

Hall. Dont work much, reads Bible and Annotations &c. 2 exempted.

Mr. Alden and Mr. Jacobs broke fellowship with the Church I belonged to, and were formerly dealt with for so doing. Mr. Green, I understand, preaches in Charlton.

Dr. Greens Society and Mr. Southgates, are in Leicester. Strict Communion, and Strict Principles.[37] Mr. Alden said He thought he missed it in giving the Charge he did to Mr. Green.

Mr. Putnam.[38] Some Learning is necessary. Learning comes not by Inspiration, great Labour and study is necessary. The Law could not intend that every Man who shall start up, should be a Minister. He is learned in his Trade no doubt, and may understand his Bible, well eno' to secure his own Salvation. But he is wrong in leading People

---

as to his beliefs and then perform the actual service of ordination. Goen, *Revivalism and Separatism* 168. The council called in Green's case seems to have already examined him informally on his appearance at the association meeting, although a formal examination may also have been held at the time of the ordination. The council apparently had the further duty of approving the organization of Green's church, which was newly formed. See note 32 above.

[36] Presumably Rev. Wightman (or Whitman) Jacobs, Pastor of the Baptist Church in Thompson, Conn. (once part of Killingly) from 1750 to 1769, when he followed many members of his congregation to Royalston, Mass., after a doctrinal split in Thompson. See 3 Backus, *Church History* 178, 261; Lilley B. Caswell, *History of the Town of Royalston, Massachusetts* 65–68, 324–325 (Royalston, 1917). The Thompson church was one of those belonging to the association by which Green was examined. See notes 34 above, 39 below.

[37] "Dr. Green" is not the plaintiff here, but Rev. Thomas Green (1699–1773), pastor of the First Baptist Church in Leicester, who was actually a medical doctor. See Estes, "Historical Discourse" 31–38. "Mr. Southgate" is undoubtedly Elder Richard Southgate (1714–1798), who preached to a Baptist society in Leicester which "was never organized as a corporate religious society; and, after the death of Elder Southgate, seems to have been merged in other societies." Washburn, *Historical Sketches of Leicester* 115. "Strict Communion," apparently the doctrine of these two societies, was the principle that no one should be admitted to communion who had not been baptized as an adult by total immersion. Opposed to it was "mixed communion," under which those baptized by sprinkling in infancy were also admitted. The difference was a major cause of dissension among Separates and Baptists. See Goen, *Revivalism and Separatism* 229–232, 258–264. Compare note 32 above. "Strict Principles" perhaps means strict adherence to Calvinism. Thomas Green's church, of which he had been pastor since its founding in 1738, was strongly Calvinistic. He was apparently on good terms with the Leicester Congregationalists; the town had remitted his taxes in 1741. See Estes, "Historical Discourse" 22, 36; Goen, *Revivalism and Separatism* 237. The evidence thus seems calculated to cast doubt on Nathaniel Green's bona fides as a minister.

[38] James Putnam, counsel for Washburn. For views similar to those here expressed by Putnam, see Petition of the Ashfield Proprietors, 27 March 1771, 4 A&R 1039–1043.

off from their legal Pastors, and forming Seperations. He seperates for trifles, I cant think 'em essential. He cant communicate with them, because they dont insist on the Formality of laying on Hands.[39] One Motive why he became a Preacher, might be, because he did not love to work.

[39] The doctrine that laying on of hands was a condition precedent to communion was adhered to by most of the General Baptist churches, which were strongest in Rhode Island and Connecticut and were known as "Six Principle" churches, this being in effect the sixth principle. The Calvinistic Particular Baptists of the Middle Atlantic states and most of the Separate Baptists of New England, including James Manning (originally a Philadelphian) and Isaac Backus, leaders of the Warren Association, rejected the doctrine. See Goen, *Revivalism and Separatism* 272 note; Burrage, *History of the Baptists* 27–30, 80–81; 3 Backus, *Church History* 59; Isaac Backus, A History of the Warren Association in New England, from its first formation to the present time (MS) 108, Backus Papers; Benedict, *General History* 453–454; Richard C. Knight, *History of the General or Six Principle Baptists* 100 and throughout (Providence, 1826) (the editors are indebted to Professor McLoughlin for the last three references). According to Backus, the association of Rhode Island and Connecticut churches which Green joined in 1763 (note 34 above), although presumably Calvinistic, was founded upon the principle of "the laying on of hands upon every member as a term of communion . . . but in two years after the most of them gave up that bar of communion, of whom Mr. Jacobs [Wightman Jacobs, note 36 above] was one." 3 Backus, *Church History* 261. The association seems to have broken up thereafter over this issue. Both Jacobs and Noah Alden moved to Massachusetts at this point and took churches which joined the Warren Association (note 18 above). Since Green also joined the Warren Association in 1768, it seems probable that all three had been among those members of the earlier association who "gave up that bar" of laying on of hands. If this is so, Putnam's statement is inaccurate as of the time of the trial, but probably it correctly describes the circumstances which led to the foundation of Green's church. Holding this belief, Green could not "communicate" (*i.e.* be in fellowship) with either the Standing Church or the Separate Church, from both of which he had separated (note 32 above). In all probability, his position would also have prevented him from "communicating" with Thomas Green's Leicester Baptist church as well. If Thomas Green were a Calvinist of "Strict Principles" (note 37 above) it is unlikely that he accepted what was essentially an Arminian doctrine. Moreover, in the church at Sutton, of which Thomas had been co-pastor before the foundation of his Leicester church, "Laying on of hands was left indifferent. Some were and some were not under h[an]ds." Journal of John Davis, 27 April 1771, Backus Papers. See also Estes, "Historical Discourse" 17–19. Thus, Putnam's point seems to be that, if it were not for this doctrinal "trifle," Nathaniel Green need never have formed his own church at all.

L. *Slavery*

EDITORIAL NOTE

"I was concerned in several Causes in which Negroes sued for their Freedom before the Revolution," Adams wrote in 1795. "The Arguments in Favour of their Liberty were much the same as have been urged since in Pamphlets and Newspapers, in Debates in Parliament &c. arising from the Rights of Mankind. . . . I never knew a Jury by a Verdict, to determine a Negro to be a Slave. They always found them free." [1]

The documentation of Adams' "slave cases" bears out his recollection, but not entirely. His minutes suggest that counsel for the slaves argued as much from precedent as from Enlightenment; and the court records show that in at least one case, *Newport v. Billing*, No. 39, the jury found the plaintiff to be a slave. It is curious that Adams should have forgotten that cause, because he was there, as in at least three other cases, of counsel for the putative master.

All the cases date from 1766 or later.[2] In that year, Adams witnessed the trial of *Slew v. Whipple*, No. 38, the first he had actually seen, although

---

[1] JA to Dr. Jeremy Belknap, 21 March 1795. MHi:Belknap Papers.

[2] JA had considered the problem tangentially some years earlier. In Feb. 1760, Jonathan Sewall wrote him: "A Man by Will gives his Negro his Liberty, and leave's him a Legacy. The Executor consents that the Negro shall be free, but refuseth to give Bond to the Selectmen to indemnify the Town against any Charge for his Support, in case he should become poor (without which, by the Province Law [see No. 39, note 5] he is not manumitted) or to pay him the Legacy. *Query*. Can he recover the Legacy, and how?"

JA replied: "The Testator intended plainly that his Negro should have his Liberty, and a Legacy. Therefore the Law will presume that he intended his Executor should do all that, without which he could have neither. That this Indemnification was not in the Testator's mind, cannot be proved from the Will. . . . I take it therefore, that the Executor of this Will, is by implication obliged to give Bonds to the Town Treasurer, and in his Refusal is a Wrongdoer and I cant think he ought to be allowed to take Advantage of his own Wrong so much as to alledge this Want of an Indemnification, to evade an Action of the Case brot for the Legacy, by the Negro himself. But why may not the Negro bring a Special Action of the Case against Executor, setting forth the Will, the Devise of Freedom, and a Legacy, and then the Necessity of Indemnification by the Province Law, and then a Refusal to indemnify and of Consequence to set free, and to pay the Legacy? Perhaps the Negro is free at common Law by the Devise. Now the Province Law seems to have been made, only to oblige the Master to maintain his manumitted ⟨slave⟩ servant, not to declare a Manumission, in the Master's Lifetime or at his Death, void. Should a Master give his Negro his freedom, under his Hand and seal, without giving Bond to the Town, and should afterwards repent and endeavor to recall the Negro into servitude, would not that instrument be a sufficient discharge against the Master?" Sewall to JA, 13 Feb. 1760; JA to Sewall, Dft, Feb. 1760; both in Adams Papers.

48

he had "heard there have been many." [3] Did the accelerated tensions of the Revolutionary movement encourage such suits? Would abolitionist pressure have developed anyway? These questions must be answered elsewhere.[4]

The cases do provide some basis for generalization. That such problems were taken to court for disposition in civil suits emphasizes the settled state of Massachusetts society at the time. A suit for trespass to the person is an exceptionally sophisticated way of testing an issue which could have been determined either by force or by flight.

It is significant that each plaintiff sought to justify his or her freedom as much on evidentiary grounds as on grounds of policy or the rights of man. As Putnam put it in *Newport v. Billing*, "Point in issue, Slave or not?" That point arose differently in different cases, depending on the twists the pleadings took and on the facts of each Negro's condition. With the exception of *Margaret v. Muzzy*, No. 40, the declarations sounded in trespass and the relief sought was damages for false imprisonment. "Freedom" was thus determined only as an incident of the right to maintain the action, much as title was tried in trespass to chattels. The form of action set the procedural frame of the case, but the facts determined counsel's pleading strategy.

In *Slew v. Whipple*, the initial skirmish centered on an attempt to abate the writ because the plaintiff had styled herself therein as a spinster. Adams' notes are cryptic, but it appears that counsel for the master argued that plaintiff's previous marriages, apparently to Negroes, had been valid, that "Jenny Slew, spinster," did not exist, and that her writ must accordingly fail. A divided court rejected that effort. The trial on the merits went forward. Here the plaintiff's case was that, although her father had been a Negro, her mother had been white; the plaintiff, therefore, ought to be a free woman. The defense was only that the plaintiff had never proved her possession of her liberty; the defendant did not or could not introduce affirmative evidence of plaintiff's slave status. The jury thereupon awarded £4 damages and costs to Jenny.[5]

In *Newport v. Billing*, apparently the first slave case in which Adams actually participated, the defendant's position was stronger. To the declaration in trespass he responded that he had purchased the plaintiff and that the plaintiff was "his own proper Negro slave." The plaintiff replied that he was "a freeman," and the burden shifted to the defendant, who put in

[3] I JA, *Diary and Autobiography* 321. No earlier suits for liberty have yet been identified, although Benjamin Kent and Judge Cushing in No. 38, referred to previous actions, as did Adams in No. 41, Doc. IV. In 1764, a Middlesex grand jury had indicted Joseph Collins and two others for forcibly taking and selling for a slave one William Benson, a free Negro, almost two years after Benson was sold to Collins. The defendants pleaded *nolo contendere*; because they had bought Benson back and freed him, the court merely imposed nominal fines. SF 147284; Min. Bk. 78; SCJ Rec. 1764–1765, fol. 155.

[4] Belknap attributed the succession of actions to publication of a "pamphlet containing the case of a negro who had accompanied his master from the West Indies to England, and had there sued for and obtained his freedom." 4 MHS, *Colls.* (1st ser.) 201 (1795–1835).

[5] SCJ Rec. 1766–1767, fol. 175; SF 131426.

evidence a bill of sale. He also argued that a Negro should be presumed to be a slave. The plaintiff urged the insufficiency of the documentary and the racial proof. Nonetheless, the jury found that Newport "was not a freeman as he alledged but the proper slave of" the defendant, and so denied him damages.[6]

Margaret v. Muzzy offered a procedural variation. Because Adams did not enter the case until late, on behalf of defendants, and because his papers contain no notes or minutes, we cannot tell why plaintiff chose to replevy herself out of defendant's possession on a writ *de homine replegiando,* or personal replevin. Once the action commenced, it proceeded as though the form were trespass; defendant pleaded not guilty and the matter went to the jury, which found for plaintiff.[7] The result was the same on the appeal and upon a writ of review.[8] The judgment in this case actually resulted in Margaret's freedom, since the plaintiff sought "possession" of her own person rather than damages.

There are no Adams minutes of *Watson v. Caesar* (May 1771) (not included here), another trespass action, but the Suffolk Files contain enough depositions and documents to disclose the story. Caesar had been a slave of Elkanah Watson of Plymouth and somehow came into the possession of the Chevalier de Drucour, a Captain in the French Navy. At Louisbourg on 1 July 1758 the Chevalier gave him his freedom and a certificate to prove it. Caesar returned to Plymouth on the sloop *Sally,* some of whose people were later to give conflicting depositions about his representations of this status, and then re-entered Watson's service.

Twelve and a half years afterward, Caesar demanded his freedom. "I am very willing he should have it," Watson wrote to Benjamin Kent, Caesar's attorney, "and should have been as willing 10 years ago or when he first came home had he ever asked me for it, or if I had ever known he had a paper." Whether Watson changed his mind, or whether they could not agree on the amount that Caesar was to be allowed for his services, Caesar commenced his action against Watson in the Plymouth Inferior Court. In April 1771, on a plea of not guilty, the jury found for Caesar. At Plymouth Superior Court in May, where Adams appeared for Watson, the jury affirmed the lower court's verdict, awarding Caesar nominal damages of 6d.[9]

---

[6] SCJ Rec. 1767–1768, fol. 284; SF 157509; 3 JA, *Diary and Autobiography* 289.

[7] "In a *Homine replegiando* the Defendant claims the Plaintiff for his Villain, and the Plaintiff pleads that he is free, and saith that the Defendant hath taken his Goods, and prays that he may gage [give] Deliverance, &c. for which the Defendant doth gage Deliverance. . . . But in a *Homine replegiando,* if the Defendant claim the Plaintiff as his Villain, the Plaintiff ought to find Sureties to deliver his Body to the Defendant, if he be found his Villain." Fitzherbert, *New Natura Brevium* 154 (1755). Compare the return on the writ in No. 40, SCJ Rec. 1768, fol. 311; SCJ Rec. 1770, fol. 216; SF 147651, 147830.

[8] See Lynde, *Diary* 200 (1 Nov. 1770): "Tryal of Manumission of Margaret, a mulatto woman"; see also Quincy, *Reports* 30–31.

[9] SCJ Rec. 1771, fol. 51; SF 142381.

Adams' last known slave case, *Caesar v. Taylor*, No. 41,[10] involved another Caesar. It appears from the documents that Taylor, Adams' client, had sold Caesar to a third party, despite an agreement that he was to be permitted to buy his freedom from Taylor. After the jury at the Newbury-port Inferior Court in September 1771 had found for Caesar (Document I), Taylor appealed. Adams, participating in the litigation for the first time, sought at the November 1771 Salem Superior Court to introduce in evidence a bill of sale from one Edward Hircom to Taylor (Document II). Plaintiff's counsel (John Lowell and Nathaniel Sargeant) objected, on the ground that defendant's plea of the general issue ("non culpabilis," or "not guilty") precluded his introducing special evidence. This was the common law rule, but the court took the matter under advisement.[11] Other minutes of the argument (Documents III and IV) indicate that plaintiff also raised evidentiary points at this time. First, he put in evidence of Taylor's agreement to sell Caesar his freedom. Second, he prevailed on his offer of evidence that Taylor's vendees had beaten Caesar, the court agreeing that the beating was what today we would call the proximate result of the initial tort, the illegal sale. Finally, plaintiff tried to convince the judges that the woman known as his wife was competent to testify; the common law rule went the other way, however, and so did the court, despite plaintiff's argument that Negroes could not legally marry and that therefore the woman was not really his wife.

At the Ipswich Superior Court in June 1772 (Document V), the court decided that a plea of the general issue barred special evidence, the new judges, Ropes and Cushing, who had been appointed since the argument, giving no opinion. Adams moved for leave to replead, which motion the court denied and brought the case on for trial. Here once again plaintiff tried unsuccessfully to have his wife testify, and Adams sought (apparently with equal lack of success) to mitigate damages by putting in evidence of Caesar's reputation as a slave. The case then went to the jury, which found in Caesar's favor in the amount of £5 13s. 4d. damages and £24 7s. 2d. costs.[12]

The final case in this collection, *Caesar v. Greenleaf*, No. 42, does not appear to be an Adams case, although the document here printed appears in the Wetmore Notes in the Adams Papers, and dates from the October 1773 Inferior Court at Newburyport. The declaration alleged trespass to which defendant pleaded not guilty, the general issue. However, to avoid the procedural cul-de-sac (or "non cul"-de-sac) which had bound Adams in *Caesar v. Taylor*, defendant's counsel here (Daniel Farnham) induced the other side (John Lowell) to stipulate that evidence of special matter would be admissible. Notwithstanding, the report does not indicate what

[10] SF 132190.

[11] See 1 Chitty, *Pleading* 491–493. On the continuance, see Min. Bk. 93, SCJ Essex, Nov. 1771, N–3. A note in the Adams Papers in JA's hand shows that he received "13s: 4d" for his services "at Salem Court 1771." Adams Papers, Microfilms, Reel No. 185.

[12] Min. Bk. 93, SCJ Essex, June 1772, C–15; SCJ Rec. 1772, fol. 91.

if any other evidence was introduced. It seems that the jury found for the plaintiff £18 damages and costs, and that there was no appeal.[13]

These cases represent only some of the "suits for liberty" which were being brought by Negroes in the years just preceding the Revolution.[14] They suggest substantial acceptance of the institution of slavery by all except perhaps its victims. It was not until the Massachusetts Constitution of 1780 and Judge William Cushing's construction of its "free and equal" clause as a prohibition of slavery in *Quock Walker's Case* (1783) that there was even a firm legal basis for manumission when on the facts the plaintiff was clearly a slave. The subsequent history of slavery indicates that it was many years after this before any substantial portion of the people of Massachusetts were ready to mount either legal or moral attacks on the institution.[15] Adams seems to have seen in recollection rather more in his early slavery cases than the records disclose.

38. Slew v. Whipple

1766

I. ADAMS' COPY OF THE DECLARATION, AND REPORT [1]

Essex Superior Court, Salem, November 1766

Essex Ss. Novr. 1766. Sup[erio]r C[our]t.

Jenny Slew of Ipswich in the County of Essex Spinster Plaintiff vs. John Whipple Jnr. of said Ipswich Gentleman, Defendant, in a Plea of Trespass, for that the said John upon the 29th January 1762 at Ipswich aforesaid, with Force and Arms, took her the said Jenny, held and kept her in servitude as a Slave, in his service, and has restrain'd her of her Liberty from that Time to the fifth of March last, without any lawful Authority or Right so to do, and did her other Injuries against the Peace, and to the Damage of the said Jenny Slew as she saith, £25.

[13] See George H. Moore, *Notes on the History of Slavery in Massachusetts* 118 (N.Y., 1866); 2 Dane, *Abridgment* 426; Joshua Coffin, *A Sketch of the History of Newbury, Newburyport, and West Newbury* 241, 339 (Boston, 1845).

[14] See Moore, *Slavery in Massachusetts* 112–121; 2 Dane, *Abridgment* 426–427; Lorenzo J. Greene, *The Negro in Colonial New England 1620–1776* 182 (N.Y., 1942).

[15] See Cushing, "The Cushing Court and the Abolition of Slavery in Massachusetts: More Notes on the 'Quock Walker Case,'" 5 *Am. Jour. Legal Hist.* 118, 131–139 (1961). The judge was the same Cushing who had sat silent in Caesar v. Taylor. Text at note 12 above.

[1] In JA's hand. Adams Papers, Microfilm, Reel No. 185. This document is in the same leaflet with Doc. II, but on a separate page. Because it repeats some of JA's minutes, it may have been written later, perhaps with a view to inclusion in a collection of forms or pleadings.

No. 38. Slew v. Whipple

Defendant pleaded, that there is no such Person in Nature as Jenny Slew of Ipswich aforesaid Spinster and this the said John is ready to verify, wherefore he prays Judgment &c.

Evidence was that she was originally called Jenny Slew, but that she had been severally Times married to slaves &c.

Writ did not abate. 2 Judges for Abatement and 2 against it. So being divided could not abate.[2]

II. ADAMS' MINUTES OF THE ARGUMENT[3]

Essex Superior Court, Salem, November 1766

Slew vs. Whipple.

Gridley. Marriage is of the Law of Nations. Justinian extends it, even to the Brutes.[4]

[2] Thomas Hutchinson, Chief Justice, and Chambers Russell were the members of the court not mentioned in JA's minute (Doc. II). But Russell was at the time of this trial out of Massachusetts; he left the Province on 16 Oct. 1766 and died in Guilford, England, 24 November. 9 Sibley-Shipton, *Harvard Graduates* 86–87. It would seem that Hutchinson, C.J., and Lynde, J., favored abatement and Oliver and Cushing, JJ., opposed.

[3] In JA's hand; a fragment only. Adams Papers, Microfilms, Reel No. 185.

[4] Jeremiah Gridley, of counsel for defendant. "Natural Law is that which nature has taught to all animals, for this law is not peculiar to the human race, but applies to all creatures which originate in the air, or the earth, and in the sea. Hence arises the union of the male and the female which we designate marriage; and hence are derived the procreation and the education of children; for we see that other animals also act as though endowed with knowledge of this law." Justinian, *Institutes* 1.2 (transl. in 2 Scott, *Civil Law* 5). Note the citation of civil law authority and the appeal to natural law. Gridley's argument was that if brutes could marry, slaves could. He may have been trying to avoid the thrust of an act of 1706 for "Better Preventing of a Spurious and Mixt Issue," 1 A&R 578: "And be it ... enacted ... that none of her majesty's English or Scottish subjects, nor of any other Christian nation within the province, shall contract matrimony with any negro or molatto. ... And no master shall unreasonably deny marriage to his negro with one of the same nation, any law, usage or custom to the contrary notwithstanding." To defeat Gridley's plea in abatement, plaintiff had to convince the court that she had never been validly married. The brief JA minutes suggest several alternative contentions. It is possible that in moving to abate, Gridley was assuming, *arguendo*, that the plaintiff was free and white; his natural-law citation was thus an answer to the argument that plaintiff's marriages with Negroes were statutorily void. It is also possible that plaintiff had argued that she was a mulatto and that the statute voided any marriage between her and a Negro. And it is possible, despite evidence of her marriage to slaves, that she was at some time married to a white man; if so, she would be justifying use of "spinster" by insisting that the statute voided that marriage also. Because of the sketchy nature of the notes, we cannot tell exactly. We cannot even be sure that Gridley was invoking natural law to control a statute; it may be that he was merely trying to regularize relationships in which (despite JA's use of the word) there had been no "marriages" at all.

The Court adjudgd at Worcester that a Married Woman could not call herself Spinster.[5]

Writ not abated.[6]

Kent. I shall not enter into the Right of some Men to enslave others.[7] This Right in some Places seems established. Not indeed a Right to Life,[8] tho this is assumed in West Indies to the shame of human Nature.

Evidence was that Jenny Slew was commonly reputed to be the Child of Betty Slew a white Woman by a Negro Man.

Mr. Goffe.[9]

Gridley. Shall Trespass be maintained? Shall not the Plaintiff who sues in Trespass for Goods be compell'd to prove his Possession and that it was by force taken out of his Possession. She has never been in Possession of her Liberty, she has been out of Possession of it for 50 years. Trespass is the highest Action of the highest Nature in Law. No other civil action in which the Party may be punished criminally.[10]

Kent. In the Case of the East Indian at Charlestown they pleaded in Bar that she was a slave, and produced the Bill of Sale. Why did not they do so here?[11]

J. Oliver. This is a Contest between Liberty and Property—both of great Consequence, but Liberty of most importance of the two.

J. Cushing. It is not long since K[ing]'s attorney brought an Action of Trespass, in such a Case as this,[12] and I think he was right, for if a Person is free he may bring Trespass at any Time.

[5] It is unclear whether Gridley refers to the Inferior or Superior Court. The case cited has not been identified.

[6] The note refers apparently not to the Worcester case, but to this one.

[7] Benjamin Kent, counsel for plaintiff. His point, echoed by Judge Cushing (text at note 13 below), was that, because Jenny's mother was a white woman, Jenny could not be a slave, no matter what her father's status.

[8] That is, the right to enslave does not give the master the right of life and death over his slaves.

[9] That is, Edmund Trowbridge, who in early life used the name of his guardian and great-uncle, Edmund Goffe. 8 Sibley-Shipton, *Harvard Graduates* 508.

[10] Trespass was a misdemeanor at common law; the tort is considered to have criminal roots, and Gridley may have been thinking of the early common law, where criminal sanctions sometimes resulted from a civil action for trespass. See Plucknett, *Concise History* 456–458; 5 Bacon, *Abridgment* 150; 3 Holdsworth, *History of English Law* 331–333. Compare Fifoot, *History and Sources* 44–56. But there is a question whether trespass was the only civil action in which the party might be punished criminally. *Id.* at 45–46.

[11] The Charlestown case has not been identified.

[12] The King's attorney would have been Trowbridge, who was Attorney General

Partus sequitur ventrem.[13] Colour is a Presumption.[14]
Lynde. Trespass has commonly been brought, I[15]

39. Newport v. Billing
1768

ADAMS' MINUTES OF THE TRIAL[1]

Hampshire Superior Court, Springfield, September 1768

Newport vs. Billing.

Strong.[2] Trespass and false Imprisonment. Plea that Plaintiff is Defendants Property—his Negro Slave.
Rep.[3] no slave but a freeman.

Bill [of] Sale 1728. 15th March from David Ingersole.
Coll. Partridge. Ingersoles Hand. Lowghtons Hand. Knew Newport to live with Billing and reputed his servant.
Mr. Dickerson. Knew him 30 Years to be the servant of Billing.

Acts of Parliament that take Notice of slaves in Plantations.[4]
Law of Province.[5]
Custom.
Every Man a Right to freedom that no Law or Usage can take away.
Forfeiture of Liberty. Wars, among them. Captives.

---

of the Province, 1749–1767. Whitmore, *Mass. Civil List* 124. The case has not been identified.
[13] The child follows the mother, *i.e.*, the child takes the mother's status. See note 7 above.
[14] In view of Cushing's apparent position favoring the action, he seems here to be saying that the plaintiff's color raised only a presumption as to her status, which presumption was rebutted by evidence of ancestry.
[15] MS breaks off at foot of page; remainder missing.

[1] In JA's hand. Adams Papers, Microfilms, Reel No. 185.
[2] Simeon Strong, counsel for defendant.
[3] "Replication"—the plaintiff's response to the plea.
[4] For example, 23 Geo. 2, c. 31 (1750): "An Act for extending and improving the trade to Africa.—Whereas the trade to and from Africa is very advantageous to Great Britain, and necessary for the supplying the plantations and colonies thereunto belonging with a sufficient number of negroes, at reasonable rates."
[5] For example, "An Act Relating to Mulato and Negro Slaves," 28 July 1703, c. 1, 1 A&R 519 (no manumission without security); "An Act to Prevent Disorders in the Night," 1 Dec. 1703, c. 11, 1 A&R 535–536 (9 P.M. curfew for Indian, Negro, and mulatto servants or slaves); "An Act for the Better Preventing of a Spurious and Mixt Issue," 5 Dec. 1706, c. 10, 1 A&R 578–579 (outlaws miscegenation and imposes a £4 per head duty on all imported Negroes).

A Right to destroy them, if necessary to secure themselves.

Right to enslave them to repay the Expences of defending ones self.

Sense of the Nation to be relyed on.

Presumption here is that an African black is a Slave.

Tax Acts.[6]

Putnam.[7] Point in issue, Slave or not?

Defendant must now prove that Plaintiff is a slave. A Negro, black &c., the only Proof. Montesquieu, flat Nose, &c.[8] Noah's Curse.[9] Dr. Newton.[10]

History, Greece and Rome. Slavery. Power of Life and death.

Not proved that he has forfeited his Liberty, by the Laws of his Country.[11]

Common Report, that they are stolen in Affrica. The Same Right for them to enslave us.

Common Law directly vs. this Principle. Villenage.[12]

[6] For example, "An Act for Apportioning and Assessing a Tax of £40,000. . . . [§3] . . . to estimate Negro, Indian, and molatto servants proportionably as other personal estate." 23 June 1767, 4 A&R 959, 973.

[7] James Putnam, counsel for plaintiff.

[8] Montesquieu, *De l'Esprit des Loix*, Liv. XV, c. V: "Ceux dont il s'agit sont noirs depuis les pieds jusqu'à la tête; et ils ont le nez si écrasé qu'il est presque impossible de les plaindre."

[9] Genesis 9:18–26: "And the sons of Noah, that went forth of the ark, were Shem, and Ham, and Japheth: and Ham is the father of Canaan. These are the three sons of Noah: and of them was the whole earth overspread. And Noah began to be an husbandman, and he planted a vineyard: And he drank of the wine, and was drunken; and he was uncovered within his tent. And Ham, the father of Canaan, saw the nakedness of his father, and told his two brethren without. And Shem and Japheth took a garment, and laid it upon both their shoulders, and went backward, and covered the nakedness of their father; and their faces were backward, and they saw not their father's nakedness. And Noah awoke from his wine, and knew what his younger son had done unto him. And he said, Cursed be Canaan; a servant of servants shall he be unto his brethren. And he said, Blessed be the Lord God of Shem; and Canaan shall be his servant. God shall enlarge Japheth, and he shall dwell in the tents of Shem; and Canaan shall be his servant."

[10] John Newton (1725–1807), English clergyman who had served when young in the ship of his father (governor of York Fort, Hudson Bay), the Royal Navy, and the slave trade. He later studied Greek and Hebrew and was ordained an Anglican priest in 1764. His *Authentic Narrative* (1764) described his early life. *DNB.*

[11] A possible reference to Smith v. Browne & Cooper, 2 Salk. 666, 91 Eng. Rep. 566, Holt K.B. 495, 90 Eng. Rep. 1172 (ca. 1707) note 13 below, in which Lord Holt held that "as soon as a Negro comes into England, he becomes free; One may be a Villein in England, but not a Slave. . . . You should have averred in the Declaration that the Sale was in Virginia and by the laws of that Country Negroes are saleable; for the Laws of *England* do not extend to *Virginia*, being a conquered Country, their Law is what the King pleases; and we cannot take notice of it but as set forth."

[12] "A base tenure, where a man holds [land] upon terms of doing whatsoever is commanded of him, nor knows in the evening what is to be done in the morning,

3 Raymond 1274. Salk. Mod. Levitic Law Exod. The master might kill his slave.[13]

May have a Right to service, during Life. But not to Life.

Province Laws might mean slaves of West indians.[14]

Sewall.[15] Painfull. Humanity, common Justice, and eternal Morality.

Conquest and Rights of War.

Plea says D. Ingersole had a Right to sell him. Rec[eip]t. Similitude of Hands.[16]

Protection. Break his Head. Indictment will lye.

Moral. Necessity to set it aside, it may be dem[onstrated?] that it is a Disadvantage to us.

Voltaire, no sugar.[17]

Wounded Consciences.

Vid. Arguments at large in 1st. Mod.[18]

---

and is always bound to an uncertain service. 1 Steph. Comm. (7th ed.) 188." Black, *Law Dictionary*.

[13] The cases cited by Putnam are probably Smith v. Gould, 2 [not 3] Ld. Raym. 1274, 92 Eng. Rep. 338, 2 Salk. 666, 91 Eng. Rep. 567 (K.B. 1705); Smith v. Browne & Cooper, note 11 above; and Chamberline v. Harvey, 5 Mod. 182, 87 Eng. Rep. 598 (K.B. 1696). In the *Gould* case it was held that trover for a Negro will not lie, "no more than for any other man; for the common law takes no notice of Negroes being different from other men." Putnam's reference to Scripture is probably a quotation from Salkeld's argument for the plaintiff in *Gould* "that a *negro* was a chattel by the law of the plantations, and therefore trover would lie for him; that by the *Levitical* law the master had power to kill his slave, and in *Exodus* xx, ver. 21 it is said, he is but the master's money." Chamberline v. Harvey was cited in the margin of both reports of Smith v. Gould. In a long opinion the court held "that no action of trespass would lie for the taking away a man generally, but there might be a special Action of Trespass for taking his Servant, *per quod Servitium amisit.*" 5 Mod. at 191. See Pleadings Book, Form XI.

[14] The argument seems to be that the word "slaves" in the various Province laws (notes 5, 6, above) ought to be taken to mean slaves on the Caribbean Islands only.

[15] Jonathan Sewall, of counsel for Newport.

[16] That is, the handwriting on the bill of sale was similar to that on another (unspecified) document.

[17] For Voltaire on slavery see "L'A, B, C, ou Dialogues entre A, B, C," 8ème Entretien, "Des Serfs de Corps": "C. . . . Montesquieu m'a fort réjoui dans son chapitre des nègres. Il est bien comique; il triomphe en s'égayant sur notre injustice. A. Nous n'avons pas, à le vérité, le droit naturel d'aller garrotter un citoyen d'Angola pour le mener travailler à coups de nerf de boeuf à nos sucreries de la Barbade, comme nous avons le droit naturel de mener à la chasse le chien que nous avons nourri: mais nous avons le droit de convention." Voltaire, *Oeuvres*, 45:67–68 (Paris, Beuchot ed., 1831). The reference to sugar may be an echo of Montesquieu. "Le sucre seroit trop cher, si l'on ne faisoit travailler la plante qui le produit par des esclaves." Montesquieu, *De l'Esprit des Loix*, Liv. XV, c. 5.

[18] This may be an inadvertence for "5th Mod." (note 13 above), where arguments are fully set forth; nothing appears on the subject in 1 Mod.

40. Margaret v. Muzzy

1768–1770

WRIT AND PLEADINGS[1]

Middlesex Inferior Court, Cambridge, May 1768

[Formal opening omitted.]

To the Sheriff of our County of Middlesex his under-Sheriff or Deputy. Greeting.

We Command you that without Delay you forthwith cause to be replevied (if she may be found within your precinct) Margaret, otherwise called Peggy, a Molatto woman now in the possession of William Muzzy of Lexington in our county of Middlesex Tanner, any claim of the said William notwithstanding, the said Margaret having found sufficient Security to prosecute her plea in this behalf against the said William. And summon the said William Muzzy (if he may be found in your precinct) to appear before our Justices of our Inferiour Court of Common pleas to be holden at Cambridge within and for our county of Middlesex on the third Tuesday of May currant then and there in our said Court to answer unto the aforesaid Margaret In a plea of taking and detaining the said Margaret whereupon she Complains that the said William Muzzy on or about the last day of August last at Lexington aforesaid unjustly took her the said Margaret and her so taken held in Servitude against her free will from the last day of August Last untill the Day of the Date hereof which is to the Damage of the said Margaret as she saith the sum of one hundred pounds which shall then and there be made to appear with other due Damages and have you there this writ with your doings herein. Witness Samuel Danforth, Esqr. at Cambridge this Second day of May in the eighth year of our Reign, Annoque Domini 1768.   Thad. Mason Cler.

Middlesex Ss. May 3d 1768. I have replevied the within named Peggy a Molatto out of the hands of the within named William Muzzy and have summoned the within named William Muzzy to appear at the time and place within mentioned by reading this writ to him.

Wm. How Dept. Sheriff

[1] Copies in SF 147651, 147830. The copy in SF 147830 has been followed, but for clarity, the deputy sheriff's return has been moved from the foot of the document to its present position.

The said William comes and Defends &c. and reserving Liberty of giving any Special matter in Evidence under the general issue and the same to avail as if specially pleaded says he is not guilty as the plaintiff complains and thereof puts himself on the Country, by Benja. Kent his Attorney:

And the said Margaret allowing the Liberty above reserved and also reserving Liberty of waiving this Demurrer on the appeal and joining the issue tendered says the said William's plea aforesaid is insufficient and prays Judgment for costs.   Jona. Sewall

And the said William consenting as above says his plea aforesaid is sufficient and prays Judgment that the said Margaret may be restored, when specially Demanded to him and for costs.

Benja. Kent

The Demurrer is waived and the Issue is joined.

Att. Saml. Winthrop Cler.[2]

41. Caesar v. Taylor

1771–1772

I. WETMORE'S MINUTES OF THE TRIAL[1]

Essex Inferior Court, Newburyport, September 1771

Cæsar v. Taylor. Trespass for detention in slavery. Plea non cul. Besides the usual proof of liberty, the plaintiff brot witnesses to prove a contract between him and defendant that he shoud be free on payment of a sum of Money and that the money was partly paid and that the Time of payment is not yet expired.

For defendant was read the province Law shewing negroes to be slaves and that they can't be manumitted without first giving bond,[2] which was not done in the present Case &c.

But answerd by Plaintiff that the Province law doth not make any negroes slaves if it did it being contra. to Laws of God and reason

---

[2] This notation on the face of the copy of the writ used on the appeal is a minute of the waiver by counsel in the Superior Court of the Inferior Court pleadings set out in the paragraphs immediately preceding in the text.

[1] Wetmore Notes. Adams Papers, Microfilms, Reel No. 184. This document, and those which follow from the Wetmore Notes contain many contractions (here mostly expanded) and little punctuation (here partly supplied). Particular passages may be difficult to interpret, but the sense is clear.

[2] "An Act Relating to Molato and Negro Slaves," 28 July 1703, c.1, 1 A&R 519.

must be void. And [...] error &c. [about?] in different matters may make [jus] but not in essentials as life liberty &c.

II. WETMORE'S MINUTES OF THE ARGUMENT [3]

Essex Superior Court, Salem, November 1771

At the Superior Court November the defendant offered to give in Evidence on plea of non Cul his right to Cæsar by purchase &c. The Council for Cæsar objected that it cou'd not be admitted on this plea and the Court doubted. It was compared to the Cases in Trials pr pais [4] and Gilbert L.E. [Law of Evidence] [5] where title agreements &c. are good evidence, when they don't go in discharge of trespass but in denial of plaintiffs declaration. And the Cause was contin'd. A special verdict was proposed.

III. WETMORE'S MINUTES OF THE ARGUMENT [6]

Essex Superior Court, Salem, November 1771

Taylor v. Cæsar. Trespass for enslaving the defendant. Plea non cul. Evidence offered was a bargain between Cæsar and Taylor that on payment of £— he woud set the boy free and proof was of payment of consid[erable] sum, and Taylor offered bill of sale in Evidence to which it was objected that its improper and doth not tend to support the plea and Trials per pais and Gilbert L. Evid. were produced. The Court doubted at first but since it was (I think June 1772) rejected by whole Court.

IV. WETMORE'S MINUTES OF THE ARGUMENT [7]

Essex Superior Court, Salem, November 1771

Trespass for enslaving Plaintiff; plea non cul. Plaintiff offered evidence of beating imprisoning and abusing the plaintiff by defendants

[3] Wetmore Notes. Adams Papers, Microfilms, Reel No. 184.
[4] 2 Duncombe, *Trials Per Pais* 549: "The Defendant may prevail on Not guilty in Trespass, by making Title to the Land."
[5] Gilbert, *Evidence* 242: "Evidence on Not guilty for the Defendant in Trespass. The Defendant may prevail in this Issue, First, By making Title to the Land; for then he satisfies the Declaration, for he proves that he did not enter into the Plaintiff's Close, but his own; and consequently that is a very just Disproof of the Plaintiff's Declaration."
[6] Wetmore Notes. Adams Papers, Microfilms, Reel No. 184.
[7] Wetmore Notes. Adams Papers, Microfilms, Reel No. 184.

vendees. As the defendant was the first cause ⟨of⟩ by illegal convey-ance the Court unanimously admitted the proof, altho' said that it cannot appear by records.

Cæsars wife offered as a witness. Objected to her as his wife and interested, and proof offered of cohabitation. Answer that there was no contract but what was dissolvable at will and said to be determined that no negro could be a bastard, but J[udge] Trowbridge said that proof of Cohabitation was proof of marriage, and evidence by wit-nesses was admitted of cohabitation for a course of years. White woman married to negro *Slave* not allowed to sue without naming him.[8]

Adams. It has been ruled in 3 cases by the Court, in Slewman, in Billings, and at Cambridge that negroes are presumed to be slaves and must make their freedom appear.[9]

Lowell.[10] Made difference between property in matter and moral beings.

Hut[chinso]n. The Evidence not admissible on the plea.

Trowbridge of the same opinion.

Oliver also, of the same opinion.

Lynde in doubt.

Cushing not in[...].

V. WETMORE'S MINUTES OF THE ARGUMENT [11]

Essex Superior Court, Ipswich, June 1772

Essex Novemr. 1771.

On motion to give property in evidence on non cul. ruled that in this case it must not be, ruled by 3 of the Justices. R[opes] and Cush-ing gave no Opinion having heard no argument.

Mr. Adams then moved for a repleader. Objected that its grantable not of right but [favor?] and its error when granted or refused wrong-fully. Its grantable in cases where the right of the suit cant be deter-mined by the issue.[12] Also objected that this is after verdict below.

[8] That is, the husband would have to be joined in the action as a plaintiff.

[9] The three cases are probably Slew v. Whipple, No. 38; Newport v. Billing, No. 39; and Margaret v. Muzzy, No. 40.

[10] John Lowell, counsel for plaintiff.

[11] Wetmore Notes. Adams Papers, Microfilms, Reel No. 184. The date heading the document refers to the term from which the case was continued, because William Cushing and Nathaniel Ropes were not appointed to the Superior Court until 15 Jan. 1772. Whitmore, *Mass. Civil List* 70.

[12] "Occasionally the Court would order a *repleader*, that is to say, that the plead-ings should start afresh, for it might turn out that owing to some error which had

J. Trow[bridge]. The diff[iculty?] is that the defendant by repleader deprives the plaintiff of the advantage. Hut[chinson]and Trow[bridge] against it because the plaintiff may lose an advantage. Cushing inclining to replead. J. Ropes says nothing. J. Oliver against a repleader.

Adams moved to ask the plaintiffs witnesses whether the plaintiff was not reputed a Slave and used as such by his master the defendant (in mitigation of Damages).

Proof was given that Taylor owned [13] a bargain between Caesar and him for his freedom for £600 O[ld] T[enor] and that part of it had been paid.

Note. J. Trowb[ridge] said in this case that the pleadings allowed the plaintiff to be a person and one able to sue. He is therefore not property which is a thing and a thing can't maintain an action. By English laws a person must be free, else no murder to kill him.

Said by Mr. Adams that Superior Court in J. Sewall's day determined from civil law authorities produced by Mr. Gridley and Pratt, that the children of a woman slave were the property of the master of the mother, and that negroes are in *classe rerum* and are Slaves in this Country.[14]

VI. ADAMS' MINUTES OF THE TRIAL [15]

Essex Superior Court, Ipswich, June 1772

Tayler vs. Cæsar. Salem Novr. 1771

contd.

Mem. examine civil Law, and Villenage, to see what Rules are to govern these Negro Causes.
Sergeant.[16]

---

been overlooked the fact on which issue had been joined did not dispose of the questions between the parties, so that the Court was after all not in a position to give judgment either way, no matter how that question of fact had been determined." Sutton, *Personal Actions* 134.

[13] That is, admitted.

[14] Stephen Sewall (1702–1760) was Associate Justice of the SCJ from 1739 to 1752, Chief Justice from 1752 to 1760. The case in question has not been identified. On Jeremy Gridley's use of civil law authority on behalf of the *defendant* in a slave case, see No. 38.

[15] Adams Papers, Microfilms, Reel No. 185. Apparently JA wrote the title of this minute and noted the continuance at the Salem Superior Court, Nov. 1771. But the notes seem to have been taken at the Ipswich Superior Court, June 1772.

[16] Nathaniel Peaslee Sergeant was Caesar's attorney.

No. 41. Caesar v. Taylor

Tim. Fuller. Known Caesar between 20 and 30 years. I bought him, about 12 years old. A new Negro, right from Guinea, could not talk English. Tayler bound him, 3 Years. He came to me to buy him when Hircum owned him. I hired him of Tayler, a Month. He gave me Liberty to hire him, and I paid the Negro. Tayler said if he behaved well and got him his Money, he should be willing to let him have his Time. I said if he did not get the Money by such a Time [17]

Indian Woman rejected because Cæsars Wife.[18]
Josh. Felt.[19] Tayler told me, that he sold him, because he behaved [20]

Trials Per Pais 538. Regula.[21] But read the Cases that follow in Illustration of the Rule, which shew that the Rule takes Place where a Person meddled with the Property of another.[22]
Wilson 254.[23] Court gave Leave to Defendant to withdraw the general Issue and Plead a Justification.

Court determined that the Master should not give in Evidence that Cæsar was a slave.

[17] The MS breaks off here. The next paragraph is in a clearer hand, suggesting that JA took time off to sharpen or replace his quill.
[18] "Husband and Wife cannot be admitted to be Witnesses for or against each other, for if they swear for the Benefit of each other, they are not to be believed, because their Interests are absolutely the same, and therefore they can gain no more Credit when they attest for each other, than when any Man attests for himself." Gilbert, *Evidence* 135–136.
[19] Josiah Phelps, according to the file. SF 132190.
[20] Sentence left incomplete by JA.
[21] "Regula. Upon the General Issue, if by the Evidence the Defendant acknowledge that he did the Wrong, and justify this, and gives the Matter that goes to discharge him of the Act by Justification, this Evidence is not good, but he ought to have pleaded it." 2 Duncombe, *Trials Per Pais* 538.
[22] "This Rule is demonstrated by those Cases, where, upon Not guilty in Trespass, the Defendant would say the Property was in a Stranger, and that by his Commandment, or as his Servant, he took the Goods." 2 Duncombe, *Trials Per Pais* 538.
[23] Taylor v. Joddrell, 1 Wils. K.B. 254, 95 Eng. Rep. 603 (1749): "Imprisonment: defendant pleaded the general issue inadvertently, and now moved to withdraw it, and for leave to plead a justification that he was master of a ship, that the plaintiff was making a mutiny therein, and so he imprisoned him. . . . *Per curiam*: There are many instances of this having been done when the court can prevent the plaintiff from suffering any inconvenience by it, as by obliging the defendant to take short notice of trial, and that if there be a verdict for the plaintiff he shall have judgment as of the present term; therefore let the defendant be at liberty to plead a justification, and the general issue also, if he pleases, upon the terms mentioned."

42. Caesar v. Greenleaf

1773

WETMORE'S MINUTES OF THE TRIAL[1]

Essex Inferior Court, Newburyport, October 1773

Cæsar v. Greenleaf

Trespass for inslaving the plaintiff.

Cæsar a molatto man (otherwise called Cæsar Hendrick) of said N[ewbury] P[ort] labourer in a plea of trespass for that the said R[ichard] G[reenleaf] at said Newbury Port on the 1 of January last, with force and arms assaulted the plaintiff then and there being in our peace, and then and there with force as aforesaid falsely imprisoned him and so with force as aforesaid and against the plaintiffs will hath then held kept and restrained him in servitude as the said Richard's slave from the same day untill the day of the purchase of this writ and many other injuries and enormities the said R.G. to the Plaintiff then and there did against our peace. Damages £50. Dated March 16. 1773.

Plea. And the said R.G. comes and defends when and where &c. and protesting that the said Cæsar is his molatto Slave and that by law he is not held to answer to the said Cæsar on his declaration aforesaid yet nevertheless the said R. for plea saith (on the plaintiffs agreeing that he the said R.G. may on the trial give any special matter in evidence for his Justification and that the same shall avail as if specially pleaded) he is not guilty in manner and form as the plaintiff hath declared, and thereof puts himself on the Country.

D. Farnham

And the Plaintiff (agreeing to the above) likewise.   J. Lowell

Farnham.
The Egyptians, Grecians, Jews, Romans, held many in slavery.
Province law. pa. 82.[2] 144–5. 152.[3] Shew there were many slaves

---

[1] Wetmore Notes. Adams Papers, Microfilms, Reel No. 184.

[2] "An Act against receiving of Stolen Goods," *Acts and Laws of the Province of Massachusetts Bay* 82 (Boston, 1759), 13 June 1698, 1 A&R 325 (receiving stolen money or goods from "Indians, Molattos, Negroes, and other Suspected Persons" made punishable by whipping).

[3] See No. 39, at note 5.

in the province at the time of making those laws, held in slavery, and not to be manumitted, without security, &c.

Lowell.

The Defendants plea acknowledgeth him a molatto and therefore must have had a white parent, either father or mother.

Certificate of his baptism and that he is a member of Mr. Parson's church,[4] read.

Admitting there are slaves in the province yet the plaintiff may be none and in fact is not one, as he will prove.

Villeins these were known in the English law. We have nothing to do with any other laws. Those of Egypt, Greece or Rome are nothing to Englishmen. At Common law partus *non* seq. ventrem, otherwise it may be in the civil law—but this law never adopted by English law in this case by the English law Villeins follow the state of the father not of the mother.

But objected by Farnham in Villeinage there was marriage, in this case none, so not applicable.

Matrimony a duty and right, and plaintiff by law of nature must provide for his issue, therefore must be free that he may discharge his duty and enjoy his right. No human tribunal can take away natural rights so fundamental.

The precepts of revealed law, golden rule of the gospel are that we are not to sell our brethren, that we are to do as we would be done unto.

He is a Christian and if held in Slavery may not perform his duties as one. His master did not object to his baptism and becoming a xtian.

Liberty is not to be taken from him by implication of law. There must be express law for it.

The province laws read establish Slavery only by implication if it does at all.

Plaintiff must be free unless a slave by common law, Statutes of G[reat] Britain, or law of the province.

But even villeinage is abolished by English law. The Common law abhors slavery.

Somersett case shews every one setting his foot on English ground to be free, wherever he came from.[5]

---

[4] Almost surely Jonathan Parsons (1705-1776), Yale 1728, of the First Presbyterian Church, Newburyport. 1 Dexter, *Yale Graduates* 389-393.

[5] Somersett's Case, Lofft 1, 19, 98 Eng. Rep. 499, 510, 20 St. Trials (N.S.) 1, 82 (K.B. 1772) in which Lord Mansfield said that slavery could exist in England only by positive law. Somersett had been the slave of Charles Stewart, an officer of the customs in Boston, and accompanied his master to England in 1769. In 1771,

Usage and custom must be for time whereof memory of man is not to the contrary, and must be reasonable, just, constant and right.

But in this country, in the Colonies, none such because records shew the beginning.

The old Colony law shews no slaves but those made by their own consent or by taking in lawful war.[6]

Sup[erio]r C[our]t hath determined this country too young for usage and custom time whereof &c.[7]

Foster Crown law, as to legality of impressing mariners, says impress had been ever Since existence of the nation, at least from William the Conqueror.[8] Yet if it was not of public necessity it ought not to be esteemed law but England being an Island there was necessity it must be guarded by ships and seamen and of Course impresses legal. But Hume in his history questions Fosters law.[9] And Foster pretends none but temporary right and while exigencies of war require.[10]

Some Legislatures So[uth]ward in the colonies have enacted, that blacks, as negroes are Slaves.[11]

---

when Somersett ran away, Stewart retook him and tried to ship him to Jamaica, there to be sold. Somersett, however, obtained a writ of *habeas corpus*, on the return of which he was freed. See George H. Moore, *Notes on the History of Slavery in Massachusetts* 116–117 (N.Y., 1866).

[6] "It is Ordered by this Court and the Authority thereof; That there shall never be any Bondslavery, Villenage or Captivity amongst us, unless it be lawful Captives taken in just Wars, as willingly sell themselves or are sold to us, and such shall have the liberties and Christian usuage which the Law of God established in *Israel* concerning such persons doth morally require; Provided this exempts none from servitude, who shall be judged thereto by Authority. (1641)." Laws and Liberties of 1672, *Colonial Laws of Massachusetts* 10 (Boston, ed. William H. Whitmore, 1887).

[7] This case has not been identified.

[8] Rex v. Broadfoot, Foster, *Crown Cases* 154 (Recorder's Court, Bristol, 1743). See No. 56, at note 102.

[9] The reference, presumably to David Hume, *The History of England, from the Invasion of Julius Cæsar to the Revolution in 1688*, published in 1754–1762, has not been identified.

[10] Rex v. Broadfoot, Foster, *Crown Cases* 154, 158 (Recorder's Court, Bristol, 1743): "I think the Crown hath a Right to Command the Service of these People, whenever the publick Safety calleth for it. The same Right that it hath to require the personal Service of every Man able to bear Arms in case of sudden Invasion or formidable Insurrection. The Right in both cases is founded on one and the same Principle, the Necessity of the Case in Order to the Preservation of the Whole."

[11] In an account of his trip to South Carolina in 1773 Josiah Quincy Jr. said: "The brutality used towards the slaves has a very bad tendency with reference to the manners of the people, but a much worse with regard to the youth. They will plead in their excuse 'this severity is necessary.' But whence did or does this necessity arise? From *the necessity* of having vast multitudes sunk in barbarism, ignorance, and the basest and most servile employ! ... From the same cause have their Legislators enacted laws touching negroes, mulattoes, and masters which savor more of the policy of Pandemonium than the English constitution:—laws which will stand eternal records of the depravity and contradiction of the human character: laws

No. 42. Caesar v. Greenleaf

Hobart 87. Act of Parliament. Jura naturæ immutabilia. An act of parliament against natural Equity, as to make one Judge in his own cause is void.[12]

The province law is to be extended only for the purpose mentioned in it, as to manumission, as to charge of supporting them &c. nothing as to the right of enslaving the negroes.

Cæsar and Greenleaf (as I suppose) the foregoing case.[13]

J[udge] Frye.[14] The defendant by the province law and by the custom of the country seems to justify his doings. The laws suppose slavery. The master by admitting the baptism &c. seems to have in a measure given the plaintiff his liberty. Shall this humanity be taken against the defendant?

N.B. This case I copied from Mr. P[ynchon's] report of it, and am uncertain whether J. Frye gave the above opinion in this case or some other.

---

which would disgrace the tribunal of Scythian, Arab, Hottentot, and Barbarian are appealed to in decisions upon life limb and liberty by those who assume the name of Englishmen, freemen and Christians: the place of trial no doubt is called a Court of Justice and equity—but the Judges have forgot a maxim of English law—*Jura naturalia sunt immutabilia*—and they would do well to remember that no laws of the (little) creature supersede the laws of the (great) creator. Can the institutions of man make void the decree of GOD? These are but a small part of the mischiefs of slavery, new ones are every day arising, futurity will produce more and greater." Howe, ed., "Journal of Josiah Quincy Jr. 1773," 49 MHS, *Procs.* 424, 456–457 (1915–1916). An editorial note states that Quincy's MS has a reference after "*Jura naturalia*" as follows: "See Hobart's Reports." Lowell used the same authority. See the following paragraph in the text, and note 12 below.

[12] Day v. Savadge, Hob. 85, 87, 80 Eng. Rep. 235, 237 (C.P. 1615). "[E]ven an Act of Parliament, made against naturall equitie, as to make a man Judge in his owne case, is void in it selfe, for *Jura naturae sunt immutabilia*, And they are *leges legum*." See No. 44, note 71.

[13] The sentence is apparently Wetmore's.

[14] Peter Frye of Salem (1723–1820), Harvard 1744, was a Judge of the Essex Inferior Court from 15 Jan. 1772 to the Revolution. 11 Sibley-Shipton, *Harvard Graduates* 399–404; Whitmore, *Mass. Civil List* 84.

M. *Admiralty— Civil Jurisdiction*

43. Doane v. Gage

1766–1769

EDITORIAL NOTE

The courts of Vice Admiralty in the colonies had been established by the Crown in 1697 primarily to provide a forum for enforcement of the Acts of Trade and Navigation, with which England sought to control colonial commerce for the benefit of the Mother Country. The courts were, of course, open for the trial of ordinary civil maritime cases, but in Massachusetts it took the earliest royal Admiralty judges nearly twenty years to overcome hostility aroused by the establishment, and unfamiliarity with the new process. Thus, although by 1720 the Admiralty had a sizable civil business, there had developed a solidly established tradition of common-law competence in maritime matters, which kept the court from realizing its full potential. The court was further hampered by the common-law power to issue writs of prohibition, with which any respondent in a case that did not actually arise on the seas, or concern the wages and discipline of seamen, could stay the Admiralty proceedings. By this means, virtually all contracts for maritime services (other than seamen's wages), as well as torts occurring within a harbor, could be excluded from the jurisdiction.[1]

Thus, even in its busiest years, the Massachusetts Vice Admiralty Court had had few cases that did not involve seamen, or other matters traditionally within its competence. The bulk of maritime torts and contracts were sued upon at common law. After 1764, when Parliament expanded and strengthened Admiralty jurisdiction of violations of the Acts of Trade, the court's business declined to fifteen or twenty cases a year. Most of these were civil in nature, but the passage of the Townshend duties in 1767 and the heightened enforcement activities of the new American Board of Customs Commissioners beginning in 1768, which sharply increased the number of revenue cases in the court, reduced its civil business to about six or eight cases a year, and, after 1770, to one or two.[2]

---

[1] For a summary of the development of the jurisdiction in Massachusetts and of the common-law restrictions, see Wroth, "The Massachusetts Vice Admiralty Court," in George A. Billias, ed., *Law and Authority in Colonial America: Selected Essays* (Barre, Mass., in press).

[2] Complete figures on the court are not available for the years 1745–1765, because virtually all of its records for that period were destroyed in the Stamp Act riot, 1765. See Wroth, "The Massachusetts Vice Admiralty Court," 6 *Am. Jour. Legal Hist.* 263–264 (1962). The business of the court, 1765–1772, can be estimated from the Minute Book for those years in the Office of the Clerk of the Supreme Judicial

As far as can be determined, Adams had no case of any kind in the Court of Vice Admiralty before 1768.[3] This may well be explained by the fact that the business of the court was so slight and the cases so unremunerative that there was no room for another advocate at its bar. He had originally brought *Doane v. Gage*, his first known Admiralty case, at common law, but decided to proceed in Admiralty, apparently for convenience. Probably because of the decline in such business he seems never to have had another civil Admiralty case.

This dispute over the ownership of a whale taken at sea shows that the civil side of the Vice Admiralty Court was not altogether defunct in the 1760's, but the case is chiefly of interest for its wealth of detail on the techniques of whaling. The whale fishery was a major industry in 18th-century Massachusetts. Vessels from Nantucket, Dartmouth, Cape Cod, and Boston had by 1775 ranged the Atlantic from Baffin Bay and Greenland in the north, eastward to the Azores and the coast of Africa, and south to Brazil and the Falkland Islands, producing an annual catch worth about £200,000.[4]

In 1765 nearly a hundred Massachusetts vessels fished the Gulf of St. Lawrence and the Straits of Belle Isle, which lie between Newfoundland and Labrador. In the fleet were a number of Cape Cod whalers, including ships captained by Joseph Doane of Chatham and Lot Gage of Harwich.[5] On 21 June the hunting was good in the Straits; a sizable number of boats from several vessels were in the water, and numerous whales had been sighted. One whale in particular had succeeded in eluding capture, until Asa Nickerson, commanding one of Doane's boats, drove his "iron" into it. The whale sounded with the line. At some point thereafter, Gage himself struck the same whale and Nickerson's line came free. Gage was able to maintain control over the whale, supervise the kill, and bring its marketable parts aboard ship.

Court for Suffolk County, Boston. See p. 102–104, notes 17, 22, 24 below. Development of the court's revenue jurisdiction is summarized at p. 98–106 below.

[3] JA first mentioned being at the Admiralty Court in a diary entry of 30 Jan. 1768, which was after the commencement of Doane v. Gage there. 1 JA, *Diary and Autobiography* 337–338; see text at note 9 below.

[4] See Edouard Stackpole, *The Sea-Hunters* 30–65 (Phila., 1953); Alexander Starbuck, *History of the American Whale Fishery* 19–77 (Waltham, Mass., 1878). For the market value, see Thomas Jefferson, "Memoranda," Oct. 1788, 14 Jefferson, *Papers*, ed. Boyd, 226–234; Thomas Jefferson, "Report to the House on the Cod and Whale Fisheries," 1 Feb. 1791, in H.R. Misc. Doc. No. 32, 42d Cong., 2d sess. (1872); Obed Macy, *The History of Nantucket* 70–72, 233 (Boston, 1835). JA was also concerned with the American whaling industry during his diplomatic career. See 3 JA, *Diary and Autobiography* 83–84.

[5] See *Boston News-Letter*, 8 Aug. 1765, p. 3, col. 1. Doane (c. 1720–1778) held a variety of public offices in Chatham, kept a public house there "of great benefit to the fishery," and found time to participate in the annual whaling voyages. See Alfred A. Doane, *The Doane Family* 136 (Boston, 1902); 17 A&R 552; 18 A&R 453, 675. He was also involved in two later JA cases, No. 57 and No. 58. Lot Gage was an incorporator of the Second Parish of Harwich in 1746. Frederick Freeman, *The History of Cape Cod*, 2:513 (Boston, 1869).

At once a dispute arose between Doane and Gage as to the ownership of the whale. There was much uncertainty as to whether Nickerson had struck it at all, and if he had, whether he had still been "fast" at the time that Gage had struck. The Cape Codders all took sides, some on the basis of long-standing political and social rivalries, others because of financial interest engendered by the flexible and temporary sharing of labor and profit among vessels known as "mateship." [6] Gage remained steadfast in the claim that the whale was entirely his, however, and some time after the return of the fleet to home waters Doane brought action against him.

Suit was commenced at law in the Inferior Court at Barnstable, where an entry in John Adams' docket dated June 1766 records that he was "spoke to," that is, asked to serve as counsel.[7] Numerous depositions were taken, but the case was not disposed of at this stage. It is possible that the common-law court declined to hear a matter so obviously within the Admiralty jurisdiction, but it seems more likely that some practical consideration, such as the desire to avoid a biased local jury, led Adams to withdraw the action at Barnstable in order to proceed in Admiralty.[8] In any event, on 6 January 1768 the case of "Joseph Doane v. Lot Gage, rela. a Whale" was entered by Adams on the docket of the Vice Admiralty Court.[9] James Otis represented the Gage interests, which apparently included his father, Col. James Otis of Barnstable.[10] Adams and Otis agreed that depositions taken for the trial in Barnstable might be used in Admiralty and that further depositions might be taken, but the case was continued from time to time.[11]

---

[6] See Stackpole, *Sea-Hunters* 42, 51. See also notes 29, 33, 45, below.

[7] JA, Docket, June 1764–Oct. 1767. Adams Papers, Microfilms, Reel No. 182. The entry, which is nearly illegible, may read "Jonathan" Doane, but if that reading is correct, it is probably an error on JA's part. That the case was first entered in the Barnstable court is established by the agreement regarding depositions from that court in note 11 below.

[8] Other whale cases in the Superior Court files are inconclusive on the jurisdictional point. Dyer v. Doane, SF 144072, SCJ Rec. 1757–1759, fol. 325 (Barnstable, 1758), was an action of trover for a whale allegedly struck by the plaintiff in Cape Cod Harbor and taken up on shore by the defendant, who won the verdict. In Bassett v. Jenkins, SF 144166, SCJ Rec. 1763–1764, fol. 245 (Barnstable, 1764), trover for a whale struck in the St. Lawrence, the defendant prevailed on a motion in arrest of judgment, apparently on a pleading defect unrelated to the jurisdictional question. The problem of location could be avoided in any event by alleging a fictitious venue within the Province, which was done in Bassett v. Jenkins.

[9] Vice Adm. Min. Bk., 6 Jan. 1768.

[10] As to Otis, see note 31 below.

[11] The agreement, dating from March 1768, provides "That Each Party shall have Liberty to use the Depositions heretofore taken to Be used in the Inferior Court of Common Pleas at Barnstable and all the Evidences heretofore Taken In Perpetuam Reis Memoriam: and to Take any others that may Be Wanted In the same Manner: and that all such Depositions shall be Considered as having the same Weight as If the Deponants were Dead Gone to Sea &c. and were Regularly taken." A supplement, dated "In Court," 15 Dec. 1768, provided that any further depositions thought necessary should be taken before two Justices of the Peace in Barnstable, "whether taken in Perpetuam or in the Common form, the Adverse Party to be notified." MHi:Waterston Collection. See note 84 below. For a discussion of the statutory

Finally, Robert Treat Paine, once briefly a whaler himself,[12] joined Otis on Gage's side, and on 22 April 1769 the parties agreed to submit the matter to arbitrators.[13] Since no notation to this effect appears in the Vice Admiralty Minute Book, it may be that the agreement was to discontinue and to arrange the arbitration privately rather than under a rule of court.

After a day of hearings in June and a further postponement in August, proceedings before the arbitrators commenced in earnest on 19 October 1769 at Brackett's tavern, with Adams arguing first.[14] The chief legal issue was the nature of the right of possession in whales, a question of vital concern to the whaling industry throughout the 19th century and to most first-year law students today. At some point before the hearing Adams had made a series of extracts of civil-law authorities standing for the proposition that property in wild animals is acquired when they are taken into possession, but lost if the animals escape from possession and regain their natural liberty. While civil-law authorities have always been of great weight at common law in such questions, the fact that this was an Admiralty proceeding probably accounts for the exclusive reliance upon them here.[15]

In the first portion of the arbitration proceedings Adams concentrated on the application of these principles to the practices of the whale fishery. His witnesses to the customary law of whaling testified that a boat was considered in possession of a whale when it was "fast" to it, that is, when its iron was still seated in the whale and the line was still in the boat's control.

A second boat striking the whale while the first was fast was entitled to a one-eighth share if it had come in at a "call" from the first; if the fast boat had not requested assistance the second striker took nothing, even though the whale ultimately cast the first iron.[16] If the whale became "loose" without having been struck a second time, the first striker lost possession and

---

rules for taking depositions, see p. xlvii above. The continuances through 28 Nov. 1768 appear in Vice Adm. Min. Bk., 6 Jan., 28 Nov. 1768. Paine notes that in Jan. 1769 the court, sitting to hear the case, adjourned until April. Paine Diary, 23 Jan. 1769.

[12] On a voyage to Greenland in 1754. See 12 Sibley-Shipton, *Harvard Graduates* 465.

[13] Paine Diary, 19 Jan., 22 April 1769.

[14] Paine Diary, 20, 21 June, 10 Aug., 19 Oct. 1769. In his own diary under the last date, JA noted, "The morning at Brackett's upon the Case of the Whale." 1 JA, *Diary and Autobiography* 344. "Brackett's" was undoubtedly the Cromwell's Head, an inn on School Street in Boston kept by Joshua Bracket, where such proceedings were commonly held. See Rowe, *Letters and Diary* 127; Thwing, *Crooked and Narrow Streets* 109; Drake, *History and Antiquities of Boston* 807. JA apparently had the assistance of an unidentified lawyer, whose notes on the case are found with his. See note 27 below.

[15] The common-law position on wild animals is typified by Kent, *Commentaries* *348–350. As to the Admiralty as a civil-law jurisdiction, see JA's argument in No. 46. From the beginning of his legal career he had read extensively in the civil law. See 1 JA, *Diary and Autobiography* 44, 55–57, 173–174.

[16] The statement in 1 JA, *Diary and Autobiography* 344 note, that Doane as first striker would be entitled only to an eighth upon losing the whale is thus erroneous.

all claim to the whale, and a subsequent striker had full possession. Except for the grant of an eighth to the second striker, these rules are similar to the code epitomized by Melville in *Moby Dick* and observed by British and American courts dealing with the Greenland whale fishery then and for a century afterward. Adams' further argument that the adoption of custom strengthened rules designed to prevent disputes has also been followed in the courts.[17]

The real problems in the case were factual. Adams' evidence tended to show that Nickerson had been fast to the whale when Gage struck, thus giving Doane possession under the rules to which earlier witnesses had testified. Adams also introduced testimony which struck at the validity of Gage's evidence, suggesting physical impossibilities, inconsistencies, and dubious motives. Paine followed Adams, first attacking Doane's case, then putting in evidence to support Gage's theory that he had struck only after Nickerson had lost the whale and was hauling in his iron. When the evidence was in, Otis summed up the testimony presented.

Altogether there had been at least 74 witnesses—34 for Doane and 40 for Gage. Whether in deference to the civil-law procedure followed in the High Court of Admiralty in England, or for convenience in a hearing four years after the event, all of the testimony seems to have been in written form—either depositions or answers to interrogatories, which each side had served upon witnesses whose depositions showed their testimony to be crucial.[18] Adams and Paine read these documents, or paraphrases of relevant portions of them, before the arbitrators, embellishing the reading with comments and arguments when appropriate. According to Paine's diary,

---

[17] Melville's formulation was:

"But though no other nation [except Holland] has ever had any written whaling law, yet the American fishermen have been their own legislators and lawyers in this matter. They have provided a system which for terse comprehensiveness surpasses Justinian's Pandects and the By-laws of the Chinese Society for the Suppression of Meddling with other People's Business. . . .

"I. A Fast-Fish belongs to the party fast to it.

"II. A Loose-Fish is fair game for anybody who can soonest catch it." Herman Melville, *Moby Dick* (Chapter 88) 393–394 (N.Y., 1950). See also William Scoresby, *An Account of the Arctic Regions*, 2:318–328 (Edinburgh, 1820). Compare Aberdeen Arctic Co. v. Sutter, 4 Macq. 355 (H.L. 1862); Addison v. Row, 3 Paton App. 334 (H.L. 1794). Different whaling areas had local customs differing from those of the Greenland fishery, but the courts have applied them on the theory enunciated by JA. See Oliver Wendell Holmes, *The Common Law* 167–168 (Cambridge, Mass., ed. Mark DeWolfe Howe, 1963), and cases there cited. See also note 32 below.

[18] For the English Admiralty practice, see No. 46, notes 35, 63. Depositions were apparently taken both during the common law proceeding and after, under the agreements cited, note 11 above. See notes 33–35 below. The interrogatories were presumably prepared during the pendency of the Admiralty proceeding and were administered to at least one witness some time during 1769. See note 59 below. In the Suffolk files are two fragments in the hand of James Otis, containing questions to be put to various witnesses. These are probably questions submitted by Otis to whoever was taking depositions in the case, to be asked of the deponent. They are set out in note 65 below.

six days were required for the hearing. Finally on 27 October he noted simply, "Whale case finished." [19] No record of the result has been found.

The materials that follow include Adams' notes of authorities (Document I) and his extensive minutes of the arbitration proceedings (Document II), as well as copies of the interrogatories prepared by both sides (Documents III, IV). The latter are of particular interest, because they show the crucial factual issues upon which counsel concentrated at the last stages of a long litigation. On the basis of these documents the reader may be able to form his own judgment as to who was entitled to the whale.

I. ADAMS' NOTES OF AUTHORITIES [20]

Court of Vice Admiralty, Boston, 1768

Doane's Whale.

Grotius B. 2, Chap. 8, §. 2. How long Beasts Birds and Fishes, may be said to be no Body's, admits of some Dispute.[21]

§. 3. "The Roman Lawyers say, We lose our Property in wild Beasts, as soon as ever they recover their natural Liberty: But in all other Things the Property acquired by Possession does not cease with the Loss of Possession. Nay it gives us a Right even to claim and recover our Possession. And Whether they be taken away from us by another, or get away of themselves, as a fugitive slave, it is all one." [22]

Inst. Lib. 2, Tit. 1, §. 12. "De rerum divisione et de [ad]quirendo [*ipsarum*] dominio. Feræ igitur Bestiæ et Volucres, et Pisces, et omnia animalia, quæ mari, Cœlo, et Terra nascuntur: simulatque ab aliquo capta fuerint, jure gentium, statim illius esse incipiunt. Quod enim ante nullius est, id, naturali Ratione, occupanti conceditur. Quicquid autem eorum ceperis, eousque tuum esse intelligitur, donec tua custodia coercetur. Cum vero tuam evaserit Custodiam, et in Libertatem naturalem sese receperit, tuum esse definit, et rursus occupantis fit. Naturalem autem Libertatem recipere intelligitur, cum vel occulos

---

[19] Paine Diary, 27 Oct. 1769.
[20] In JA's hand. Adams Papers, Microfilms, Reel No. 184.
[21] Hugo Grotius, *The Rights of War and Peace* (London, 1738). The passage reads: "And to this Head [the Seizure or Possession of Things that have no Owner], in the first Place, is referred the Catching of Beasts, Birds, and Fish. But how long all these may be said to be no Body's, admits of some Dispute." *Id.* at 248. The remainder of the section deals with the question whether the owner of an enclosed forest or lake has a property in the wild animals therein.
[22] Grotius, *War and Peace*, bk. 2, ch. 8, §3. Quotation marks supplied.

tuos effugerit vel ita sit in Conspectu tuo ut difficilis sit ejus Perse-
cutio." [23]

§. 13. "Illud quæsitum est, an si Fera Bestia ita vulnerata sit, ut
capi possit, statim tua esse intelligatur. Et, quibusdam placuit, statim
esse tuam et eousque tuam videri donec eam persequaris. Quod si
defieris persequi: definere esse tuam, et rursus fieri occupantis. Alii
vero putaverant non aliter tuam esse quam si eam ceperis. Sed posteri-
orem sententiam nos confirmamus, quod multa evidere soleant ut eam
non capias." [24]

Vid. same Law in same Words: Digest Lib. 41. Tit. 1. "De adquirendo Rerum Dominio." [25]

§. 5. "Naturalem &c. illud quæsitum est an fera bestia, quæ ita
vulnerata sit, ut capi possit statim nostra esse intelligatur. Trebatio
placuit statim nostram esse, et eo usque nostram videri donec eam
persequamur. Quod si defierimus eam persequi: definere nostram esse,
et rursus fieri occupantis. Itaque si per hoc tempus, quo eam persequi-
mur, alius eam ceperit eo animo ut ipse lucrifacerit: furtum [*videri*]

[23] This and the next paragraph are from the *Institutes* of Justinian, that *summa*
of the Roman law which is the basis of all civilian studies. The edition used by JA
cannot be determined, but the fact that he also quoted the *Digest*, note 25 below,
indicates that he had access to a copy of the *Corpus Juris Civilis*, in which all of the
works attributed to Justinian are contained. The passages here have been collated
with *Corpus Juris Civilis* (Altenburg, ed. C. H. Freiesleben, 1751). Quotation
marks have been supplied. The translation of the passage quoted here follows, with
a sentence omitted by JA given in brackets. "Of the different kinds of things and of
acquiring dominion of them. . . . Wild animals, birds, and fish, that is to say all the
creatures which the land, the sea, and the sky produce, as soon as they are caught by
any one become at once the property of their captor by the law of nations; for
natural reason admits the title of the first occupant to that which previously had no
owner. [So far as the occupant's title is concerned, it is immaterial whether it is on
his own land or on that of another that he catches wild animals or birds, though it
is clear that if he goes on another man's land for the sake of hunting or fowling, the
latter may forbid him entry if aware of his purpose.] An animal thus caught by you
is deemed your property so long as it is completely under your control; but so soon
as it has escaped from your control, and recovered its natural liberty, it ceases to be
yours, and belongs to the first person who subsequently catches it. It is deemed to
have recovered its natural liberty when you have lost sight of it, or when, though it
is still in your sight, it would be difficult to pursue it." *The Institutes of Justinian*
37 (Oxford, transl. J. B. Moyle, 1913).

[24] The translation of bk. 2, tit. 1, §13 of the *Institutes* is as follows: "It has been
doubted whether a wild animal becomes your property immediately you have
wounded it so severely as to be able to catch it. Some have thought that it becomes
yours at once, and remains so as long as you pursue it, though it ceases to be yours
when you cease the pursuit, and becomes again the property of anyone who catches
it: others have been of opinion that it does not belong to you till you have actually
caught it. And we confirm this latter view, for it may happen in many ways that you
will not capture it." *Institutes*, transl. Moyle, 37.

[25] Justinian, *Digest*, bk. 41, tit. 1, also collated with the text of Freiesleben, note
23 above. The first four paragraphs of Title 1 repeat the beginning of §12 of the
Institutes quoted by JA, note 23 above.

nobis eum commisisse. Plerique non aliter putaverunt eam nostram esse, quam si eam ceperimus: quia multa accidere possunt, ut eam non capiamus: quod verius est." [26]

II. ADAMS' MINUTES OF THE ARBITRATION [27]

Boston, October 1769

Doane vs. Gage.

Our Depositions [28]

Silvanus Snow and Amos Knowles. Captains. Have been long acquainted with the Customs of Whaling. If A. strikes a Whale, and B. puts in a 2nd. Iron upon a *Call* or *Swing,* from A. or *otherwise* and A's Iron draws, the Whale is in the *Possession of A.* the first striker.

Knowles to the Mateship and Value of the Whale.[29]

Gamaliel and Barzillai Smith. It was the Custom 1765 at Streights of Bellisle, *that if A. struck a Whale, and made a Swing, B. getting an Iron in was intituled to an Eighth.* Several Instances last Year, of Whales struck with only *an Iron and naked Warp,* and they that struck em again *had 1/8,* by arbitration. The Custom also, that *if A struck a Whale,* and she *drawed* his Iron *he had no Right, except B's Iron was in before she was loose, by a Call.* The common Custom, *the first Striker is in Possession* while he *is fast* if it were but for a *Minute.*

[26] *Digest,* bk. 41, tit. 1, §5. The sentence which JA sums up as "&c." is the same as the last sentence of §12 of the *Institutes,* note 23 above. The remainder of the paragraph is an elaboration of §13 of the *Institutes,* note 24 above: "The following question has been asked: when a wild beast is so wounded that it could be taken, does the person [who wounded it] immediately become owner? Trebatius was of opinion that he did immediately, and that he must be held to retain the ownership so long as he kept on following the animal up, but that, if he relinquished the pursuit, his ownership ceased and the animal would once more become the property of whoever took it; so that if, at any moment while the pursuit lasted, some other person should capture it with a view to his own profit, he must be held to have committed a theft on the person first mentioned. A good many authorities hold that the party does not become owner unless he captures it, because there is a considerable chance of the capture not being made; and this is a better view to take." *De Adquirendo: Translation of Justinian's Digest, Book 41, Title I,* 3 (Cambridge, transl. C. H. Monro, 1900).

[27] In JA's hand. Adams Papers, Microfilms, Reel No. 184. Appended to the minutes are notes made by JA and an unidentified assistant on several of Gage's depositions. These have been printed as footnotes at the appropriate points below.

[28] That is, depositions in Doane's favor. The text to note 47 below is apparently the material from which JA argued.

[29] That is, Captain Knowles' deposition is also pertinent on these two questions. See JA's Interrogatories (Doc. III) on mateship and custom.

Nathan Hopkins saith, there was a Dispute or Controversy between Doane and Gage, about a Whale killed the day before, and Gage had in Possession. Doane said *He was the first Striker* and that his Boat was *fast to her*, when Gage put in his Iron. Gage said she was a *loose Whale* when he struck her. Doane desired to leave it to *Whalemen on the Spot.* Gage refused. Doane *demanded* his Part according to *Custom* would not be at *Charge* for *Trying, Freight,* or *Barvell.*[30] Gage would do nothing, but said his *owner* might *dispute* it at Home. Deponent and David Welts called as Witnesses to the *offer and Demand.* Custom that 2d. Iron called by 1st has an 1/8.

David Welts to the same Purpose.[31]

These 5 deponents sufficient to ascertain the Custom. The Customs of Whaling are certain Regulations dictated by observation, Experience, of Common Sense among Whalemen. They are the Result of the Common Sense of Whalemen. And this Regulation among the Whalemen at the Streights seems to be a wise, prudent, and equitable one. Some Rule, and Law, they must have, to avoid everlasting Contention. What better Rule can they have than this that the first striker shall have the Game?[32]

[30] Trying: "The process of extracting oil from blubber by heat." *OED.* Barvell: "A leather apron." *OED.* See Andrews, ed., " 'State of the Trade,' 1763," 19 Col. Soc. Mass., *Pubns.* 384 note (1918). Presumably here, by extension from the leather apron worn in cutting up the whale, the term means the process of cutting up.

[31] Apparently the same David Welts, or Welch, who testified for the other side also. See note 42 below. The notes of JA's assistant on Welch's deposition for Gage are as follows:

"Davd. Welch. ⟨Otis⟩ Gages witness when summoned by them says some said the whale belonged to Doane some to Gage. He Cant Tell which was the most and at the Time he Gave Evidence before he heard Jno. Whelden say the whale belonged to Coll. Otis—that Disputes used to be settled by arbitration—that Claimers Gave in their Claims and that sometimes bad Judgment was given and that the Doanes was Reconed Just men in the whaleing bussiness—in answer To Coll. Otis's Question. And that when he Claimed by the head of his Iron no boate was fast to the whale and no other thing To Claim by for the whale had Ran Loose above a mile. And that if he had held tow till another Iron was in he need not produced his Iron head. And the 2d striker Could have had no more than his Call or 8th if his Iron had been in before the Deponent's broke or Drawed out. And further says that in the whaleing bussiness he has heard of Instances of puting in Iron on the presumtion of Gaining a Call or 8th but then in that Case it Lyeth with the 1st striker Either To Give or not but saith if he is the first striker and another Iron is put in before he is Loose the possession Remains in the first striker. And that the whale in which his broken Iron was was not mortally wounded. But said Iron, was in the whales small. He Got a Quarter altho she was Cut of when Runing away." Adams Papers, Microfilms, Reel No. 184. The small of a whale is "the part of the tail in front of the flukes." *OED.*

[32] Lord Mansfield was said to have argued similarly for the application of custom: "I remember the first case upon that usage [the Greenland practice], which was tried before Lord Mansfield, who was clear, that every person was bound by it, and said, that were it not for such a custom, there must be a sort of warfare perpetually

Witnesses to the Facts. 8 in Point. Jesse Newcomb and John Chase.

Robert Newcomb. Hove his Iron at her, did not fasten, *hawled in his Iron.* Nickerson shot in, and struck her, his Boat not more than *8 or 10* fathoms from mine. Nickersons *Iron Pole* the *whole length above the Water.* Nick. *hove over his Coils* of Warp and *shipped his oars.* Whale went down, in *about a minute shot up again so near* to Gage that I thought she would *have stove* his Boat. I, *40 yds.* distance from Gage. Gage hove his Iron into her. Nothing parting *us and Gage* from *the Whale* but *Nickersons Boat. Nick and Gage towed away together.* About 4 Boat length 104 foot. *Both fast to said Whale at the same Time,* cant say how long. When Nick. struck her he saw the *Whale and Iron Pole go down together.*

Silas Newcomb. We hove at a Whale, but did not fasten, so we *haled in our Iron.* Nick. shot in, and *struck her,* and *hove over* his *Coils of Warp.* The Whale went down, and as she rose, Gage met her, and *hove his Iron into her.* Nothing parting us and Gage but the *Whale and Boat.* Nick. and Gage *towed away together 2 boats Length.* Nick.'s Iron struck the Whale *above Water* his Boat *12 or 15 fathoms* from ours. Gage 40 Yds. when he put his Iron. When Nick. struck I saw the *Whale and Iron Pole go down together.* I saw the shank of Nick's Iron was bent as if it had been fastend in a Whale.[33]

---

subsisting between the adventurers." Fennings v. Lord Grenville, 1 Taunt. 241, 248, 127 Eng. Rep. 825, 828 (C.P. 1808) (Opinion of Chambre, J.), cited in Holmes, *Common Law* 168. See note 17 above.

[33] Compare the deposition of Silas Newcomb, 4 April 1766, SF 172973:

"Silas Newcomb of lawful age testifyeth and saith that he being on a whaling voiage at the Labradore Shore and sometime the latter Part of June or the beginning of July last past I fell in Chase of a whale and we hove at her But did not fasten to her so we hauled in our Iron and Asa Nickerson Shot in upon her and struck her and hove over his Coils of warp. Then the whale went down, and as she Rose again one Gage met her and hove his Iron into her, nothing parting us and Gage But the whale and Boat. And Nickerson and Gage towed away together about Two Boats length. We Rowed up and asked them what they would give and I heard no answer, then we asked again and I heard Gage say I forbid any person to Touch that whale for she was in his Possession. Then we Eased away and I saw that Nickerson *was loose from the whale.* Further I saw that when Nickerson's Iron struck the whale the Iron hit the whale above water and Judge Nickersons Boat was then about Twelve or fifteen fathoms from our Boat when he said Nickerson Put his Iron Into said Whale and Gage I judge was about forty Yards from our Boat when he put his Iron Into the whale. And further saith that one Thomas Mayo of Harwich struck the same whale in his Judgment before said Nickerson did and held to her near a quarter of a Mile or more before his Iron drew and after that the said whale ran a Mile and half at least before said Nickerson struck her, and further saith that when Nickerson struck said Whale he saw the whale and Iron pole Go down Together and that he did not see said Iron or pole afterwards: further after Gage had forbid any Body's Medling with the whale Jashur Tayler came up, Eased away, and asked who struck the whale and I Told him Asa Nickerson. Then he answered Capt. Gage is fast to her and he is our mate Boat and then pulld away."

Atkins Smith. In the Boat with Silas Newcomb. *Hove and missed and hawled in our Warp.* Nick. shot in, and *struck her* and *hove over* his *Coils of Warp.* The Whale went down and as she rose, Gage met her and hove his Iron into her, nothing parting Gage and us, but *Whale and Nickersons Boat.* I then saw *both tow.* Then several Questions and answers passed before *Gage forbid* any Person, and *after that* We saw Nickerson loose. Saw Nick. Boat *come in Tow after the Whale with the oars shipped in.* They *both towed together*, and then I [lookd?] off.[34]

Edward Cook. In *the Boat with Silas Newcomb.* Hove and missed. *Hawled in the Iron.* Nick. shot in and struck her and *hove over his Coils of Warp that lay on the Head of the Boat.* Then the Whale *went down*, and as she *rose again* Gage *met her* and hove his Iron into her, nothing parting Us, and Gage, but Whale and Nickersons Boat. Saw Nick's Boat *come in Tow* after the Whale with his *oars shipped in*, and *Nick and Gage towed away together 2 Rods at least* while I looked on.

Note these 4. Witnesses, Rob. and Silas Newcomb, Atkins Smith and Ed. Cook. are all direct and possitive to the Point. They were all in one Boat—all very near to the Whale and to Nick. and Gage: it was a Whale that they had hove at but a minute before, and therefore the more likely to observe attentively. They all agree, that they hove at the Whale first, missed and haled in their Iron—that Nickerson instantly upon their missing of her, shot in upon her—hove at her ⟨and⟩ struck her and fastened to her. That the Whale upon being struck by Nickerson went down under Water, and soon after came up near Gage's Boat—so near that they thought she would have stove him as Rob. Newcomb swears—that Gage threw his Iron into her, without any Call from Nick. and both Boats towed away together. They can none of them say exactly how long.

Joseph Cable. In Newcombs Boat. Silas Newcomb steersman and Robert Harponier. Our Harp[oon] hove and misst. *Nick. hove his Iron into the Whale and made fast to her.* Gage came up, in 2 minutes and hove his in. *The Whale run*, and *both Boats towed sharp for a minute and half.* Then Nicks *Iron drew. Plain to be seen*—within 30 Yds. of the Whale.[35]

[34] See the deposition of Atkins Smith, Truro, 6 March 1766. SF 172962.
[35] See the deposition of Joseph Cable, Eastham, 17 Feb. 1768, SF 173117, in which there is the further statement "that the said Newcombs contended about their

Edmund Freeman. A Dispute between Doane and Gage. Newcomb said he was *close by,* and looked *right on* and saw both under Tow together. Dispute whether an Indian or Nickerson was Endsman, and Newcomb right and Gage wrong. Custom to leave such disputes to Arbitration.

Archelaus Harding. Mayo's Steersman. *Nick. struck the Whale* sometime *before Gage,* and *continued fast to her untill Gage was fast and sometime after Whale winded Nickersons Boat round,* and *upon a Turn the Whale hove out Nicks Iron.* Still he followd and *worked upon her till dead.* I viewed her, and *found an Iron Hole in which was no Iron. A warps Length off when Nick. struck. Whelden farther off.*

From this Deposition it seems that Gages putting in his Iron, made the Whale shift her Course turn Nickersons Boat quite round, and in turning, hove out his Iron. So that Gage's striking the Whale when in Nickersons Possession was the Cause why his Iron drew and if Gage had not struck her Nickerson would probably have continued fast till he could have put in more Irons.

Elisha Linnell in Wheldens Boat with him and Eldridge. Saw Gage put in his Iron, several other Boats near, one of them being Nick. Not above *15 fathoms* from Gages Boat when Gage struck the Whale. *Never saw Nick hawling in his Iron*—nor heard Whelden *say so.* Not till We arrived at N. England. Nick. *pursued and assisted in killing* the Whale and insisted she was his Property as the first striker. And fast when Gage put in his Iron.

Vid. Saml. Linnells Deposition vs. this.[36]

Captn. Joshua Harding. In Conversation with Jno. Wheelden, a few days after the whale was killed Wheelden told him, that if the Dispute was left to him as an Arbitrator, *he should give Part of the Whale to Mayhew*[37] *and Part to Doane.* He saw an Hole, that he thought and still thinks an Iron Hole.

Josh. Bassitt, Harponier to Jno. Crowell, and belonged to Wheel-

being fast to the same Whale untill Nickerson Struck her and they saw their own Iron pole at the Stern of the Whale boat."

[36] See Paine's summary of Samuel Linnell's deposition, text following note 60 below. See also note 65 below.

[37] This probably refers to Thomas Mayo, who was fast to the whale and then lost her before Nickerson struck. See note 33 above.

dens Vessell. Swears, that *when the Boats were close upon the Whale, he was 200 Rods distant, and that he could not know one Boat, nor Man from another.* Near 30 Boats between him and Whale. And he saw Nickerson, with Gage and others at Work on the Whale after he came up. Heard none of the Crew say, that Nicks Iron was out when Gage struck, or that the whole whale belongd to Gage.[38]

James Wallace. An oarsman to Crowell. By Reason of the Distance could not know ⟨one Man nor Boat from another, when the whale was struck⟩ who struck the Whale. On his coming on Board, the People in Wheeldens Boat told him the Whale belonged to the Doans. Elisha Linnell told him so in particular.

Captn. Micajah Sears. Wheelden or some of his Head Men on board their Vessell told me, that they were nigh the Whale when struck, and by what they saw, they thought she belonged to Captn. Doane. This was the general Talk on board Captn. Wheeldens Vessell, at that Time, and no Contradiction to it.

Robt. Homer. Master of a Voyage. In a Boat with Seth Baker and Jno. Cash. *1/3 of a Mile off, and 10 or 12 Boats nearer than ours. We were not near enough to distinguish the Persons, or know one Man or Boat from another.* Took it to be the opinion *of the whole Crew that the whale belongd to the Doans and heard Wheelden and others say so. And fully expected that Wheeldens Evidence would have been for Doane.*

Jesse Newcomb, now a Master. He was in the Boat with the 2 Newcombs. *Nickerson hove and fastend above Water. Saw 2 Boats tow, one of 'em the Indian Boat.*[39] *I thought I saw the Iron enter the Whale.* Saw 2 Boats tow together about 50 Yards. The general Voice of the People it was Doanes Whale in other Boats besides his.

Jno. Chase. Saw Nick. deliver his Iron at the Whale and throw the Coils out of the Head of his Boat. And saw Gage give the 2d. Iron. Then saw Nicks Boat, wheeled or winded round. *Heard Gage I think say Nickerson veer out your Warp.*[40] Both towed away together about 100 yards. Then saw Nick. loose. Nick killed the Whale by lancing her. Saw him launce her in a good Place, and she spouted Blood immediately.

Vid. Depositions of Saml. Howland, Benja. Bussley, Elijah Blush

[38] Bassett also gave a deposition for Gage in which he apparently sought to qualify his testimony here. See text at note 72 below. See Otis' question apparently aimed at Bassett's credibility, note 65 below.

[39] That is, Nickerson's boat, one of the crew of which was an Indian. See note 63 below.

[40] Slack off your line. See *OED.*

vs. Jno. Chase's deposition. Attempts to prove him distracted but no Lyar. Blush says, never heard any Body say but Chase was a Man of Truth.[41]

David Welts. Heard Doane offer Gage to leave the Dispute to Men.

Additional Evidence. Examine this Deposition if reyled on of the other side.[42]

Timothy Right, Simeon Tobey and Jona. Child, to be put in Ballance vs. Amos Otis's Deposition.[43]

Captn. Nat. Ellis. Vox Populi.
Benja. Fessenden. Adams blamed Gage for not leaving the affair to Men because several Persons on the Spot were positive that Nickersons Iron was fast when Gage hove in his. Edd. Dillingham Ditto.
Chillingsworth Foster. Never heard but Chase was a Man of Truth.
Thos. Mayo. Gage took the whale away by Force.

Nathl. Bassett a Deacon, Jabez Crowell and Barnabas Eldridge Depositions vs. Zechariah Smalleys Deposition.

Reuben Doane, Barnabas Chase, and [*blank left in MS*] against James Gages Deposition about the general Talk and something said by Joseph Doane that he should not have stirred but for setters on.

Saml. Burgess. Gage said there was Nickersons Boat and his and they wanted no Help. And that Nickerson claims Part in the Whale then spouting Blood.

Mem. Captn. Jasher Taylor confessed before the arbitrators last June[44] that Richard Godfrey one of Nickersons Mate Boats[45] did put an Iron into the Whale after Nickersons drew, and it remained in till she was dead.

David Okelly, one of Gages Depositions[46] says that Nicks Boat and Gage's Boat were partly crossing each other, just before he heard

[41] See these depositions as summarized by Paine, text at notes 58–60 below. Compare Howland's interrogatories, note 59 below.
[42] Welts or Welch apparently gave a deposition for each side. See note 31 above.
[43] See the deposition of Amos Otis as summarized by Paine, text at note 57 below.
[44] Taylor's earlier appearance was at the two-day hearing held on 20–21 June 1769. See note 14 above. His testimony does not seem to have been relied on by either side, but he would probably have been favorable to Gage. See note 33 above.
[45] That is, a boat from a ship with which Nickerson's ship was "mated." See note 6 above.
[46] See O'Kelly's deposition, text at note 56 below.

Captn. Tayler say that Gage was fast. *Which agrees with our Witnesses and militates with theirs.*

Mr. Paine.[47] One Rule in our favor. We are in Possession and Possession is a good Title, untill a Person demands who has an absolute Right.

Q. Who the first Occupant?

Custom. Evidence dont support the Proposition. The Witnesses seem to evade the Point. Odd Custom. (Meaning I suppose not reasonable).

Inconsistencies and Contradictions in our [48] Depositions. Sufficient to destroy them.

6 Witnesses in the same Boat, not so good, as in different Boats.

Rob. Newcombs Deposition. Inconsistency in the situation. 40 yards distance. Nothing parting us and Gage from the Whale but Nick[er]sons Boat. In the after Questions,[49] We were a little quartering upon the Whale. Answer Gage was a broad side of us. Dont know whether starboard or larboard. How is this possible.

Nickersons [50] transient View, of Nickersons halling in his Warp.

Silas Newcombs Account different about parting &c. us and Gage from the Whale, &c.

Confused and disorderly in that Boat, so that they could not observe truly.

Differ about the Distance, the fathoms.

Silas says he never saw the Iron Pole afterwards.

Answer, not till I saw Nickerson hawl it into his Boat. Then the Iron was bent.[51] *Contradiction.*

Robt. *saw the Iron Pole the whole Length above Water. This Otis says inconsistent with Silas's Account of the Whale and Iron Pole going down together.*[52]

Silas says 60 or 70 foot from Nick. when he hawl'd in his Iron, 12 or 15 fathom when he struck, 60 or 70 fathom.

[47] JA's notes of the arguments of Paine and Otis for Gage comprise the remainder of Doc. II.

[48] That is, Doane's.

[49] Probably referring to the questions asked during the taking of the deposition, following the deponent's statement.

[50] Apparently an inadvertence for Newcomb.

[51] Silas Newcomb's deposition, set out, note 33 above, contains only the statement that he never saw the iron afterwards, and not the remark that the iron was bent. JA noted the latter, but not the former, statement, however. See text at note 33 above. The remark is thus either from a subsequent deposition given by Newcomb or, possibly, from his answers to interrogatories, neither of which we have.

[52] Apparently James Otis' comment on the testimony.

Iron might be bent, i.e. might be fastend and bent and drawn before Gage enterd. Answer true, but prooves the fastening. Might be bent on Purpose. Needle and Barn.[53]

Silas says 18 yds. Rob. 36. Silas 50. That the 2 Boats towd together.

Arch. Harding. No. 7. Differs from all in Newcombs Boat, about the Position. *He says Nick. and Gage met the Whale Head and Head.* This Deposition a finished Piece of Cookery.

There might be an Iron Hole, and yet Nick. never fast, for Mayo might have been fast to her.

Mayo did not know who struck. Harding did. How could this be— one says a quarter of Mile, the other a Warps *Length.*

Jno. Chases dont mention the Whales going down. Whalemen remember as exactly as Hunters.

Their Witnesses to invalidate ours.[54]

Mayo and Harding. *Barnabas Tayler.* A Minor. *Mayo said He would clear from Doane for a Trifle.* Never heard Mayo say he saw an Iron hole. *Saw Adams &c. try several Holes* &c. Did not hear any Body talk about an Iron Hole.

Jacob Hawes, a Lad. 3 Papers. Tayler desired Doane to come and view and see if he could find an Iron Hole, to claim her by. I search'd, *and found no Holes, but what Irons were taken out at.* Nick. worked, 'tho forbid. Saw Nick. and Indian change Ends. *Saw Godfrey offer to tow,* being a Party to Doane's side. *Gage refused unless a free will offering.*[55]

Levi Bearse, No. 16, a Lad in Adams's Boat. *See Nick', launce her diverse Times, and heard that Godfrey put an Iron in.*

David OKelly, a Lad. No. [...] Evidence. *Whale and Nickersons Boat crossing each other.* Militates with Wheelden.[56]

Josa. Knowles. No. 8. with Syl Hopkins. Silas Newcomb in a Passion. Damning the freemasons.

Thos. Chase. No. 28. Heard Silas Newcomb say, *he did say the D—l take the freemasons.* Hawld in his steering oars.

[53] Thus in MS. The reference is unclear.

[54] That is, Gage's to invalidate Doane's.

[55] JA's assistant says of this deposition: "In the same boate with Clark. Viz. Taylor a party."

[56] See notes on this witness by JA, text at note 46 above. His assistant's notes on this deposition follow:

"David OKelly a minor in Capt. Jasher Taylors boate millitates with Wheeldens Deposition and all his Company as to the Distance of Nickerson and Gages boates when strikeing the whale together with the scituation of their position and the Distance of time and thereby Corroborates the Newcombs Depositions and their boats Crew &c. Notes made on the Coppy [*i.e.* of the deposition] more fully. This to compare with Jacob Hawes' Deposition allso."

Abner Chase the same as Thos. Chase. *Said he did not row any farther to the best* of my Remembrance.

Amos Knowles Jnr. No. 22. *Robt. and Silas Newcomb both told me,* Whale turned off, and Lot Gage *struck the Whale directly.* Nothing of Nick's striking *in March 1766 in Kings Road that Doanes Boat struck her &c. They said that Doane was so unfair with them that they had rather Gage should have the Whale than they.*

Amos Otis. Have since understood, that Adams run foul of Lot Gage. And heard a Voice to Adams to veer Warp. *The Whale as near again to the Newcombs as they to me.* Yet heard the Disturbance in their Boat. *Adams told him he ran foul of Gage—did not see Gage fast—that Adams and Gage both in one—Newcomb more noisy than common. Heard several People say there come the crazy Newcombs.* Heard Silas was crazy, after he came home.[57]

Saml. Howland vs. *Jno. Chase.* Same Boat—*thought Nick's was not fast.* No Way ahead.[58] *Saw Nick. hauling Warp when Gage struck. Jno. Chase out of his Head sometimes—jumped overboard. Not a lying fellow*—behaved well that day. *To the best of my Remembrance he seemed to signify, that Gage had the best Right.*[59]

---

[57] The notes of JA's assistant on this deposition follow:

"Amos Otis' Deposition proves that the Newcombs was up aboute as near the whale as they say in their Deposition: but it appears he Did not observe when Either Nickerson or Gage struck the whale. See Right Childs and Tobey, Depn."

[58] That is, Nickerson's boat was not making way through the water, which it would have done had it been fast to the moving whale.

[59] The notes of JA's assistant on Howland's answers to unidentified interrogatories follow:

"Saml. Howland sworn 1769 has Lived in the midst of the whalers of Gages party aboute 3 years and an half since the Suite was Commenced first and brought to Give his Evidence at Last which Does not appear verey fair and Consistant.

"He says the head of their boate was toward the whale's head. He says he saw Nickerson Dart   A. Yes.   Did he fasten   A. He thought not.

"He Did not see Nickerson Tow and his Answer To Question 9 is Saw Nickerson hawling in his warp Before Gage struck: and his Answer is To Question 10 that to the best of his Remembrance he thinks it was the same whale that Nickerson flung his Iron at and that he is Verey sure of it: and that he saw Gage strike her after he saw Nickerson hawling in his warp, which is his answer To Question 11th. Then he Goes on and says their people wondred the Contending parties Did not Leave the affair to *masters of Vessels To settle it as Usual* and that their people said they *Reconed that the whale was a Loose Whale when Gage struck her but* Cant Remember he heard Chase say any thing aboute her nor Cant Remember that Chase was present at the Conversation. Goes on to say that at sometimes John Chase Drank To much and Did not behave well for he Kept a Journal and said he Could Keep as Good a one as the Master. And that he went in to swim with his Cloath on once or twice and that he struck the Deponent with his fist &c. but Cant say Chase's memory is bad nor that he is not a man of Truth &c. nor Can he pretend to say near the Time of Day the whale was first Discovered wether in the morning noon or Towards night. But a Good many boats in pursuit of her near her in Chase upon her allmost up with her. Answer To 42 Question when he first saw the whale she was Comeing Right at us he says and we was Rowing toward her. I saw Gage fast to her and

Elijah Blush. No. 36. vs. Jno. Chase. Never call'd a Lyar that I know of.

Lem'. Crocker. Chase got overboard, stripped off his Cloaths &c. Asa Croker to the same fact.

Jona. Bassett. No. 30. vs. Jno. Chase. With Josa. Godfrey. Jno. Chase Harpoonier. *Never heard Chase say that Nick struck. Knew nothing of Chases Truth &c.*

⟨W⟩ ⟨*Boat came along close to our Boat*⟩

Whale came along with Gage close to our Boat no other fast to her. Saw no 2d Iron put in.

Benja. Busseley No. 17 vs. Jno. Chase. Heard Josa. Godfrey ask who struck first &c. and him and Jno. Chase talk about it after. *I heard him Godfrey say, he could not tell who would get the Whale, but he believd it belonged to Gage.* Chase said it was devlish strange, they could not tell who struck at first. *One time he said he believd that Gage struck the Whale first. Understood by him or others, that Gage was up or near up in the Chase. Paine says he said he was far off.*[60]

Saml. Linnell Junr. [. . . .] No. 26. vs. Elisha Linnell. Elisha told me that he saw Doanes Boat hawl in his Iron as Gage dart[ed] and that the Whale belonged to Gage.

Their Witnesses off the fact.

John Wheelden. No. 1. 3 Papers. Vid.[61] and Vide Micajah Siers. As explicit as any of our side, and Wheelden wasnt.[62]

Nickerson hawleing in his warp. He saw him Dart and see him hawleing in his warp. He saw Gage heave in his Iron: he afterwards says he was aboute 80 or 100 fathoms from her. Cant tell whether Rowing or Lying on their oars. Query whether he Could Clearly Distinguish boats and presisely whether a boat Veered warp or halled in Especially in the Direction of head To head, the boats and whale, the oarsmen, back to [*i.e.* because facing aft].

"He saw no Iron put in after Gages as he says. And he saw her a few minutes after she past them Even To Rowing 80 or 100 fathom. I am at a Lost to know which way the boat Could turn so as for the Deponent not to have a much Clearer View than he had when meeting the whale: Query whether this agrees with the witnesses on the same side that say in aboute 1 minute after Gage struck that Adams second[ed] an Iron. He says he observed Gage from the time he fastened to her. Cant tell whether he made a General Call or not and answers To Question 61 that he is Verry sure he saw Nickerson hawleing in his warp when Gage struck and thinks the warp was in the pins or Chocks. He says it was Verry soon a small space of time after Nickerson hove his Iron when Gage struck but Cant say how Long. Believes the same Riseing of the whale and is pretty sure it was—and never saw the whale Go Down from the Time Nickerson Darted till Gage was fast all which millitates with Wheelden and Tarrow and others of the same side who say the whale Run the Distance of 80 or 100 fathom between Nickersons and Gages Darting at the whale and some of them say a Greater Distance."

[60] Comment by Paine on the testimony.

[61] JA's notes on this deposition are as follows:

"Captn. John Wheelden. [Heard?] Barn. Eldridge saw Mayo strike a Whale. She

Barnabas Eldridge. No. 2. Not acquainted with Nick at that time. Indian in the Head when I first saw that Boat. *Both Nicks and Newcombs 6 handed Boats.*[63]

——————

towed sharp 1/4 Mile. Iron drew. 2 Whales together when Mayo struck. One kept along shore. I thought it the same Mayo struck. But since found I was mistaken, for Tayler told me no Iron hole. Newcombs Harponier hove at the Whale and missed. *As he stoppd to hale in his Iron We got by.*

"Nickerson flung at her. His Boat *shot ahead a little and then he hawled in his Iron and Warp.* As I went by Nickersons Boat, I saw them *hawling in their Iron and Warp and* think their *oars not shipped*, and the *Iron Pole came above Water as we passed 'em at his stern.* The Whale run after that 2 *shot of Warp* [i.e. two segments of line probably of 120 fathoms each] before Lot Gage put his Iron into her. 140 fathom. Upon his striking he made a *general Call.* He said *get in your Iron as soon* as you can, but in less than a Minute Adams seconded in an Iron, and *Gage and he towed away* together. When Gage fastened, *Nickerson 70 fathoms off* and *Newcombs a great deal farther off.* Newcombs did not mention Nickersons striking. Nickerson said he had not his Warp in the Pins, and in such a Hurry he had not Time to call before Gage struck. Saw Nickerson work on her, and Gage forbid him. When Nick. hove, he was *about 20 fathoms* from Deponent."

The following comments were appended in the hand of JA's assistant:

"Observe that the whale Runing above 50 Rood after Nickerson was Loose if fact must put the matter in Dispute so Intirely out of the Question that it seems to me Mr. Wheelden must utterly mistake with Respect to the boates Engaged: or must mistake the time when Gage first put his Iron in the Whale. Jno. Wheelden finds himself mistaken aboute 2 whales because Taylor Told him so. Why Did not Whelden Contradict Asa Nickerson when he Queried with him."

The assistant also commented as follows on Whelden's answers to interrogatories:

"John Wheldins Interogatories

"Observe Wheldens answers. Remarkable with Respects to his particular observations of what Past in the Newcombs boate when in pursuite which Generally is full of noise and bustle and when Whelden was Rowing full speed. He says Robert Whelden Called 3 times the Last time To swear Back on those that had Contradicted his Deposition and so it might be add Infinitum."

[62] Comment by JA.

[63] The notes of JA's assistant on this deposition are as follows:

"Barnabas Eldrige Mr. Wheldens Harpooner was in Chase of a whale with Newcombs and others whose Back was Toward the whale in the time of Chase: says that after Sometime Newcombs Harpooner Darted at the whale. Does not observe that he saw it. After which Wheelden told him Nickerson had hove at the whale and was fast. *He Looked Round and Replied* he was not fast and soon after Wheelden said so too. The Reason of his opinion was Because Nickerson boate had not such way on head as is usual for a fast boate to have. *Did not believe he had any head way but what his oars gave him.* And the whale Run 60 or 70 fathom before Gage struck her *and then is Quite* Clear in it that the whale was Loose when Gage struck and that Gage made a Call and in Less than a minute Edwd. Adams shot in a second Iron and Gage and Adams Towed away together. When Gage struck the whale the Deponent was the nearest boate and Does not Remember to have seen Asa Nickerson near at that time and the first time he saw Nickerson afterwards he was behind Gage. He Did not see the Indian untill he saw him in the head."

The assistant also made the following observations, apparently on Eldridge's answers to interrogatories:

"Barnabas Eldridge says Whelden said Nickerson ⟨Swears the Newcombs Did not⟩ was fast to the whale. The first he saw Nickerson [. . .] the Indian was in the head of his boate. He heard on that Day the whale was killed by Samle. Howes one of

John Tarrow. No. 3. With Wheelden. *The Whale went under Water, 8 or 10 Minutes.* Saw no Boat fast when Gage struck.[64]

Jno. Wheelden Junr. No. 4. Not fast for Boat had no Way a head. The Whale under swift way. Clear that the loose Whale.[65]

Jno. Crowell.[66] No. 5. 3 Papers. In another Boat in the Stern. *According to my apprehension Nick. missed, because not under tow.* About 50 or 60 fathom, before Gage struck. Wallace's Character not

---

Gage's mates. The Vessells 4 Leages apart. A sure mark of a boats being fast if she Tows after the whale. And says he Does not Remember that he heard Robt. Homer say any thing aboute it. Cash and Baker men of Probity never Disputed. By the way he allso says Homer is a man of truth. As to the Quarrel knows nothing to the purpose."

[64] The notes of JA's assistant on this deposition are as follows:

"John Tarrow saw somebody thro[w] at a whale which he understood afterward was Asa Nickerson but Concludes Did not fasten because his boate Did not seem to be under such way a head as fast boats have. In two or three minutes after *I saw said Nickerson* hawling in his Iron. Then in 5 or 6 minutes after *saw* Gage strike a whale no boate in Tow after her as *he saw* which he thinks was the same *that Nickerson threw at* and the Distance of time 8 or 9 minutes after Nickerson hove before Gage struck. His Judgment Is that they was 30 or 40 fathoms from Nickerson when he hove his Iron. And that soon after Gage was *fast Wheelden asked him what he would Give. He answered nothing as* his mate boates was all Round him and that the Deponent says he Does not know Silas or Robert Newcombs and that he saw no other person thro[w] at said whale but Nickerson before Gage struck her.

"Observe the Deponent Did not know Nickerson in nor Newcombs. So Comparing the Distance of time between the persons throwing his Iron that he afterward ⟨was told⟩ *understood to be Nickerson must be the Newcombs. He allso millitates with the other witnesses in Wheeldings boate the same he was in*: with Respect to Gages *Giveing a Call &c. and Repeats Gages answer when asked for a peice by Wheelden.*"

[65] Thus in MS. The notes of JA's assistant on this deposition are as follows:

"John Wheelden Jnr. Deposition: says he heard his father say that Newcombs had missed the whale after which he said Asa Nickerson was fast but himself and Eldrige both thought him not fast after which he Gives some matter of othere opinion with Regard to the Distance the whale Run ⟨after⟩ before Gage put in his Iron which he suposes to be a Quarter of a mile but Does not Declare that he saw what passed nor is it Likely he should as his back must be toward the whale."

See notes in the hand of James Otis (described, note 18 above):

"Questions to ask younge Wheldon wheither he heard any Talke on Board the Vessel while Elisha Lenel [Linnell?] was Present. What it was that was said about her [*i.e.* the whale?]. Do you think that Stephen Linel's Capacity and Understanding is Equal to Common men in General. Was James Wallis Reconed to be a man of Truth By your vessels Company In General." SF 173972.

"Question. Are [*you*] Quite Clear in it that the whale Gage Struck was a loose whale when he fastened to her. Did you during your voiage or Since talke with Joseph Basset about a whale. What did he say to you. Ask Wheldon as to his Conversation with Nickerson why he did not make a General Call. His answer was he could not get his [hemp?] for the [. . . .]" SF 173914 (Verso: "Question to be asked Young Whelden, Joshua Harding, Jesse Newcomb, John Chase").

[66] See an undated deposition by John Crowell 3d, SF 174202, repeating in substance this statement to the phrase "before Gage struck." JA's assistant says: "John Crowels at a greate Distance."

good for Truth.[67] *Boats all round cant tell the Number. Afterwards told it was Nickerson.* Dispute between Wheelden and Homer.[68]

Silvanus Hopkins. Conclude missed her because his Iron Pole when [*i.e.*, went?] all under Water. Mem. knows nothing of Nickerson.[69]

Wm. Clark, same Boat No. 7. Saw Gage fast and no other.[70]

Seth Baker, in another Boat. Jno. Cash his Harpoonier. Dont know Nick. Knows there was no Boat fast when Gage struck. Vid. this Deposition (*Mem. not the same Whale*). Saw no Indian in that Boat, that struck and hawld in Iron before Gage struck.

Jno. Cash. 2 Papers. No. 13. Encouraged to row, by being told several had hove and missed. *No other Boat fast but Gage,* no other towed away with him. Steersman said he saw one quoiling in his Warp. Heard of Difference between Homer and Baker.[71]

Zechariah Smalley. Nota. And several Depositions vs. this.

Levi Bearse. Additional Evidence, No. 16. *A Man said We had better go aboard and git some Victuals for we were* never fast. Nick—d—n *your Blood hold your Tongue.* Q. *Who was that Man, that was so hungry.* 1/4 *an Hour after the Whale was dead.* Mem. never mentioned it before to any Body.

[67] Wallace's testimony for Doane appears in text following note 38 above. See also note 65 above.

[68] See the questions regarding Homer in Gage's interrogatories, Doc. IV. Homer's testimony, indicating a prior inconsistent statement by Wheelden, appears in text following note 38 above.

[69] The notes of JA's assistant on this deposition are as follows:
"Silvanus Hopkins says ⟨he heard⟩ he saw somebody thro[w] at a whale. He Did not see Nickerson neither thro[w] at the whale nor no other. He millitates with John Whelden, Barnabas Eldridge, Jno. Whelden Jnr., and Jno. Tarrow with Regard to the Distance that Newcombs was from Gage when Gage fastened."

[70] The notes of JA's assistant on this deposition are as follows:
"Willm. Clark says in fact nothing to the purpose his Depn. being wholly negitive or hear say with Respect to what the Newcombs said. Viz: that Sometime that Day they or some one in their boat said Gage struck the whale. If he heard such Talk it is Reasonable To Suppose he might mistake them by heareing them say Gage is now fast or to that purpose or might not attend to all that was said."
The assistant's notes on Clark's answers to interrogatories are:
"Clark swears somebody hove at the whale as his stearsman Told him but Called one boate and another boate but [*sentence incomplete in MS*]."

[71] The notes of JA's assistant on the depositions of Baker and Cash are as follows:
"Seth Baker and John Cash says that he saw several Boats Dart at the whale. He thinks none was fast but Gage when Gage struck but that several boats was near the whale. After some time saw 2 boats Tow away. Did not see when the other put his Iron in. The 2 boats he saw Tow was Likely to be Nickerson and Gage. The Reason is he soon Turned his back To them. His harponeer Cash says he saw no other boats fast at all and he had much the best Chance to see as they Rowd away for his face was then Toward the whale and it was probably the time between Nickersons Iron Drawing and Adams puting in his Iron that Cash perce[ive]d no other boate fast.
"Homers Deposition To Encounter these."

Jno. Bartlet, David Rider, Thos. Rider, Jno. Thatcher all to Wheeldens Character. *Bartlett* rather to shew that he told the same story 3 years before.

Isaiah Eldridge. 14 Years an Endsman, a Boat would go 15 Rods, after the oars still, in a smooth sea.

Nathl. Delano. 12 or 16 Rods and have considerable Force.

Saml. Tayler, a Minor, Son to Jasher. Doane said I would not give a Copper for our Chance, but We may scare 'em and make em leave it to Men. *Mem. at Law.*

Gideon Baty. Sears said they did not ⟨strike⟩ fasten so as to bring the Boat fairly under tow.

John Lothrop. A Minor. Doane desired Tayler to search the Whale well when he cutt her up.

James Gage. Doane said, if it had not been for setters on he should not have been concerned. *Would not give a Copper for an Iron Hole.* Brother to Lot Gage.

Jno. Gage Jnr.

Joh. Bassett. Did not know Nick. Explanatory of his Deposition of our side.[72] In the Boat with Crowell.

Seth Whelden Jnr. about Homer &c. Dispute between Homer and Whelden.

David Welts.[73] Custom vid. &c.

Paine. 2 Boats Newcombs and Wheeldens the most positive.

Our Boat the nearest. In the best situation to observe, calm &c. Newcombs, disappointed, tumultuous and inattentive.

Whelden a Man of good Character for Truth.

Our Witnesses as positive, as explicit, as circumstantial as theirs and more so.

More necessary to suppose our Witnesses perjured, if their accounts not true, than to suppose theirs so, if theirs not.

Iron being bent. Silas mistaken. For no Person takes Notice of this but Silas. Oar crooked coming out of Water.

Calling to Adams or to Nick. [to] veer warp, contradictory and counterpoised.

---

[72] JA's notes of this deposition appear in text following note 37 above. His assistant's notes on this deposition are as follows: "Joseph Basset says at a Greate Distance.

"Mere Guess and tho he swears he saw Asa Nickerson miss the whale he says afterward he was told so." See note 65 above.

[73] See notes 31, 42, above.

The Iron Pole above Water. Mem. Hopkins concluded one missed because his Iron Pole went under Water.

4. Witnesses in Wheeldens Boat, and more to be believed than our 8. ⟨*Crowell says that the Whale went 50 or 60 fathom before Gage struck, and concludes Nick missed because*⟩ &c.

Hopkins says she was a loose Whale.

Haws saw Nick hawl in his Iron before somebody told him that Gage was fast.

Cash says Whale towed Gage and no other Boat.

Seth Baker says, Gage was the first that fastnd, and that no other Boat was in Tow.

S. Howland in the Boat with Chase—thought Nick. not fast and saw Nick. hawl in his Warp before Gage struck.

11. Witnesses from 5 or 6 Boats. Positive to the fact in Paines favour he says.

All the rest of the Evidence to corroborate or invalidate these Testimonies.

Mayo's Evidence of the Iron hole.

Turning or winding round, she might have a sheer given her.

Doane would not examine for Iron Holes.

Zech. Smalleys Deposition. Vid.

Mr. Otis. ⟨*Gage*⟩ [74] if by Custom then not by Equity.

The Rule about positive and Negative Witnesses,[75] has Exceptions, e.g. 20 Witnesses that heard no Pistol 2 did &c.

Our Witnesses have recollected themselves at a great Distance from the Time.

But one Witness that saw the Iron Pole sticking up above Water, and but one that saw the Iron bent. Impossible but that other People should have seen these facts if true.

Towed away together. They speak of this in a manner and in Language that all Whalemen must laugh at.

Eldridge *looked round, therefore was up and might have seen the Iron Pole above Water.* [...] Nearest when Gage struck. Whelden so too. *Nota.* Iron Pole came above Water as we pasd Nickerson. Mistakes Newcombs.

Tarrow, an Indian with Whelden. Missed because not a sufficient way of Head. Mem. liable to mistake Newcombs for Nick. not know-

---

[74] This may be an inadvertence for Doane, or JA may not have recorded Otis' thought completely in the following phrase.

[75] See Gilbert, *Evidence* 157: "One affirmative Witness countervails the Proof of several Negative, because the Affirmative may swear true, and the Negative also."

ing either at the time. Tarrow dont agree with Whelden about the general Call.

Stray of the Warp, as streight as an arrow, enough for a Rope dancer.

Jesse Newcomb, thinks she ran 1/4 of a Mile.

Jno. Crowell in the stern of Jo. Bassetts Boat. Saw a Man which afterwards proved to be Nick. Missed because not way of Head enough. Vid. James Wallace's Deposition.

Syl. Hopkins. Missd. because Iron and Pole went all under Water. Newcombs. Soon after saw Gage. Never saw Nick throw. Proof that he had a very care⟨full⟩less View.

Otis says, if Nick. struck so notoriously, he must have seen it and the Iron Pole above Water. I say, it proves he had no good View.[76]

Josa. Knowles, and a No. of Witnesses swear that Silas was d——g the freemasons and his Boat in Confusion.

David OKelly a Minor with Jasher Tayler. Whale and Nicks Boat crossing each other. Nicks no Way of Head. Tayler desird Doane to come and see her cutt up and search for Iron Holes.

Otis confounds Nick. with Doane, when he blames for not viewing the Whale for Iron Holes.[77]

Why did not they view the Whale.

We fail in the essential fact that both Boats fast together. No Evidence of this. Answer 8 Witnesses are some Evidence.[78]

Jacob Hawes. A Minor. At the stern Nick pulling his Iron into the Boat. Saw Newcombs at a considerable distance to the stern of our Boat. Offer to come and view, when cut up, or turnd over.

Saml. Howland in Godfreys Boat with Chase. Very sure *Nick hauling in his Warp before Gage struck.*

Seth Baker ⟨Harponier⟩ Steersman to Jno. Cash. Whale run a Quarter of a Mile. &c. Knows not Nick nor Gage. Saw em haul in his Iron. Round by the last Boat that hove before Gage, while she was coiling in her Warp in the Bow of the Boat. Much about Robert Homer.

Jno. Cash. Much about Robert Homer. &c.

Amos Otis. These advantageously sit[uate]d. to see. Answer—vid. Homer's Deposition.[79]

Zech. Smalley. What Nick. told him. Did not care to say, he was fast.

[76] These two sentences are a comment by JA, perhaps for use in rebuttal.
[77] Comment by JA.
[78] The last phrase is a comment by JA.
[79] The last phrase is a comment by JA. For Homer, see note 68 above.

Levi Bearce, a Minor. In Adam's Boat. About 40 Rods from the Whale when Gage struck. Mayo said if they would give him a Piece he would prove the Doanes were not fast. This Deposition confirmed by OKelly and Haws's.

Busseley to Wheldens Character and Consistency.

Bartlett Ditto.

Josa. Eldridge [80] and Delano. Construction of a Whale boat.

Amos Knowles Jnr.

22. to the Character of Whelden and that Newcomb said Gage struck her directly, after they missd her. Rather Gage should have her than Doane.

Saml. Tayler. Doane said he would not give one Copper for our Chances, *but We may scare 'em to leave it to Men.*

Baty. Something like the former.

Jno. Lothrop. Heard Tayler tell Doane to come and search the Whale, and Doane said Well Well, do you search her well.

Saml. Linnell. Vs. Elisha Linnell. Heard Elisha say he saw Doanes Boat halling in his Iron and that she was Gages clear enough.

Barnabas Tayler. Like OKelly's.

Thos. Chase 28. vs. Silas Newcomb. D—l take the Freemasons. Otis said bro't to shew that Newcomb told a different story. But no such matter.[81]

Jona. Bassett. Did not see any Boat fast, when Gage struck.

Lem. Crocker 31. vs. Jno. Chase that he was delirious at Times. But no Lyar.

James Gage. General ⟨Gage's⟩ Talk. Dont care for an Iron Hole.

Jno. Gage. *The Iron came up at the Stern of the Boat of Newcombs not Nicks.*

Jo. Bassett. Both sides.

Elisha Blush.[82] General Talk.

37. Seth Whelden. Conversation with Homer and general Talk.

38. David Welts. Custom. I took it from Jno. Wheelden that she belonged to Coll. Otis.

Jno. Lothrop 39. The same day or a day or two after the Whale was killd I heard Whelden say that Gage killed the Whale and that she belonged to him.

[80] Apparently Isaiah Eldridge, whose testimony appears with that of Delano in text following note 71 above.

[81] The last two sentences are a comment by JA.

[82] That is, Elijah Blush. See text following note 59 above.

No. 43. Doane v. Gage

III. INTERROGATORIES FOR DOANE[83]

Court of Vice Admiralty, Boston, 1768

Interrogatories

1. Was you on Board a Whale Boat with Asa Nickerson, on or about the 21st. of June 1765, in the Streights of Bellisle, and to what Vessell did said Boat belong, and who was Master of said Vessell?

2. Did you see the said Asa Nickerson, strike any Whale or Whales, on or about that Time in said Streights, if you did in what manner, declare all you know herein.

3. How and from what Circumstances do you know the said Asa did strike a Whale at said Time, declare in particular what you know relating thereto.

4. Was there at that Time any and what Boats near the Boat on which you was, and whose Boats were they, and at what Distance from your Boat, when said Nickerson struck said Whale?

5. Did you afterwards See any other Person put an Iron into said Whale, and who?

6. How long was it after said Nickerson had struck the said Whale, before you saw any other Person put an Iron into her?

7. Was said Nickersons Iron in said Whale when you saw the Iron put into her by Lott Gage, declare all you know herein.

8. Did said Whale, after She was struck tow said Nickersons Boat any Distance, and what other Boat, and for how long did you see them tow together?

9. Did said Nickerson with his Boats Crew, together with any other Boats Crew and what, help to kill said Whale?

10. Did you hear any Person forbid said Nickerson and his Crew to assist in killing said Whale?

11. Did you after said Whale was killed, hear any Person and whom forbid Said Nickerson from towing said Whale?

12. Did you see any Boat after said Whale was struck by said Nickerson foul of Said Nickersons Boat and whose and how long after?

13. † Did the Iron struck into said Whale by said Nickerson, remain any, and what Length of Time, in said Whale. † Omit this Q.

14. How long was it, after said Gage, put his Iron into said Whale, before said Nickersons Iron drew out of her? Declare all you know.

15. At what Distance was you from Nickersons Boat when he struck the whale?

[83] In JA's hand, undated, SF 172907. See note 18 above.

16. Of What Bigness and Value was said Whale according to your best Judgment?

17. In what Direction was Nickersons Boat to the said Whale when he struck her?

18. Did said Boat shoot a head after the said Nickerson struck said Whale or did she veer round. Was it occasioned by the oars or the towing of the Whale by the way. Declare particularly all you know herein.

19. Have you been for any Time and how long acquainted with the Whale Fishery and the Customs thereof.

20. What, according to the Customs of Whalers, gives the Possession of a Whale? Declare particularly all you know herein.

21. After the first Strike of a Whale, and while his Iron is in her, if any other Person by Calling or Swinging to or of his own accord, put another Iron into her and then the first Strikers Iron Draws, Does the first Striker loose his Possession according to the Customs of Whaling and Right to said Whale? Declare particularly all you know herein. Quære of this Q.

22. Is it, or is it not necessary, according to said Custom to give the Possession and Right of a Whale to the first Striker, that his Stroke should give her a mortal Wound, or that his Iron should remain in her untill She be dead, declare all you know herein.

23. Did you ever hear Joseph Doane Demand of Lott Gage said Whale and when and where, and what was the Answer of the Said Lott Gage, declare all you know herein.

24. Did you ever hear the Said Joseph Doan request the Said Lott Gage to refer it to indifferent Men, well acquainted with the Customs of Whaling to decide whose Said Whale, immediately on the Spot, and When and Where and what was the answer of Said Gage?

25. Did you see Said Whale after she was dead, did you See any Hole or Holes in Said Whale, made by an Harpoon, or how many or any when the Iron was drawn?

26. Do you know there was a Mateship between Joseph Doane Senr., Joseph Doane Jnr., Stephen Sears, and Thomas Jones, while they were whaling, in the Streights of Bellisle, on the Labradore shore in the Year 1765.

27. Was it generally understood that there was such a Mateship?

Commission [to] David Gorham Esq. and John Freeman, Esq. if [need be].[84]

---

[84] These were Barnstable County justices of the peace before whom the answers could be sworn. See Whitmore, *Mass. Civil List* 146. Compare note 11 above.

IV. INTERROGATORIES FOR GAGE [85]

Court of Vice Admiralty, Boston, 1768

Interrogatories In the Behalf of Lot Gage and Partners In the Case of Joseph Doane and others against him and Partners.

1st. Was you on a Whaling Voyage In the Streights of Bellisle on or about the 21st. of June 1765.

2. What Boat was you in and what Vessel did you belong to.

3. Do you remember that on or about that time there was a Whale Killed by Lot Gage and others the Property of which whale has Since been disputed by Joseph Doane and others.

4. Did you see Lot Gage Faste to said Whale.

5. Was there any other Boat fast to her when Lot Gage Struck her.

6. How Near was you to Said Whale when Gage Struck her.

7. Did you Sit down or stand up tell all you Know about it.

8. Did you see Asa Nickerson that day.

9. Did you See him or his harpooner Dart at said Whale.

10. Did he fasten to her or Not.

11. Did you See him hawling in his Iron and Warp before Gage Struck the Whale he fastned too. Tell all you Know about it.

12. Did you at that time Know Silas and Robert Newcomb.

13. Did you see them at the time Gage was fast to the Whale or before.

14. What was the Newcombs Conduct on that Voyage according to your observation.

15. Did you observe that when you fell in Chase of Whales with the Newcombs they were more Noisey then [than] Common.

16. Did that Boat the Newcombs was in go by the Name of the Crasey Newcombs that Voyage.

17. Did you hear that Silas Newcombs was Crasey since he got home from that Voyage at any time.

18. Did you hear Josiah Godfrey your Stearsman say (at the time Mentioned In your Deposition) any thing on Board your Vessel about this Whale and what he Said.

19. Was Josiah Godfrey your Stearsman present at the Conversation aboard your Vessel as mentioned in your Deposition. Tell what you Know about it.

20. Was Robert Homer a Whaling with you in the Year 1765 at the Streights of Bellisle about the 21st of June.

[85] In an unidentified hand, without date, SF 172906. Endorsed: "Interrogatorys on the Deft's side." See answers of Samuel Howland to some similar interrogatories, note 59 above.

21. Had you any Conversation with him about the Whale In Controversy and what was it.

22. What was the Capacity that he went in.

23. Was he Not Looked on as a very Raw hand by your Crew and one that had Little or No knowledge about Whaling.

24. Did he Ever Mention to you or the Crew you belonged to any Conversation that he had with John Whelden or his Crew about this Whale.

25. Did you hear any man on Board the Vessel that John Whelden was in say the Whale In Controversey between Joseph Doane and others and Lot Gage and others belonged to the Doanes.

26. Did you hear any Man say so on Board the Vessel you Belonged to.

27. What was the general opinion while you was on the Voyage of the people a Board your Vessel and John Weldens vessel who said Whale belonged to whether to Gage or to whom.

28. Was you a Whaling with Seth Baker in the Year 1765 at the Streights of Bellisle on or about the 21st of June that Year.

29. What did you hear him say when he Come on Board the Vessel you was in about the Whale In Controversy that Same day said Whale was Kill'd or Soon after. Tell what you Know about it.

30. Did you go in an End of a Boat and which End.

31. What was the General Talk of the People at the Streights of Bellisle about the Whale in Controversy that is who she Belonged to tell all you Know about it.

32. Did you hear Samuel Howes talking with John Whelden about the Whale In Controversy very soon after the Whale was Killed Relate The talk Whelden had about her at that time.

33. Had you ever any Conversation with Silas Newcomb about the Whale in Controversy, tell all you heard him Say about it and when and where it was.

34. Had you Ever any Conversation with Captn. Joseph Doane about the Whale In Controversy. Tell all you remember of it.

35. Are you Acquainted or do you Know Asa Nickerson.

36. Had you Ever any Conversation with him about the Whale In Controversy Between Captn. Joseph Doane and others and Captn. Lot Gage and others. Relate the Conversation and tell what you Remember of it.

37. Did you hear any person in Asa Nickerson Boate at the Time Lot Gage was fast to the Whale now in Controversy say that they the said Nickersons boate was not fast to said Whale and that they had

Better go on Board their Vessel and Get some Victuals and not Contend about her or words to that Effect. Tell all you know about it.

38. Can you tell how Near Seth Bakers Boate that you was in was to the Whale In Controversy when Lot Gage struck her.

39. Was you at one Oar with your Back Toward the Whale.

40. Was not Robert Homer In the same Boat at the same Time.

41. Did he stand up to Look at the Whale and Boats that you Observed.

42. Do you Know of any Boats Besides Gages that was Nearer to the Whale when he struck then your Boat.

43. Was you Near Enough to Gages Boat or the Whale to Know one man from another.

44. How long after you Perceivd the Whale to be fast before you Quitted the Chace.

45. Did you Ever hear it said on Board your Vessel that the Whale In Controversy Belonged to the Doanes.

46. Did you Ever tell any Body so.

47. Did you hear any of the Crew on Board your Vessel say so.

48. Was it not the General Voice of your Vessels Crew that she Belonged to Gage.

49. Did you Ever Suggest to Robert Homer or say any thing like it that you should or Could be an Evidence in Doans favour.

50. Did you Ever Say to Robt. Homer or in his hearing that said Whale Belonged to the Doanes.

51. Was you in the Boat with John Chase at the Streights of Bellisle on or about the 21st. of June 1765.

52. Did you see any thing of the Transactions of Asa Nickerson or Lot Gage at that time. Relate all you know about them.

53. Do you Know Seth Baker.

54. What is his Charecter as to Probity and Truth.

55. Do you Know John Cash.

56. What is his Charecter as to Probity and Truth.

57. Have you heard of any Contention or Quarrel Between Robert Homer and John Whelden or Family, tell all you Know about it.

N. *Admiralty—Revenue Jurisdiction*

EDITORIAL NOTE

The majority of John Adams' cases in the Court of Vice Admiralty involved breaches of the British Acts of Trade. The Acts were a coherent body of legislation, enacted between 1660 and the Revolution, which regulated the flow of colonial trade, laid duties on some aspects of it, and established a system of enforcement. The basic regulatory provisions were: that vessels engaged in the plantation trade had to be English- or colonial-built, owned, or manned; that certain enumerated goods produced in the colonies could be shipped only to England or to another colony; and that most European goods could be shipped to the colonies only from English ports.[1]

This system was designed primarily to aid the English merchant and shipbuilder by creating monopolies in the colonial trade, but it did benefit colonial shipbuilders, and at least some colonial merchants, by assuring them of markets. The system also was an indirect producer of revenue for the Crown, since goods flowing through English ports were subject to duties to be paid there by the importer or exporter. The only duties levied in the colonies before 1764 had their primary effect as measures to support or encourage trade with England, rather than as direct revenue-producers. Thus, although the Plantation Duties Act of 1673, laying duties upon enumerated goods shipped from one colony to another, had the effect of equalizing the tax burden between English and colonial consumers of colonial goods, its principal aim was to make shipment of these goods to England more economical for the exporter than intercolonial shipment. Similarly, the heavy duties laid upon the importation of foreign colonial sugar products by the Sugar Act of 1733 were designed to put British West Indian sugar producers in a favorable position.[2]

Enforcement of these measures was in the hands of customs officials in the colonies who were responsible to the Commissioners of the Customs in England.[3] The colonial officers administered a complicated documentary control system designed to insure compliance with both regulatory and

---

[1] These provisions were first enacted in the statutes, 12 Car. 2, c. 18, §§1, 18 (1660), and 15 Car. 2, c. 7, §6 (1663). For a summary of later statutory modifications, see Harper, *Navigation Laws* 388–390, 395–404. For provisions applicable to colonial manufacturing, see Knollenberg, *Origin of the American Revolution* 169–171.

[2] See the Plantation Duties Act, 25 Car. 2, c. 7, §§2, 4 (1673); the Sugar Act, 6 Geo. 2, c. 13 (1733). For discussion of these Acts and the legislative purpose, see Barrow, Colonial Customs 26–32, 283–286.

[3] Provision for a colonial customs service was first made in the Plantation Duties Act, 25 Car. 2, c. 7, §3 (1673). Its existence was confirmed and the officers' powers strengthened by 7 & 8 Will. 3, c. 22 (1696).

revenue provisions. The basis of the system was the requirement that vessels arriving from or bound for parts beyond the seas enter and clear with the customs officers at each port.[4] This practice permitted a constant check on each vessel's compliance with the Acts, as evidenced by certain required documents. For example, the nationality of vessels and crews was controlled through the ship's register, a certified copy of the master's or owner's oath that the vessel was English built, owned, and manned.[5] A vessel carrying enumerated goods had to give bond on clearing that they would be landed only in an English or colonial port; if a certificate of compliance were not returned within a certain time, the bond was forfeit.[6] To ensure that European goods had been shipped in England, the master was required to submit a manifest, showing the nature, amount, and origin of his cargo before his vessel could enter and unload. The payment of duties was also controlled through the manifest and through certificates of the officers on entry and clearance that duties had been paid.[7]

To prevent violations, the customs officers had broad powers to search vessels, as well as premises ashore, for contraband, and to seize such goods.[8] Violators were subject to a variety of penalties, ranging from small fines for failure to comply with administrative rules to forfeiture of vessel and goods for breach of the substantive requirements of the Acts. Although in England such offenses were within the jurisdiction of the Court of Exchequer, in the colonies many of them could be sued upon in the Courts of Vice Admiralty, which had been established in 1697 primarily for this purpose. The customs officers were allowed to bring suit for penalties and forfeitures, receiving a share of the proceeds upon condemnation. Jurisdiction of these actions was concurrent at common law, but in Massachusetts at least, the officers preferred to proceed in Admiralty, where recovery was not subject to the whim of a jury friendly to the offender.[9]

[4] See 15 Car. 2, c. 7, §8 (1663); 13 & 14 Car. 2, c. 11, §§2, 3 (1662), made applicable in the colonies by 7 & 8 Will. 3, c. 22, §6 (1696). For cases involving the requirement of entry, see No. 46 and No. 48.

[5] See 7 & 8 Will. 3, c. 22, §§17–21; No. 51; No. 45, note 34.

[6] See 12 Car. 2, c. 18, §19 (1660); 7 & 8 Will. 3, c. 22, §13 (1696); Harper, *Navigation Laws* 161–165. For further discussion, see No. 45, note 34.

[7] See 15 Car. 2, c. 7, §8 (1663); 13 & 14 Car. 2, c. 11, §§2, 3 (1662), made applicable in the colonies by 7 & 8 Will. 3, c. 22, §6 (1696); *Instructions by the Commissioners for Managing and Causing to be levyed and collected His Majesty's Customs, Subsidies, and other Duties in England, to   who is Established Collector of His Majesty's Customs at   in America* ([London], ca. 1733). For a case on European goods, see No. 52.

[8] 13 & 14 Car. 2, c. 11, §§4–11, 15–20, 32–34 (1662), made applicable in the colonies by 7 & 8 Will. 3, c. 22, §6 (1696). See No. 44, No. 45, No. 50.

[9] As to the establishment of the Vice Admiralty Courts, see Barrow, *Colonial Customs* 124–127, 145–150; Wroth, "The Massachusetts Vice Admiralty Court," in George A. Billias, ed., *Law and Authority in Colonial America* (Barre, Mass., in press). As to doubts about the scope of the jurisdiction before 1764, see Knollenberg, *Origin of the American Revolution* 266–268. The various penalties and forfeitures, and the mechanics of suit run through all the statutes and are discussed in most of the cases that follow. See especially No. 46. A search of the records of the Massachusetts Superior Court and the Suffolk County Inferior Court files has revealed no

There was some opposition to this system at its inception, but after about 1725 the furor generally died down. Historians have seen this reaction as an indication that the colonists had come to accept the benefits which they received in trade with England as compensation for some of the disadvantages which regulation imposed. This was undoubtedly a factor, but it is clear that colonial acceptance was made easier by the fact that after 1725 English policy seemed to be one of deliberately ignoring violations of the system. Revenue collections from the colonies were small, in part because of the regulatory purpose of the revenue measures, but to an even greater extent because of a widespread laxity of enforcement that was known to and condoned by Parliament. Presumably a similar laxity pervaded the enforcement of other provisions of the Acts.[10]

Adams came upon the scene just as this policy of laxness was being abandoned. New England's trade with the enemy during the Seven Years' War had reached such heights that the Crown made determined efforts to control it through strict enforcement of the Acts of Trade. There was an immediate reaction among the Boston merchants against the Admiralty court and the customs officials, which manifested itself in several ways, including opposition to the officers' application for writs of assistance (general search warrants). Adams attended the first of two arguments on the question, held before the Superior Court at Boston in February 1761. Although he was not of counsel, he produced a report which was widely circulated and of some importance in later political struggles. Boston's resistance to the application, although unsuccessful, marked the first step in an opposition to the Acts which was to culminate in the American Revolution.[11]

At the conclusion of the war in 1763 England was both financially strained and sharply aware of the extent of colonial evasion of the Acts of Trade. The American Act of 1764 was directed at both problems. For the first time duties were levied on colonial imports for the express purpose of raising a revenue. To prevent violation of this and other Acts, various holes in the enforcement system were plugged with requirements for ad-

actions at law under the Acts of Trade after 1764. An incomplete search for the earlier period has produced only a few revenue suits, and these were matters in which the power of the Admiralty Court was being tested by writ of prohibition. See, for example, Robinson v. Patriarch, SCJ Rec. 1725–1730, fol. 59 (Suffolk, 1726) (Dismissed on exceptions); Robinson v. Patriarch, SCJ Rec. 1725–1729, fols. 97–99 (Essex, 1726) (Quashed because summons said "Suffolk SS" instead of "Essex SS"); Lambert v. Bardin, SCJ Rec. 1730–1733, fol. 202 (Suffolk, 1732) (Verdict for forfeiture. Vessel ordered sold, with seamen's wages also to be paid). As to distrust of the jury, see No. 46, note 61.

[10] For the view that the system of duties and regulation prior to 1764 was agreeable to the colonists and that only changes made in that year and after (notes 12, 15, below) caused opposition, see Harper, *Navigation Laws* 365–378; Dickerson, *Navigation Acts* 208. These and earlier studies of the problem are admirably summarized in Barrow, Colonial Customs 1–17, 512–524, where the conclusion is reached that the entire system from 1660 on was inimical to colonial interests, and that lax enforcement between 1725 and 1764 was the key to colonial acceptance. The debt of the editors to this work here and elsewhere should be evident.

[11] See No. 44.

I. HARRISON GRAY, BY JOHN SINGLETON COPLEY

1768
October 29 Jer. Lovall Esqr vs John Lorrington

1769 March 25. The Advocate General pray leave to Retract this Information & says our Sovereign Lord the King will prosecute no further herein — Allowed

Same vs Daniel Malcom

1769 March 26. The Advocate General may leave to Retract this Information & says our Sovereign Lord the King will prosecute no further herein — Allowed

Same vs Benjamin Burt

1769 April 13. The Lord the King will prosecute no further herein

Same vs Jos. Healy Esqr
Claim not heard

Same vs Francis Richey

1769 March 25. The Advocate General pray leave to Retract the Information & says Sovereign Lord the King will prosecute no further herein — Allowed

November 21. Jer Lovall Esqr Adv Genl vs John Lorrington
Claim not closed

Same vs Nathaniel Barnard
Claim not closed

1760
November 20 Joseph Jeans & vs Lot Gage

November 18. Robert Trail Esqr & vs Schooner Friendship
Adjudged Forfeit — The Claimant to Pay Cost

1764 March 21. Adjudged Forfeit — The Claimant to Pay Cost

December 6th. Joseph Dowse Esqr vs 19 Casks of Molasses
Adjudged Forfeit, no Person appearing to claim the same.

December 6. Thos. Grosvr Esqr vs Schooner Earl of Gloucester

1769 March 15. No Person appearing to claim the Schooner
Called — Adjudged Forfeit

December 8. Viz. Breed adm'r vs Benj. Goodwin
Not to appear the 9 inst
The Judge gave his Decree as on file

1769 January 17. Will McBuddington Esqr vs Sloop Ranger
one Cask of Tea
1769 March 20. His Honor the Judge Decreed that this Information so far as it Relate to said Sloop to be Dismissed.
The Cask of Tea adjudged Forfeit.

ditional bonds and certificates and a closer check by the customs officers. Heavy pecuniary penalties against offenders were set in addition to the previous system of forfeitures, and it was made clear that all violations of the Acts could be sued upon in colonial Admiralty courts. In these suits the prosecuting officers were given certain procedural advantages. Finally a new superior court of Admiralty was created to hear cases from any province.[12]

Before the effect of these new measures could be felt, Parliament passed the Stamp Act of 1765, a provision for further revenue to be levied by a tax upon a variety of documents and printed matter. Colonial objections to the American Act were submerged in a sudden rush to defy the Stamp Act. In Boston, violence and the threat of violence prevented the distribution of the stamps. One result was that the courts, which required stamped paper for their documents, were closed. Adams appeared before the Governor and Council in December 1765 for the Town of Boston to pray that the courts be opened without stamps. Although his arguments took account of the political nature of the body which he was addressing, his notes show that he backed up rhetoric with authority, relying upon the kind of argument that had earlier been made against writs of assistance. The petition was denied on the ground that the question was a judicial one, but the Inferior Court soon opened in acquiescence to popular pressures. The Superior Court was formally opened, but did only token business until news of the Stamp Act's repeal was received in May 1766.[13]

Along with repeal, most of the duties of 1764 were reduced to acceptable levels.[14] The enforcement provisions were not repealed, however. Calm temporarily prevailed until a change of governments in England brought Charles Townshend, long a proponent of colonial taxation, to the post of Chancellor of the Exchequer. The Townshend Acts of 1767 again laid duties upon American imports, to be used in part to pay colonial officials independently of the legislatures. The Acts renewed the drive for strict enforcement by authorizing the appointment of an American Board of Customs Commissioners to sit at Boston and exercise the powers formerly

[12] The American Act, 4 Geo. 3, c. 15 (1764). For a summary of its provisions, see Knollenberg, *Origin of the American Revolution* 150–152, 176–181; compare Barrow, Colonial Customs 376–390. See also No. 46, No. 47, No. 52. Earlier a wartime practice had been extended by a measure providing for the seizure at sea by naval vessels of offenders against the Acts of Trade. 3 Geo. 3, c. 22, §4 (1763). See No. 51, note 1. As to the new Admiralty court, see Ubbelohde, *Vice-Admiralty Courts* 44–54. The court was given power to hear appeals from the provincial Admiralty courts by the Stamp Act, 5 Geo. 3, c. 12, §58 (1765).

[13] JA's notes of his argument, now in the Adams Papers, are printed in 2 JA, *Works* 159 note. See also JA's diary entry for 20 Dec. 1765, 1 JA, *Diary and Autobiography* 266–267. Compare Quincy's account of the argument, Quincy, *Reports* 200–214. For further discussion, see No. 44, note 48; No. 46, note 68. See also Edmund S. and Helen M. Morgan, *The Stamp Act Crisis* 139–143 (Chapel Hill, 1953).

[14] 6 Geo. 3, c. 52 (1766). The Act did tighten enforcement regulations in other respects, and did not affect the duties on wines. See Barrow, Colonial Customs 443–444; No. 46, note 17; No. 47, note 1.

held by the English Commissioners.[15] At the same time the superior court created in 1764 was superseded by four new district courts of Admiralty, to sit at Halifax, Boston, Philadelphia, and Charleston, and exercise both original and appellate jurisdiction over surrounding provinces.[16]

Adams does not seem to have tried a revenue case in the Court of Admiralty before 1768. In that year, however, the activities of the Commissioners inevitably drew him into such matters. Their immediate application of the new enforcement policy increased the number of actions in Admiralty to the point where there was need for additional lawyers. Further, the Commissioners' policy aroused an immediate opposition among the merchants who seemed determined to spare no effort in resistance. Accordingly, Adams' first such case, *Folger v. The Cornelia*, No. 45, which was a direct confrontation between the Commissioners and those who had found the previous administration more agreeable, marked the beginning of a busy year and a half in the Court of Admiralty.[17]

The seizure of John Hancock's sloop *Liberty* in June 1768 provided the focus for the attack upon the Commissioners. Adams was deeply involved in this affair, both as counsel for Hancock in an action brought against him for penalties, and as a draftsman of political manifestos for the Town of Boston.[18] At the same time there was a steady stream of less important revenue litigation in which Adams participated, perhaps because he was in court on Hancock's business.[19] Although Adams was politically committed to opposition to the Acts of Trade, he was of counsel for Crown officers in two cases in the spring and summer of 1769.[20] As a lawyer, he had a right, if not a duty, to give his services to those who sought them. In view of the political situation, however, it is likely that he was under heavy pressure from the Crown to yield a more permanent allegiance. In his Autobiography, Adams wrote that sometime

[15] 7 Geo. 3, c. 41 (1767); *id.*, c. 46. As to the Commissioners, see No. 45. The Acts also tightened the entry requirements and clarified the status of the writ of assistance. 7 Geo. 3, c. 46, §§9, 10. See No. 44, note 29.

[16] 8 Geo. 3, c. 22 (1767). See Ubbelohde, *Vice-Admiralty Courts* 130–133. See also No. 46, notes 41–43.

[17] In 1767 there had been 15 actions on the docket of the Vice Admiralty Court, of which one can be definitely identified as a revenue case and 2 are suits under the White Pine Acts (p. 247–253 below). The rest are presumably ordinary civil maritime actions. In 1768, out of 33 actions, 12 entries were *in rem* actions under the Acts of Trade, and 12 were *in personam* actions, the latter the Hancock and Malcom prosecutions (see No. 46, note 26). In 1769, out of 55 actions, 21 were under the White Pine Acts (see No. 54), 18 were *in rem* actions under the Acts of Trade and 10 were *in personam* prosecutions, including those arising out of Dowse v. 33 Hogsheads of Molasses, No. 47. See Vice Adm. Min. Bk. To the extent that the figures here and in notes 22, 24, below, differ from those in Wroth, "Massachusetts Vice Admiralty Court," 6 *Am. Jour. Legal Hist.* 367, the latter are erroneous.

[18] See No. 46.

[19] See Nos. 47, 48, 49.

[20] See Nos. 50, 54. At the same time JA was of counsel for the accused in Rex v. Corbet, No. 56, a trial before a Special Court of Admiralty for the killing of a naval officer at sea, which had political implications.

during 1768 Jonathan Sewall had asked him to take over his position as advocate general in Admiralty. Adams reported that he had had no trouble in refusing this offer, since he wished to be under no obligation to those whose political principles he opposed. There is other evidence that some such episode took place. Perhaps Adams' legal activities for the Crown indicate that he gave Sewall's proposal more serious consideration than he was later willing to admit.[21]

The uproar over the *Liberty* led the Crown to send troops to Boston. The presence of soldiers and continued tension over the Commissioners' activities led at length to the Boston Massacre in March 1770 (Nos. 63, 64). In the aftermath of this episode the troops were withdrawn, and the Commissioners, who were accused of instigating both the Massacre and the earlier shooting of a small boy by their employee Ebenezer Richardson (No. 59), greatly moderated their tactics. The Boston merchants, feeling a revulsion against civil disobedience, in the fall abandoned the policy of nonimportation with which they had reacted to the Townshend Acts. Parliament had contributed to the atmosphere of conciliation in March by repealing all of the Townshend duties except the tax on tea.

So far as is known, Adams had no Admiralty cases for nearly three years after the summer of 1769. Although he may have withdrawn from practice in the court in disgust at the political ramifications, there are other possible explanations. In 1769 his business in the common-law courts drastically increased to the level where it was to remain until the Revolution. At the same time the atmosphere of conciliation following the Massacre had greatly reduced the number of customs cases and diminished the political tension which had surrounded such matters. A balance of interests in favor of the economics of the profession probably accounts for Adams' abandonment of the Admiralty.[22]

[21] For the passage in the Autobiography, see 3 JA, *Diary and Autobiography* 287–289. Hutchinson's statement that JA was offered the position of justice of the peace is discussed in *id.* at 289 note. In his diary for 22 Sept. 1772, JA noted that in the service of his "Country" he had sacrificed "Time, Peace, Health, Money, and Preferment, both of which last have courted my Acceptance, and been inexorably refused, least I should be laid under a Temptation to forsake the Sentiments of the Friends of this Country." 2 *id.* at 63. That Sewall was dissatisfied with his post as early as the summer of 1768 seems clear from the story of his dealings with Samuel Venner. In Nov. 1768 he learned that he had been appointed Judge of the new Admiralty court at Halifax, which would have given him valid ground to look for a successor. See No. 46, notes 20, 27, 41–43. He was actually in Halifax on business at the time of the trial in Butler v. The *Union*, No. 50. Samuel Fitch was finally appointed to the post in March 1770. See No. 51, note 2. For the later relations between JA and Sewall, see 2 JA, *Diary and Autobiography* 67–68, and 1 *Adams Family Correspondence* 135–137.

[22] In 1770 there were 13 actions in the Vice Admiralty Court, of which 5 were for breaches of the Acts of Trade and 2 were under the White Pine Acts. In 1771 out of 17 actions, 15 were for breaches of the Acts of Trade. See Vice Adm. Min. Bk. For the end of nonimportation, see Miller, *Origins of the American Revolution* 309–311. The Townshend Acts repeal was 10 Geo. 3, c. 17 (1770). As to JA's 1769 practice, see vol. 3:335–337 below. He had moved to Braintree in April 1771 after his exhausting defense of the Massacre defendants (Nos. 63, 64). See

Whatever the reason, he does not seem to have appeared there again until February 1772, when he was retained in the first appeal brought before the Boston District Court of Admiralty since its creation in 1768. Robert Auchmuty, previously judge for the Province, had been appointed to the new court, but he had apparently continued to sit in his former capacity also, thus rendering appeals of doubtful value in Massachusetts. The decision in this case had been given by Auchmuty's deputy in New Hampshire, however. In his diary Adams noted that "as it is a new Thing the Judge has directed an Argument, and a Search of Books concerning the Nature of Appeals by the civil Law. I found Time to look into Calvins Lexicon Title Appellatio and Provocatio, and into Maranta, who has treated largely of Appeals. Borrowed Ayliff, but there is no Table and could find nothing about the Subject. Domat I could not find." The appeal and another from the condemnation of a vessel belonging to John Langdon of New Hampshire, were decided in favor of the Crown, presumably in spite of the efforts of Adams, who was probably on the side of the claimants.[23]

Adams did undertake at least two revenue cases in 1772 and 1773. Although the burning of the revenue cutter *Gaspee* in Rhode Island and the special tribunal appointed to investigate the incident had awakened political responses in him and in many others, his later cases had no particular political relevance, except as further evidence to the colonists of the oppressiveness of the system.[24] The tax on tea, left unrepealed in 1770, finally led to the events which terminated whatever uneasy truce remained and took political dispute beyond the confines of the courtroom. In 1773 Parliament had saved the East India Company from collapse by an Act allowing it a full drawback of English duties on tea shipped to the colonies, and permitting it to ship directly to colonial consignees, instead of dealing through English tea merchants. With these advantages, the Company could now compete with the smugglers who had been evading the duty regularly since 1770. An increase in the sales of legally imported tea meant an increase in duties. More revenues meant more funds to be applied under the Townshend Acts to pay the salaries of royal officials. This threat aroused Boston, and other colonial ports, to action.[25]

---

2 JA, *Diary and Autobiography* 6–7. Health is usually given as the reason for his departure. See *id.* at 7 note; 3 *id.* at 296. Compare 2 *id.* at 65–66. There is also reason to think, however, that he had had his fill of politics. *Id.* at 63.

[23] See 2 JA, *Diary and Autobiography* 56. As to these cases, see Ubbelohde, *Vice-Admiralty Courts* 157. See Cutt v. Meservey, Vice Adm. Min. Bk., 23 Jan. 1772; Baker v. Meservey, *id.*, 9 March 1772.

[24] For Adams' cases, see Nos. 51, 52. As to the *Gaspee*, and the reaction to the incident, see No. 46, note 22; Miller, *Origins of the American Revolution* 325–329. For JA's reactions see 2 JA, *Diary and Autobiography* 73, 75–76. Although the records of the Vice Admiralty court are incomplete, there is some evidence that the Commissioners increased their activities in 1772. The existing docket of the court, through March 1772, shows 16 actions, of which at least 10 were customs cases. Vice Adm. Min. Bk. See also, Receipts from Seizures of Ships, 1772–1773, MBAt:Price Papers, which contains receipts of 19 forfeitures and one composition between May 1772 and Sept. 1773. A check of the Boston newspapers reveals at least 10 seizures between Sept. 1773 and Feb. 1776.

[25] The Tea Act was 13 Geo. 3, c. 44 (1773). See generally Benjamin W. Labaree,

The first of the tea ships, the *Dartmouth*, arrived in Boston harbor on 28 November, and, apparently at the request of the Committee of Correspondence, came up to the town on the 30th, taking a berth at Griffin's Wharf the next day. There she was soon joined by other vessels. The ships had apparently entered at the Custom House soon after arrival, but none of the tea was unloaded. The "Body," the *ad hoc* mass meeting which purported to speak for Boston, demanded that the ships be sent home with cargo still intact, but the owners were unable to comply. The customs officers refused to issue clearances until the tea had been unloaded, and Governor Hutchinson would not allow the province naval officer to give the vessels a pass to leave the port without a clearance.

In this state of things the owners of the *Dartmouth* sought counsel from Adams and Sampson Salter Blowers. The owners probably wanted both arguments to use before the customs officials and Hutchinson, and advice on the potential liability of the *Dartmouth* and her cargo for seizure. The account of the vessel's master shows that Adams and Blowers were paid a total of £7 4s. for "advice," but no indication of its nature has survived.[26] Under the applicable statutes duties were due upon "importation" and goods could be seized if duties remained unpaid twenty days after entry. The principal questions were probably whether there had been an "importation" within the Act when bulk had not been broken, and if there had, whether the customs officers could nevertheless clear out vessel and cargo without payment of duties.[27] Before these questions could be raised in any legal proceeding, events made them moot. On 16 December Hutchinson refused a last request for a pass and an immortal band of Indians proceeded to dump the tea into Boston Harbor, in what Adams described in his diary as "the most magnificent Movement of all." [28]

In reaction to this act of defiance, Parliament passed the Boston Port Act and other coercive measures designed to punish the Town and its supporters by terminating its trade and abridging provincial self-govern-

---

The Boston Tea Party 58–109 (N.Y., 1964). See also Dickerson, "Use Made of the Revenue from the Tax on Tea," 31 *NEQ* 232 (1958).

[26] See account of James Hall, in Francis S. Drake, ed., *Tea Leaves* 352 (Boston, 1884). See generally, Labaree, *Boston Tea Party* 118–137. For Hutchinson's account, see 3 Hutchinson, *Massachusetts Bay*, ed. Mayo, 307–312.

[27] The basic provision was the Sugar Act, 6 Geo. 2, c. 13, §§2, 3 (1733), incorporated by the Townshend Act, 7 Geo. 3, c. 46, §4 (1767). The High Court of Admiralty had held that under the Act prohibiting European goods "importation" occurred upon arrival. See No. 52, note 5. The Privy Council, however, had held in another case that "importation" did not occur until bulk had been broken. Smith, *Appeals to the Privy Council* 496. The practice was thus presumably not fixed in the colonies and varied from port to port. That the officers did not consider that they had power in the ordinary course to clear out a vessel in such circumstances appears in an episode in 1774 at Salem, where tea was permitted to be sent on to Halifax only after bond for the duties had been given. Salem Custom Officers to Commissioners, 5 Dec. 1774, Salem Custom House Letter Book Outwards, 1772–1775, Office of the U.S. Collector of Customs, Boston, Mass. For a full discussion of this phase of the question, see Labaree, *Boston Tea Party* 126–127.

[28] For JA's comment, see 2 JA, *Diary and Autobiography* 85. See generally Labaree, *Boston Tea Party* 137–145.

ment.[29] Adams does not seem to have had further cases in the Vice Admiralty Court, but he was at least present to report a case in which the Port Act was put to the test there in the summer of 1774 (No. 53). In the meantime the colonies had begun to move toward union, revolution, and independence. The First Continental Congress sat at Philadelphia in September 1774, with Adams among its members.[30] Before independence was formally declared, the British sought to bring the colonies to heel by Act of Parliament, extending the Port Act to other colonial ports. Finally Britain laid a total embargo on colonial commerce in a statute that was not an Act of Trade, but a measure regulating the taking and distribution of prizes. Adams' only contact with this later legislation was in the somewhat different context of prize litigation during the Revolution.[31]

44. Petition of Lechmere
(Argument on Writs of Assistance)
1761

EDITORIAL NOTE

In February 1761 John Adams was present at an event which his later descriptions have firmly implanted in the mythology of the American Revolution. The arguments of James Otis before the Superior Court on the granting of writs of assistance to royal customs officials are generally known as one of the earliest statements of colonial opposition to parliamentary regulation. The scene itself, so vividly described by Adams in a letter to William Tudor nearly sixty years later, is surely part of the common vision of this period: In the Council Chamber of what is now the Old State House in Boston "near the Fire were seated five Judges, with Lieutenant Governor Hutchinson at their head, as Chief Justice, all in their new fresh Robes of Scarlet English Cloth in their Broad Bands, and immense judicial Wiggs. In this Chamber were seated at a long Table all the Barristers of Boston and its neighbouring County of Middlesex in their Gowns, Bands, and Tye Wiggs. They were not seated on ivory Chairs, but their dress was more solemn and more pompous than that of the Roman Senate, when the Gauls broke in upon them."

There also sat Samuel Quincy and John Adams. "John was the youngest. He should be painted looking like a short, thick, fat Archbishop of Canterbury, seated at the Table with a pen in his hand, lost in Admiration, now and then minuting those despicable Notes which you know that Jonathan Williams Austin your fellow student in my office, stole from my desk and

[29] The Port Act was 14 Geo. 3, c. 19. As to the rest of the legislation, see Miller, *Origins of the American Revolution* 355–376. See also Labaree, *Boston Tea Party* 178–203.

[30] See 2 JA, *Diary and Autobiography* 97–160. Compare No. 53, note 5.

[31] As to these Acts and JA's concern with them, see No. 58, notes 14, 173.

printed in the Massachusetts Spy, with two or three bombastic expressions interpolated by himself; and which your Pupil, Judge Minot has printed in his history."

Jeremiah Gridley, for the Crown, and Oxenbridge Thacher, for the merchants of Boston, argued well and eloquently, but it was Otis, also for the merchants, whom Adams hailed so many years later. "Otis was a flame of Fire! With the promptitude of Clasical Allusions, a depth of Research, a rapid Summary of Historical Events and dates, a profusion of legal Authorities, a prophetic glare [i.e. glance?] of his eyes into futurity, and a rapid Torrent of impetuous Eloquence, he hurried away all before him; American Independance was then and there born. The seeds of Patriots and Heroes to defend the non sine Diis animosus infans, to defend the vigorous Youth, were then and there sown. Every man of an [immense] crowded Audience appeared to me to go away, as I did, ready to take up Arms against Writts of Assistants. Then and there was the first scene of the first Act of Opposition to the arbitrary Claims of Great Britain. Then and there the child Independance was born. In fifteen years, i.e. in 1776, he grew up to manhood, declared himself free." [1]

By this and other letters to his old student, Adams sought to recreate a great moment of his youth. In the course of his efforts he put into Otis' mouth the entire body of arguments against the power of Parliament developed over the whole of the next decade. The inaccuracies and exaggerations of these letters have been ably summarized elsewhere; further comment on them must await The Adams Papers edition of that portion of Adams' correspondence.[2] Here we deal only with the legal situation as it can be recreated from Adams' original notes of the argument and other sources.

The arguments which Adams heard turned on the nature of the writ and the construction of three Acts of Parliament and a Province statute. The term "writ of assistance" had originally been applied to process in favor of a particular litigant in the Exchequer or in Chancery, enabling him to obtain the sheriff's help in collecting a debt or gaining possession of property to which he was entitled.[3] The writs sought by the Crown officials

[1] JA to William Tudor, 29 March 1817. LbC, Adams Papers. Printed with some variations and omissions in 10 JA, Works 244–249. The letter had first appeared in 14 Niles' Weekly Register 137–140 (25 March 1818), and was printed again in Novanglus and Massachusettensis 244–247 (Boston, 1819). JA, in a contemporaneous report of the proceedings in Congress on the Declaration of Independence, referred to "the Argument concerning Writs of Assistance, in the Superiour Court, which I have hitherto considered as the Commencement of the Controversy, between Great Britain and America." JA to AA, 3 July 1776, 2 Adams Family Correspondence 28.

[2] As to the inaccuracies, see notes 20, 22, below; they are fully discussed in Horace Gray's appendix to Quincy's Reports [hereinafter to be cited as Quincy, Reports (Appendix)] at p. 408–411, 416–417, 469. See also Joseph R. Frese, Writs of Assistance in the American Colonies, 1660–1776, p. 1–19 (Harvard Univ. doctoral dissertation, 1951). The principal letters are in 10 JA, Works 244–362; see also id. at 362 note.

[3] See Quincy, Reports (Appendix) 395–396. The examples cited by Thacher,

in Boston in 1761, however, were general standing warrants, good from the date of issue until six months after the death of the issuing sovereign, which permitted the holder to enter any house by day, with a constable or other officer, and there search for smuggled goods without special application to a court.[4]

The earliest relevant statute, an Act of Parliament passed in 1660, authorized the issuance "to any person or persons" of a warrant to enter any house to search for specific goods, upon oath made of their illegal entry before "the lord treasurer, or any of the barons of the Exchequer, or chief magistrate of the port or place where the offense shall be committed, or the place next adjoining thereto."[5] Both the language and the legislative history of this enactment make reasonably clear that its purpose was to authorize a special search warrant of limited extent, under control of a higher authority.[6] The statute central to the controversy was the Act of 1662, which, in setting up a comprehensive scheme of customs administration for the British Isles, first used "writ of assistance" to describe a customs search warrant. The act provided that "any person or persons, authorized by writ of assistance under the seal of his majesty's court of exchequer," might enter any premises in the day time, with a constable or other officer, using force if necessary, and there seize any contraband goods found.[7] It has been argued on the basis of the language and legislative history of this and other contemporary acts, that the Act of 1662 was intended to incorporate no more than the special warrant embodied in the Act of 1660.[8] The language of the two statutes is open

---

note 56 below, are writs of this kind, in aid of Chancery decrees. The process is still known in England. See 16 *Halsbury's Laws of England*, tit. Execution, §100 (London, 3d edn., 1956). In the United States the equitable writ of assistance is found in a number of states and, under Federal Rule of Civil Procedure 70, is available after an order for the delivery of possession. See Note, 8 *Arkansas Law Review* 92–100 (1954); James W. Moore, *Federal Practice*, 7:2503 (Albany and N.Y., 2d edn., 1955).

[4] See the examples, text at note 100 below, and Doc. III.

[5] 12 Car. 2, c. 19, §1 (1660). The warrant so issued enabled the holder "with the assistance of a sheriff, justice of peace or constable, to enter into any house in the day-time where such goods are suspected to be concealed, and in case of resistance to break open such houses, and to seize and secure the same goods so concealed; and all officers and ministers of Justice are hereby required to be aiding and assisting thereunto." The Act limited entries under it to one month after the offense was supposed to have been committed and gave any party injured by a false information an action of trespass against the informer. *Id.* §§2, 4.

[6] See Frese, "Early Parliamentary Legislation on Writs of Assistance," 38 Col. Soc. Mass., *Pubns.* 318–326 (1959); Frese, Writs of Assistance (dissertation) 41–56.

[7] 13 & 14 Car. 2, c. 11, §5(2) (1662), set out in text at note 92 below as JA copied it. For confusion introduced by variant spellings of "assistance," see note 93 below. §4 of the Act provided for search of vessels at any time without a warrant.

[8] See Frese, "Legislation on Writs of Assistance," 38 Col. Soc. Mass., *Pubns.* 327–352; Frese, Writs of Assistance (dissertation) 97–106. See also Quincy, *Reports* (Appendix) 530–532.

to the contrary construction, however, and, since the parliamentary debates contain no affirmative statement on the precise point in question, contrary inferences may also be drawn from the legislative history.[9] The actual intent of Parliament in the Act of 1662 thus cannot be determined.

Whatever the legislative intent, a course of practice under the statute soon developed which was a surer guide to construction in the courts than ambiguous language and incomplete history.[10] There are some indications

[9] The language of 13 & 14 Car. 2, c. 11, §5(2) (1662), standing alone seems to envision a general warrant, if the term "writ of assistance" is not held to incorporate the ancient process. See note 12 below. The statute, 12 Car. 2, c. 19 (1660), was continued and confirmed long after 1662, however, leading to the conclusion that the Act of 1662 included only the special warrant of the 1660 Act. Frese, "Legislation on Writs of Assistance," 38 Col. Soc. Mass., *Pubns.* 335; compare Quincy, *Reports* (Appendix) 531–532. It could nevertheless be argued that the Act of 1660, which provided for the issuance of warrants by officers other than the Barons of the Exchequer (who had the sole power under the 1662 Act), was retained as an additional weapon in the battle against illicit trade. The other Acts chiefly relied upon to support the special warrant theory are 13 & 14 Car. 2, c. 3, §14 (1662), a provision of the Militia Act that general warrants might issue to search for illegal arms; and 13 & 14 Car. 2, c. 33, §§15, 19 (1662), which provided such warrants for searches for unlicensed printed matter. See Frese, "Legislation on Writs of Assistance," 38 Col. Soc. Mass., *Pubns.* 336–351. Father Frese points to the contrast between the battle required to pass even these measures, which were limited by numerous exclusions, and the ease with which the less limited writs of assistance provision was passed, as evidence that the latter embodied only special warrants. *Id.* at 351–352. This difference might also be accounted for by a difference in the nature of the evils sought to be remedied by the various acts. Insurrection and sedition are political crimes; measures designed to control them may affect the liberties of the entire populace. Smuggling is a crime with a financial motive; its suppression is more likely to be localized in effect, harming only those who habitually live close to or beyond a rule of law accepted by the majority. Other legislation of the same Parliament provided for search without special warrant. See 13 & 14 Car. 2, c. 7, §§7, 14 (Search of London leather workers' shops for prohibited leather); 13 & 14 Car. 2, c. 5, §8 (Search of Norfolk and Norwich shops and other locations for defective yarns); 13 & 14 Car. 2, c. 32, §9 (Search of West-Riding shops and other locations for illegally imported cloth). Father Frese argues that the matters involved in these acts are too minor and local to be analogous to the Customs Act; moreover, they do not authorize use of force. Frese, Writs of Assistance (dissertation) 99–104. Although the latter objection has some merit, it could be argued that a customs measure bears greater resemblance to this last class of statutes than to the Militia and Printing Acts, thus accounting for a uniform silence as to the general search powers. In any event, it is clear that the 1662 Parliament did not hesitate to convey such powers when the occasion required.

[10] For the general proposition that long-continued usage can control the construction of a statute, see Sir Peter B. Maxwell, *The Interpretation of Statutes* 308–314 (London, 9th edn., Sir G. H. B. Jackson, 1946). The printed *Journals* of the House of Commons and House of Lords, upon which Father Frese's legislative history (notes 8–9 above) is chiefly based were published in about 1742, but there is no evidence that they were known in Massachusetts. See L. A. Abraham and S. C. Hawtrey, *A Parliamentary Dictionary* 104 (London, 1956). Even if the *Journals* had been available, it is possible that the Massachusetts court might have refused to consider them in construing the statute. The familiar English doctrine barring legislative history as an aid in this process was not clearly formulated until 1769, however, and legislative materials were so used by Lord Camden in Entick v. Carrington, 2 Wils. K.B. 275, 95 Eng. Rep. 807 (C.P. 1765), a famous decision

that in the years after 1662 searches were carried out under special warrant, probably as a result of an attempt to follow the former practice under the Act of 1660.[11] Apparently, however, the view prevailed that the Act of 1662 had created a new process, limited neither by the earlier statute nor by practice under the ancient equitable writ. There is no reported decision on the point prior to the argument at Boston in 1761, but before 1685 a form of the writ granting unlimited powers of general search seems to have been in use in the Exchequer.[12] Other evidence indicates that from some time in the first half of the 18th century, the writ was established as a general standing warrant issued by the Exchequer on the application of the Commissioners of Customs, to be held by the principal customs officers for use by them or their subordinates as the occasion demanded. Abuses of the instrument were probably avoided by virtue of the fact that ordinarily the principal officers required the same showing of information and probable cause that a justice would have required for the issue of a special search warrant.[13] Furthermore, even with probable

---

against general warrants, handed down in the course of the Wilkes controversy (text at note 33 below), cited in Plucknett, *Concise History* 335–336; see also Maxwell, *Interpretation of Statutes* 27–30.

[11] Frese, Writs of Assistance (dissertation) 160–161 note.

[12] See the form of a writ dating from between 1676 and 1685, published in William Brown, *Compendium of the Several Branches of Practice in the Court of the Exchequer* 358–361 (London, 1688). It is more fully discussed in notes 57, 68, below. This form bears little or no resemblance to the ancient writs of assistance (note 3 above). It has been suggested that the source may have been either the sheriff's "Patent of Assistance" (a general command to others to aid this officer), or, by analogy, the general warrants authorized by 13 & 14 Car. 2, c. 33, §15 (note 9 above), which gave the bearers power, "with a constable, to take unto them such assistance as they shall think needful." See Quincy, *Reports* (Appendix) 397–398, 530–531 note. "Writs of assistance" were known in the colonies before the Act of 1696 (note 15 below), but these were apparently special warrants. Frese, Writs of Assistance (dissertation) 127–177. In England, however, the evidence is ambiguous. The materials cited by Frese (note 11 above) indicate the use of special warrants, but there was a second edition of Brown's *Compendium* in 1699, containing the form of the general writ. Reissues of the first edition in 1689 and 1692 presumably were likewise unchanged. See 1 Sweet and Maxwell, *Legal Bibliography* 319. Since special warrants could still be obtained under 12 Car. 2, c. 19 (1660), note 5 above, it is possible that warrants of both kinds were used during this period.

[13] See Hoon, *English Customs* 63, 272–273; Quincy, *Reports* (Appendix) 532 note; note 25 below. Writs of assistance were among those processes which would survive the death of the sovereign by six months under 1 Anne, stat. 1, c. 8, §5 (1702), cited in notes 80, 85, below. No English case has been found in which the validity of the writs was directly raised, but their existence as general warrants was recognized and seemingly approved in a series of cases after 1765. See text and note 33 below; Quincy, *Reports* (Appendix) 533–534 note. Gray suggests that the writ first came to the notice of the English judges through Hutchinson's application to the ministry in 1761. *Ibid.* See also cases cited, notes 59, 62, below. The writ remained in use in England throughout the 19th century in substantially its earlier form. Wolkins, "Writs of Assistance in England," 66 MHS, *Procs.* 357–360 (1936–1941). It is today authorized by the Customs and Excise Act of 1952, 15 & 16 Geo. 6 & 1 Eliz. 2, c. 44, §296, which permits entry with a writ by day or night

cause, the officer who searched and found nothing was liable in damages for the trespass.[14]

The use of the writ in the colonies depended upon a third statute, the Act of 1696, by which colonial customs control was generally strengthened and reorganized, and colonial customs officials were given the powers of their English counterparts, whatever those might be.[15] In Massachusetts, both before and after the passage of this act, the powers of search granted to customs officers by statute and inherent in their commissions were exercised, but there is little affirmative evidence that general warrants were issued in support of these powers.[16] According to Thomas Hutchinson, however, Governor Shirley, in office from 1741 until 1757, issued what were apparently general warrants to the customs officers. When Hutchinson himself pointed out the illegality of this practice, the Governor directed "the officers to apply for warrants from the superior court; and from that time, writs issued, not exactly in the form, but of the nature of writs of assistance issued from the court of exchequer in England." [17]

---

on "reasonable grounds to suspect that anything liable to forfeiture under the customs or excise Acts" is concealed on the premises. The presence of a constable is required only when the entry is at night. The special search warrant is clearly distinguished, being covered in a separate paragraph. For an account of the practice in 1930, when writs were in the custody of principal customs officers for use when circumstances did not permit a special warrant, see Wolkins, "Writs of Assistance in England," 66 MHS, *Procs.* 362; *Ham's Year Book 1930* 180 (London, 1930). In Canada the writ is still issued to officers charged with the enforcement of customs, excise, food and drug, and narcotics control acts. See Trasewick, "Search Warrants and Writs of Assistance," 5 *Crim. Law Quart.* 341, 345–349, 356–363 (1962).

[14] See note 62 below.

[15] 7 & 8 Will. 3, c. 22, §6(2), set out as JA copied it in text at note 94 below. The legislative history of this provision, while inconclusive, offers no affirmative evidence that Parliament intended to establish warrants in the colonies. See Frese, "Legislation on Writs of Assistance," 38 Col. Soc. Mass., *Pubns.* 352–359. There were, however, several measures in the same Parliament which provided general search powers in commercial situations like those in note 9 above. Frese, Writs of Assistance (dissertation) 117–125.

[16] See Frese, Writs of Assistance (dissertation) 127–179. It was later argued that the power to search was actually conveyed by 13 & 14 Car. 2, c. 11, §5(2) (1662), note 7 above, and that the writs were merely for identification purposes. Opinion of Attorney General DeGrey, 20 Aug. 1768, Quincy, *Reports* (Appendix) 454; compare Frese, Writs of Assistance (dissertation) 171 note. This theory is borne out by the fact that the form of the writ used after 1676 contained authority for searches aboard ship as well as ashore, although the 1662 Act did not require a writ for cases of the former class. See the writ at note 100 below; compare Doc. III. For a copy of a commission, see Commission of Benjamin Hallowell as Comptroller of Boston, 9 March 1764, Quincy, *Reports* (Appendix) 433 note. One 18th-century colonial law book contains only a special search warrant for customs officers. Frese, Writs of Assistance (dissertation) 179 note; see *Conductor Generalis: or the Office, Duty and Authority of Justices of the Peace* 91–92 (Phila., 2d edn., 1749). The latter work, intended for justices of the peace, would not contain the form of the writ of assistance, which could issue only from the Exchequer or an equivalent.

[17] 3 Hutchinson, *Massachusetts Bay*, ed. Mayo, 67. That the writs were general appears from Hutchinson's description of the event. This conclusion is supported

This development brought a fourth act into play—a Province law of 1699 which conveyed to the Superior Court the powers of the Exchequer. In 1754 the court had expressly refused to exercise the equitable branch of this jurisdiction, but it seemed to find no objection to the issuance of a writ ancillary to the Exchequer's revenue powers.[18] On the application of Charles Paxton a writ of assistance issued in August 1755, and the files of the court reflect that thereafter until 1760 general writs of assistance were granted to seven other officers.[19]

The death of George II in October 1760 touched off the controversy which led to the argument in 1761. Since the existing writs survived the sovereign's death by only six months, it was necessary for the customs officers to procure new ones.[20] The absence of records obscures the procedure by which the case came up, but probably Paxton and several other

---

by a phrase in Otis' argument at note 67 below, as well as by Hutchinson's remarks in the second writs of assistance argument in Nov. 1761. Quincy, *Reports* 52. Shirley was probably acting under the authority given to the governor, or one delegated by him, to seize illegally entered goods under 6 Geo. 2, c. 13, §3 (1733). He may also have relied, as "chief magistrate," on the provisions of 12 Car. 2, c. 19, §1 (1660), which permitted search of any premises for specific goods. See text at note 5 above.

[18] The Province law was the Act of 26 June 1699, c. 3, § 1, 1 A&R 370, set out in note 98 below. For the 1754 refusal to act, see note 61 below. The Superior Court could be said to have had a jurisdiction equivalent to that of the Exchequer over breaches of the Acts of Trade in England, because the acts applicable to the colonies gave concurrent jurisdiction of breaches there to the Courts of Vice Admiralty and the common-law courts. The Superior Court also had jurisdiction of breaches of provincial revenue acts. See 15 Car. 2, c. 7, §§6, 8 (1663); Act of 31 Jan. 1761, c. 20, §§14, 15, 20, 4 A&R 407. No evidence of a significant exercise of the jurisdiction under the English statutes has been found in the records or files of the Superior Court, however, and there seem to have been few actions under the Province acts. See p. 99, note 9, above; note 82 below. For Parliament's later efforts to meet the problem of a general colonial lack of Exchequer jurisdiction, see note 29 below.

[19] See Paxton's petition and writ in text at notes 99, 100, below. For the record references to the allowance of his and the other petitions, see Quincy, *Reports* (Appendix) 402–406. See also the petition of Francis Waldo, April 1758, SF 78370, and that of James Nevin, Jan. 1759, SF 79409.

[20] By virtue of 1 Anne, stat. 1, c. 8, §5 (1702), note 13 above. Hutchinson stated that the argument which followed had been called for in part because Samuel Sewall, "the late chief justice, who was in high esteem, had doubts of the legality of such writs." 3 Hutchinson, *Massachusetts Bay*, ed. Mayo, 68. JA later concurred as to Sewall's doubts and further stated that the February argument was before that Justice. JA to Tudor, 29 March 1817, 10 JA, *Works* 247. There is some question whether Sewall in fact had doubts. See Malcolm Freiberg, Prelude to Purgatory: Thomas Hutchinson in Provincial Massachusetts Politics, 1760–1770, p. 13 note (Brown Univ. doctoral dissertation, 1950). Whatever his views, he had died in Sept. 1760, so that he could not have heard the Feb. 1761 argument. See Whitmore, *Mass. Civil List* 70; Quincy, *Reports* (Appendix) 409. Since Hutchinson was commissioned as chief justice on 13 Nov. 1760 and took his seat on the bench on 30 Dec., only three days after George II's death was known in Boston, it would seem that JA was also in error in stating that Hutchinson was appointed expressly to decide the writs question in the Crown's favor. See Quincy, *Reports* (Appendix) 408–411 note.

officers applied in the form followed in the prior reign. This time, however, there was opposition, apparently as part of a general attack then being mounted on the customs and the Admiralty under the guidance of Benjamin Barons, disaffected collector of the port, and James Otis.[21] Thomas Greene and other Boston merchants petitioned to be heard on the question. Thomas Lechmere, Surveyor General of the Customs, then stepped into the case both for the Crown and his men, petitioning the court "to be heard on the same subject: And that Writs of Assistants may be granted to himself and his officers as usual." The proceeding seems to have gone forward as a hearing on these petitions, rather than on the application of any single officer.[22]

[21] Barons, appointed in 1759, had immediately begun to cause trouble, apparently because of a long-standing vendetta with Charles Paxton, surveyor and searcher at Boston. Barrow, Colonial Customs 261–262, 352–353. According to Paxton, Barons was behind not only the opposition to writs of assistance but also the efforts of the merchants to alter the practice whereby the charges of the informer in condemnations in the Court of Admiralty were paid out of the Province share of the proceeds. Quincy, *Reports* (Appendix) 425–426, 542. In the latter controversy James Otis represented the merchants at legislative hearings in Dec. 1760, which led the General Court to authorize Province Treasurer Harrison Gray to sue Paxton for specific sums he allegedly received in this fashion. *Id.* at 541–543. See note 130 below. Gray, with Otis as counsel, first lost on a plea in abatement upheld because he had sued in his own person. See *id.* at 541–547; 1 JA, *Diary and Autobiography* 210–212; SF 172289, 172353. In a new action in the name of the Province, Paxton obtained verdict and judgment at the Feb. 1762 term of the Superior Court. Quincy, *Reports* (Appendix) 548–552; SF 100183. At the Aug. 1761 Superior Court, John Erving, a Boston merchant and councilor, had obtained judgment against Collector George Cradock for money paid under a composition (consent decree) of a libel brought in Admiralty for duties—despite the court's instructions that the Admiralty decree was binding. *Id.* at 553–557. In the meantime, Barons had finally been removed from his post, in June 1761. See No. 45, note 44. Since he had brought three actions against those responsible for his removal which, with Gray v. Paxton and Erving v. Cradock, were all pending in the Suffolk Inferior Court in July 1761, it is little wonder that Governor Bernard saw the entire problem as the result of a plot fomented by Barons, Erving, and Otis. Bernard to Lords of Trade, 6 Aug. 1761, quoted in Quincy, *Reports* (Appendix) 426, 545, 555. It is more likely, however, that the opposition derived strong support from all the merchants because of their resentment toward a tightening of customs control insisted on by Pitt in Aug. 1760 as a means of halting illicit trade with the enemy. See *id.* at 407–408; Lawrence H. Gipson, *The British Empire before the American Revolution*, 10:111–131 (N.Y., 1961); King, "Judicial Flotsam in Massachusetts Bay," 27 *NEQ* 366, 371–374 (1954); Freiberg, Prelude to Purgatory 9 note. Otis was allegedly involved against the Crown because of wrath at the appointment of Hutchinson to the Superior Court in lieu of Otis' father. See 11 Sibley-Shipton, *Harvard Graduates* 252; note 20 above; note 128 below.

[22] JA's "Abstract," at note 105 below, reports that the case came up on the petition of James Cockle, Collector at Salem, at the Nov. 1760 term of the Essex Superior Court, an assertion which JA repeated in later writings. See, for example, JA to Tudor, 29 March 1817, 10 JA, *Works* 246–247. Cockle's petition has not been found, and there is no indication in the appropriate Minute Book that he, or any other officer, had applied for a writ in Nov. 1760. Quincy, *Reports* (Appendix) 409. Moreover, since the news of George II's death was not received in Boston until 27 Dec. 1760 (*Id.* at 411), the application certainly was made at a later date. That Paxton was first to apply is indicated by the facts that his was the

The argument actually began on 24 February 1761, and, according to later accounts, lasted for several days. Whether these recollections are accurate, and if they are, how many hours per day were spent in oratory, cannot now be determined.[23] Adams' on-the-spot report indicates that Gridley spoke first for the Crown, but whether through enthrallment, inattention, or nonattendance, Adams took virtually no notes of this portion of the argument. Thacher and Otis then appeared and Gridley gave what was apparently a rebuttal. It is these last three arguments which Adams preserved, at least in part. How much else was said we can only speculate, perhaps more misled than guided by Adams' later recollections.

Gridley's position was clear-cut. Parliament, he argued, had empowered the Exchequer to issue "writs of assistance"; authority showed these to be general writs. Parliament had given colonial customs officers the powers of the English customs; and the Superior Court had the powers of the Exchequer; thus the writ could issue. If the practice seemed to infringe upon individual liberties, there were ample English and colonial precedents for such infringement in the name of the exigencies of collecting the revenue. Thacher cast doubt upon the existence of a proper precedent for the writ and contended that the powers given by the Act of Parliament were too broad to be exercised under a general warrant. The bulk of his argument as recorded by Adams was addressed to the power of the Superior Court to act as the Court of Exchequer. Not only had this jurisdiction been renounced in a prior case, but the Massachusetts court lacked many of the powers with which the Exchequer could control English customs officers.

Otis alone seems to have raised broader questions. After a bombastic introduction, which may be a subsequent contribution by Adams,[24] he insisted that, while special writs might be allowed by necessity, a general writ violated the fundamental principle that a man should be secure in

---

first writ granted, and that Quincy's account is entitled "Paxton's Case." See note 27 below. Hutchinson also says that an officer applied first. 3 Hutchinson, *Massachusetts Bay*, ed. Mayo, 68. There are no Minute Books for the 1761 terms of the Suffolk Superior Court, but the files and records support the conclusion that the petitions of Greene et al. and Lechmere were filed at the Feb. term 1761, and that the final decision reached at the Nov. adjournment of the Aug. term was on these petitions. See Petition of Greene et al., Petition of Lechmere, SF 100515b, printed in Quincy, *Reports* (Appendix) 412–414. See entries, "Greene et al. Petn.," and "Lechmere, Survr. Genl. his petition," on otherwise blank leaves, SCJ Rec. 1760–1761, fols. 225–226; and see, generally, Quincy, *Reports* (Appendix) 412–418.

[23] Francis Bernard in 1765 said that the argument lasted three days, but it is unclear whether he referred to the Feb. or Nov. argument. Quincy, *Reports* (Appendix) 416. JA, in his Autobiography, characterized the argument as "several days" and in a letter in 1818 said that Otis' speech against the Acts of Trade alone lasted four or five hours. 3 JA, *Diary and Autobiography* 276; JA to William Tudor, 1 June 1818, 2 JA, *Works* 314. The argument has been dated by virtue of the fact that it was held on the second Tuesday of the term. See note 104 below. The term began on the third Tuesday of the month, 17 Feb. 1761.

[24] This portion of Otis' remarks does not appear in JA's actual minutes (Doc. I), but is part of his later "Abstract" (Doc. II).

his own house. He disparaged the source of Gridley's authority, then argued that if it were valid, the courts did not have to follow a precedent offensive to fundamental principles. In an often-cited passage he urged that an Act of Parliament which sought to make the courts act in violation of these principles was void. He then went on to show various flaws in the writ contended for and to argue that on a proper construction the statutes cited authorized only special warrants. He closed with a reiteration of Thacher's attack on the Exchequer powers of the Superior Court.

The only question about which the court seems to have been in doubt was that of the nature of the warrants actually used in England. Accordingly, judgment was suspended pending an inquiry by Hutchinson into the Exchequer practice. The reply was that general writs were granted freely upon the application of the Commissioners of Customs to the clerk of the Exchequer,[25] but the whole matter was reargued at Boston in November 1761 at an adjournment of the August term. After the second hearing, the court decided unanimously in favor of the writ.[26] No record or minute book entry has been found. The decision seems to have been not an order allowing the issuance of a writ to a specific officer, but a kind of declaratory ruling, in effect granting the prayer of Lechmere's petition, that the writ might thereafter issue upon due application in accordance with the English practice. Thus, the first writ granted after the argument was given to Paxton on 2 December 1761, upon the application of the Surveyor General in his behalf. Similar procedure was followed for each writ subsequently issued in Massachusetts.[27]

[25] 3 Hutchinson, *Massachusetts Bay*, ed. Mayo, 68; Quincy, *Reports* (Appendix) 414–416; Freiberg, Prelude to Purgatory 15 note. The inquiry was apparently directed by Hutchinson to William Bollan, former Massachusetts agent in London. According to Bollan's memorial of 1766, seeking preferment from the Duke of Newcastle, Hutchinson desired "to know whether such writs of assistance ever issue from the exchequer, except upon special information, and confined either to particular houses, or to particular goods of which information is made." Bollan replied by sending him a copy of the writ from the Exchequer, which was similar to that used in Massachusetts in 1755, reproduced in text at note 100 below. Bollan also noted that "These writs upon any application of the commissioners of the customs to the proper officer of the court of Exchequer are made out of course by him, without any affidavit or order of the court." Wolkins, "Bollan on Writs of Assistance," 59 MHS, *Procs.* 415, 420 (1925–1926). See, as to the English practice, note 13 above.

[26] See Quincy, *Reports* 51–57; compare *Boston Gazette*, 23 Nov. 1761, reprinted in Quincy, *Reports* (Appendix) 486–487. A summary of the arguments, apparently by Otis, appeared in the *Boston Gazette* for 4 Jan. 1762. It is reprinted in Quincy, *Reports* (Appendix) 488–494.

[27] See the applications (1762–1769) in SF 100515b, printed in Quincy, *Reports* (Appendix) 416–434. Quincy styled the second argument "Paxton's Case of the Writs of Assistance," but the evidence of the court records suggests that he, like JA in the first argument, simplified the nature of the proceedings. See Quincy, *Reports* 51; note 22 above. Hutchinson's draft of the writ which issued is printed as Doc. III. For the reaction and subsequent history of the writ in Massachusetts, see Quincy, *Reports* (Appendix) 416–468, 495–499; Wolkins, "Malcom and Writs of Assistance," 58 MHS, *Procs.* 5 (1924–1925); Frese, "James Otis and Writs of Assistance," 30 NEQ 496, 499–508 (1957); Frese, Writs of Assistance (disserta-

The importance which Adams attached to this case has been disputed. It has been suggested that oral argument delivered before a relatively small audience could not of itself have had the inspirational effects attributed to it.[28] Certainly the efforts of Otis and Thacher did not change the orthodox view of what the law was. Writs were allowed to issue, and the practice was continued thereafter. Moreover, when in 1767 Parliament came to revise the statutes to effect the issuance of writs of assistance in all the colonies, the problem with which it was concerned was not the constitutionality of a general warrant, nor the power of the courts to deal with an unconstitutional Act, nor even the nature of the practice in the Exchequer, but merely an assurance to the high courts of judicature in the colonies that they could exercise Exchequer powers.[29]

The role of Otis' argument in the larger political and constitutional developments that were to follow is less easily dismissed. It is true that questions of Exchequer practice and Superior Court powers are not the stuff of revolution. As to the validity of general warrants, it is probably also true, as modern historians contend, that continuing colonial opposition to writs of assistance was not a direct response to Otis' oratory at Boston in 1761. Presumably the renewed efforts of customs officers to obtain writs after 1767 produced the widespread resistance to general warrants which led ultimately to the prohibition against unreasonable searches and seizures in the Fourth Amendment to the United States Constitution.[30]

---

tion) 202–235, 251–257, 273; Freiberg, Prelude to Purgatory 19–22. See also note 30 below.

[28] See Dickerson, "Writs of Assistance as a Cause of Revolution," in R.B. Morris, ed., *The Era of the American Revolution* 40 (N.Y., 1939). Compare Frese, Writs of Assistance (dissertation) 21–26; Frese, "Otis and Writs of Assistance," 30 *NEQ* 496 (1957).

[29] The Townshend Act, 7 Geo. 3, c. 46, §10 (1767), provided that, doubts having arisen about the legality of the use of writs of assistance in the colonies through the failure of the Act of 7 & 8 Will. 3, c. 22, to authorize any particular court to issue them, "such writs of assistance . . . shall and may be granted by the said superior or supreme court of justice having jurisdiction within such colony or plantation respectively." The doubts had been expressed in a series of opinions of the Attorney General in England, which did not squarely face the question presented by the Exchequer jurisdiction of the Massachusetts superior court. See Wolkins, "Malcom and Writs of Assistance," 58 MHS, *Procs.* 5 (1924–1925); Frese, "Otis and Writs of Assistance," 30 *NEQ* 496, 503–505. Compare Opinion of Attorney General DeGrey, 20 Aug. 1768, Quincy, *Reports* (Appendix) 452–454.

[30] The passage of 7 Geo. 3, c. 46, note 29 above, and the creation of a new board of American Customs Commissioners to enforce it (No. 45, notes 10–14), marked the beginning of a concerted effort by the customs officials in all colonies to obtain and enforce writs of assistance. For the difficulties which they encountered, even with the new enactments, see Dickerson, "Writs of Assistance," *Era of the Revolution* 49–75; Frese, Writs of Assistance (dissertation) 225–293. For earlier problems in Massachusetts, see sources and authorities cited in note 27 above. The 14th Article of the Declaration of Rights in the Massachusetts Constitution of 1780, substantially drafted by JA, is an early and explicit demonstration of the reaction: "Every subject has a right to be secure from all unreasonable searches and seizures of his person, his houses, his papers, and all his possessions. All warrants, therefore, are contrary to this right, if the cause or foundation of them be not previously

Nevertheless, in this struggle Otis' ideas, published in the newspapers and circulated by the bar, continued to stimulate resistance.[31]

Otis' argument had its greatest significance in questions of legislative and judicial power. By 1761 the doctrine of absolute parliamentary sovereignty, which is today the foundation of the British constitution, had become generally accepted in England. As Blackstone said in 1765, "if the parliament will positively enact a thing to be done which is unreasonable, I know of no power that can control it." [32] In the latter year the doctrine was applied to writs of assistance. Litigation arising out of the problems of John Wilkes and the *North Briton* had led to a series of rulings in which the English courts held that general warrants were invalid as an intrusion on rights guaranteed by the common law. There had been no statutory authority for the warrants in those cases, however, and in the leading formulation of the position, Lord Mansfield was careful to distinguish writs of assistance as authorized by act of Parliament.[33]

In the 1761 argument, the theory of parliamentary sovereignty was implicit in the Crown's position.[34] Otis, however, urged that acts of Parlia-

---

supported by oath or affirmation, and if the order in the warrant to a civil officer, to make search in suspected places, or to arrest one or more suspected persons, or to seize their property, be not accompanied with a special designation of the persons or objects of search, arrest, or seizure; and no warrant ought to be issued but in cases and with the formalities prescribed by the laws." 4 JA, *Works* 226–227. As to JA's role in the framing, see *id.* at 215–217; 2 JA, *Diary and Autobiography* 401 note. The Fourth Amendment to the United States Constitution is of similar purport: "The right of the people to be secure in their persons, houses, papers, and effects, against unreasonable searches and seizures, shall not be violated, and no Warrants shall issue, but upon probable cause, supported by Oath or affirmation, and particularly describing the place to be searched, and the persons or things to be seized." The first United States Customs Act provided that officers might search vessels upon reasonable suspicion at any time without warrant, but that premises ashore could be searched only with a warrant obtained on representation of suspicion to a Justice of the Peace. Act of 31 July 1789, c. 5, §24, 1 Stat. 43.

[31] For newspaper publication in Boston after the Nov. 1761 argument and reaction there, see notes 26, 27, above. In many other colonies arguments similar to those of Otis were used; in 1773 JA's version of his argument as printed in the *Massachusetts Spy* (Doc. II and notes 103, 122, below) was sent to the Connecticut Committee of Correspondence. Frese, "Otis and Writs of Assistance," 30 NEQ 506–508.

[32] 1 Blackstone, *Commentaries* *91. As to the 18th-century position generally, see J. W. Gough, *Fundamental Law in English Constitutional History* 174–191 (Oxford, rev. edn., 1961); Plucknett, "Bonham's Case and Judicial Review," 40 *Harv. L. Rev.* 58–60 (1926). Even Lord Camden, a friend to America, took the same position in 1768. Quincy, *Reports* (Appendix) 516–517. For the modern British view, see Edward McWhinney, *Judicial Review in the English-Speaking World* 31–48 (Toronto, 2d edn., 1960).

[33] Money v. Leach, 3 Burr. 1742, 1766, 97 Eng. Rep. 1075, 1088 (K.B. 1765). See generally, 10 Holdsworth, *History of English Law* 659–672. The existence of the writ in England today (note 13 above) emphasizes the continuing force of the constitutional doctrine.

[34] See Gridley's arguments, text following note 83 below; compare his position in Nov. 1761. Quincy, *Reports* 56–57. Hutchinson expressly adopted this position at a later date. See his charge to the Grand Jury, March 1769, quoted in note 72

ment "against the Constitution" and "against natural Equity" were void, and that "the executive courts must pass such Acts into disuse." Adams' notes show that in support of this position Otis cited the well-known language of Coke's opinion in *Bonham's Case*: "When an Act of Parliament is against Common Right and Reason, or repugnant, or impossible to be performed, the Common Law will controll it, and adjudge such Act to be Void." [35]

Modern scholars have concluded that in context this passage states a familiar common law canon of construction, rather than a constitutional theory.[36] Coke's view of the constitution was that a supreme Parliament (the "High Court") and the courts of justice both participated in the process of declaring and applying the same body of unchangeable, pre-existing law; a kind of sovereignty, the prerogative, resided in the Crown, subject to the limitations of that law. The issue to which constitutional arguments were directed was the clash between the powers of the Crown on the one hand and the powers of Parliament and the courts on the other.[37] Since the power of the Crown was not in question in *Bonham's Case*, the issue there raised was procedural, not constitutional.

For Coke, *Bonham's Case* was thus a conflict between private interests regulated by a statute which had to be interpreted, rather than a direct challenge to the power of Parliament to make the statute.[38] The standard by which the statute was to be measured was the basic reasonableness, the common sense, of the common law. This quality was not a "higher law" by which Parliament was to be kept in check, but a guide by which statutes, presumably intended by the makers to conform to the reason of the common law, were to be construed. If, in the process of construction, an act was adjudged "void," the court was not acting as a separate branch of government with a power to control Parliament by declaring acts unconstitutional, but was only applying the law of Parliament, necessarily

---

below; Hutchinson to Richard Jackson, 12 Sept. 1765, 26 Mass. Arch. 153, quoted in Quincy, *Reports* (Appendix) 441 note.

[35] Bonham's Case, 8 Co. Rep. 113b, 118a, 77 Eng. Rep. 646, 652 (C.P. 1610), quoted more fully, note 73 below. For Otis' citation of the case and the other phrases quoted here, see text at notes 71–73 below.

[36] See Thorne, "Dr. Bonham's Case," 54 *L.Q. Rev.* 543 (1938); MacKay, "Coke—Parliamentary Sovereignty or the Supremacy of Law," 22 *Mich. L. Rev.* 222–231 (1924); Gough, *Fundamental Law* 10–11, 31–40. It has also been argued that Coke intended to state a broader proposition of fundamental law. See Plucknett, "Bonham's Case," 40 *Harv. L. Rev.* 31–48; Corwin, "The 'Higher Law' Background of American Constitutional Law," 42 *Harv. L. Rev.* 373 (1929).

[37] See Gough, *Fundamental Law* 40–65.

[38] In a sense, *Bonham's Case* involved the public interest, since it concerned the statutory powers of the London College of Physicians to license practitioners. However, the form of the proceeding was an action of trespass for false imprisonment brought by Dr. Bonham against the members of the Board of Censors of the College, who had imprisoned him for contempt of their orders; such actions were considered as ordinary civil actions, the concept of review of administrative action by certiorari not having been developed. See Jaffe and Henderson, "Judicial Review and the Rule of Law: Historical Origins," 72 *L.Q. Rev.* 350–352 (1956); compare Gough, *Fundamental Law* 49. See also No. 24, note 4; No. 27, notes 4–9.

general in effect, so as to do justice in the circumstances of a particular case.

Otis' argument in 1761, by contrast, was a constitutional one, addressed directly to the questions of the limits of legislative power and the power of the judiciary to enforce those limits. In the latter half of the 17th century, as Parliament increasingly acquired the sovereignty formerly attributed to the Crown, *Bonham's Case*, taken out of its private law context, had often been relied upon in political and constitutional argument to support the proposition that there was a higher law to which Parliament must bow.[39] Other authorities cited by Otis indicate that he quoted Coke's words in this constitutional sense, rather than as a canon of construction. The contrast between construction and constitution is emphasized by the fact that Otis also argued in conventional fashion that the statute should be read narrowly to permit only the special search warrant known at common law. If, however, the court insisted on treating the act as "made in the very words of this petition," that is, as embodying the language of the writ of assistance itself, then he argued that the act would be void not only under *Bonham's Case*, but by virtue of "natural equity" and "the Constitution." [40]

These terms do not denote the "reason of the common law," but instead refer to fundamental principles of equity and justice embodied in a British constitution that a century and a half of political development had made into a formal, if still invisible, instrument of government. They are thus "higher law" in something like the sense used by modern constitutional theorists. Otis drew these ideas from sources which demonstrate the breadth of his argument. His pamphlet, *Rights of the British Colonies*, published in 1764, invoked Locke's description of a government in which legislative sovereignty ultimately was a grant from the people and so could not be absolute. In a passage strongly reminiscent of his writs of assistance argument, Otis cited the Swiss publicist Emmerich de Vattel, as well as *Bonham's Case* and other common law precedents, for the proposition that Parliament could not make a statute against natural equity or the British constitution. In all probability he cited the same authorities and made the same appeal to higher law before the Superior Court in 1761.[41]

[39] See Gough, *Fundamental Law* 104–105, 111; Plucknett, "Bonham's Case," 40 *Harv. L. Rev.* 61–63.

[40] See text at notes 71–73 below. Compare Adams' "Abstract," text at note 148 below.

[41] See James Otis, *The Rights of the British Colonies Asserted and Proved* 72–73 (Boston, 1764), reprinted with the original pagination in Bernard Bailyn, *Pamphlets of the American Revolution*, 1:419–482 (Cambridge, Mass., 1965): " 'Tis hoped it will not be considered as a new doctrine that even the authority of the Parliament of *Great Britain* is circumscribed by certain bounds which if exceeded their acts become those of mere *power* without *right*, and consequently void. The judges of England have declared in favor of these sentiments when they expressly declare that *acts of Parliament against natural equity are void*. That *acts against the fundamental principles of the British constitution are void.* ‡ This doctrine is agreeable to the law of nature and nations, and to the divine dictates of natural and revealed religion." (See also *id.* at 70.) In a footnote at the dagger Otis quoted a long

Both the writs argument and *Rights of the British Colonies* also suggest that Otis saw the courts in a constitutional role not envisioned in *Bonham's Case*. The phrase, "the executive courts must pass such acts into disuse," reported by Adams, contains a hint of a power that went beyond Coke's words. This hint is borne out by a passage in the pamphlet. Otis there argued the existence of two remedies when an act of Parliament clashed with equity and justice. Repeal might be sought, or, "If the reasons that can be given against an act plainly demonstrate that it is against *natural* equity, the executive courts will adjudge such act void. It may be questioned by some, though I make no doubt of it, whether they are not obliged by their oaths to adjudge such act void. If there is not a right of private judgment to be exercised, so far at least as to petition for a repeal, or to determine the expediency of risking a trial at law, the parliament might make itself arbitrary, which it is conceived it cannot by the constitution." [42] In voiding acts of Parliament, the courts were not merely interpreting statutes incident to the decision of private disputes. They were obligated by the nature of their office to pass judgment on legislation, and this function was itself a vital element of the constitution.

The power which Otis urged for the courts fell short of the later American doctrine of judicial review. His pamphlets show that he still saw Parliament as supreme, and so not bound to yield to a court's decision adverse to a statute. The point was that, although Parliament might err, it was benevolent and sought to act within the constitution; it would therefore accept the judicial determination, even though not compelled to.[43] The courts thus did not occupy their modern position as a separate governmental branch of coordinate authority with the legislature, having express power to declare the law. Lacking this power, a court could not

---

passage on legislative power from Emmerich de Vattel, *Law of Nations*, bk. 1, c. 3, §34 (London, 1760), to the effect that the legislature could not change "the constitution of the state." The footnote also cited Bonham's Case; Day v. Savadge, Hobart 85, 80 Eng. Rep. 235 (C.P. 1615) (possibly cited in argument; see note 71 below); Thornby v. Fleetwood, 10 Mod. 113, 88 Eng. Rep. 651 (C.P. 1713); and City of London v. Wood, 12 Mod. 669, 88 Eng. Rep. 1592 (K.B. 1701). The last three were all cases which repeated the *Bonham* principle. For Otis' reliance on Locke, see, for example, *Rights of the British Colonies* 22–23; see also Corwin, "Higher Law," 42 Harv. L. Rev. 399. JA, years later, asserted that *Rights of the British Colonies* did contain the authorities cited in the writs argument. JA to Tudor, 21 Aug. 1818, 10 JA, *Works* 351.

[42] Otis, *Rights of the British Colonies* 41. For a passage in JA's "Abstract" which may also convey this idea, see text at note 149. In a newspaper statement of the arguments, attributed to Otis, *Bonham's Case* was not cited, and it was merely argued that the English construction of the Act should not be followed in Massachusetts. *Boston Gazette*, 4 Jan. 1762, printed in Quincy, *Reports* (Appendix) 491–492.

[43] See Otis, *Rights of the British Colonies* 60, citing Jeremiah Dummer, *A Defence of the New England Charters* 41 (Boston, 1745). See generally 1 Bailyn, *Pamphlets* 415–417. Otis' concept of a supreme Parliament complying with law of its own volition is related to Coke's ideas. *Id.* at 412–413; Gough, *Fundamental Law* 40–50. For Otis, however, it was the necessity for maintaining the constitution, rather than undefined moral obligation, which enjoined compliance.

totally annul an act, but could only decide the case before it. The modern court does no more in form, but its constitutional eminence gives its decisions an effective force beyond the confines of a particular case. Nevertheless, Otis' notion that the courts have some kind of constitutional function in controlling Parliament was surely one source of the modern concept of their power.[44]

In his argument, Otis was far from proclaiming revolution, and he did not singlehandedly create American constitutional law. He was, however, ahead of the revolutionary pamphleteers in confronting the orthodox idea of Parliamentary sovereignty with the notion that there might be a rule of law superior to Parliament; [45] and he did suggest that it might be a function of the courts to enforce compliance with that rule. These ideas appeared in his later writings, but other problems, theoretical, political, and emotional, so obscured them, that Otis undoubtedly did not realize their full import, and certainly did little to argue them in a consistent and coherent manner.[46] Nevertheless, he had put them into play. Other writers, more aware of political realities, carried his ideas to their logical extreme— the justification of the overthrow of parliamentary authority and the subsequent establishment of a new government in which the legislature was limited by an express fundamental law.[47]

The argument of 1761 did not of itself lead to these great ends, but if it marked for Otis a first opportunity to formulate and express ideas which were later to circulate throughout the colonies in his pamphlets, then it

[44] See Charles G. Haines, *The American Doctrine of Judicial Supremacy* 22–25 (Berkeley, 1932); Henry Rottschaefer, *Handbook of American Constitutional Law* 32–36 (St. Paul, Minn., 1939); Andrew C. McLaughlin, *A Constitutional History of the United States* 26–27 (N.Y., 1935); Corwin, "Higher Law," 42 *Harv. L. Rev.* 375, 379, 408–409. Corwin seems to read too much into Adams' report of Otis' words when he says, "Then and there American constitutional law was born, for Otis' contention goes far beyond Coke's: an ordinary court may traverse the specifically enacted will of Parliament, and its condemnation is final." *Id.* at 398. The history of judicial review in the colonies suggests many roots, including the activities of the colonial courts and the judicial functions of the Privy Council. See Haines, *Judicial Supremacy* 44–66; Smith, *Appeals to the Privy Council* 522–653. For references to the idea in Massachusetts, see Quincy, *Reports* (Appendix) 527–528 note; note 42 above; note 48 below. JA spoke of "telling the jury the nullity of acts of Parliament," but this was after the British had left Boston. JA to William Cushing, 9 June 1776, 9 JA, *Works* 390–391.

[45] 1 Bailyn, *Pamphlets* 121; Charles F. Mullet, *Fundamental Law and the American Revolution* 80–81 (N.Y., 1933).

[46] Otis' writings contained much ambiguity, which gave rise to the correspondingly ambiguous reactions among his contemporaries. See 1 Bailyn, *Pamphlets* 121–123, 409–417. In *Rights of the British Colonies* 22–23, he quoted, apparently with approval, Locke's theory that revolution was justified when the sovereign arbitrarily assumed absolute power. He expressly rejected revolution as a solution to the existing problems of the colonies, however. *Id.* at 50–51. Later he retreated even further. 1 Bailyn, *Pamphlets* 122, 546–552.

[47] See Corwin, "Higher Law," 42 *Harv. L. Rev.* 394–409. The power of the courts to enforce the supremacy of the United States Constitution was not express, but was established by Chief Justice Marshall in Marbury v. Madison, 1 Cranch (5 U.S.) 137, 173–180 (1803). See also 1 Bailyn, *Pamphlets* 102–105.

cannot be said that his words stopped at the door of the Council Chamber. And if, when John Adams said sixty years later that "Then and there the child Independence was born," he really meant that the suggestion that Parliament's power was not absolute started the intellectual process which was to lead him to the forefront of the revolutionary movement, then surely the argument of 1761 was a vital predecessor of those of 1776.[48]

The documentary history of the materials which follow is nearly as tortuous as their intellectual history. Document I is the booklet of "despicable notes" which Adams actually took down at the argument. They are hastily written and certainly do not touch all points covered in the course of a hearing of at least several hours' duration. Appended to them are Adams' extracts of the statutes involved and copies of the petition and writ issued to Paxton in 1755. These were apparently made by him for use in the more elaborate abstract of the argument which is reproduced as Document II.

It is this document which creates problems, since no copy of it in Adams' hand has been found. In his diary for 3 April 1761, he reported showing to Colonel Josiah Quincy "an Abstract of the Argument for and against Writts of Assistance." Quincy cried, "did you take this from those Gentlemen as they delivered it? You can do any Thing! You can do as you please! Gridley did not use that Language. He never was Master of such a style! It is not in him—&c." [49] This description is ambiguous, the more so because it occurs in a passage in which Adams is dubious of the sincerity of the Colonel's flattery on this and other points. It seems, on balance, to refer not to the rough notes made in court but to a more careful treatment written out at a later date. Description of the piece as an "Abstract" seems to imply work of more finished quality than that of notes made on the spot; moreover, praise such as that given by Quincy would have seemed extravagant and suspect in the extreme if applied to the fragmentary jottings that are the notes.[50]

In his Autobiography, and in the passage from his letter to Tudor quoted at the beginning of this note, Adams spoke of his notes of the argument as having been printed in the *Massachusetts Spy* and in Minot's *History of Massachusetts Bay*.[51] The material printed is not the rough notes, but a comparison of the texts shows that it was drawn from those notes. Other versions of the arguments, in virtually identical language, exist in

[48] See JA's comment of 3 July 1776 in note 1 above. For an example of his use of the fundamental law principle, see his argument before the Governor and Council on the closing of the courts during the Stamp Act crisis. Quincy, *Reports* 200–202. JA's own notes for this argument suggest that he was citing *Bonham's Case* in a narrow sense. 2 JA, *Works* 159 note. In another well-known case where the validity of an act denying jury trial was in question, JA argued for strict construction only. No. 46, text at notes 65–66.

[49] 1 JA, *Diary and Autobiography* 210.

[50] See 1 JA, *Diary and Autobiography* 211 note; 10 Gipson, *British Empire* 122–123 note.

[51] For the letter, see text at note 1 above. The passage in the Autobiography is in 3 JA, *Diary and Autobiography* 276.

circumstances linking them to Adams. It therefore may be concluded that Adams composed a longer version of his notes and that it was this work which circulated among the bar and was preserved in the *Spy* and in Minot's *History*. On the basis of these conclusions, Document II is offered as the first collation of all known versions of Adams' "Abstract of the Argument." [52]

In the "Abstract" Adams has made the remarks of Gridley the opening argument, although from their position in his notes they would seem to have been a rebuttal. This argument and that of Thacher, which follows it, are taken with almost literal exactness from the rough notes. It is in Otis' often reprinted argument that Adams seems to have exercised artistic license. No doubt Otis said all that is attributed to him and much more; but the "Abstract" seems to be a combination of Adams' notes and his impressions of the larger questions that is peculiarly his own. The bones of the legal arguments which appear in the notes are there, but in pruning legal complexities and in adding fervor, Adams created a minor work of political propaganda. Perhaps the inspiration that produced this epitome of a famous address is the best evidence we have of the birth of "the child Independence" in 1761.

Document III is Hutchinson's draft of the writ issued after the November argument.

I. ADAMS' MINUTES OF THE ARGUMENT [53]

Suffolk Superior Court, Boston, 24 February 1761

Writs of Assistance

Gridley. The Constables distraining for Rates.[54] More inconsistent with English Rights and Liberties than Writts of assistance. And Necessity authorizes both.

Thatcher. I have searched, in all the ancient Repertories of Prece-

---

[52] Details of the provenance of the materials printed are in note 103 below. For one example of the "Abstract's" circulation, see note 31 above. Further evidence is provided by the existence of the Hawley and Keith versions, note 103 below. It is worth noting that the brief accounts of the argument in 3 Hutchinson, *Massachusetts Bay*, ed. Mayo, 68, and 1 Gordon, *History of Independence* 141–142, suggest that their authors may have at least read the "Abstract," probably in the *Massachusetts Spy*.

[53] In JA's hand, one large sheet folded three times to make a pocket-size gathering of sixteen pages; seven pages are blank. Adams Papers, Microfilms, Reel No. 185. Printed by CFA in 2 JA, *Works* 521–523, and, with extensive annotation, in Quincy, *Reports* (Appendix) 469–476. For the dating, see note 23 above.

[54] That is, the procedure for taking and selling property for nonpayment of taxes authorized under Province Law. Act of 3 Oct. 1730, c. 1, §§12, 13, 2 A&R 552–553.

dents, in Fitzherberts Natura Brevium,[55] and in the Register (Q. what the Register is) and have found no such Writt of assistance as this Petition prays. I have found two Writts of assistance in the Register but they are very different from the Writt pray'd for.[56]

In a Book, intituled the Modern Practice of the Court of Exchequer[57] there is indeed one such Writt, and but one.

By the Act of Parliament any other private Person may as well as a Custom House Officer take an officer, a sherriff, or Constable &c. and go into any shop, store &c. and seize: any Person authorized by such a Writt, under the seal of the Court of Exchequer, may. Not Custom House officers only.[58] Strange.[59]

Only a temporary Thing.

The most material Question is, whether the Practice of the Exchequer, will warrant this Court in granting the same.

The Act impowers all the officers of the Revenue to enter and seize in the Plantations, as well as in England. 7. & 8. Wm. 3, c. 22, §6. gives the same as 13. & 14. of C[harles][60] gives in England. The Ground of Mr. Gridleys argument is this, that this Court has the

[55] Anthony Fitzherbert, *New Natura Brevium* (various edns.: French, ca. 1531–1635; English, 1652–1793).

[56] The *Registrum Brevium*, or Register of Writs, a semi-official compilation based on the medieval manuscript registers kept by clerks of Chancery and practitioners. See Percy H. Winfield, *The Chief Sources of English Legal History* 298–302 (Cambridge, Mass., 1925). The writs to which Thacher refers are found in *Registrum Brevium tam Originalium quam Judicialium*, Appendix 46–47 (London, 4th edn., 1687). Gray points out that they direct the sheriff to assist a "party to a suit in chancery to get possession, under a decree of the Court, of lands withheld from him by another party to the suit." Quincy, *Reports* (Appendix) 396.

[57] As the remarks of Otis and Gridley, notes 69, 86, below, indicate, the work referred to here is William Brown's *Compendium of the Several Branches of Practice in the Court of Exchequer at Westminster* (London, various edns., 1688–1725). The writ in question, found at p. 358–361 in the 1688 edition, is set out in full in Quincy, *Reports* (Appendix) 398–399. See an extract, note 69 below. See also notes 12 above, 68 below. A work entitled *The Modern Practice of the Court of Exchequer* (London, 1731) contains nothing even resembling a writ of assistance.

[58] 13 & 14 Car. 2, c. 11, §5(2) (1662), extracted by JA, text at note 92 below. The section cited bears Thacher out, but it probably should be read with 13 & 14 Car. 2, c. 11, §15, providing that no goods "shall be seized as forfeited" except by persons authorized by the Customs Commissioners, the Treasury, or the Crown.

[59] Presumably Horne v. Boosey, 2 Str. 952, 93 Eng. Rep. 963 (K.B. 1733): Trover held to lie against a tidesman (a minor official charged with searching vessels for prohibited goods), who had seized goods ashore and had them condemned in the Exchequer. The Court noted a distinction between a seizure by "a proper officer," which could be attacked only in the Exchequer, and the seizure by this defendant, "who could not enter a house without a writ of assistance and a peace officer, the words of his warrant being so restrained." See Quincy, *Reports* (Appendix) 470 note.

[60] That is, 13 & 14 Car. 2, c. 11, note 58 above. For the Act of 7 & 8 Will. 3, see note 15 above.

Power of the Court of Exchequer. But This Court has renounced the Chancery Jurisdiction, which the Exchequer has in Cases where either Party is the Kings Debtor. Q. into that Case.[61]

In England all Informations of uncust[om]ed or prohibited Importations, are in the Exchequer. So that the Custom House officers are the officers of that Court. Under the Eye and Direction of the Barons.

The Writ of Assistance is not returnable. If such seisure were brot before your Honours, youd often find a wanton Exercise of their Power.

At home, the officers seise at their Peril even with Probable Cause.[62]

Otis. This Writ is against the fundamental Principles of Law. The Priviledge of House. A Man, who is quiet, is as secure in his House, as a Prince in his Castle, not with standing all his Debts, and civil Prossesses of any kind.—But

For flagrant Crimes, and in Cases of great public Necessity, the

---

[61] Gray has identified this case as McNeal v. Brideoak, SCJ Rec. 1754, fol. 150 (Suffolk, Feb. 1754), in which the complainants, Ann and Mary McNeal of Dublin, proceeded as "Debtors and Accountants to his Majesty." The action, described as a "Bill in Equity," was dismissed and the complainants were allowed an appeal to the King in Council, of which no record has been found. Quincy, *Reports* (Appendix) 470–471 note. Compare Quincy, *Reports* 54. See Min. Bk. 67, SCJ Suffolk, Nov. 1752, N–137; Feb. 1754, C–26. The Exchequer jurisdiction in question, either legal or equitable, arose from a writ known as *quominus*, because the plaintiff made a fictional allegation that he was debtor to the King for the amount of his claim and was "by which less" able to meet his debt. The court acted by virtue of its power in matters affecting the royal purse. See 3 Blackstone, *Commentaries* *45–46; Plucknett, *Concise History* 160–161, 170. The Massachusetts court's refusal to act would seem to be a reflection more of its lack of equity powers than of any desire to disclaim the powers of Exchequer, conferred on it by statute. Act of 26 June, 1699, c. 3 §1, 1 A&R 370, set out, note 98 below. The writ of assistance was part of the Exchequer's common-law revenue jurisdiction, rather than an equitable process. See Quincy, *Reports* (Appendix) 538–539; Brown, *Compendium* 28–29; note 18 above; note 82 below.

[62] Thacher here seems to be citing Leglise v. Champante, 2 Str. 820, 93 Eng. Rep. 871 (K.B. 1728) where in an action at law against a customs officer for the seizure of goods which the Exchequer had found not liable to forfeiture, "it was held, that in these cases the officer seizes at his peril, and that a probable cause is no defense." The authority of this case is cast in doubt by the statute, 19 Geo. 2, c. 34, §16 (1746), continued to 29 Sept. 1764 by 32 Geo. 2, c. 18, §1 (1759), which made a court's certification of probable cause a bar to any suit against the seizing officer. See 12 Viner, *Abridgment* 173. It seems to have been well established in England, however, that in case of a wrongful search as distinct from a wrongful seizure, probable cause was not a defense to an action, even when the search had been carried out by virtue of a writ of assistance. See authorities cited in Quincy, *Reports* (Appendix) 533–534 note. These cases were all decided after 1761, but even if this had clearly been the rule when Thacher argued, it would seem to cut against his position, since it demonstrates that the power given by the writ could be curbed by the courts.

Priviledge may be [encroached?] [63] on. For Felonies an officer may break upon Prossess, and oath—i.e. by a Special Warrant to search such an House, sworn to be suspected, and good Grounds of suspicion appearing.

Make oath coram Ld. Treasurer, or Exchequer, in England or a Magistrate here, and get a special Warrant, for the public good, to infringe the Priviledge of House. [64]

General Warrant to search for Felonies, Hawk. Pleas Crown. [65] Every petty officer from the highest to the lowest. And if some of em are ⟨comm[issioned], others⟩ uncom[missioned] others are uncomm[issioned]. [66] Gov[ernor and?] Justices used to issue such perpetual Edicts. [67] (Q. with what particular Reference?)

But one Precedent, and that in the Reign of C. 2, when Star

---

[63] Illegible in the MS. Gray's reading is "incroached." Quincy, *Reports* (Appendix) 471 note. It is textually more likely, but hardly more satisfactory than CFA's reading of "infringed." 2 JA, *Works* 521.

[64] For the powers of customs officers to enter on special warrant see 12 Car. 2, c. 19 (1660) quoted, note 5 above. In a number of situations the General Court granted provincial customs and other officers power to obtain a special search warrant to search specific premises upon giving information to a justice of the peace. See for example, Act of 13 Feb. 1760, c. 28, §25, 4 A&R 311 (Collector of excise to search for liquors sold without permit); Act of 3 Feb. 1764, c. 28, §5, 4 A&R 684 (Sheriff or constable to have warrant to search for flesh or skins of moose and deer killed out of season). Prior to the Import Act of 20 April 1756, c. 47, §§18–20, 3 A&R 936, province customs officers had the right to search in all suspected places "for illegally imported goods." In the 1756 act and thereafter the general provision was retained, but officers with a warrant on oath of information could force an entry to search. Compare Act of 27 June 1755, c. 1, §§18, 19, 3 A&R 845. See Frese, Writs of Assistance (dissertation) 179 note, 181 note.

[65] Hawkins, *Pleas of the Crown* 82. "But it seems to be very questionable whether a Constable can justify the Execution of a general Warrant to search for Felons or stolen Goods, because such Warrant seems to be illegal in the very face of it; for that it would be extremely hard to leave it to the discretion of a common Officer to arrest what Persons, and search what Houses he thinks fit. And if a Justice cannot legally grant a blank Warrant for the Arrest of a single Person, leaving it to the Party to fill it up, surely he cannot grant such a general Warrant, which might have the effect of an Hundred blank Warrants."

[66] Gray's suggestion that JA meant to write, "If some of em are commissioned others are uncommissioned," seems sound in context, although the MS also supports CFA's reading of "common" and "uncommon." Quincy, *Reports* (Appendix) 472 note; 2 JA, *Works* 522.

[67] This is apparently a reference to the prior practice in Massachusetts. See text and note 17 above. Gray reads the passage as "Government Justices" and suggests that it is a reference to the 17th-century English practice under which justices of the peace would issue warrants authorizing a general search for stolen goods upon the complaint of one who had been robbed. Quincy, *Reports* (Appendix) 472 note. See also 2 JA, *Works* 522. There is a passage in JA's "Abstract," at note 135 below, in which Otis goes on at some length about the former powers of Justices of the Peace to issue general warrants. The use of the phrase "perpetual Edicts" in the present text, however, surely indicates a writ giving a general power of search, rather than the more limited Justice's warrant.

Chamber Powers, and all Powers but lawful and useful Powers were pushd to Extremity.[68]

The Authority of this Modern Practice of the Court of Exchequer. It has an Imprimatur. But what may not have? It may be owing to some ignorant Clerk of the Exchequer.[69]

But all Precedents and this among the Rest are under the Control of the Principles of Law. Ld. Talbot. Better to observe the known Principles of Law than any one Precedent, tho in the House of Lords.[70]

As to Acts of Parliament. An Act against the Constitution is void: an Act against natural Equity is void: and if an Act of Parliament should be made, in the very Words of this Petition, it would be void.[71]

[68] Probably a reference to the form of a writ in Brown's *Compendium*. See note 57 above, note 86 below. Although this work was not published until 1688, the form recites that the customs officers therein given writs were commissioned by virtue of Letters Patent dated "anno regni nostri vicesimo septimo" (in the twenty-seventh year of our reign), which could refer to no English monarch ruling between Elizabeth I and George II except Charles II. The date of the form would thus be between 1676 and 1685, the year of Charles II's death.

[69] Gray notes that the language of the writ is "so curious a justification of Otis's suggestion" that he reprints it in full. Quincy, *Reports* (Appendix) 398–399. As the following extract may suggest, it is certainly an interesting example of the degeneration of Latin: "Ac etiam in tempore diurno unacum Constabular' Praeposito Anglice HEADBOROUGH aut alio publico officiario prope inhabitan' intrare & ire in aliquas Cellas Anglice VAULTS Cellur' Repositor' Anglice WAREHOUSES Shopas vel alia loca scrutare & videre utrum aliqua bon' res vel merchandizas. . . . Ac aperire aliquos riscos Anglice TRUNCKS cistas pixid' fardell' Packs fatt' vel de la Bulke quecunque in quibus aliqua bona res vel merchandiz' erint suspect' fore paccat' vel concelat.' " *Id.* at 399. The translated form, issued to Charles Paxton in Massachusetts in 1756, is printed in text at note 100 below.

[70] See Clare v. Clare, Talb. 21, 26–27, 25 Eng. Rep. 638, 640 (Ch. 1734) (Talbot, Lord Chancellor): "The case of *Higgins* versus *Dowler* is very imperfectly reported; and was upon a Demurrer, where Things are not argued with that Nicety which they are upon arguing the Merits of a Cause. That of *Stanley* and *Lee* has not been particularly mentioned; so that what we have of it is only upon memory: And I think it much better to stick to the known general rules, than to follow any one particular precedent which may be founded on reasons unknown to us: Such a proceeding would confound all Property. . . . The Case of *Lady Lanesborough* versus *Fox* is the strongest authority that can be; and even, had it not been in the House of Lords, I should have thought myself bound to go according to the general and known Rules of Law." Compare Quincy, *Reports* (Appendix) 473 note 17. Otis here makes use of two of the loopholes available in the 18th century to ensure that precedent did not stifle the orderly growth of the law. These were the inadequacy of the source of the asserted precedent and an appeal to principles variously described as those of common law, natural law, reason, and common sense. See 12 Holdsworth, *History of English Law* 150–158; C. H. S. Fifoot, *Lord Mansfield* 214–218 (Oxford, 1936).

[71] Probably an inadvertence for the writ itself. A statute in the language of the petitions upon which the case came up would have been neither unconstitutional nor effective. See text at note 22 above. The petition of Charles Paxton for a writ in 1755, printed at note 99 below, even if it had been urged in this case, is scarcely less neutral in tone. But compare Quincy, *Reports* (Appendix) 474 note. Gray suggests that the phrase "natural equity" means that Otis cited Lord Hobart's

The executive Courts must pass such Acts into disuse.[72] 8. Rep. 118.
from Viner. Reason of the Common Law to control an Act of Parliament.[73] Iron Manufacture. Noble Lord's Proposal, that we should
send our Horses to England to be shod.[74]

If an officer will justify under a Writ he must return it. 12th. Mod.
396.[75] Perpetual Writ.

language in Day v. Savadge, Hobart 85, 87, 80 Eng. Rep. 235, 237 (C.P. 1615):
"Even an act of Parliament, made against naturall equitie, as to make a man
judge in his owne case, is void in it selfe, for *Jura naturæ sunt immutabilia*, and they
are *leges legum*." See Quincy, *Reports* (Appendix) 521–524. See note 41 above.

[72] That is, the courts of justice, which "execute" the law. See Quincy, *Reports*
(Appendix) 474 note; No. 46, text at note 92. Compare Hutchinson's Charge to
the Grand Jury, March Term, Suffolk, 1769: "We, Gentlemen, who are to execute
the Law, are not to enquire into the Reason and Policy of it, or whether it is constitutional or not. . . . We, and you, Gentlemen, as the Executive Body, are to enquire
what is Law, and see that the Laws are inforced. If we step over this Line, and
judge of the Propriety or Impropriety, the Justice or Injustice of the Laws, we
introduce the worst sort of Tyranny:—the most absolute Despotism being formed
by a Union of the Legislative and Executive Power." Quincy, *Reports* 307–308.

[73] Bonham's Case, 8 Co. Rep. 113b, 118, 77 Eng. Rep. 646, 652–653 (C.P.
1610), here cited by Otis from the extract of it in 19 Viner, *Abridgment* 512–513,
tit. Statutes (E. 6, p. 15), which is as follows (variations in Coke's text being
indicated in brackets): "It appears in our Books, That in several [many] Cases the
Common Law shall [will] controul Acts of Parliament, and sometimes adjudge them
to be utterly void; For when an Act of Parliament is *against Common Right and
Reason*, or *repugnant, or impossible to be performed*, the *Common Law shall* [will]
controul it, and *adjudge it* [such act] to be void, and therefore in 8 E. 3. 30. a. b.
THOMAS TREGOR's Case upon the Statute of Westm. 2. cap. 38 & Artic. super
Cartas cap. 9 Herle said, that Sometimes [some] Statutes are made contrary to
[against] Law and Right which the Makers of [those who made] them perceiving
will not put them in Execution." For discussion of this passage, see text at notes
35–44 above.

[74] The reference has not been identified, but it is presumably to the debates in
Parliament on 23 Geo. 2, c. 29 (1750) prohibiting iron manufacture in the colonies.
See Quincy, *Reports* (Appendix) 474 note. This is the only mention of the statutes
regulating colonial trade and manufacture in either of JA's contemporary accounts.
In his later letters, however, JA described Otis' massive attack of "four or five
hours" on these Acts. See 10 JA, *Works* 315–350. He also told Tudor in a letter of
21 Aug. 1818 that "Mr. Otis asserted all these acts to be null and void by the law
of nature, by the English constitution, and by the American charters, because
America was not represented in Parliament." *Id.* at 351. This statement would
not seem to be justified by the bare reference here.

[75] Freeman v. Bluet, 12 Mod. 394, 396, 88 Eng. Rep. 1403, 1404 (K.B. 1700),
an action against a court officer who had seized goods in replevin under a precept
from the sheriff directing a return. In upholding a demurrer to a plea of justification, on the ground that it did not allege a return, Holt, C.J., said, "in all *Capias's
ad Respondend*, or other mean Process to [the] Sheriff [or other immediate officer],
if Trespass or false Imprisonment be brought against him for executing them, he
cannot justify without showing a Return . . . for, he that has not shewed to the
Court that he has done his Duty in what the Process of the Court required him,
shall not be justified by the Process." Otis seems to be arguing that since the writ
of assistance does not require a return the court has no control over its use. See
his argument, text at note 137 below. Compare Thacher's argument, text at notes
61–62 above.

Stat. C. 2.[76] We have all as good Right to inform as Custom House officers. And any Man may have a general, irreturnable ⟨Writ⟩ Commission to break Houses.

By 12. of C. on oath before Ld. Treasurer, Barons of Exchequer, or Chief Magistrate to break with an officer.[77] 14th. C. to issue a Warrant requiring sherriff &c. to assist the officers to search for Goods not enterd, or prohibited.[78] 7 & 8th. W. & M. gives officers in Plantation same Powers with officers in England.[79]

Continuance of Writts and Prossesses proves no more, nor so much as I grant a special Writ of assistance on special oath, for special Purpose.[80]

Pew indorsd Warrant to Ware. Justice Walley searchd House.[81] Law Prov. Bill in Chancery. This Court confind their Chancery Power to Revenue, &c.[82]

Gridley. By the 7. & 8. of Wm. c. 22. §. 6th.[83] This authority, of breaking and Entring ships, Warehouses Cellars &c. given to the Customs House officers in England by the statutes of the 12th. and 14th. of Charl. 2d.[84] is extended to the Custom House officers in the Plantations: and by the statute of the 6th. of Anne,[85] Writts of assistance

---

[76] That is, the statutes of Charles II referred to in the next paragraph. Compare Thacher's remark, text at note 58 above.

[77] 12 Car. 2, c. 19, §1 (1660), discussed, note 5 above.

[78] 13 & 14 Car. 2, c. 11, §5(2) (1662), text at note 92 below.

[79] 7 & 8 Will. 3, c. 22, §6 (1696), text at notes 94–97 below.

[80] That is, 1 Anne, stat. 1, c. 8, §5 (1702), providing for continuation of the writ of assistance and other processes after the death of the sovereign. JA's notes may be somewhat garbled, but Otis seems to be saying that this statute is of equal force whether the writs are special or general in nature. See his remarks in JA's "Abstract," text at notes 134–136, and following note 148 below.

[81] These incidents are more fully described in JA's "Abstract," text at notes 140–144 below.

[82] Otis is here apparently rehearsing Thacher's arguments, text at note 61 above, that the Superior Court had renounced the Exchequer powers given it by province law (note 98 below). The last sentence, which may be inaccurately reported by JA, seems to mean that the only Exchequer powers which the court retained were those given it by provincial and parliamentary Acts of Trade and Revenue over violations of their provisions. See note 18 above. If this is the argument, it may prove too much. For, while the provincial statutes contained sharply limited search provisions (see note 64 above), in cases under English statutes it could well be argued that the power to issue writs of assistance was a power incident to the revenue jurisdiction, rather than an inherent chancery power which the court had renounced.

[83] At notes 94–97 below.

[84] The 12th of Charles II is quoted, note 5 above. For the "14th" (i.e. 13th & 14th) of Charles II, see text at note 92 below.

[85] Apparently an inadvertence for 1 Anne, stat. 1, c. 8, §5 (1702). The confusion, whether in Gridley's argument or JA's reporting, may perhaps be explained by the fact that the duration of Parliament and the Privy Council and the tenure of all

are continued, in Company with all other legal Proscesses for 6 months after the Demise of the Crown.—Now What this Writ of assistance is, we can know only by Books of Precedents. And We have producd, in a Book intituld the modern Practice of the Court of Exchequer,[86] a form of such a Writ of assistance to the officers of the Customs. The Book has the Imprimatur of Wright, C.J. of the King's Bench which is as great a sanction as any Books of Precedents ever have, altho Books of Reports are usually approvd by all the Judges.[87] And I take Brown the Author of this Book to have been a very good Collector of Precedents. I have two Volumes of Precedents of his Collection, which I look upon as good as any, except Coke and Rastal.[88]

And the Power given in this Writ is no greater Infringement of our Liberty, than the Method of collecting Taxes in this Province.[89]

Every Body knows that the subject has the Priviledge of House only against his fellow subjects, not vs. the King either in matters of Crime or fine.[90]

Crown officers was extended for six months after the death of the sovereign by 6 Anne, c. 7, §§4, 8 (1707).

[86] That is, Brown's *Compendium*, cited in note 57 above.

[87] Under the various Licensing Acts which controlled the British press during the greater part of the 17th century, the imprimatur was a required proof that permission to publish had been granted. See 6 Holdsworth, *History of English Law* 367–378. Upon occasion, however, the judges used it to convey some opinion of a book's value. See John William Wallace, *The Reporters* 34 note (Boston, 1882). The *Compendium* bears no such judgment, but only the statement, "Imprimatur, R. Wright, May 1st, 1688." This was Sir Robert Wright, Chief Justice of the King's Bench, 1687–1688. Gray suggests that Wright's incompetence weakens the value of his imprimatur, relying largely on the judgment of Roger North, whose brother, Baron Guilford, was Wright's personal enemy. Quincy, *Reports* (Appendix) 477 note. See 6 Holdsworth, *History of English Law* 507–508, 530, 534. Both Wright's rise to judicial eminence and his conduct upon the Bench under the Stuarts were politically tainted, as was his end, which came in Newgate in 1689 while under indictment for high treason and bribery. He was nevertheless a lawyer of long experience, having entered Lincoln's Inn in 1654, been made serjeant in 1679, and been appointed a Baron of the Exchequer in 1684. DNB.

[88] That is, Sir Edward Coke, *Booke of Entries; containing perfect and approved Presidents of Counts, Declarations, etc.* (London, 1614), and William Rastell, *Colleccion of entrees, of declaracions, of barres, replicacions, rejoinders, issues, verdits, and divers other matters and fyrst an Epistle, with certayne instructions* (London, 1566). As to these two basic works on common law pleading, see 5 Holdsworth, *History of English Law* 384, 461. The volumes of Brown which Gridley owned were probably his *Formula bene placitandi; a Book of Entries, containing Precedents* (London, 1671), and *Methodus Novissima intrandi Placita Generalia* (London, 1699). See 5 Holdsworth, *History of English Law* 385–386; 6 *id.* at 600, 683, 686.

[89] See note 54 above.

[90] See Dalton, *Country Justice* 404: "The Officer, upon any Warrant from a Justice, either for the Peace or Good Behaviour, or in any other Case where the King is a Party, may by Force break open a Man's House to arrest the Offender." Compare 2 Hale, *Pleas of the Crown* 82, 92, to the effect that an officer may break

Extracts from the Acts of Parliament.[91]

14. Car. 2nd.[92] "And it shall be lawful to and for any Person or Persons authorized by *Writ of assistants,*[93] *under the seal of his Majesties Court of Exchequer,* to take a Constable, Headborough, or other public officers inhabiting near unto the Place, and in the day time to enter and go into any House, shop, Cellar, Warehouse or Room or other Place, and in Case of Resistance to break open Doors, Chests, Trunks and other Package, there to seize and from thence to bring any Kind of Goods, or Merchandize what soever prohibited and uncustomed and to put and secure the same in his Majesties store House, in the Port [*next*] to the Place where such seizure shall be made."

7. & 8th. Willm. 3rd.[94] "And that the officers for collecting and managing his Majesties Revenue and inspecting the Plantation Trade in any of the said Plantations shall have the same Powers and authorities &c.[95] as are provided for the officers of his Majesties Customs in

---

a house to arrest a suspect felon, "for it is a proceeding for the king by persons by law authorized"; but that a private person does so at his peril. But see 2 Hawkins, *Pleas of the Crown* 86–87: "But where one lies under a probable suspicion only, and is not indicted, it seems the better Opinion at this Day, That no one can justify the Breaking open Doors in Order to apprehend him."

[91] The material following is in a more careful hand and was evidently added to the foregoing by JA at some time after the argument.

[92] That is, 13 & 14 Car. 2, c. 11, §5(2) (1662). Quotation marks supplied; italics are JA's.

[93] There was considerable confusion between this spelling and "assistance." In the Nov. 1761 argument Gridley urged that "assistants" was correct, and that it signified the controlling power which a constable could exercise in the search. Quincy, *Reports* 56–57. Contemporary sources indicate that the original spelling was "assistance." See, for example, Thomas Manley, ed., *A Collection of the Statutes Made in the Reigns of King Charles I and King Charles II* 131 (London, 1667); J. Keble, ed., *Statutes at Large* 1216 (London, 1676); compare 5 *Statutes of the Realm* 394 (London, 1819). Although this spelling was followed in the index to the 1688 edition of Brown's work on Exchequer practice (note 57 above), "assistants" is found in all editions of the *Statutes at Large* published between 1681 and 1758. See, for example, Keble, ed., *Statutes at Large* 1218 (London, 2d edn., 1681); William Hawkins, ed., *Statutes at Large,* 2:583 (London, 1735). In editions of 1758 and after, however, the spelling is once again "assistance." See John Cay, *Statutes at Large,* 2:708 (London, 1758); Owen Ruffhead, *Statutes at Large,* 3:237 (London, 1763). It seems probable that the confusion was due to an error in Keble's 1681 edition of the *Statutes at Large.* According to R. C. Jarvis, present Intelligence Officer and Librarian, H.M. Customs and Excise, "assistance" is merely an archaic form of "assistants," meaning a body of official helpers. Letter of 8 Nov. 1963 and memorandum in Adams Papers editorial files. Compare *OED.* If this interpretation is correct, Gridley's view is sound, regardless of the spelling adopted.

[94] That is, 7 & 8 Will. 3, c. 22, §6(2) (1696). Quotation marks supplied. Passages omitted by JA are set out in notes 95 and 96 below from Hawkins, *Statutes at Large.*

[95] JA has here omitted the following: "for visiting and searching of ships, and taking their entries, and for seizing and bringing on Shoar any of the Goods prohibited to be imported or exported into or out of any of the said Plantations or for

England by the said last mentioned Act made in the 14th. Year of the Reign of K. Char. 2d. and also to enter Houses or Warehouses to search for and seize any such Goods.[96] And that the like assistance shall be given to the said officers in the Execution of their office, as by the said last mentiond Act is provided, for the officers in England." [97]

Prov. Law. Page 114.[98] Be it enacted &c. that there shall be a Superiour Court of Judicature, Court of Assize and General Goal &c. over this whole Province &c. who shall have Cognizance of all Pleas Real, Personal or mixt, as well all Pleas of the Crown &c. and generally of all other matters as fully and amply to all Intents and Purposes whatsoever as the Courts of Kings Bench, Common Pleas, and *Exchequer* within his Majesties Kingdom of England, have or ought to have.

Petition. To the honorable &c.[99]
Humbly shews,

---

which any Duties are payable or ought to have been paid, by any of the aforementioned Acts."

[96] JA has here omitted the following: "And that all the Wharfingers, and Owners of Keys and Wharfs, or any Lightermen, Bargemen, Watermen, Porters, or other Persons assisting in the Conveyance, Concealment or Rescue of any of the said Goods, or in the hindring or Resistance of any of the said Officers in the Performance of their Duty, and the Boats, Barges, Lighters or other Vessels, employed in the Conveyance of such Goods shall be subject to the like Pains and Penalties as are provided by the same Act made in the Fourteenth Year of King Charles the Second, in relation to prohibited or uncustomed Goods in this Kingdom."

[97] The section continues with provisions for penalties upon officers who violate the Act and for special pleading on their behalf in actions brought against them for performance of their duties. See note 62 above.

[98] That is, Act of 26 June 1699, c. 3, §1, 1 A&R 370. JA's reference here may be to the text of the Act in *Acts and Laws of His Majesties Province of Massachusetts Bay* 114 (Boston, 1726), where it appears as 11 Will. 3, c. 3. The relevant section is as follows: "[T]here shall be a Superior Court of Judicature, Court of Assize and General Goal Delivery, over this whole Province, to be Held and Kept Annually at the respective Times and Places in this Act hereafter mentioned and expressed, by One Chief Justice, and Four other Justices to be Appointed and Commissionated for the same. Any Three of whom to be a *Quorum*, who shall have Cognizance of all Pleas, Real, Personal or Mixt, as well all Pleas of the Crown, and all matters relating to the Conservation of the Peace, and Punishment of Offenders; as Civil Causes or Actions between party and party; and between His Majesty and any of His Subjects, whether the same do concern the Realty, and relate to any Right of Freehold and Inheritance; or whether the same do concern the personalty, and relate to matter of Debt, Contract, Damage or personal Injury; and also all mixt Actions which concern both realty and personalty brought before them by Appeal, Review, Writ of Error, or otherwise as the Law directs. And generally of all other Matters as fully and amply to all intents and purposes whatsoever, as the Courts of Kings Bench, Common Pleas and Exchequer within His Majesty's Kingdom of *England*, have, or ought to have. And are hereby Impowred to give Judgment therein, and award Execution thereupon."

[99] JA has here copied the form of petition used by Charles Paxton in applying

4. TIMOTHY FOLGER, BY JOHN SINGLETON COPLEY

3. RICHARD DANA, BY JOHN SINGLETON COPLEY

5. JAMES OTIS, BY JOSEPH BLACKBURN

That he is lawfully authorized to execute the office of surveyor of all Rates, Duties, and Impositions, arising and growing due to his Majesty, at Boston in this Province and cannot fully exercise said office in such manner as his majesties service and the Laws in such Cases require Unless your Honours, who are vested with the Power of a Court of Exchequer for this Province will please to grant him a Writt of assistants, he therefore prays he and his Deputties may be aided in the Execution of said office within his District by a Writ of assistants under the seal of this superior Court in legal Form and according to Usage in his Majestys Court of Exchequer and in Great Britain. C.P.

Province of the Massachusetts Bay } George the second by the Grace of God of Great Britain France and Ireland King, Defender of the Faith &c.[100]

To all and singular Justices of the Peace, sherriffs and Constables, and to all other our officers and subjects within said Province and to each of you

Greeting.

Whereas the Commissioners of our Customs have by their Deputation dated the 8th. day of Jany. 1752, assignd Charles Paxton Esqr. surveyor of all Rates, Duties, and Impositions arising and growing due within the Port of Boston in said Province as by said Deputation at large appears, We therefore command you and each of you that you permit the said C.P. and his Deputies and servants from Time to time at his or their Wi[ll] [101] as well in the day as in the Night to enter and go on board any ship, Boat or other Vessel riding lying or being within or coming to the said Port or any Places or Creeks appertaining to said Port, such ship, Boat or Vessell then and there found to View and search and strait to examine in the same, touching the Customs and subsidies to us due, and also in the day Time together with a Constable or other public officer inhabiting near unto the Place to enter

---

for a writ in 1755. The original, printed by Gray, was captioned, "To the Honourable his Majestys Justices of his Superior Court for said Province to be held at York in and for the County of York on the third Tuesday of June 1755." The writ was issued by order of the Superior Court in August 1755. See Quincy, *Reports* (Appendix) 402–403 and notes. The document is now in MHi:Misc. MSS.

[100] JA has here copied the form of the writ issued to Paxton. The original has not been found. As Gray, who printed JA's copy, notes, it is a translation of the form in Brown's *Compendium*, note 57 above. Quincy, *Reports* (Appendix) 404 note.

[101] Missing in worn margin of the MS. This is Gray's reading. The Latin is "volunt'." Quincy, *Reports* (Appendix) 399, 404.

and go into any Vaults, Cellars, Warehouses, shops or other Places to search and see, whether any Goods, Wares or Merchandizes, in the same ships, Boats or Vessells, Vaults, Cellars, Warehouses, shops or other Places are or shall be there hid or concealed, having been imported, ship't or laden in order to be exported from or out of the said Port or any Creeks or Places appertaining to the same Port; and to open any Trunks, Chests, Boxes, fardells or Packs made up or in Bulk, whatever in which any Goods, Wares, or Merchandizes are suspected to be packed or concealed and further to do all Things which of Right and according to Law and the statutes in such Cases provided, is in this Part to be done: and We strictly command you and every of you that you, from Time to Time be aiding and assisting to the said C.P. his Deputties and servants and every of them in the Execution of the Premisses in all Things as becometh: Fail not at your Peril: Witness Stephen Sewall Esqr.[102] &c.

II. ADAMS' "ABSTRACT OF THE ARGUMENT"[103]

Ca. April 1761

Boston Superior Court February 1761.[104]

On the second Tuesday of the Court's sitting, appointed by the rule of the Court for argument of special matters, came on the dispute on

[102] As to Sewall, see note 20 above.

[103] The text that follows is the most complete rendition possible today of JA's "Abstract of the Argument for and against the Writts of Assistance," probably made by him sometime in the spring of 1761. See text at note 49 above. Five versions of this famous document are here brought together: (1) The text of the Gridley and Thacher arguments from Israel Keith's Common Place Book, as printed in Quincy, *Reports* (Appendix) 479–482, from a document then (1864) in the possession of John Newell of Pittsford, Vt., and Boston, which recent extensive search has not located; (2) the text of the Gridley and Otis arguments from the Joseph Hawley Common Place Book now in NN:Hawley Papers; (3) the text of the Otis argument as printed in the *Massachusetts Spy*, 29 April 1773, p. 3, cols. 1–3; (4) the text of the Otis argument as printed in George Richards Minot, *Continuation of the History of the Province of Massachusetts Bay*, 2:91–99 (Boston, 1803), with paraphrases of the arguments of Gridley and Thacher; (5) Minot's text of the Otis argument as reprinted by CFA with some further minor corrections and the elimination of phrases which JA had described as interpolations, in 2 JA, *Works* 523–525. All five versions are closely related. The *Spy* and Minot texts of Otis differ only in corrections of grammar and style, apparently made by Minot, and CFA follows the latter, except for the interpolations. The Hawley version of Otis and that in the *Spy* are identical, with the exception of material apparently omitted in copying by Hawley and certain touches of style omitted, perhaps for editorial reasons, from the *Spy*. Gray did not print Keith's text of Otis, but we

the petition of Mr. Cockle[105] and others on the one side, and the Inhabitants of Boston on the other, concerning Writs of Assistance. Mr. *Gridley* appeared for the former, Mr. *Otis* for the latter. Mr. *Thacher* was joined with him at the desire of the Court.

---

have his testimony that it closely followed Minot. Quincy, *Reports* (Appendix) 482. A similar identity prevails among the various texts of the Gridley and Thacher arguments, including Minot's paraphrase.

Although no copy in JA's hand has been found, the evidence that his was the common parent of these five versions seems overwhelming. The similarity in content and phraseology to JA's rough notes has already been pointed out, as have his later recollections that it was his notes which appeared first in the *Spy*, then in Minot's *History of Massachusetts Bay*. See text and note 51 above. For other circulation of the "Abstract," see note 52 above. The best independent evidence of JA's authorship is the Keith Common Place Book. Keith, Harvard 1771, served in the Continental Army and was admitted an attorney in the Superior Court for Suffolk County in March 1780. No record of his clerkship has been found, but he undoubtedly studied law in Boston both before and after his military service. His Common Place Book was said to contain not only the argument on the writs, but other legal notes known to have come from JA. Quincy, *Reports* (Appendix) 478. On the basis of this evidence it seems a fair conclusion that Keith copied both the argument and the other materials either from JA's own papers, or from a copy by someone who had clerked for him. The history of the Hawley version cannot be so readily traced, but since Joseph Hawley was JA's friend and contemporary at the bar, it seems likely that he too copied the arguments from JA. The only other reasonable hypothesis would seem to be that the Keith and Hawley texts were copied from a summary of the argument which another (perhaps Jonathan Williams Austin, whom JA accused of the 1773 "theft" of the materials, text at note 1 above) had made on the basis of JA's on-the-spot notes, which are indubitably the source of the longer version. This theory seems refuted by the evidence of the diary entry, note 49 above, and by JA's later taking credit for the *Spy* and Minot texts.

The basic texts followed here are Gray's rendition of the Keith version of Gridley's and Thacher's arguments, and the *Massachusetts Spy* version of the Otis argument. These are textually the most complete versions and are probably also closest to the missing original. In the footnotes, variations with the other versions have been noted where they seem significant, either as touches of style that might have been JA's, or as examples of later editorial practice.

[104] The following text of Gridley's and Thacher's arguments is from Quincy, *Reports* (Appendix) 479–482. See note 103 above. Gray pointed to the first paragraph, placing the argument on the second Tuesday of the term, as corroboration of the Keith document's "antiquity and authenticity," since an order of court at the August term 1759 had provided that "the special pleadings shall come on the second Tuesday in each term." *Id.* at 479; see Min. Bk. 71, SCJ Suffolk, Aug. 1759, following N–73. The *Massachusetts Spy's* version of the Otis argument began with the first sentence of this introduction (erroneously dated Feb. term, 1771), and added that Gridley "endeavoured to support the legality of Writs of Assistance by force of several statutes and precedents in England, but his chief stay he acknowledged was *the necessity of the case*, and in the course of his arguments he discovered himself to be an ingenious lawyer." *Massachusetts Spy*, 29 April 1773, p. 3, col. 1.

[105] James Cockle, Collector of Customs at Salem from 1760 to 1764. See Quincy, *Reports* (Appendix) 422–424. That Cockle was one of the officers who sought writs seems certain from the fact that one was granted to him shortly after the second argument in Nov. 1761. *Id.* at 422. Paxton was probably the first to apply, however, and the matter was actually heard on the petitions of the merchants and the Surveyor General. See notes 22, 27, above.

Mr. Gridley.[106] I appear on the behalf of Mr. Cockle and others, who pray "that as they cannot fully exercise their Offices in such a manner as his Majesty's Service and their Laws in such cases require, unless your Honors who are vested with the power of a Court of Exchequer for this Province will please to grant them Writs of Assistance. They therefore pray that they and their Deputies may be aided in the Execution of their Offices by Writs of Assistance under the Seal of this Court and in legal form, and according to the Usage of his Majesty's Court of Exchequer in Great Britain."

May it please your Honors, it is certain it has been the practice of the Court of Exchequer in England,[107] and of this Court in this Province, to grant Writs of Assistance to Custom House Officers. Such Writs are mentioned in several Acts of Parliament, in several Books of Reports; and in a Book called the Modern Practice of the Court of Exchequer, We have a Precedent, a form of a Writ, called a Writ of Assistance for Custom house Officers, of which the following[108] a few years past to Mr. Paxton under the Seal of this Court, and tested by the late Chief Justice Sewall is a literal Translation.[109]

The first Question therefore for your Honors to determine is, whether this practice of the Court of Exchequer in England (which it is certain, has taken place heretofore, how long or short a time soever it continued) is legal or illegal. And the second is, whether the practice of the[110] Exchequer (admitting it to be legal) can warrant this Court in the same practice.

In answer to the first, I cannot indeed find the Original of this Writ of Assistance. It may be of very antient, to which I am inclined, or it may be of modern date. This however is certain, that the Stat. of the 14th. Char. 2nd. has established this Writ almost in the words of the Writ itself. "And it shall be lawful to and for any person or persons *authorised by Writ of Assistance under the seal of his Majesty's Court of Exchequer* to take a Constable, Headborough, or other public Officer, inhabiting near unto the place, and in the day time to enter and go into any house, Shop, Cellar, Warehouse, room, or any other

---

[106] The Hawley MS is headed "Substance of Mr. Gridley's Argument Before the Superior Court in favor of Writs of Assistance." The argument begins: "May it please your honors."
[107] Hawley: "Great Britain" for "England."
[108] Hawley here supplies the inadvertent omission of "given."
[109] Hawley omits the writ. According to Gray, who also omitted it from his rendition of the Keith MS, it was the writ granted to Paxton in 1755, printed in text at note 100 above, which JA had apparently copied from the court files. See Quincy, *Reports* (Appendix) 480.
[110] Hawley here supplies "Court of."

place, and in case of Resistance, to break open doors, Chests, Trunks and other Package, and there to seize any kind of Goods or Merchandize whatever prohibited, and to put the same into his Majesty's Warehouse in the Port where Seisure is made." [111]

By this act and that of 12 Char. 2nd.[112] all the powers in the Writ of Assistance mentioned are given, and it is expressly said, the persons shall be authorised by Writs of Assistance under the seal of the Exchequer. Now the Books in which we should expect to find these Writs, and all that relates to them are Books of Precedents, and Reports in the Exchequer, which are extremely scarce in this Country;[113] we have one, and but one that treats of Exchequer matters, and that is called the "Modern practice of the Court of Exchequer," and in this Book we find one Writ of Assistance, translated above. Books of Reports have commonly the Sanction of all the Judges, but books of Precedents never have more than that of the Chief Justice. Now this Book has the Imprimatur of Wright, who was Chief Justice of the King's Bench,[114] and it was wrote by Brown, whom I esteem the best Collector of Precedents; I have Two Volumes of them by him, which I esteem the best except Rastall and Coke. But we have a further proof of the legality of these Writs, and of the settled practice at home of allowing them; because by the Stat. 6th Anne which continues all Processes and Writs after the Demise of the Crown, *Writs of Assistance are continued among the Rest.*

It being clear therefore that the Court of Exchequer at home has a power by Law of granting these Writs, I think there can be but little doubt, whether this Court as a Court of Exchequer for this Province has this power. By the Statute of the 7th. & 8th. W. 3d., it is enacted "that all the Officers for collecting and managing his Majesty's Revenue, and inspecting the Plantation Trade in any of the said Plantations, shall have the same powers &c. as are provided for the Officers of the Revenue in England; also to enter Houses, or Warehouses, to search for and seize any such Goods, and that the *like Assistance* shall be given to the said Officers as is the Custom in England." [115]

Now what is the Assistance which the Officers of the Revenue are to have here, which is like that they have in England?[116] Writs of

---

[111] 13 & 14 Car. 2, c. 11, §5(2). See JA's copy, text at note 92 above. The text of the statute is omitted by Hawley.

[112] 12 Car. 2, c. 19, note 5 above.

[113] Hawley: "Province" for "country."

[114] Hawley here adds "&c." and omits the remainder of the present sentence.

[115] 7 & 8 Will. 3, c. 22, §6. See JA's copy, text and notes 94–97 above. Hawley omits some portions quoted here.

[116] It has been suggested that "like assistance" in 7 & 8 Will. 3, c. 22, §6, may be

Assistance under the Seal of his Majesty's Court of Exchequer at home will not run here. They must therefore be under the Seal of this Court. For by the law of this Province 2 W. 3d. Ch. 3 [117] "there shall be a Superior Court &c. over the whole Province &c. who shall have cognizance of all pleas &c. and generally of all other matters, as fully and [amply] [118] to all intents and purposes as the Courts of King's Bench, Common Pleas and *Exchequer* within his Majesty's Kingdom of England have or ought to have."

It is true the common privileges of Englishmen are taken away in this Case, but even their privileges are not so in cases of Crime and fine. 'Tis the necessity of the Case and the benefit of the Revenue that justifies this Writ. Is not the Revenue the sole support of Fleets and Armies abroad, and Ministers at home? without which the Nation could neither be preserved from the Invasions of her foes, nor the Tumults of her own Subjects. Is not this I say infinitely more important, than the imprisonment of Thieves, or even Murderers? yet in these Cases 'tis agreed Houses may be broke open.

In fine the power now under consideration is the same with that given by the Law of this Province to Treasurers towards Collectors, and to them towards the subject. A Collector may when he pleases distrain my goods and Chattels, and in want of them arrest my person, and throw me instantly into Goal. What! shall my property be wrested from me!—shall my Liberty be destroyed by a Collector, for a debt, unadjudged, without the common Indulgence and Lenity of the Law? So it is established, and the necessity of having public taxes effectually and speedily collected is of infinitely greater moment to the whole, than the Liberty of any Individual.

Thacher. In obedience to the Order of this Court I have searched with a good deal of attention all the antient Reports of Precedents, Fitz. N. Brev.[119] and the Register, but have not found any such Writ as this Petition prays. In the latter indeed I have found Two Writs which bear the Title of Brev. Assistentice, but these are only to give possession of Houses &c. in cases of Injunctions and Sequestration in Chancery. By the Act of Parliament any private Person as well as

---

a reference to 13 & 14 Car. 2, c. 11, §32, providing that royal officers and others concerned were to "be aiding and assisting" the customs officers in performance of their duties. Frese, "Early Parliamentary Legislation on Writs of Assistance," 38 Col. Soc. Mass., *Pubns.* 318, 354 note (1959). While "like assistance" certainly does not literally refer to the writ of assistance, the phrase is broad enough to include it as well as the aid and assistance of other officers.

[117] That is, 11 Will. 3, c. 3, 1 A&R 370. See JA's copy, text at note 98 above.

[118] Apparently supplied by Gray. See Quincy, *Reports* (Appendix) 481.

[119] Fitzherbert's *New Natura Brevium.* See note 55 above.

Custom House Officer may take a Sheriff or Constable and go into any Shop &c. and seize &c. (here Mr. Thacher quoted an Authority from Strange which intended to shew that Writs of Assistance were only temporary things).[120]

The most material question is whether the practice of the Exchequer is good ground for this Court. But this Court has upon a solemn Argument, which lasted a whole day, renounc'd the Chance of [Chancery][121] Jurisdiction which the Exchequer has in Cases where either party is the King's Debtor.

In England all Informations of uncustomed or prohibited Goods are in the Exchequer, so that the Custom House Officers are the Officers of that Court under the Eye and Direction of the Barons and so accountable for any wanton exercise of power.

The Writ now prayed for is not returnable. If the Seizures were so, before your Honors, and this Court should enquire into them you'd often find a wanton exercise of power. At home they seize at their peril, even with probable Cause.

[Otis:][122]

May it please your Honours,

I was desired by one of the court to look into the books, and consider the question now before the court,[123] concerning Writs of Assistance. I have accordingly considered it, and now appear not only in obedience to your order, but also in behalf of the inhabitants of this town, who have presented another petition, and out of regard to the liberties of the subject. And I take this opportunity to declare, that whether under a fee or not, (for in such a cause as this I despise a fee) I will to my

[120] Horne v. Boosey, note 59 above. This helps to establish that the "Abstract" is from JA's rough notes, although the case may not have been cited for this proposition.
[121] Correction apparently by Gray. See Quincy, *Reports* (Appendix) 482. Compare JA's rough notes at note 61 above. Interestingly enough, the same error appears in Minot's paraphrase. 2 Minot, *History of Massachusetts Bay* 90.
[122] The text of Otis' argument, up to the sentence at note 149 below, is from the *Massachusetts Spy*, 29 April 1773, p. 3, cols. 1–3. The argument was introduced as follows: "For the MASSACHUSETTS SPY. Mr. Thomas, As the public have been lately alarmed with the evil and wicked effects of the power lodged in custom-house officers, by virtue of that most execrable of all precepts, a Writ of Assistance: And as I conceive it to be more immediately destructive of the liberty of the subject, than any other innovation of power: The following is offered to the public, being taken from the mouth of that great American oracle of law, JAMES OTIS, Esq; in the meridian of his life."
Then follows the material quoted in note 104 above, concluding with "Mr. Otis appearing for the inhabitants of Boston, with his usual zeal for the common liberties of mankind, spoke as follows, viz."
[123] Minot substitutes "them" for "the court," a change typical of his minor improvements of style, most of which will not be noted herein.

dying day oppose, with all the powers and faculties God [124] has given me, all such instruments of slavery on the one hand, and villainy on the other, as this writ of assistance is. It appears to me (may it please your honours) the worst instrument of arbitrary power, the most destructive of English liberty, and the fundamental principles of the constitution,[125] that ever was found in an English law-book. I must therefore beg your honours patience and attention to the whole range of an argument, that may perhaps appear uncommon in many things, as well as points of learning, that are more remote and unusual, that the whole tendency of my design may the more easily be perceived, the conclusions better descend,[126] and the force of them better felt.

I shall not think much of my pains in this cause as I engaged in it from principle. I was sollicited to engage on the other side.[127] I was sollicited to argue this cause as Advocate-General, and because I would not, I have been charged with a desertion of my office; to this charge I can give a very sufficient answer, I renounced that office,[128] and I argue this cause from the same principle; and I argue it with the greater pleasure as it is in favour of British liberty, at a time, when we hear the greatest monarch upon earth declaring from his throne, that he glories in the name of Briton, and that the privileges of his people are dearer to him than the most valuable prerogatives of his crown.[129] And as it is in opposition to a kind of power, the exercise

[124] Hawley here adds "almighty."

[125] Minot: "law" for "the constitution."

[126] This word apparently is illegible in the original. Hawley read it as "answered." CFA has changed Minot's reading of "descend" to "discerned," which is probably correct.

[127] Minot omits this sentence.

[128] In 1769, Otis published in the *Boston Gazette* a deposition alleged to be Paxton's, dated 28 Feb. 1761, which indicates that a more direct cause of his resignation as Advocate General of Admiralty was the attack upon the Vice Admiralty Court that resulted in the case of Gray v. Paxton, note 21 above. See Quincy, *Reports* (Appendix) 542 note. Robert Auchmuty was shortly thereafter appointed to the position. See the latter's biography in 12 Sibley-Shipton, *Harvard Graduates* 12–16.

[129] George III, in his accession speech on 18 Nov. 1760, had actually said: "Born and educated in this country, I glory in the name of Briton; and the peculiar happiness of my life will ever consist in promoting the welfare of a people, whose loyalty and warm affection to me, I consider as the greatest and most permanent security of my throne; and I doubt not, but their steadiness in those principles will equal the firmness of my invariable resolution to adhere to, and strengthen, this excellent constitution in church and state; and to maintain the toleration inviolable. The civil and religious rights of my loving subjects are equally dear to me with the most valuable prerogatives of my crown: and, as the surest foundation of the whole, and the best means to draw down the divine favour on my reign, it is my fixed purpose to countenance and encourage the practice of true religion and virtue." This speech was reprinted in its entirety in the *Boston News-Letter*, 15 Jan. 1761, p. 1, cols. 2–4. In his diary for 9 Feb. 1761, JA set down his favorable reaction to the speech, con-

of which in former periods of English history, cost one King of England his head and another his throne. I have taken more pains in this cause, than I ever will take again: Although my engaging in this and another popular cause [130] has raised much resentment; but I think I can sincerely declare, that I cheerfully submit myself to every odious name for conscience sake; and from my soul I despise all those whose guilt, malice or folly has made my foes.[131] Let the consequences be what they will, I am determined to proceed. The only principles of public conduct that are worthy a gentleman, or a man are, to sacrifice estate, ease, health and applause,[132] and even life itself to the sacred calls of his country. These manly sentiments in private life make the good citizen, in public life, the patriot [133] and the hero.—I do not say, when brought to the test, I shall be invincible; I pray GOD I may never be brought to the melancholy trial; but if ever I should, it would be then known, how far I can reduce to practice principles I know founded in truth.—In the mean time I will proceed to the subject of the writ. In the first,[134] may it please your Honours, I will admit, that writs of one kind, may be legal, that is, *special writs, directed to special officers*, and to search *certain houses*, &c. *especially set forth in the writ*, may be granted by the Court of Exchequer at home, *upon oath made before* the Lord Treasurer by the person, who asks, *that he suspects such goods to be concealed in* THOSE VERY PLACES HE DESIRES TO SEARCH. The Act of 14th Car. II. which Mr. Gridley mentions proves this. And in this light the writ appears like a warrant from a justice of peace to search for stolen goods. Your Honours will find in the old book, concerning the office of a justice of peace, precedents of general warrants to search suspected houses.[135] But in more modern books you will find only special warrants to search such and such houses specially named, in which the complainant has before sworn he suspects his goods are concealed; and you will find it adjudged *that special warrants only are legal*. In the same manner I rely on it, that the writ prayed for in this petition being general is illegal. It is a power

cluding "These are sentiments worthy of a King—a Patriot King." 1 JA, *Diary and Autobiography* 200–201.

[130] As Gray points out, this "popular cause" was probably Gray v. Paxton. Quincy, *Reports* (Appendix) 482. See note 21 above.

[131] This clause was rendered by Hawley, "whom guilt, malice or folly has made my foes," and by Minot, "whose guilt, malice or folly has made them my foes."

[132] Hawley: "worthy a gentleman, a man of sense, or a Christian, are, to sacrifice estate, ease, health, honor, applause."

[133] Hawley: "the patriot, the man and the hero."

[134] Hawley and Minot supply "place."

[135] See text at note 65 above.

that places the liberty of every man in the hands of every petty officer. I say I admit that *special* writs of assistance to search *special* houses,[136] may be granted to certain persons on oath; but I deny that the writ now prayed for can be granted, for I beg leave to make some observations on the writ itself before I proceed to other Acts of Parliament.

In the first place the writ is UNIVERSAL, being directed "to all and singular justices, sheriffs, constables and all other officers and subjects, &c." So that in short it is directed to every subject in the king's dominions; every one with this writ may be a tyrant: If this commission is legal, a tyrant may, in a legal manner also, controul, imprison or murder any one within the realm.

In the next place, IT IS PERPETUAL; there's no return, a man is accountable to no person for his doings, every man may reign secure in his petty tyranny, and spread terror and desolation around him, until the trump of the arch angel shall excite[137] different emotions in his soul.[138]

In the third place, a person with this writ, IN THE DAY TIME may enter all houses, shops, &c. AT WILL, and command all to assist.

Fourth, by this not only deputies, &c. but even THEIR MENIAL SERVANTS ARE ALLOWED TO LORD IT OVER US—What is this but to have the curse of Canaan with a witness on us, to be the servant of servants, the most despicable of GOD's creation.[139] Now one of the most essential branches of English liberty, is the freedom of one's house. A man's house is his castle; and while he is quiet, he is as well guarded as a prince in his castle. This writ, if it should be declared legal, would totally annihilate this privilege. Custom house officers may enter our houses when they please—we are commanded to permit their entry—their menial servants may enter—may break locks, bars and every thing in their way—and whether they break through malice or revenge, no man, no court can inquire—bare suspicion without oath is sufficient. This wanton exercise of this power is no chimerical suggestion of a heated Brain—I will mention some facts. Mr. Pew had one

---

[136] Minot: "places" for "houses."

[137] Hawley: "raise" for "excite."

[138] The preceding clause, beginning "until the trump," is one omitted by CFA, on the basis of JA's comments. The presence of both this and the other omitted passage (note 139 below) in the Keith and Hawley MSS supports Gray's suggestion that in repudiating them JA "was guided by his taste rather than his notes or his memory." Quincy, *Reports* (Appendix) 479. JA's notation that these passages were interpolations may be seen in his copy of Minot's *History of Massachusetts Bay* at p. 95–96, now among his books in the Boston Public Library.

[139] This sentence, beginning "What is this," is the second passage omitted by CFA because disclaimed by JA. See note 138 above.

of these writs, and when Mr. Ware succeeded him, he endorsed this writ over to Mr. Ware, so that THESE WRITS ARE NEGOTIABLE from one officer to another, and so your Honours have no opportunity of judging the persons to whom this vast power is delegated. Another instance is [140] this.—Mr. Justice Wally had called this same Mr. Ware before him by a constable, to answer for a breach of the Sabbath day acts, or that of profane swearing. As soon as he had done,[141] Mr. Ware asked him if he had done, he replied, yes. Well then, says he,[142] I will shew you a little of my power—I command you to permit me to search your house for unaccustomed [143] goods; and went on to search his house from the garret to the cellar, and then served the constable in the same manner.[144] But to shew another absurdity in this writ, if it should be established, I insist upon it EVERY PERSON by 14th of Car. II. HAS THIS POWER as well as Custom-house officers; the words are, "it shall be lawful for any person or persons authorized, &c." What a scene does this open! Every man prompted by revenge, ill humour or wantonness to inspect the inside of his neighbour's house, may get a writ of assistance; others will ask it from self defence; one arbitrary exertion will provoke another, until society will be involved in tumult and in blood. Again these writs ARE NOT RETURNED. Writs in their nature are temporary things; when the purposes for which they are issued are answered, they exist no more; but these monsters in the law [145] live forever, no one can be called to account. Thus reason and the constitution are both against this writ. Let us see what authority there is for it. No more than one instance can be found of it in all our law books, and that was in the zenith of arbitrary power, viz. In the reign of Car. II. when Star-chamber powers were pushed in extremity by

[140] Hawley telescopes this entire episode into "where the same Mr. Ware from a principle of revenge went on to search a number of houses from Garret to Cellar."
[141] Minot: "finished."
[142] Minot: "said Mr. Ware."
[143] Minot: "uncustomed" — no doubt a proper correction.
[144] Compare the account in the version of the argument in the *Boston Gazette* for 4 Jan. 1762, attributed to Otis. Quincy, *Reports* (Appendix) 490. Jonathan Pew (or Pue) (d. 1760) was Searcher and Surveyor of the Port of Boston from 1735 until he was succeeded by Paxton in 1752. At the latter date he entered into the same office at Salem, where he served until his death. Book of Charters, Commissions, Proclamations, &c., fols. 80, 173–175, M–Ar; Wolkins, ed., "The Boston Customs District in 1768," 58 MHS, *Procs.* 418, 430 (1924–1925). Nathaniel Ware was Comptroller of Customs for the Port of Boston from 1750 until 1764. Book of Charters, &c., fols. 79–80; Wolkins, "Boston Customs District," 58 MHS, *Procs.* 418, 430. Abiel Walley was appointed a Justice of the Quorum in Suffolk County, 5 Nov. 1740. Whitmore, *Mass. Civil List* 128. No documentation of these incidents has been found.
[145] Minot omits "monsters in the law."

some ignorant clerk of the Exchequer. But had this writ been in any book whatever it would have been illegal. ALL PRECEDENTS ARE UNDER THE CONTROUL OF THE PRINCIPLES OF THE [146] LAW. Lord Talbot says, it is better to observe these [147] than any precedents though in the House of Lords, the last resort of the subject. No Acts of Parliament can establish such a writ; Though it should be made in the very words of the petition it would be void, "AN ACT AGAINST THE CONSTITUTION IS VOID." Vid. Viner.[148] But these prove no more than what I before observed, that *special* writs may be granted *on oath* and *probable suspicion*. The Act of 7th and 8th of William III. that the officers of the plantations shall have the same powers, &c. is confined to this sense, that an officer should show probable grounds, should take his oath on it, should do this before a magistrate, and that such magistrate, if he thinks proper should issue a *special warrant* to a constable to search the places. That of 6th of Anne can prove no more.[149]

It is the business of this court to demolish this monster of oppression, and to tear into rags this remnant of Starchamber tyranny—&c.

The court suspended the absolute determination of this matter. I have omitted many authorities; also many fine touches in the order of reasoning, and numberless Rhetorical and popular flourishes.[150]

III. THOMAS HUTCHINSON'S DRAFT OF A WRIT OF ASSISTANCE [151]

December 1761

Prov. of ⎫ George the third by the grace of God of Great Britain
Mass. Bay ⎭ France and Ireland King Defender of the faith &c.

[SEAL] To all and singular our Justices of the Peace Sheriffs Constables and to all other our Officers and Subjects within our said Province and to each of you Greeting.

---

[146] Minot omits "THE."

[147] Hawley adds "principles of law."

[148] Hawley omits the remainder of this paragraph.

[149] The next sentence appears only in the Hawley MS. See note 103 above. It may be an elaboration of the well-known passage, "the executive courts must pass such acts into disuse." See notes 42, 72, above.

[150] This paragraph appears in the Hawley MS. At least the first sentence of it also appears in the Keith MS. Quincy, *Reports* (Appendix) 482. See note 103 above.

[151] In Hutchinson's hand, Dec. 1761. Adams Papers, Microfilms, Reel No. 185. It is unclear how this document found its way into the Adams Papers. Gray printed it, identifying it as from the court files. Notations on the back of the writ as to the

No. 44. Petition of Lechmere

Know ye that whereas in and by an Act of Parliament made in the ⟨thir⟩ fourteenth year of the reign of the late King Charles the second ⟨it is declared⟩ the Officers of our Customs and their Deputies are authorized and impowered to go and enter aboard any Ship or Vessel outward or inward bound and for the Purposes in the said Act mentioned and it is ⟨also⟩ in and by the said Act further enacted and declared that it shall be lawful to or for any person or persons authorized by Writ of assistants under the seal of our Court of Exchequer to take a Constable Headborough or other Publick Officer inhabiting near unto the Place and in the day time to enter and go into any House Shop Cellar Warehouse or Room or other Place and in case of resistance to break open doors chests trunks and other package there to seize and from them to bring any kind of goods or merchandize whatsoever prohibited and uncustomed and to put and secure the same in ⟨his Majestys⟩ our Store house in the port next to the place where such seizure shall be made.[152]

And where as in and by an Act of Parliament made in the seventh and eighth year of the reign of the late King William the third there is granted to the Officers for collecting and managing our Revenue and inspecting the Plantation trade in any of our Plantations the same powers, and authority for visiting and searching of Ships and also to enter houses or warehouses to search for and seize any Prohibited or uncustomed goods as are provided for the Officers of our Customs in England by the said last mentioned Act made in the fourteenth year of the reign of King Charles the second, and the like assistance is required to be given to the said Officers in the execution of their office as by the said last mentioned Act is provided for the Officers in England.[153]

And whereas in and by an Act of our said Province of Massachusetts bay made in the eleventh year of the reign of the late King William the third it is enacted and declared that our Superior Court of Judicature Court of Assize and General Goal delivery for our said Province shall have cognizance of all matters and things within our said Prov-

---

issuance of writs to individuals between 1763 and 1769, in the hand of Superior Court Clerk Samuel Winthrop, not printed here, confirm this suggestion. Perhaps Gray, who had access both to the court files and to the Adams Papers, inadvertently effected a transfer. See Quincy, *Reports* (Appendix) 418–421, 434. It is photographically reproduced in Wolkins, "Writs of Assistance in England," 66 MHS, *Procs.* 362 (1936–1941). See Freiberg, Prelude to Purgatory 18 note. Hutchinson's draft was undoubtedly used as the basis for all subsequent writs issued. Compare the writ issued to Nathaniel Hatch, 3 June 1762, in SF 100515b.

[152] 13 & 14 Car. 2, c. 11, §5(2), text at note 92 above.
[153] 7 & 8 Will. 3, c. 22, §6(2), text at notes 94–97 above.

ince as fully and amply to all intents and purposes as our Courts of King's Bench Common Pleas and Exchequer within our Kingdom of England have or ought to have.[154]

And whereas our Commissioners for managing and causing to be levied and collected our customs subsidies and other duties have by Commission or Deputation under their hands and seal dated at London the 22d. day of May in the first year of our Reign deputed and impowered Charles Paxton Esqr. to be Surveyor and Searcher of all the rates and duties arising and growing due to us at Boston in our Province aforesaid and in and by said Commission or Deputation have given him power to enter into any Ship Bottom Boat or other Vessel and also into any Shop House Warehouse Hostery or other Place whatsoever to make diligent search into any trunk chest pack case truss or any other parcell or package whatsoever for any goods wares or merchandizes prohibited to be imported or exported or whereof the Customs or other Duties have not been duly paid and the same to seize to our use In all things proceeding as the Law directs.[155]

Therefore we strictly Injoin and Command you and every one of you that, all excuses apart, you and every one of you permit the said Charles Paxton according to the true intent and form of the said commission or deputation and the laws and statutes in that behalf made and provided, as well by night as by day from time to time to enter and go on board any Ship Boat or other Vessel riding lying or being within or coming to the said Port of Boston or any Places or Creeks thereunto appertaining such Ship Boat or Vessel then and there found to search and oversee and the persons therein being strictly to examine touching the Premises aforesaid and also ⟨*according to the form effect and true intent of the said commission or deputation*⟩ in the day time to enter and go into the vaults cellars warehouses shops and other places where any prohibited goods wares or merchandizes or any goods wares or merchandizes for which the customs or other duties shall not have been duly and truly satisfied and paid lye concealed or are suspected to be concealed, according to the true intent of the law to inspect and oversee and search for the said goods wares and merchandizes, And further to do and execute all things which of right and according to the laws and statutes in this behalf shall be to be done. And we further strictly Injoin and Command you and every one of you that to the said Charles Paxton Esqr. you and every one of you from time to time be aiding assisting and helping in the execution of

[154] Act of 26 June 1699, 1 A&R 370, text at note 98 above.
[155] As to Paxton's commission, see Quincy, *Reports* (Appendix) 421 note.

the premises as is meet. And this you or any of you in no wise omit at your Perils. Witness Thomas Hutchinson Esq. at Boston the day of December in the Second year of our Reign Annoque Dom. 1761.[156]

> By order of Court
> N.H. Cler.[157]

45. Folger v. Sloop *Cornelia*

1768

EDITORIAL NOTE

In this, Adams' earliest known appearance in an Admiralty action for a violation of the Acts of Trade, he and James Otis argued for Timothy Folger, Searcher and Preventive Officer at Nantucket. The lawyers were not engaged on the side of royal authority, however. Folger was a native of the island, sympathetic to Massachusetts mercantile interests. Arrayed against him were the customs officers of the port of Boston, backed by the newly created American Board of Customs Commissioners.

The Boston customs establishment, like that in other English and colonial ports, was under the joint control of a Collector and a Comptroller. Until 1767 these officers were appointed by the Commissioners of Customs in England,[1] and were responsible to John Temple, Surveyor General of the Customs for the Northern District, also an appointee of the Com-

---

[156] The last three words are in another hand, perhaps that of Nathaniel Hatch, a clerk of the Superior Court. See Quincy, *Reports* (Appendix) 418.

[157] The initials (standing for Nathaniel Hatch) are in Hutchinson's hand, but "Cler." (for Clerk) is not; Gray suggests it is in Samuel Winthrop's hand. See Quincy, *Reports* (Appendix) 418.

[1] For the statutory authority of the Commissioners, see notes 51 and 52 below. The collector was primarily responsible for gathering the revenue; entering, registering, bonding, and clearing vessels; and prosecuting violations of the Acts. The comptroller checked the collector's performance of these duties and audited his accounts. In Boston these officers were assisted by a surveyor and searcher and a tide surveyor (both also commissioned by the Customs Commissioners), who were charged with boarding and searching vessels for illegal goods. There were also a deputy collector and about a dozen waiters, tidesmen, boatmen and the like, all appointed locally. See *Instructions by the Commissioners of His Majesty's Customs to   who is established Collector of His Majesty's Customs at   4* (London, ca. 1764); 4 Andrews, *Colonial Period* 204–212; letter of Joseph Harrison and Benjamin Hallowell to American Customs Commissioners, 30 April 1768, PRO, Treas. 1:465, fols. 179–193, printed in Wolkins, ed., "The Boston Customs District in 1768," 58 MHS, *Procs.* 418, 429–432 (1924–1925). As JA suggests, text at note 40 below, the statutes did not even attempt to limit the numbers of these officers or to define their duties. Their titles and functions were modeled on the English establishment, which had evolved from medieval administrative practice without benefit of parliamentary control. See Hoon, *English Customs* 5–25; 4 Andrews, *Colonial Period* 178–221.

missioners. Temple was empowered to exercise disciplinary control over inferior officers and add his efforts to theirs in the control of illicit trade throughout the northern colonies. Acting in this capacity, he had commissioned Folger to serve at Nantucket in 1764.[2]

The Boston officers, Joseph Harrison, Collector, and Benjamin Hallowell, Comptroller, later claimed that they had always disapproved of Folger's position,[3] and there is reason to believe that this claim was not entirely the product of hindsight. In the first place, there was a serious legal question whether Temple had power to appoint such an officer. Secondly, on a more immediate level, Nantucket was traditionally within the port of Boston, so that Folger's presence deprived Harrison and Hallowell of a portion of the income from fees and forfeitures which was a substantial part of their compensation.[4]

Finally, and most important, Folger represented a threat to the security of the revenue. Temple, who took office at the time of the writs of assistance controversy in 1761 (No. 44), had at first won a reputation as a dedicated and successful officer. From the beginning he had shown sympathy with the position of the Boston merchants, however, and his feelings soon manifested themselves in an open feud with Governor Bernard of Massachusetts and in doubts of the wisdom and efficacy of parliamentary efforts to raise a revenue in the colonies. Yet, although his brush with Bernard, in which he had dismissed James Cockle, Collector at Salem, on charges of corruption, had won him the acclaim of the merchants, it had also been approved by his superiors in England.[5]

[2] As to the surveyor general's powers, see 4 Andrews, *Colonial Period* 202–204. This office was also modeled on the English system. See Hoon, *English Customs* 113–114, 190–191. For Folger's deputation, see note 45 below.

[3] In April 1768, after Folger had been dismissed, and again in July 1769, Harrison and Hallowell reported that their doubts of Folger stemmed from the beginning of his tenure. Wolkins, "Boston Customs District," 58 MHS, *Procs.* 433–434; Harrison to Commissioners, 27 July 1769, PRO, Treas. 1:471, fols. 189–190.

[4] The legal problems are discussed in text at notes 24–26 below. The position of Nantucket is described in Wolkins, "Boston Customs District," 58 MHS, *Procs.* 421, 428–429. For the importance of fees, see *id.* at 438, 445; Harrison to Temple, 30 May 1766, 1 *Bowdoin-Temple Papers* (9 MHS, *Colls.*, 6th ser.) 74–75 (1897); Barrow, Colonial Customs 272–274; *Instructions by the Commissioners* 1 (1764); 6 W. & M., c. 1, §5 (1694); 5 Geo. 3, c. 45, §27 (1765). Compare Sewall's comment, text at note 65 below.

[5] Temple, born in Boston, but raised in England, was appointed surveyor general in Dec. 1760, but did not arrive in Boston until Nov. 1761. Treasury Warrant, 1 Dec. 1760, PRO, Treas. 11:26, p. 5 (a reference furnished the editors by Thomas C. Barrow). See 1 *Bowdoin-Temple Papers* xv–xvii; Quincy, *Reports* (Appendix) 428 note; Temple to Commissioners, Jan. 1762, Temple Letter Book, 1762–1768, fols. 7–9, MHi; Temple's Memorial, undated, *id.* at fol. 187. His early zeal is commended in Thomas Whately to Temple, 18 June 1764, *id.* at fols. 19–21. For the Cockle-Bernard affair, see Barrow, Colonial Customs 406–408; Ubbelohde, *Vice Admiralty Courts* 58–60; Whately to Temple, 5 Nov. 1764, 1 *Bowdoin-Temple Papers* 36–39; Joseph Harrison to Temple, 12 June 1765, *id.* at 57–58; Commissioners to Temple, 9 March 1765, 1 Bowdoin-Temple MSS, fol. 60, MHi. The feud with Bernard and opposition to the customs service seem to have begun with Temple's sympathy toward Benjamin Barons, dismissed as Collector in 1761. See note 44 be-

No. 45. Folger v. Sloop Cornelia

While Temple thus remained in favor, his appointment of Folger in 1764 is consistent with an intent to use his powers to mitigate the effect of the new duties and enforcement measures imposed by the American Act of that year.[6] There was both practical justification and precedent for the appointment of an officer at Nantucket. The distance of the island from Boston made customs enforcement difficult and meant a long voyage around Cape Cod for vessels seeking to enter or clear. As a result, for at least forty years an officer appointed either by the Surveyor General or the Collector of Boston had been stationed there.[7] Folger's background suggests other purposes, however. Descended from one of Nantucket's oldest families and deep in local politics, he had been master or part-owner in numerous whaling and trading voyages, and kept a store in which imported goods were sold. In addition he was engaged in extensive dealings in whale oil with various merchants, including John Hancock.[8] Whether Temple in-

---

low; Barrow, Colonial Customs 358–359; No. 44, note 21. For Temple's adverse reactions to the American Act, 4 Geo. 3, c. 15 (1764), and the Stamp Act, 5 Geo. 3, c. 12 (1765), see Temple to Whately, 10 Sept. 1764, 1 Bowdoin-Temple Papers 24–28. Temple and Bernard also could not agree on procedures for clearing vessels without stamps. See Edmund S. and Helen M. Morgan, The Stamp Act Crisis: Prologue to Revolution 134–139 (Chapel Hill, 1953).

[6] 4 Geo. 3, c. 15 (1764). Folger was commissioned on 17 Aug. 1764. See note 45 below. For fears of the Boston customs officers, expressed in April 1768, see Wolkins, "Boston Customs District," 58 MHS, Procs. 434–435. Temple had previously appointed several minor functionaries in the port of Boston, and had made one "Mr. Hubbard" deputy collector at Stamford, Conn., but these seem to have been ordinary dispensations of patronage. See id. at 418, 431–432; Harrison to Temple, 30 May 1766, 1 Bowdoin-Temple Papers 74–75. In 1764 and 1765, in addition to Folger, he appointed his brother-in-law, John Fenton, deputy collector at Albany; Edward Winslow, deputy collector at Plymouth; James McCobb, searcher and preventive officer at "the port of Kennebec"; and other similar officers at Charleston, Annapolis, Cape Breton, and Canso. Wolkins, "Boston Customs District," 58 MHS, Procs. 418, 435–436; 1 Bowdoin-Temple Papers 66–70; PRO, Treas. 1:471, fols. 192–193; Book of Commissions, 1677–1774, fols. 44–45, 48, M–Ar; Temple to Commissioners, 10 April 1766, Temple Letter Book, 1762–1768, fol. 155. MHi. His appointments may all represent an effort to place favorably disposed men in strategic locations. For Temple's defense of the appointments, see Temple to Treasury, 10 Aug. 1769, 7 Bowdoin-Temple MSS 18–27, MHi.

[7] Wolkins, "Boston Customs District," 58 MHS, Procs. 432–433. See note 78 below.

[8] On the Folger family, see Alexander Starbuck, The History of Nantucket 113, 740–755 (Boston, 1924), where the Timothy Folger in question here (1732–1814) is genealogically confused with his uncle at p. 749. Compare 1 Vital Records of Nantucket, Massachusetts, to the Year 1850 509 (Boston, 1925); 3 id. at 472 (Boston, 1927); 5 id. at 280 (Boston, 1928). Folger was appointed coroner in 1762. Whitmore, Mass. Civil List 159. His mercantile interests are catalogued in Joseph Harrison's Report to the American Customs Commissioners on Folger's memorial, PRO, Treas. 1:471, fols. 472–474. See also 1 Commerce of Rhode Island (69 MHS, Colls.) 97–98 (1914). For the connection with Hancock, see, for example, Folger to Hancock, 28 June 1764, 2 Hancock Papers 165, MB; list of debts to Hancock, 4 May 1769, id. at 227. See also W. T. Baxter, The House of Hancock 169–174, 226–231 (Cambridge, Mass., 1945); Abram E. Brown, John Hancock His Book 274 (Boston, 1898); Edouard A. Stackpole, The Sea-Hunters 88 (N.Y., 1953). For his subsequent career, see note 31 below.

tended it or not, there now existed at Nantucket a sizable loophole for evaders of the Acts of Trade.

If the Boston customs officers had borne Folger's appointment with misgivings, they had made no formal protest. Temple was not only their superior, but a dangerous opponent, as his contest with Bernard had shown. Moreover, the political lines were still vague enough so that, despite his opinions, Temple could not be characterized as an enemy of the revenue.[9] The Townshend Acts, passed in the summer of 1767, changed both of these conditions. Temple's post as Surveyor General was eliminated in the creation of the American Board of Customs Commissioners, a five-man body which was to sit at Boston and carry out the functions of control and management previously within the province of the English Customs Commissioners. Temple was made a Commissioner, but his former authority was now to be exercised by a majority of the Board.[10]

At the same time the political situation was solidified by the colonial reaction to the import duties laid by the Acts.[11] Inspired by the vote of the Boston town meeting in the fall of 1767, a drive for the nonimportation of British goods developed, uniting and defining the opposition to royal authority. Folger, elected to an unruly House of Representatives in 1767, was clearly a part of this opposition. In January 1767 Temple had married Elizabeth, daughter of James Bowdoin, a prominent merchant and member of the Council, who became one of the leaders in the fight for nonimportation. Whatever his prior vacillations, Temple too was now definitely aligned with the Boston faction.[12] The other Commissioners saw as their first duty

[9] Harrison, appointed collector in 1766, was doubtless further inhibited by the fact that he had obtained his position in part through Temple's influence, and had assisted in presenting Temple's case in the matter of Cockle in England. See Temple to Whately, 3 Oct. 1764, 1 *Bowdoin-Temple Papers* 29; Harrison to Temple, 12 Jan. 1765, *id.* at 42–45; 12 July 1765, *id.* at 62–64. Moreover, Harrison may have had some sympathy for the colonial view himself. See William Molineux to ———, June 1768, 3 Chalmers New England MSS 1, MH. Temple's strength was dependent in great part upon his family connection with the Grenvilles, who had been his patrons during his early years in England and continued to ease the way for him. See 1 *Bowdoin-Temple Papers* 1, and materials cited in note 5 above. See also Charles Paxton to George Townshend, 6 Nov. 1769, 56 MHS, *Procs.* 351–352 (1922–1923).

[10] The Commissioners were authorized by 7 Geo. 3, c. 41 (1767). For their commission, see note 41 below. See also Clark, "The American Board of Customs, 1767–1783," 45 *AHR* 777–785 (1940). The offices of all the colonial surveyors general were abolished and their commissions revoked when the Board was commissioned. *Id.* at 783; Samuel Venner to Thomas Bradshaw, 28 March 1768, PRO, Treas. 1:465, fols. 250–251.

[11] 7 Geo. 3, c. 46, §§1–7 (1767).

[12] On nonimportation, see Arthur M. Schlesinger, *The Colonial Merchants and the American Revolution, 1763–1776* 106–111 (N.Y., 1918). Folger sat for a single term in the House at this time. Starbuck, *History of Nantucket* 635; 18 A&R 225. For Temple's marriage, see 30 Boston Record Commissioners, *Reports* 329 (1903); 1 *Bowdoin-Temple Papers* 80–81. The Commissioners and Hutchinson both blamed Temple's opposition on his marriage, which brought him also into close relationship with James Pitts and John Erving, patriot members of the Council.

the plugging of procedural loopholes that encouraged smuggling. Temple, who felt that compliance could be obtained without undue restrictions, was from the beginning of their deliberations an articulate but ineffective minority of one.[13] The Boston customs officers now had both higher authority to support them in opposing Folger and a clear-cut political basis for doing so.

After the Commissioners took office on 16 November 1767 they occupied themselves in clarifying the scope of the new statutes, which were to take effect on 20 November, and in determining the extent of their new domain and the current state of the customs establishment. From the moment when three of them arrived from England on 5 November in the midst of a well-behaved but hostile Pope Day celebration, they had been aware of the opposition to them; they thus seemed determined to move carefully.[14]

The first call to action came on 29 January 1768 when Folger reported that a week previously he had seized the sloop *Cornelia,* William Summers master, at Tarpaulin Cove in the Elizabeth Islands, the easterly boundary of Buzzards Bay. The vessel was ostensibly bound for New York from the Dutch island of St. Eustatia with a cargo of eighteen casks of Bohea tea, a commodity that could be imported only by way of England and upon pay-

---

See Hutchinson to ———, Dec. 1769, 26 Mass. Arch. 417; Commissioners to Treasury, 6 Jan. 1769, PRO, Treas. 1:471, fols. 438–439, 452.

[13] For the disputes between Temple and the Commissioners, see Clark, "American Board of Customs," 45 *AHR* 782, 790–791. Temple dissented in the Board's determination to flee to Castle William after the *Liberty* riots in June 1768 (No. 46) and in the dismissal of John Fisher, collector at Salem, for corruption in July 1768. In the latter case, he was upheld by the Lords of the Treasury, who ordered Fisher reinstated. See No. 47, note 7. Finally in Feb. 1769 the other four members of the Board complained formally and at length to the Treasury about Temple's continuing opposition to their doings. PRO, Treas. 1:471, fols. 429–430. See also sources on Temple's marriage, note 12 above. For a sympathetic view of Temple's position, see Memorial of Samuel Venner to the Duke of Grafton, 1 May 1769, PRO, Treas. 1:471, fols. 495, 497. As to Venner, see note 16 below. Temple was finally dismissed in the fall of 1770, but he soon obtained a position in the English customs and lived to be British consul at New York after the Revolution. Clark, "American Board of Customs," 45 *AHR* 791; 1 *Bowdoin-Temple Papers* xvi–xvii, 151–152, 281–282.

[14] See Commissioners to Lords of Treasury, 12 Feb. 1768, PRO, Treas. 1:465, fols. 330–334; Charles Paxton to George Townshend, 24 Feb. 1768, 56 MHS, *Procs.* 348–349 (1922–1923). For examples of their activities, see opinions of the solicitor general on construction of the statutes, 15 Dec. 1767 and 18 Jan. 1768, PRO, Treas. 1:465, fols. 138–144; extracts of general letters to the collector of each port, 10 Dec. 1767 and 11 Jan. 1768, *id.,* 1:471, fols. 177, 179. The Minute Book of the Vice Admiralty Court shows that no seizures were prosecuted between Nov. 1767 and the entry of Folger's suit, note 17 below. The arrival of the Commissioners is described in Clark, "American Board of Customs," 45 *AHR* 785–786. Following the formula prescribed for the English Commissioners in 6 W. & M., c. 1, §5 (1694), Temple and Henry Hulton, "the first two named in the Commission," took oath in the Superior Court, "before the Barons of the Exchequer," on 16 Nov. 1767. See Minutes of the Commissioners, 16 Nov. 1767, 7 Bowdoin-Temple MSS 147, MHi; compare Min. Bk. 86, SCJ Suffolk, Aug. 1767, following N-115.

ment of the new duties.[15] He had brought the *Cornelia* to Nantucket, sequestered her cargo in his house, and now sought advice on how to proceed. The Commissioners referred him to their solicitor, Samuel Fitch, for legal assistance and directed him to report the seizure to Harrison and Hallowell.[16]

These officers at once raised the question of Folger's authority to seize the vessel and, after consulting with Jonathan Sewall, Advocate General in Admiralty, informed Folger that his commission was invalid and that the seizure would fail if a claim were entered for the vessel or cargo. They offered, however, to let him accompany them to Nantucket to seize her again under proper authority. According to Harrison's later account, Folger agreed to do so and to join with them in the forfeiture proceedings in exchange for a substantial share as informer. When the time came to leave for the island, however, Folger backed out, explaining that his "friends" had advised him not to join, and that he was determined to file an information in his own right. Knowing that James Otis was one of Folger's "friends," Harrison immediately dispatched Hallowell and George Lyde, Surveyor and Searcher of the port, to Nantucket, where they seized the *Cornelia* and cargo. Upon their return they found that Folger had, on 4 February, filed his information in the court of Admiralty. A new attempt to win him over failed, and, on 12 February, Harrison, Hallowell, and Lyde joined in a second information against vessel and tea.[17]

[15] The import restrictions were laid by 7 Geo. 1, Stat. 1, c. 21, §9 (1721), and the duties by 7 Geo. 3, c. 46 (1767).

[16] Letters of Folger to Commissioners, 29 Jan., 1 Feb. 1768, PRO, Treas. 1:471, fols. 171–174; Minutes of the Commissioners, 29 Jan., 1 Feb. 1768, 7 Bowdoin-Temple MSS 147, MHi. Compare the account of the Commissioners replying to Folger, 24 July 1769, PRO, 1:471, fol. 363. According to Samuel Venner, writing after his dismissal as secretary to the Commissioners (No. 46, notes 20, 27), almost as soon as the Board was constituted, the Commissioners had begun a concerted attack on Temple by questioning the legality of a list of his former appointments which he had submitted. Upon the seizure of the *Cornelia*, "the Board having consulted Mr. Samuel Fitch, then acting as their Soliciter, he reported that a Libell should be filed in the Court of Vice Admiralty against the Vessel and Goods. But the Commissioners apprehending that this would give a Sanction to such Officers [*i.e.* Temple's appointees], immediately declared that Mr. Folger had no Power to make such Seizure, and directed the Collector and Comptroller of the Port of Boston to reseize the Vessel and Cargo." Venner to Duke of Grafton, 1 May 1769, PRO, Treas. 1:471, fol. 496. The chief materials cited here and in note 17, above, supporting the view that Harrison and Hallowell took the initiative to reseize, were prepared by the Commissioners or the officers, and are thus as liable to prejudice as Venner's account. Temple's own copy of the Commissioners' Minutes indicates that he did not submit a list of his appointees until 14 March, however. 7 Bowdoin-Temple MSS 151, MHi. Folger's Memorial to the Treasury, 24 Nov. 1768, states that it was the collector and comptroller who declared the seizure illegal. PRO, Treas. 1:471, fols. 366–367. Although the Commissioners were probably unofficially aware of what was going on, the fairest conclusion seems to be that their opposition to Temple's appointments was brought about by Folger's case, rather than that the opposition to Folger was a calculated part of a scheme directed against Temple.

[17] Folger v. The *Cornelia* and 18 Casks of Tea, Vice Adm. Min. Bk., 4 Feb.

Hearings in both actions were set for 29 February, then continued.[18] In the meantime other pressures were building up. On 26 February, with Folger voting in the majority, the House approved nonimportation resolutions, which pledged it, among other things, "to discountenance the use of foreign superfluities, and to encourage the manufactures of this province."[19] The Customs Commissioners met on 7 March and dismissed Folger, determining that a nominee of the Boston collector should be appointed in his stead. There was an immediate outcry in the press that Folger had been dismissed solely because of his vote on the resolves. The Board, in a later statement of its position, admitted asking him about his vote, but insisted that "he had been before charged with being concerned in Trade, and he was only told that the Board had no further service for him." The Commissioners also suggested that direct opposition to the principal officers of the port and open alliance with the antigovernment faction did not constitute the conduct expected in the customs service.[20] For whatever reason, Folger was no longer searcher and preventive officer when the case of the *Cornelia* came to trial.

Both proceedings were tried in the court of Admiralty on 21 and 26 March before Judge Robert Auchmuty, probably in a combined hearing.[21]

1768; Harrison v. The *Cornelia* and 18 Casks of Tea, *id.*, 12 Feb. 1768. See notices of monitions, *Boston Gazette*, 18 Feb. 1768, p. 1, col. 1. For accounts of the maneuvering prior to the filing of suit, see the materials cited above, note 16; Harrison and Hallowell to Commissioners (extract), 8 March 1768, PRO, Treas. 1:471, fols. 181–182; Folger's Memorial, 24 Nov. 1768, *id.*, fols. 366–367; Harrison to Commissioners, 21 June 1769, *id.*, fols. 472–475. Harrison's fears about Otis are substantiated by the latter's familiarity with Folger's commission in the incident of 11 Feb., described below, note 60. It was Harrison's letter of 21 June 1769, containing the reference to Folger's "friends," which started the bad blood between Otis and the customs officials leading to Otis' disastrous fight with Commissioner John Robinson. See Minutes of the Commissioners, 4 Aug. 1769, 7 Bowdoin-Temple MSS 188, MHi. As to the fight and subsequent litigation in which JA was of counsel for Otis, see 2 JA, *Diary and Autobiography* 47–48.

[18] Vice Adm. Min. Bk., 4 Feb., 12 Feb. 1768.

[19] Mass. *House Jour.* 1767–1768, p. 198–199. *Boston Gazette*, 29 Feb. 1768, p. 2, col. 2. See American Commissioners to Lords of Treasury, 28 March 1768, PRO, Treas. 1:465, fols. 363–364.

[20] See Minutes of Commissioners, 7 March 1768, PRO, Treas. 1:471, fol. 159; *Boston Gazette*, 14 March 1768, p. 3, col. 1; Commissioners to Treasury, 24 July 1769, PRO, Treas. 1:471, fols. 364–365. Compare Hutchinson to ———, Dec. 1769, 26 Mass. Arch. 417, 418. Temple did not dissent from Folger's dismissal, but on 10 May 1768, he wrote a testimonial for him. PRO, Treas. 1:465, fols. 248–250. There was a specific prohibition against engaging in trade and an injunction to report any such activity by inferior officers in the Collector's instructions. *Instructions by the Commissioners* 6 (1764). Most of Temple's other appointees were reappointed. See note 78 below. As late as 12 March the Commissioners were willing to offer Folger a settlement. Minutes of the Commissioners, 12 March 1768, 7 Bowdoin-Temple MSS 153, MHi.

[21] Vice Adm. Min. Bk., 4 Feb., 12 Feb. 1768. See Rowe, *Letters and Diary* 157, 158. Interrogatories on Folger's behalf were served on the Commissioners. After taking Fitch's advice, they directed him to except to the interrogatories. Minutes of the Commissioners, 24, 25 March 1768, 7 Bowdoin-Temple MSS 155–157, MHi. It is not known whether the exceptions were filed, or what the result was.

No claim for vessel or goods appears to have been filed in either suit, but Adams and Otis were opposed by Jonathan Sewall, who had intervened in Folger's proceeding on behalf of the Crown and was doubtless of counsel for Harrison and his associates in their information. Adams' role is perhaps unfairly minimized in the later report of the Commissioners that Folger "having Mr. Otis for his Lawyer, the Cause was contested with great Spirit." [22]

The three documents printed here are: (I) Adams' minutes on the depositions of several witnesses as to Folger's performance of his functions; (II) Adams' minutes of the arguments on both sides; and (III) Auchmuty's opinion and decree in the case, an unusual report which summarizes the arguments and deals with the questions involved in great detail.

Sewall's position was, first, that by statute only a duly commissioned customs officer could seize; second, that Folger had not been duly commissioned; and, third, that if his commission were valid, it had been terminated when Temple's office was merged in that of the American Board of Customs Commissioners. In reply Adams and Otis contended that no commission was necessary for the seizure, first, because under applicable statutes evidence of reputation as an officer was sufficient; second, because Folger had been a *de facto* officer whose acts were valid despite lack of authority. Then they argued in the alternative that Folger's commission was properly given by Temple, did empower him to make seizures, and was still in force despite the establishment of the American Customs Commissioners.

On 2 April, Auchmuty handed down his opinion and decree, dismissing Folger's information. He found that the statutes allowing reputation evidence created only a presumption, rebutted by the production of the invalid commission under which Folger had acted. Further, the common law rules validating the acts of a *de facto* officer were intended to protect innocent third parties who had relied upon the officer's apparent status; they could not be taken advantage of for his own profit by the officer himself. As for the commission, Auchmuty held that Temple had no power to create new officers, and, although he might have created a deputy, he had not done so in this case, thus making it unnecessary to consider in detail the effect of the creation of the American Commissioners.

Auchmuty's argument on the reputation statutes seems a proper construction. As for the *de facto* argument, he managed to turn Otis' own authority against him in pointing out the distinction between Folger's case and the cases chiefly relied on. If the arguments that Folger acted in good faith and that the proceeds of the forfeiture were a kind of compensation for his efforts might have altered the result, at least in a modern view, they do not seem to have been made by counsel.[23]

[22] Commissioners to Treasury, 24 July 1769, PRO, Treas. 1:471, fol. 364.

[23] The rule at common law in the United States in the 19th century was that a *de facto* officer was not entitled to compensation (except, perhaps, his expenses), even when he had acted in good faith. Floyd R. Mechem, *A Treatise on the Law of*

The question of the commission is more difficult. As Adams seems to have argued, the statutes establishing the customs were vague as to the types and duties of officers, and ambiguous as to the source of the power to appoint.[24] Temple's general powers probably could have been read as implying an authority to create lesser officers to implement them; if so, it would seem unduly restrictive to require that this authority be exercised only through the formal creation of a deputy surveyor general. The real question was whether an officer so created had the power to seize, in view of the statutory limitation on that power. As an original matter, the language of that limitation, "officers of his majesty's customs for the time being," [25] could be stretched to include a person situated as Folger was, but the point does not seem to have been pressed by Adams or Otis, and Auchmuty did not address himself to the question. Even if Folger were duly empowered to seize, however, another ground supported Auchmuty's decision.

This ground was the fact that not only had Temple been removed from office but that the office itself had been abolished. The analogy to officers whose powers survive the death of the principal, urged by Otis, was thus inapposite. Here, the existence of the authority which had created the lesser office, rather than the life of the individual who had made the appointment, had terminated; it seems obvious that lesser offices also should cease to exist, barring express confirmation or ratification.[26] Adams and Otis urged certain statutes as confirmatory, but these acts clearly applied only to appointments by the English Commissioners. They apparently did not argue that the American Commissioners had ratified Folger's appointment by keeping him on after November 1767, or even by dismissing him as unfit, rather than as a usurper. Thus, despite the obvious political advantage in a finding against Folger, Auchmuty's opinion seems on the merits to be sound.

Having dismissed Folger's information, Auchmuty on 4 April decreed in favor of Harrison, Hallowell, and Lyde in the other proceeding.[27] Fol-

---

Public Offices and Officers §§331–334, 342 (Chicago, 1890). More recently some courts have allowed compensation, even where there is a rightful claimant, if the *de facto* officer has acted in good faith. Eugene McQuillin, *The Law of Municipal Corporations*, vol. 4, §12.181 (Chicago, 3d edn., 1949); Charles S. Rhyne, *Municipal Law* 145 (Washington, 1957).

[24] See JA's argument, text at notes 40–44 below. The statutes, 25 Car. 2, c. 7, §3 (1673), and 7 & 8 Will. 3, c. 22, §11 (1696), which deal with the power of the English Commissioners over the colonial customs, are quoted in notes 51, 52, below. For the narrower question whether the Commissioners themselves were authorized to appoint under these Acts without warrant from the Treasury, see No. 50 at notes 3–8.

[25] 13 & 14 Car. 2, c. 11, §15 (1662), quoted in note 68 below.

[26] There was authority to this effect in the 18th century. See 16 Viner, *Abridgment*, tit. Officers and Offices, O. 4, pl. 7. For similar modern authority, see Mechem, *Public Offices* §407; 3 McQuillin, *Municipal Corporations* §§12.115, 12.121.

[27] Vice Adm. Min. Bk., 12 Feb. 1768. See Harrison and Hallowell to Commissioners, 8 April 1768, PRO, Treas. 1:471, fol. 183.

ger appealed both decisions to the High Court of Admiralty, but the result is not known. In any event, the vessel was sold, and the governor received his one-third share.[28] The victory can have been small consolation to the Commissioners, however; they were almost at once embroiled in the disastrous consequences of the seizure of John Hancock's sloop *Liberty* (No. 46), which demonstrated that countering colonial resistance was more than a matter of plugging loopholes.

Not satisfied with the ordinary appellate process, Folger sailed to England in August 1768. There he petitioned the Lords of the Treasury for relief, asserting that the *Cornelia* and his position had both been unjustly taken away from him and that, as he had given up his position as shipmaster to serve as a customs officer, he was "now out of all employ whatsoever." The last was a manifest exaggeration since he had been master on the voyage that brought him to England.[29] His memorial was referred to the American Board of Customs Commissioners, who finally replied on 24 July 1769, denying the validity of Folger's complaints and pointing out his relations with the antigovernment faction.[30] No record has been found of further action on the matter, but Folger was doubtless able to survive his losses, thanks to various maritime and mercantile ventures, which, despite his protestations, he never seems to have abandoned completely. That he did not fall out of political favor altogether appears in his appointment as

[28] Vice Adm. Min. Bk., 4 Feb., 12 Feb. 1768. See order of sale, *Massachusetts Gazette*, 15 April 1768, p. 3, col. 2. Andrews suggested that the Minute Book must be in error in recording that this appeal was to the High Court, because he believed that after 1766 Vice Admiralty appeals lay only to the Privy Council. Andrews, "Vice Admiralty Courts in the Colonies," in *Records of the Vice Admiralty Court of Rhode Island, 1716–1752* 22 note (Washington, ed. Dorothy S. Towle, 1936). Subsequent research has disclosed that the High Court and the Privy Council continued to exercise concurrent jurisdiction in appeals, at least in cases under the Acts of Trade, after 1766. See Smith, *Appeals to the Privy Council* 191–192. A newspaper correspondent reported that "The first Civilian in this Kingdom has undertaken for Capt. Folgier in his Appeal from your [*i.e.* the Boston] Court of Admiralty; and it is expected that he will not only succeed in the appeal, but also have a handsome appointment." *Boston News-Letter*, 12 Jan. 1769, p. 2, col. 2.

[29] Rowe, *Letters and Diary* 173. *Boston News-Letter*, 25 Aug. 1768, p. 2, col. 3. Commissioners to Treasury, 24 July 1769, PRO, Treas. 1:471, fol. 365. Folger's memorial, received on 24 Nov. 1768, is found in *id.* at fols. 366–368. It was accompanied by Temple's testimonial, note 20 above.

[30] American Commissioners to Treasury, 24 July 1769, PRO, Treas. 1:471, fols. 363–365. The reply was accompanied by much documentation, including statements of the customs officers, earlier letters from their records concerning the surveyor general's powers, and Auchmuty's opinion and decree (Doc. III). The documents, which have been heavily relied on in this account, are scattered throughout PRO, Treas. 1:465, 471. Folger returned to Massachusetts in April 1769. *Massachusetts Gazette*, 27 April 1769, p. 1, col. 3. In June he applied to the Commissioners for reinstatement, but action was deferred pending reply to the Memorial. Minutes of the Commissioners, 6, 20 June 1769, 7 Bowdoin-Temple MSS 180, MHi. Temple, who apparently saw the attack on Folger as an attack on himself, wrote at length to the Treasury in Folger's behalf, asserting the power of the surveyor general to appoint inferior officers and the legality of seizures made under such appointments. Temple to Bradshaw, 10 Aug. 1769, 7 Bowdoin-Temple MSS 18–27, MHi.

Justice of the Peace for Nantucket County in 1771. Thereafter, he went on to play a leading role in that peculiar mixture of seamanship and diplomatic intrigue which was Nantucket's brief flirtation with neutrality during, and for a decade or so after, the Revolution.[31]

I. ADAMS' MINUTES OF THE TESTIMONY[32]

Court of Vice Admiralty, Boston, March 1768

Folger vs. Tea

James Athern Esqr.
Joshua Gardiner.[33] Folger has entered and cleared Vessell I am concerned in to and from London. Commonly reputed a Custom House Officer at Nantucket. Have seen a Plantation Certificate signed by him, the Governor and Peleg Gardiner Naval Officer.[34]

[31] As to Folger's commercial activities, see notes 8, 29, above. For his appointment as Justice, see Whitmore, *Mass. Civil List* 148. The adventures of Folger and Nantucket from 1775 to 1795 are chronicled in Stackpole, *Sea Hunters* 66–144. See also Starbuck, *History of Nantucket* 206–259, 384–414. In 1785 Folger served again as a Representative to the General Court. *Id.* at 636. He was related to Benjamin Franklin and in 1771 provided him with a map of the Gulf Stream, upon which Franklin relied in later scientific writings. *Id.* at 374–375. For Folger's later contact with JA, see No. 58, note 9.

[32] In JA's hand. Adams Papers, Microfilms, Reel No. 185.

[33] The deponent may have been the junior partner in Folger & Gardner, Folger's whale oil business. See sources in note 8 above.

[34] The term "Plantation Certificate" may here refer to the certificate of registry, required for every vessel by the statute 7 & 8 Will. 3, c. 22, §§17, 18 (1696), in which the governor and collector attested that oath of the vessel's place of construction and ownership had been made by the master or owner before them. Although there was no requirement that the naval officer join in this procedure, that official was the governor's appointee charged with general responsibility for maritime matters and oath was often actually taken before him, the governor's name probably being affixed to certificates in blank beforehand. See Register of the *Lusanna*, 28 June 1773, cited in No. 58, note 16; compare 3 Hutchinson, *Massachusetts Bay*, ed. Mayo, 311–312; *Instructions by the Commissioners*, Form I (1764). As to the naval officer, see generally, 4 Andrews, *Colonial Period* 187–189. It is perhaps more likely that the reference is to one of the certificates that bond had been given or other export requirements complied with, issued as part of the vessel's clearance. 7 & 8 Will. 3, c. 22, §13; 4 Geo. 3, c. 15, §24 (1764). The term seems to have been so used on occasion. See *Instructions by the Commissioners for Managing and Causing to Be Levyed and Collected His Majesty's Customs, Subsidies, and other Duties in England, to   who is established Collector of His Majesty's Customs at   in America* 13 (London, ca. 1733). The signature of the governor was required only on the certificates attesting that pig iron, hemp and flax, and hewn timber were the produce of the colonies. 23 Geo. 2, c. 29, §5 (1750); 4 Geo. 3, c. 26, §3 (1764); 5 Geo. 3, c. 45, §2 (1765); *Instructions by the Commissioners*, Forms XXVII, XXIX (1764). In the more usual certificates the collector and naval officer alone seem to have signed. See certificates of the *Lusanna*, cited in No. 58, note 17; compare certificates of the *Rebecca*, Pensacola, 28 Feb. 1765, SF 101107.

Jno. Handcock Esqr.[35] Cleared two Vessells that Deponent is concernd in for London, since the arrival of the Commissioners.[36] And has acted in all Respects, with the Regard to my Navigation at Nantucket, as the officers of the Customs do here. Commonly reputed an officer of the Customs. I know of his Acting, by his clearing my Vessells. I cant say I ever saw a Clearance of his signing, or saw him sign one. I know of his Clearing my Vessells by the Consequences for that the Vessells were admitted to an Entry in London. And others here by the Officers here.

Thos. Gray. Dep. vide

Mr. Sheaf. Have seen Papers of his signing, as Searcher and preventive Officer at Nantucket. Coasting Clearances. I acted under Sir H. Frankland, as Deputy Collector for this Port, for some Years.[37] Mr. Harrison the present Collector, wrote a Letter to Mr. Folger giving him Instructions about a Vessell with sugars at Nantucket.[38]

Captn. Partridge. Used [to] London Trade. Made many Voyages there. Papers are demanded of Us, on our Arrival by the Custom House Officers. Clearance from the Customs demanded. Once admitted to an Entry without producing my Clearance, but was soon sent for by the Clerk and told by the Clerk that he had done wrong, and that the Clearance was his only Security, for Entering me. Never

[35] For Hancock's business relations with Folger, see note 8 above.

[36] The American Board of Customs Commissioners, who landed on 5 Nov. 1767 and took office on 16 November. See text and note 14 above.

[37] William Sheaffe (1706–1771), Harvard 1723, a familiar figure in the Boston customs office since 1731. Not only had he served as Frankland's deputy, but after the latter's dismissal in 1759 he acted as collector until Benjamin Barons was appointed to the post by the English Commissioners. In Jan. 1762, in the aftermath of Barons' dismissal (note 44 below), Sheaffe was again made acting collector, this time by John Temple. This tenure was also brief, Roger Hale taking office under an appointment from the Commissioners in July. Sheaffe served as deputy to both Hale and his successor, Joseph Harrison. He was also appointed a port waiter by Temple sometime before Oct. 1766 and was acting in both capacities at the time of this proceeding. In 1769, he was placed upon the establishment as an "Officer of the Customs," and remained deputy collector until his death. See Quincy, *Reports* (Appendix) 424–429; Stark, *Loyalists of Mass.* 439; Wolkins, "Boston Customs District," 58 MHS, *Procs.* 431, 436; PRO, Treas. 1:471, fol. 161, 461–463; 7 Sibley-Shipton, *Harvard Graduates* 253.

[38] Perhaps a reference to an episode in April 1767 in which Folger sought to collect the duties on a vessel arrived at Nantucket from the Spanish sugar port of Monti Christi, which had not entered at Boston. When Harrison asked Temple for guidance, the latter replied, "Capt. Folger has no Authority to Enter or clear any Goods that are Dutiable and the Vessel he mentions I think ought to be Entered at Boston before anything is discharged; after she is so Entered, I have no objection to her unloading at Nantucket under the Inspection of Mr. Folger, or if you think necessary send an Officer from Boston to inspect her unlading, which Officer they must pay." Letters of Harrison and Temple, both dated 13 April 1767, PRO, Treas. 1:471, fols. 185, 188.

admitted upon Producing Manifest and Register, except in the above Instance.

II. ADAMS' MINUTES OF THE ARGUMENT[39]

Court of Vice Admiralty, Boston, March 1768

Folger vs. Hallowell.

The Affairs and Transactions of the Customs and Revenue, are very loose. Customs and Duties and subsidies, have from Time to Time been granted by Parliament to his Majesty and the Collection and Management of them has been committed by Parliament to his Majesty, in short the Crown seems to have been entrusted with a discretionary Power ⟨by the Parli⟩ of appointing as many Sorts of Officers and as many in Number, as are or shall be thought convenient. We hear of Surveyors, Collectors, Searchers, and Comptrollers but there is not any act of Parliament, which describes and limits their Provinces and Powers.[40]

Compare the Commission of the Commissioners with the Act of Parliament on which it is grounded. How small the Foundation! How mighty the super Structure! Are there no Powers in the Commission which are not pointed out in the Act? [41]

[39] In JA's hand. Adams Papers, Microfilms, Reel No. 185. The first four paragraphs seem to be JA's notes for an argument that in the absence of specific statutory language an officer's authority was to be found in his commission or in customary practice. See the statutes in notes 51 and 52, below. Compare note 1 above. The notes were probably written out at leisure before Sewall's argument, which ensues.

[40] See note 1 above.

[41] Presumably the American Board of Customs Commissioners, notes 10, 14, above. The act authorizing their positions provided that the customs in the plantations might "be put under the management and direction of such commissioners, to reside in the said plantations, as his Majesty, his heirs, and successors, by his or their commission or commissions under the great seal of *Great Britain*, shall judge to be most for the advantage of trade, and security of the revenue of the said *British* colonies." The commissioners, "or any three or more of them," were to "have the same powers and authorities for carrying into execution the several laws relating to the revenues and trade" of the colonies as other acts gave to the English commissioners, and it was to be lawful for the King "in such commission or commissions, to make provision for putting in execution the several laws relating to the customs and trade of the said *British* colonies." 7 Geo. 3, c. 41, §§1, 2 (1767). Their commission, which is set out in Book of Commissions, 1677–1774, fols. 83–92, M–Ar, was detailed, providing not only the general powers conveyed by the Act, but power to appoint and suspend inferior officers (see No. 50, note 15); power to apply the funds collected to rewards and salaries; power to administer oaths, to enter and search vessels and buildings, to compound forfeitures, to compel obedience from inferior officers and assistance from other officials; and authority to oversee the accounts of the entire system. In addition the Commissioners were granted salaries, were relieved of liability for the defaults of inferior officers, and were freed from

Compare the Act that empowers the King to constitute Commissioners at Home, with the Powers exercisd by them,[42] and by the late Surveyors General as Representatives of them.[43] The Commission empowers to suspend, and remove &c. Does the Act of Parliament enable the K. to give such Powers to Commissioners?

Where did Mr. Lechmere get his Authority to suspend Mr. Barons as Collector of this Port? He claimed an Authority, and exercised it of suspending.[44] Yet there is no Act of Parliament in the whole Statute Book, that enables the K. or Commissioners of Customs or any Body else to create such an officer as Surveyor General.

Sewall.

Folgiers Commission. Preventive officer. In my behalf.[45] All Temples

---

obligations for jury service and other local offices. Part of the text is quoted in No. 50, notes 15, 16.

[42] The English Customs Commissioners were first appointed by royal patent in 1671 and seem to have functioned by that authority until the passage of 9 Geo. 1, c. 21, §1 (1722), which, to remedy a defect in the Act of Union with Scotland of 1707, provided that "the customs and other duties, now under the management of the several and respective commissioners of the customs of *England* and *Scotland,* shall and may be put under the management of one commission of the customs for the whole united kingdom, or under the management of several commissions of the customs for *England* and *Scotland* respectively, from time to time, as his Majesty shall judge to be most for the advantage of trade and security of his revenues." The Act also made it lawful for the King "in such commission or commissions to make provision for putting in execution the several laws relating to the customs." *Id.* §2. See Hoon, *English Customs* 56–57. The very extensive powers actually granted in the commissioners' patents, including the appointment and dismissal of inferior officers, are summarized in *id.* at 59–60. For their authority over the colonial customs, see notes 51, 52, below.

[43] That is, John Temple and the surveyors general for the other continental districts, whose commissions were revoked upon the appointment of the American Board of Customs Commissioners. See note 10 above. For their powers, see text at note 2 above.

[44] Benjamin Barons, appointed Collector in 1759, was already on bad terms with the rest of the customs establishment, and sought to turn the system to his own profit by allying himself with the Boston merchants. In June 1761 he was dismissed by Thomas Lechmere, the Surveyor General, on charges of interfering with the Admiralty courts and the customs officers; he was not reinstated, despite the appeals of the merchants and the tacit support of Temple, who succeeded Lechmere in the midst of the squabble. See notes 5, 37, above. The dispute produced extensive litigation, including the case of the writs of assistance (No. 44), and the cases of Gray v. Paxton and Erving v. Cradock. Quincy, *Reports* (Appendix) 425–426, 541–557. See generally Barrow, Colonial Customs 262, 352–360; see also No. 44, note 21. As to the Surveyor General's power to suspend and appoint, see note 77 below.

[45] The text of Folger's commission, dated at Boston, 17 Aug. 1764, and signed by Temple, is as follows: "To all People to whom these presents shall come, Know ye, That I the Surveyor General of his Majesty's Customs in the Northern District of America, By Vertue of the Power and Authority to me given, Do hereby appoint Timothy Folger to be Searcher and preventive Officer in his Majesty's Customs at the Island of Nantucket in the Province of Massachusetts Bay and by Vertue of these

No. 45. Folger v. Sloop Cornelia

Authority ceased, on Arrival of Commissioners. Made vs. Claimers.[46]
Exclusion of officers and [their?] dues.[47]

Reputation and Exercise sufficient. 6. G. 1, c. 21, §24.[48] 11. G. 1,
c. 30, §32.[49]

---

presents he hath Power to enter any Ship, Bottom, Boat, or any other Vessel, as
also into any Shop, House, Warehouse, Hostry, or other Place whatsoever, to make
diligent Search into any Trunk, Chest, Pack, Case, Truss, or any other Parcel or
Package whatsoever, for any Goods, Wares or Merchandize, prohibited to be Imported or Exported, or whereof the Customs or other Duties have not been duly
paid, and the same to Seize (in my behalf) to his Majesty's Use, and also put in
Execution all other the lawful Powers and Authorities for discharging the Trust
reposed in him as an Officer of the Customs In all things proceeding as the Law
directs; Hereby praying and requiring all Officers both Civil and Military In the
Province of the Massachusetts Bay to be aiding and assisting to him the said Timothy
Folger in all things as becometh." Book of Commissions, 1677–1774, fol. 39, M–Ar.
Folger took the necessary oaths before Governor Bernard on 18 August. *Ibid.*

[46] Probably an argument by Sewall that Folger's defenses under the Acts of 6 and
11 Geo. 1, notes 48, 49, below, might properly have been made against parties
claiming the vessel, but were not valid against other royal officials. Compare Auchmuty's opinion, text following note 71 below.

[47] The reference is not clear. The phrase may simply echo the thought expressed in
text at note 65 below, or it may refer to the practice of exempting customs officers
from local obligations such as the payment of provincial taxes, jury duty, and
military service. See note 41 above. See the complaint of the Commissioners to the
Lords of the Treasury that the Province assessors were seeking to levy on their
salaries, 27 July 1769, PRO, Treas. 1:471, fols. 459–460; see also 4 Andrews,
Colonial Period 204.
   There follows a gap of half a page in the MS. The materials which follow in text
through note 53 were probably JA's notes for his own argument.

[48] 6 Geo. 1, c. 21, §24 (1719), provided that "if upon trial or trials of or in any
information, action, suit or prosecution whatsoever relating to his Majesty's duties of
customs and excise, or to either of them, or to any other his duties whatsoever, or to
any seizure or seizures, penalty or penalties, forfeiture or forfeitures, relating to the
said duties, or any of them, or if upon any trial or trials of or in any action, suit or
prosecution whatsoever against any person or persons, for anything done by virtue
or in pursuance of any act or acts of parliament relating to the said duties, any or
either of them, any question or questions shall be made, or any doubt or doubts,
dispute or disputes, shall arise or happen, touching or concerning the keeping of any
office or offices of excise in any city or cities, town or towns, or touching or concerning any one or more defendants being an officer or officers of or for the said
duties, any or either of them, that in every such case and cases proof shall and may
be made, or evidence given, either of the actual keeping of such office or offices of
excise in such city or cities, town or towns, or of such one or more defendants actually exercising of and being employed and intrusted in such office or offices respectively, before and at the respective time and times when the matter or matters in
question upon such trial or trials shall happen to have been done or committed, or
omitted, or neglected to have been done or performed, without producing any particular person or persons to prove the names of the particular and respective commissioners to any commissions in the respective cases before-mentioned, any or either
of them, to be of their own hand-writing; and that in every such case and cases
respectively such proof and evidence shall be deemed and taken to be legal and
sufficient evidence, unless or until by other evidence the contrary shall or do appear."

[49] 11 Geo. 1, c. 30, §32 (1724), simplified the language and clarified the cover-

Continuance of Deputations &c. after Death of Commissioners. 12. Ann. St. 2, c. 8, §13.[50]

Comrs. of Customs. 25th. Car. 2, Chap. 7 §3.[51]

Comrs. of Customs and Lds. of Treasury to appoint officers. 7. & 8. W. 3. Chapt. 22 §11.[52]

age and procedure of the Act of 6 Geo. 1, note 48 above. After reciting the failure of the earlier act, it provided that if, in the same categories of actions, as well as "upon the trial of any information or indictment for assaulting, resisting or obstructing any officer or officers of the customs, excise or duties upon salt, or other duties due and payable to his Majesty, in the execution of his or their respective office or offices, or for rescuing any goods or merchandizes seized or to be seized by any such officer or officers; any question shall arise, whether any person be an officer of his Majesty, his heirs or successors, of or for any of the said duties: in every of the said cases, proof shall and may be made and admitted, that such person was reputed to be and had acted in, and in fact exercised such office, and at the respective time and times, when the matter or matters in controversy upon such trial or trials shall happen to have been done or committed, or omitted to have been done or performed, without producing or proving the particular commission, deputation, or other authority, whereby such officer was constituted and appointed, and that in every such case such proof shall be deemed and taken by the judges or justices before whom any such trial shall be had, to be good and legal evidence, unless by other evidence the contrary shall be made to appear; any law or usage to the contrary hereof notwithstanding."

[50] 12 Anne, Stat. 2, c. 8, §13 (1713), continued by 5 Geo. 1, c. 7 (1718), provided that all "collectors, surveyors, or other inferior officers" appointed by the Commissioners of the Customs "shall be deemed to remain and continue in their respective offices and imployments, notwithstanding the death or removal of any of the commissioners of the customs who deputed and appointed such officers, until the deputations of such officers respectively shall be by the said commissioners, or any other superior authority, revoked, annulled, or made void."

[51] An undated MS copy of this section in JA's hand reads: "And for the better Collection of the several Rates and Duties aforesaid imposed by this Act, be it enacted and it is hereby further enacted by the Authority aforesaid, that this whole Business shall be ordered and managed, and the several Duties hereby imposed shall be caused to be levyed by the Commissioners of the Customs in England now and for the Time being, by and under the Authority and Directions of the Lord Treasurer of England or Commissioners of the Treasury for the Time being." Adams Papers, Microfilms, Reel No. 185. The section is part of the Act of 1673 which first imposed duties to be collected in the colonies; it served as the basis for the first organized establishment of a colonial customs service, although isolated officials had been sent out before. See A. Berriedale Keith, *Constitutional History of the First British Empire* 76 (Oxford, 1930); Barrow, Colonial Customs 37–41.

[52] An undated MS copy of the relevant portion of this section in JA's hand reads: "And for the better executing the several Acts of Parliament relating to the Plantation Trade, be it enacted, that the Ld. Treasurer, Commissioners of the Treasury, and the Commissioners of the Customs in England for the Time being, shall and may constitute and appoint such and so many officers of the Customs in any City, Town, River, Port, Harbour, or Creek, of or belonging to any of the Islands Tracts of Land and Properties, when and as often as to them shall seem needfull." Adams Papers, Microfilms, Reel No. 185. This statute, passed in 1696, consolidated and defined the authority of the colonial customs service, gave its officers the powers and duties of their English counterparts, and facilitated placing them upon the English establishment. See Barrow, Colonial Customs 118–130, 133–136; 4 Andrews, *Colonial Period* 163–165, 213–215; No. 44.

No. 45. *Folger v. Sloop* Cornelia

7. G. 3d.[53]

Mr. Otis. Admitted an officer De Facto, and therfore have given up their Cause. Distinction between King De Jure and De Facto.[54] Maxim officers to be favoured.

Viners Abridgment Tit. Officers, and Offices G, Plea 2. Keeper of Goal De Facto, and De Jure.[55] Mayor De Facto.[56] G. 4, Plea 2. All Judicial Acts shall be good.[57] Colour of Election all Judicial and Ministerial Acts good.[58]

[53] Presumably a reference to 7 Geo. 3, c. 41, §3 (1767), which provided that "all deputations, and other authorities, granted by the commissioners of the customs in England before the passing of this act, or which may be granted by them before any commission or commissions shall issue in pursuance of this act, to any officer or officers acting in the said colonies or plantations, shall continue in force as fully, to all intents and purposes, as if this act had not been made, until the deputations or other authorities, so granted to such officer or officers respectively, shall be revoked, annulled, or made void, by the high treasurer of *Great Britain*, or commissioners of the treasury for the time being." See Auchmuty's discussion of this point, text at note 79 below.

[54] According to Blackstone, when Edward IV assumed the throne, "after a breach of succession that continued for three descents, and above threescore years, the distinction of a king *de jure*, and a king *de facto* began to be first taken; in order to indemnify such as had submitted to the late establishment, and to provide for the peace of the kingdom by confirming all honors conferred, and all acts done, by those who were now called the usurpers, not tending to disherison of the rightful heir." 1 Blackstone, *Commentaries* *204; see also 4 *id.* at *77–78; compare 1 Hale, *Pleas of the Crown* 101–103 notes. If Otis here referred to Blackstone's formulation, he was on treacherous ground, since the doctrine seems intended to protect those who had relied upon a usurper, but not to support the claims of the usurper against those of the rightful "heir"—in this case the *de jure* officers.

[55] "The Words Sheriff, Gaoler, &c. in the Statute 13 E. 1. cap. 11. extend to all Keepers of Gaols; and therefore if one hath the keeping of a Gaol by Wrong or De facto, and *suffers an Escape*, he is within this Statute as much as he that has the keeping of it De Jure. 2 Inst. 381, 382." 16 Viner, *Abridgment*, tit. [Officers and] Offices, G. 3, pl. 2.

[56] "An *Action* will lie against a Mayor de Facto *for a false Return* upon a Writ of Mandamus. Lutw. 519. Trin. 6 W. & M. in Case of Knight v. the Corporation of Wells." 16 Viner, *Abridgment*, tit. [Officers and] Offices, G. 3, pl. 3.

[57] "Acts done by an Officer De Facto, and not De Jure, are good; As if one being created *Bishop*, the former Bishop not being deprived or removed, *admits one to a Benefice upon a Presentation, or collates by lapse*, these are good and not avoidable. Arg. Quod Curia Concessit; for the *Law favours Acts of one in a reputed Authority*, and the inferior shall never inquire if his Authority be lawful. Cro. E. 699. Mich. 41 & 42 Eliz. B.R. in Case of Harris v. Jays. [*In the margin:*] S.P. Where the Bishop De Facto *made a Lease* which was confirmed by the Dean and Chapter, and after the Bishop De Jure died in the Life of the Bishop De Facto; it was resolved, that he not being lawful Bishop, and this Lease being to charge the Possessions of the Bishoprick, it is void; altho' all *Judicial Acts*, as Admissions, Institutions, Certificates, &c. shall be good; but not such *voluntary Acts as tend to the Depauperation of the Successor*, and so affirmed a Judgement given in B.R. in Ireland. Cro. J. 552, 554. Reuan Obrian & al. v. Knivan." 16 Viner, *Abridgment*, tit. [Officers and] Offices, G. 4, pl. 2.

[58] "If one *is elected Mayor of a Corporation without being duly qualified* accord-

Evidence that he was in Fact an officer, an officer De Facto.

If it should appear that the King was deceived [59] in his Grant and issued a Commission to the Commissioners that was void, would it be pretended that all their Acts and Orders through the Continent were void? No. Their Reputation And Exercise, sufficient to make their Acts and orders good.

All the Officers Comptrollers, Searchers Inspectors and even Commissioners them selves are only Preventive officers, none of them are to collect his Majesty's Duties.

Wonderfull Parenthesis (in my Behalf). [60] These Words cant make Folger a Deputy, merely Surplussage, currente Calamo, and may go out again without injuring the Commission.

If not rejected as surplusage, yet capable of several Constructions that will not vitiate or render void the Commission.

Whether the Surveyor General had, and the Commissioners have a Power to dismember a Port, or to make any Alterations in a Port, Yet if they will undertake to do it, it must be good till set aside by superiour Authority.

Lechmere went to England and appointed Coll. Brinley his Deputy in his Absence, and many of the officers got him to allow them salaries &c. Wages, Fees or some thing that they never could get before, and particularly the present Commissioner Paxton got a large sum at that Time. [61]

---

ing to a late Charter, to be chose into that Office, and after such Election he *puts the Seal of the Corporation to a Bond*, this Obligation is good: For by his coming into the Office by Colour of an Election, he was thereby Mayor De Facto, and all Judicial and Ministerial Acts done by him are good; and tho' the Corporation might have removed and displaced him, yet this not being done he had Power to seal the Bond. Lutw. 508. 519. Trin. 6 W. & M. Knight v. the Corporation of Wells." 16 Viner, *Abridgment*, tit. [Officers and] Offices, G. 4, pl. 3.

[59] For this usage, see No. 55, note 14.

[60] That is, the parenthetical phrase in Folger's commission, note 45 above. Otis had earlier had to defend this phrase in a coffeehouse gathering when William Molineux, the radical leader, attacked Temple and Folger, asserting that the latter had been appointed only to provide profit for the former. When a question was raised as to the validity of Folger's commission, "Mr. Otis said the commission, he thought, was very Good, but that there was one Expression in it that some People Hesitated about and Repeated the Sentence in the Commission which Runs thus—and in my Behalf to seize for his Majesty's Use—Upon repeating of this Sentence Mr. Mollineux [said] 'Now Gentlemen, you see that I am Right in what I said,' and seemed to lay great Stress upon these words—in my Behalf—signifying that whatever seizures were made by Folger, he, the said Folger, was not to have the profit arising from such seizures but the Surveyor General and that the Surveyor General gave him his Commission on these terms." Rowe, *Letters and Diary* 150–151 (11 Feb. 1768). The commissions which Temple gave to Edward Winslow as deputy collector at Plymouth and James McCobb as searcher and preventive officer at Kennebec omitted the phrase. Book of Commissions, 1677–1774, fols. 44–45, 48, M-Ar.

[61] Further documentation of this incident has not been found. Brinley was un-

No. 45. Folger v. Sloop Cornelia

A Deputy Sherriff would be liable to an Action if he should act after the death of his Principal, but this is not the Case of the Custom House officers. Their Deputations or other Authorities, are not nullified by the Demise of the Crown, any more than the Judges.[62]

2 Lev. 131. 10. Co. ——— [63]

Sewall. General Question, whether Mr. Folger had any Authority to make the Seizure.

The supposition of his having another Commission besides this from Temple.

Q. whether I have not offered such Evidence of his Having no Authority, as shall oblige Folger to produce ⟨his⟩ some other Commission.

The Act of 6. G. 1, c. 21, §24.[64] intended for the security of the Officers and off the Revenue. It is inconsistent with Common sense to suppose that the Legislature had any such Case in View, as this before your Honour.

This Act not extended to America.

I believe there is no Bottom to this Affair of the Customs.

By fair Contract the officers entituled to all the Fees within Their District.[65]

---

doubtedly Col. Thomas Brinley (d. 1765), a leading resident of Roxbury, whose son, Thomas, Harvard 1744, was a loyalist who fled to Halifax in 1776. 11 Sibley-Shipton, *Harvard Graduates* 366–367. Since Lechmere should have obtained permission from England for his trip and the appointment of a deputy, it is possible that Brinley was acting with the sanction of the Commissioners. See Barrow, Colonial Customs 296–298.

[62] By statute every "office or employment, civil or military," was continued for six months after the death of the sovereign, unless revoked by the successor. 1 Anne, stat. 1, c. 8, §2 (1701). A requirement subsequently imposed by 6 Anne, c. 7, §18 (1707), that all such officers take a new oath before continuing in office was replaced by 1 Geo. 2, c. 5, §2 (1727), and *id.*, stat. 2, c. 23, §7 (1728). See Samuel Baldwin, *A Survey of the British Customs*, part 2, p. 195 (London, 1770). Compare 12 Anne, stat. 2, c. 8, §13, note 50 above.

[63] Otto v. Selwin, 2 Lev. 131, 83 Eng. Rep. 483 (K.B. 1675), citing The Case of the Marshalsea, 10 Co. Rep. 68b, 77 Eng. Rep. 1027 (C.P. 1612). *Otto* held, per Hale, C.J., that an officer of the Court of Admiralty, pleading the warrant of that court in justification in an action of trespass and false imprisonment against him, need not plead and prove that the Admiralty had jurisdiction of the original cause. *The Case of the Marshalsea* had held that the warrant of a court lacking jurisdiction of the cause was not a defense in an action of false imprisonment; Hale distinguished that case on the ground that the lack of jurisdiction had there appeared (it was in fact conceded *arguendo*). Otis seems to be citing *Otto* for the proposition that when the actions of an officer are justified by a document regular on its face, the burden of proving an underlying irregularity lies with the opposing party.

[64] Note 48 above.

[65] That is, the officers appointed by the English Customs Commissioners are en-

In my Behalf, intended to make him Deputy, not to make a new office or officer. No Person can make a Deputy but the Principal. No Surveyor General can make a Deputy Collector, any more than I, as Advocate can make a Deputy Judge of Admiralty, or than your Honour can make Deputy Advocate General.

Surveyor and Searcher.[66]

III. AUCHMUTY'S OPINION AND DECREE[67]

Court of Vice Admiralty, Boston, 2 April 1768

Information

Timothy Folger vs. Sloop Cornelia and Eighteen Casks Tea. On this information the Advocate general in behalf of the King intervened.

In determining this cause, I shall consider the matters on each side of the question principally relied on by the Gentlemen in their arguments and much in the same order as proposed.

The Advocate general in behalf of the King urged, that none but the Officers of the Customs could seize in cases similar to this, relying on the 14 Car. 2d. for this point.[68] That the informer, who in the information, calls himself searcher and preventive Officer in the Island of Nantuckett never was an Officer of the Customs, and that granting he was, his Authority ceased on the commissioners of the Customs in North America entering upon the Execution of their Office. Because the Informer was authorized and appointed, as by an authenticated copy of his Commission exhibited by the said advocate appears, by the

---

titled to all the fees without competition from officers appointed by other sources. See text and note 4 above.

[66] The MS breaks off here and the reference is unexplained. The office of Surveyor and Searcher is described in note 1 above. George Lyde, the incumbent, had accompanied Hallowell in reseizing the *Cornelia* and was a party to the action. See text at note 17 above.

[67] MS, endorsed: "Copy. Decree in the Court of Admiralty at Boston in the Case of Folger &ca. vs. Sloop Cornelia, and 18 Casks of Tea." Subscribed: "A true copy. Att[estatu]r Ez. Price D. Regr." PRO, Treas. 1:471, fols. 152–158 (photostats in DLC:British Reproductions).

[68] 13 & 14 Car. 2, c. 11, §15 (1662) provided that no ship or goods were to be seized for violations of the Acts of Trade "but by the person or persons who are or shall be appointed by his majesty to manage his customs, or officers of his majesty's customs for the time being, or such other person or persons as shall be deputed and authorized thereunto by warrant from the lord treasurer or under-treasurer, or by special commission from his majesty under the great or privy seal." Seizures by others were to be void. This section was presumably made applicable in the colonies by 7 & 8 Will. 3, c. 22, §7 (1696). It was interpreted strictly in England. See Hoon, *English Customs* 271–272.

Honble. John Temple Esqr. late surveyor general of the northern district; whose office was entirely vacated and made void by the said commissioners executing their said Office, which was prior to the seizure set fourth in said Information. That the three known principal officers of the Customs in the port of Boston, of which the said island of Nantuckett is a member, had seized and informed against the same vessel and goods which information was pending in this Court; wherefore on his Majesty's behalf said advocate prayed that the libel of the said informer might be dismissed unless he could shew his authority to seize.

To all which it was answer'd by James Otis and John Adams Esqrs. advocates for the informer, first that he was not held to produce any commission to authorize him to make or hold said seizure, because it was sufficient to prove himself a reputed Officer of the Customs, by acting as such at the time of seizing. To support which the statutes of the 6 Geo. 1 and the 11. of the same reign were produced.[69] Secondly, that considering the exhibits, proofs and Advocate's concession in the case, it evidently appeared, the Informer was either an Officer of the Customs de facto, or de jure or both. If the latter a right of seizing must undoubtedly have been in him. If only the informer,[70] yet even by the rules of the common law, without the aid of the Statutes, it was sufficient. Thirdly, that the Informer was an Officer de jure by his commission from the said late surveyor general, produced by the advocate and by the Court allowed to be filed as evidence and lastly, that the Authority granted by said commission did not cease on the Surveyor generals office being vacated by the appointment of the Commissioners of the customs in North America, and their Executing their office. To prove which the 12. Ann. and the 7. Geo. 3. were cited and relied on.[71]

The force and operation of the two statutes of Geo. 1. must be considered in order to determine whether the same comprehend the present case, Those were formed to guard the revenue, by protecting the real Officers thereof against certain inconveniences. A construction therefore of the statutes different from that design or exceeding such Inconveniences must be erroneous: In the first act by the perview which immediately relates to the section under consideration it clearly appears, the mischiefs intended to be remedied were, the trouble and expence Officers were necessarily at in procuring the condemnation of

[69] Notes 48, 49, above.
[70] Apparently an inadvertence for "former."
[71] Notes 50, 53, above.

Goods seized, and in consequence thereof the enacting part enables officers to give proof of their actually exercising and being imployed and entrusted in an Office, without producing evidence to prove the names of the Commissioners to any Commission to be their hand writing. But there are only two Cases in which such proof of reputation is Admissible, First, when the trial is between the Officer seizing and the Claimer. Secondly when the Officer is prosecuted for any thing done by virtue of any act relating to duties. If therefore the present dispute is not such an instance as is pointed out by the Act, it cannot be within it Because this Act, which is enlarged by the 11. Geo. 1. but for the same purposes, gives a remedy not known at common law, in particular cases. Therefore by the rules of law relative to the constructions of Acts, such remedies cannot be extended to alter the Common law in any others than those particular instances mentioned in the Act. This rule is founded on the deference always justly paid to the common law by the Judges in construing statutes and by which the common law is preserved from Constructive innovations. It is indisputable that the present controversy is not a Trial between an Officer and Claimer, or a civil action or other process brought against an Officer by a Subject, but a litigation founded on the intervention of the Kings Advocate in behalf of his Majesty, The point is now between the King and one who claims to be an Officer of the Customs under his Majesty: therefore to extend the said Acts or either of them to such a case would be both absurd and illegal. Illegal, because by so construing the Act, the King himself would be thereby affected, tho' not mentioned therein, and tho' considering the nature and tendency of the Act, he cannot consistently with the rules of law, be constructively included. Absurd because it would be foreclosing his Majesty from whom all the powers of Officers mediately or immediately flow from trying whether one asserting to be his Officer was so, and notwithstanding the admission of such an enquiry, it appears to me, the letter as well as the spirit of the Acts will be preserved entire; and so no reason presents why it should not be granted. I am sensible, it is objected that the trial now is founded on an information, and relates to a seizure, and from thence concluded to be within the express words of the Acts. To this it may be answered, that those Acts are not to be construed by the different modes of prosecution therein enumerated, nor by the general expressions pointing out the causes of such prosecutions; but by the mischeifs intended to be remedied, and not guarded against by the common law, and therefore, tho' a Case in one sense may depend on a seizure and information, yet if none of the mischeifs mentioned in and designed to be redressed by said acts, attend it, the law will not adjudge such a Case to be within the Acts. It is an established rule that tho' a Case be within the letter of an Act, if not within the real meaning thereof, it cannot be included therein, A construction different from that I have given would make said Acts productive of a very great repugnancy, by forcing the same to operate in favour of persons, without an enquiry whether they were or were not properly Officers of the Crown to the prejudice of others duly appointed, for the protection and advantage of whom said statutes most undoubtedly were designed. And lastly, that by the duly authenticated Copy of the Informers commission exhibited by the Advocate, evidence appears to the contrary of the informers being an Officer of right at the time of making the seizure, as far as a negative can. The reservation in the Acts made in these Words, "unless by other Evidence the contrary shall be made to appear," entitles even a claimer, a fortiori his Majesty, to prove if he can; that the Officer seizing, notwithstanding his being reputed and acting as such, really was not, otherwise the statutes are justly chargable with one of the greatest irregularities known in the law, in preferring the lowest kind of evidence to the highest. To support the words "other evidence to the contrary" intend to confine the evidence to a persons being an Officer de facto, in exclusion of an enquiry if one de jure, must render the Acts totally ridiculous. Because when once the fact of his being an Officer de facto is established by positive evidence, it must be impossible negatively to prove the contrary. In short, tho' the acts give great releif to Officers even claimers are not by force thereof left remediless, nor do the Acts place persons proving their reputation as Officers absolutely beyond the inspection and reach of law. But the burthen of Strict legal proof is by force of the same acts removed from the Officer, in certain Cases; and if the Claimer or prosecutor would avail himself against the proof resulting from reputation, he is obliged to produce legal evidence, that notwithstanding such reputation the person seizing either was never commissioned, or if he was, the authority thereby conferred was determined, or he had exceeded his Authority. Therefore I do adjudge and decree, that said Acts are not sufficient to authorize the informer to prosecute said information without shewing a further right so to do.

I shall next determine what influence the rules of the common law touching Officers de facto ought to have in this cause.

Those rules appear to me to be calculated only to make such as presume to act as Marshall or Mayor &c. without being completely qualified, answerable for their own misconduct, in cases where the Interest

of others is concerned, but not to extend to such as immediately tend to
their own private advantage.[72] They are institutions to prevent mischeifs happening to some, through an undue exercise of power by
others, rather than to give a sanction to it for the sole benefit of the
Actors. It is but just that he who undertakes as a publick Officer the
Execution of any thing without a full Authority for so doing, and of
which he is to be the judge in the first instance, and does it in such a
manner as renders another a sufferer, should be adjudged accountable
therefor. But It by no means follows that such an undertaker should
advance his own Interest by his own wrong Act, in direct opposition to
the legal Officer: Therefore the law cases above alluded to and the one
in trial materially differ from each other. Also the cases of the parson
and bishop appear to me not applicable to the present dispute, for the
same and other reasons.[73] In both the latter instances their acts which
may be considered as judicial, are allowed good for the benefit of others
their inferiours in the law sense and so not obliged to know the legality
of the induction of the parson, or the deprivation or removal of the
Bishop; Where a Bishop de facto does an act which charges the possession of the bishoprick, as a lease of lands, it is void.[74] The true
reason of which I take to be, he shall not by any act advance his own
private interest, and thereby deprive an Officer de jure of his. This
case is more applicable to the present dispute than any of the others.
And indeed without observing this rule all distinction between Officers
de facto and de jure must cease. But to close this subject the very
making of the acts [75] evidently shew that at common law, Officers of
the Customs could not be sufficiently guarded by proving themselves
such de facto: then consequently none of those rules abstractedly were
able to support the doings of such an Officer, even when the contest was
not between him and the King, but a Claimer. So that tho' by the
Exhibits in the case it is both proved and granted that the informer was

[72] A reference to the cases from Viner cited by Otis, notes 55–58 above. At the
same place in the *Abridgment* it is also stated, "He who occupies as *Marshal* in B.R.
be he Officer of Right or by Tort, shall be *charged with the Escapes*. Br. Escape, pl.
18, cites 39 H. 6. 33." 16 Viner, *Abridgment*, tit. [Officers and] Offices, G. 3, pl. 1.

[73] The case of the parson is evidently the following passage in Viner not taken
down by JA: "Where an *Abbot or Parson* is inducted *erroneously*, and makes a Grant
or Obligation, and after is *deprived or dereigned for Precontract* or such like, this
shall bind; because *he was an Abbot* or Parson in *Possession*, but *a Usurper* who
usurps before Installation, or Induction, or Presentation, where another Abbot or
Parson is Rightfully in Possession, or if one enters, and occupies in the Time of
Vacation *without any Election* or Presentation, the Deed of such is void. Br. Non est
Factum, pl. 3, cites 9 H. 6. 32." 16 Viner, *Abridgment*, tit. [Officers and] Offices,
G. 4, pl. 1.

[74] See note 57 above.

[75] The statutes of Geo. 1, notes 48, 49, above.

an Officer de facto, yet as the Statutes allow of proof being made against his being one de jure, and the common law does not avail him in this point, I am next to enquire what proof there is of his being the latter.

The proof of this point arises out of his Commission and the Authority of the late surveyor general to grant the same. It is certain the informer was by said commission created, if any thing, either a New Officer, or deputy surveyor general. It could not be a deputation as searcher and preventive Officer, if there had been any such Office known, because the surveyor general could not make a deputy to another Officer, that power being lodged only in the principal. As to the first, considering that the Island of Nantuckett is a member of the port of Boston, it is necessary to examine whether the late surveyor general had any authority, without positive orders or instructions from the Commissioners of the Customs in England under the direction of the Commissioners of the treasury to create new Officers, when there were proper Officers of the port duly commissioned and acting; and secondly if not, whether by the said Commission the Informer was deputy surveyor general.

As the statute did confine the appointment of the Officers of the Customs to the Lord treasurer Commissioners of the treasury and Commissioners of the Customs in England for the time being,[76] it is impossible that any surveyor general could legally appoint or create new Offices and Officers without an authority for so doing from those who by the law had that power. It was said in the argument, that the late surveyor general had equal authority with the Commissioners of the Customs in England but it was neither attempted or possible to be proved on an inspection of his instructions as far as relate to this enquiery and consideration thereof.[77] I do not perceive any thing which

---

[76] 7 & 8 Will. 3, c. 22, §11 (1696), note 52 above. Compare No. 50.

[77] Temple's instructions and commission have unfortunately not been found. For the powers of surveyors general, see note 2 above.

When Temple's predecessor, Thomas Lechmere, suspended Benjamin Barons in 1759 (prior to his dismissal in 1761, note 44 above), he appointed George Cradock temporary collector, relying on the powers given him by the Commissioners of Customs "for managing and causing to be levied and collected His Majesty's customs," and "to appoint officers that may be for the service of His Majesty's Revenue." See Cradock's commission, 13 Dec. 1759, SF 172363. Lechmere used this formula in other appointments. See Book of Commissions, 1756–1767, fols. 80–81, 203, M-Ar. Temple contented himself with reciting "the Powers and Authority to me given." See Folger's commission, note 45 above, and examples cited, note 6 above. Accompanying the American Commissioners' reply to the Treasury on Folger's memorial in 1769 (note 30 above), were extracts from letters of the English Commissioners in 1740 and 1765 in which they had questioned not the Surveyor General's authority to appoint deputy collectors, but the wisdom and propriety of

proves or has a tendency to prove a power in him to create new Offices or Officers. His power of suspending for misbehavior, and appointing others in the places of the persons so suspended or of such as decease by no means can be extended to create new officers ad libitum. The former is a contracted and limitted power, and was usually lodged with all surveyor generals by the Commissioners of the Customs, and founded in necessity. The latter comprehends almost all the powers of both the Commissioners of the treasury and Customs and it is not to be supposed they ever delegated such Authority to any person whatsoever, there being neither necessity or law for so doing. It was urged in favor of such appointments of the Surveyor generals, that great inconveniences will follow if they are not adjudged valid, as many have been made, particularly one at Plymouth a member of this port.[78] If the fact is so, of which there is no evidence excepting the instance at Plymouth, it ought not to regulate a judgment on the validity of such appointments, because that would be Establishing a practice not founded in law, in opposition to law. Nor can I conceive it the duty of [a] judge to depart from the law to cure inconveniences resulting from the misapprehensions of any other Officer, without something very express to warrant his so doing. Secondly if the late surveyor general had authority to appoint a deputy, which is very supposeable though not proved, it is clear he has not executed that power in the appointment of the informer, but attempted one entirely different, and therefore it is not a deputation as Surveyor general. These two points being determined makes a minute enquiry into the objection of the said commissions being superceded by the appointment of the Commissioners of the Customs in North America and

his doing so without consulting them. PRO, Treas. 1:471, fols. 192–193; Wolkins, "Boston Customs District," 58 MHS, *Procs.* 432–433. This material does not seem to have been put in evidence, perhaps because it dealt with the office of collector, rather than that of preventive officer.

[78] See Temple's appointments, including that of Edward Winslow at Plymouth, in note 6 above. The "inconvenience" was simple enough to remedy. The Commissioners confirmed Winslow in his office and either confirmed or replaced other Temple appointees. Samuel Proctor was appointed to Folger's place, but was forced from the island in the fall of 1768. PRO, Treas. 1:471, fols. 461–463; *Boston News-Letter*, 11 Aug. 1768, p. 2, col. 1; Minutes of the Commissioners, 15 March 1768, 7 Bowdoin-Temple MSS 151–153, MHi; *Massachusetts Gazette*, 3 Nov. 1768, p. 1, col. 3. Although it does not seem to have been put in evidence, Temple's predecessors had been appointing officers at Nantucket since at least 1740, a fact which was relied on in this case by both sides in their memorials to the Treasury. Folger claimed that it showed the antiquity of the practice; the Commissioners pointed out that the English Commissioners had often rejected such appointments. See Wolkins, "Boston Customs District," 58 MHS, *Procs.* 432–433; PRO, Treas. 1:471, fols. 363–365, 366–367; Minutes of Commissioners, 15 March 1768, 7 Bowdoin-Temple MSS 152–153, MHi.

their exercise of that Office, needless; I shall therefore only say, that neither the statute of Ann, or of his present Majesty extend to any deputations save those granted by the Commissioners of the Customs in England.[79] These acts also prove the legislature never conceived of or had in contemplation any other appointments then such as were made by the Commissioners of the Customs in England as aforesaid. If they had, doubtless the death and removal of surveyor generals would have been guarded against, as well as that of the commissioners. Those who made the last act must certainly have known, that the Office of surveyor general was merged in that of the Commissioners: therefore it is against reason to imagine, it was intended first to destroy the Office of principal, and secondly, to secure his deputys, or to extend the words of the proviso expressly mentioning certain Officers, to others probably not known, and if known, certainly not noticed. Therefore haveing fully heard the Kings Advocate and the Advocates for the informer and after a mature consideration of their arguments and of all the statutes and authoritys quoted and used, proofs allegations and exhibits adduced in the cause, I decree the information against the aforesaid sloop and tea filed by the said Timothy Folger to be dismissed.   Rob[ert] Auchmuty Judge
April 2d. 1768.

46. Sewall v. Hancock

1768–1769

EDITORIAL NOTE

In November 1768 Adams undertook the defense of John Hancock in what, politically, was his most important case until the Boston Massacre trials (Nos. 63, 64). Jonathan Sewall, the advocate general, had sued Hancock in Admiralty for penalties incident upon the alleged smuggling of wine from the latter's sloop *Liberty*. The circumstances of this prosecution and portions of Adams' defense were carried in a variety of contemporary newspapers and played a leading part in the development of colonial opposition to the British customs system and Vice Admiralty courts.

The case arose in a Boston already antagonized by the activities of the recently formed American Board of Customs Commissioners. The fate of Timothy Folger and the sloop *Cornelia* (No. 45), must have convinced the town, if proof were needed, that the Commissioners had no interest in the

---

[79] 12 Anne, Stat. 2, c. 8, §13 (1713), note 50 above; 7 Geo. 3, c. 41, §3 (1767), note 53 above.

kind of benign administration that might have permitted an accommodation between the stringencies of the Townshend Acts of 1767 and the realities of commercial life. In the forefront of mounting opposition to the Board and the Acts was Hancock, leading merchant, Boston selectman, and representative to the General Court, who must have been pleased to find that he could so easily combine his zest for politicking with pursuit of his commercial interest. His political tactics included a variety of threats, boasts, and social snubs, nicely calculated both to offend the Commissioners and to arouse the public.[1]

On the commercial side, Hancock's opposition was less flamboyant, but no less determined. In early April, he had found Owen Richards, one of two tidesmen sent to supervise the discharge of his brigantine *Lydia,* poking around in the hold of that vessel. Hancock ordered Richards forcibly brought topside, making clear that he considered the deck to be the limit of the officer's jurisdiction.[2] Attempts to prosecute Hancock in the Superior Court for this incident were frustrated when Jonathan Sewall gave his opinion as attorney general that no offense had been committed and refused to put the matter in suit. The Commissioners wrote to England asking that Sewall be overruled.[3] Before a reply could be received, the affair of the *Liberty* gave them a better opportunity to make an example of their chief tormentor.

The sloop had arrived in Boston from Madeira on 9 May; next day, Nathaniel Barnard, her master, made entry of twenty-five pipes of madeira wine, upon which the duties were paid.[4] According to the later testimony of various royal officials, Hancock had boasted that he would land wine from his vessel without payment of duties, and rumors were rife that he had done so.[5] The customs officers had to be satisfied with rumor until, on

---

[1] See W. T. Baxter, *The House of Hancock* 260–263 (Cambridge, Mass., 1945). For one customs officer's view of the situation, see Joseph Harrison to the Marquis of Rockingham, 17 June 1768, in Watson, "Joseph Harrison and the Liberty Incident," 20 *WMQ* (3d ser.) 585, 587–589 (1963).

[2] See deposition of Owen Richards and Robert Jackson, 11 April 1768, PRO, Treas. 1:465, fols. 351–353; Ubbelohde, *Vice Admiralty Courts* 119–121. Richards was to suffer more violent physical opposition to his role. See *Richards v. Doble*, Pleadings Book, Form VI.

[3] See the Memorial of the Commissioners, 12 May 1768, enclosing the depositions of Richards and Jackson, note 2 above; the opinion of Samuel Fitch, Solicitor to the Commissioners, in favor of prosecution; and the opinion of Sewall, PRO, Treas. 1:465, fols. 348–360. Sewall's opinion, 23 April 1768, is reprinted in Dickerson, "Opinion of Attorney General Sewall of Massachusetts in the Case of the *Lydia*," 4 *WMQ* (3d ser.) 499, 501–504 (1947). Thomas Hutchinson also questioned the wisdom of prosecution in the matter. See Hutchinson to ———, 17 April 1768, 26 Mass. Arch. 299–300. In Oct. the Commissioners again ordered Hancock's prosecution in the Superior Court, but no record of any action has been found. Minutes of the American Board of Customs Commissioners, 20 Oct. 1768, 7 Bowdoin-Temple MSS 167, MHi.

[4] The duty had been levied since 1764. See note 86 below.

[5] The arrival and entry of the *Liberty* and Hancock's boasts are described in Opinion of William DeGrey, 25 July 1768, PRO, Treas. 1:463, fol. 85, printed in Wolkins, "The Seizure of John Hancock's Sloop 'Liberty,'" 55 MHS, *Procs.* 239, 273

10 June, Thomas Kirk, a tidesman who at the time of the *Liberty's* arrival had reported nothing amiss, now made affidavit to a different story. On the night of 9 May, he testified, one Captain Marshall came aboard and, after failing to persuade Kirk to allow several casks of wine to be unloaded before the vessel's entry the next day, locked him in the steerage. Confined for about three hours, Kirk "heard a Noise as of many people upon deck at Work hoisting out Goods," as well as "the Noise of the Tackles." He was released when the activity ceased, but Marshall's dire threats had kept him silent; Marshall had since died, and Kirk no longer feared to come forward.[6]

Joseph Harrison, Collector of the port, presented Kirk's affidavit to the Commissioners. Corroboration was impossible, Kirk's fellow tidesman being variously reported as asleep or drunk during the hours in question, but the Commissioners and their solicitor determined that the affidavit was grounds for a seizure of the *Liberty* for violation of the statutory provisions against unloading before entry. Harrison and Benjamin Hallowell, the Comptroller, were ordered to make the seizure. To avoid the possibility that the townspeople might rescue the vessel, the Commissioners suggested that the officers obtain the assistance of H.M.S. *Romney*, which had arrived in the harbor on 17 May in response to the urgent pleas of the Board that it could not enforce the laws without such assistance.[7]

At about sunset on the 10th, with the tide near full, Harrison, Hallowell, and a number of lesser officers proceeded to Hancock's wharf, where the *Liberty* lay, loaded with two hundred barrels of oil and a few barrels of tar. According to a contemporary account, these goods were not cargo for another voyage, but had been put aboard for storage, there being no room in the warehouses along the wharf.[8] The officers boarded the sloop,

---

(1921–1922); Thomas Hutchinson to Richard Jackson, 16 June 1768, 26 Mass. Arch. 310–312, printed in 55 MHS, *Procs.* 281; Examination of Benjamin Hallowell, Treasury Chambers, 21 July 1768, *American Gazette* (No. 6) 449 (London, 2d edn., 1770); Testimony of Joseph Harrison, 27 June 1770, 5 *Acts, Privy Council* (*Col.*) 254; see also Baxter, *Hancock* 263 note.

[6] Deposition of Thomas Kirk, 10 June 1768, PRO, Treas. 1:465, fol. 72; Opinion of William DeGrey, 55 MHS, *Procs.* 273–274. Marshall, one of Hancock's captains, died on 10 May, allegedly from overexertion in the unloading. *Boston Gazette*, 16 May 1768, p. 3, col. 1. See Andrew Oliver to Francis Bernard, 3 Dec. 1769, 12 Bernard Papers 164, MH; Oliver, *Origin and Progress* 69.

[7] For the decision to seize the vessel and seek aid from the *Romney*, see Minutes of the Commissioners, 13 June 1768, PRO, Treas. 1:465, fol. 67; letter of Harrison and Hallowell to Commissioners, 11 June 1768, *id.* at fol. 88; letter of Harrison to John Powell, 13 June 1768, 3 Chalmers New England MSS 2, MH; Harrison to Rockingham, 17 June 1768, 20 *WMQ* (3d ser.) 589–590 (1963); Examination of Hallowell, 21 July 1768, *American Gazette* (No. 6) 449; Testimony of Harrison, 27 June 1770, 5 *Acts, Privy Council* (*Col.*) 255. For the requests of the Commissioners for naval support and the arrival of the *Romney*, see Samuel Venner (Secretary of the Board) to Thomas Bradshaw, 3 June 1768, PRO, Treas. 1:465, fol. 149; *Boston Gazette*, 23 May 1768, p. 3, col. 1; Wolkins, "Liberty," 55 MHS, *Procs.* 239, 246 note, 248, 271–272.

[8] As to the lading, see *Boston News-Letter*, 16 June 1768, p. 2, col. 1; *Boston Evening-Post*, 20 June 1768, p. 2, col. 1. Sunset was at 7:33 P.M. and high tide

went through the formalities of seizing her, and signaled the *Romney*, at anchor nearby. Two boats of marines and sailors came to the wharf and set about taking the *Liberty* in charge. Meanwhile a crowd, including Captain Daniel Malcom (long an enemy of the revenue) and a number of other waterfront figures known to be friendly to Hancock, had gathered. Despite assurances from the mob that there would be no interference with the seizure, and efforts to hold the vessel to the wharf, the marines cut her loose and, with the consent of Harrison and Hallowell, towed her out into the harbor, where she was moored under the guns of the *Romney*.[9]

A small riot then ensued, in the course of which Harrison and Hallowell were roughed up, windows in their houses were smashed, and the Collector's pleasure boat was burned on the Common.[10] The Commissioners, fearing that they would be next, went into hiding and the next day transferred their operations to the *Romney*. Harrison began to negotiate with Hancock for the return of the *Liberty* in exchange for a bond for her value to abide the outcome of proceedings against her in the Court of Admiralty.[11] Meanwhile, Boston remained in an uproar, stimulated by a series of town meetings at which fiery orations were delivered. John Adams' first connection with the case was his service upon a committee appointed by the Town to draw up instructions to its representatives.[12] Hancock at length

---

at 7:38 P.M. on 10 June. John Mein and John Fleeming, *Register . . . 1768* 18 (Boston, 1768). The accounts in note 9 below vary as to the time of the seizure according to the politics of the declarant. In question was a mistaken understanding that the limitation in the writ of assistance to daylight activities applied to seizures. 3 Hutchinson, *Massachusetts Bay*, ed. Mayo, 138 note; *Boston Gazette*, Supp., 23 Jan. 1769, p. 1, col. 3. Actually no writ was necessary to board, search, and seize a vessel. See 13 & 14 Car. 2, c. 11, §§4, 5 (1662); 7 & 8 Will. 3, c. 22, §6 (1696). The time was doubtless dictated in part by a delay in making the decision to seize, and in part by a desire to catch the tide. See Harrison to Powell, 13 June 1768, 3 Chalmers New England MSS 2, MH.

[9] See the following accounts of the seizure: *Boston News-Letter*, 16 June 1768, p. 2, col. 1; Deposition of Harrison, 11 June 1768, PRO, Treas. 1:465, fol. 74; Deposition of Hallowell, 11 June 1768, *id.* at fol. 76; Harrison to Rockingham, 17 June 1768, 20 *WMQ* (3d ser.) 590 (1963); Testimony of Harrison, 27 June 1770, 5 *Acts, Privy Council (Col.)* 255; Affidavits accompanying Boston, "A Letter from Boston to a Gentleman in London," *American Gazette* (No. 2) 97–110 (London, 2d edn., 1768). As to Malcom, see Wolkins, "Daniel Malcom and Writs of Assistance," 58 MHS, *Procs.* 14–15 (1924–1925).

[10] For the riot, see sources cited in note 9 above.

[11] Harrison to Rockingham, 17 June 1768, 20 *WMQ* (3d ser.) 592 (1963); Examination of Hallowell, 21 July 1768, *American Gazette* (No. 6) 450; Minutes of the Commissioners and other materials, 12–14 June 1768, PRO, Treas. 1:465, fol. 67–107; Testimony of Hallowell, 26 June 1770, 5 *Acts, Privy Council (Col.)* 250. For the negotiations and an account of events in Boston generally, see John Cary, *Joseph Warren* 74–79 (Urbana, Ill., 1961). The flight to the *Romney* marked John Temple's open break with the rest of the Board. Thereafter he participated in their routine activities, but opposed them on all political matters. See Barrow, *Colonial Customs* 480–487. All subsequent references to "the Board" or "the Commissioners" refer to the four-man majority, exclusive of Temple.

[12] PRO, Treas. 1:465, fols. 70–71, 92–93, 112–113; 16 Boston Record Commissioners, *Reports* 253–259 (Boston, 1886). The Instructions, of which JA claimed

declined to stipulate for the vessel, apparently on the theory that her continued presence in the harbor would serve to keep the Town reminded of the incident.[13] After the failure of this step at conciliation, the Commissioners chose to view the situation in Boston as one of serious emergency; and, when Governor Bernard reported that he could not guarantee their personal safety in town, they took up residence at Castle William in Boston Harbor. From this retreat the North American customs were managed until mid-November, when the presence of troops and Governor Bernard's assurances finally eased the Commissioners' fears.[14]

While the Commissioners languished, Jonathan Sewall on 22 June filed a libel in behalf of Joseph Harrison against the *Liberty* and the oil and tar aboard her at the seizure.[15] Although no papers in the suit have survived, the grounds were probably three: (1) landing goods before entry, as Kirk had sworn; (2) loading the oil and tar without having given bond; and (3) loading the oil and tar without having a sufferance from the Collector. For the first, the penalty was forfeiture of the vessel;[16] for the

the authorship and which were adopted by the Town on 17 June, were first printed in the *Boston Gazette*, 20 June, and reprinted in 3 JA, *Works* 501–504. See 3 JA, *Diary and Autobiography* 291; Cary, *Joseph Warren* 77–78.

[13] See sources cited, note 11 above. On 15 June Hancock's warehouse was burgled and his papers "displaced." *Massachusetts Gazette*, 16 June 1768, p. 1, col. 1. This may have been an effort on the part of the Commissioners to find evidence linking him with the *Liberty*'s alleged cargo. See Dickerson, *Navigation Acts* 243.

[14] See Commissioners to Governor Bernard, 12 June 1768, PRO, Treas. 1:465, fols. 86–87; 13 June 1768, *id.* at fols. 100–101; Bernard to Commissioners, 13 June 1768, *id.* at fol. 102; Collector and Comptroller to Commissioners, 14 June 1768, *id.* at fols. 106–107; Commissioners to Commodore Hood, General Gage, Col. Dalrymple, 15 June 1768, id. at fols. 108–111. The troops were requested in July; two regiments arrived in Boston at the end of Sept., and two in early November. It was not until the second week of Nov. that the Commissioners felt sufficiently sure of their safety to venture back to Boston. Commissioners to Treasury, 11 July 1768, PRO, Treas. 1:465, fol. 420; Venner to Bradshaw, 26 Nov. 1768, *id.* at fols. 127–138; *Massachusetts Gazette*, 10 Nov. 1768, p. 1, col. 3; Rowe, *Letters and Diary* 175–176. It is possible that they were awaiting the public reaction to the *in personam* suits against Hancock and the others, in which process was served on 3 November. See note 30 below.

[15] Joseph Harrison Esq. v. The Sloop *Liberty*, 20 Barrels of Tar, 200 Barrels of Oil, Vice Adm. Min. Bk., 22 June 1768. See *Boston News-Letter*, 23 June 1768, p. 2, col. 1. Samuel Fitch was also of counsel for the Crown, and David Lisle, solicitor to the Commissioners, assisted in the preparation for trial. Minutes of the Commissioners, 8 Aug. 1768, PRO, Treas. 1:471, fol. 7.

[16] 15 Car. 2, c. 7, §8 (1663), set out in No. 48, note 10. See Opinion of William DeGrey, PRO, Treas. 1:463, fol. 87, printed in 55 MHS, *Procs.* 276. The violation of a statutory requirement that entry be made before unlading was the only possible basis for proceeding against the *Liberty* on the alleged smuggling. The statutes levying penalties for landing goods without payment of duties provided for the forfeiture of the goods alone (6 Geo. 2, c. 13, §3, made applicable by 4 Geo. 3, c. 15, §5), or for pecuniary penalties against the smugglers themselves (4 Geo. 3, c. 15, §37). For proceedings under the former, see No. 47; the latter was the basis of the later *in personam* proceedings against Hancock; see notes 26, 82, below. A suit based on 6 Geo. 2, c. 13, was presumably impossible, the wines having been dispersed. 4 Geo. 3, c. 15, presented evidentiary problems, as subsequent events demonstrated. See text

second, vessel and goods were forfeit; [17] and for the third the goods alone were forfeit.[18] The second and third counts would have been included to justify seizing the oil and tar and retaining it aboard the *Liberty* as she lay under the *Romney's* protection. To have brought the sloop back to the wharf for discharge would have exposed her to rescue. These counts, of course, had the additional value of further harassing Hancock by complicating the suit and by tying up his goods pending the outcome.

The identity of Hancock's counsel in this *in rem* proceeding is not known. He may well have been Adams, who had recently tried Timothy Folger's action against the sloop *Cornelia* (No. 45), in which Hancock was a witness. Adams was doubtless on hand in the summer of 1768, since he had recently moved to Boston [19] and had no cases on circuit with the Superior Court in June or July. Whoever Hancock's lawyer was, he did not let the forfeiture go by default. An appearance was entered on 7 July and, after several continuances, Hancock's claim was filed on the 29th. Counsel had earlier agreed that witnesses should be examined by the Register upon interrogatories filed by the parties. On 4 August, Judge Auchmuty himself attended the examination of two witnesses, Captain Malcom and William Mackay. Auchmuty gave his decree on 17 August, declaring the *Liberty* forfeit, but releasing the oil and tar.[20] No copy of the decree exists, but it

at note 44 below. Moreover, under both acts proof had to be made that dutiable goods had been landed, whereas under 15 Car. 2, c. 7, §8, only the landing before entry need be shown. The statute 1 Eliz. 1, c. 11, §2 (1558), forbidding landing of goods except in the daylight would also have been ineffective, since it provided for seizure of goods, not vessel. See No. 49, notes 14–17.

[17] Vessel and goods were forfeit if either enumerated or nonenumerated goods were loaded before bond was given. 12 Car. 2, c. 18, §19 (1660); 22 & 23 Car. 2, c. 26, §11 (1670); 6 Geo. 3, c. 52, §30 (1766). Tar was enumerated and oil was not. 3 & 4 Anne, c. 10, §8 (1704); Samuel Baldwin, *A Survey of the British Customs,* pt. 2, p. 201 (London, 1770).

[18] 4 Geo. 3, c. 15, §29 (1764).

[19] At the end of April. Elizabeth Smith to Isaac Smith Jr., 13–18 April 1768, 1 *Adams Family Correspondence* 63–66.

[20] See Harrison v. The *Liberty,* et al., Vice Adm. Min. Bk., 22 June 1768. The date and substance of the decree are known only from a contemporary newspaper report that "Wednesday the 17th the Hon. Robert Auchmuty Esq. Judge of Admiralty for this province, decreed the sloop Liberty, seized the 10th of June last, to be forfeited; but the 200 barrels oil, and six barrels tar, which were on board her when seized, were cleared." *Boston Chronicle,* 22 Aug. 1768, p. 331, col. 3; *Boston Post-Boy,* 22 Aug. 1768, p. 1, col. 3. This result is confirmed by the order of sale, dated 31 Aug. 1768, which dealt with the vessel alone. *Massachusetts Gazette,* 1 Sept. 1768, p. 1, col. 2. Sewall's conduct of the cause, although successful, was not vigorous enough to suit the Commissioners. They found that he had been dragging his feet because he had been informed by Samuel Venner, their secretary, that they had criticized his conduct in the matter of the *Lydia* to the Treasury. This episode apparently had something to do with the delay in prosecuting Hancock *in personam* and may even have affected the outcome of that suit. See notes 27–28, 42, below. Although Sewall remained in favor, Venner was finally suspended by the Board. See Minutes of Commissioners, 8 Aug. 1768, PRO, Treas. 1:471, fols. 7–8. Other materials are in *id.* at fols. 1–88, 303–312, 435–436, 492–502. See also Clark, "American Board of Customs," 45 *AHR* 791 note; Dickerson, "John Hancock," 32 *MVHR* 517, 532–534 (1946).

apparently condemned the *Liberty* for unlading without entry, and cleared the oil and tar as having been loaded for storage rather than shipment.[21] On 6 September, the sloop was put up for sale and purchased by Harrison for the Commissioners, who proceeded to have her fitted out as a revenue cutter. In this capacity she served until July 1769, when a Rhode Island

[21] It has been argued that the *Liberty* was seized and condemned solely for having loaded oil and tar without bond or permit, a technical offense against a requirement that had not previously been enforced in Boston. The loading is said to have been made the basis for the suit, because it provided ground for condemnation more readily provable than unloading before entry, and at the same time allowed the customs officers and Governor Bernard to take the proceeds of the cargo as well as of the vessel. Dickerson, *Navigation Acts* 237–238. See also Lovejoy, "Rights Imply Equality: The Case against Admiralty Jurisdiction in America, 1764–1776," 16 *WMQ* (3d ser.) 459, 478 (1959); Ubbelohde, *Vice Admiralty Courts* 121–122. This view was followed in 3 JA, *Diary and Autobiography* 306 note. The files of the Vice Admiralty Court are lost, but secondary materials support the contrary position on several grounds: (1) There is complete unanimity in the contemporary accounts of the various royal officials concerned that Kirk's deposition of 10 June as to the unloading and the opinion of the Board's solicitor thereon provided the immediate impetus for the seizure. See materials cited in notes 7, 9, above; also, Commissioners' Minutes, 8 Aug. 1768, PRO, Treas. 1:471, fols. 7, 8; Bernard to Lord Hillsborough, 11 June 1768, 6 Bernard Papers 311, MH; Hutchinson to Richard Jackson, 16 June 1768, 55 MHS, *Procs.* 281. The case was presented to Attorney General DeGrey for his opinion on this basis. Opinion of William DeGrey, 25 July 1768, 55 MHS, *Procs.* 273–276. (2) The only accounts which mention the failure to secure bond or permit indicate that this was an alternative ground for the seizure. *Boston News-Letter*, 16 June 1768, p. 2, col. 1; 3 Hutchinson, *Massachusetts Bay*, ed. Mayo, 137 (The latter states expressly that the vessel was seized for false entry, and the goods for lack of a permit). (3) Dickerson's argument that the use of a writ of assistance to search the *Liberty* shows that her present cargo, rather than her past misdeeds, was the basis for the seizure, seems to be based on a misreading of Hutchinson's account of the question raised by the fact that the seizure was at sunset. See note 8 above. No contemporary account mentions a writ of assistance. (4) If the suit had been based only on loading without bond or permit, the oil and tar would certainly have been condemned with the vessel. The release of the goods (note 20 above) indicates that there was no violation of the bond and sufferance provisions at all. See also Hutchinson to ——, ca. 3 Nov. 1768, 26 Mass. Arch. 324–325. (5) In all the furor which the Town of Boston produced in print as a result of the seizure and its aftermath, there is not a single complaint that the cause of seizure was the technical, and therefore unjust, one of loading without bond or permit. Boston's position was that the employment of the *Romney*, already despised for the impressment activities of her captain, brought on the riot of 10 June; this was the basis of all subsequent complaints. See Instructions to Boston Representatives, 17 June 1768, 16 Boston Record Commissioners, *Reports* 258; "A Letter from Boston to a Gentleman in London," 15 June 1768, *American Gazette* (No. 2) 97–110; *An Appeal to the World, or a Vindication of the Town of Boston* 14–17 (London, 1770); *Letters to the Right Honorable the Earl of Hillsborough from Governor Bernard, General Gage, and the Honorable His Majesty's Council* 44 (London, 1770); *Observations on Several Acts of Parliament* 19 note (Boston, 1769). See also Cary, *Joseph Warren* 75–76. (6) One contemporary account favorable to Boston states that the seizure and condemnation of the *Liberty* were "for a non-entry of a part of her cargo of Madeiria wines." "A Journal of the Times," 3 Nov. 1768, in Dickerson, *Boston under Military Rule* 18. An early historian of the Revolution, who had access both to documents and personal accounts in Boston, states that the seizure was for a false entry. 1 Gordon, *History of Independence* 231.

mob seized and burned her at Newport in wrath over the enforcement activities of her commander, Captain William Reid.[22]

The focus now shifted to those responsible for running the wine and fomenting riot. Efforts to indict the rioters before the Suffolk Grand Jury in August were effectively forestalled when Boston returned Captain Malcom and other alleged participants as jurors.[23] On 2 September the Commissioners directed their solicitor to consult with the advocate general as to prosecuting "the master of the Sloop Liberty and all persons concerned in running the cargo for treble the value of the goods run." [24] During the summer, in response to a request from the Lords of the Treasury for an opinion on a memorial submitted by the Commissioners, William DeGrey, Attorney General in England, had found that there was not only a basis for proceeding against the vessel, but that "Actions may likewise be brought against the Persons concern'd in the unshipping the Goods, and in obstructing the Seizure." [25] Emboldened or coerced by this opinion, Sewall on 29 October filed informations against Hancock and five others, including Nathaniel Barnard, master of the *Liberty*, and Daniel Malcom.[26]

[22] On the sale, see *Massachusetts Gazette*, 1 Sept. 1768, p. 1, col. 2; *Boston Evening-Post*, 12 Sept. 1768, p. 3, col. 1. Governor Bernard received his third on 9 Nov. 1768. Vice Adm. Min. Bk., 22 June 1768. The *Liberty* sold for £102 15s. 1/2d; the expense of fitting her out as a cutter was £813 18s. 9d. Commissioners to Treasury, 28 July 1769, quoted in Wolkins, "Liberty," 55 MHS, *Procs.* 261 note 3. Full details regarding her destruction may be found in PRO, Treas. 1:471, fols. 200–225, 289–292, 371–385. See also *Boston Gazette*, 24 July 1769, p. 2, col. 3; Quincy, *Reports* (Appendix) 456–457; Wolkins, "Liberty," 55 MHS, *Procs.* 261 note. Baxter is incorrect in identifying the *Liberty* with the *Gaspee*, destroyed below Providence in June 1772. Baxter, *Hancock* 268. See Edward Channing, *A History of the United States*, 3:125 (N.Y. 1912).

[23] See Bernard to Hillsborough, 9 Sept. 1768, 7 Bernard Papers 26, 27, MH. The *venire* for the Aug. term of the Superior Court in Suffolk County includes Daniel Malcom among the Grand Jurors from Boston. SF 101222.

[24] Minutes of the Commissioners, 2 Sept. 1768, 7 Bowdoin-Temple MSS 166, MHi.

[25] Opinion of William DeGrey, 55 MHS, *Procs.* 273–276. The memorial of the Commissioners, which with its enclosures, is found in PRO, Treas. 1:465, fols. 67–121, was carried to England by Benjamin Hallowell, who presented the case personally to the Treasury. See Examination of Benjamin Hallowell, 21 July 1768, *American Gazette* (No. 6) 450; Dickerson, *Navigation Acts* 241, 261 note; Wolkins, "Liberty," 55 MHS, *Procs.* 260. DeGrey's opinion could not have reached Massachusetts in time to affect the *in rem* proceeding, but it was undoubtedly the basis for the *in personam* actions. See Hillsborough to Bernard, 13 Aug. 1768, 11 Bernard Papers 285, MH.

[26] Vice Adm. Min. Bk., 29 Oct. 1768. See "A Journal of the Times," 31 Oct. 1768, Dickerson, *Boston under Military Rule* 16. The other respondents were John Matchet, William Bowes, and Lewis Gray. Vice Adm. Min. Bk., 29 Oct. 1768. The citation against Barnard was not served, no doubt because he had gone to sea. *Id.*, 21 Nov. 1768. He was lost on a voyage from Madeira in June 1769. A. Oliver to F. Bernard, 3 Dec. 1769, 12 Bernard Papers 164, MH; *Boston Gazette*, 17 July 1769, p. 3, col. 2. On 29 Oct. Sewall also brought actions against Malcom and three others for unloading wines from the schooner *Friendship* in Feb., after Malcom had unsuccessfully sought a reduction in duties from the customs. In these informations £2400 was sought from each respondent and bail was set at £800. Vice Adm. Min. Bk., 29 Oct. 1768; *Observations on Several Acts of Parliament* 19 note (Boston,

His delay had probably resulted, at least in part, from a prudent desire to wait until excitement over the arrival of the first troops in September had died down and they were in place and ready to be of assistance.[27]

The suits were based on a provision of the American Act of 1764 that persons "assisting or otherwise concerned" in landing goods without payment of duties should forfeit treble the value of the goods in a proceeding in the Court of Admiralty. Despite a certain vagueness in the language of the information, it is clear that Sewall brought the actions as informer. In this capacity he was entitled to a third of the proceeds, which may have been the price of his abandonment of an earlier reluctance to proceed in such an unpopular cause.[28] The information against Hancock alleged that he had aided and assisted in landing one hundred pipes of Madeira wine valued at £30 sterling each, knowing that the duties had not been paid. The penalty sought was £9,000, treble the value of the wine. Judge Auchmuty set bail at £3,000 and ordered a warrant to issue for Hancock's appearance on 7 November.[29] According to the patriot propaganda sheet, "A Journal of the Times," the warrants were served on 3 November by "Mr. Arodi Thayer, marshal of the Court of Admiralty for three provinces, with a hanger at his side." After offers of property and Massachusetts currency for bail were refused, Hancock and the others produced the amount demanded in sterling.[30]

1769); Minutes of Commissioners, 10 Oct. 1768, 7 Bowdoin-Temple MSS 167, MHi; Bernard to Shelburne, 21 March 1768, 6 Bernard Papers 289–290, MH. These suits were dismissed with Hancock's on 25 March 1769. See note 40 below. The *Friendship* was seized on 31 Oct. and adjudged forfeit in March. Trail v. The *Friendship*, Vice Adm. Min. Bk., 18 Nov. 1768; *Massachusetts Gazette*, 24 Nov. 1768, p. 2, col. 1.

[27] So General Gage suggested. Gage to Hillsborough, 5 March 1769, quoted in Dickerson, *Navigation Acts* 262 note. The delay may also be related to the Sewall-Venner affair, note 20 above. Sewall had refused to reveal Venner's name to the Commissioners. Apparently with Sewall's tacit consent, Hutchinson told the Commissioners that Venner was the informant in a letter dated 29 Oct. 1768. PRO, Treas. 1:471, fol. 43; see Hutchinson to Commissioners, 3 Jan. 1769, *id.* at fol. 81. The delays both in the suits and in revealing Venner may have been occasioned by Sewall's reluctance to proceed until he had some kind of assurance of the Commissioners' support.

[28] See 4 Geo. 3, c. 15, §§37, 41, 42 (1764), quoted, text at notes 82, 93, 96, below. In England the Attorney General would proceed for penalties owed the Crown, but where forfeitures were divided between informer and Crown, the usual form was the *qui tam* action brought by the informer for himself and other parties. See 3 Blackstone, *Commentaries* *160, 261–262; 4 *id.* at *303–304. The form of the information shows that Sewall was proceeding in the latter capacity. See note 80 below. It has been suggested that retainers of £72 each paid to Sewall and Fitch in Oct. and Feb. for "sundry causes" disguise a single large fee necessary to get them to take on Hancock's case. Dickerson, *Navigation Acts* 263 note. The suggestion is refuted by the fact that on the docket of the Vice Admiralty Court at this period were seven forfeiture actions pending, as well as three penal suits. Vice Adm. Min. Bk., Oct. 1768–Feb. 1769. See, for example, No. 47, No. 48, No. 49. See also note 26 above.

[29] The information and order are set out in text at notes 79–82 below.

[30] "A Journal of the Times," 3 Nov. 1768, Dickerson, *Boston under Military Rule*

When the court sat on 7 November, the informations were read and the matter continued until the 28th.[31] Thus began a lengthy trial, in which Adams served as counsel for Hancock and probably the other respondents as well. Years later in his Autobiography he said of Hancock's case: "and a painfull Drudgery I had of his cause. There were few days through the whole Winter, when I was not summoned to attend the Court of Admiralty. It seemed as if the Officers of the Crown were determined to examine the whole Town as Witnesses. Almost every day a fresh Witness was to be examined upon Interrogatories. They interrogated many of his [Hancock's] near Relations and most intimate Friends and threatened to summons his amiable and venerable Aunt, the Relict of his Uncle Thomas Hancock, who had left the greatest Part of his Fortune to him. I was thoroughly weary and disgusted with the Court, the Officers of the Crown, the Cause, and even with the tyrannical Bell that dongled me out of my House every Morning." [32]

The cases were further continued from time to time until 2 January 1769.[33] The trials seem to have proceeded together without objection from any party. Interrogatories had been filed on 13 December, and now the first of many witnesses for the Crown was called.[34] For many weeks Auchmuty continued to examine witnesses both in court and in chambers, an Admiralty practice that, like the constant continuances and long delays, offended the common-law practitioners.[35] Finally on 16 February the

---

18. The account of the trial which follows is largely based on this source. Political bias casts doubt on the "Journal's" treatment of events, but its dating is probably accurate and is corroborated by what little other information there is.

[31] "A Journal of the Times," 7 Nov. 1768, Dickerson, *Boston under Military Rule* 19.

[32] 3 JA, *Diary and Autobiography* 306. The sheer length of the proceeding was a source of contemporary complaint also. See note 35 below; JA's Instructions to the Boston Representatives, 14 May 1769, 3 JA *Works* 509. In his Autobiography JA wrongly dated the suit as beginning in 1773 and being "suspended at last only by the Battle of Lexington." 3 JA, *Diary and Autobiography* 305–306. He also stated that the action against Hancock was "upon a great Number of Libells for Penalties, upon Acts of Parliament, amounting to Ninety or an hundred thousand Pounds Sterling." *Id.* at 306. Either JA here added a zero to the sum involved, or else he meant that Hancock had undertaken to make good any liability imposed upon the other respondents. Hancock's account with JA, beginning in March 1769 and receipted 21 Dec. 1771, contains the following statement in JA's hand, but lined out, which probably refers to his fees in this case: "The Affair in the Admiralty is omitted for the Present, Mr. Price [Deputy Register of the Vice Admiralty Court] has promised to give me the Particulars Tomorrow. I had much rather leave that to Mr. Hancocks Pleasure, but if he chooses to have me make an Account of it I will do it tomorrow."

[33] "A Journal of the Times," 28 Nov., 5 Dec., 14 Dec., 1768, Dickerson, *Boston under Military Rule* 28–34.

[34] "A Journal of the Times," 14 Dec. 1768, 2 Jan. 1769, Dickerson, *Boston under Military Rule* 34, 43. Further interrogatories were filed on 7 Jan. *Id.* at 46.

[35] See the entries in "A Journal of the Times" for 5 Jan., 7 Jan., 23 Jan., 28 Jan., 30 Jan., 11 Feb. 1769, Dickerson, *Boston under Military Rule* 44–64. Critical comments on the practice of the Admiralty Court are appended to these entries. See *id.* at 43 (number of witnesses); *id.* at 46 (Star Chamber method of interroga-

respondents' witnesses were examined, and the case was set for argument on Tuesday the 21st. On that date, however, the Crown sought, and was granted, leave to examine additional witnesses "for the whole of this week," which prompted "A Journal of the Times" to conclude that the respondents' evidence had seriously damaged Sewall's case.[36]

On the 24th Adams tried to impeach one Joseph Maysel, apparently a key witness for the Crown, by questioning another witness in an effort to prove that Maysel was a fugitive from justice, guilty of a "heinous crime." The Crown opposed the line of questioning, pointing to the common-law rules that only a witness' general character for truth was admissible as oral testimony, and that a written record of conviction was necessary to establish a specific crime. Adams argued that the civil law, which he said would permit his evidence, should be followed, since this was a Court of Admiralty.[37] On 1 March, Auchmuty, in an interlocutory decree, ruled that the question objected to should be withdrawn on the grounds that even under civil-law rules the evidence was inadmissible, but that in any event the common law controlled this matter in a statutory proceeding.[38]

As far as can be determined, no further sessions of the court were held. Sometime in March the Suffolk County Grand Jury reportedly indicted Maysel for perjury, but, according to "A Journal of the Times," he was spirited out of the jurisdiction by the Commissioners, and the indictment was not brought to trial.[39] Finally, on 25 March 1769 Sewall moved that the informations against Hancock and the other respondents be withdrawn.[40] There has never been a satisfactory explanation for the Crown's action, although in the "Journal" the withdrawal was implicitly linked with the reading of Auchmuty's commission as Judge of Admiralty for the new, enlarged district centered at Boston.[41] Since Sewall at the same time had been commissioned Judge of Admiralty at Halifax, it has been sug-

---

tion and exercise of jurisdiction on land); *id.* at 54 (examination in chambers); *id.* at 56 (powers and perquisites of the judge); *id.* at 57 (length of trial); *id.* at 64 (length of trial). JA may have supplied some or all of these comments. See note 74 below.

[36] "A Journal of the Times," 17, 18, 23 Feb. 1769, Dickerson, *Boston under Military Rule* 66–67.

[37] "A Journal of the Times," 24 Feb. 1769, Dickerson, *Boston under Military Rule* 68, quoted, note 126 below. The "Journal" here paraphrased a portion of JA's argument. See note 74 below.

[38] "A Court of Admiralty relative to Mr. Hancock's libels, sat yesterday.—It is said the judge has given his decree upon the question mentioned in our last Journal [i.e. 24 Feb., note 37 above]." "A Journal of the Times," 2 March 1769, Dickerson, *Boston under Military Rule* 72. See JA's copy of the decree and comments on it, text at notes 127–134 below.

[39] "A Journal of the Times," 27 March, 22 April 1769, Dickerson, *Boston under Military Rule* 84, 92. No copy of the indictment or record of trial has been found in the Suffolk Files.

[40] "The Advocate General prays leave to retract this information and says Our Sovereign Lord the King will prosecute no further hereon. Allowed." Vice Adm. Min. Bk., 25 March 1769.

[41] "A Journal of the Times," 26 March 1769, Dickerson, *Boston under Military Rule* 83. Vice Adm. Min. Bk., 25 March 1769.

gested that Auchmuty and he, now assured of fixed salaries, were willing to forgo the expected profits from these actions.[42] It might just as well have been that Sewall now felt himself sufficiently independent of the Customs Commissioners to withdraw actions which he had instituted only under pressure from them. Neither theory explains why the actions were not dropped when the commissions were actually received in Boston on 20 January.[43] It seems more likely that the departure of Maysel and a failure of other evidence were the reasons for the withdrawal.[44] It is also possible that the actions were settled in some way, although there is no evidence of such a result. Whatever the fact, the withdrawal probably coincided with the reading of Auchmuty's commission only because the opening of court for that purpose provided a convenient opportunity for Sewall's motion.

The trial of Hancock and the others was an event of major political importance in the colonies. Its very length played into the hands of the revolutionary propagandists. From November 1768 until the following summer, "A Journal of the Times," which appeared in a variety of colonial newspapers, carried periodic accounts of the proceedings, interspersed with tart comments on the twin themes of the venality of the Customs Commissioners and the arbitrary injustice of the Court of Admiralty.[45] These attacks helped to establish the Commissioners as obnoxious at the very beginning of their tenure. Their effectiveness was permanently damaged and they served until the Revolution in an atmosphere of constant hostility.[46]

The attack on the Admiralty Court was buttressed by a portion of Adams' draft argument in the case, which was widely circulated as part of his Instructions to the Boston Representatives of May 1769.[47] These and other responses to the prosecution of revenue cases brought the Vice Admiralty courts under the disapprobation of the colonists. The jurisdiction was more and more invoked only in enforcement of the Acts of Trade, and ordinary civil maritime cases were tried in the common-law courts.[48] A multitude

[42] Lovejoy, "Rights Imply Equality," 16 *WMQ* (3d ser.) 459, 481–482. See also Dickerson, *Navigation Acts* 245–246. These authorities also suggest that the impending recall of Bernard and the Treasury's disapproval of the activities of the Customs Commissioners led to the withdrawal. The evidence on this point is at present inadequate. The new judges were created pursuant to a statute providing for superior Admiralty courts of both original and appellate jurisdiction to sit in the colonies. 8 Geo. 3, c. 22 (1767). The salaries were fixed at £600 to be paid out of the King's share of fines and forfeitures, or from the sale of old naval stores in England if the former was insufficient. Ubbelohde, *Vice Admiralty Courts* 133.

[43] "A Journal of the Times," 20 Jan. 1769, Dickerson, *Boston under Military Rule* 53. News of the commissions was received in Boston on 29 Nov. 1768. *Id.* at 28.

[44] One contemporary historian found lack of evidence to be the reason. 1 Gordon, *History of Independence* 240–241.

[45] See notes 30–41 above.

[46] See Barrow, Colonial Customs 487–511; Clark, "American Board of Customs," 45 *AHR* 787–790.

[47] See note 93 below; text at note 74 below.

[48] See Wroth, "The Massachusetts Vice Admiralty Court and the Federal Ad-

of revenue cases in each port served to stir up local feeling; *Sewall v. Hancock* helped to unite this feeling and to produce the single impulse against the courts which increased steadily until its manifestation in the Declaration of Independence.[49]

Recently it has been argued that the whole affair of the *Liberty* is proof that the Commissioners were in fact as venal, and the Admiralty Courts as arbitrary, as the colonists contended. Hancock is pictured as the innocent victim of a prosecution carried on by "customs racketeers" bent on "plunder," who sought to obtain their evil ends in an arbitrary and oppressive mockery of a trial.[50]

Hancock's innocence is open to question. His reported boasts that he would defy the Commissioners and the rumors that he had done so may be dismissed as the self-serving statements of interested royal officials, but there remains the fact that the *Liberty* was condemned for unloading cargo before entry.[51] Without court files it is difficult to evaluate that decision, but on balance it was probably justified. In the first place, the problem of proof was relatively simple. The issue was only the fact of unloading, not the complicity of Hancock or anyone else. Secondly, Kirk's deposition, which has been attacked as vague and perjured,[52] was probably not the only evidence for the Crown. During the eight weeks of trial interrogatories were filed and the court examined several witnesses, presumably including Kirk. In any event, his original deposition, if believed, was persuasive ground for condemnation, regardless of the testimony of Hancock's witnesses, who had the difficult job of proving a negative.[53] Even if the deposition could not be corroborated by other testimony, Kirk could have been further examined to ascertain his credibility, and character witnesses could have been called.[54]

To argue that Auchmuty decided the case against the weight of the

---

miralty Jurisdiction," 6 *Am. Jour. Legal Hist.* 250, 360–364, 367 (1962); p. 102–104, notes 17, 22, 24, above.

[49] The Declaration spoke out against judges independent of colonial legislatures, as well as against trial without jury. For a summary of the much more detailed attacks between 1769 and 1774, see Ubbelohde, *Vice Admiralty Courts* 142–147, 189–190.

[50] Dickerson, *Navigation Acts* 231–246; see also Lovejoy, "Rights Imply Equality," 16 *WMQ* (3d ser.) 459, 478–482.

[51] See note 21 above.

[52] Dickerson, *Navigation Acts* 239–240.

[53] Opinion of William DeGrey, 25 July 1768, 55 MHS, *Procs.* 273–276. As to the problem of weighing evidence, see Gilbert, *Evidence* 150, 157–158.

[54] The location of the burden of proof depends on the statute, 4 Geo. 3, c. 15, §45 (1764), providing that "if any ship or goods shall be seized for any cause of forfeiture, and any dispute shall arise whether the customs and duties for such goods have been paid, or the same have been lawfully imported or exported, or concerning the growth, product, or manufacture of such goods, or the place from whence such goods were brought, then and in such cases, the proof thereof shall lie upon the owner or claimer of such ship or goods." Assuming that goods landed before entry were not "lawfully imported" within this statute, Hancock bore the burden. He thus could have failed either because his evidence was insufficient on its face, or because Kirk's testimony outweighed it.

evidence is to say that he either was wrong in believing the witnesses or was influenced by prejudice. Both are possible, but the presumption is surely the other way. At least as to testimony given in his presence, only Auchmuty could weigh credibility, and there is no actual evidence of prejudice. Moreover, if the condemnation had not been supported by the evidence it is hard to believe that there would not have been some outcry. Not only was none forthcoming, but the few mentions of this phase of the case which are found support the view that the forfeiture was justified.[55] A conclusion that the *Liberty* was justly condemned for unloading before entry does not convict Hancock of smuggling; it does indicate that wine or other goods were smuggled from the *Liberty* on the night of 9 May. It seems unlikely that Hancock would have been so out of touch with his affairs as not to have been involved.

If the Commissioners were reasonable in believing that Hancock was not innocent, then they were justified in proceeding against him with all the weapons they could command. They had been sent to Boston to implement a new policy of strict enforcement of the Acts of Trade. Hancock led the opposition to the new establishment, both with his political attacks and with the example of his own violation. If the law could be applied strictly to him, others would fall into line. The procedures used to gain this end were harsh, but they were neither extortion nor persecution. All were prescribed by the law which the Commissioners had sworn to uphold, and all were dictated by the position of outright defiance which Hancock had taken.

The forfeiture of the *Liberty* and the penalties sought in the *in personam* actions were not "plunder" unless that term is understood to include rewards sanctioned by law. It was common 18th-century practice to divide the proceeds of such suits, a third each to Governor, informer, and Crown. In many situations fees and forfeitures were used to encourage an element of private enterprise which helped to keep salaries low and place the cost of government on those who invoked its powers. In the area of the customs the practice was especially necessary to encourage effective enforcement in the face of firm opposition.[56] This system could certainly be abused if

[55] JA in his argument, text following note 86 below, conceded that the wines were smuggled, although this may have been a recognition either of the principle of *res judicata*, or of the practical futility of rearguing this point before the same court. See also the language of his Autobiography, admittedly many years later, that "a great Uproar was raised in Boston, on Account of the Unlading in the Night of a Cargo of Wines from the Sloop Liberty from Madeira, belonging to Mr. Hancock, without paying the Customs." 3 JA, *Diary and Autobiography* 305–306. See also Gordon, 1 *History of Independence* 231, 240–241. Some of the colonial writings which might have raised an objection, but did not, are cited in note 21 above.

[56] This system had been incorporated in all of the Acts of Trade from the beginning. See, for example, 12 Car. 2, c. 18, §§1, 3 (1660); 4 Geo. 3, c. 15, §42 (1764). See also Hoon, *English Customs* 275–276, 285–289. In England it had been standard practice in a variety of situations since the 15th century. See 9 Holdsworth, *History of English Law* 240. One of the earliest of such statutes provided that a customs officer who embezzled duties should be liable for treble the value of the goods, with a third to the informer who sued. 3 Hen. 6, c. 3 (1424).

profit, rather than enforcement, became the sole aim of the officials involved. There was no abuse in the seizure of the *Liberty*, however. The
cause was not a breach of some technical and previously unenforced requirement, but a violation that amounted to the very kind of smuggling
which the Commissioners had been sent to root out.[57]

Nor were the penalties in the *in personam* proceedings an abuse. The
statute under which they were sought had been enacted precisely because
forfeitures alone were not sufficient to deter violators.[58] The substantial
amount asked for here was necessary to make an impression upon a man
of Hancock's wealth, power, and obstinacy. Although the figure of one
hundred pipes alleged to have been smuggled was doubtless chosen arbitrarily to raise the stakes, there could be no unlawful exaction, because the
fines which would have been paid if Sewall had obtained a decree were
based upon the quantity and value of the wine smuggled, matters of fact
which the Crown had to prove at the trial. The ultimate penalty thus
would not have been dictated by the allegations in the information, but
would have been computed according to the offense, as authorized by
statute.[59]

The principal result of the high *ad damnum* was that a high bail was
levied. There is some justice to complaints on this point, as the rule at common law in England seems to have been that only the fictitious common
bail was required in an action on a penal statute. The figure itself was not
excessive, however. Although it might have seemed so in a criminal action,
where bail was proportioned to the gravity of the offense, this was a quasi-
civil proceeding, in which the purpose of bail was to provide security for
the amount sued for, rather than merely for the defendant's appearance.
In a civil action at law the plaintiff could demand that the sheriff take
security in the full amount of the *ad damnum*, and full bail was required
in an *in personam* civil suit in the English High Court of Admiralty.[60] The

---

The process was commonly followed in Massachusetts penal acts. See, for example,
Act of 26 Feb. 1768, 4 A&R 983 (All penalties and forfeitures for breach of
Province customs laws to be paid one-half to Province and one-half to informer).

[57] See note 21 above.

[58] 4 Geo. 3, c. 15, §37 (1764), text at note 82 below. See Barrow, Colonial
Customs 323, 473–474. For use of penalties in England, see Hoon, *English Customs* 288–289.

[59] See 2 Hawkins, *Pleas of the Crown*, c. 26, §75. It should be noted that the sum
sued for was required to be in sterling by 4 Geo. 3, c. 15, §41 (1764).

[60] 3 Blackstone, *Commentaries* *289–291, Appendix III, §5; 1 Bacon, *Abridgment* 209–210; 12 Geo. 1, c. 29 (1725); Francis Clerke, *Praxis Curiae Ad-
miralitatis Angliae*, tit. 4 (London, 3d edn., Latin and English, 1722). (The
Harvard Law School's copy of this work bears the following notation on its title
page in the hand of Simon Greenleaf: "This book belonged to the late Prest. John
Adams, whose autograph was stolen as above appears, *after* I gave it to the Law
Library. S.G." The page is cut at the top.) The Massachusetts practice has not been
determined, but in the absence of statute the English procedure was presumably
followed. For the English rule on bail in suits on penal statutes, see Presgrave v.
————, 1 Comyns 75, 92 Eng. Rep. 966 (K.B. 1700); St. George's Case, Yelv. 53,
80 Eng. Rep. 38 (K.B. 1604); Gilbert, *Common Pleas* 37. The statute embodying
this rule was specifically limited to cases arising in the common-law courts at

court here was more lenient, requiring bail for only one third of the amount sought.

The procedure followed in the *in personam* actions was unusual and, no doubt, tended to Hancock's disadvantage, but it was not persecution invented arbitrarily by the Commissioners for political revenge or financial gain. The statute provided the choice of proceeding at common law or in Admiralty, because it was a truism that no jury could be found to convict for violation of the Acts of Trade.[61] After the recent failure to indict the *Liberty* rioters, the Commissioners can hardly be blamed for accepting truism as truth and exercising the option to proceed in Admiralty. Since the trial was in Admiralty, it was by information, not indictment; [62] it was before a judge sitting without a jury; and the whole range of civil law procedure followed in the High Court of Admiralty in England was invoked—interrogatories, irregular sessions, secret examination of witnesses, and the rest.[63] Whether these procedures were "illegal" depended not on their inherent qualities but upon the power of Parliament to place violations of the statute within the Admiralty jurisdiction. There was much dispute on this point, and it is not surprising that the Commissioners upheld the parliamentary side of a constitutional question which was resolved only by the Revolution.[64]

Westminster, however. 29 Eliz. 1, c. 5, §21 (1587). Even if the case law could be deemed applicable in the colonies, it would not bind the Court of Admiralty. See a proceeding under the White Pine Acts in New York in which the "Defendent" was held to bail. Wentworth v. Dean, Hough, *Reports* 227, 228 (N.Y. Vice Adm. 1769). The complaint about bail was thus in effect only another complaint about the latter jurisdiction. See "A Journal of the Times," 2 March 1769, Dickerson, *Boston under Military Rule* 72; see notes 63, 64, below.

[61] 4 Geo. 3, c. 15, §§41–42 (1764). See Anthony Stokes, *A View of the Constitution of the British Colonies in North America* 360–361 (London, 1783); Barrow, *Colonial Customs* 322–323.

[62] In England such proceedings were by information, although at common law. 4 Blackstone, *Commentaries* *303; Hoon, *English Customs* 279–280. In his opinion in the case of the *Lydia*, note 3 above, however, Sewall had expressed a great reluctance to proceed by information in the Superior Court, noting that this method had "seldom been used [in Massachusetts] without the consent of the Judges, except in cases where the offense has been clearly against Law and the public Good has evidently required it." 4 *WMQ* (3d ser.) 504. The implication is clear that if the Commissioners had wished to proceed at common law in the *Liberty* case, they would have had to obtain an indictment.

[63] For the English Admiralty practice, see Arthur Browne, *A Compendious View of the Civil Law*, 2:396–443 (London, 2d edn., 1802).

[64] One basic issue was the power of Parliament to pass such legislation without colonial representation. See JA's Argument, text following note 89 below. The colonial position, which had at first been that there should be no taxation without representation, gradually broadened after 1765 into a denial of all parliamentary power over the colonies; moreover, the remedy sought became not representation in Parliament, but colonial home rule. Needless to say, the orthodox English view was opposed to the colonial stand. Miller, *Origins of the American Revolution* 225–231. Equally critical was the question of the power of Parliament, however constituted, to interfere with what the colonists claimed as fundamental rights. In his argument for Hancock, JA urged that trial in Admiralty was an interference with the right of trial by jury, and others argued, if he did not, that such statutes were void. See

188

No. 46. Sewall v. Hancock

Hindsight suggests that wiser administrators than the Commissioners might have sought to gain compliance through friendship and understanding rather than in an outright confrontation which they were bound to lose. A different course could have slowed or even prevented what became a headlong rush toward American independence. The British policy in accordance with which the Commissioners acted was based upon an unrealistic appraisal of the proper role of the colonies, which the colonial constitutional arguments were intended to correct. To recognize the justice of the colonial position, however, is not to say that the actions of the Commissioners were immoral or illegal. Hancock had defied authority. As representatives of that authority they were duty-bound to react to his defiance. Their reaction was not the only possible one, but it was a proper, if ultimately ineffective, course.

The document printed below from Adams' Admiralty Book concerns only the *in personam* action against Hancock. It consists of a copy in Adams' hand of the information and statutes involved, followed by a draft of his argument in Hancock's behalf. In this argument Adams approached the case as presenting a problem in statutory construction. Conceding that wine had been landed from the *Liberty* without payment of duties, he first argued that Hancock could not be said to fall within the statutory description of one "assisting or otherwise concerned" unless his knowing complicity in the unloading could be directly proven. Sewall must have been equally aware that Hancock's liability turned on the question of his knowledge and participation. Only this could account for the flood of friends, relations, employees, and business associates who were called as Crown witnesses, doubtless to be interrogated on possible links between Hancock and the nocturnal activities of the late Captain Marshall. Sewall's decision to abandon the action may well have turned on his inability to produce evidence of this vital element in his case.

Adams' basic argument was supported by a plea that the act be strictly

---

text at notes 92–104 below. The English position was that Parliament could not be controlled in this regard. No. 44, notes 32–34. There was a further problem in the effect of the statutes, 13 Ric. 2, c. 5 (1389), and 15 Ric. 2, c. 3 (1391), limiting the Admiralty jurisdiction to matters not arising "within the bodies of the counties," which had been relied upon at common law in both England and the colonies to restrict the Admiralty courts in ordinary civil matters to things "done upon the sea." The common-law courts used the writ of prohibition to halt Admiralty proceedings that exceeded these statutory limits. See 1 Holdsworth, *History of English Law* 552–559. In Massachusetts the Superior Court seems to have interfered in customs suits only when the Vice Admiralty Court acted beyond the jurisdiction given it by the Acts of Trade, indicating an understanding that the latter legislation abrogated the statutes of Richard II *pro tanto*. See Wroth, "The Massachusetts Vice Admiralty Court," in George A. Billias, ed., *Law and Authority in Colonial America: Selected Essays* (Barre, Mass., in press). Perhaps for this reason, JA did not touch upon the issue in Hancock's case. It was raised by others in Massachusetts and elsewhere, however, implying that the ancient acts had attained the stature of fundamental law. See, for example, "A Journal of the Times," 7 Jan. 1769, Dickerson, *Boston under Military Rule* 46; Ubbelohde, *Vice Admiralty Courts* 188–190; Henry Laurens, *Extracts From The Proceedings Of The Court Of Vice-Admiralty In Charles-Town, South Carolina* 18–19 ([Phila.], 1768), discussed further, note 73 below.

construed in Hancock's favor. Presumably this meant that "assisting or otherwise concerned" should not be expanded to include any kind of constructive or circumstantial implication of Hancock in the unloading. There was, of course, a familiar canon of construction that penal acts were to be construed narrowly,[65] but Adams' argument was unusual in the reasons which he assigned for calling this statute penal. Not only was there an obvious disproportion between offense and penalty, but there were two grave constitutional defects in the act: (1) Adams' "Clyent Mr. Hancock never consented to it," through his own vote or that of his actual representative; (2) its penalties were to be recovered in Admiralty courts, which deprived Hancock of the right to trial by jury, a defect all the more grievous because comparable offenses in England were to be tried to a jury in the Exchequer.

Here, like Otis in the famous argument on writs of assistance (No. 44), Adams attacked a statute as an intrusion upon fundamental rights. Unlike Otis, Adams did not make this invasion the basis for a demand that the court repudiate the statute altogether. *Bonham's Case*, upon which Otis grounded his argument that "the Executive Courts must pass such Acts into disuse," held only that a statute should be construed to avoid a result in conflict with common-law principles.[66] Adams' position neatly tied his broad political and constitutional arguments in with a similar narrow theory of construction: a penal statute conflicting with basic principles should be construed in every instance in favor of the subject.

In the light of later theorizing on the question whether Otis had foreshadowed the doctrine of judicial review,[67] it is interesting that Adams' argument was so much more in accord with traditional English legal theories. Perhaps he had not understood Otis to have gone beyond those theories; or, if Otis had gone farther, Adams might now have come to realize that this was not a correct statement of the law. Otis' appeal to *Bonham's Case* could be rationalized in a narrow view, because he was urging invalidity in the application of a statute; the statute here, if void, was void on its face, a much more drastic flaw. Whatever the force of these considerations, Adams undoubtedly felt the need to ask for relief in terms acceptable to the judge trying the case. Auchmuty could hardly be persuaded as a loyal servant of the Crown that the act was void, but he might be convinced that in the circumstances it should not be applied harshly to Hancock.[68] The structure of the argument may also be explained by an intention on Adams' part to make political use of the draft—a possibility discussed more fully below.

[65] See No. 51, notes 16–21, text at notes 33–35.

[66] See Bonham's Case, 8 Co. Rep. 114, 118a, 77 Eng. Rep. 647, 652 (C.P. 1610); No. 44, notes 35–38.

[67] See No. 44, note 44.

[68] In making what was really a political appearance before the Governor and Council to argue for the opening of the courts during the Stamp Act crisis of 1765, Adams urged the invalidity of the Act in the strongest terms. Quincy, *Reports* 200–202; 2 JA, *Works* 158–159 note. See No. 44, note 48. See also 1 JA, *Diary and Autobiography* 263–267.

The remainder of the draft deals with the question of the application of the civil law. Although Auchmuty had held that common-law rules governed the questioning of an impeaching witness, that opinion was based on alternative grounds and could have been limited to the issue there raised. Adams here argued for the civil-law approach on a broader front, buttressing his position with an array of citations from the *Digest* and other appropriate authorities. Conviction must be on the evidence of two or more witnesses whose credibility the court must establish. If oral testimony of Maysel's criminal record was not admissible on the question of credibility, his present condition, as well as his own testimony as to his past should be taken into account. The civil law also supported Adams' previous contention that harsh laws should be construed strictly, especially in criminal cases. The draft ends with the unexpected insertion of a summary of the earlier arguments and decree on the impeachment question. In this material was the crux: If the court was to apply some common-law rules, it should apply all, including the jury. If it was to follow the civil law in matters such as interrogatories, it should not omit those civil-law rules which favored Hancock.

Adams may have delivered this argument in open court, but no direct evidence of such a dramatic event has been found, and there is reason to believe that it never occurred. As already noted, argument on the merits had been set for 21 February but was postponed until after 1 March by the Crown's call for further witnesses and the subsequent controversy over the impeachment of Maysel. In all probability Maysel's indictment and disappearance led to further postponements, so that there was no occasion to hold argument prior to the withdrawal of the actions on 25 March.[69] In any event, "A Journal of the Times," which faithfully recorded these and other stages of Hancock's trial, made no mention of an argument. If Adams had addressed the court in the eloquent and politically provocative terms of his draft, it seems likely that the "Journal" would have reported it, perhaps embellishing the account with passages supplied by Adams from his own text.

The state of the manuscript is ambiguous on this point. The draft contains textual errors of a sort suggesting that at least the portions of it dealing with the constitutional issues were copied from an earlier, rougher draft.[70] At the same time, the less organized and less careful manner in which the extracts from civil-law sources were entered, the sudden insertion of the impeachment materials, and the lack of a formal conclusion on the civil-law issues indicate that this is not a final draft. If there had been an argument on the merits, the draft could be either a copy or expansion of the text from which Adams argued, or it could be an intermediate state from which he prepared a now missing final version for presentation to the court.

In view of the likelihood that there was no argument on the merits,

---

[69] See text at notes 36–44 above.
[70] See, for example, text at notes 89, 91, 105, below.

another explanation is called for. Adams may well have prepared an argument on the constitutional points for presentation on 21 February, and copied the first part of the present draft from it into his Admiralty Book, perhaps in expanded form. Possibly inspired by the issues raised in the impeachment argument, he doubtless added the civil-law extracts during the latter part of February or early in March. Then, "disregarding order," he inserted the material on "the Controversy We had last Week."—that is, the impeachment [71]—some time after Auchmuty's 1 March decree. His failure to complete the draft may be ascribed to the fact that at some point in March he learned that it would not be needed in court.

Whether or not the argument was ever presented, there are many indications that Adams intended his draft to serve a purpose beyond mere advocacy in court. "A Journal of the Times" twice promised a full account of *Sewall v. Hancock*, although none ever appeared.[72] Adams had earlier turned law reporting to partisan advantage with his "Abstract" of the argument on the writs of assistance (No. 44, Document II), and he now had before him a recent example of this technique in the pamphlet attack which Henry Laurens of Charleston had launched upon the activities of the South Carolina Vice Admiralty Court.[73] Adams may have intended to use his draft as the basis for a similar pamphlet, which would fulfill the "Journal's" promises, graphically demonstrating Boston's grievances and presenting the Town's legal position in its quarrel with the Customs Commissioners and the Admiralty Court.

Whether termination of the trial, the press of other business, or another reason caused Adams to leave his draft unfinished, a gap of ten pages before the next entry in the Admiralty Book (*Rex v. Corbet*, No. 56, tried in May and June 1769) suggests that he intended to return to it. The work that he had done did not go to waste, whatever his intentions. As previously noted, he used his arguments on the right to jury trial almost verbatim in his Instructions to the Boston Representatives in May 1769. This document was carried in the newspapers as well as in "A Journal of the Times," and so played a political role. The passage on impeachment was similarly adapted for the "Journal." [74]

[71] See text at note 126 below.
[72] "Journal of the Times," 7 Jan., 26 March 1769, Dickerson, *Boston under Military Rule* 46–47, 83–84.
[73] Laurens' pamphlet, *Extracts From The Proceedings Of The Court Of Vice-Admiralty In Charles-Town, South-Carolina*, was first published in Philadelphia late in 1768. A portion of it entitled "General Observations on American Custom House Officers and Courts of Vice Admiralty" appeared in the *Boston Gazette* for 9 Jan. 1769, p. 2, cols. 1–3. An expanded version of the pamphlet, *Extracts from the Proceedings of the High Court of Vice Admiralty upon Six Several Informations*, published in Charleston, in Feb. 1769, may also have been available to JA. See T. R. Adams, "American Independence," Nos. 57a–c; "A Journal of the Times," 7 Jan. 1769, Dickerson, *Boston under Military Rule* 46–47; Ubbelohde, *Vice Admiralty Courts* 109–112.
[74] See text at note 47 above; text and notes 93, 126, below. Horace Gray suggested that these passages show JA's hand in the "Journal." Quincy, *Reports* (Appendix) 457. JA's comment in June 1771 that he had "not wrote one Line in a

No. 46. Sewall v. Hancock

If these partisan uses of portions of the draft suggest that it was as much a political as a legal document, its content provides firm ground to support such a theory. In the first place, both Adams' use of court documents with appended comments and the general tone of his arguments indicate a desire to emulate Laurens' South Carolina pamphlet.[75] More important, Adams' draft stands in its own right as skilled political writing.

The language and style of his political and constitutional arguments, which might have impressed a jury but would have been wasted on a hostile judge, suggest the intention to reach a wider audience. In fact, the portion on Magna Carta, later used in the May 1769 Instructions, shows great similarity to a passage in Adams' "Clarendon Letters" of 1766, attacking the Stamp Act.[76] His juxtaposition of broad constitutional positions with a plea for strict construction gives rise to an irony more appropriate in political writing than in legal argument. To call a statute merely "penal" when it has been enacted by an improperly constituted legislature and invades a basic constitutional right is the kind of understatement which implies a more drastic conclusion: The statute is invalid and the political system which produced it must be changed. Even the civil-law argument seems calculated less for legal advantage than as a means of emphasizing the deprivation of jury trial and the unfair manipulation of the law in the Admiralty court.[77] The case was to be tried on the facts; these arguments were for the world.

Adams' "Abstract" of the writs of assistance argument was the transformation of a legal argument into a political tract. His argument in *Sewall v. Hancock* is a much more subtle and accomplished piece of craftsmanship. Here, political theory is manipulated within a legal framework in such a way that the case is presented both at the level of the court room and at the level of the public forum in which broader constitutional issues are discussed. Whatever the purpose for which it was written, the argument deserves recognition as an unfinished contribution to the political literature of its time.

Newspaper these two Years" (2 JA, *Diary and Autobiography* 39), has been taken to mean that he probably did not participate in the "Journal." Arthur M. Schlesinger, *Prelude to Independence* 312 (N.Y., 1958). JA's statement would not have excluded his supplying both the impeachment materials and other commentary on the trial (note 35 above) to the "Journal," however, since these accounts were published no later than May 1769. Dickerson, *Boston under Military Rule* 82.

[75] Laurens' pamphlet (note 73 above) consisted chiefly of papers from the files of the court in the seizure of his ship *Ann*, with comments. Compare JA's text at notes 79–82, 127–134, below. For political similarities, compare JA's argument with Laurens' "General Observations." JA did contemplate a report of this nature based on his notes in *Rex v. Corbet*, also in his Admiralty Book. See No. 56, note 24.

[76] The Earl of Clarendon to William Pym, *Boston Gazette*, Supp., 13 Jan. 1766, in 3 JA, *Works* 470–472. See also 1 JA, *Diary and Autobiography* 273–275. Compare text at notes 97–102 below.

[77] Compare note 132 below. The political significance of JA's argument is discussed in Lovejoy, "Rights Imply Equality," 16 WMQ (3d ser.) 459, 478–484 (1959).

ADAMS' COPY OF THE INFORMATION AND DRAFT OF HIS ARGUMENT [78]

Court of Vice Admiralty, Boston, October 1768—March 1769

Jonathan Sewal vs. John Hancock

Prov. &c.[79] Before the Honorable Robert Auchmuty Esqr.

Be it remembered, that on the 29 day of October in the Ninth Year of the Reign of his Majesty George the Third, Jonathan Sewall Esqr. Advocate General for the said Lord the King, in his proper Person comes and as well on behalf of the said Lord the King, as of the Governor of this Province,[80] gives the said Court to understand and be informed, that on the ninth day of May last, a certain Sloop called the Liberty, arrived at the Port of Boston in said Province, from the Islands of Madeira, having on Board, one hundred and twenty seven Pipes of Wine of the Growth of the Madeira's; of which said Sloop, one Nathaniel Barnard was then Master, and that in the Night Time of the same day the said Nathaniel Barnard with Intent to defraud the said Lord the King of his lawfull Customs, did unlawfully and clandestinely unship and land on shore in Boston aforesaid one hundred of the aforesaid Pipes of Wine [81] of the Value of Thirty Pounds Sterling Money of Great Britain, each Pipe, the Duties thereon not having been first paid, or secured to be paid, agreable to Law. And that John Hancock of Boston aforesaid Esqr. was then and there *willfully and unlawfully aiding and assisting in unshipping and landing* the same one hundred Pipes of Wine, he the said John Hancock, at the same Time *well knowing, that the Duties thereon were not paid or secured* and that the unshipping and landing the same, as aforesaid, was with Intent to defraud the said Lord the King as aforesaid, and contrary to

[78] In JA's hand, in his Admiralty Book, Adams Papers, Microfilms, Reel No. 184. Apparently a copy from an earlier state now lost. See text at note 70 above. Portions of the MS were printed in Quincy, *Reports* (Appendix) 457–463, and 2 JA, *Works* 215. For the dating of the MS, see text following note 70 above.

[79] An abbreviated form for the usual caption, probably "Province of Massachusetts Bay / Court of Vice Admiralty."

[80] The usual form of the *qui tam* information used to prosecute these divided forfeitures. See notes 28, 56, 62, above. The name derives from the full Latin phrase, "qui tam pro Domino Rege quam pro seipso" (who [sues] as well for our Lord the King as for himself). See 2 Hawkins, *Pleas of the Crown*, c. 26, §17. Sewall omitted the usual last phrase "for himself," but it is clear from the form of the information as a whole that he was suing as informer. See form used in New York, Hough, *Reports* 272–274.

[81] According to testimony, note 5 above, twenty-five pipes were entered at the Custom House. It is not known whether the two additional pipes alleged here are the correct figure or represent counsel's margin for error.

No. 46. Sewall v. Hancock

Law; against the Peace of the said Lord the King and the Form of the Statute in such Case made and provided, whereby and by Force of the same Statute, the said John has forfeited Treble the value of the said Goods, so unshipped and landed as aforesaid, amounting in the whole to the Sum of Nine Thousand Pounds Sterling Money of Great Britain, to be divided, paid and applied in manner following, that is to say, after deducting the Charges of Prosecution, one Third Part thereof to be paid into the Hands of the Collector of his Majesty's Customs for the said Port of Boston, for the Use of his Majesty, his Heirs and Successors, one Third Part to the Governor of said Province, and the other Third Part to him that informs for the same.

Whereupon as this is a matter properly within the Jurisdiction of this Honorable Court, the said Advocate General prays the Advisement of the said Court in the Premises, and that the said John Hancock may be attached and held to answer to this Information, and may by a Decree of this honourable Court be adjudged to pay the aforesaid Sum of Nine Thousand Pounds to be applied to the uses aforesaid.

Jon. Sewall Advocate for the King

Octr. 29, 1768. Filed and allowed and ordered that the Register of this Court or his Deputy issue out a Warrant for the Marshall of this Court or his Deputy to arrest the Body of the said John Hancock and him keep in safe Custody so that he have him at a Court of Vice Admiralty to be holden at Boston on the Seventh day of November next at Nine of Clock before noon and that he take Bail for Three Thousand Pounds Sterling money of G. Britain.   Robert Auchmuty Judge &c.

Upon what Statute is this Libel founded? Is it on 4 G. 3, C. 15, §37.[82] Be it enacted, &c. "if any Goods or Merchandizes whatsoever, liable to the Payment of Duties in any British Colony or Plantation in America, by this or any other Act of Parliament shall be *loaden on Board any Ship or Vessel outward bound*, or shall be *unshipped or landed from any ship or Vessell inward bound*, before the respective Duties due thereon are paid, agreable to Law; or if any prohibited Goods whatsoever shall be imported into, or exported out of, any of the said Colonies or Plantations contrary to the true Intent and meaning of this or any other Act of Parliament; *every Person who shall be assisting, or otherwise concerned*, Either in the Loading outwards, or in the *Unshipping or landing Inwards*, such Goods, *or to whose Hands the same shall knowingly come* after the Loading or unshipping there-

---

[82] The American Act of 1764, 4 Geo. 3, c. 15, §37. Quotation marks supplied.

of, shall for *each and every offence* forfeit *treble the Value of such Goods*, to be estimated and computed according to the best Price that each respective Commodity bears at the Place where such offence was committed; and all the Boats, Horses, Cattle, and other Carriages whatsoever, made Use of, in the Loading, Landing, removing, Carriage or Conveyance of any of the aforesaid Goods, shall also be forfeited and lost, and [*shall and*] may be seized and prosecuted, by any officer of his Majestys Customs, as hereinafter mentioned." [83]

There is a Clause similar, in most respects to this in 8. Ann, C. 7, §17.[84] "And for preventing the Frauds, which may be practised in *unshipping to be landed* any Pepper, Raisins, Mace, Cinnamon, Cloves, Nutmegs, Snuff, or any other *Sort of Goods whatsoever, subject to the Payment of Duties without paying the same* as also to hinder the Importation of any Sort of prohibited Goods into Great Britain, Be it further enacted by the Authority aforesaid, that if any Pepper, Raisins, Mace, Cinnamon, Cloves, Nutmegs, Snuff, *or any other Sort of Goods whatsoever, liable to the Payment of Duties*, shall be unshipped, with Intention to be laid on Land (customs and other Duties, not being first paid or secured) or if any prohibited Goods whatsoever, shall be imported into any Part of Great Britain, then not only the said *un-customed* and *prohibited* Goods, shall be forfeited and lost, but also the Persons who shall be *assisting*, or *otherwise concerned* in the *un-shipping* the said prohibited and uncustomed Goods, or to whose Hands the same shall knowingly come, after the unshipping thereof, shall forfeit Treble the value thereof, together with the Vessells and Boats, and all the Horses, and other Cattle and Carriages whatsoever, made use of in the Landing, removing, Carriage, or Conveyance of any of the aforesaid Goods," &c.[85]

Madeira Wines are Goods and Merchandises, liable to the Payment of Duties in this British Colony or Plantation.[86] Admitting it

---

[83] That is, in a court of law or of Admiralty, the proceeds to be divided equally among the Crown, the governor of the province in which the case was tried, and the informer. 4 Geo. 3, c. 15, §§41, 42.

[84] 8 Anne, c. 7, §17 (1709). Quotation marks supplied.

[85] The remainder of the section provides that half of the penalties and forfeitures levied go to the Crown and the other half to the informer, "to be recovered by bill, plaint, or information, wherein no essoin, protection, or wager of law shall be allowed." The latter clause, which in other similar acts had been held to limit the jurisdiction to the common law, and the seeming limitation on the face of the act to imports into England, indicate that this statute could not have been the basis of the action. See Chalmers, *Opinions* 500.

[86] A duty of £7 per tun was levied on Madeira wine by the American Act of 1764, 4 Geo. 3, c. 15, §1; Knollenberg, *Origin of the American Revolution* 176–177.

proved that a Quantity of such Wines were unshipped and landed, from the sloop Liberty inward bound, before the Duties due upon it, were paid, agreable to Law. What shall be the Construction of the Words *"assisting or otherwise concerned," in the Unshipping or Landing inwards.* The Labourers, the Porters, and Sailors, who manage the Tacles and with their own Hands, hoist out the Pipes, are no doubt, concerned, and the Master who oversees and gives orders, is no doubt assisting. But is the owner Either concerned or assisting in it, if he does not know of it. He may be asleep in his Bed, and not so much as know or dream that any Body is unshipping and landing his Wines. Is he then concerned or assisting? Can it be proved that Captain Barnard was concerned? Can it be proved that Captn. Marshall was? What then? Can it be proved that Captn. Marshall asked Leave of Mr. Hancock? Can it be proved that Mr. Hancock knew of this Frolick? If he neither consented to it, nor knew of it, how can he be lyable to the Penalty? [87]

I must beg the Indulgence of the Court, while I consider the Character of this Act of Parliament. There is a great Variety in the Characters of Laws as well as Men. A benign and beneficial Law is to receive a liberal and benign Construction. A rigorous and severe Law is to receive a strict and severe Construction. And the more penal it is the more severe must the Construction of it be, and the more tenderly must it be carried into Execution. It will not be impertinent therefore to shew in some Detail the Circumstances, that render this Law the most rigid and severe, or in other Words the most pœnal of almost any Law in the whole British Pandect.

The Degree of severity in any Pœnal Law is to be determined only

According to Webster's *New Collegiate Dictionary* (Springfield, Mass., 1949), a tun was equal to two pipes, or about 250 gallons.

[87] This represents the general common-law rule on the liability of a principal for the misdemeanor of an agent, at least in the absence of the principal's negligence. See William L. Clark and William L. Marshall, *Law of Crimes* §8.12 (Chicago, 6th edn., M. F. Wingersky, 1958). As to Captains Barnard and Marshall, see text at notes 4–6 above. In Attorney General v. Woodmass, Bunbury 247, 145 Eng. Rep. 662 (Exch. 1727), an information on 8 Anne, c. 7, §17, note 84 above, "for being assisting or otherwise concerned in unshipping five hundred gallons of brandy," some of the brandy "run" was ultimately "carried to the defendant's house; but it did not appear the defendant was present either at the time of running or removing the goods to his house; but he afterwards paid the cobblemen for running these goods." The court held that "this was a being concerned within the statute, if the jury were of opinion that the defendant employed the persons to run the goods on his account, and paid them for that purpose." Verdict for the Crown. See also Attorney General v. Flower, Bunbury 227, 145 Eng. Rep. 656 (Exch. 1726); Attorney General v. Lake, Bunbury 277, 145 Eng. Rep. 673 (Exch. 1729). William Bunbury's *Reports of Cases in the Court of Exchequer* was first published at London in 1755. 1 Sweet and Maxwell, *Legal Bibliography* 322.

by the Proportion between the Crime and the Punishment. Treason is justly punished with death because it is an attempt to overthrow the whole Frame of the Government, and the Government can never be overturned without the slaughter of many Hundreds of Lives and the Ruin of many Thousands of Fortunes. If a Man will murder his Fellow subject it seems but equall that he should loose his own Life. But in this Case what is the Crime? Landing a few Casks of Wine. Admitting the Crown to have the clearest Right to the Duties it is but unjustly taking away a small sum of Money from the Crown, and one would think that the forfeiture of £100 would be an equal Punishment for withholding £100 in Duties.[88] But surely the Forfeiture of an whole Cargo of Wines worth Ten Thousand Pounds, for withholding one hundred Pounds in Duties would be a great Disproportion between the Crime and Punishment. To carry it one step further, and subject the ship, as well as Cargo to Confiscation, but above all to subject the Master to £1000,[89] and every Person concerned to a forfeiture of threble value, is such a stretch of security as renders this Act more Penal, than any Statute vs. Rape, Robbery, Murder or Treason.

But among the Groupe of Hardships which attend this Statute, the first that ought always to be mentioned, and that ought never to be forgotten is

1. That it was made without our Consent. My Clyent Mr. Hancock never consented to it. He never voted for it himself, and he never voted for any Man to make such a Law for him. In this Respect therefore the greatest Consolation of an Englishman, suffering under any Law, is torn from him, I mean the Reflection, that it is a Law of his own Making, a Law that he sees the Necessity of for the Public. Indeed the Consent of the subject to all Laws, is so clearly necessary that no Man has yet been found hardy enough to deny it. And The Patrons of these Acts allow that Consent is necessary, they only contend for a Consent by Construction, by Interpretation, a virtual Consent.[90] But this is

---

[88] The duties on 100 pipes, or 50 tuns, would have been £350. See note 86 above.

[89] Thus in MS. The penalty on a master permitting dutiable goods to be loaded aboard his vessel for unlawful entry in the Plantations was actually £100. 6 Geo. 2, c. 13, §7 (1733), made applicable by 4 Geo. 3, c. 15, §7 (1764). It would seem that the master would also be liable under the broader provisions of 4 Geo. 3, c. 15, §37, note 82 above. Sewall did proceed against the master of the *Liberty*. See note 26 above.

[90] The doctrine of virtual representation, by which a member of Parliament was held to represent the interests of the Empire as a whole, rather than those of his constituents, was used by the English to justify their own system of limited franchise and rotten boroughs, as well as colonial nonrepresentation. See Miller, *Origins of the American Revolution* 212–215.

only deluding Men with Shadows instead of Substances. Construction has made Treasons where the Law has made none. Constructions, in short and arbitrary Distinctions, made in short only for so many by Words,[91] so many Cries to deceive a Mob have always been the Instruments of arbitrary Power, the means of lulling and ensnaring Men into their own Servitude. For whenever we leave Principles and clear positive Laws, and wander after Constructions, one Construction or Consequence is piled up upon another untill we get at an immense distance from Fact and Truth and Nature, lost in the wild Regions of Imagination and Possibility, where arbitrary Power sitts upon her brazen Throne and governs with an iron Scepter. It is an Hardship therefore, scarcely to be endured that such a pœnal Statute should be made to govern a Man and his Property, without his actual Consent and only upon such a wild Chimæra as a virtual and constructive Consent.

But there are greater Proofs of the Severity of this statute, yet behind.

2. The Legislative Authority by which it was made is not only grievous, but the Executive Courts [92] by which it is to be carried into Effect is another. In the 41st section of this Act 4 G. 3, c. 15.[93] we find that "All the Forfeitures and Penalties inflicted by this or any other Act [*or Acts*] of Parliament, relating to the Trade and Revenues of the said British Colonies or Plantations in America, which shall be incurred there, shall and may be prosecuted, sued for, and recovered, in any Court of Record,[94] or *in any Court of Admiralty*, in the said Colonies or Plantations where such offence shall be committed, or in any Court of Vice Admiralty, which may or shall be appointed over all America, (which Court of Admiralty or Vice Admiralty, are hereby respectively authorized and required to proceed, hear, and determine

[91] Thus in MS. Compare 2 JA, *Works* 215 note. The garbled text here suggests that JA was copying from notes or an earlier draft.

[92] That is, the courts of justice, which "execute" the laws, as distinguished from legislative "courts," such as the General Court, which make them. See No. 44, note 72.

[93] American Act of 1764, 4 Geo. 3, c. 15, §41. Opening quotation mark supplied. The text following, through note 104, was used by JA with some revision in his "Instructions of the Town of Boston to their Representatives," 15 May 1769, 3 JA, *Works* 508–509, 16 Boston Record Commissioners, *Reports* 285–289, abbreviated in "A Journal of the Times," 14 May 1769, Dickerson, *Boston under Military Rule* 99. The MS, in JA's hand, is in the Boston Public Library. The instructions were published in full in the *Boston Gazette*, 15 May 1769, p. 1, cols. 1–3. See text at notes 47, 74, above. Important variations between the text of the argument and that of the "Instructions" are noted below, but a detailed comparison must await publication of the "Instructions" in Series III of *The Adams Papers*.

[94] In quoting the statute in his "Instructions" JA omitted all clauses dealing with the concurrent jurisdiction at common law.

the same), at the Election of the Informer or Prosecutor." Thus, these extraordinary Penalties and Forfeitures, are to be heard and try'd,— how? Not by a Jury, not by the Law of the Land, [but] by the civil Law and a Single Judge. Unlike the ancient Barons who unâ Voce responderunt, Nolumus Leges Angliæ mutari,[95] The Barons of modern Times have answered that they are willing, that the Laws of England should be changed, at least with Regard to all America, in the most tender Point, the most fundamental Principle. And this Hardship is the more severe as we see in the same Page of the Statute and the very preceeding section §40, "That all Penalties and Forfeitures, herein before mentioned, which shall be incurred in Great Britain, shall [*and may*] be prosecuted, sued for and recovered in any of his Majestys Courts of Record in Westminster or in the Court of Exchequer in Scotland respectively." [96]

Here is the Contrast that stares us in the Face! The Parliament in one Clause guarding the People of the Realm, and securing to them the Benefit of a Tryal by the Law of the Land, and by the next Clause, depriving all Americans of that Priviledge. What shall we say to this Distinction? Is there not in this Clause, a Brand of Infamy, of Degradation, and Disgrace, fixed upon every American? Is he not degraded below the Rank of an Englishman? Is it not directly, a Repeal of Magna Charta, as far as America is concerned. It is not att all surprising that the Tryals of Forfeiture and Penalties are confined to the Courts of Record at Westminster, in England. The Wonder only is that they are not confined to Courts of common Law here.

The People of England are attached to Magna Charta.[97] By the 29th Chapter of that Statute, "Nullus liber Homo capiatur, vel imprisonetur, aut disseisietur de libero tenemento [*suo*], vel libertatibus, vel liberis Consuetudinibus [*suis*], aut utlagetur, aut exuletur, aut aliquo modo destruatur, nec super eum ibimus nec super eum mittemus, nisi per

[95] Translated in JA's "Instructions" as "who answered with one voice, 'We will not that the laws of England be changed.'" This famous line is the reply of the barons to the request of the bishops that they be permitted to follow the canon law by certifying children born before marriage as legitimate. Statute of Merton, 20 Hen. 3, c. 9 (1234). The phrase appears in slightly different form in the text of the statute itself, but JA followed Coke's rendition of Bracton's version. 2 Coke, *Institutes* *98. See 2 Holdsworth, *History of English Law* 218. In Coke's text, the active voice of the infinitive "mutare" (to change) is used. JA's probably inadvertent use of the passive, "mutari," is carried over into his translation, changing the barons' denial of a request for legislation into a legislative principle.

[96] American Act of 1764, 4 Geo. 3, c. 15, §40.

[97] This and the preceding three sentences were omitted in the "Instructions," and the two paragraphs were telescoped into a single sentence, "Is it not with respect to us a Repeal of the 29th Chapter of *Magna Charta?*" 3 JA, *Works* 509.

legale Iudicium Parium Suorum vel per Legem Terrae."[98] This 29. Chap. of Magna Charta, has for many Centuries been esteemed by Englishmen, as one of the noblest Monuments, one of the firmest Bulwarks of their Liberties—and We know very well the Feelings and Reflections of Englishmen whenever this Chapter has been infringed upon even in Parliament. One Proof of them has been given us by Lord Coke, in his Exposition of this Chapter.[99] 2. Inst. 51. "Against this ancient and fundamental Law, and in the Face thereof I find an Act of Parliament made, that as well Justices of Assize as Justices of Peace without any finding or presentment of 12 Men, upon a bare Information for the King before them made, should have full Power and Authority by their Discretions," &c.[100]

Lord Coke after mentioning the Repeal of this Statute and the Fate of Empson and Dudley, concludes with a Reflection, which if properly attended to might be sufficient even to make a Parliament tremble.[101] "The ill success of this Statute and the fearfull End of these 2 oppressors, should deter others from committing the like, and should admonish Parliaments, that instead of this ordinary and precious Tryal Per Legem Terræ, they bring not in absolute and partial Tryals by Discretion."[102]

[98] Translated by JA in his "Instructions," 15 May 1769, as "No freeman shall be taken or imprisoned or disseised of his freehold or liberties or free customs or outlawed or exiled or any otherwise destroyed, nor will we pass upon him nor condemn him, but by lawful judgment of his peers or the law of the land." 3 JA, *Works* 509. The text is that of Magna Carta, 9 Hen. 3, c. 29 (1225), quoted from the version given by 2 Coke, *Institutes* *45. Quotation marks and omitted words supplied. It is this text, approved by Henry III at his majority, rather than that granted by John at Runnymede in 1215, which actually has the force of law today. See Plucknett, *Concise History* 23. The differences between the two documents are slight, however, and are not material in this section. See William S. McKechnie, *Magna Carta* 181–183, 436, 445–446 (Glasgow, 1905). For changes in translation brought about by modern scholarship, see *id.* at 436–448; 1 Holdsworth, *History of English Law* 59–63.

[99] This and the preceding sentence are rendered in the "Instructions" as "Englishmen are inviolably attached to the important right expressed in this clause, which for many centuries has been the noblest monument and firmest bulwark of their liberties. One proof of this attachment, given us by a great sage of the law, we think proper to mention, not for your information, but as the best expression of the sense of your constituents." 3 JA, *Works* 509.

[100] 2 Coke, *Institutes* *51. Quotation marks supplied. Coke's sentence continues, "to heare and determine all offenses, and contempts committed, or done by any person, or persons against the forme, ordinance, and effect of any statute made, and not repealed, &c." The Act, 11 Hen. 7, c. 3 (1494), excepted treason, murder, and felony from its provisions. See 4 Coke, *Institutes* *40–41. In his "Instructions" JA quoted Coke as saying "by their discretions to hear and try men for penalties and forfeitures." 3 JA, *Works* 509.

[101] In the "Instructions" the last phrase is "to discourage such attacks upon fundamental principles." 3 JA, *Works* 509.

[102] 2 Coke, *Institutes* *51. 11 Hen. 7, c. 3, was repealed by 1 Hen. 8, c. 6 (1509),

These are the Reflections of an Englishman, upon a Statute which gave to Justices of Assize, and Peace, the Tryal of Penalties and Forfeitures, which by the 29. C[hapter] of Magna Charta ought to be tryed by Jury. The Statute 4 G. 3. takes from Mr. Hancock this precious Tryal Per Legem Terræ, and gives it to a single Judge.[103] However respectable the Judge may be, it is however an Hardship and severity, which distinguishes my Clyent from the rest of Englishmen, and renders this Statute, extremely pœnal.[104]

I have mentioned this Particular, not merely to shew the Hardship

---

which, according to Coke, recited that under the earlier act, "it was manifestly known, that many sinister, and crafty, feigned and forged informations, had been pursued against divers of the kings subjects to their great damage, and wrongful vexation." 2 Coke, *Institutes* *51. This is a reference to the doings of Sir Richard Empson and Edmund Dudley, councilors of Henry VII employed in the collection of taxes and forfeitures due the Crown, who were purported to have abused the power of proceeding by information under 11 Hen. 7, c. 3. On the accession of Henry VIII they were thrown into the Tower, accused of various oppressive tactics; while there, they were charged with and convicted of having compassed the death of the new king, and were executed on these grounds in 1510. 1 Howell, *State Trials* 283–288; see *DNB* under both names. JA used this episode in his Clarendon Letters of 1766, attacking the use of the Admiralty courts in the Stamp Act. See note 76 above.

[103] Coke does not deal with the problem under the clause "Iudicium Parium suorum," or judgment of peers, the traditional source of the right to jury trial. He seems to view that clause merely as a confirmation of the nobility's right to a trial by their peers. 2 Coke, *Institutes* *48–50. Instead, his "reflections" are a gloss on the clause "per Legem Terrae," to which he gives the meaning "due process of law." His criticism of 11 Hen. 7, c. 3, seems to be based more on the fact that no indictment was required, than on the absence of a trial jury. *Id.* at 50–51; but see 4 Coke, *Institutes* *41. Modern scholars are agreed that in granting a trial by judgment of peers, Magna Carta granted not the modern trial by jury but rather the right to trial in a court of peers instead of in the King's court. There is disagreement as to whether "the law of the land" means due process, or simply the usual medieval modes of trial—battle, ordeal, and compurgation. See 1 Holdsworth, *History of English Law* 59–63; 2 *id.* at 214–215. Whatever the correct interpretation, Parliament does not seem to have regarded summary trial as a deprivation of due process. No general measure was ever enacted again, but by the middle of the 18th century certain customs violations and at least 200 other specific offenses against statutory regulation, punishable corporally or by fines ranging up to £500, were to be tried by one or more justices of the peace sitting without a jury. Frankfurter and Corcoran, "Petty Federal Offenses and the Constitutional Guaranty of Trial by Jury," 39 *Harv. L. Rev.* 917, 922–934 (1926); Hoon, *English Customs* 277, 280. A similar range of offenses was within the jurisdiction of Massachusetts justices, but there was a theoretical right to a jury through an appeal procedure much hedged in with restrictive security requirements. 39 *Harv. L. Rev.* 938–942. Moreover, in England the proceeding by information, rather than indictment, was a common one for many misdemeanors even when trial was to a jury. See note 62 above.

[104] In the "Instructions" the preceding paragraph is summed up in the sentence, "Such are the feelings and reflections of an Englishman upon a statute not unlike the statute now under consideration, and upon courts and judges not unlike the courts and judges of admiralty in America." 3 JA, *Works* 509.

of this Statute and Prosecution, and that my Client is therefore in a favourable Case,[105] but for another Purpose, vizt. to shew the Nature of the Evidence, that is required in this Case. We are here to be tryed by a Court of civil not of common Law, we are therefore to be tryed by the Rules of Evidence that we find in the civil Law, not by those that We find in the common Law. We are to be tryed, both Fact and Law is to be tryed by a single Judge, not by a Jury. We therefore claim it as a Right, that Witnesses not Presumptions nor Circumstances are to be the Evidence.

We are to enquire what is the Evidence required by the civil Law, ⟨*in Criminal Cases*⟩ in order to convict a Person of a Crime and to Subject him to a Penalty. New Inst. civil Law. Page 316.[106] 2. "The Number of Witnesses ought to be two at the least to make a full Proof, and these must be free from all Exceptions, Either as to their Persons or their Depositions. For the Testimony of a single Witness is of no Validity, tho the Person is of a great Character," &c.[107] "For one Witness may mistake or lie, and be corrupted, and yet be consistent with himself, and so remain undiscovered; whereas two or three Witnesses may more easily be found in a Conspiracy by a prudent Judge if they are separately examined; and tho many Criminals would escape and many might loose their Right for Want of two Witnesses, yet it would be a lesser Evil than to trust so much Power to the Mistakes or Malice of one Person."

Dig. Lib. 22. Tit. 5. §12. De numero Testium. "Ubi numerus testium non adjicitur, etiam duo sufficient. Pluralis enim elocutio duorum numero contenta est." [108]

Codicis Lib. 4. Tit. 20. §9, §1. "Simili modo sanximus, ut unius testimonium nemo Iudicum, in quacunque causa facile patiatur ad-

---

[105] This may be another garbled passage showing that JA copied from notes. See text at note 70 above. Or it could mean that Hancock's "Case" was to be considered "favourable" in the sense that the hardships were extenuating circumstances which entitled him to favorable consideration. See *OED.*

[106] Wood, *New Institute of the Civil Law* 316. Quotation marks supplied.

[107] JA has here omitted the following passage: "unless he swears of his own Fact, and where there are other Circumstances to concur or corroborate, or unless he is a publick Officer; as a Notary, &c. deposing by Vertue of his Office. This is founded upon very good reason." Wood, *New Institute of the Civil Law* 316.

[108] Justinian, *Digest*, bk. 22, tit. 5, §12. Quotation marks supplied. For translation see 5 Scott, *Civil Law* 235: "Where the number of witnesses is not specified by law, two are sufficient, for the term 'several' is embraced in the number two."

[109] Justinian, *Codex*, bk. 4, tit. 20, §9, §1. Quotation marks supplied. See 13 Scott, *Civil Law* 37: "In like manner, we have ordered that no judge shall in any case readily accept the testimony of only one witness; and now We plainly order that the evidence of only one witness shall not be taken, even though he should be distinguished by senatorial rank."

mitti. Et nunc manifeste sanximus, ut unius omnino testis responsio non audiatur, etiamsi præclaræ Curiæ honore prefulgeat." [109] Vide Note 32. "Unus testis, nullus testis. Unius Testimonium non admittitur. Vox Unius, Vox nullius est." [110] In this Respect the civil Law conforms to the divine Law. Deut. 19. 15. "One Witness shall not rise up against a Man for any Iniquity, or for any Sin, in any sin that he sinneth: at the Mouth of two Witnesses, or 3, shall the matter be established." [111]

But in Hancock's Case, if there were 2 or ten such Witnesses as Mezle,[112] they would not amount to Proof sufficient for Condemnation. Because there are against him, the strongest legal Exceptions. 1. His Condition. New Inst. civ. Law. 315. "Indigent Persons and Beggars ought to be suspected, because they are easily corrupted." [113] Dig. 22. 5. 3. "Testium Fides diligenter examinanda est: Ideoque in Persona eorum exploranda, erunt in primis, Conditio, cujusque; utrum quis decurio an Plebeius sit; et an *honestæ et inculpatæ vitæ*, an vero *notatus quis*, et reprehensibilis. An locuples vel egens sit ut lucri causa quid facile admittat: vel an inimicus ei sit, adversus quem testimonium fert; vel amicus ei sit, pro quo testimonium dat:" &c.[114] Vide Note 22. "In Testibus hac sunt inquiranda, Conditio, Vita, Facultates, Inimicitiæ, vel amicitiæ, suspicio denique &c." [115]

Calv. Lex. Testes. "Callistratus, testium Fidem, Conditionem, Vitam anteactum, Fortunam, Æstimationem, atque dignitatem diligenter exquirendam esse præcipit." [116]

---

[110] The edition used by JA has not been found. For this passage, see 2 *Corpus Juris Civilis* 176, note 18 (Antwerp, 1726).

[111] Deuteronomy 19:15. Quotation marks supplied. The reference appears at the page in Wood's *New Institute*, cited in note 106 above.

[112] As to Mezle, or Maysel, see text at notes 37–39 above.

[113] Wood, *New Institute of the Civil Law* 315.

[114] Justinian, *Digest*, bk. 22, tit. 5, §3. Quotation marks supplied. See 5 Scott, *Civil Law* 232–233: "The integrity of witnesses should be carefully investigated, and in consideration of their personal characteristics, attention should be, in the first place, paid to their rank; as to whether the witness is a Decurion or a plebeian; whether his life is honorable and without blame, or whether he has been branded with infamy and is liable to censure; whether he is rich or poor, lest he may readily swear falsely for the purpose of gain; whether he is an enemy to him against whom he testifies, or whether he is a friend to him in whose favor he gives his evidence." The concluding sentence of the above translation, which was omitted by JA, is, in the Latin, "Nam si careat suspicione testimonium, vel propter personam, a qua fertur, quod honesta sit: vel propter causam, quod neque lucri neque gratiae, neque inimicitiae causa sit: admittendus est."

[115] See 1 *Corpus Juris Civilis* 436 note 38 (Antwerp, 1726).

[116] Johannes Calvinus, *Lexicon Juridicum Juris Cæsarei Simul et Canonici* 905, tit. "Testis," (Cologne, 1622). Quotation marks supplied. The editors' translation: "Callistratus decreed that the good faith, condition, previous life, lot, reputation, and rank of witnesses should be diligently inquired of."

Fortescue De Laudibus Legum. C. 31. page 38. "It will not always happen that they [*i.e.* perjured witnesses] are or can be known by the Party, Defendant in the Cause, in order to call in Question their Life and Conversation, that as Persons of a profligate Character, they might be cross examined; upon which account their Evidence might be set aside."[117]

The general Character of this Witness cant be known. We can have no Citation to the Mountains of Switzerland, or the Fens of Holland or the Plains of Cape Francois,[118] for Witnesses to his general Character for Truth. We ought to know therefore all that can be known of his History from his own Mouth. Life and Conversation, Fides, Vitam anteactam, inculpatæ et honestæ Vitæ are Expressions, that denote more than a general Character for Truth or falshood.

The civil Law seems to lean to the side of Mercy, as much as the common Law. Wood Inst. 310. "In Criminal Cases the Proofs ought to be as clear as the Sun at Noon day:"[119]

Domat. V. 1. Page 13. Preliminary Book. Tit. 1. Sect. 2. N. 15.[120] "The Laws which restrain our natural Liberty, such as those that forbid any Thing that is not in itself unlawfull or which derogate in any other manner from the general Law, the Laws which inflict Punishments for Crimes and offences, or Penalties in civil matters; those which prescribe certain Formalities; *the Laws which appear to have any Hardship in them*" &c.[121] "are to be interpreted in such a manner, as not to be applied beyond what is clearly expressed in the Law," &c.[122] "We ought to give to such Laws all the Temperament of Equity and Humanity, that they are capable of." Notæ: "Interpretatione Legum Pœnæ molliendæ sunt, potius quam asperendæ. In Pœnalibus Causis benignius interpretandum est. In levioribus Causis proniores at Lenitatem Judices esse debent, in gravioribus Pœnis, Severitatem Legum, cum aliquo temperamento benignitatio subsequi."[123]

[117] Sir John Fortescue, *De Laudibus Legum Angliæ* 38 (London, 1741). Quotation marks supplied. Fortescue was actually pointing to this as a defect in civil-law procedure. His *De Laudibus*, written about 1468, and first published in the 16th century, was intended to demonstrate the great superiority of the English to the Roman law. See 2 Holdsworth, *History of English Law* 569–570.

[118] Maysel was evidently of European origin. See note 126 below.

[119] Wood, *New Institute of the Civil Law* 310. Quotation marks supplied.

[120] Jean Domat, *The Civil Law In Its Natural Order*, 1:13–14 (London, transl. Strahan, 1722). Quotation marks supplied.

[121] JA here omitted "those which permit Disinheriting and others the like."

[122] JA here omitted: "to any consequences to which the Laws do not extend. And on the contrary . . ."

[123] The preceding three sentences are in a note at the end of the passage from Domat, cited, note 120 above. They are quoted from the following sections of Justinian, *Digest*: bk. 48, tit. 19, §42; bk. 50, tit. 17, §155(2); bk. 48, tit. 19, §11.

Codicis. Lib. 4. Tit. 19. §.25. De Judiciis criminalibus. "Sciant cuncti accusatores eam se rem deferre in publicam notionem debere quæ munita sit idoneis Testibus, vel instructa apertissimis documentis vel indiciis ad probationem indubitatis et luce clarioribus expedita." [124] Vide Notes also.[125]

But disregarding order, for the present let me record the Controversy We had last Week, Concerning the Rules of Law which were to govern this Case.[126] The Court of Admiralty is originally a Civil Law Court. Jurisdiction of a Crime, is given to it in this Case by Act of Parliament. The Question is whether it is to proceed by the civil Law? If it is, We have a Right to examine the Witnesses whole past Life, and his Character at large. A Son cannot be examined against the Father nor the Father against the Son, and other Relations are disqualified to be Witnesses. All Persons under Twenty are disqualified, under 20 years of age I mean, from being Witnesses. Servants and dependants

---

See 11 Scott, *Civil Law* 124: "By the interpretation of the laws, penalties should rather be mitigated than increased in severity." *Id.* at 312: "In penal cases, the most benevolent construction should be adopted." *Id.* at 115: "It is clear that in cases of minor importance, judges should be inclined to lenity; and where heavier penalties are involved, while they must comply with the stern requirements of the laws, they should temper them with some degree of indulgence."

[124] Justinian, *Codex*, bk. 4, tit. 19, §25. See 13 Scott, *Civil Law* 36: "All accusers are hereby notified that they cannot bring a criminal charge for anything which has been established by reliable witnesses; or clearly proved by documentary evidence; or shown to be true by undoubted testimony clearer than light." A better translation of the first clause might be "charge unless a thing has been established." This section is cited in the margin of the passage in Wood's *New Institute*, cited, note 119 above.

[125] The notes in 2 *Corpus Juris Civilis* 175, notes 24–26 (Antwerp, 1726), reiterate the sense of the text quoted at note 124 above.

[126] According to "A Journal of the Times," on 24 Feb. "The advocates for Mr. Hancock, offered evidence to prove that a witness, who had been before examined for the proponent, was a *fugitive* from his native country, to *avoid the punishment* due to a very *heinous crime*. The advocates for the crown objected to this evidence as improper, urging that by common law, nothing could be proved against a witness but his general character for falsehood. The advocates for the respondent replied, that the Court of Admiralty proceeded according to the *civil law*, whereby a witnesses whole life and conversation ought to be examined. And they insisted upon knowing by what law their client was to be tried." Dickerson, *Boston under Military Rule* 68. The passage continues with a close paraphrase of the text here, adding a few phrases from JA's earlier notes on the civil law. The English common-law rule at this time was basically that asserted by the Crown. A witness' general moral character and character for truth were admissible to impeach, but evidence of specific misconduct could be admitted only in the form of a record of criminal conviction. See Wood, *Institute of the Laws of England* 597; 2 Bacon, *Abridgment* 288, 296; Gilbert, *Evidence* 157–158. The distinction was doubtless due to the fact that those guilty of felony and other crimes involving falsehood were altogether excluded as witnesses. *Id.* at 142–145.

are not to be Witnesses. Nay. Mr. Fitch says we must adopt the Method of Torture, among the rest.

On the Contrary I argue, that if We are to be governed by the Rules of the common Law We ought to adopt it as a whole and summon a Jury and be tryed by Magna Charta. Every Examination of Witnesses ought to be in open Court, in Presence of the Parties, Face to Face. And there ought to be regular Adjournments from one Time to another.

What other Hypothesis shall we assume? Shall We say that We are to be governed by some Rules of the common Law and some Rules of the civil Law, that the Judge at his Discretion shall choose out of each system such Rules as please him, and discard the rest. If so Misera Servitus est. Examinations of witnesses upon Interrogatories, are only by the Civil Law. Interrogatories are unknown at common Law, and Englishmen and common Lawyers have an aversion to them if not an Abhorrence of them. Shall We suffer under the odious Rules of the civil Law, and receive no advantage from the beneficial Rules of it? This, instead of favouring the Accused, would be favouring the Accuser, which is against the Maxims of both Laws.

Interlocutory Decree [127]
Advocate General vs. John Hancock, Esqr.

The Substance of the Point before the Court, is, whether a Witness shall be examined to charge another Witness in the Cause with a particular infamous Crime.

It is urged by the Advocates offering the first mentioned Witness, first, that this is a civil Law Court, and secondly, by that Law such Evidence is admissible. To the last Point several authorities were cited, but the principal one from the Digest 22. 5. 2. 3.[128]

---

[127] Probably given on 1 March 1769. See note 38 above.

[128] Though partly overwritten, this refers to bk. 22, tit. 5, §§2, 3. For §2, see 5 Scott, *Civil Law* 232: "The rank, the integrity, the manners and the gravity of witnesses must be taken into consideration, and therefore those who make contradictory statements, or who hesitate while giving their evidence, should not be heard." "Manners" (Latin "*mores*") might be better translated as "morals." The first part of §3 appears in text at note 114 above. The section goes on to provide that the judge should determine credibility; that all available kinds of proof should be investigated; that the judge should examine the witnesses if possible, allowing them their costs; and that witnesses should not be summoned from afar unless it is the custom of the region. The passage most relevant here would seem to be the following: "It is proved by the *Lex Julian* relating to violence, that those shall not be permitted to give testimony against a defendant who has [i.e. have] been freed by him or his father; or who have not yet arrived at puberty, or anyone who has been condemned for a public crime, and has not been restored to his former condition,

To which it was answered by the Advocates on the other side that
this is not a civil Law Court in such Cases as the present. And that the
Authorities produced were not to be understood in the Sense contended for by the Respondents Advocates. In support of the last, the
Notes under the aforesaid 3 Law in the Digest were read and relyed
on.¹²⁹ It was also urged, that admitting the civil Law to be as contended
for, the argument would prove too much, because it would exclude
relations in certain Degrees, intimate Friends, Persons under the age
of Fourteen &c. from testifying.

I take the Sense of the Authority first mentioned, to be no more
than a general description of what are good objections against persons
being admitted to their Oaths as Witnesses without describing the
mode whereby such disqualifications are to be ascertained. If said
Authority is not so construed, it certainly clashes with the notes,
which clearly relate not to the Admission of Witnesses, but the
Credit or Refutation of their Evidence. The reason why proof by
record ought to be exhibited against a Witness, when charged with a
Crime, appears clear from the Question put in the Note, under D. 22.
Tit. 3. "Quis enim, si sufficiat accusasse, innocens fiet?"¹³⁰ Such a
reading reconciles the Text and comment in the Digest to each other,
and the former to Reason. I am therefore of opinion the motion is not
well supported, even by the Rules of the civil Law. In addition to
which, when I consider the process now in question, is founded on an
Act of parliament, originally intended to be guided by the Rules of the
common Law,¹³¹ that the Practice of the Court has ever been to hear
and determine similar cases, according to those rules, the manifest and
great inconveniences which must accrue, by the Admission of such

---

or who is in chains, or in prison, or has hired himself out to fight with wild beasts;
or any woman who openly prostitutes herself, or has already done so; or anyone who
has been sentenced or convicted of having received money for giving or witholding
testimony." *Id.* at 233–234.

¹²⁹ For the notes, see 1 *Corpus Juris Civilis* 436–437 (Antwerp, 1726). See note
130 below.

¹³⁰ 1 *Corpus Juris Civilis* 437 note 1, a note to the latter part of Justinian, *Digest,*
bk. 22, tit. 5, §3. Editors' translation: "Who, however, will be found innocent, if
it be sufficient to have been accused?" The preceding sentence is, in translation, "In
the refutation of a witness, it is not enough that he be accused of a crime; it is necessary that he be convicted." See also, 1 *Corpus Juris Civilis* 436, note 73, an annotation to the passage quoted in note 128 above concerning those who are in chains or
in prison, which states that such persons are not rejected as witnesses unless they
have been convicted, seemingly because chains and prison alone are not a sign of
infamy.

¹³¹ Compare "A Journal of the Times," 24 Feb. 1769: "If therefore the court is
to adopt the common law, because the jurisdiction was created by Act of Parliament;
it ought to adopt it as a system." Dickerson, *Boston under Military Rule* 68.

evidence, I am clearly of opinion, the Question put is improper, and therefore Decree the same to be withdrawn.[132]

Robt. Auchmuty Judge &c.

Obsirve, The Expressions. The *Substance of a Point.* A Point has not Parts, therefore is indivisible, therefore to talk of the substance of it, is not the neatest or most elegant. But to omit Criticism, let me make a few Observations upon the ⟨Reasoning⟩ substance of the Decree.

1. The Advocates for the Crown, did not argue that our Argument would exclude Relations, Friends, Persons under 14. &c. But the Advocates for the Respondent, insisted that all those Rules of the civil Law ought to be adopted, because they were beneficial to the subject the Respondent. We had no difficulty at all in Admitting the Consequence as far as it is here mentioned. So far from it that we desired it, because Mr. Hancock's Relations, Friends, and many Persons under age have been examined in this Case. It is true Mr. Fitch did argue that our Principle would justify the Introduction of Torture and this he thought was proving too much, and this was well observed by Mr. Fitch and was the best argument I have heard in the Case.[133]

2. The Judge has totally mistaken the "Sense" of the Authority, for instead of being a Description of Objections against Persons being admitted to their Oaths it is wholly confined to those who are already sworn. It is Testium Fides examinanda est,[134] not Personarum Fides, and as a Witness in English implies the Competency of the Person, so

---

[132] For a somewhat similar argument, see Stokes, *Constitution of the British Colonies* 361. In "A Journal of the Times," 2 March 1769, Auchmuty's point that the evidence would be inadmissible even under the civil law was not mentioned and the decision was said to have turned upon "the usage of the court, and the inconveniencies that would attend the introduction of the rules of the civil law, in cases of this nature." The writer asked upon what usage this unique case could be based, and went on to point out that the court had not been deterred by inconvenience in using interrogatories, in sitting without regular adjournments, in issuing compulsory citations to witnesses, and in ordering arrest and high bail for immediate appearance. After noting that only the judge's discretion determined which law would apply, the account continued, "It is reported that the advocates for Mr. Hancock, had no solicitude about the question they put to the witness, but they thought that if the court would proceed by such rules of the civil law *as pleased the officers of the revenue,* they had a right to *such rules* of the same law, *as made* in favour of *Mr. Hancock.*" Dickerson, *Boston under Military Rule* 72.

[133] This point was turned to good account in the entry in "A Journal of the Times," note 132 above. As a consequence of the judge's discretion to determine the applicable law, "if a case should happen that should require it, or if the C[om-missio]n[e]rs should give their mandate to the court, supposing them *hereafter* to get a judge fit for the purpose, why might he not gently put *parties* or *witnesses* to the torture, and extend them on the rack? Donec eorum rumpuntur nervi, et venae in sanguinis fluenta prorumpunt." Dickerson, *Boston under Military Rule* 72.

[134] That is, in the passage in the *Digest* in text at note 114 above.

Testis in Latin implies the same, and a Person cannot be Testis, untill he is admitted, to tell what he knows, i.e. to give Evidence.[135]

47. Dowse v. Thirty-three Hogsheads of Molasses
1768–1769

EDITORIAL NOTE

While the affair of John Hancock's *Liberty* (No. 46) drew public attention, a steady flow of other cases of illicit importation kept merchants, customs officers, and lawyers busy. On 6 September 1768, Joseph Dowse, surveyor and searcher of the customs for the port of Salem and Marblehead, seized thirty-three hogsheads and four tierces of molasses which had allegedly been landed in Gloucester without entry or payment of duties.[1] Although another seizure which Dowse had made on Cape Ann was rescued at about this time by the inhabitants, he managed to retain control of the molasses. Jonathan Sewall filed an information against it for him in the Court of Admiralty on 26 October, with claimants cited to appear on 7 November.[2]

Since Adams was to appear in court for Hancock on the latter date,[3] it is probable that he was of counsel for David Plumer of Gloucester, who claimed the molasses. In any event, Adams' minutes, printed below, show that when the case came on to trial, probably some time in December, Plumer sought to establish that the molasses had been imported, duty-paid, in August on his schooner *Earl of Gloucester*. Unfortunately, this vessel, after earlier evading the officers, had been seized on 22 October for the illicit importation of forty hogsheads of molasses on the same August voyage. An *in rem* proceeding was begun against her on 6 December.[4]

[135] Both the abrupt termination of his argument at this point without a formal conclusion and the state of the manuscript suggest that JA intended to continue this paper.

[1] The duties, of a penny a gallon on all molasses imported except from the island of Dominica, were imposed by 6 Geo. 3, c. 52, §4 (1766). Forfeiture, as provided by 6 Geo. 2, c. 13, §3 (1733), was the penalty for landing without entry and payment of duties, because §12 of the 1766 Act had incorporated prior statutes. As to Dowse, see Quincy, *Reports* (Appendix) 428.

[2] Dowse v. 33 Hogsheads and 4 Tierces of Molasses, Vice Adm. Min. Bk., 26 Oct. 1768; *Massachusetts Gazette*, 27 Oct. 1768, p. 1, col. 3. The rescue, "at Squam" in Gloucester occurred at midnight on 11 September. In Nov. the Commissioners offered a reward of £50 for the culprits, which was supported by a proclamation of Governor Bernard. *Id.*, 10 Nov. 1768, p. 1, col. 1. Dowse was still searching for these or other goods at Squam in the middle of October. Quincy, *Reports* (Appendix) 428 note. See also Dowse v. Nineteen Casks of Molasses, No. 49.

[3] No. 46, note 31.

[4] Grason v. The *Earl of Gloucester*, Vice Adm. Min. Bk., 6 Dec. 1768; *Massachusetts Gazette*, 8 Dec. 1768, p. 2, col. 2; "A Journal of the Times," 24 Oct. 1768,

The Commissioners also sought to impose penalties upon the individuals responsible for the alleged smuggling. At the end of December, Sewall filed *in personam* actions against seven men, including Plumer and Moses Bray, master of the *Earl of Gloucester*. On 3 February 1769 the citations were returned not served.[5] It is possible that the respondents entered into a settlement whereby they agreed to withdraw their opposition in the forfeiture proceedings in exchange for an undertaking not to press the penal actions. Whatever the reason, the molasses, condemned earlier, was ordered sold on 2 March; on 18 April the *Earl of Gloucester* was adjudged forfeit, no claim having been entered for her.[6]

If Plumer did not voluntarily withdraw his claim for the molasses, there were other reasons why his defense might have failed. Adams' minutes indicate that Plumer produced witnesses to establish an identity between the molasses in suit and certain molasses covered by a cocket certifying legal entry on payment of duty, which had been signed by John Fisher, Collector at Salem. At the end of September, however, Fisher had been suspended by the Commissioners of the Customs on a number of charges,

---

Dickerson, *Boston under Military Rule* 10. Commissioners' General Letter, 14 Oct. 1768, Salem Custom House Record Book, 1763–1772, p. 254, MSaE. The *Earl of Gloucester* was informed against by her former master, Samuel Fellows, who apparently had a grievance against the owners. Minutes of the Commissioners, 30 March 1769, 7 Bowdoin-Temple MSS 173, MHi; "A Journal of the Times," 16 Dec. 1768, Dickerson, *Boston under Military Rule* 36. See R. Reeve to Salem Customs Officers, 28 Jan. 1769, Salem Record Book, 1763–1772, p. 262. By way of reward, Fellows was given a position aboard a customs vessel and was soon in trouble. In May he led several men to rescue a member of his crew from a Salem deputy sheriff, firing on the officer in the process. Commodore Hood turned him over to the civil authorities, and at Ipswich Superior Court in June he was fined £10 and ordered to give £50 bond to keep the peace for two years. "A Journal of the Times," 20 May, 3 June, 2 July 1769, Dickerson, *Boston under Military Rule* 100–101, 105–106, 113–114; *Massachusetts Gazette*, 25 May 1769, p. 1, cols. 1–2; *Boston News-Letter*, 1 June 1769, p. 1, col. 2; Min. Bk. 85, SCJ Essex, June 1769; SCJ Rec. 1769, fol. 71; SF 131768.

[5] Advocate General v. David Plummer, Moses Bray, Daniel Plummer, Peter Clowning, Daniel Trew, Joseph Eveleth, and Thomas Corbin, Vice Adm. Min. Bk., 3 Feb. 1769; "A Journal of the Times," 28 Dec. 1768, Dickerson, *Boston under Military Rule* 40. The Commissioners had asked the Salem customs officers for these names in a letter of 13 Sept. 1768. Salem Record Book, 1763–1772, p. 237.

[6] For the molasses, see Notice of Sale, *Massachusetts Gazette*, 2 March 1769, p. 1, col. 3. The sale was set for 16 March. Only thirty hogsheads are included in the order, but it is not clear whether this was a typographical error, or whether in fact only thirty were condemned. Governor Bernard was paid his share of the proceeds on 8 June. Vice Adm. Min. Bk., 26 Oct. 1768. The *Earl of Gloucester* was first condemned along with her lading of a hogshead of rum, 1000 feet of white pine boards, and 3000 shingles, on 15 March 1769, and sale was set for 21 March. Grason v. The *Earl of Gloucester*, Vice Adm. Min. Bk., 6 Dec. 1768; *Massachusetts Gazette*, 16 March 1769, p. 1, col. 3. Perhaps because the buyer failed to pay, or else for some technical error in the proceedings, the vessel was then seized again on 10 April and declared forfeit on 18 April, this time with a cargo of 488 planks and 13,000 shingles. No order of sale or distribution of proceeds has been found. Vice Adm. Min. Bk., 10 April 1769; *Massachusetts Gazette*, 13 April 1769, p. 1, col. 2.

including that of crediting merchants with more duties than they had actually paid.[7] The court thus may well have found the cocket fraudulent, or may not have accepted the evidence of Plumer's witnesses.

ADAMS' COPY OF THE LIBEL AND REPORT OF THE TRIAL[8]

Court of Vice Admiralty, Boston, October 1768–March 1769

Dowse vs. Thirty Three Hdds. Molosses

Libel

Be it remembered that on the 26 October 1768 Joseph Dowse of Salem in the County of Essex Esqr., Surveyor and Searcher for the Port of Salem and Marblehead in said Province, who prosecutes as well &c.[9] comes and gives the Court to be informed that on the Sixth day of September last at Glocester in the Port aforesaid, he Seized as forfeited, one Third to the King &c.[10] Thirty Three Hogsheads and four Tierces of Molasses, for that the same, on the same day was *illegally imported*, in some Ship or Vessell to the said Informant unknown, from *foreign Parts*, and was *illegally unshipped and landed* on Shore in Glouster aforesaid, *no Report or Entry* thereof having been first made and the Same being customable Goods and the *Dutys thereon* not having been *first paid*; against the Form of the Statute in that Case made and provided;[11] whereby the Same Molasses is become forfeit to the Uses aforesaid. Whereupon as this is a matter properly within the Jurisdiction of this honorable Court, the said Joseph Dowse prays the Advisement of the Court in the Premises, and that the same may by proper Process from this Court, be taken into Custody of the

---

[7] Fisher had been appointed in 1765 at the behest of John Temple, then Surveyor General of the Customs. His case was sent to the Treasury in London, who reversed the Commissioners and ordered them to reinstate him in Aug. 1769. Full documentation of the matter appears in PRO, Treas. 1:465, fols. 285–328, 389–391; 1:471, fol. 438. See also Quincy, *Reports* (Appendix) 451; Barrow, Colonial Customs 483–487. As to cockets, see note 12 below.

[8] In JA's hand, in his Admiralty Book, Adams Papers, Microfilms, Reel No. 184.

[9] Omitted in MS is the remainder of the usual form of words in the *qui tam* information, "on behalf of the said Lord the King and of the Governor of this Province, as for himself." See No. 46, note 80.

[10] The omitted language is presumably "One Third to the Governor of said Province, and one Third to him that informs and sues for the same," the statutory scheme of distribution. See 4 Geo. 3, c. 15, §42 (1764), applicable here. See also No. 46, note 56.

[11] See note 1 above.

Marshall of the same Court and by Decree be adjudged and decreed to remain forfeit to the Uses aforesaid.

Jona. Sewall Advo. for said Dowse &c.

David Plumer of Glocester in the County of Essex Merchant produces a Cockett from the Custom House in Salem 20 Aug. 1768 signed by Fisher Collector Mascarene Comptroller and John Turner Jr. Navall officer, for Thirty Three Casks of foreign Molasses, 3089 Gallons imported from St. Eustatia in the Earl of Glocester, duties paid by Moses Bray, now on board the Schooner Olive Branch Wm. Low Master, bound for Boston.[12]

And said Plumer proves by Witnesses that the Molasses now libelled against is the Same, that is mentioned in the above cockett.

48. Sheaffe v. The *Triton*

1768

EDITORIAL NOTE

The documents that follow tell all that is known about this forfeiture proceeding in Admiralty. The basis of the suit was apparently the same statutory prohibition against unloading cargo before entry upon which John Hancock's *Liberty* had been condemned.[1] The parties were cited to appear on 7 November, the date on which the *in personam* actions against Hancock and others involved in the *Liberty* affair began. Adams was thus certainly in court to make the brief minute of Otis' argument printed here as Document IV, and may also have been of counsel for Solomon Davis, the owner. The Minute Book entry (Document III) does not report the outcome, but presumably the *Triton* was acquitted, since no notice of sale was published in the Boston newspapers, and the Minute Book does not indicate a distribution of the proceeds of condemnation.

[12] A cocket was a document required for intercolonial shipment of goods, showing their quantity and quality, shipper, consignee, and where and when duties had been paid. 4 Geo. 3, c. 15, §29 (1764); 5 Geo. 3, c. 45, §25 (1765). Auchmuty had ruled in Dawson v. Lighter and Molasses (May 1768) that a cocket was not needed for shipments from port to port within a colony, but the Commissioners had asked for a ruling from the Treasury in London. The opinion of the attorney general upholding Auchmuty was not given until 8 Sept. See sources cited in Dickerson, *Navigation Acts* 214–215; Oaks v. Dawson, SF 101809. As to Fisher, see note 7 above. John Mascarene had been appointed comptroller of the port of Salem and Marblehead in Aug. 1764. See Quincy, *Reports* (Appendix) 434, 450–451. As to the Naval Officer, see No. 45, note 34.

[1] 15 Car. 2, c. 7, §8 (1663), set out in note 10 below. As to the *Liberty*, see No. 46, note 16.

Legal Papers of John Adams

I. "A JOURNAL OF THE TIMES" [2]

24 October 1768

This day the brig Tryton, owned by Mr. D——s, a merchant of this town,[3] was seized by order of the Board of Customs, on supposition it is said, that she had some time ago been employed in an illicit trade; and that they may oblige the owner to prove where and how she has been employed.—*This seizure exhibits another instance of the generosity of the Commissioners, and their friendly disposition towards trade, in as much as it is said, that they have not now any more cause of suspicion than they had four months past; during which time she has remained in port undisturbed till the owner had spent £100 sterling in repairs, and had taken a freight for Hull, the insurance of which has been some time past wrote for by the several freighters.*[4]

II. MINUTES OF THE
CUSTOMS COMMISSIONERS' PROCEEDINGS [5]

27 October 1768

Read a Letter of the 25 Instant from the Collector and Comptroller of Boston. Ordered that the Solicitor do attend the Advocate General, and give him Instructions for prosecuting the Brigantine Tryton formerly called *The Popet* for Breach of the Acts of Trade.

III. VICE ADMIRALTY COURT MINUTE BOOK ENTRY [6]

29 October 1768

Wm. Sheaffe, Esqr.,[7] Dy. Collector &c. vs. Brigt. Triton. Sewal [8]

Cited to appear 7 Novr.

His Honor the Judge gave his Decree as on file.

[2] Printed in Dickerson, *Boston under Military Rule* 9, from the *New York Journal*, 10 Nov. 1768.
[3] Solomon Davis.
[4] The italicized portion was omitted in the *Boston Evening-Post* publication of the item. Dickerson, *Boston under Military Rule* 9 note.
[5] 7 Bowdoin-Temple MSS 169, MHi.
[6] Vice Adm. Min. Bk., 29 Oct. 1768.
[7] As to Sheaffe, see No. 45, note 37.
[8] That is, Jonathan Sewall, who filed the information as Advocate General.

214

IV. ADAMS' MINUTES OF THE ARGUMENT[9]

Court of Vice Admiralty, Boston, November 1768

Sol. Davis's. Triton.

Otis. 15. C. 2, c 7, §. 8.[10]

49. Dowse v. Nineteen Casks of Molasses

1768

EDITORIAL NOTE

September 1768 was a busy month for Joseph Dowse. On the night of 6 September, in which he seized the goods involved in *Dowse v. Thirty-three Hogsheads of Molasses*, No. 47, nineteen additional casks were allegedly landed in Salem from the schooner *Neptune*, which had entered on 19 August. Dowse seized them on the 7th. In November the Commissioners of the Customs asked their solicitor to consult with Jonathan Sewall about filing a libel against the *Neptune* and her contraband in the name of Rowland Savage, "Land waiter, Weigher and Gauger at Salem," who had apparently seized the vessel.[1] No action was taken against the *Neptune*,

[9] In JA's hand. Adams Papers, Microfilms, Reel No. 185.
[10] 15 Car. 2, c. 7, §8 (1663). The pertinent portion of the section provides: "(2) and no ship or vessel coming to any such land, island, plantation, colony, territory or place [i.e. royal colonies in Asia, Africa, or America, except Tangier. 15 Car. 2, c. 7, §6], shall lade or unlade any goods or commodities whatsoever, until the master or commander of such ship or vessel shall first have made known to the governor of such land, island, plantation, colony, territory or place, or such other person or officer as shall be by him thereunto authorized and appointed, the arrival of the said ship or vessel, with her name, and the name and surname of her master or commander, and have shewn to him that she is an *English-built* ship, or made good by producing such certificate, as abovesaid [i.e. that required by 12 Car. 2, c. 18, §10 (1660)], that she is a ship or vessel *bona fide* belonging to *England, Wales*, or the town of *Berwick*, and navigated with an *English* master, and three fourth parts of the mariners at least *Englishmen*, and have delivered to such governor or other person or officer a true and perfect inventory or invoice of her lading, together with the place or places in which the said goods were laden or taken into the said ship or vessel; (3) under the pain of loss of the ship or vessel, with all her guns, ammunition, tackle, furniture and apparel, and of all such goods of the growth, production or manufacture of *Europe*, as were not *bona fide* laden and taken in *England, Wales*, or the town of *Berwick*, to be recovered and divided in manner aforesaid" (i.e. in "any of his Majesty's courts" in the colony, one third to the Crown, one third to the Governor, and one third to the informer. 15 Car. 2, c. 7, §6).

[1] Minutes of the Commissioners, 18 Nov. 1768, 7 Bowdoin-Temple MSS 169, MHi. See Commissioners' letter, 9 Sept. 1768, ordering seizure of molasses. Salem Custom House Record Book, 1763–1772, p. 238, MSaE. According to the notice of monition, note 2 below, the seizure was on 7 September. Dowse was informed of the entry by Thomas Rowe, tidesman. Popular displeasure at this led to a riot on

perhaps because of legal doubts as to Savage's authority to seize. On 6 December, Sewall filed an information in Dowse's behalf against the molasses alone.[2]

On 14 December no claimant appeared and the molasses was decreed forfeit.[3] Adams, who was then spending most of his time in the Admiralty Court as counsel in *Sewall v. Hancock*, No. 46, apparently contemplated making a claim in behalf of the consignee of the molasses. His notes, printed below, show that he had made a study of the statutes requiring an officer's warrant for goods to be landed, which, the information alleged, had not been obtained. He probably intended to argue that these Acts did not apply in an *in rem* proceeding against the goods, since they provided only for monetary fines against those involved in the landing or for the forfeiture of any small craft used. The decision not to file a claim may have been based on a desire to avoid exposure to an *in personam* action for these or the much more serious penalties imposed for entry without payment of duties, which were the basis of the suit against Hancock.[4]

ADAMS' COPY OF THE INFORMATION AND STATUTES INVOLVED[5]

Court of Vice Admiralty, Boston, December 1768

Josh. Dowse Esq. vs 19 Casks of Molasses. Gardiners.[6]

For that the same Molasses on 19 Aug. last, was imported and brought into the Port of Salem and Marblehead, from the Island of Guadaloupe, in a certain Schooner called the Neptune, Phillip Saun-

---

8 Sept. in which Rowe was injured. See Commissioners to Salem Customs Officers, 13 Sept. 1768, 2 Feb. 1769, Salem Record Book, 1763–1772, p. 237, 264.

[2] Joseph Dowse v. 19 Casks of Molasses, Vice Adm. Min. Bk., 6 Dec. 1768. See the notice of monition in *Massachusetts Gazette*, 8 Dec. 1768, p. 2, col. 2. For the statutes involved, see notes 8–20 below. Savage had been appointed by the American Commissioners of Customs on 30 March 1768. Salem Record Book, 1763–1772, p. 61. The question of the power of such officers to seize remained open until it was apparently decided in the negative in July 1769. No. 50. There may have been doubt previously, however, in view of the decision in Folger v. The *Cornelia*, No. 45, against the power of an appointee of the surveyor general.

[3] Vice Adm. Min. Bk., 6 Dec. 1768. See Notice of Sale, dated 3 Jan. 1769, for sale on 11 Jan. 1769. *Boston News-Letter*, Postscript, p. 2, col. 1. Governor Bernard received his third of the proceeds on 9 June 1769. Vice Adm. Min. Bk., 6 Dec. 1768.

[4] No. 46, note 28 and text at note 83. The Commissioners sought those responsible, apparently in contemplation of such suits. See Commissioners to Salem Customs Officers, 13 Sept. 1768, 26 Nov. 1768, Salem Record Book, 1763–1772, p. 237, 258.

[5] In JA's hand, in his Admiralty Book, Adams Papers, Microfilms, Reel No. 184.

[6] Presumably "Gardiner" was consignee and potential claimant of the molasses. Possibly Joshua Gardiner, a considerable merchant in Boston and a commercial partner of John Hancock. See No. 45, note 33.

ders Master, and in the Night Time between the 6. and 7. days of September last, the said 19 Casks of Molasses were fraudulently and clandestinely landed from on board the said Schooner, and put on Shore in Salem aforesaid, with Intent to defraud the said Lord the King of his customary Duties thereon; neither the said Master nor any other Person having first duly entered and paid the legal Duties for the same, and without having first duly entered and paid the legal Duties for the same,[7] and without having first obtained a Warrant from a proper officer, for the landing the same against the Form of the statutes in such Case made and provided,[8] whereby the same is become forfeited as aforesaid.

13. 14. C. 2, C. 11, §. 7.[9] Be it enacted that [*if*] any Wharfinger, or his servant, shall take up or land, &c. or suffer to be waterborn &c. any prohibited Goods &c.[10] without the Presence of some officer, &c. or at Hours and Times, not appointed by Law (1. Eliz.)[11] &c. he shall forfeit 100£.—and if any Goods or Merchandizes shall be taken in from the shore &c., into any Bark, Hoy, Lighter &c.[12] without a Warrant, and the Presence of an officer, the Bark &c. shall be forfeited and the Master, Boatswain, Mariner[13] &c. consenting shall forfeit the value of the Goods.

1. Elisabeth. C. 11, §. 2.[14] Not lawfull for any Person to lade or put off or from any Wharf, Key, or other Place on the Land &c. or to take up, discharge and lay on Land, out of any Lighter, Ship, Crayer or Vessell any Goods, Wares or Merchandises &c.[15] but only in the Day light, i.e. from March to Sept., between Sun setting and Sun rising,

[7] Thus in MS. Either a copying error on JA's part, or an example of extreme nicety in pleading.

[8] For the statutes requiring the duties and entry, see No. 47, note 1; No. 46, note 16. A warrant was required by 13 & 14 Car. 2, c. 11, §7 (1662), made applicable in the colonies by 7 & 8 Will. 3, c. 22, §6 (1696), which are set out in the text immediately following.

[9] 13 & 14 Car. 2, c. 11, §7 (1662). Pertinent omissions are supplied in footnotes.

[10] The statute also included goods "whereof any custom, subsidy or other duties are due and payable unto the King's majesty." 13 & 14 Car. 2, c. 11, §7.

[11] That is, 1 Eliz. 1, c. 11, §2 (1558), set out immediately following in the text, which establishes times and places for the loading and unloading of cargo. The reference in 13 & 14 Car. 2, c. 11, §7, is actually to an exception made in the Act of Elizabeth for the town of Hull.

[12] "To be carried aboard any ship or vessel outward bound for the parts beyond the seas, or laden or taken in from or out of any ship or vessel coming in and arriving from foreign parts," 13 & 14 Car. 2, c. 11, §7.

[13] "The master, purser, boatswain, or other mariner of any ship inward bound." 13 & 14 Car. 2, c. 11, §7.

[14] 1 Eliz. 1, c. 11, §2 (1558). Pertinent omissions are supplied in footnotes.

[15] "Whatsoever . . . to be brought from any the parts beyond the sea." 1 Eliz. 1, c. 11, §2.

&c.[16] and in some open Place that shall be appointable,[17] upon Pain of Forfeiture of all such Goods &c.

7. 8. W. 3, C. 22, §.6.[18] For the more effectual preventing of Frauds and regulating abuses in the Plantation Trade, be it enacted that all Ships coming into or going out of, any of the said Plantations and lading or unlading any Goods or Commodities, whether Ships of War or Merchant Ships and the Masters and Commanders thereof and their Ladings, shall be subject and liable to the same Rules, Visitations, Searches, Penalties and forfeitures, as to the Entering, lading, or discharging their respective Ships and Lading, as Ships and their ladings and the Commanders and Masters of Ships, are subject and liable unto in this Kingdom, by 14 Car. 2d. &c.[19] and the officers shall have the same Powers and be subject to the same Regulations, as officers in England by that act.[20]

50. Butler v. The *Union*

1769

EDITORIAL NOTE

In this forfeiture proceeding, as in *Folger v. The Cornelia*, No. 45, Adams argued in favor of the power of an inferior officer of the customs to seize a vessel. In this case, however, he was defending the interests of an officer appointed by the Commissioners of Customs. On 12 May 1769 Jonathan Sewall had filed a libel against the brigantine *Union* in behalf of John Butler, tide surveyor in the port of Salem, who had earlier seized the vessel at Marblehead. Claimants were cited to appear on 22 May, at which time an exception attacking Butler's authority was evidently filed, and the case continued for argument.[1]

[16] "And from the last of *September* until the first of *March,* between the hours of seven in the morning and four at the afternoon." 1 Eliz. 1, c. 11, §2.

[17] That is, an "open place, key or wharf," designated by the Crown within London or certain other named ports, or at any such place in any other port in which there had been a customs officer resident for the preceding ten years. 1 Eliz. 1, c. 11, §2. By 13 & 14 Car. 2, c. 11, §14 (1662), the Crown was given the power to establish the limits of all ports and appoint landing places within them.

[18] 7 & 8 Will. 3, c. 22, §6 (1696). Paraphrased with insignificant omissions.

[19] That is, 13 & 14 Car. 2, c. 11 (1662).

[20] The sections of both statutes regarding the powers of officers are set out in No. 44, at notes 92–97.

[1] Butler v. The *Union*, Vice Adm. Min. Bk., 12 May 1769; *Massachusetts Gazette,* 18 May 1769, p. 1, col. 3. The *Union* was seized for an alleged unloading of molasses before entry on a former voyage in March 1768. On learning of the seizure the Commissioners directed that she be libeled in Butler's name and that prosecutions be commenced against her master, Edward Hales, and one John Gary, for aid-

No. 50. Butler v. The Union

On 22 June the Commissioners directed their solicitor "to engage Mr. Adams and Mr. Quincy to assist the Advocate General in supporting the Libel" against the *Union*. This action is doubtless accounted for by the fact that, from 24 June to 12 July, Sewall was on a trip to Halifax, the seat of his new jurisdiction as Judge of Admiralty.[2] The trial was probably held during Sewall's absence, because Adams' minutes, printed below, do not mention the Advocate General and indicate that Adams himself argued the case for Butler. James Otis appeared for the claimants.

Butler had been commissioned by the American Commissioners of Customs without warrant from the Treasury. By statute, only the Commissioners themselves, "officers of his majesty's customs for the time being," or others appointed by Crown or Treasury, could make a valid seizure.[3] Adams argued first that Butler was *de jure* an "officer of his majesty's customs" because the American Commissioners had by statute and commission all the powers of their English counterparts to appoint such officers. His second point was that, by statute, exercise of office made Butler a *de facto* "officer" regardless of his commission. Despite these arguments, the libel was dismissed, presumably on the theory that the seizure was void because Butler lacked authority.[4]

Although the statutes and other instruments involved are ambiguous, there are reasonable grounds for such a result. The statute establishing the colonial customs system had provided that "officers of the customs" should be appointed by the Treasury *and* the Commissioners.[5] It had long been the rule for the English Commissioners to make such appointments only upon warrant from the Treasury, a practice which the patent of the American

---

ing in the unloading contrary to 4 Geo. 3, c. 15, §37, the act under which Hancock was prosecuted. See No. 46, notes 82–83; Commissioners to Salem Customs Officers, 5 May 1769, Salem Custom House Record Book, 1763–1772, p. 285, MSaE. Butler, appointed "Customs Officer" in March 1768, had immediately made himself so disliked that the customs boat in his charge was burned by a mob. In spite, or perhaps because, of this he was appointed Tide Surveyor of the Port in Aug. 1768, with the function of inspecting cargoes. He served in this capacity until at least Jan. 1775. See *id.* at 63–64, 227–234, 241–242; note 17 below. See also Salem Custom House Letter Book Outwards, 1772–1775, 9 Jan. 1775, Office of the U.S. Collector of Customs, Boston, Mass.

[2] Minutes of the Commissioners, 22 June 1769, 7 Bowdoin-Temple MSS 180, MHi. It is not clear whether the reference was to Samuel or Josiah Quincy Jr. Sewall voyaged to Halifax and back aboard the *Rose*, the vessel involved in Rex v. Corbet, No. 56, which at this time was engaged in removing a portion of the British garrison from Boston. *Boston News-Letter*, 22 June 1769, p. 2, col. 1; *Massachusetts Gazette*, 13 July 1769, p. 1, col. 2. See "A Journal of the Times," 25, 29 June 1769, Dickerson, *Boston under Military Rule* 112–113.

[3] See notes 11, 12, below.

[4] Vice Adm. Min. Bk., 12 May 1769. Dismissal suggests a disposition on such a preliminary question. See Folger v. The *Cornelia*, No. 45, Doc. III, where the information was dismissed in a case similar to that here. Likewise, in Dawson v. The *Dolphin*, No. 51, Doc. II, the libel was dismissed on the ground that it did not state a cause of action. Compare Dawson v. Lighter and Molasses, cited in No. 47, note 12, where the decree upheld the libel as to part of the seizure and adjudged the remainder not forfeit.

[5] See text at note 13 below.

Commissioners confirmed.[6] It was thus sound construction to hold that the "officers of his majesty's customs" empowered to make seizures were only those officers appointed upon warrant.[7] If this view were adopted, the portion of the Commissioners' patent cited by Adams which gave their lesser employees power to enter vessels and premises "to Search and Survey" and do all other necessary acts "agreable to the Laws and Statutes relating to the said Revenues," [8] would be expressly limited by the statutory provisions to powers other than that of making seizure. Insofar as Butler's commission gave him such a power, it would thus be void.

The question of Butler's statutory *de facto* authority was controlled by the holding in *Folger v. The Cornelia* that the statutes in question created only a presumption, which could be rebutted by evidence of lack of authority. The principles of that case, which had concerned an officer friendly to local mercantile interests, thus seem to have been applied evenhandedly where the officer was loyal to the Crown.[9]

ADAMS' NOTES AND MINUTES OF THE TRIAL [10]

Court of Vice Admiralty, Boston, July 1769

Butler vs. Brigg Union.

14. Car. 2d, c. 11, §.15. Seizures confined to Officers of his Majestys Customs, for the Time being.[11]

[6] See note 15 below. In colonial appointments the English Commissioners had followed the system used in England, whereby they in practice recommended candidates for principal positions within their jurisdiction, but made the actual appointments only upon Treasury warrant. Hoon, *English Customs* 195–198. Failure to remedy this lack of control over appointments was a major error in the creation of the American Board which led to much of its later difficulty. Clark, "The American Board of Customs," 45 *AHR* 777, 795–797. The one major exception to this practice was the commissioning of naval personnel as customs officers. See Hoon, *English Customs* 272. In a case in the Massachusetts Vice Admiralty Court in 1763, with Auchmuty as Advocate General, counsel for the claimants of a vessel seized by an officer of the navy had argued that the statute's conjunction of Treasury *and* Commissioners required a warrant. Nevertheless, the vessel was condemned. Bishop v. The *Freemason*, Quincy, *Reports* 387 (Mass. Vice Adm., 1763). On appeal in the High Court of Admiralty, it seems to have been argued that there was a standing order from the Treasury authorizing such commissions. The condemnation was affirmed without comment on this point. The *Freemason* v. Bishop, Burrell 55, 167 Eng. Rep. 469 (High Ct. Adm., 1767). See No. 51, note 1; No. 52, note 5.
[7] This was the English interpretation. Hoon, *English Customs* 195. Apparently, however, the need for securing seizures sometimes caused the rule to be overlooked in practice. *Id.* at 198, 271–272.
[8] See note 16 below.
[9] No. 45, Doc. III. In Nov. 1772 Butler was allowed to join in the successful prosecution of a vessel which he had seized under the direction of the Collector. Commissioners to Salem Customs Officers, 30 Nov., 14 Dec. 1772, Salem Letter Book Inwards, 1772–1775. The authority to seize in this case was undoubtedly the Collector's.

7. & 8. W. 3, c. 22, §. 6. Officers in America the same Power.[12]
§.11. Treasury, and Commissioners may constitute *such* and *so many*
officers of the Customs in any Port &c., when and as often as to them
shall seem needfull.[13]

7. G. 3. American Commissioners vested with such Powers as are
now exercised by Commissioners in England by Laws in being. May
be put under the Management and direction of Commissioners. Expressly any 3 of em to have the same Powers with Commissioners in
England.[14]

Commission. 2d. page. All the Powers expressly given that were
exercised by the Commissioners in England, and particularly to
constitute Inferiour officers in any Ports.[15] 4. page. Other Officers,
Power to enter Houses, and ships, and do all Things agreeable to
Law.[16]

[10] In JA's hand. Adams Papers, Microfilms, Reel No. 185. The material to note
18 below is on a separate page.

[11] 13 & 14 Car. 2, c. 11, §15 (1662), set out in No. 45, note 68.

[12] 7 & 8 Will. 3, c. 22, §6 (1696), set out in No. 44, notes 94–97.

[13] 7 & 8 Will. 3, c. 22, §11 (1696), set out in No. 45, note 52.

[14] 7 Geo. 3, c. 41 (1767), the act creating the American Board of Customs
Commissioners, set out in No. 45, note 41.

[15] Commission of the American Board, 12 Sept. 1767, Book of Commissions,
1677–1774, fols. 83–92, at 84–85, M-Ar.: "And we do hereby give and grant unto
you our said Commissioners during our pleasure as aforesaid or to any three or more
of you full power and authority to cause to be duly observed and executed within
the Limits of this your Commission [i.e. the geographical limits] all and singular
the Laws and Statutes and all and every the powers, directions and Clauses in them
or any of them contained touching or concerning the Collecting, Levying, receiving
or Securing any of the said Duties hereby committed to your charge, and to do or
cause to be done all other matters and things whatsoever touching or relating to the
Revenues and Trade of the British Colonies in America within the Limits aforesaid
as were before the passing of the said Act [i.e. 7 Geo. 3, c. 41] Exercised by the Commissioners of the Customs in England by virtue of any Act or Acts of Parliament in
force at the time of the passing thereof. And we do hereby further impower and
authorize you our said Commissioners or any three or more of you from time to time
to Constitute and appoint by any writing under your hands and Seals or under the
hands and seals of any three or more of you Inferior officers in all and singular the
ports within the Limits of this your Commission (other than such officers as are or
may be Constituted by Letters Patent of us our Heirs and Successors) according to
such warrants as you shall from time to time receive from the Commissioners of
our Treasury or our High Treasurer for the time being, and at such salaries as by
the said Warrants shall be directed, and them from time to time to suspend, remove
and displace as to you our said Commissioners or any three or more of you shall be
thought necessary and expedient to our service in the premises." JA's page references,
here and at note 16 below, are to a form of the Commission printed—apparently at
Boston—from this record. A copy is in MBAt: Tracts, A–24. See also No. 45, note 41.

[16] Commission, fols. 86–87: "We have further given and Granted, and by these
presents do give and Grant unto you our said Commissioners or any three or more
of you, and to all and every the Collectors, Deputy Collectors, Ministers, Servants
and other officers serving and attending in all and every the ports or other places
within the limits of this your Commission aforesaid," power "as well by night as by

Butlers Commission. Full Power to search and seize.[17]

6. G. 1, c. 21, §.25. 11. G. 1, c. 30, §.22. Evidence of Officers Authority as of a Fact.[18]

Mr. Otis. Common Practice, for the principal Officers of the Port to seize, not for the Inferiour Officers to seize.

King cant erect new Courts. They must be established by Act of Parliament. Therefore if the Powers in the Commission exceed the Act, they are void.

Q. whether within the Acts, Butler can seize. By the Act of C[harles] [19] he is not appointed by his Majesty, nor an officer of the Customs. He is merely a preventive officer.

Commissioners Commission. Inferiour Officers. No Warrant from the Treasurer. No Authority without.

Is he constituted by the Treasury and Customs in England.

No such officer has ever done ay [20] one Thing about the Custom[s].

---

day to enter and go on Board any Ship, Boat or other Vessel . . . to Search and Survey and the persons therein being strictly to Examine touching or concerning the premises, and also in the daytime to enter and go into any House, Warehouse, Shop, Cellar and other place where any Goods, Wares or Merchandizes lye concealed or are suspected to lye concealed whereof the Customs and other Duties have not been or shall not be duly paid . . . and the said House, Warehouse, Shop, Cellar and other place to Search and Survey, and all and every the Trunks, Chests, Boxes and packs then and there found to break open and to do all and every other the matters and things which shall be found necessary for our service in such Cases and agreable to the Laws and Statutes relating to the said Revenues."

[17] Butler's commission as Tide Surveyor, dated 22 Aug. 1768, was in a standard form conveying powers to enter ships and, with a writ of assistance, buildings, to search for prohibited goods, "and the same to seize to his Majesty's use." Salem Record Book, 1763–1772, p. 67. See also his instructions, 23 Aug. 1768, which deal with his authority to board vessels and "rummage" cargo, but contain no express power to seize. *Id.* at 68. There is no notation that this Commission was sworn, although it is clear (note 1 above) that Butler acted as Tide Surveyor. No objection on this point seems to have been made at the trial. If it had been, Butler might have been held to have seized under his earlier commission as "Customs Officer," which conveyed the same powers. *Id.* at 63–64.

[18] The correct citations are 6 Geo. 1, c. 21, §24 (1719), and 11 Geo. 1, c. 30, §32 (1724). These statutes provided that in trial upon forfeitures, penalties, and other matters relating to the customs, proof of the actual exercise of office at the time in controversy was sufficient to create a rebuttable presumption that the officer was authorized. They are set out in No. 45, notes 48, 49. See also *id.*, text at note 75.

[19] That is, 13 & 14 Car. 2, c. 11, §15, note 11 above.

[20] Thus in MS. Perhaps JA started to write "any thing." This sentence is in a thicker ink and appears more hurriedly written.

51. Dawson v. The *Dolphin*

1772–1773

EDITORIAL NOTE

On 14 October 1772 George Dawson, an officer of the royal navy, who since at least 1768 had been commissioned to assist in the enforcement of the Acts of Trade off the New England coast, seized the sloop *Dolphin* and her cargo at Holmes Hole, Martha's Vineyard.[1] The cause of the seizure was a defect in the vessel's papers. She had been built and registered in Marshfield, Massachusetts, in 1759, but in the meantime had been sold to new owners in that port. Unfortunately the requirement of the Act of 1696 that the transfer be endorsed on the register was overlooked. The *Dolphin* was thus in technical violation of a provision of the statute which had not previously been enforced. Samuel Fitch, now the Advocate General, brought a libel against vessel and cargo in Dawson's behalf on 4 November.[2]

The parties had been cited to appear on 11 November, but the argument was probably had early in February 1773. In the interim, vessel and

[1] Dawson's commission has not been found. For an early example of his activity, see Dawson v. Lighter and Molasses, Vice Adm. Min. Bk., 26 April 1768, discussed in No. 47, note 12. See also No. 52 (1773). His activities against American shipping in the early years of the Revolution are reported in William Bell Clark, *George Washington's Navy* 113–114, 125–128, 159–160 (Baton Rouge, 1960). Officers of the navy had long aided in enforcing the Acts of Trade, although the scope of their authority was sometimes questioned. See, for example, 12 Car. 2, c. 18, §1 (1660); Harper, *English Navigation Laws* 177–179. The Navy's success in halting trade with the enemy during the French wars led, after 1763, to expanded authorization for naval officers to seize vessels violating the Acts of Trade. 3 Geo. 3, c. 22, §4 (1763); 4 Geo. 3, c. 15, §42 (1764); 5 Geo. 3, c. 45, §26 (1765); see Ubbelohde, *Vice Admiralty Courts* 38–44, 116. The authority for their commissions was not in the statutes, however. The Privy Council presumably directed the Commissioners of the Customs to deputize naval officers. See Lord Egremont to Governor Bernard, 9 July 1763, 10 Bernard Papers 120–121, MH. Their shares of seizures were established by Order in Council, 8 July 1763, Book of Charters, Commissions, Proclamations, &c., 1628–1763, fols. 254–257, M-Ar. Probably the American Commissioners acted under the same authority after 1767. The High Court of Admiralty in that year affirmed a decision of the Massachusetts Vice Admiralty Court condemning a vessel seized by the first of these officers to present his commission in Massachusetts in 1763. The question of the power to seize had been raised in the lower court and seems to have been discussed on the argument in the High Court, although the reported opinion there dealt with other questions. Bishop v. The *Freemason*, Quincy, *Reports* 387, 389–390 (Mass. Vice Adm., 1763), affirmed *sub nom.* The *Freemason* v. Bishop, Burrell 55, 167 Eng. Rep. 469 (High Ct. Adm., 1767). See No. 50, note 6; No. 52, note 5.

[2] *Massachusetts Gazette*, 5 Nov. 1772, p. 3, col. 2. For the statute, see note 15 below. As to previous enforcement, see note 26 below. Fitch had been appointed Advocate General on 4 March 1770 to replace Sewall, who had finally resigned his post to undertake his new duties as Judge of Admiralty at Halifax. See "Boyle's Journal of Occurrences in Boston, 1759–1778," 84 NEHGR 263 (1930).

goods were released on stipulation to the owners.[3] When the case came on, Adams, making his first known appearance in a forfeiture proceeding since 1769,[4] was of counsel for the claimants. Fitch argued for Dawson. Adams' notes (Document I) set forth the statutory provisions upon which the case turned, as well as several authorities on the question of statutory construction.[5] The opinion and decree of the court (Document II) show that Judge Auchmuty resolved the case into three issues: (1) If there were a violation, did the provision of the Act making an improperly registered vessel liable to forfeiture "as any foreign ship" bring into play the section dealing with foreign vessels, under which cargo too was forfeit, or was the penalty forfeiture of the vessel only? [6] (2) Was this a penal statute which must thus be construed strictly? (3) Did the penalty of forfeiture, which clearly attached for failure to obtain the new registration required in the event of change of name or sale to new owners in a different port, apply to a sale to new owners in the same port? [7]

Auchmuty decided all three questions in favor of the claimants in a detailed and lengthy piece of statutory construction. His opinion on the first two points is relatively clear. On the last question, which was conclusive in the case, his language is somewhat muddy, but he seems to have found two bases for the result: (1) That no penalty attached for violation of the home-port sale provisions, whatever the nature of the sale. (2) That if, as Fitch argued, these provisions only covered the sale of a part interest in the vessel, then no provision of the Act covered the case of the *Dolphin,* which was a sale of the entire vessel within the home port. On whatever ground, on 2 March, Auchmuty decreed that the libel be dismissed as a matter of law. He found probable cause for the seizure, however, which meant that the claimants were required to pay their own costs.[8]

[3] See note 38 below. The trial has been dated on two grounds: (1) The use of a stipulation suggests a delay in the proceedings, which usually followed the filing of the libel by a week or less. Since Dawson was a naval officer, delay may have been necessitated by his other duties. (2) Auchmuty's decree which might have been expected to follow trial by a week or so was given on 2 March 1773, and would have been given "some days sooner," except for a petition for rehearing. See text following note 40 below.

[4] He had participated in the trial of an Admiralty appeal in Feb. 1772. See p. 104 above.

[5] In the Adams Papers there is an undated MS in JA's hand entitled "Construction of Statutes," which contains extracts from many of the authorities cited by JA at notes 16–21 below. Adams Papers, Microfilms, Reel No. 185. In all probability these notes were made in preparation for this case.

[6] 7 & 8 Will. 3, c. 22, §§2, 18 (1696), notes 10, 12, below.

[7] 7 & 8 Will. 3, c. 22, §21, note 15 below.

[8] The finding also barred any action against the seizing officer. 4 Geo. 3, c. 15, §46 (1764). These advantages had long been given to English customs officers under statutes which presumably were not applicable in the colonies. See 19 Geo. 2, c. 34, §16 (1746), discussed in No. 44, note 62. It is usually held that the Act of 1764 marked the introduction of this privilege in the colonies. See Ubbelohde, *Vice Admiralty Courts* 50–51; Dickerson, *Navigation Acts* 179–184; Knollenberg, *Origin of the American Revolution* 179. As this case shows, the provision did not throw the entire cost of litigation upon the claimant. The purpose was to alter the familiar

No. 51. *Dawson v. The* Dolphin

I. ADAMS' NOTES OF STATUTES AND AUTHORITIES[9]

Court of Vice Admiralty, Boston, February 1773

George Dawson Esqr. vs. The Sloop Dolphin,
Walson, Lothrop and others owners.

This Vessell was seized merely for the omission of an Indorsement upon her Register.

7. & 8. W. 3d, c. 22. An Act for preventing Frauds and regulating Abuses in the Plantation Trade.

§.2: Be it enacted, that after 25th March 1698—"*No Goods or Merchandises, shall be imported into or exported out of, any Colony or Plantation, to his Majesty in Asia, Africa, or America, belonging, or in his Possession,* or which may hereafter belong unto, or be in the Possession of his Majesty, his Heirs or Successors, or shall be laden in, or carried from any one Port or Place in the said Colonies or Plantations, to any other Port or Place in the same, the Kingdom of England, Dominion of Wales, or Town of Berwick upon Tweed, *in any Ship or Bottom but what is, or shall be of the built of England, or of the Built of Ireland or the said Colonies or Plantations, and wholly owned by the People thereof,* or any of them, and navigated with the Masters, and three fourths of the Mariners of the said Places only" (except Prize ships &c. and foreign ships employed for 3 years to bring in naval Stores) "*Under Pain of Forfeiture of Ship and Goods*" 1/3 to the King, 1/3 to the Governor, 1/3 to the Informer.[10]

§.17. "For the more effectual Prevention of Frauds which may be used to elude the Intention of this Act by colouring Foreign Ships under English Names;" be it further enacted, &c. that, "*No Ship, or Vessell, shall be deemed or pass, as a Ship of the Built of England, Ireland, Wales, Berwick, Guernsey, Jersey, or any of his Majestys Plantations in America so as to be qualified to Trade to, from, or in, any of the said Plantations* untill the Person, or Persons, claiming Property in such Ship or Vessell *shall register the same* as follows, that is to say, if the Ship, at the Time of such Register doth belong to

---

practice whereby the losing party bore the entire cost of suit. See 4 Holdsworth, *History of English Law* 536–538.

[9] In JA's hand, in his Admiralty Book, Adams Papers, Microfilms, Reel No. 184. For the dating, see note 3 above.

[10] 7 & 8 Will. 3, c. 22, §2 (1696). Quotation marks supplied. Italics are JA's. The last clause of the section is "and the other third part to the person who shall inform and sue for the same, by bill, plaint or information, in any of his Majesty's courts of record at *Westminster,* or in any court in his Majesty's plantations, where such offense shall be committed."

225

any Port in England, Ireland, Wales, or to the Town of Berwick upon Tweed, then Proof shall be made upon oath of one or more of the owners of such Ship or Vessell, before the Collector, and Comptroller, of his Majestys Customs in such Port; or if at the Time of such Register, the Ship belong to any of his Majestys Plantations in America, or to the Islands of Guernsey or Jersey, then the like Proof to be made before the Governor, together with the Principal officer of his Majesty's Revenue residing on such Plantation or Island" &c.

Form of the oath.[11]

§.18. "Which Oath, being attested by the Governor or Custom officer, respectively who administered the same, under their Hands and Seals, shall after having been registered by them, be delivered to the *Master of the Ship for the Security of her Navigation*, a Duplicate of which Register shall be immediately transmitted to the Commissioners of Customs in the Port of London, in order to be entered in a general Register to be there kept for this Purpose, with *Penalty* upon any Ship or Vessell trading to, from, or in any of his Majesty's Plantations in America" &c. "and not having made Proof of her Built and Property, as is here directed that she shall be liable, and she is hereby made liable, to such Prosecution and Forfeiture, as any foreign ship" (except Prizes &c.) "would for trading with those Plantations by this Law be liable to."[12]

Prize ships to be registered &c.[13] Fisher Boats, Hoys &c. Lighters &c. not to be registered.[14]

§. 21. "That No Ships Name registered shall be afterwards changed, without registering such Ship de Novo, which is hereby required to be done, upon any Transfer of Property to another Port, and delivering up the former Certificate to be cancelled, under the same Penalties,

---

[11] 7 & 8 Will. 3, c. 22, §17 (1696). Quotation marks supplied. Italics are JA's. The section concludes, "which oath the said governors and officers of the customs respectively are hereby authorized to administer in the tenor following, viz. "JURAT" A.B. *That the ship* [name] *of* [port] *whereof* [master's name] *is at present master, being a* [kind of built] *Of* [burthen] *tuns, was built at* [place, where] *in the year* [time when] *and that* [owners name] *of and of, &c. are at present owners thereof; and that no foreigner, directly or indirectly, hath any share, or part, or interest therein.*" As to the administration of this provision, see Bernard and Lotte Bailyn, *Massachusetts Shipping 1697–1714* 1–12 (Cambridge, Mass., 1959).

[12] 7 & 8 Will. 3, c. 22, §18 (1696). Quotation marks supplied. Italics are JA's.

[13] 7 & 8 Will. 3, c. 22, §19 (1696), providing that ships condemned as prize in the High Court of Admiralty in England are to be specially registered, with oath made as to their capture and condemnation, rather than their building.

[14] 7 & 8 Will. 3, c. 22, §20 (1696), providing that such craft need not be registered if they are used only for river or coastwise navigation.

226

and in the like Method, as is herein before directed; and that *in Case there be any alteration of Property in the same Port, by the Sale of one or more Shares in any Ship after registering thereof, such Sale shall always be acknowledged by Indorsement on the Certificate of the Register before two Witnesses, in order to prove that the entire Property in such Ship remains to some of the Subjects of England, if any dispute arises concerning the same.*" [15]

Rules of Construction. Woods Inst. 8.[16]—3. Rep. 7.b.[17]—4. Inst.

[15] 7 & 8 Will. 3, c. 22, §21 (1696). Quotation marks supplied. Italics are JA's.

[16] This reference is ambiguous, since rules of statutory construction appear on page 8 of both Thomas Wood, *An Institute of the Laws of England* (London, 9th edn., 1763), and of Thomas Wood, *A New Institute of the Imperial or Civil Law* (London, 1704). While it is possible that JA used the latter work because of the civil-law nature of the court of Admiralty (See No. 46, note 126), the rules in the former are more directly concerned with the interpretation of acts of Parliament, the problem here; moreover, the authorities cited in notes 17, 18, and 21, below, appear in the first cited work, which is also quoted in JA's other notes on construction. See note 5 above. Following are pertinent passages from Wood, *Institute of the Laws of England* 13–14:

"The Preamble or Rehearsal of a Statute is to be taken for Truth; therefore good Arguments and Proofs may be drawn from the Preamble or Rehearsal . . . .

"A Sentence, which begins and ends with specifying Persons and Things of an inferior Rank ought not to be extended by *General Words* to those that are Superior; as by these general Words, (*viz.*) *And no other Person or Act whatsoever, &c.* shall not include superior *Persons* or *Things* that were not particularly expressed.

"Statutes must be interpreted by reasonable Construction, according to the Meaning of the Legislators.

"It is natural to construe one part of a Statute by another.

"They may be construed according to Equity; especially where They give Remedy for Wrong; or are for Expedition of Justice, or to prevent Delays; for Law-makers cannot comprehend all Cases . . . .

"A Penal Statute regularly ought to be construed strictly. But it *may* be construed beneficially; for what is out of the Mischief, is out of the Meaning of a Law, though it is within the Letter. [The preceding two sentences appear in JA's notes on construction, note 5 above.] And on the contrary, what is within the same Mischief, shall be within the same Remedy, tho' it be out of the Letter of the Law . . . .

"It [a Statute] must be construed that no innocent Man may by a literal Construction receive [i.e. sustain] Damages.

"Statutes made to prevent and suppress Fraud ought to have a favourable Interpretation . . . .

"Custom or Usage is a good Interpreter of a Law."

[17] Heydon's Case, 3 Co. Rep. 7a, 7b, 76 Eng. Rep. 637, 638 (Exch. 1584), held that a copyhold estate was an estate for life within the meaning of 31 Hen. 8, c. 13 (1540), a statute intended to prevent religious orders from avoiding dissolution by making new leases of lands when estates were already in being in those lands. "[F]or the sure and true Interpretation of all Statutes in general (be they penal or beneficial, restrictive or enlarging of the Com. Law,) four things are to be discerned and considered.

"1. What was the Common Law before the making of the Act.

"2. What was the Mischief and Defect for which the Common Law did not provide.

"3. What Remedy the Parliament hath resolved and appointed to cure the Disease of the Commonwealth.

330.[18]—4 Bac. Abr. 652.[19] 1 Blackst. Com. 87. 88.[20]—1. Inst. 11.b.[21]

"And 4. The true Reason and Remedy; and then the Office of all the Judges is always to make such Construction as shall suppress the Mischief, and advance the Remedy, and to suppress subtil Inventions and Evasions for Continuance of the Mischief, and *pro privato commodo*, and to add Force and Life to the Cure and Remedy, according to the true Intent of the Makers of the Act, *pro bono publico."*

[18] 4 Coke, *Institutes* 330: "Every Statute ought to be expounded according to the intent of them that made it, where the words thereof are doubtful and incertain, and according to the rehearsal of the Statute; and there [i.e. in Year Book, 4 Edw. 4, fols. 4, 12] a general statute is construed particularly, upon consideration had of the cause of making of the Act, and of the rehearsal of all the parts of the Act. To conclude this point with a general rule allowed by all laws in construction of statutes, Quamvis lex generaliter loquitur, restringenda tamen est, ut cessante ratione et ipsa cesset: cum enim ratio sit anima vigorque ipsius legis, non videtur legislator id sensisse quod ratione careat etiamsi verborum generalitas prima facie aliter suadeat."

[19] 4 Bacon, *Abridgment* 652 contains several authorities to the effect that despite the rule of strict construction, the intent of the legislature must be observed. Compare note 34 below. There follows a series of "other rules" to be followed in statutory construction which are more favorable to JA's case. For example,

"Acts of Parliament are to be so construed, that no Man, who is innocent or free from Injury or Wrong, be punished or endamaged.

"No Statute shall be interpreted so as to be inconvenient, or against Reason."

In JA's notes on construction, note 5 above, appears the following extract from 4 Bacon, *Abridgment* 651:

"4. Bac. Abr. 651. 9. Penal Acts of Parliament are to be strictly construed. The Rules of the Common Law will not suffer the general Words of a Statute to be restrained, to the Prejudice of him upon whom a Penalty is to be inflicted: But there are a Multitude of Cases, where such general Words shall be restrained in his favour."

[20] 1 Blackstone, *Commentaries* *87–88, part of a discourse on "the rules to be observed with regard to the construction of statutes." In JA's notes on construction, note 5 above, appear abstracts of the following passages:

"1. . . . Let us instance again in the same restraining statute of the 13 Eliz. [i.e. 13 Eliz. 1, c. 10]. By the common law ecclesiastical corporations might let as long leases as they thought proper: the mischief was, that they let long and unreasonable leases, to the impoverishment of their successors: the remedy applied by the statute was by making void all leases by ecclesiastical bodies for longer terms than three lives or twenty one years. Now in the construction of this statute it is held, that leases, though for a longer term, if made by a bishop, are not void during the bishop's life; or, if made by a dean and chapter, they are not void during the life of the dean: for the act was made for the benefit and protection of the successor. The mischief is therefore sufficiently suppressed by vacating them after the death of the grantors; but the leases, during their lives, being not within the mischief, are not within the remedy. . . .

"3. Penal statutes must be construed strictly. Thus the statute 1 Edw. VI. c. 12. having enacted that those who are convicted of stealing *horses* should not have the benefit of clergy, the judges conceived that this did not extend to him that should steal but *one horse*, and therefore procured a new act for that purpose in the following year. And, to come nearer our own times, by the statute 14 Geo. II, c. 6, stealing sheep, *or other cattle*, was made felony without benefit of clergy. But these general words, 'or other cattle,' being looked upon as much too loose to create a capital offence, the act was held to extend to nothing but mere sheep. And therefore in the next sessions, it was found necessary to make another statute, 15 Geo. II, c. 34. extending the former to bulls, cows, oxen, steers, bullocks, heifers, calves, and lambs, by name."

[21] Coke, *Littleton* 11b: "From statutes his arguments and proofs are drawn. 1.

No. 51. Dawson v. The Dolphin

II. AUCHMUTY'S OPINION AND DECREE [22]

Court of Vice Admiralty, Boston, 2 March 1773

George Dawson Esqr. vs. Sloop Dolphin and Cargoe.

This Libel is bottomed on the Act of the 7. & 8. Will. 3 Cap. 22. Those parts therefore of the Act, which relates to the present case must be thoroughly considered.

The facts either proved, or granted, by the Advocates on both sides are, that said sloop was built at Marshfield in this province by inhabitants of the same, and by them owned. In the Year 1759 was duly registered, afterwards by the original was sold to the present owners and claimants, who are inhabitants of the same port with her former owners, that she has been always navigated with three fourths, at least, of english subjects, and that her original name has never been changed. But that on the transferr to the present owners, there was neither a new register taken out, nor any indorsement on the certificate of the old one, and that said Vessell and Cargo being inward bound were seized by said Dawson at a place called Holmes's hole within the port of Boston.

The Advocate General insisted, that a vessel and cargo under the abovementioned circumstances are forfeited by force of the said Statute. Because all vessels, together with their Cargoes, trading to or from the plantations, which are not qualified as the Act directs, are thereby declared forfeit. That the words used in the seventeenth section thereof "deemed or pass" signify adjudged or decreed, and therefore taken in that sense, must relate to a Court and not to Custom Officers.[23] That this Act ought not to be considered as a penal one, because the forfeiture therein given is not annexed to any crime, for which the Actor is to suffer corporally, but only to a neglect. And therefore, the rules urged by the gentlemen on the other side touching the construction of penal Statutes, are not applicable to the present case. That the importance of this Act, resulting from its great public

From the rehersal or preamble of the statute. 2. By the body of the Law diversly interpreted. Sometime by other parts of the same statute, which is *benedicta expositio & ex visceribus causae.* Sometime by reason of the Common Law. But ever the general words are to be intended of a lawful Act, and such interpretation must ever be made of all statutes, that the innocent or he in whom there is no default may not be damnified."

[22] NN: Samuel Adams Papers. Copy attested in the hand of Ezekiel Price, Deputy Register of the Court of Vice Admiralty.

[23] See text following note 10 above. The argument seems to be that the court is required to find that an unregistered vessel is not a vessel belonging to the colonies or England.

utility ought to draw such a construction, as will operate very Severely against Claimants. That the last clause in the Act relates only to a partial transfer of a vessel, the words being "and that in case of any alteration of property in the same port, by the sale of one or more Shares in any ship after registering thereof, such sale shall always be acknowledged by indorsement on the certificate of the register before two witnesses" &c.[24] That by using those words "one or more Shares," it is evident only a partial transfer was intended. That this last clause must be taken as part of the general plan of the Act, and therefore must be construed as connected with and relative to the penal parts of it. That the Statute does not say a subject shall forfeit his vessell for not registering her but that she shall not be qualified to trade, and therefore if she does without being registered, she ought, to all intents and purposes, be adjudged a foreign vessell, and so the Cargo condemnable as much as if seized on board a trading vessel actually belonging to foreigners.[25]

By the Gentlemen on the other side, it was urged, that as indorsements on the Certificates of the register were not practiced till of late nor even required at the Custom houses, it would be against equity now to mark such instances with the utmost severity.[26] That, as there is not the least Shade of proof, or even a suggestion of fraud, in this case, it is not within the mischief intended to be remedied by the Statute.[27] That the words "deemed or pass" ought not to be construed adjudged or decreed, but more properly are to be understood only as directory to Officers of the customs in the entering and clearing of vessels. That penal Statutes ought not constructively to be extended, because such a practice is against the well known and established rules of law, and in Support of which they produced several good authorities.[28] That as no fraud was either committed or designed in this case, the Statute ought not to be construed Strictly against them, even if it was not penal.[29] But that the same is penal and therefore a fortiori

---

[24] 7 & 8 Will. 3, c. 22, §21, note 15 above.

[25] 7 & 8 Will. 3, c. 22, §§2, 18, notes 10, 12, above.

[26] This position is confirmed by a public notice from the Commissioners dated 12 Dec. 1772, reciting that there had been great neglect on the part of ship owners in complying with the provisions of 7 & 8 Will. 3, c. 22, §21 (note 15 above), requiring new registers or endorsements, and warning that ships failing to comply in the future "will be liable to the same Prosecutions and Penalties as if such Vessels were owned entirely by Foreigners." *Massachusetts Gazette*, 7 Jan. 1773, p. 4, col. 1.

[27] See authorities cited, notes 16, 17, 20, above. Compare the preamble of the pertinent sections, text following note 10 above.

[28] See authorities cited, notes 16, 20, above.

[29] See authorities cited, notes 16, 19, 21, above.

it cannot. That the last clause in the Act has no penalty annexed to it, nor can that clause consistent with the Authorities mentioned be made by construction to relate to the preceeding parts of the Statute mentioning penalties. But if at all it must be confined to the forfeiture expressed in the eighteenth section,[30] which extends only to the vessell. These were the principal matters mentioned and relied on by the gentlemen on both sides; some of which do not appear to me to deserve much notice in the present case.

In determining this cause first great care must be taken in making a true distinction between such parts of the Act, as relate entirely to vessels the property of foreigners, and those which only respect english built and owned vessels, tho' not registered pursuant to the directions of the Act. Because on a supposition, that the vessel now libelled against is forfeit a question will Arise, whether the Cargo is also, which question entirely rests on that distinction.

Secondly, whether this Act is to be considered as penal. Because, the rules of construing such Acts, are variant from those which relate to, and govern Acts which are not. And lastly, what is the legal construction of the words contained in the last clause of said Act.

In the second section of the Act Ship and goods are both declared forfeited.[31] But then it must be recollected, that the whole of that section entirely relates to foreign built vessels, owned by foreigners and navigated by such. Indeed that section contains nothing more than a repetition of the capital act of navigation, the 12. Car. 2. excepting some additional prohibition touching the plantations.[32] In this section there is not any mention of vessels really english built, owned by english Subjects or navigated by such: therefore such cannot be the objects of that clause not being therein mentioned. But the contrary will evidently appear by considering those subsequent parts of the same act, wherein notice is particularly taken and directions given how they shall be qualified, under a certain, and in part, a different penalty. I can not therefore conceive how, consistent with propriety or justice, the said second section, guarded by the forfeiture of ship and Cargo, and calculated for a certain express purpose can relate or be extended to a distinct detach'd part of the same Act, clearly made to regulate cases totally different and under a different forfeiture. Compare the

[30] See text at note 12 above.
[31] See text at note 10 above.
[32] 12 Car. 2, c. 18, §1 (1660). The only differences with 7 & 8 Will. 3, c. 22, §2 (1696) are the provisions in the latter barring foreign ships in the intercolonial trade and making exceptions for foreign prizes and mast ships. See text at note 10 above.

abovementioned section with the Eighteenth, and not only the difference in point of forfeiture but the reason of it, I apprehend, will appear obvious. In the second section the Act goes entirely on the supposition, that the vessel so trading is owned by foreigners of foreign built, and not navigated by three fourths english. Doubtless if such a practice was permitted, it would have a direct tendency to enrich foreigners and prevent the increase of English shipping and seamen; therefore in such instances both vessel and cargo are declared forfeit. But in the eighteenth section, the Legislators have no such foreign vessel in view, having already made provision for such, but are guarding against certain mischiefs which might arise among their own Subjects. As the dangers and loss to goverment, where the vessell is really of english built, owned and navigated by english subjects, though not registered pursuant to the Act, can not be so great as in the Case of foreign vessels trading in the plantations, so neither ought the penalty to be. The greater the injury done to a State or an individual, the higher the punishment ought to Arrise. This I take to be one of the two great reasons for varying the penalties in the aforementioned clauses. There is also another very obvious one for the parliament's not annexing the same penalty to the two sections. For had they done it, in some instances very great loss, and in others, total ruin might thereby have fallen upon innocent subjects; a consequence which that Legislature have always Studiously avoided, and where from the necessity of using general expressions, such an instance has come within the express letter of an Act, the common law Judges have in conformity to the designs and desires of parliament ruled it not to be within the meaning of it.[33] This rule however is not perhaps to be taken as unlimited, but only applicable where such an exemption may safely be made, and the Act remain in its full intended force. The case alluded to is plainly that of freighters. The wisdom or justice of parliament ought never to be so impeached, as to suppose that, for the omission of an Owner, the innocent freighter who could not, in the nature of things, be privy to it, should suffer perhaps to his total ruin. Such a doctrine if once established, I imagine, would be very destructive to trade and Commerce, and therefore instead of promoting the Public interest, would have a quite contrary effect. And in Addition to what has been observed, I may safely assert, there never was, and I hope never will be found among the english law rules of construing Statutes, that a Judge shall extract the penalty from the first part of a law, calculated for one express evident purpose only, and annex it to another part of the

[33] See authorities cited, notes 16, 19, 21, above.

same Act, which relates entirely to a different case and governed by different reasons; especially, when in such other part, a penalty is given in an as express terms as that Contained in the first part, though not so great. Granting an english vessel and Cargo to be seized which came within the express provision of the Eighteenth Section, and surely thats as strong a case as the present, could a Judge make an addition to that Part of the Act by condemning both vessel and Cargo, when the Act itself declares only the former liable to forfeitures. On the whole, I am clear in opinion, on supposition the vessel now libelled by law ought to remain forfeit, her Cargo ought not.

In order to determine whether an Act is penal within the sense of the Law, it must first be enquired, whether the Common law is thereby altered, and Secondly, whether there is any penalty expressly annexed to such Act, either pecuniary or corporal. To conclude all Acts not penal, except such as inflict the latter, is contradicting rules too well established to be even called in question. Nor will it do to suppose that the general utility of an Act can exempt it from being Classed among penal Statutes; because such a conclusion proves too much. All public Statutes are made to supply some omission, or correct some defect in the common law, and in their nature must be founded in, and designed for the public Good; therefore as the law has not yet pointed out to what degree of public good such Acts must attain to prevent their being construed as penal ones, they must all remain so, which come under the first mentioned rules, or more. To affirm the latter, in direct contradiction to the many law Authorities, proving the contrary, is what I neither dare or wish to do. When a severe corporal punishment is enacted, the Argument drawn from importance and public utility, seems to me, will be stronger, for such Acts are made to prevent the most atrocious crimes, and therefore those Statutes may justly be said to be of the greatest importance and utility to the community. This doctrine however has never prevailed, nor never can untill the well known and established rules of law are entirely altered.[34] And it is equally clear, from all the books treating on this Subject, that very many Acts, to the breach of which there is not any corporal punishment fix'd, but only a fine or forfeiture, have

[34] There is authority for the proposition that penal statutes tending to the public good, at least where the offense is a felony or heinous crime, should be freely construed, in 4 Bacon, *Abridgment* 652, the same page in which JA's authority, note 19 above, appears. To the contrary, however, see the cases cited by Blackstone, note 20 above. See also a passage extracted by JA in his notes on construction, note 5 above, from Wood, *Institute of the Laws of England* 561: "Penal Statutes shall not be extended by Equity: The Words may be construed beneficially, according to the Intent of the Legislators; but things out of the Words shall not be taken by Equity."

always been esteemed penal, and received constructions applicable to such Statutes. To enumerate instances of this kind to convince Lawyers would be a misspence of time.[35] On a due and thorough consideration of this point, I am of opinion, that the Act in question is and must be, notwithstanding its general importance, which undoubtedly is very great, and ought in every part to be punctually complied with, determined penal, and liable to the rules of construction relative to such Acts.

My next business is to endeavour to disclose the true meaning of the last words in the Statute,[36] on which this Case rests.

I have already attempted to shew a distinction between those parts of the Act which relate to foreigners, and those which appertain to English Subjects, not conforming to the express requisites of the Statute. I shall now also attempt to shew a difference between cases coming under the last paragraph of said Statute, supposing this to be one of that class for the present, and such as are within the words immediately preceeding said paragraph. Whenever an Act is introductory of new rules for the regulation of commerce, ordaining what shall be done by the subject, and the manner of doing it, namely under oath, establishing a certain penalty for the neglect thereof, and then immediately goes on to regulate cases under other and different circumstances, without mentioning any penalty or oath, it must be supposed, that the Legislators did not conceive the latter instances of such importance as the former: otherwise they would have guarded the one as strongly as the other. On no other principle can the different modes pointed out by the Act be accounted for. This is exactly the present case. The Act very clearly orders a register de novo on a vessel's name being changed. Also on any transfer of property to another port, under, as I construe it, the forfeiture of the vessel. Then follows the last clause Vizt. "And that in case of any alteration of property in the same port, by the sale of one or more shares &c. such sale shall always be acknowledged by indorsement on the certificate of the register" &c. Is it possible, on due consideration of these two clauses to suppose, that the Parliament conceived there was in both cases a like necessity of a new register, supposing the words "one or more shares" include an entire transfer, and yet in the one, command it expressly, and in the other, which immediately follows, order a different mode. Or can it be imagined, that by guarding the first part, which they have ma-

[35] See, for example, 4 Bacon, *Abridgment* 651, note 19 above; 1 Blackstone, *Commentaries* *87–88, note 20 above.
[36] 7 & 8 Will. 3, c. 22, §21, note 15 above.

terially differed from the last, with a certain penalty, they thereby
intended the penalty should be extended by implication to the last;
especially since its beyond all doubt, that the sanction of an Oath is
required by the first and omitted in the last. It's natural to conclude,
had not the intention of the law makers been to have discriminated
between the cases, they would have inserted those words about trans-
fering one or more Shares in the same port before the penalty; and
thereby have brought the three cases under the same predicament.
By admitting the indorsement before two witnesses to be one complete
mode of evidence to prove the property english, and that not under
the sanction of an Oath, the Strongest bond of society, it is evident
they did not think there was equal danger in such cases of evading the
Act, as in the others. This, I think, must be the reason why they
omitted, in the last part of the Statute, that strong requisite and the
penalty. In my Opinion it is equally justifiable to condemn, where an
entire transfer is made in the same port (tho' the words share or
shares only extended to a partial Sale) because there was not a new
register taken out, under colour of promoting the main Scope and
purpose of the Act, as to extend a penalty clearly designed for certain
cases, and expressly annexed thereto, to others, apparently in the contemplation of the Legislators, of much less consequence; and whereto
they did not think proper, in express terms at least, to fix any. This
would not be construing an Act in conformity to any rules of law, but
in fact, giving a decree in addition to an Act. Such a power would be
subversive of the authority of parliament, and of all Acts.[37] For by the
same reason that a Judge could add to, he might diminish from any
act, so that it would be in his power to mould them ad libitum. If the
words, "any one or more Shares," are taken as relative to and meaning
a partial transfer, then the true sense of them is, that when the fact
is known to the officers of the Customs, they shall have power to refuse
entering or Clearing till the indorsement is made. And where it is
done and produced, it shall amount, prima facie, to satisfactory evidence of the property's being wholly english; and thereby put an end
to disputes about it, and prevent great delays in business. From this
view of the words, the reason why the Compilers of the Act, did neither
extend the penalty or require a new register in such partial transfers,
is evident. First, there is not in such instances equal danger of the

[37] The argument is somewhat cloudy, but Auchmuty seems to refer to his position
below, that the case of an entire sale within a port is not covered by the statute, and
to say that extending to one section penalties clearly affixed to another would be a
vice equal to extending a statute to cover a case which the legislature had omitted.
See note 16 above.

Act's being evaded, with impunity, as where a vessel is wholy trans-fer'd to another Port or where her name is changed. And secondly, because considering the vast numbers of transfers of quarters eighths sixteenths and other small proportions or shares of vessels, it would be laying a heavy burthen on trade, not only of the pecuniary, but troublesome kind, to require in every such instance a new register. This construction, tho' not clear of all doubts, is much the most natural and easy, it being vastly more consistent with the other parts of the Act, than the one last contended for by the Advocate General.

I will now particularly consider that Gentleman's construction of this last part of the Act, and see how well his own doctrine will serve his purpose. He very Strenuously and repeatedly urged, that the words "any one or more Shares", therein used, manifestly pointed out the meaning of Parliament. That thereby, I take his own words, "it is evident to any one, who has the least Idea of the force of english words, only a partial transfer was intended, and not an entire and complete one." So far I incline to his Opinion. But in the Close of his Argument, he as strongly contended, that this very last part of the Act must be taken as part of the general System intended to be formed by the Act, must be connected with, and relate to the penal parts of it; and therefore as this vessel was not qualified to trade, that part of the Act, which gives the forfeiture of both vessel and Cargo, must be applied to this last part; And consequently, in the present case both are for-feited. This reasoning can not be right, because by his own doctrine the words, "any one or more Shares" mean no more than a partial transfer, which is not pretended in the present case, but the Contrary has been by him all along acknowledged, Vizt. an entire Sale of the said vessel. So that supposing his first argument right, the present case, beyond all possibility of doubt, is casus omissus. And it is equally certain granting it to be such, that it is not in any Judge's power to remedy that inconvenience, any more than to make a new law.

Upon the whole, as I can not find any Law by which either vessel or cargo ought to be condemned, I adjudge and decree, that the said libel be dismissed, and it is accordingly hereby dismissed, saving the right to both parties of appeal. I do not decree a restitution of said Sloop and cargo, because the same have been already delivered to the Claimant, by virtue of a writ of delivery they first having duly stip-ulated for the value thereof agreable to the practice of the Court.[38]

[38] Delivery of vessel and goods on stipulation for their value was a familiar Ad-miralty practice which was used in the Massachusetts court in revenue cases. See 2 Browne, *Civil Law* 411–412; Harrison v. The *Chance*, Vice Adm. Min. Bk., 10 March 1769. It was presumably this practice, rather than the statutory "Writ of

I also certify, that as the Seizing officer could not possibly know whether the transfer was in the same port, or who were the real Owners, there was a probable cause for making said Seizure.[39] As to the costs, I decree each party to pay his own.

Robert Auchmuty Comr. &c.[40]

Boston March 2d. 1773

The above decree would have been given some days sooner, had there not been an application for another argument which application is now waived.   Robt. Auchmuty Comr. &c.
March 2d. 1773

52. Dawson v. The *Jenny*

1773

EDITORIAL NOTE

The *Jenny*, owned by Elisha Doane, long one of Adams' clients, was stopped inward bound to Boston on 3 March 1773 by George Dawson, the naval officer involved in the case of the *Dolphin*, No. 51. Finding that she had goods aboard of European origin that had not been shipped in Great Britain as required by statute, Dawson seized her and had her brought into port. On 24 March, Samuel Fitch, the Advocate General, filed a libel in the Court of Vice Admiralty against vessel and cargo. Doane claimed the *Jenny* and at least a portion of the goods seized, and argument was had on the case sometime in April. John Adams and Sampson Salter Blowers were of counsel for Doane; Fitch and James Otis argued for Dawson.[1]

Delivery" permitted in the Exchequer where goods were perishable or the informer delayed his suit, that was followed here. See 13 & 14 Car. 2, c. 11, §30 (1662).

[39] See note 8 above.

[40] That is, "Commissary Deputy and Surrogate of the Court of Vice Admiralty of Boston in the Province of Massachusetts Bay." See No. 54, note 4.

[1] *Massachusetts Gazette*, 25 March 1773, p. 3, col. 1. Doane, a wealthy Cape Cod shipowner, was to be Adams' client in the case of the *Lusanna*, No. 58. See also 2 JA, *Diary and Autobiography* 61. As to Dawson, see No. 51, note 1. That the *Jenny* was inward bound may be inferred from the award of pilotage to Dawson on her condemnation as well as from the size of his share in her proceeds. See note 7 below. In a letter of 22 April 1773 to Arthur Lee, Samuel Adams remarked that "Otis yesterday was engaged in a cause in the admiralty on the side of Dawson, commander of one of the king's cutters." Adams reported that the tories considered this a victory, but he wondered how they could "boast of the acquisition of one, whom they themselves have been ready to expose as distracted." Harry A. Cushing, ed., *The Writings of Samuel Adams*, 3:36–37 (N.Y., 1907). Otis, who had been intermittently confined and released, was at this point in a decline. 11 Sibley-Shipton, *Harvard Graduates* 281–284.

As Adams' minutes, printed below, indicate, Blowers opened the case for Doane, presumably because under the Acts of Trade the claimant had the burden of proof as to the origin of the goods.[2] Two statutes were involved. Under the Staple Act of 1663 if goods "of the growth, production, or manufacture of Europe," were "imported" into the colonies without having been loaded in England, vessel and goods were forfeit.[3] A provision of the American Act of 1764 tightened enforcement of this regulation by permitting the seizure at sea of any goods found aboard a vessel "arriving from any part of Europe," for which there were no papers showing that the goods had been taken aboard at a British port.[4]

In 1767 the High Court of Admiralty had upheld a decision of the Massachusetts Vice Admiralty Court that a vessel which had been seized in Boston Harbor when still three miles from port had "imported" goods within the meaning of the 1663 Act.[5] The facts in the *Jenny's* case were apparently within this decision because the question does not seem to have been raised at the trial. In order to avoid forfeiture of the vessel, Blowers and Adams thus had to show that none of her cargo was of European "growth, production, or manufacture"; if this was impossible, then at least all goods of non-European origin might be kept from condemnation, if it could be proved that the *Jenny* had cleared from a non-European port.

Blowers attempted to meet this burden by introducing evidence to the effect that the cargo had been loaded at Tangier. This fact, if established, would at least save non-European goods, and might allow an inference that the entire cargo, having been loaded in Africa, was of African origin. The evidence consisted of the testimony of several witnesses, probably members of the crew; the certificates of one Meshod Meguiers, apparently English Vice Consul at Tangier, that the goods had been loaded there; and the master's manifest, presumably also to the same effect.

Otis and Fitch seemed to have no direct evidence in rebuttal, but launched a telling counterattack both on the credibility of Blowers' evidence and on the inferences which he hoped to draw from it. The witnesses were all connected with Doane, and their testimony was full of inconsistencies; the certificates were incomplete, inconsistent, and of doubtful probative value; the manifest was rendered doubtful by evidence that Doane had tampered with it, and by one witness who indicated that the harbor of Tangier did not have adequate facilities for taking on cargo. In addition, much of the cargo was patently European in origin. In all likelihood the *Jenny* had actually cleared from Gibraltar, across the straits from Tangier.

Adams must have closed the case for Doane, but he has left us no record of his arguments. Whatever they were, they failed to convince the court completely. On 12 May the *Jenny* and at least part of her cargo,

[2] 4 Geo. 3, c. 15, §45 (1764), set out in No. 46, note 54.
[3] 15 Car. 2, c. 7, §6, note 9 below.
[4] 4 Geo. 3, c. 15, §30, note 10 below.
[5] Bishop v. The *Freemason*, Quincy, *Reports* 387 (Mass. Vice Adm., 1763), affirmed *sub nom.* The *Freemason* v. Bishop, Burrell 55, 167 Eng. Rep. 469 (High Ct. Adm., 1767). See No. 50, note 6; No. 51, note 1.

consisting of raisins, wine, cotton and silk stockings, and several pieces of silk, were ordered to be sold. Since not all of the goods mentioned in Fitch's argument appear in the notice of sale, it is possible that the court found some items to have been non-European, both in origin and point of shipment.[6] In any event, the sale on 20 May produced an adequate return for Dawson's efforts. The court's receipt book shows that his half of the proceeds amounted to £773 16s. 11 1/2d.[7]

ADAMS' MINUTES OF THE ARGUMENT[8]

Court of Vice Admiralty, Boston, April 1773

Captn. Dawson. vs. Jenny.

Blowers. Libel, claim, 15 Car. 2, c. 7, §.6.[9]

Hillman, and Cato.

Certificates. Goods claimed, taken in at Tangier.

[6] *Massachusetts Gazette*, 13 May 1773, p. 3, col. 1. A literal interpretation of 4 Geo. 3, c. 15, §30, note 10 below, would have allowed condemnation of all goods not shipped in England, even though properly shipped outside Europe, if the vessel made a European stop prior to landfall in the colonies. Fitch's argument, text at note 24 below, suggests a looser construction, however. It is possible that some of the *Jenny*'s cargo may not have been claimed, and may have been sold separately under an order of 14 April 1773, for the sale of a small quantity of lemons and olives, and 1409 "raw hides" also seized by Dawson, for "illegal importation." *Massachusetts Gazette*, 16 April 1773, p. 2, col. 3.

[7] Receipts from Seizures of Ships, 2 July 1773, MBAt:Price Papers. Dawson also received £43 for "Pilotage, Information money and cash paid Mr. Otis." *Ibid.* "Information money" may have covered either Fitch's fees or a payment to an informer. Dawson was entitled to a half, rather than a third, because the seizure was "at sea," which was defined to include seizures "in or upon any river . . . not actually made on shore." The Governor was thus not entitled to a share. 4 Geo. 3, c. 15, §42 (1764); 5 Geo. 3, c. 45, §26 (1765).

[8] In hands of JA and Sampson Salter Blowers. Adams Papers, Microfilms, Reel No. 185. See notes 17, 20 below.

[9] The Staple Act of 1663, 15 Car. 2, c. 7, §6: "[N]o commodity of the growth, production or manufacture of *Europe*, shall be imported into any land, island, plantation, colony, territory or place to his Majesty belonging, or which shall hereafter belong unto or be in the possession of his Majesty, his heirs and successors, in *Asia*, *Africa*, or *America* (*Tangier* only excepted,) but what shall be *bona fide*, and without fraud, laden and shipped in *England*, *Wales*, or the town of *Berwick* upon *Tweed*, and in *English* built shipping, or which were *bona fide* bought before the first day of *October* one thousand six hundred sixty and two, and had such certificate thereof as is directed in one act passed in the last sessions of this present parliament intituled, *An Act for preventing frauds, and regulating abuses in his Majesty's customs*; and whereof the master and three fourths of the mariners at least are *English*, and which shall be carried directly thence to the said lands, islands, plantations, colonies, territories or places, and from no other place or places whatsoever; any law, statute or usage to the contrary notwithstanding," under penalty of forfeiture of ship and goods, one third to the Crown, one third to the Governor of the colony, and one third to the informer. Salt for the New England and Newfoundland fisheries, Madeira and Azores wines, and certain Scottish and Irish commodities

Captn. Brace. Hides cured in the Hair with salt.
Brooke and Guthrie. Fez, Morocco.
Downes's Manifest.

Mr. Otis. Reads Libel, Claim, and Answer. 15 C[ar.] 2, c. 7, §. 6.
4. G. 3, c. 15. page 291. No Vessell shall be cleard out in England
unless the whole Cargo was shipped in ⟨*England*⟩ Great Britain.[10]

Onus on the Claimant.[11] No attempt to prove the Goods grown in
Affrica.

Bishop [Burnet?] said he always presumed a [Priest?] to be a Rogue
untill the contrary is proved.[12] Doane has been catched. And therefore
must be presumed to be a Smuggler, untill he proves himself a fair
Trader.

This Vessell as curious a Voyage as St. Paul made to Rome.[13]

Pieces of Silks.

Mr. Hallowell tasted one Quarter Cask, it has the Taste of Malaga
Wines, not so sweet as some Malaga.[14]

were excepted. *Id.* §7. As to Tangier, see note 21 below. For the construction of
"imported," see text at note 5 above.

[10] 4 Geo. 3, c. 15, §30 (1764), after reciting that British vessels had been
carrying whole cargoes of goods shipped in Europe direct to the colonies under a
clearance covering a few articles shipped in Britain, provided that no "ship or vessel
shall, upon any pretence whatsoever, be cleared outwards from any port of this
kingdom, for any land, island, plantation, colony, territory, or place, to his
Majesty belonging, or which shall hereafter belong unto or be in the possession or
under the dominion of his Majesty, his heirs, or successors, in *America*, unless the
whole and entire cargo of such ship or vessel shall be *bona fide*, and without fraud,
laden and shipped in this kingdom; and any officer of his Majesty's customs is hereby
impowered to stop any *British* ship or vessel arriving from any part of *Europe*, which
shall be discovered within two leagues of the shore of any of the said *British*
colonies or plantations in *America*, and to seize and take from thence, as forfeited,
any goods (except as hereinafter mentioned) for which the master or other person
taking the charge of such ship or vessel shall not produce a cocket or clearance from
the collector or proper officer of his Majesty's customs, certifying that the said goods
were laden on board the said ship or vessel in some port of *Great Britain.*" Salt,
wines of the Madeiras and Azores, and certain Irish commodities were excepted
from the last provision. *Id.* §31.

[11] See text at note 2 above.

[12] The allusion has not been identified, but the remark undoubtedly should be
attributed to Gilbert Burnet (1643-1715), Bishop of Salisbury and ecclesiastical
prime mover of the Revolution of 1688, whose best known work is his *History of
His Own Times* (London, 1723-1734). DNB.

[13] A reference to Paul's voyage from Judaea to make his appeal to Caesar at
Rome, in the course of which he was driven all over the Mediterranean by contrary
winds and shipwrecked at Malta before attaining his goal. Acts 27-28.

[14] Malaga wines are Spanish, and thus not within the exception in the statutes,
notes 9, 10, above. The taster was probably Robert Hallowell, commissioned Comptroller of the Port of Boston in 1770, when his brother Benjamin, who held that
office since 1764, was made a Customs Commissioner in place of John Temple.
Jones, *Loyalists of Mass.* 158-160.

Jona. Wild[15] would blush at mentioning the Supposition, that C[aptain] Dawson procurd these silks to carry about to take in a fair Trader.

It appears on Record that a Number of Packages were thrown over. Negatur.

French Chart. Shews that C[aptain] Brace was mistaken in many things.

500 Cattle, an over load for the Ark. [...] to an Horse.[16]

Ballances the Testimonies of Mathews, Hillman and Cato.

Harrison and Hallowell, about Downes's Manifest.

Major Doane required the Master to swear differently from what he first intended.[17] A strong mark of fraud.

The Conversation between Major Doane and Mr. Waterhouse and Hallowell, can by no means help them for it appears clear the Major did not follow his Advice.

As to the *Conculs* Papers produced, tho I am willing to allow them authentick, yet they can prove nothing for every Body knows those Certificates can be obtained when askd for.

Advocate General.

The Cause rest[s] on two distinct points, the first is on the 15 Car 2d.[18] That the Goods on board her were not of the Growth &c. of Europe.

The other is that this Vessell came from some parts of Europe, and has produced no Cocket or Clearance.[19]

The Burthen of proof on the Claimants.

Remarks on the Statutes.

1. The Act of Charles, of the utmost national Service.[20]

---

[15] The archrogue of the 18th century and hero of Henry Fielding's ironic novel, *The Life of Mr. Jonathan Wild* (London, 1743).

[16] The reference is unclear, but it apparently is a reflection on the testimony of Hillman, Cato, and Mathews, who seem to have described a loading operation at Tangier, perhaps involving live cattle. See text at note 23 below.

[17] This sentence and the following text through note 20 are in Blowers' hand. JA was apparently called away during the argument. The point here seems to be that Doane had required the master to submit an altered manifest on entry at Boston. For another example of Doane's casual attitude toward shipping documents, see No. 58, note 27. Compare *id.,* note 167.

[18] 15 Car. 2, c. 7, §6, note 9 above.

[19] 4 Geo. 3, c. 15, §30, note 10 above.

[20] Probably the beginning of an argument for a construction of the Act favoring the Crown. Compare Fitch's argument in Dawson v. The *Dolphin*, No. 51, text following note 23, and text at note 34. The remainder of the minutes are in JA's hand, suggesting that some of the argument may have been lost in the process of his resumption of note-taking.

Captn. McNeal. No Harbour at Tangier, no shelter since the Pier blown up. An open Bay.[21]

The Act. 4. G. 3. whole Cargo must be relanded and reshipped. p. 291.

No Proof that any one Article, the Produce of Africa. Only consequential.

Certificate from Mr. Meshod Meguiers.

Salt not exported from Africa.

Oyl. 26 Boxes. Figgs, Capers &c.

Pampo[u]ses.

Honey. Matts. Silks never exported from Africa.[22]

Our Witnesses, their Connection with the Claimant.

Cato talks of a Xebec 3 Masts. Hillman a Schooner, with 2 Masts.

Cato believes 'em to be Spaniards. Cato's 200 could not be Hillmans 200 therefore 400.

Mathews 900. 1st. did not know.[23]

Unwillingness and forgetfulness of Hillman. At a Loss as to Time how long, &c. when the Mate died &c.

Pampouses, shipd in Europe, tho produced in Africa must be shipped in England by the statute 4. G.[24]

The Wine.

Certificate.

Doane and his V[ice] Consul dont agree. D. says not shippd, Consul that they were at Tangier.

The only unerring Guide is Truth.

Masters Manifest. From Tangier, should have been from Gibralter.

---

[21] Tangier was a British possession from 1662 until 1684. In the latter year the English abandoned it, blowing up the mole and fortifications which they had constructed. Commercial relations were maintained, however, primarily as a source of provisions for Gibraltar. Louis Sauveur de Chenier, *The Present State of the Empire of Morocco*, 1:20–21, 2:202, 355–356 (London, 1788).

[22] One 18th-century account states that among the goods shipped at Tangier were "oils, gums, wax, elephants-teeth, ... raw hides and wool." 2 Chenier, *Present State of the Empire of Morocco* 356. The reading "pampouses" has been adopted on the supposition that the goods in question were slippers made of undressed cowhide. See *OED*: "pampootie," "papoosh, or papouche." The word might also be "pamponses," perhaps a form of "pompon" or "pompion," a kind of melon said to grow in the Indies, Java, and India. *OED*. Melons were a product of the Mediterranean. See John M. Baker, *A View of the Commerce of the Mediterranean* 100 (Washington, 1819). Some variety of the fruit might have been shipped to Boston in dried form, perhaps as gourds.

[23] See text and note 16 above.

[24] See note 6 above.

53. Ross' Case

1774

EDITORIAL NOTE

On 25 March 1774, aroused at the presumption which Boston had earlier displayed in dumping the East India Company's tea into the harbor, Parliament passed the Boston Port Act. This was the first of a series of harsh measures known as the Coercive, or Intolerable, Acts, which were designed to bring Massachusetts to heel. Instead they stirred an immediate storm of resistance, which produced that final colonial union necessary to make the fight for independence a reality.[1] Adams' minutes of the arguments in a case arising in the first days of the Port Act's operation, which are printed below, are hardly prophetic of these later developments.

The Act, which was to remain in force until the Town had paid for the tea and made good other damage incurred through its rebelliousness, provided that after 1 June 1774 no goods other than food or fuel shipped coastwise could be loaded or unloaded in Boston Harbor, except by vessels which were there on or before that date. Even these ships were to depart by 14 June. Other vessels found moored or hovering in the Harbor, or within a league of it, could be seized as forfeit if they did not depart within six hours after being warned by a naval or customs officer. Violations of the Act were to be prosecuted in the same manner as offenses against the Acts of Trade, which meant at common law or in Admiralty at the option of the prosecutor.[2]

All that is known of the case which Adams minuted has been deduced from his notes. Some time in April 1774, one Ross, master of a vessel of unknown name, sailed from an unknown port bound for New York with a cargo which included indigo and wrought plate. When about 1500 miles from Boston, the vessel was seriously damaged, presumably through stress of weather. Finding his condition such that he could not make New York, Ross put into Boston although he had heard "in his Passage" that the port was closed. The date of his arrival cannot be calculated with any certainty; the best guess is that it was about the middle of June, but it could have been as late as mid-July.[3] Apparently recognizing this as a genuine case of distress, Admiral Montagu and the customs officers allowed Ross to

[1] For the Tea Party and the Coercive Acts, see p. 105–106 above.

[2] 14 Geo. 3, c. 19 (1774). As to the latter provision, see note 12 below.

[3] One Ross entered at Boston from St. Croix early in May. *Massachusetts Gazette,* 5 May 1774, p. 2, col. 3. Since under 14 Geo. 3, c. 19, §4, a ship arriving before 1 June could have entered and would have had until 14 June to clear, it is unlikely that this was the Ross in question here. The dates in the text are consistent with the assumption that the hearing was held between 15 July and 10 August. See note 5 below. This would have been three to four weeks after the vessel's arrival, allowing her two or three weeks in port before seizure and a week to ten days between seizure and trial. A June arrival seems more likely because of Ross' "April" embarkation.

enter the port for repairs. But Ross overstayed his welcome. After an indeterminate period, probably two to three weeks, his ship was still not ready to sail, and he had begun to offer some of his cargo for sale, perhaps to raise necessary funds.

The Crown now acted, presumably by seizing the vessel and libeling her in the Admiralty Court. In view of the local reaction to the Port Act, it is unlikely that the customs officers would have entrusted any case under it to a jury, and there is no record of any proceeding at common law.[4] Daniel Leonard argued the case for the Crown and William Tudor appeared for Ross, who had presumably filed a claim for the vessel. Adams' minutes show that he attended the argument. It thus could have taken place before he left for the eastern circuit on 20 June, but it was probably held between his return from the eastward on about 18 July and his departure on 10 August to attend the Continental Congress at Philadelphia.[5] The question chiefly agitated at the hearing was whether Ross had been diligent in getting his ship ready to put to sea. No record has been found of the result, but it seems most probable that the vessel was acquitted, because no notice of her sale as forfeit appeared in the Boston newspapers.

ADAMS' MINUTES OF THE ARGUMENT[6]

Court of Vice Admiralty, Boston, June or July 1774

Leonard. Port Bill, Lex Talionis. Punishment of Boston the main Object.

There is an Exception where by the Act of God, there is an Impossibility of getting out.[7] A Necessity.

She had no Right to Stay to repair and refit for a Voyage.

She might have gone out, if not in 6 Hours,[8] yet in two or three days.

She was not in a worse situation than she had been.

[4] For accounts of several proceedings in Admiralty under the Act between 30 Sept. and 21 Nov. 1774, see "Letters of John Andrews," 8 MHS, *Procs.* 371, 378, 386 (1864–1865).

[5] See 2 JA, *Diary and Autobiography* 96–97. The hearing was probably three or four weeks after the vessel's arrival. Since she must have arrived after 1 June, there probably would not have been time for trial before 20 June. See note 3 above. JA's return from Maine can be estimated on the basis of the fact that the Superior Court at Falmouth adjourned on 13 July. SCJ Rec. 1774, fol. 225.

[6] In JA's hand. Adams Papers, Microfilms, Reel No. 185. For the dating, see notes 3, 5, above.

[7] There is no such exception within the Port Act. 14 Geo. 3, c. 19 (1774). Leonard may here refer to a doctrine of statutory construction that excuses liability for actions forced by acts of God. See 4 Bacon, *Abridgment* 649. Or he may be incorporating by analogy an exception in cases of necessity to the provision of the Act of 1764 requiring foreign vessels to leave colonial waters on warning. 4 Geo. 3, c. 15, §33. See note 8 below.

[8] Six hours was the grace period allowed to vessels after being warned to leave by naval or customs officers. 14 Geo. 3, c. 19, §3.

She might have hired assistance.

The Part the Crown officers have acted is extreamly fair and legal.

The Admiral could not allow him to stay compleatly to refit. Tho he seemed to understand that he had leave to do so.

Mr. Gray [9] tells us that the whole might have been had in a Week. J. Hall thinks 7 or 8 days. Compasses were done in 4 days.

If she is not now fit for sea that is not an excuse.

He is shewing Specimens of his Indigo &c. and brings on shore some of his Wrought Plate. This comes within another Act.[10]

Plate—Goods, Wares or Merchandise.[11]

She was in the same Condition in which she came 500 Leagues.

Tudor. The Rules that govern other Acts, are to rule this.[12]

Ross Sail'd in April. Heard in his Passage that Boston Port was shut.[13]

Holrode describes their distress. Bound to N. York. Shut. And Middleton says, Distress. Mier, and Dodge.

John Hall. Mate of the Mercury [14] describes her distress, no Masts, sails tattered.

James Hall. We have invalidated his Testimony.

[9] Perhaps John Gray, the proprietor of Gray's ropewalk.

[10] Under 15 Car. 2, c. 7, §8 (1663), set out, No. 48, note 10, unloading goods before entry was a cause of forfeiture. Ross had presumably made no entry, because the customs officers had moved to Plymouth with their records. Warren, "The Colonial Customs Service in Massachusetts in its relation to the American Revolution," 46 MHS, *Procs.* 440, 471–472 (1913). In addition, if the goods were European in origin, they could be forfeited if they had not been shipped in Great Britain. See No. 52.

[11] The Port Act forbade the loading of "any goods, wares, or merchandise whatsoever, to be transported or carried into any other country, province, or place whatsoever, or into any other part of the said province of the *Massachuset's Bay*, in *New England*," or the unloading of goods, wares or merchandise "to be brought from any other country, province, or place, or any other part of the said province of *Massachuset's Bay* in *New England*," under penalty of forfeiture of goods, vessel, and small craft used in the process. 14 Geo. 3, c. 19, §1.

[12] The Act, 14 Geo. 3, c. 19, §6, provided that forfeitures were to be prosecuted "in like manner as other penalties and forfeitures inflicted by any act or acts of parliament relating to the trade or revenues of the *British* colonies or plantations in *America*, are directed to be prosecuted," under 4 Geo. 3, c. 15, §§41–47 (1764) and 8 Geo. 3, c. 22 (1768). For authorities favoring strict construction of these Acts in favor of the claimant, see No. 51. In addition, there were provisions in some of the statutes for leniency toward unintentional violations. See, for example, 4 Geo. 3, c. 15, §22 (1764), excusing from liability goods improperly imported into England with no intent to defraud.

[13] The Port Act was passed on 25 March 1774. News of it reached Boston on 11 May. Miller, *Origins of the American Revolution* 359–360.

[14] One of the British warships on station off Boston to enforce the Act. See Rowe, *Letters and Diary* 273 (29 May 1774). Perhaps the *Mercury* had intercepted Ross' vessel and escorted her into port.

Jack the Pilot. Distress enough.

It was Ross's Duty to come in here.

Q. Whether Ross used his utmost Endeavour to get out?

Hall says Ross did Use a reasonable Dilligence. Middleton &c. Mier says Ross hurried them.

In Town. Mr. Hutchinson. Very dilligent. Concernd about lying at Expence.

His Landlady. Anxious to get away.

Ruggles the Sail maker. Up at Gun firing [hiring us?].[15] Worked on the Mast when the Weather would permit. Employd as Many Hands as could be employed.

[15] Illegible in MS. If the editors' reading is correct, the meaning may be "up at sunrise assembling a crew."

O. Admiralty—White Pine Acts Jurisdiction

EDITORIAL NOTE

Colonial forests were a natural resource upon which Britain depended for a vital element in her naval strength. The towering white pines which had grown untouched in the woods of northern New England for centuries were unequaled throughout the world as mast timber. Moreover, the supply from this source did not depend upon the vicissitudes of foreign trade or war and peace. The royal mast contractors met severe competition, however, because these same mighty trees were attractive to the colonists both for maritime uses and for the humbler purposes of the settler. To protect the forests from local depredations, the British developed a statutory conservation scheme, enforced in the Vice Admiralty Courts, which led to a running battle with the colonists through most of the 18th century.[1]

The basis of the scheme was the Massachusetts Charter of 1691, which combined the former colonies of Plymouth, Massachusetts Bay, Maine, Nova Scotia, and certain lands lying between the latter two, into a single province. In the Charter "all Trees of the Diameter of Twenty Four Inches and upwards of Twelve Inches from the ground" growing on land "not heretofore granted to any private persons" were reserved to the Crown, to be cut only by royal license; a penalty of £100 for each tree cut without license was established.[2] To implement this provision a system of licensing certain royal mast contractors was established, and a Surveyor General of the Woods was appointed to oversee their operations and to put down unlicensed activity.[3] After a series of only partly successful enforcement attempts, Parliament in 1711 embodied the Charter language in the

---

[1] For an admirable treatment of the naval and economic considerations, and a summary of the 18th-century struggle, see Robert G. Albion, *Forests and Sea Power* 231–280 (Cambridge, Mass., 1926). The cutting and shipment of masts to England was further encouraged by the grant of bounties to importers, and the inclusion of masts and other naval stores in the list of "enumerated" colonial products that could be shipped only to an English or colonial port. The latter provision did not prevent the development of an illicit trade in these materials. *Id.* at 250–251, 264–265; see note 17 below.

[2] Province Charter of 1691, 1 A&R 20, set out in pertinent part in No. 55, Doc. III, text and note 28. England had relied on colonial masts through most of the 17th century, but the Charter of 1691 was the first formal effort at regulation. It seems to have resulted from a combination of pressures exerted by the commencement of hostilities with the French and a mercantilist desire to protect the English woolen industry by encouraging colonial initiatives in other directions. Albion, *Forests and Sea Power* 233–240. Compare Board of Trade to Governor Shute, 16 Aug. 1722, *Cal. State Papers* (Col.), 1722–1723, §263. Although there was no enforcement provision in the Charter, actions under it were brought in the common-law courts. See materials cited in Albion, *Forests and Sea Power* 265 note; Usher to Secretary of State, 25 Nov. 1710, 9 Maine Hist. Soc., *Colls.* (2d ser.) 305 (1907).

[3] Albion, *Forests and Sea Power* 235–238, 242–248.

first of the White Pine Acts, which provided that no "white or other pine tree" meeting the Charter qualifications should be cut in any province or colony north of New Jersey. Penalties in the amount set in the Charter were to be sued for before the nearest justice of the peace and to be divided equally between the Crown and the informer.[4]

These provisions produced more controversy than conservation. The popular faction in the Massachusetts House, led by Dr. Elisha Cooke, a life-long opponent of royal authority, denied that the Charter and Act bound the unincorporated Province lands in the timber-rich Gorges patent in Maine, claiming that the royal grant of this tract to Sir Ferdinando Gorges in 1639 brought it within the exception for lands granted to private persons.[5] In 1718 Counsel for the Board of Trade held that the conveyance of these lands from the Gorges interests to the Massachusetts Bay Colony in 1678 and the vacation of the colony charter in 1684 revested the lands in the Crown and took them out of the exception.[6] The focus then shifted

[4] 9 Anne, c. 17, §1 (1711), set out in No. 55, Doc. III, at note 31. For the enforcement efforts, see Albion, *Forests and Sea Power* 242–249 and materials cited in note 2 above. An earlier statute had protected "pitch, pine trees, or tar trees, not being within any fence or actual inclosure, under the growth of twelve inches diameter, at three foot from the earth." Penalties of £5 "for each offense" were to be sued for before the nearest justice of the peace, to be divided equally between Crown and informer. 3 & 4 Anne, c. 10, §6 (1704). The purpose of the latter act seems to have been to protect trees useful for naval stores such as tar, rather than mast trees. Albion, *Forests and Sea Power* 249. See Bridger to Board of Trade, 9 Maine Hist. Soc., *Colls.* (2d ser.) 266, abstracted in *Cal. State Papers* (*Col.*), 1708–1709, §428. However, it did have the further effect of serving as a long-range conservation measure by assuring future growth of the great pines. The exception for trees within a fence or enclosure seems to have been intended to permit cutting for the purposes of clearing land for settlement only. Albion indicates that this limitation was continued in the White Pine Act of 1729, note 17 below. *Id.* at 258. It is probable, however, that the latter act, and that of 1721, note 13 below, which covered white pines of every size, and together limited unlicensed cutting to private property within township bounds, were considered to have repealed 3 & 4 Anne, c. 19, §6 *sub silentio* and not to embody its narrower limits. JA did not use its language in the information which he drafted for John Wentworth in 1769. No. 54, Doc. II.

[5] The Gorges Patent, or Province of Maine, which ran from the New Hampshire border to the Kennebec River, had been conveyed by Gorges' heir through a straw to the Massachusetts Bay Colony in 1678. See the deeds in 2 Maine Hist. Soc., *Colls.* (1st ser.) 257–264 (1847). As to the Gorges Patent, see No. 55, notes 6, 17. The Massachusetts argument was that the Province title derived from the 1639 grant to Gorges through the title of the Bay Colony, which had allegedly been confirmed by another provision of the 1691 Charter (No. 55, note 22). See "The right of Massachusetts to the Province of Maine, vindicated," 9 Maine Hist. Soc., *Colls.* (2d ser.) 388–414. Cooke had a personal interest in this phase of the struggle against the Crown, for he had bought up at least two grants of land made by the Bay Colony General Court before 1678 which had never been laid out, and had proceeded to lay them out as a large tract within the Gorges Patent, which the Province General Court confirmed. John Bridger to ———, 8 April 1720, 10 *id.* at 134–135; 2 Mass., *House Jour.* 24, 66–67. As to Cooke generally, see 4 Sibley-Shipton, *Harvard Graduates* 349–356; No. 5, note 14.

[6] The question reached the Board of Trade on the petition of John Bridger, Surveyor General of the Woods, whom Cooke had personally attacked as part of his

to the trees themselves. In 1721 the House claimed and exercised the power to seize for the Province logs that had been cut into twenty-foot lengths. The justification advanced by Cooke was that the Charter reserved only timber fit for use as masts. This stand was the basis of one of the charges of usurpation of the prerogative which Governor Shute success-fully prosecuted against the House before the Privy Council in 1725.[7]

The Act of 1711 also proved inadequate in its enforcement provisions. Jurisdiction of offenses under it had been given to justices of the peace

---

campaign (note 5 above). The House had approved these strictures against Bridger in Dec. 1718, Cooke having spent the session on the sidelines as a result of the Governor's negative of his election to the Council. See Bridger to Board of Trade, 14 July 1718, *Cal. State Papers (Col.)*, 1717–1718, §616; 1 Mass., *House Jour.* 272; 2 *id.* at 3, 47, 52, 53, 108–109. By this time, however, Richard West's opinion, adopted by the Board of Trade, had destroyed the legal foundation of the Province arguments, since it meant that any conveyance of the Gorges lands from the Province General Court after 1691 could have been made only by virtue of a title derived from the 1691 Charter and must be subject to the reservation in that instrument. Opinion of Richard West, 12 Nov. 1718, Chalmers, *Opinions* 133–137; *Cal. State Papers (Col.)*, 1717–1718, §§744, 755. See generally, Albion, *Forests and Sea Power* 256–257; Knollenberg, *Origin of the American Revolution* 132–133. Knollenberg argues that on a strict construction of the Charter language, West's opinion is unsound; since the only requirement was that the lands have been *granted* previously to private persons, the subsequent history of the title was irrelevant. *Ibid.* West's ruling that the Bay Colony title was revested in the Crown in 1684 had some sanction in English corporate law, however, and it was supported by a decision of the Privy Council on Gorges' application in 1691. See 9 Holdsworth, *History of English Law* 67–68; 9 Maine Hist. Soc., *Colls.* (2d ser.) 390–392; *Cal. State Papers (Col.)*, 1689–1692, §1677. The 1691 Charter confirmed titles under pre-vious grants in language which limited the confirmation to grantees actually holding title at the time of the Charter, thus excluding the Bay Colony. See No. 55, note 22. When the Charter's exception of lands previously granted to private persons is read with this confirmation clause, it would seem that the Crown could not have in-tended to save private rights in trees growing on lands to which it did not at the same time confirm the title. The problem raised by the Gorges patent is thus to be distinguished from the case of the Kennebec Company's claims, which were based on a title that had not revested in the Crown in 1684 and was thus confirmed in 1691. See text and notes 33–41, below.

[7] See generally, Albion, *Forests and Sea Power* 256–267. For the House action, see 2 Mass., *House Jour.* 362–366, 381, 383, 386, 388; 3 *id.* at 30–32, 42, 154, 159, 174, 186. For Cooke's justification, see 3 *id.* at 31–32, 40. See also 2 Hutchin-son, *Massachusetts Bay*, ed. Mayo, 190–191. Shute's charges were the result of a struggle that had been going on between him and the House since his arrival in 1716. Cooke, who was involved in all of the questions, traveled to England to argue the case for the House. He tried to maintain that they had acted so as to pre-serve the King's rights, but he was confronted with the defiant resolutions of the House, and after an adverse report by the hearing officers, was forced to abandon this and several other points. He ultimately prevailed before the Privy Council on the questions whether the Governor had the power to negative him as Speaker of the House, and whether the House could adjourn without the Governor's consent. The Explanatory Charter of 1726 was a direct result of Cooke's activities. See *Cal. State Papers (Col.)*, 1722–1723, §§683, 704; *id.* 1724–1725, §346 i; 3 *Acts, Privy Council (Col.)* 94–95, 102–104; John Colman to Rev. Dr. Colman, 18 May 1724, 2 MHS, *Colls.* (1st ser.) 32 (2d edn., 1810); *Boston Chronicle*, 7–11 Jan. 1768, p. 33, cols. 1–3; 1 A&R 21–23.

to avoid the hazards of jury trial, but the local interests of the justices made them of little more value than juries in obtaining convictions of violators.[8] There were other impediments to prosecution: The Crown bore the burden of proving that trees had been cut on reserved land; [9] the rigid and complicated common-law process, which was under the control of reluctant local courts and sheriffs made it difficult to obtain execution when penalties were awarded; [10] there was no express authority for the *in rem* seizure and forfeiture of trees felled within the prohibited areas.[11]

The Naval Stores Act of 1722, which was the basis of enforcement until the Revolution, sought to deal with all of these problems. It repealed the Act of 1711 and replaced its provisions with a prohibition against the unlicensed cutting of "any white pine trees, not growing within any township," in the colonies from New Jersey north, with penalties varying in amount according to the size of the tree. The bulk of the Gorges tract, being unincorporated, was thus covered, whatever the state of the title.[12] The problem of locally oriented courts was solved by a provision that the penalties were to be recovered "before the judge of the admiralty, or his deputy, within the colony or plantation where such pinetree shall be

[8] For troubles with juries before 1711, see materials cited, note 2 above. For later instances, see *Cal. State Papers (Col.)*, 1720–1721, §118; *id.* 1722–1723, §132; *id.* 1728–1729, §118; 6 *Acts, Privy Council (Col.)* §399. The situation was further complicated in Massachusetts by the fact that there was an appeal as of right from the decision of a single justice to the Court of General Sessions, which sat with a jury. 1 A&R 368–369. This provision was presumably applicable even where jurisdiction was conferred by Parliament, in the absence of any expression to the contrary.

[9] Surveyor General Bridger urged that "The owners [i.e. onus] probandi must be on the cutters," after losing on a failure of proof. *Cal. State Papers (Col.)*, 1720–1721, §118; see *id.* §179 i. For similar but more conventional comments, see *id.* §§319, 352 ii; 9 Maine Hist. Soc., *Colls.* (2d ser.) 267.

[10] For Bridger's difficulties with fraudulent conveyances, faulty returns, inadequate jails, and the like, see Bridger to Lords of Trade, 14 July 1718, 9 Maine Hist. Soc., *Colls.* (2d ser.) 420; Bridger to Popple, 26 June 1719, 10 *id.* at 119–120 (1907).

[11] Such seizures had been carried out at least as early as 1709, probably on the authority of the Surveyor General's commission or instructions, or perhaps by special warrant from the Admiralty. Logs so seized were apparently not forfeit without the approval of the Lords of Admiralty in England, however, which meant that difficult questions of fact and title had to be decided by a body far from the scene and unacquainted with local practice. As a result the chance of forfeiture was very uncertain, and the logs more than likely to rot where they lay before they could be condemned. See Bridger to Board of Trade, 27 March 1709, 9 Maine Hist. Soc., *Colls.* (2d ser.) 268; same to same, 17 Aug. 1709, *id.* at 298; Bridger to Lord Dartmouth[?], 21 May 1711, *Cal. State Papers (Col.)*, 1710–1711, §846. Bridger to ———, 8 April 1720, 10 Maine Hist. Soc., *Colls.* (2d ser.) 137. The common-law courts could also interfere by treating a seizure as an attachment in a suit for penalties and ordering delivery on failure of conviction. *Ibid.*; *Cal. State Papers (Col.)*, 1720–1721, §§57, 82, 118, 127, 179.

[12] 8 Geo. 1, c. 12, §§5, 6 (1722), set out in No. 55, at notes 32–35. The reservation of all trees outside township bounds was an idea of Bridger's directed specifically against Cooke's claims to unincorporated lands. Bridger to ———, 8 April 1720, 10 Maine Hist. Soc., *Colls.* (2d ser.) 135–137.

cut." [13] Other complaints about the judicial process were remedied by placing the burden of proof of the trees' location upon the claimant and by providing stringent measures for execution by distress and sale.[14] To meet the contention that cut logs were not Crown property and to end the difficulties experienced in enforcing seizures, the statute further provided that all illegally-cut "white pine-trees, masts or logs made from such trees," should "be forfeited and seized for the use of his Majesty." [15]

[13] 8 Geo. 1, c. 12, §5. See No. 55, note 33. See the materials cited, note 8 above. Little consideration seems to have been given to the legal basis for this extension of the Admiralty jurisdiction to an area that was geographically far from its usual purview. Objections were occasionally made in a political context. See *Cal. State Papers* (Col.), 1722–1723, §4. However, no case has been found in which a plea to the jurisdiction was offered. See Wentworth v. Dean, Hough, *Reports* 227, 229, 233 note (N.Y. Vice Adm., 1769) (Respondent complained of "Hardship of the Prosecution in the Admiralty" and being held to bail; but no jurisdictional objection made). It may have been generally accepted that the Admiralty was a proper forum in which to litigate the King's right to royal property of a maritime nature, on an analogy to droits of Admiralty (great fish and other unclaimed objects cast up from the sea, which belonged to the Crown). The proceeds of the droits were granted to the Lord High Admiral and litigation concerning them was carried on in the Admiralty Courts. 1 Holdsworth, *History of English Law* 559–561. If this was the basis of the extension, the Crown interest must have been the chief justification, since ordinarily even today in delictual actions, some element of maritime location is usually necessary for jurisdiction. Grant Gilmore and Charles L. Black, *The Law of Admiralty* 18–30 (Brooklyn, 1957). There was also a clear administrative justification for the jurisdiction since the Lords of the Admiralty, who were the authority constituting the colonial Vice Admiralty Courts, had ultimate control of timber policy, having in fact previously supervised the process of seizure and forfeiture. See Albion, *Forests and Sea Power* 42–43; note 11 above. Although the *in personam* actions for penalties involved the same questions of title to royal property, colonial complaints about deprivation of the jury had more force here. They could be met, however, by the argument that in England countless such petty offenses were triable before justices of the peace, who sat without a jury, a practice which had doubtless been the model for the statute 9 Anne, c. 17 (note 4 above). See No. 46, note 103.

[14] 8 Geo. 1, c. 12, §5. As to burden of proof, see note 9 above. Problems concerning execution are covered, note 10 above. The act provided that if a convicted offender failed to pay the penalties assessed within twenty days, the judge was authorized to have the amounts due levied by distress and sale of the offender's goods (presumably through the office of Marshal of the Admiralty Court, rather than the sheriff), or to imprison him for three to twelve months. For this provision in action, see Wentworth v. Dean, Hough, *Reports* 227, 232–233 (N.Y. Vice Adm., 1769).

[15] 8 Geo. 1, c. 12, §5. See No. 55, note 34. For the problems concerning property in the logs and the enforcement of seizures, see notes 8, 11, above. The statute did not expressly provide that such seizures should be prosecuted in Admiralty, but no case has been found in which an objection to the jurisdiction based on the statutory language was made. It may have been felt that the Admiralty's right to the logs made the jurisdiction clear. See note 13 above. In any event, the grant of jurisdiction over penalties could be read to include seizures. 8 Geo. 1, c. 12, §5. It is also not clear how the forfeited logs were to be dealt with, once condemned. The statutory language, and that of JA's information, No. 54, Doc. II, indicate that the logs or their proceeds were to go solely to the Crown. See also Wentworth v. Dean, Hough, *Reports* 227 (N.Y. Vice Adm., 1769), where the action for penalties is entitled Wentworth qui tam v. Dean, but the action against the logs is entitled Our Lord The

It was soon argued that the Act of 1722 had rendered void the Charter reservation. The Crown law officers ruled that the reservation was still in force, but repeal of the Act of 1711 meant that, except in Massachusetts, trees of the reserved size were protected only if they grew outside township bounds. Within Massachusetts the Charter covered trees in the towns, but its enforcement was again at the mercy of common-law juries.[16] These loopholes were closed by the Act of 1729, which provided that in all of the American colonies no white pine trees should be felled (except by licensed cutters) even within a township's bounds unless they were "the property of private persons," and that in Massachusetts white pines within the Charter reservation should not be cut unless they were on lands granted to private persons before 1690. The penalties and recovery machinery of the 1722 statute were to be applicable to violations.[17]

The construction which the Crown gave to the rules applicable in the Province of Massachusetts may be summarized as follows: (1) White pine trees of the size reserved in the Charter could not be cut without license unless they grew (a) within a township at the time of cutting, and (b) on land granted to private persons before 1690. (2) White pine trees of lesser size could not be cut without license unless at the time of cutting they were (a) within a township, and (b) the property of private persons.[18] Until the Revolution this scheme was criticized as bad conservation and commercial policy, as well as an unjust taking of property without compensation. It was also attacked before the courts. Despite the best efforts

---

King v. Three White Pine Trees. After condemnation, if the timber had been cut into logs too short for masts, it might be sold, with the proceeds going to the Surveyor General for the Crown, subject to a charge for his expenses. See Benning Wentworth v. Logs, SF 157245 (Mass. Vice Adm., 1763); Mayo, "The King's Woods," 54 MHS, *Procs.* 50, 54 (1920–1921); Bridger to Board of Trade, 27 March 1709, 9 Maine Hist. Soc., *Colls.* (2d ser.) 268; same to same, 17 Aug. 1709, *id.* at 298. If the seized logs were fit for use as masts, at least in earlier practice they were taken *in specie* by the Crown. *Ibid.* That this remained the practice is suggested by the fact that no notices of sale appear in the Boston newspapers for John Wentworth's successful seizures in 1769–1772.

[16] See Opinion of Francis Fane, 19 July 1726, Chalmers, *Opinions* 137; *Cal. State Papers (Col.)*, 1726–1727, §226; Opinion of Attorney General Yorke and Solicitor General Talbot, 23 Dec. 1726, Chalmers, *Opinions* 139; *Cal. State Papers (Col.)*, 1726–1727, §386. For the opposition to enforcement, including the necessity of a resort to common law, which these loopholes provoked, see *id.* 1724–1725, §§352, 771; *id.* 1726–1727, §§48, 172, 227, 290, 498; *id.* 1728–1729, §§627 i, 892 i, 1018; *id.* 1730, §§288, 402 ii. The problem was further aggravated by a sudden proliferation of new townships in the white pine country. See Albion, *Forests and Sea Power* 255–256; *Cal. State Papers (Col.)*, 1726–1727, §335.

[17] 2 Geo. 2, c. 35, §§1, 2 (1729), set out by JA in No. 55, notes 38–43. That the Act was the result of the problems in note 16 above, appears in *Cal. State Papers (Col.)*, 1726–1727, §§498, 771; *id.* 1728–1729, §§50, 118, 755. The statute also revived the system of bounties and enumeration enacted in 3 & 4 Anne, c. 10 (1705), which had lapsed in 1725. 2 Geo. 2, c. 35, §§3–17. See note 1 above.

[18] Opinion of Richard Jackson, 5 June 1771, Chalmers, *Opinions* 157. In 1773 JA argued that the reservation of trees outside of township bounds was not meant to apply to Massachusetts. See No. 55, text at notes 36–37.

of men seriously interested in a sound forest policy, the attacks on policy grounds brought no change. The court battles provided a constant accompaniment to sporadic efforts at strict enforcement.[19]

These efforts and resultant opposition, legal and otherwise, continued steadily until 1743 when Benning Wentworth, Governor of New Hampshire, succeeded in becoming Surveyor General of the Woods, a fitting appointment, since the mast contract for the northern woods was also in the Wentworth family. Enforcement now subsided, perhaps because the wide-ranging family timber interests were able by different means to satisfy the demand for naval stores as well as for commercial lumber.[20] Apparently moved both by new demands for enforcement from the Crown and by the encroachment of commercial rivals on the family preserve, Wentworth in 1763 suddenly began to enforce the Acts in a series of suits for logs brought in the Admiralty Court at Boston. These suits continued until his resignation, in 1766, as Governor of New Hampshire and as Surveyor.[21]

John Wentworth, nephew of Benning, and successor to both his titles, brought to his new positions a desire to enforce the laws and an enthusiastic interest in the welfare of his native New England. He was in office until the Revolution, and was always active in the surveying phase of his commission, which required him to locate trees suitable for masts and to mark them with the King's broad arrow. He also worked continually to remove colonial objections to the laws.[22] From the beginning, however, he was engaged in the task of enforcement. In July 1767 and again in September he brought libels in the Vice Admiralty Court at Boston for the forfeiture of illegally cut logs and masts which he had seized.[23] Thereafter he was not a suitor in that court until April 1769, although he may have brought

[19] For the failure of various well-intentioned efforts to change the colonial forest policy and the difficulties in enforcement, see Albion, *Forests and Sea Power* 258–269; Knollenberg, *Origin of the American Revolution* 130–131, 133–134.
[20] Albion, *Forests and Sea Power* 253; Knollenberg, *Origin of the American Revolution* 134–135.
[21] See Albion, *Forests and Sea Power* 253; Knollenberg, *Origin of the American Revolution* 135–137; Lawrence S. Mayo, *John Wentworth* 23–24, 47–51 (Cambridge, Mass., 1921). For instances of Benning Wentworth's activities in 1763 and after, see Wentworth v. Logs, SF 157245 (Mass. Vice Adm., 1763); Wentworth v. Loggs, Vice Adm. Min. Bk., 19 April 1766. See Governor Bernard's Proclamation, 9 July 1763, calling on all to aid the Surveyor General of the Woods. Book of Commissions, 1756–1767, fols. 339–340, M-Ar.
[22] For Wentworth's role as Surveyor General, see Albion, *Forests and Sea Power* 253–254, 268–271; Mayo, *John Wentworth* 51–60. Born in 1737, he was a Harvard classmate of JA's, and a man of considerable education. He was one of the most sympathetic and effective colonial administrators, but remained loyal to the Crown at the Revolution. In 1782 he was reappointed Surveyor General of the Woods and took up residence in Nova Scotia, where he served as Lieutenant Governor from 1792 until 1808. He was knighted in 1795 and died in 1820. See generally, Mayo, *John Wentworth.*
[23] Wentworth v. Loggs, Vice Adm. Min. Bk., 28 July 1767; Wentworth v. Masts and Bowsprit, *id.* 7 Sept. 1767. Wentworth did not arrive in Portsmouth to take up his duties until 13 June 1767. Mayo, *John Wentworth* 28–30.

forfeiture actions in the Portsmouth Admiralty Court, held by William Parker, deputy of Robert Auchmuty, Judge of Admiralty at Boston.

In the spring of 1769 Wentworth was about to proceed in the Portsmouth court when Auchmuty suspended Parker from office; Wentworth therefore turned again to Boston. In a letter of 10 April he sent several "informations" against violators to Joshua Loring Jr., one of his deputy surveyors general, with directions to put them in suit before Auchmuty. (No. 54, Document III). At about the same time, John Hurd, one of the Governor's staff, forwarded other informations that had already been "under Consideration of Mr. Parker." (No. 54, Document I). In his letter to Loring, Wentworth suggested that his old friend and Harvard classmate, John Adams, be retained to prosecute the suits. Wentworth spoke warmly of Adams and their somewhat neglected friendship, and ordered that Loring "Present the Lawyer rather a generous fee."

Wentworth's letter may represent one of the influences which were brought to bear on Adams at about this time in an effort to draw him to the side of government.[24] Adams, however, seems to have proceeded in the case more out of pleasant regard for his old companion (and perhaps for the "generous fee") than from any conscious political motive. On 24 April he wrote Wentworth, reporting on his progress in drawing several libels, and asking for information necessary to complete others. (No. 54, Document IV). The letter concludes with a personal message, briefly reminiscent of the baroque style of Adams' youthful correspondence, which seems to express a longing for the freedom and innocence of their old friendship, while recognizing that in present circumstances it could never again exist.

Whatever his motive, Adams drafted an information praying forfeiture of 606 logs and nine masts seized by Wentworth in various locations in York and Cumberland Counties, Maine. (No. 54, Document II). Although Adams' draft is dated 20 April, the libel was filed on 1 May, and claimants were cited to appear on the 24th. The logs and masts were decreed forfeit on 1 June, apparently without a claim's being filed.[25]

In the months before and after the forfeiture, twenty *in personam* actions, some of them involving several respondents, were entered in the Court of Vice Admiralty on Wentworth's behalf. The Minute Book of the court shows that Adams filed three of these on 4 September 1769; penalties of £50 to £100 were decreed against the respondents upon their default on 20 November.[26] Fifteen years later, in describing the White Pine Acts to the Maréchal de Castries, the French Minister of Marine, Adams wrote that at Wentworth's request he had "commenced and prose-

---

[24] As to other possible efforts to subvert JA, see p. 103 above. His early friendship with Wentworth is amply documented in 1 JA, *Diary and Autobiography* 4, 19, 115, 355, 360, 2 *id.* at 308, 4 *id.* at 85–86. See also Mayo, *John Wentworth* 166–167, 189–190.

[25] Vice Adm. Min. Bk., 1 May 1769; *Massachusetts Gazette*, 11 May 1769, p. 2, col. 1.

[26] Wentworth v. Noyes, Wentworth v. Frost, Wentworth v. Knight, Vice Adm. Min. Bk., 4 Sept. 1769.

cuted a great number of libels in the court of admiralty at Boston against transgressions of those acts of parliament." [27] This statement and Adams' letter to Wentworth indicate that Adams was responsible for most, if not all, of the remainder of the twenty suits as well.[28] The Minute Book shows that, in addition to the three defaults, forfeitures were decreed in only two other actions. Of the rest, two were settled, one was dismissed, and in twelve the respondents were not served.

After 1769 Wentworth's enforcement activities seemed to subside, at least as they were reflected in Admiralty actions at Boston. Perhaps he was trying to encourage compliance through persuasion and negotiation, rather than by legal process.[29] His dealings with the Kennebec Company which preceded his action against logs found on the lands which it claimed in Maine (No. 55) suggest an effort to reach an understanding.

In the summer of 1769, the Company, one of Adams' most important clients, had won three significant actions against other claimants to that famous tract, the Kennebec Purchase.[30] Perhaps encouraged, the Proprietors, all of whom were important figures in the Boston financial community, wrote to Wentworth on 16 October 1769, asserting their claim to the Kennebec lands, and protesting the entry thereon of the royal mast contractors, but expressing a willingness to furnish masts to the Crown on their own terms. Wentworth replied that he could not decide the validity of their title himself, but that he was as eager as they were to have a correct determination of it. He offered either to bring an action in Admiralty that would decide the question, or to transmit to England a state of the Proprietors' claim for a ruling. Although he could not "relinquish the Royal Claim either in honor or Justice," he would in the meantime "endeavor to prevent tho' I have no power to refuse the Cutting Masts on the premises." [31] The Proprietors apparently hoped to avoid either variety of determination, perhaps relying on their social acquaintance with Wentworth to produce a favorable result. They thus wrote to him in May 1770, sug-

[27] JA to the Maréchal de Castries, 9 Dec. 1784, 8 JA, *Works* 216.
[28] Wentworth was present in Boston during June 1769 as a member of the Special Court of Admiralty convened for Corbet's Case, in which JA was of counsel for the accused. See No. 56. An agreement for JA to take on more of the logs cases may have been made at this point.
[29] For Wentworth's own account of a successful attempt at persuasion along the Androscoggin in the summer of 1769, see Mayo, *John Wentworth* 52–54. The best known of his prosecutions, Wentworth v. Dean, Hough, *Reports* 227, was tried and decided in the New York Court of Vice Admiralty during the fall of 1769. See Mayo, *John Wentworth* 56–61; Ubbelohde, *Vice Admiralty Courts* 177–178. See also notes 13–15 above.
[30] See JA to AA, Falmouth, 1 July 1769, 1 *Adams Family Correspondence* 67. JA's notes of two of these cases, Bowdoin v. Springer and Gardiner v. Tyng, show that the opposing claims were based at least in part on the Gorges Patent (notes 5, 6, above). Adams Papers, Microfilms, Reel No. 185.
[31] Wentworth to the Committee of the Kennebec Purchase, 19 Oct. 1769, PRO, Treas. 1:471, fols. 149–150. The Proprietors' letter is in 1 Kennebec Purchase Letter Book 26–27, MeHi. For another statement of their position, see James Bowdoin to Thomas Pownall, 29 Sept. 1772, 1 *Bowdoin-Temple Papers* (9 MHS, Colls., 6th ser.) 296 (1897).

gesting that he submit the question to counsel for an opinion. Wentworth refused to be trapped, pointing out in reply that his position was based on the opinion given on Cooke's claims in 1718, to which he must conform, and that the question was beyond his competence. He renewed his offer to forward the Company's state of its claim, however.[32]

About a year later, Richard Jackson, counsel for the Board of Trade, was asked to decide the matter on the basis of a letter from Wentworth, stating the Kennebec claim. Jackson refused to decide the question of title involved, but stated that if the trees in question grew within a township, and if the claim of the Kennebec Company to a title derived prior to 1690 were established, the trees could be cut without penalty.[33] The Proprietors were still reluctant to submit their title to the courts, however, probably fearing the effect of an adverse determination on other claims which might be brought for the lands. In December 1771 they petitioned the Admiralty and Treasury, not for complete relief, but for compensation for logs taken from their lands, stating that they wished to avoid litigation, "the entering into a Law Suit having the appearance of refusing the Masts for His Majesty's service." Wentworth himself recommended this solution to the Treasury, "not as a matter of right, but as a Gratuity for the Timber being found well preserved upon their Land." [34] The petition, which had not been acted upon by the fall of 1772,[35] was probably tabled, because the question was finally submitted to litigation.

Perhaps expecting efforts at settlement to fail, the Proprietors had already begun to prepare for litigation. At a meeting on 8 January 1772, James Bowdoin, James Pitts, Sylvester Gardiner, Benjamin Hallowell, and

[32] Wentworth to the Committee of the Kennebec Purchase, 29 June 1770, PRO, Treas. 1:471, fol. 150. See the Proprietors' letter in 1 Kennebec Purchase Letter Book 35–36, MeHi. For the 1718 opinion, see note 6 above. The Proprietors had replied to Wentworth's earlier letter (note 31 above) by asserting their claim in fuller detail, threatening to prosecute the "mast men," and pointing out that they should at least have compensation for their efforts and expenditures in opening the country. Proprietors to Wentworth, 8 Nov. 1769, 1 Kennebec Purchase Letter Book 27, MeHi.
[33] Opinion of Richard Jackson, 23 May 1771, Chalmers, *Opinions* 155–156. See also Opinion of same, 5 June 1771, *id. at* 157–158.
[34] For the petition to the Admiralty, 18 Dec. 1771, and letters requesting Wentworth, Governor Hutchinson, and Admiral Montagu to forward it, see 1 Kennebec Purchase Letter Book 55–72, MeHi. Wentworth's comment is quoted in Albion, *Forests and Sea Power* 258. In an earlier letter, commenting upon a proposal by Hutchinson that the General Court curb the unlicensed destruction of timber in Maine, James Bowdoin of the Proprietors had stated their wish to cooperate in providing masts, if their title was made clear. Bowdoin to Thomas Pownall, 12 Nov. 1770, 1 *Bowdoin-Temple Papers* 234. See notes 31, 32, above. See also 3 Hutchinson, *Massachusetts Bay*, ed. Mayo 244–245. Hutchinson's family had long been active in Maine land speculation under claims opposed to those of the Kennebec Company. See Malcolm Freiberg, Prelude to Purgatory 119 and notes (Brown Univ. doctoral dissertation, 1950); *Remarks on the Plan and Extracts of Deeds Lately Published by the Proprietors of the Township of Brunswick* 6–7 (Boston, 1753). Later Bowdoin wrote that the Company's motive for avoiding litigation was financial. Bowdoin to Pownall, 29 Sept. 1772, 1 *Bowdoin-Temple Papers* 295–296.
[35] Bowdoin to Pownall, 29 Sept. 1772, 1 *Bowdoin-Temple Papers* 296.

William Bowdoin were constituted "lawful attorneys," who were empowered, among other things, "to appear, and the Person of us said Proprietors Constituant to represent before any Governor, Judges, Justices, Officers and Ministers of the Law whatsoever, in any Court or Courts whatsoever, and there on our behalf to answer, defend, and reply unto all Actions, Matters and things whatsoever," with power to appoint attorneys under them. Since the previous grant of such a power to a committee had authorized only the appointment of an "Attorney for the proprietors to appear for them in any Courts of Law or Equity in New England or Great Britain," the 1772 vote indicates an awareness that the controversy with Wentworth would be tried in Admiralty. At the same meeting Adams, who had been acting for the Company since 1769, was formally voted "Attorney in all Causes, Real, personal, or Mixt, moved and to be moved for us or against us." [36]

On 14 July 1772 an information was filed in the Court of Admiralty at Boston against a total of 573 logs, 424 pieces of hewn timber and 70,000 feet of pine board, alleged to have been seized on the Kennebec River and at various locations within the claimed lands to either side of it.[37] The action seemed calculated to produce a determination both of the Kennebec claim and of the question whether the statutes applied to dressed timber (other than masts) and sawn boards, as well as to trees, masts, and logs.[38] Adams appeared for the Kennebec Company and filed a claim, which apparently asserted its title. The case was argued on what Adams in his minutes described as a "demurrer" (No. 55, Document II), but which in Admiralty practice is more properly known as an exception. The effect was that of a demurrer, however, which admitted all the facts as to the chain of title pleaded in the claim, leaving in issue only questions of law as to the validity of the title and the construction of the White Pine Acts.[39]

[36] See the 1772 votes in 3 Kennebec Purchase Records 78–79, MeHi. The earlier power was granted on 19 Jan. 1764 to the same committee and Thomas Hancock. 2 *id.* at 341–342. JA's appointment seems to have been only a formal step, coincident with the withdrawal of William Cushing from the same post, which he had held since 1760. See *id.* at 255; Cushing's Account, Aug. 1761–Sept. 1771, Kennebec Purchase Waste Book 131–140, MeHi. Cushing was appointed to the Superior Court bench on 15 Jan. 1772. Whitmore, *Mass. Civil List* 70.

[37] *Massachusetts Gazette*, 16 July 1772, p. 3, col. 2. In a letter of 22 July, the Proprietors asked Jonathan Bowman to find out whose were the logs mentioned in this notice and stated that if the owners would apply, the Company would defend for them. 1 Kennebec Purchase Letter Book 73, MeHi.

[38] See Knollenberg, *Origin of the American Revolution* 131–132.

[39] On 23 Oct. 1772 JA received a fee of £4 16s. "for his Appearing at the Court of Admiralty to claim Logs." On 28 Nov. he received an additional £7 4s. No other payments for this case have been found. See Accounts of Henry Alline, Kennebec Purchase Bills, Receipts, &c., MeHi. The term "exception" covers all preliminary objections including those in the nature of a demurrer. See 2 Browne, *Civil Law* 362. Despite JA's statement as to the effect of a demurrer here (No. 55, Doc. II), the Company obtained a Commission from the court to take depositions and obtain record copies at Plymouth in April 1773. Alline's Accounts, Kennebec Purchase Bills, Receipts, &c., MeHi.

The case was heard in March 1773. James Otis and Samuel Fitch, the Advocate General, argued for the Crown. Adams appeared for his old clients, undoubtedly with a colleague whose identity is not known. Printed below in No. 55 are a list of questions of law apparently drawn for the hearing (Document I), Adams' minutes of the Crown argument (Document II), and Adams' notes of his own argument (Document III).

The Kennebec Company traced its title back to the Council for New England, or Council of Plymouth, established in 1620 by a royal patent which conveyed to it all of New England from 40° to 48° North Latitude. In 1630 the Council had granted to William Bradford, moving spirit in the Plymouth Colony, the so-called Plymouth Patent, which conveyed both the lands which the Pilgrims had occupied in Massachusetts and a tract on either side of the Kennebec to be used for trading purposes. In 1641 Bradford had "surrendered" to the colony his interest and that of his associates in the patent. Plymouth sought to improve the Maine lands, leasing the trading rights there periodically and adding further tracts acquired by deed from the Indians. Finally in 1665 the colony conveyed the land to four individuals. The heirs and successors of these grantees organized in 1749 as "the Proprietors of the Kennebec Purchase from the late colony of New Plymouth," an arrangement given legal sanction by a Province Act of 1753 permitting the proprietors of undivided lands lying outside of organized townships to act as a body.[40]

The basic position of the Proprietors was that the chain validated their title and that at least the conveyance out of the Plymouth colony in 1665 was a grant to private persons before 1690, within the meaning of the Charter and statutes. Otis and Fitch attacked the Kennebec position along two lines: First, that the grants were made not to "private persons," but to corporate bodies or to tenants in common of undivided lands, who as proprietors held in a capacity other than private. Second, that the chain of title was defective, so that even if the grantees were private persons, they did not hold by virtue of a grant, but by adverse possession. Even if the Proprietors' arguments on these points prevailed, only trees growing within townships would be protected.[41] Fitch argued that the 1722 act had been

[40] For documentation of the title, see No. 55, notes 2, 3, 17, 18. For the history of the Kennebec Company see Gardiner, "History of the Kennebec Purchase," 2 Maine Hist. Soc., *Colls.* (1st ser.) 269–294 (1847); L. C. Wroth, "The Thomas Johnston Maps of the Kennebeck Purchase," in Walter M. Whitehill, ed., *In Tribute to Fred C. Anthoensen, Master Printer* 77–107 (Portland, Maine, 1952); Philip C. Olsson, The Kennebec Purchase from the Colony of New Plymouth, 1749–1765 (Harvard Univ. B.A. Honors Paper, 1962). For the Proprietorship Act, see 3 A&R 669. See also 4 Dane, *Abridgment* 70–72.

[41] At least six townships had been granted within the Kennebec Purchase before 1772; Pownalborough, 1760, 4 A&R 287; Bowdoinham, 1762, 4 A&R 600; Hallowell, 1771, 5 A&R 129; Winthrop, 1771, 5 A&R 132; Vassalborough, 1771, 5 A&R 135; Winslow, 1771, 5 A&R 136. These grants had not been confirmed by the Crown, however, a Charter requirement for lands north and east of the Sagahadoc River, which arguably included Pownalborough, part of Hallowell, part of Vassalborough, and part of Winslow. See 3 Hutchinson, *Massachusetts Bay*, ed. Mayo 244–245; Bowdoin to Pownall, 29 Sept. 1772, 1 *Bowdoin-Temple Papers* 295; 1 A&R 18–19.

construed to mean that trees growing outside of township bounds were reserved, regardless of ownership. Adams met the argument with the proposition that the Charter excepted grants to private persons, regardless of township bounds, and that the exception was not narrowed by the Act of 1722, which was intended to apply only in other royal provinces in which all unincorporated lands of necessity belonged to the Crown.

Adams' arguments must have been successful, because on 3 May 1773 Wentworth's libel was dismissed. The Surveyor General appealed to the Privy Council, and in September 1774 his petition was referred to the Council's Committee for Hearing Appeals, which finally set the case for hearing on 3 August 1775.[42] No record of the result has been found. If the petition was not withdrawn, the Order in Council resulting can have had little effect, since Boston was by the time of its issuance the besieged stronghold of the last vestiges of British authority in New England.

54. Surveyor General v. Logs

1769

I. JOHN HURD TO JOSHUA LORING JR.[1]

Dear Sir   Portsmo. 13th. April 1769
   The inclosd Informations were preparing by Mr. Claggett,[2] and under Consideration of Mr. Parker the Deputy Judge of Admiralty,

---

[42] 5 *Acts, Privy Council (Col.)* §304. Robert Auchmuty, Judge of the Admiralty Court, had been of counsel to the Company in important land actions in the prior decade. In June and Dec. 1774 he received payments totaling £282 0s. 12d., apparently for these services. No objection seems to have been raised on this ground, however. See 2 Kennebec Purchase Records 422; Accounts of Henry Alline, Kennebec Purchase Bills, Receipts, &c., MeHi.

[1] RC, presumably in Hurd's hand. Adams Papers, Microfilms, Reel No. 185. Docketed by JA: "Mr. Hurd's Letter." Enclosures not found. Hurd (1727–1809), Harvard 1747, was the son of Jacob Hurd, Boston goldsmith. After an unstable commercial career in Boston he developed New Hampshire land interests, became Wentworth's personal secretary, and held other administrative positions. He became an early settler in the upper Connecticut Valley and at the Revolution was a patriot. After losing in several political struggles, he returned to Boston in 1779, where he finished his life in the commercial community. 12 Sibley-Shipton, *Harvard Graduates* 164–171. Loring (1744–1789) was Deputy Surveyor of the Woods, as well as the last royal sheriff of Suffolk County. A tory, he is best known as General Howe's Commissary of Prisoners, a post for which he has received much abuse. Stark, *Loyalists of Mass.* 424–425; Jones, *Loyalists of Mass.* 199–200.

[2] Wyseman Clagett (1721–1784), Attorney General of New Hampshire from 1765 to 1769. Son of an English barrister, he had been admitted an attorney in the King's Bench before his emigration to Antigua in 1748. He came to Portsmouth in 1758, where he took up practice and was soon made a justice of the peace. His severity with petty offenders was such that "I'll Clagett you," became a popular threat. In 1769, as Hurd's postscript, below, indicates, he moved to England. Upon

when he received a Letter from the Honorable Judge Auchmuty suspending him from the Office.[3] Mr. Claggett returnd them to the Surveyor General, and by his directions I forward them to you, to be laid before Mr. Auchmuty, who will know best to putt them in proper order; and if he thinks the Evidence sufficient forward them for Execution, as the Governor has already advisd. There will be further and more particular Information soon collected from some of the principal people at Law which shall be immediately sent along. I am with great Esteem and regard Dear Sir Your Most hum Servt.

John Hurd

Mr. Claggett is about leaving Us and sails soon for England. We shall miss him in some of our Affairs.

P.S. You have also inclosd a Diary of Willm. Ham Assistant Deputy, which may be of some use; after shewing it to the Judge You'll please to return it to the Surveyor General's Office.

II. ADAMS' DRAFT OF THE INFORMATION [4]

Court of Vice Admiralty, Boston, 20 April 1769

Province of the Massachusetts Bay Court of vice Admty. 20th. April 1769	To the Honble. Robert Auchmuty Esqr. Judge ⟨*of his Majestys said Court or to his lawfull Deputy*⟩ Commissary Deputy and surrogate of the Court of Vice Admiralty of Boston in the Province of the Massachusetts Bay

his return in 1771, he took up the patriot cause, serving in the Provincial Congresses and later on the State Committee of Safety and Council. From 1781 to 1784 he was a special Justice of the New Hampshire Superior Court and Solicitor General. *DAB.*

[3] William Parker (1703–1781), Harvard A.M. (hon.) 1763, Deputy Admiralty Judge for the Province of New Hampshire. Admitted to the bar in 1732, Parker served in a variety of legislative and judicial posts, ending his active career as a Justice of the New Hampshire Superior Court (1771–1775). Charles H. Bell, *The Bench and Bar of New Hampshire* 26–28 (Boston, 1894). Since New Hampshire was under the jurisdiction of the Massachusetts Vice Admiralty Judge, Parker owed his authority to a deputation from Judge Auchmuty. He was apparently also commissioned by Governor Wentworth. See Ubbelohde, *Vice Admiralty Courts* 153–154; Jeremy Belknap, *The History of New Hampshire*, 1:421 (Dover, 2d edn., 1831). The cause of his suspension has not been determined, but he was still in office in 1773. *Ibid.* He had also sat on a case appealed from New Hampshire to Auchmuty's new District Court of Vice Admiralty at Boston in 1772. Lawrence S. Mayo, *John Langdon of New Hampshire* 42 (Concord, 1937). See p. 104 above.

[4] Copy in JA's hand. Adams Papers, Microfilms, Reel No. 185. Docketed by JA: "Wentworth vs. Logs. Form." The caption of the document indicates that Auchmuty sat on the case in his capacity as Judge of the Massachusetts provincial court, rather

6.   ROBERT TREAT PAINE, BY RICHARD A. BROOKS

8. DR. SYLVESTER GARDINER, BY JOHN SINGLETON COPLEY

7. JOHN WENTWORTH, BY JOHN SINGLETON COPLEY

John Wentworth Esqr. Surveyor General of all and singular his Majestys Woods on the Continent of North America shews that on the Twenty fourth day of March last he seized for his Majestys Use, at the several Places hereafter mentioned in said Province, the following white pine Logs; vizt at a Place called little Ossipee in the County of York in said Province Three hundred white Pine Logs from twenty four to fifty four Inches Diameter, and from Eighteen to Twenty four Feet long; at a Place called Narragansett in the County of York in said Province Three Logs from twenty five to Thirty Inches Diameter; at Faybans Mills so called in Scarborough in the County of Cumberland, Three hundred Logs.

At a Place called Dunstons Landing in Scarborough aforesaid, two Masts, vizt one of forty Inches Diameter and fifty seven Feet long, another of forty four Inches Diameter and Eighty seven feet long.

At a Place called Blue Point in Scarborough aforesaid one Mast of forty four Inches Diameter and Ninty three feet long, one of twenty Eight Inches Diameter and Eighty Eight feet and an half long; At a Place called Pepperellborough in the County of York aforesaid one Mast forty two Inches in Diameter and Sixty feet long, one of forty two Inches in Diameter and Eighty four feet long, one of Thirty Six Inches in Diameter and Eighty four feet long, one of forty two Inches in Diameter and fifty seven feet long, one of Thirty Six Inches Diameter and fifty seven feet long. At Narragansett in the County of York aforesaid Three Logs from twenty five to Thirty Inches Diameter; All cutt out of Trees growing in this Province, and not in any Township, or within the Bounds Lines or Limits thereof, or if growing within the Limits of any Town, those of twenty four Inches Diameter at twelve Inches from the Ground, not growing within any Soil or Tract of Land granted to any private Person before the Seventh Day of October Anno Domini 1690, and those under Twenty four Inches Diameter, not being the Property of any private Person or Persons, and felled by some evil minded Persons within Six Months last past, without his Majestys royal Licence first had and obtained; and by them removed to the aforesaid Places, contrary to the Laws in that Case made and provided.[5]

Wherefore as this matter is within the Jurisdiction of this Honorable Court the said John Wentworth prays sentence for the Forfeiture of said Logs to his Majestys Use, agreable to Law.

---

than as Judge of the new district court to which he was appointed in the fall of 1768. See No. 46, notes 41–43; p. 102, note 16, above. Compare Ubbelohde, *Vice Admiralty Courts* 148–155.

[5] For the statutes, the requirements of which are neatly summarized in the foregoing sentence, see No. 55, notes 32–35, 38–43.

III. JOHN WENTWORTH TO JOSHUA LORING JR.[6]

Sir   Portsmouth 10th April 1769

Inclosed are informations against sundry Tresspassers upon the King's woods, in the (late called) Province of Main. Which I request you will immediately in my name enter Complaint of, before the Honorable Robert Auchmuty Esq. and pray that process may immediately issue thereon, for recovery of the penalty. The Trees were not seized mentioned in the information No. 5, As the offenders by violence and menaces rendered it too dangerous for any single Officer to perform, but I am determined in May next to go myself and convince them that Threats and wicked Intents are not enough to prevent any service being done;[7] that is committed to my care. Whatever may be the Event, I will assuredly attempt and persevere in my duty. As Mr. Sewall is now (I am glad for him) constituted Judge,[8] I am at a Loss who to direct to as Advocate, If he does not still act, I desire you'd employ John Adams Esq. in my behalf to prosecute and aid and advise in these suits. He was my Cotemporary at Cambridge, and will I dare say oblige me by his greatest care and assiduity herein, which I hope will give me opportunity to convince him that our Friendship long since commenced is still the object of my pleasing respect. I wou'd observe to you, That these People, Vizt. Ross, Ross, Denning and particularly Thompson, have thus, trespassed in open avowed defiance and contempt of the Law, publickly declaring they have done it, will persist, and that no Officer shall come among them; it is therefore necessary that a trusty, resolute and experienced Marshal be entrusted by the Court, to execute these Precepts.[9] If they fail then adieu to all public reservations to the Crown, or private property of individuals. I therefore hope they'l be properly supported by the Sheriffs and other civil officers—it is too important to bear even a thought of disappointment, in bringing them to legal trial. I am resolv'd to carry this prosecution to effect, Mr. Adams will therefore be pleased to pursue the exact rules of the Law, and on our side I'le promise him the

[6] RC in Wentworth's hand, addressed to "Joshua Loring Junr. Esq." Adams Papers. This letter, and that printed as Doc. IV, appear out of chronological order because they were discovered after the rest of the documents in this case had been set in type.

[7] See p. 255, note 29 above.

[8] That is, Jonathan Sewall, commissioned as Judge of the Vice Admiralty Court at Halifax. See No. 46, text at notes 41–43.

[9] Libels in Wentworth's name against Robert Ross, William Ross, James Denning, and Samuel Thompson, were entered in the Vice Admiralty Court on 26 May 1769, but the respondents were not served. Vice Adm. Min. Bk., 26 May 1769.

most steady and vigorous support. Hitherto I have not been able to collect the additions[10] to the names complain'd against, but am daily expecting them; these will be sufficient I presume to ground the respective process, and I shall be glad Mr. Adams will write me what further will be requisite to support our Complaints and informations. By the next post I shall send some further Evidence. I have this day wrote to the Judge on this subject, requesting to you, all necessary and legal Assistance. I beg you'd lose no time in these matters, for they are of the greatest consequence to the preservation of the Woods.

Have you yet heard any thing further from Albany of Colo. Bs. supposed tresspasses? We will now make a thorough business of reformation by the Vigor of Law, since these and these only are no other ways to be reclaim'd.[11]

I am exceedingly oblig'd by your good Father's interest to get the Young man discharg'd, it has made a Family very happy here. If this favor was asked in my name of Commodore Hood, I beg He would be so kind to make my most respectful acknowledgments for his politeness, which I shall at all times rejoice to retaliate. I was uncertain, therefore cou'd not mention anything about it, in a Letter I've lately had occasion to write to Commodore Hood.

My best regards attend your good Parents. I suppose your Father is quite a Farmer and you a Gardener—happy life indeed—and if completely so, long may it be continued to you. Pray be so good to make my Respects to Mr. Adams, I fear myself indebted to him a Letter from Worcester, but hope soon to repay him—better late than never.[12]

I am with great esteem my dear Sir, your very sincere friend and most hble servt.,   Wentworth
PS. Present the Lawyer rather a generous fee, I'le reimburse.

IV. JOHN ADAMS TO JOHN WENTWORTH[13]

Sir   Boston April 24. 1769

I have prepared Eight Libells, and shall compleat the rest immediately. Those I mean whose Additions and Abodes are made known to me. The others must remain undone till I receive Directions con-

[10] That is, the degree or occupation and place of abode of the party, a necessary element in a pleading. See vol. 1, p. 32, note 19.

[11] See p. 255, note 29 above.

[12] Probably JA's letter to Wentworth from Worcester dated Sept. 1756; Photostat of FC in Adams Papers Files.

[13] FC in JA's hand. Adams Papers. Addressed to "His Excellency Governor Wentworth."

cerning the Persons. Should be glad if any further Informations are sent, to have the Names, Occupations, and Places of Abode of the Persons, that is, the Towns and Countys they live in. The Number of Trees they have cutt, not the Number of Logs, because if we prosecute for Penalties, those Penalties are to be measured by the Number of Trees, not of Logs, according to the Statutes.[14] And also the Town and County where the Trespasses were done. As to the Riot or Assault upon Mr. Ham the officer, you desired that the Rioters might be rigorously prosecuted, but this cannot be done in the Court of Admiralty, which has no Jurisdiction of such Crimes, but must be left to the Kings Attorney and the grand Jury at the next Circuit of the Court of Assize.

In the Informations against Ross, Ross, Denning, and Thompson, I have put fifty Trees for each. In the Minutes I received it is Said they had cut 400 Logs each. It is possible that 50 Trees may not make so many as 400 Logs. But I thought that 50 Trees would probably be 25 times so much as the Culprits were worth, and therefore an omission of 100 Trees or so, would be of no Consequence to the Parties nor to the Crown.

I have given this Business all the Dispatch in my Power, encumbered as I have been during the whole of it, with the Hurry and Confusion of a Court in a wild, noisy, Smoaky Town. I wonder from my Soul what Fiend possessed me, when I left the ⟨calm⟩ Tranquility of Braintree for the Fatigue and Dissipation of Boston? But, hush my murmuring Imagination! I see more and more there is no disputing with Fate and Fortune. These inexorable Deities will dragg, if they cannot lead, and therefore the best Way is to trip it along as light as you can.

You see I feel a great Inclination to be upon a Footing with your Excellency and to be chatting about my self as I used twelve years ago. But I cant conceive what Business I have with a Wife and three Children when I am conversing with your Excellency. Excuse this Freedom and believe me, with great Respect and Esteem, your Excellency's most obedient, huml Servt.,   John Adams

[14] 8 Geo. 1, c. 12, §5 (1722); 2 Geo. 2, c. 35, §2 (1729). See No. 55, text at notes 33, 43.

55. Surveyor General v. Logs, Kennebec Company, Claimant

1772–1773

I. QUESTIONS PRESENTED [1]

Court of Vice Admiralty, Boston, March 1773

Questions.

1. Whether King James's Letters patent to Lodowick Duke Lenox and others,[2] are allowed to be good and sufficient to vest the lands thereby granted in the Grantees in Fee simple?

2. Whether their grant to Bradford is also good, and sufficient to vest the lands thereby granted either in him and his heirs in fee simple, or in the Colony of New Plymouth so called, by virtue of the said grant and his surrender.[3]

---

[1] In an unidentified hand. Adams Papers, Microfilms, Reel No. 185.

[2] That is, the patent of 3 Nov. 1620, to Lenox and other worthies, by which James I incorporated them as "the Councill established at Plymouth, in the County of Devon, for the planting, ruling, ordering, and governing of New-England, in America," and granted to this council "and their Successors and Assignes forever," all of New England from 40° to 48° North Latitude, and "from Sea to Sea, . . . to be holden of Us, our Heires, and Successors, as of our Manor of East-Greenwich, in our County of Kent, in free and common Soccage and not in Capite, nor by Knight's Service; yielding and paying therefore," one-fifth of all gold and silver found to the Crown for "all Dutys, Demands and Services whatsoever." 3 Thorpe, *Federal and State Constitutions* 1827–1840.

[3] In Jan. 1630 the New England Council, reciting its patent, note 2 above, granted to "Wm. Bradford, his heires associates and assignes for ever," both the lands in Massachusetts on which the Plymouth Colony was settled, and a tract "which lyeth within or between and Extendeth it self from the utmost of Cobest-cont alias Comasecont Which adjoyneth to the River Kenibeck alias Kenebeckick towards the Westerne Ocean and a place called the falls of Nequamkick in America aforesaid and the Space of Fifteen English milles on Each Side of the said River Commonly called Kenebeck River and all the said River Called Kenebeck that Lyes within the said Limitts and Bounds Eastward Westward Northward and Southward Last afore mentioned." The grantees were to pay one fifth of all gold and silver found to the Crown, and another fifth to the grantors, "for all Services and demands Whatsoever." Morison, "The *Mayflower's* Destination and the Pilgrim Fathers' Patents," 38 Col. Soc. Mass., *Pubns.* 387, 407–413 (1959). See 1 Andrews, *Colonial Period* 293–296. Bradford held directly from the King by virtue of the requirement of the Statute of *Quia Emptores*, 18 Edw. 1 (1290), which had not been waived in the 1620 patent. *Id.* at 335. Known as the "Plymouth Patent," this grant was the foundation of the Kennebec Company's land claims in the 18th century. See Doc. II below. The "surrender" of the patent was the act by which Bradford, on 2 March 1641, "by the free and full consent, approbacion, and agreement of the . . . old planters," who had joined him in financing the early days of the colony, did "surrender into the handes of the whole Court, consistinge of the freemen of this

3. Whether it is granted that there are now living lawfull heirs of the said Bradford.

4. Whether it is contended, that private persons, mean private persons in opposition to Tenants in common or joint Tenants? [4]

5. Whether the Duke of Lenox et al. are to be considered as private persons within the meaning of the Charter and Statutes?

6. If a mere Trespasser should cut Masts on land, which was indisputably the property of private persons before 1690, and was, by the King, prosecuted for the penalty could he legally, give in evidence, that the soil on which such trees grew, was the property of private persons before the 7 of October 1690,[5] and thereby prevent the Statutes operating against him?

7. If lands were duly granted to a private person or persons before 7 Octr. 1690 and one, not the Owner of such lands, should cut Masts on said lands, could the King by virtue of the Charter and Statutes recover said trees or masts?

8. Whether the Council of Plymouth ever surrendered their patent,[6] and when?

9. Whether it is conceded that by force of the Charter or the Stat-

---

corporacion of New Plymouth, all that ther right and title, power, authorytie, priviledges, immunities and freedomes granted in the said lettres patentes by the said right honorable counsell for New England, reserving his and their personall right of freemen, together with the said old planters aforesaid, except the said lands before excepted [certain tracts previously agreed to be reserved for the old planters], declareing the freemen of this present corporacion, together with all such as shalbe legally admitted into the same, his associates." *Records of the Colony of New Plymouth*, 2:10–11 (Boston, ed. N. B. Shurtleff, 1855). The patent was actually surrendered "in publick Court" and returned to Bradford for safekeeping. *Id.* at 11. See Morison, "Pilgrim Fathers' Patents," 38 Col. Soc. Mass., *Pubns.* 397–398.

[4] That is, "private persons" in the language of the Charter of 1691 and applicable statutes, text at notes 28, 38, below. For earlier arguments that land held by proprietors in common was not held by "private persons," see Knollenberg, *Origin of the American Revolution* 131.

[5] The date set by statute. See text at note 42 below.

[6] Presumably, "the Councill established at Plymouth, in the County of Devon," note 2 above, rather than the Plymouth Colony. The Council surrendered its patent to the Crown on 7 June 1635. *Records of the Council for New England* 75–80 (Cambridge, Mass., 1867). This action was part of an effort by Sir Ferdinando Gorges, moving force in the Council, to halt the infringement of the Massachusetts Bay Company upon his domains in New England. Charles I accepted the surrender in July 1637, shortly after the Crown had obtained a judgment in *quo warranto* in the King's Bench against the Massachusetts Bay charter. Gorges' plan was to divide the Council's patent among its members, the whole to be under a royal government loyal to the Crown. Only Gorges' own patent for a part of Maine was confirmed, however, as the onset of the civil war involved the other participants in different concerns. See 1 Andrews, *Colonial Period* 417–424; Barnes, "Land Tenure in English Colonial Charters," in *Essays in Colonial History Presented to Charles McLean Andrews* 29–30, 34–35 (New Haven, 1931).

utes, the Claimants are obliged to derive their title from a date prior to 7 October 1690?

II. ADAMS' MINUTES OF THE ARGUMENT[7]

Court of Vice Admiralty, Boston, 8 March 1773

Surveyor General vs. Loggs.
Kennebec Company. March 8. 1773.
Claim and Demurrer—which admits all in the Claim.[8]

Mr. Otis. In Event, as important a Cause as ever was decided in America.

The Navy, an important Object, without offence to any Sect or Party.

Charter. Reservation in it.[9] We hold all we have under this Charter. No Gentleman will dispute the Validity of this Reservation.

A great deal of Talk and Scribbling about mutual Compact. Should as soon expect good and sound Law from N. Hampton in a N.W. Wind.[10]

Indian Natives had under God a Right to the Soil. That no good Title could be acquired by sovereign or subject, without obtaining it from the Natives.

No Man has a Right to a Foot of Land, who has not a good Purchase from the Natives, by a Licence from his lawfull Prince.

Proposal of large Forrests to be set apart, by Act of P[arliament] in Secula Seculorum.[11]

8. G. 1, c. 12, §5. 1721.[12]

2. G. 2, c. 35, §1. 2. No Trees to be cutt, excepting such as are the Property of private Persons. 1729.[13]

Plymouth Patent.

[7] In JA's hand. Adams Papers, Microfilms, Reel No. 185.
[8] See p. 257, note 39 above.
[9] The Province Charter of 1691, set out, text at note 28 below.
[10] Perhaps a reference to Joseph Hawley, Northampton lawyer, who was disbarred from 1767 to 1769.
[11] Such proposals, intended to free large tracts of forest for general use, had been made periodically during the 18th century. The most recent effort, by Wentworth himself, had received some support in England in 1769, and by 1773 the Surveyor General had made extensive preliminary surveys for it. Robert G. Albion, *Forests and Sea Power* 268–272 (Cambridge, Mass., 1926). Otis' point here would seem to be that until such a plan received legislative sanction, all forest lands were subject to the laws.
[12] 8 Geo. 1, c. 12, §5 (1722), extracted by JA, text at notes 32–33 below.
[13] 2 Geo. 2, c. 35, §§1, 2 (1729), extracted by JA, text at notes 38–43 below.

Not in the Power of the King to grant *Royalties*. King deceived.[14]
Lit. §117. Socage Tenure. 1. Inst. 85. b.[15]
Sir F. Barnards Doctrine about holding as of our Manor of East
Greenwich in the County of Kent.[16]

[14] Both the patent of the Council for New England (note 2 above) and the Plymouth Patent (note 3 above) included a grant of "Royalties," or royal rights and privileges. See Cunningham, *Law Dictionary*, tit. Royalties. Otis here seems to be meeting an argument that this grant included the timber reserved to the Crown by the 1691 Charter and later statutes. Presumably he does not mean that the patentees "deceived" King James, but is using the term in the sense intended in Coke, *Littleton* 27a: "If the King by his Letters Patents giveth Lands or Tenements to a man, and to his heires males, the grant is void, for that the King is deceived in his grant, in as much as there can be no such inheritance of Lands or tenements as the King intended to grant." Compare No. 45, text at note 59.

[15] That is, Coke, *Littleton* §117, appearing in 1 Coke, *Institutes* 85b: "Tenure in Socage, is where the Tenant holdeth of his Lord the tenancie by certain service for all manner of services, so that the service be not Knights service: As where a man holdeth his land of his Lord by Fealty and certaine rent, for all manner of services: or else where a man holdeth his Land by homage, fealty, and certain rent, for all manner of services, for homage by it selfe maketh not Knights service. The patent of the New England Council (note 2 above), the Plymouth Patent (note 3 above), and the Plymouth deed of the Kennebec lands (note 18 below), were all grants in socage, one of the four ancient feudal tenures. At this period the tenures had largely lost their military and political significance and were only descriptive of differing proprietary relationships. When they could, English rulers were glad to grant lands by Knight Service, which had profitable incidents such as scutage and wardship and marriage. Socage, under which there were few fixed requirements of service, had become much more common, however, especially in grants like these, where some inducement was necessary for the grantees. See Sir William Holdsworth, *Historical Introduction to the Land Law* 21–29 (London, 1927); Haskins, "Gavelkind and the Charter of Massachusetts Bay," 34 Col. Soc. Mass., *Pubns.* 483–484, 496 (1943); Barnes, "Land Tenure," *Essays in Colonial History* 7, 10, 33.

[16] The reference to "Sir F. Barnard" remains unclear. The language is that of the New England Council's patent of 1620, note 2 above. Since the Plymouth patentees of 1630 (note 3 above) were "assignes" of the New England Council under its 1620 patent, it would seem that Haskins is in error in his conclusion that the Plymouth grant "was not as of East Greenwich." As he notes, the leaders of the colony thought that they so held. Haskins, "Gavelkind," 34 Col. Soc. Mass., *Pubns.* 487 note. Moreover, the colony's grant of the Kennebec lands in 1661 was as of East Greenwich. See note 18 below. This was the common form of grant, designed to make clear that the tenant did not hold *in capite*, that is, "as of the Crown." Although the King made the grant and received services in both cases, the fiction that the grant was from a lesser lord was adopted where the potential grantee had the bargaining power because, as in the case of tenure by socage, note 15 above, the incidents were far less onerous. Such grants had been made in England since the 16th century, with the "Manor of East-Greenwich" employed in most cases apparently as a convenient form, adopted because it was a favorite royal resort. The form was also used in about a dozen other colonial charters. *Id.* at 483–484, 489, 494–496; Barnes, "Land Tenure," *Essays in Colonial History* 4–11. Modern historians generally agree that its only significance was as the description of a convenient relationship, and that there was no intention to incorporate the peculiar Kentish custom of gavelkind, or partible inheritance, a practice which made its way to some of the colonies independently. Haskins, "Gavelkind," 34 Col. Soc. Mass., *Pubns.* 483–498; 1 Andrews, *Colonial Period* 86–87 note; Goebel, "King's Law and

Uncertain where the Bounds of the Patent are. What then?

Will it be said that the Patent is a Grant to private Persons? If so the Grant to Massachusetts, Province of Maine &c. are Grants to private Persons.[17]

1665 Grant to Boies &c.—a private Transaction.—Mem. by the Way Otis concedes tacitly at least we are within the Exception of Grants made to private Persons. Is forced to deny this to be a Grant to private Persons.[18]

This no Grant at all. No Estate passed by it. It is void.

Viner. Tit. Corporations B. pl. 1. "None but the King can make a Corporation."[19]

E. pl. 1. a Name.[20]

Local Custom in Seventeenth Century New England," 31 *Colum. L. Rev.* 416 (1931). But see Richard B. Morris, *Studies in the History of American Law* 103–120 (Phila., 2d edn. 1959).

[17] That is, the Massachusetts Bay Charter of 1629, and the grant of the Province of Maine to Sir Ferdinando Gorges in 1639. (As to the latter, see note 6 above.) In the former the grant was to individual patentees, who were then incorporated into the Massachusetts Bay Company. 1 *Records of the Governor and Company of the Massachusetts Bay in New England* 3–20 (Boston, ed. N. B. Shurtleff, 1853). In the latter the grant was to Gorges personally, but the lands were first constituted a Province or County Palatinate. 1 *Province and Court Records of Maine* 9–29 (Portland, ed. C. T. Libby, 1928). The Plymouth Patent, note 3 above, was, of course, in form only to individuals, with leave to incorporate themselves. See note 23 below. The patent of the New England Council, note 2 above, was even less "private," since the grant was in form to the Council which the patent had created. As to earlier claims for logs based on the Gorges patent, see p. 248, notes 5, 6, above.

[18] Otis refers to the deed by which the General Court of Plymouth Colony conveyed the Kennebec lands to Antipas Boies, Edward Tyng, Thomas Brattle, and John Winslow, the predecessors in interest of the Kennebec Company. See p. 258, at note 40 above. The instrument, dated 27 Oct. 1661, but not delivered until 15 June 1665, had been recorded in Plymouth, probably on the latter date, and was recorded in York County, Maine, 22 Oct. 1719. After reciting the New England and Plymouth patents (notes 2, 3, above) and a consideration of £400, it proceeded to grant the lands conveyed to Plymouth by the New England Council, as well as lands in the same area which the colony had acquired by two Indian deeds, "with All our said lawful right in the lands Abovementioned Either by Purchase or Patent with All and Singular the Appurtenances priviledges and Immunitys thereunto belonging to Appurtaine to them the said [named grantees] to them and Every of them their and Every of their heirs and Assigns forever to be holden of his Majesty [as of] his Mannor of East Greenewick in the County of Kent in free And Common Soccage And not in Capite Nor by Knights Service by the rents and Services thereof and thereby due and of right Accustomed." The grant was warranted against all claims that might be made under the colony's title. 9 *York Deeds*, fols. 226–228 (Portland, 1894). The sale was ratified by the General Court on 3 June 1662. 4 *Plymouth Colony Records* 17. See also *id.* at 38. JA's note to himself seems to mean that Otis has conceded that Boies et al. were "private persons" and is now forced to attack the sufficiency of the grant.

[19] 6 Viner, *Abridgment* 259, tit. Corporations, B. 1. Quotation marks supplied.

[20] 6 Viner, *Abridgment* 261, tit. Corporations, E. 1: "There ought to be a Name by which it ought to be incorporated."

Mr. Fitch. 8. G.[21] secures all Trees, let them be whose Property they will.

Boies had no Title.

Bradford—His associates could not take by the Grant. No Name of a Corporation.

The surrender is no Deed, nor Conveyance. Mem. our Law and Clause in the Charter.[22]

No Colony of New Plymouth.[23]

1. Inst. 295. b. "Confirmation doth not strengthen a void Estate." [24]

Duely made, or any other lawfull Title.[25]

Law of Prov. 13. Wm.[26]

[21] 8 Geo. 1, c. 12, §5, text at notes 32–34 below.

[22] The last phrase is apparently JA's note of his own position made during Fitch's argument. The charter clause is presumably the provision of the Province Charter of 1691, by which the Crown, after granting all the lands formerly part of the colonies of Plymouth, Massachusetts Bay, Maine, and Nova Scotia to the inhabitants of the newly created Province, confirmed the titles to all lands "which any person or persons or Bodyes Politique or Corporate Townes Villages Colledges or Schooles doe hold and enjoy or ought to hold and enjoy within the bounds aforesaid by or under any Grant or estate duely made or granted by any Generall Court formerly held or by vertue of the Letters Patents herein before recited [those to the New England Council, note 2 above, and from the Council to the Massachusetts Bay Company] or by any other lawful Right or title whatsoever," to be "by such person and Persons Bodyes Politique and Corporate Townes Villages Colledges or Schooles their Respective Heires Successors and assignes forever hereafter held and enjoyed" according to the terms of the original grant. 1 A&R 9–10. The "law" to which JA referred was probably the Act of 30 Oct. 1697, 1 A&R 299–301, which provides that "every person or persons who were possessed in his and their own proper right of any houses or lands within this province," on 1 Oct. 1692, and their successors in interest, who continued in undisturbed possession until 1 Oct. 1704, should thereafter have title in fee simple, "*provided, always,* that there shall be a saving of his majesty's rights, and all publick lands belonging to the province not orderly disposed of." An exception that titles in the Maine lands should remain open until five years after the conclusion of King William's War, then in progress, is not material, because that war ended on 30 Oct. 1697 with the Treaty of Ryswick, which was proclaimed at Boston on 10 Dec. of that year. See 1 A&R 767 note.

[23] This argument is presumably based on the fact that the Plymouth colony was not directly constituted by the Crown; the Plymouth Patent of 1630 was in form a grant to William Bradford and his associates. See note 3 above. The colony was recognized as such by the Crown in various dealings, including the Massachusetts Charter of 1691, however, so that it may be said to have had some sort of *de facto* status. See 1 Andrews, *Colonial Period* 296 note; 1 A&R 8. Moreover, the government of the colony was sanctioned by both the so-called "Peirce Patent" of 1621 and the 1630 grant to Bradford. Morison, "Pilgrim Fathers' Patents," 38 Col. Soc. Mass., *Pubns.* 402–403, 411. There was thus a corporate body in existence to take title to the lands, even if it was not technically a colony.

[24] Coke, *Littleton* 295b. Quotation marks supplied. Coke adds, "for a Confirmation may make a voidable or defeasable estate good, but it cannot work upon an estate that is void in Law." *Ibid.* Fitch is arguing that the confirmation of all titles in the Charter of 1691, note 22 above, is of no effect here. The Charter did provide, however, that no grant should fail for want of form. 1 A&R 10.

[25] The language of the Charter of 1691, note 22 above.

[26] Presumably the Act of 26 June 1701, 1 A&R 471, which provided that grants

III. ADAMS' NOTES FOR HIS ARGUMENT [27]

Court of Vice Admiralty, Boston, March 1773

Prov. Charter. Last Clause. "We do hereby reserve to Us, our Heirs and Successors, *all Trees of the Diameter of 24 Inches* and upwards of 12 Inches from the Ground, *growing* upon any *Soil* or *Tract of Land* within our said Province or Territory, *not heretofore granted to any private Persons.*" [28] The Old Charter of Mass. Bay, was a Grant to private Persons. [29]

"Growing" when? At the date of the Charter? According to this no Tree was reserved, but such as were then standing and 24 Inches diameter.

No Trees, growing on any "Soil" theretofore granted to any private Persons, are within this Reservation.

The Question is what is meant by the Words "granted to any private Persons"? Granted by whom? And who are private Persons?

Answer, granted by the general Court either of Mass. Bay, or New Plymouth? To any individual, or Number of Individuals.

All the Lands in the Province, had been granted to Persons, and to private Persons, by the Council at Plymouth. The Patent to Bradford and his associates was certainly a Grant to private Persons [30]—not to any Corporation according to Mr. Fitch's Doctrine.

1710. 9. Ann, c. 17, §1. "No Person, or Persons &c., do or shall presume to cutt, fell, or destroy, any white or other sort of Pine Tree, fit for Masts, *not being the Property of any private Person,* such Tree being of the Growth of *24 Inches Diameter,* and upwards at 12 Inches from the Earth." Penalty £100, before a Justice of Peace. [31]

---

of land obtained "by any person or persons whatsoever" from the Indians without license of the General Court of Massachusetts or New Plymouth were void unless in confirmation of other valid titles in the purchasers. Fitch is arguing that the Kennebec Company's title cannot be supported on Indian deeds of the land in question to the Plymouth Colony. See note 18 above.

[27] In JA's hand. Adams Papers, Microfilms, Reel No. 185. Docketed by JA: "Masts".

[28] The Province Charter of 7 Oct. 1691, 1 A&R 20. Opening quotation mark supplied. Emphasis is JA's. The Charter continues, "And Wee doe restraine and forbid all persons whatsoever from felling cutting or destroying any such Trees without the Royall Lycense of Us Our Heires and Successors first had and obteyned upon penalty of Forfeiting One Hundred Pounds sterling unto Ous Our Heires and Successors for every such Tree soe felled cutt or destroyed without such Lycense had and obteyned in that behalfe any thing in these presents conteyned to the contrary in any wise Notwithstanding." *Ibid.*

[29] See note 17 above.

[30] See note 3 above.

[31] 9 Anne, c. 17, §1 (1711). Closing quotation mark supplied. Emphasis is JA's. JA has omitted at the "&c." a recital of the areas in which the statute was

1721. 8. G, c. 12, §5. "No Person or Persons, &c. do or shall presume to cutt, fell, or destroy *any white Pine Trees, not growing within any Township*, or the Bounds, Lines or Limits thereof," &c. without Licence, &c.[32]

Penalties. 12 Inches and under 3 feet from the Ground £5. From 12 to 18 Inches £10. From 18 to 24, twenty Pounds. From 24 and upwards £50—before the Admiralty.[33]

Trees, Masts or Logs, found cutt, or felled, forfeited and seized to his Majestys Use.[34]

§6. repeals 9. Ann, c. 17. So much of it as relates to cutting &c. such White Pine Trees.[35]

"Not growing" when? In 1721 or at the Time of cutting.

Here a Question is what the Legislature meant by a "Township"? This Law was intended for the other Colonies, not for this Province. Not supposed that it could affect any private Property. In N. Hampshire, and N. York, where the K's Governor was giving away and selling Townships where he had not made a Township, it remained Crown Land.[36]

30 years intervened, between the Charter and the Act of 1721. Many Townships were erected in the mean Time which were not private Property before the act 1690. Therefore in all these Townships Trees might be cutt, even of 24 Inches Diameter, and upwards, for the Penalty in the Charter was void.[37]

---

applicable: The "colonies of New Hampshire, the Massachusetts Bay, and Province of Main, Rhode Island, and Providence Plantation, the Narragansett Country or King's Province, Connecticut in New England, and New York and New Jersey." The penalty was £100 "for each such offense" unless royal license had been obtained. It was to be sued upon within six months before the nearest justice of the peace, and was to be divided, half to the Crown and half to the informer. The act was repealed as to white pine trees by 8 Geo. 1, c. 12, §6 (1722). See note 35 below.

[32] 8 Geo. 1, c. 12, §5 (1722). Quotation marks supplied. Emphasis is JA's. JA omitted a recital of the colonies in which the act was effective, which was identical to that in note 31 above, with the addition of Nova Scotia.

[33] 8 Geo. 1, c. 12, §5. Abstracted by JA. The figures in inches are the diameters of the trees. The penalties could be "sued for within six months after the offence committed, by plaint or information, upon the oath of one or more credible witness or witnesses, before the judge of the admiralty or his deputy, within the colony or plantation, where such pine tree shall be cut, felled or destroyed." They were to be divided, half to the Crown and half to the informer.

[34] 8 Geo. 1, c. 12, §5. Abstracted by JA. See p. 251, notes 14, 15, above.

[35] 8 Geo. 1, c. 12, §6, repealing 9 Anne, c. 17, §1, note 31 above, as far as it applied to white pine trees.

[36] That is, there were no private claims to the unincorporated lands. In these provinces a reservation of mast trees was contained in township grants. Mayo, "The King's Woods," 54 MHS, *Procs.* 51.

[37] For rulings of English law officers in 1726 that the Act of 8 Geo. 1 did not

1729. 2. G. 2, c. 35, §1. reciting the 8. G, c. 12. and that great Tracts, to evade the Act, had been erected into Townships, enacts that "No Person or Persons, do or shall presume to cutt, fell, or destroy any white Pine Trees, *except only such as are the Property of private Persons*, notwithstanding the said Trees do grow within the Limits of any Township, laid out, or to be laid out." &c.[38]

But no Penalty, nor any Forfeiture, by this Clause, nor any Seizure to the Kings Use. This Exception defeats the Provision.[39]

§. 2.[40] recites the Reservation in the Massachusetts Charter, "of all Trees of 24 Inches Diameter and upwards at 12 Inches &c. growing upon any Soil or Tract of Land, &c. not theretofore granted to any private Person:" to make the *Reservation more effectual*, enacted that "No Person or Persons within said *Prov. of Mass. Bay*, or *N. England*, do or shall presume to cutt, or destroy, any white Pine Trees of 24 Inches and Upwards at 12 Inches &c., not growing within *some Soil or Tract*, &c. *granted to some private Person, or Persons*, before 7. Oct. 1690.

"And every Person so cutting &c. such white Pine Trees, *not being the Property of private Persons*, in any of the Colonies &c.[41]

"And likewise every Person cutting &c. any white Pine Trees of the Diameter of 24 Inches or upwards at 12 Inches &c., growing in any Tract &c. in said Prov. of N. England or Mass. Bay, *not granted to some private Person or Persons* before 7 Oct. 1690, &c.[42] shall be subject to such and the like Penalties and Forfeitures respectively, as

---

affect the charter reservation, and the problem of new townships, see p. 252, note 16, above.

[38] 2 Geo. 2, c. 35, §1 (1729). Closing quotation mark supplied. Emphasis JA's. JA has omitted a clause reciting the areas in which the Act applies, which extends coverage from that in prior acts (notes 31, 32, above), to "any other province or country in America, that now belongs or hereafter shall belong to the Crown of Great Britain." The final "&c." covers the omission of "in any of the said colonies or plantations, without his Majesty's royal license for so doing first had and obtained."

[39] The last sentence is an insertion by JA with a different pen, suggesting that it was an afterthought. It may refer either to the exception for "the Property of private Persons," in the statute, or to the lack of a forfeiture provision in the section. Section 2 of the act, which is quoted by JA below, is ambiguous, but arguably was intended to provide a penalty for section 1. See note 41 below.

[40] 2 Geo. 2, c. 35, §2, set out by JA in this and the next two paragraphs. Quotation marks supplied. Emphasis is JA's.

[41] JA has here omitted: "abovementioned." This reference to section 1 of the Act, as well as the use of the phrase "Property of private persons" from that section, suggests that this clause was intended to provide a penalty for section 1. See note 39 above.

[42] JA has here omitted: "or who shall be abiding and assisting therein, or in drawing away the said pine trees, after the same shall have been so cut and felled."

are provided in 8. G. 1. for such Persons as cutt &c. Pine Trees, not growing in any Township &c." [43]

If the Words in the Charter "not herefore granted to any private Persons," should be construed to mean only, not granted by Titles which were then good, valid and legal, the Words will mean nothing. For if the Vacation of the Charter [44] dissolved the Basis and superstructure together, there was not at the Time of the Charter an Inch of private Property in the Province, it all being revested in the Crown, and the Consequence is that every Pine Tree in the Prov. 24 Inches, is reservd to the Crown.

On the contrary, if they mean, ever granted, and by any means, all the Trees in the Province are excepted out of the Reservation, and the Crown has no Right to one Tree.

The Clause in 2. G. 2, c. 35. "not growing within some soil &c. granted to some private Person or Persons before 7 Oct. 1690," is liable to all the Difficulties in the Clause in the Charter, and to the same Construction. The Intention must have been, to except out of the Reservation all the Lands which had at any Time before been granted by any General Court, Either of Mass. or N. Plymouth, to private Persons, in short. Many had made great Improvements upon Lands, had cleared them, built Houses upon them &c.

[43] JA has here omitted: "the said forfeitures to be recovered and applied in the same manner, as in the said act is particularly set forth and enacted." For the penalties and enforcement provisions of 8 Geo. 1, c. 12, see text and note 33 above. In the MS a half-page is left blank. The notes resume on the facing page.
[44] That is, of the old Charter of Massachusetts Bay, in 1684.

P. Admiralty—Criminal Jurisdiction

EDITORIAL NOTE

The Vice Admiralty Courts had jurisdiction over a multitude of petty criminal offenses committed at sea by masters and mariners, as well as power to punish contempt of their own authority.[1] Offenses that amounted to felony and the crime of piracy were within the competence of a different forum.

In England, since the time of Henry VIII, the trial of "all treasons, felonies, robberies, murders and confederacies," committed upon the seas, or elsewhere within the Admiralty jurisdiction had been given to royal commissioners, who were to sit within the realm and try such offenses "after the common course of the laws of this realm, used for treasons, felonies, murders, robberies and confederacies of the same, done and committed upon the land within this realm." Trial was to be upon indictment of a grand jury, before a petit jury to be summoned by the commissioners.[2] By the middle of the 18th century, procedure under this statute had become formalized as an Admiralty Session at the Old Bailey, where the judges of the common law courts, who were appointed commissioners, sat with a jury for the trial of maritime offenses, dispensing substantially the same brand of justice that shoregoing offenders received.[3]

Since the distance of the colonies from England made transportation of offenders apprehended there a matter of great difficulty, provision was made in a statute of 1700 for the trial in the colonies of "all piracies, felonies, and robberies" committed upon the seas. Commissioners to be appointed by the Crown in each colony were given authority to remit suspected persons to custody and to call a Special Court of Admiralty, which would have power to summon and try offenders "according to the civil law, and the methods and rules of the admiralty." The statute provided a procedure for the court, defined certain offenses, and gave the commissioners under it or the Act of Henry VIII exclusive jurisdiction of such offenses within the colonies.[4] To prevent a possible jurisdictional doubt, an act of

[1] See Wroth, "Massachusetts Vice Admiralty Courts," 6 *Am. Jour. Legal Hist.* 347–348 (1962). For an exercise of the contempt power, see Rex v. Bethune, Vice Adm. Recs. 1718–1726, fol. 1 (1718).

[2] 28 Hen. 8, c. 15, §§1, 2 (1536). Portions of the act are set out in No. 56, at notes 34, 40–43.

[3] See 2 Stephen, *History of the Criminal Law* 18–20; 1 Holdsworth, *History of English Law* 550–552; 2 Browne, *Civil Law* 457–460. For correspondence and other material dealing with these sessions, 1767–1774, see PRO, Adm. 1:3679.

[4] 11 & 12 Will. 3, c. 7 (1700), made perpetual by 6 Geo. 1, c. 19, §3 (1719). Portions of the Act are set out in No. 56, at notes 44–49 and in No. 57, note 57.

1717 provided that all offenses under the 1700 statute might be tried according to the method laid down in the Act of Henry VIII.[5]

During the 18th century the Crown issued standing commissions in each colony or Admiralty district for trial under the provisions of the Act of 1700. The commissioners were a roster of all of the political leaders of the colony or district involved, usually including the Governor, Lieutenant Governor, Secretary, Chief Justice, Judge of Admiralty, members of the Council, officers of the royal navy within the district, and various customs officers.[6] In Massachusetts when the time came to issue a new commission after the death of George II in 1760, this practice was varied. The Council was no longer included, allegedly because Governor Bernard had complained to the Admiralty that its members had joined with the House in opposing the activities of the Vice Admiralty Court.[7] The commission that was issued on 14 January 1762 covered Massachusetts, Rhode Island, and New Hampshire, and so included appropriate officers from all of those colonies.[8] It was before Special Courts of Admiralty called pursuant to this commission that Adams tried two of his most unusual criminal cases, *Rex v. Corbet*, No. 56, and *Rex v. Nickerson*, No. 57.

56. Rex v. Corbet

1769

EDITORIAL NOTE

British impressment of American seamen, a grievance normally associated with the War of 1812, actually antedated even the Revolution, as the present case shows. Early in the morning of Saturday, 22 April 1769, H.M. Frigate *Rose*, patrolling on the high seas off Marblehead, intercepted and stopped the brig *Pitt Packet* (Thomas Power master), owned by Robert "King" Hooper, manned with a crew of Irishmen, and homeward bound

[5] 4 Geo. 1, c. 11, §7 (1717), set out in No. 56, at note 53.

[6] See J. Franklin Jameson, ed., *Privateering and Piracy in the Colonial Period* 577 note (N.Y., 1923).

[7] Samuel Dexter to William Bollan, 26 July 1769, 2 Bowdoin-Temple MSS, fol. 25, MHi. Compare "A Journal of the Times," 31 May 1769, Dickerson, *Boston under Military Rule* 104–105.

[8] See Samuel Seddon, Solicitor to the Admiralty, to Philip Stephens, Secretary of the Admiralty, 26 Aug. 1772, Jameson, *Privateering and Piracy* 578–580. The commission gave to the Commissioners "jointly or severally by warrant under the hand and seal of you or any one of you full power and authority to commit to safe custody any person or persons against whom information of piracy, or robbery or Felony upon the sea or as accessory or accessories to any piracy or robbery shall be given upon oath (which oath you or any one of you shall have full power and are hereby required to administer), and call and assemble a Court of Admiralty on Shipboard or on the land when and as often as occasion shall require which court our will and pleasure is shall consist of 7 persons at the least and if so many of you our said Commissioners cannot conveniently be assembled any 3 or more of you." Book of Charters, Commissions, Proclamations, etc., 1628–1763, fols. 231–238. M-Ar.

from Cadiz, Spain, with a cargo of salt.[1] Henry Panton, the lieutenant, or executive officer, of *Rose*, came aboard with some sailors and marines, asked for the vessel's papers, and commenced a search. In the forepeak, a small space under the weather deck between the stem and the main hold, he discovered crewmen Michael Corbet, Pierce Fenning, John Ryan, and William Conner, variously armed with fish gig, musket, hatchet, and harpoon. To Panton's threats and entreaties, they remained obdurate and menacing; even when the officer secured reinforcements from *Rose* and commenced to have the bulkhead torn down, they refused to budge.

According to John Adams' later reminiscences of the testimony at trial, Corbet drew a line in the salt and told Panton, " 'If you step over that line, I shall consider it as a proof that you are determined to impress me, and by the eternal God of Heaven, you are a dead man.' 'Aye, my lad,' said the lieutenant, 'I have seen many a brave fellow before now.' Taking his snuff-box out of his pocket, and taking a pinch of snuff, he very deliberately stepped over the line, and attempted to seize Corbet. The latter, drawing back his arm, and driving his harpoon with all his force, cut off the carotid artery and jugular vein, and laid the lieutenant dead at his feet." [2]

But the truth, at least according to the actual testimony at the trial, set out in Document V, suggests that Panton, rather than striding into danger, was sitting on the salt, there being no room to stand, and that Corbet, like his friends, was "pushing" at the men who were tearing apart their fortress. At least one pistol had been fired into the forepeak, and it could be only a matter of time before someone was seriously hurt. In the confusion, Corbet thrust with his harpoon, striking Panton, who was carried topside where he bled to death within two hours. Corbet and the others meanwhile were gradually subdued, and that only because, it was rumored, they had drunk themselves into a stupor.[3]

Now the authorities faced the serious problem of properly dealing with the sailors. It was clear that they could not be indicted and tried in one of the common law courts, because the offense had not been committed within the bounds of any county, but the statutes providing for Admiralty jurisdiction of such offenses left the question of jury trial in doubt. The

[1] See Rowe, *Letters and Diary* 186–187. "Not one American belonging to the Brig." *Boston Gazette*, 5 May 1769, p. 1, cols. 1–2; *Boston Chronicle*, 27 April 1769, p. 135, cols. 2–3. As to the *Pitt Packet's* cargo, see Customs Commissioners to Salem Customs Officers, 27 April 1769, Salem Custom House Record Book, 1763–1772, fols. 280–281, MSaE.

[2] "The Inadmissible Principles of the King of England's Proclamation of October 16, 1807, Considered," 9 JA, *Works* 312, 318. See JA to JQA, 8 Jan. 1808, 44 MHS, *Procs.* 422, 424 (1910–1911).

[3] See *Boston Chronicle*, 27 April 1769, p. 135, col. 2; *Boston Gazette*, 1 May 1769, p. 1, cols. 1–2; "A Journal of the Times," 4 May 1769, Dickerson, *Boston under Military Rule* 94–95. "About noon two of the people delivered themselves up, and soon after they seized Corbet. They were all carried on board the Rose. It must be observed the man who was wounded came out soon after Mr. Panton was killed. N.B. It has been said the Brig's men were drunk, but they did not appear so when they were carried on board the Rose." *Boston Chronicle*, 1 May 1769, p. 139, cols. 2–3.

original Act of Henry VIII specified a jury trial before a special Admiralty court in England;[4] a statute passed in the time of William III indicated that trial in the colonies ought to be without a jury.[5] Finally, an Act of George I seemed to restore the jury right.[6] Predictably, the defendants pressed for a jury trial, while the Crown advocates tried to bar it.

But even if the mode of trial were settled, there still remained two knotty issues: Of what crime should the men be accused, and by what substantive law should they be tried? Adams, who with James Otis defended the sailors, was in later years to claim that the successful result of the trial hinged on his discovery of a statute which forbade impressment of American seamen, and on the court's fear that it might have to apply that statute.[7] It is certainly true that the statute in question seemed to render *Rose*'s press gang illegal; that being so, then Panton had no authority to threaten or attempt to seize Corbet, and the killing could be justified on grounds of self-defense. But the issue appears to have been current long before the trial. If one can believe "A Journal of the Times," the loyalists were contending as early as 5 May 1769 that Panton had gone aboard, not to search for seamen, but to inspect for contraband,[8] an argument which the Crown advocates, Samuel Fitch and Jonathan Sewall, were to echo at the trial. And indeed, almost a year before Panton's death, the "Instructions of the Town of Boston to their Representatives," written by Adams himself, had set out the entire relevant section of the act.[9]

Much depended on the question of the applicable substantive law. If the common law applied, then, unless the homicide were justifiable, the accused would be liable to conviction of manslaughter; and the statutes left it unclear whether in trials before the Special Admiralty Court the benefit of clergy could be pleaded, as it could have been at common law. If the trial were, on the other hand, to be held according to the civil law (which usually controlled ordinary Admiralty proceedings), the killing was

[4] 28 Hen. 8, c. 15 (1536).

[5] 11 & 12 Will. 3, c. 7 (1700).

[6] 4 Geo. 1, c. 11 (1717). This statute, and those in notes 4 and 5, are discussed at p. 275–276, notes 2, 4, 5, above, and are set out in part at notes 34, 40–49, 52–53, below. See also No. 57, note 57.

[7] 6 Anne, c. 37, §9 (1707); see JA to William Tudor, 30 Dec. 1816, 2 JA, *Works* 224, 225. Of Otis, JA later said, "[H]is unhappy distemper was then in one of its unlucid intervals, and I could hardly persuade him to converse with me a few minutes on the subject; and he constantly and finally refused to appear publicly in the cause." *Id.* at 224.

[8] "A Journal of the Times," 5 May 1769, Dickerson, *Boston under Military Rule* 95. As to the veracity of the "Journal," see No. 46, notes 30–41, text at note 45. The *Pitt Packet*, having been seized and "rummaged" at Boston, was ordered admitted to entry at Marblehead by the Customs Commissioners, with a few prohibited goods in stores. The officers of the port were ordered to search carefully, however, lest there be further prohibited goods concealed beneath her cargo of salt. See Commissioners to Salem Officers, 27 April 1769, Salem Record Book, 1763–1772, fols. 280–281, MSaE; note 96 below. As to impressment, see note 102 below.

[9] 3 JA, *Works*, 501, 503–504. The "Instructions" are dated 17 June 1768. Impressment had been a Boston grievance at the time of the *Liberty* riot in June 1768. See No. 46, notes 12, 21.

punishable by death only if it was murder; there was no death penalty for the crime which the common law called manslaughter (intentional, unjustifiable, inexcusable homicide without malice).

The Crown officers proceeded carefully. Panton was barely in his King's Chapel grave [10] when Governor Bernard, Lieutenant Governor Hutchinson, Commodore Samuel Hood, Province Secretary Oliver, and Admiralty Judge Auchmuty, Commissioners for the Trial of Piracies, went aboard *Rose* to confer with Captain Caldwell.[11] Shortly thereafter, an account of the affair, based, as it later developed, on the various depositions of *Rose's* people, appeared in the tory *Boston Chronicle* and so angered the patriots that they attempted to counter it with a rehash of an earlier version which everyone, including the *Chronicle*, had already published.[12]

In the face of conflicting documents, Adams' shifting memory, and the disappearance of the pleadings, the exact chronology of the litigation is hard to trace. However, the following seems probable. "Articles" were drawn up against each defendant by Ezekiel Price, Register (Clerk) of the Court of Vice Admiralty. On Tuesday, 23 May 1769, the Special Court of Admiralty, called pursuant to the Commission for the Trial of Piracies, convened. In addition to the five Commissioners who had visited *Rose*, the court consisted of Governor John Wentworth and Councilors Jonathan Warner and George Jaffrey of New Hampshire; Judge John Andrews of the Rhode Island Court of Vice Admiralty; Collectors Joseph Harrison of Boston, John Nutting of Salem, and Robert Trail of Portsmouth. However, at the first session, only Bernard, Hutchinson, Hood, Auchmuty, Oliver, Trail, and Nutting attended.[13] The jury-right issue having been raised early, the court adjourned to Thursday, 25 May, meanwhile hearing argument (Document II); then it further adjourned to Monday, 29 May, when Adams filed his plea to the jurisdiction (Document III), upon which the court "thought proper to take the same under consideration," and adjourned to 14 June.[14]

Finally, on Wednesday, 14 June 1769, the trial commenced in the Court House. "No trial had ever interested the community so much before, excited so much curiosity and compassion, or so many apprehensions of the fateful consequences of the supremacy of parliamentary jurisdiction, or the intrigues of parliamentary courts. No trial had drawn together such crowds of auditors from day to day; they were as numerous as those in the next year, at the trials of Preston and the soldiers." [15]

The court quickly announced that it had overruled the pleas, and pro-

[10] *Boston Chronicle*, 1 May 1769, p. 140, col. 1.

[11] *Boston Gazette*, 8 May 1769, p. 2, col. 1. The visit took place on 29 April.

[12] *Boston Chronicle*, 1 May 1769, p. 139, cols. 2–3; see note 3 above.

[13] See *Boston Gazette*, 29 May 1769, p. 3, col. 1; *id.*, 19 June 1769, p. 1, col. 3.

[14] *Boston Gazette*, 29 May 1769, p. 3, col. 1; *Boston News-Letter*, 1 June 1769, p. 3, col. 1.

[15] JA to Jedidiah Morse, 20 Jan. 1816, 10 JA, *Works* 204, 209–210. The trial was among the first held in the newly built court house on Queen (now Court) Street. See Thwing, *Crooked and Narrow Streets* 95.

ceeded to trial.[16] The taking of evidence commenced immediately and continued for three days; the testimony seems to be substantially reproduced in Adams' minutes (Document V). In contrast to the common-law practice, the evidence was "taken down by the clerk and the counsel in writing." [17] It should be noted that none of the accused testified. There is no evidence that any attempt was made to call any of them as witnesses on behalf of any of the others. Of course, no accused could testify in his own behalf, even at common law; but it was customary at common law when a number of prisoners were tried on the same facts for the court to acquit those whom the evidence did not materially affect, in order that the others might call them as witnesses.[18]

On Saturday, 17 June, Adams rose to make the argument which is detailed in Document VI. He had barely commenced, and had begun to argue that the killing was only justifiable homicide, when, as he loved to tell in later years, Hutchinson moved for adjournment. The court retired for four hours, then returned with its decree: Justifiable homicide, and the prisoners set at liberty. Although Adams insisted that it was fear of the nonimpressment statute which swayed the court, Hutchinson gave a different reason: "It appeared that neither the lieutenant nor any of his superior officers were authorized to impress, by any warrant or special authority from the lords of the admiralty; and the court (the commanding officer of the king's ships being one of the commissioners) was unanimously of opinion that the prisoners had a good right to defend themselves, and, though the fact of killing was fully proved, that they ought to be acquitted of murder, with which they were charged, and that, at common law, the killing would not have amounted to manslaughter." [19] In other words, Adams' substantive legal argument prevailed.

Immediately upon the acquittal, Ryan, whose arm had been broken by a pistol ball in the fracas, brought an action against Midshipman William

[16] *Massachusetts Gazette*, 15 June 1769, p. 1, col. 3; *Boston Gazette*, 19 June 1769, p. 1, col. 3. It is interesting to speculate that in coming to its conclusion the court may have contemplated an item from the *Boston Chronicle*, 25 May 1769, p. 167, col. 2, describing the trial in New York, "before a court of Admiralty held in the City hall, consisting of his Excellency the Governor, the gentlemen of his Majesty's Council &c.," of Joseph Andrews, accused of piracy and murder in Aug. or Sept. 1766. He was convicted and condemned to be hanged.

[17] *Boston Chronicle*, 19 June 1769, p. 195, col. 2; JA to Jedidiah Morse, 20 Jan. 1816, 10 JA, *Works* 204, 207. The procedure, particularly the questioning of witnesses by the court and by the accused, suggests 18th-century naval court-martial procedure. See, for example, Owen Rutter, *The Court-Martial of the Bounty Mutineers* (London, 1931). Hood was president of the *Bounty* trial (1792).

[18] This point arose in the *Bounty* trial, and resulted in the reversing of one of the convictions. See Rutter, *The Court-Martial of the Bounty Mutineers* 53–54.

[19] 3 Hutchinson, *Massachusetts Bay*, ed. Mayo, 167. For JA's versions, see sources cited in notes 7, 15, 17, above. JA's recollection, JA to William Tudor, 30 Dec. 1816, 2 JA, *Works* 224, 225–226, that the court considered its decree overnight, is probably erroneous in light of the contemporary note that the court consulted from 9 to 1 P.M. on Saturday, 17 June. *Boston Chronicle*, 19 June 1769, p. 195, col. 2. It is possible, however, that JA began to argue and was interrupted late on Friday, and the court adjourned to consider on Saturday.

Peacock, who had fired the shot. The Sheriff rowed out to *Rose* and seized Peacock personally, taking £300 bail in lieu of an arrest.[20] Commodore Hood himself sought vainly to buy Peacock's peace, writing Adams (who represented Ryan) and offering his client a cook's place in the fleet, which, with its perquisites, was worth £30 a year. But Ryan refused "because he had fallen in love and would be married," and the matter was finally settled for £30.[21]

Adams always remembered Corbet's case warmly. He considered it more important than the Massacre trials,[22] and he never forgot the honest testimony of the British sailors (some of whom testified in behalf of the prisoners) and their apparent abhorrence of the press gang.[23] At one time, he contemplated publishing a report of the case. Characteristically, he noted: "A great Variety of useful Learning might be brought into an History of that Case—and the great Curiosity of the World after the Case, would make it sell. I have half a Mind to undertake it." [24] Apparently,

[20] *Boston News-Letter,* 22 June 1769, p. 2, col. 1. SF 101703.
[21] JA to JQA, 8 Jan. 1808, 44 MHS, *Procs.* 422, 424; Hood to James Bowdoin, Halifax, 24 April 1770, 1 *Bowdoin-Temple Papers* (9 MHS, *Colls.,* 6th ser.) 175, 176 (1897); Hood to James Bowdoin, 7 Aug. 1770, *id.* at 210. Ryan's release, in SF 101703, is here set out in full to illustrate how little personal injury litigation has changed in two centuries:

Know all Men by these presents that I John Ryan late of Marblehead in the County of Essex, now of Boston in the County of Suffolk and Province of the Massachusetts Bay Mariner, for and in Consideration of the Sum of Thirty pounds Lawful Money of the Kingdom of Great Britain, to me in Hand paid before the Executing of these presents by William Peacock of his Majesty's Ship Rose, now in said Boston Gentleman, the Receipt whereof I do hereby acknowledge; Do by these presents fully and absolutely Release Remise and for ever acquit and Discharge the said William Peacock his Heirs, Executors and Administrators of and from all and all Manner of Action and Actions Cause and Causes of Action, Suits, Sum and Sums of Money, Controversies Variances, Damages, Trespasses, Claims and Demands Whatsoever in Law and Equity which against the said William Peacock I the said John Ryan ever had, now have or which I, my Heirs, Executors or Administrators hereafter can shall or may have for, upon, or by Reason of any Matter, Cause, or Thing whatsoever from the Begining of the World to the Day of the Date of these Presents: More especially a Certain Action of Trespass brought by me the said John Ryan against the said William Peacock and which is now depending in the Superiour Court of Judicature &c. now holden at Said Boston in and for said County of Suffolk; which said last mentioned Action, and the Cause thereof being settled, I hereby Release and Discharge the same and all Costs thereon, and acquit and Discharge him the said William Peacock therefrom forever: In Witness whereof I have hereunto set my Hand and Seal this thirtieth Day of August in the Tenth Year of the Reign of his Majesty George the third of Great-Britain &c. King Annoque Domini 1770.

John Ryan

[22] JA to Jedidiah Morse, 20 Jan. 1816, 10 JA, *Works* 204, 210: "Panton and Corbet ought not to have been forgotten. Preston and his soldiers ought to have been forgotten sooner."
[23] See letters cited in notes 2 and 22 above.
[24] Diary, 23 Dec. 1769, 1 JA, *Diary and Autobiography* 347. JA's plan for a report consisting both of the record of the case and a statement of the broader arguments involved (*ibid.*) resembles that of Henry Laurens, *Extracts From the Proceedings*

he did take some steps along those lines, because the documents here set out, particularly Documents II and VI, indicate careful expansion of legal jottings and courtroom minutes. Document I seems to be the rough notes on which he based his argument, expanded in Document II. Document III is the plea, and Document IV additional pleadings in the nature of demurrer and joinder. Adams' actual trial minutes are Document V, while his final argument is Document VI.

The editors have decided to place the litigation materials in roughly chronological order, and have therefore divided some of Adams' documents at appropriate places. The MS trial minutes (Document V) contain also a series of eight leaves in Adams' hand which Brooks Adams called "supplementary notes." [25] They appear, in fact, to be Adams' digest of the various witnesses' depositions. Thus the summary of Hugh Hill's testimony commences: "Like the Master's till . . . ." And John Roney's starts: "As the Master." In the present arrangement of the materials these have been placed as footnotes to each respective witness' trial testimony.

It is tempting to speculate that these notes are evidence of pre-trial discovery techniques not usually associated with traditional Admiralty practice.[26] However, a more probable view is that, all the witnesses being mariners, each deposition had been taken *in rei perpetuam*, against the possibility of the witness' being at sea when the case came to trial.[27]

I. ADAMS' NOTES OF AUTHORITIES [28]

Special Court of Admiralty, Boston, May 1769

28. H. 8, c. 15. For Pirates.

The Statute on which this Court is founded is 11th. & 12th. Wm. 3rd, C. 7. An Act for the more effectual suppression of Piracy.

6. Ann, c. 37, §9. Impresses in America prohibited. This act perpetual. 1. because of the Title. 2. the Preamble, in two Parts, for Ad-

---

of the Court of Vice-Admiralty In Charles-Town, South-Carolina (Phila., 1768). See No. 46, notes 73, 75. JA may also have contemplated such a report of Hancock's case. *Id.,* text at notes 72–77.

[25] Appendix to BA, "The Convention of 1800 with France," 44 MHS, *Procs.* 377, 429 (1910–1911). Because the stitching in JA's paper booklet recording the evidence wore away long ago and allowed the leaves of the MS to get out of order, BA printed some of the testimony in an improper sequence; the order of the documents in the Adams Papers microfilms is also wrong. What is with little doubt the correct order of the evidence on both sides has been restored below. See also note 95 below.

[26] See Miner v. Atlass, 363 U.S. 641 (1960).

[27] See "An Act for Taking of Affidavits out of Court," 12 Dec. 1695, 1 A&R 225, 226.

[28] In JA's hand. Adams Papers, Microfilms, Reel No. 184. Because most of the authorities are expanded in Docs. II and VI, full annotations have been deferred until those documents. On the first page of the notes, to which JA gave no caption, "Corbit's Case" is written in pencil in an unidentified hand.

vancement of Trade, and increase of Shipping and Seamen. 4. the same Clauses in their Nature temporary, yet others perpetual. Others expressly limited to the duration of the War. This § not §4. No limitation in the Act itself to Years, or other Term. 4. G, c. 11, §7. Sugar Colonies Act. 19. G. 2, c. 30, §1.[29]

Fosters Crown Law.

Necessary Homicide. 2. Domat. 638 §6. Woods Inst. civ. Law 270. Cod. Lib. 9. Tit. 16. 2. 3. 4 &c.

Civil Law, relative to Defense and Provocation.

2. Domat 638. §6. Woods Inst. civ. Law 270. Cod. Lib. 9. Tit. 16. 2. 3. 4. &c. Note 46. Gail Page 503. Maranta Page 49, Pars 4. ⟨*Dig. 1.*⟩ Dist. 1. 77.

Com. Law justifiable self Defense.

1. Hawk. 71. §4. middle. §21. killing ravisher. page 72 §23. towards the End. §24. page 75. §14.

Keyling page 128. bottom page 136. Top. Buckners 136. 3. bottom. 3dly. 59. Hopkin Huggetts. 2. Ld. Ray. Tooleys Case. Holt 485. 484. Foster 312–316–vid. Foster 292, the smart &c. for Manslaughter, also 296.

Calvin. Tit. Culpa.[30]

7. W. 3, c. 4. An Act for Grand Jurors serving at Quarter Sessions. Clerk of the Peace of each County shall annually 15 days before the day for holding the Court issue out Writs to the Constables of Towns, to warn a Meeting of the Inhabitants, for chusing one or more Grand Jurors.[31]

Grand Jurors Oath 4. W. & Mary. c. 16.[32]

[29] "An Act for the Better Encouragement of the Trade of His Majesty's Sugar Colonies in America," 19 Geo. 2, c. 30 (1746). Section 1 exempts from impressment all mariners "who shall serve on board, or be retained to serve on board any privateer, or trading ship or vessel, that shall be employed in any of the British sugar colonies in the West Indies, in America."

[30] John Calvin, *Magnum Lexicon Juridicum,* 1:406–409 (Geneva, 1734), discusses guilt.

[31] Act of 16 March 1695, 1 A&R 193.

[32] Act of 25 Nov. 1692, 1 A&R 78, 79: "You as foreman of this inquest for the body of this county of S., you shall diligently enquire and a true presentment make of all such matters and things as shall be given you in charge, the king and queen's majesties' counsel, your fellows' and your own you shall keep secret; you shall present no man for envy, hatred or malice, neither shall you leave any man unpresented for love, fear, favor or affection, or hope of reward, but you shall present things truly as

Temp[orary] Laws. 23. G. 2, c. 2. better regulating the Choice of Petit Jurors.[33]

28. H. 8, c. 15. For Pirates. After the common Course of the Laws of this Realm. Commissioners to enquire, by the Oaths of 12 good and lawfull Inhabitants, in the *Shire limited in their Commission*, as if such Crimes committed on Land. And Tryal by 12 lawfull Men, inhabited in the shire limited within such Commission. Expressly excluded clergy. Tryals in 5. Ports shall be ⟨in⟩ by Inhabitants,[34] &c.

11. & 12. W. 3, c. 7. Act for more effectual suppression of Pyracy. 4. G. c.

18. G. 2, c. 30.[35]

Otis. 2 Salk. The Word "may," shall be construed "shall." Tit. Statutes and their Construction.[36]

Tryal of Stede Bonnett, before Judge Trott.

1718. 5. G. 1. V. 6. 156.[37]

Consent of Parties would cure all Difficulties, Vin. Tit. Tryal.[38]

---

they come to your knowledge, according to the best of your understanding. So help you God. The same oath which your foreman hath taken on his part, you and every one of you on your behalf shall well and truly observe and keep. So help you God."

[33] "An Act for the Better Regulating the Choice of Petit Jurors," 12 Aug. 1749, 3 A&R 474. Renewed 13 Oct. 1756, 3 A&R 995; 29 March 1760, 4 A&R 318; 20 March 1767, 4 A&R 920.

[34] 28 Hen. 8, c. 15, §6 (1536): "Provided alway, that whensoever any commission shall be directed unto the five ports for the inquisition and trials of any the offences expressed in this act, that every such inquisition and trial to be had by virtue of such commission, shall be made and had by the inhabitants in the said five ports, or the members of the same." The "five ports" or "cinque ports" were "those special havens that lie toward France," generally thought to be Dover, Sandwich, Rumney, Winchelsea, and Rye. They had "many privileges, liberties, and franchises." Their governor, or Lord Warden of the Cinque Ports, had a special Admiralty jurisdiction. See Cunningham, *Law Dictionary*, tit. Cinque Ports.

[35] 18 Geo. 2, c. 30 (1745) extends the Act of 11 & 12 Will. 3, c. 7 (1700) to British subjects committing nautical treason.

[36] Presumably Otis refers to 2 Salk. 610–613: "Statutes, and the Exposition thereof." But none of the cases there reported treats the issue here framed. The other reference may be either to 4 Bacon, *Abridgment* 644: "Rules to be Observed in the Construction of Statutes"; or to 19 Viner, *Abridgment* 511: "Construction of Statutes."

[37] Rex v. Bonnet et al., 6 State Trials 156 (S.C. Vice Adm., 1718).

[38] Possibly 21 Viner, *Abridgment* 386: "The Jury is not to inquire of that which is agreed by the Parties."

II. ADAMS' ARGUMENT AND REPORT [39]

Special Court of Admiralty, Boston, May 1769

Case of Michael Corbit and others, charged with
the Murder of Lt. Panton on the High Seas

28th. Hen. 8th. c. 15. "For Pirates." [40] Where *Traytors, Pirates, Thieves, Robbers, Murtherers*, and *Confederates* upon the Sea, many times escaped unpunished, because the Tryal of their offences, hath heretofore been ordered, judged and determined before the *Admiral,* or his *Lieutenant* or *Commissary*, after the Course of the civil Laws, the Nature whereof is, that before any Judgment of Death can be given against the offenders, either they must plainly *confess their offences,* (which they will never do, without Torture or Pains) or else their offences be so plainly and directly proved by Witness indifferent, such as saw their offences committed &c.[41] for Reformation whereof be it enacted, That all *Treasons, Felonies, Robberies, Murthers*, and *Confederacies*, hereafter to be committed *in or upon the Sea*, or in any other *Haven, River, Creek,* or *Place* where the Admiral or Admirals, have or pretend to have Jurisdiction, Authority, or Power, shall be *enquired, tried, heard, determined*, and *Judged*, in such Shires and Places in the Realm, as shall be limited, by the Kings Commission, &c. as if the Offence done upon Land, &c. after the common Course of the Laws of this Realm.[42]

§. 2d. to enquire by the Oaths of twelve good and lawfull Men &c. in the shire limit in the Commission.[43]

11. and 12. W. 3, c. 7. An Act for the more effectual Suppression of Piracy.[44]

All Pyracies, Felonies, and Robberies, committed in, or upon the

---

[39] In JA's hand, in his Admiralty Book, Adams Papers, Microfilms, Reel No. 184. Printed in 2 JA, *Works*, Appendix B, 526–528.

[40] That is, 28 Hen. 8, c. 15 (1536). Emphasis is JA's.

[41] JA omits this apparently relevant material: "which cannot be gotten but by chance at few times, because such offenders commit their offences upon the sea, and at many times murder and kill such persons being in the ship or boat where they commit their offences, which should witness against them in that behalf; and also such as should bear witness be commonly mariners and shipmen, which, because of their often voyages and passages in the seas, depart without long tarrying and protraction of time, to the great costs and charges as well of the King's highness, as such as would pursue such offenders."

[42] JA omits several unimportant phrases.

[43] This section of the statute details procedure for jury indictment and jury trial.

[44] That is, 11 & 12 Will. 3, c. 7 (1700). Emphasis is JA's.

Sea, or in any Haven, River, Creek, or Place, where the Admiral or Admirals have Power, Authority, or Jurisdiction, may be examined, enquired of, tried, heard, determined, and adjudged, [according to the directions of this act,] and in any Place at sea, or upon the Land, in any of his Majestys Islands, Plantations, Colonies, Dominions, Forts or Factories to be appointed for that Purpose by the K's Commission &c. under the great seal of England, or the Seal of the Admiralty of England, directed to all or any of the Admirals, Vice Admirals, Reer Admirals, Judges of Vice Admiralties, or Commanders of any of his Majestys Ships of War, and also to all or any such Person or Persons as his Majesty shall please [45] to appoint; &c. which said Commissioners shall have full Power jointly or severally, by Warrant under the Hand and seal of them or anyone of them to commit to Safe Custody, any Person &c. vs. whom Information of Pyracy, Robbery or Felony upon the Sea shall be given upon oath &c.[46] and to call and assemble a Court of Admiralty on shipboard, or upon the Land &c.[47] and such Persons so assembled, shall have full Authority, *according to the Course of the Admiralty*, to issue Warrants for bringing any Person accused of Piracy or Robbery before them, to be tried &c.[48] to summon, and examine Witnesses &c. and to do all Things necessary for the Hearing and final Determination of any Case of Piracy, Robbery, and Felony; and to give Sentence and Judgment of Death, and to award Execution [of the offenders convicted and attainted as aforesaid], *according to the civil Law*, and the *Methods and Rules of the Admiralty*; [49]

This Statute is the Foundation of the Special Commission, and of the present Proceeding, and upon it a Question has been made by Mr. Otis whether the Prisoners have not a Right to a Jury? He says that Magna Charta, in a Case of Life, at least must be expressly repealed, not by Implication, or Construction only. And that in England a Jury is summoned every day for the Tryal of such offences committed at sea. But I think that the statute of 28th H.8. before cited explains this Difficulty. And this Case seems to be but one Instance among many others, of the partial Distinctions made between British subjects at Home and abroad. The *civil Law*, The *Course of the Admiralty*, and

[45] The statute says: "think fit."

[46] JA omits: "(which oath they or any one of them shall have full power, and are hereby required to administer)."

[47] JA omits: "when and as often as occasion shall require; which court shall consist of seven persons at the least."

[48] JA omits: "heard, and adjudged"; he also paraphrases the next clause, which says: "and to summon witnesses, and to take informations and examinations of witnesses upon their oath."

[49] The text from note 47 to this point comes from §4 of the statute.

the *Methods and Rules of the Admiralty*, will be construed to take away the Benefit of a Jury.—†Turn to the last Leaf but one.[50]

† Mr. Otis, from his first Retainer in the Cause, has been very sanguine, to move for a Jury. He has mentioned his Resolution in all Companies, [and] last Week at Plymouth he mentioned it to the Lt. Govr. and the rest of the Judges.[51] Mr. Fitch happening to hear of our Design to move for a Jury, went to rummaging up Acts of Parliament to satisfy himself, and found the 4. of G, c. 11. An Act for the further preventing of Robbery &c. and for declaring the Law upon some Points relating to Pirates.[52] In the 7th section of this statute "It is hereby *declared*, that all and every Person and Persons who have committed or shall commit any offence, or offences, for which they ought to be adjudged, deemed and taken to be *Pirates, Felons,* or *Robbers,* by an Act made in the Parliament holden in the 11. and 12. Years of [the reign of his late majesty King] Wm. 3d, intituled 'An Act for the more effectual suppression of Piracy' may be tried and judged for every such offence, *in such Manner and Form* as in and by an Act 28. H. 8. is directed and appointed for the Tryal of Pirates."[53] This statute Fitch discovered to Sewall and Sewall shewed it to the Governor and Lt. Govr., and the rest of the Court, the first Morning of the Courts sitting, in the Council Chamber. They were all struck and surprised, and the Lt. Govr. observed that this Statute cleared up, what had always to him appeared a Mistery. In the State Tryals, the Tryal of *Stede Bonnet* before Judge Trott at Carolina 1718. 5. G. 1.—V. 6. 156. It being the next Year after the statute, Bonnett had a Grand and Petit Jury.[54]

In the Council Chamber the Court, however agreed, that they would go into the Court House and take the oaths &c. and then the Court would publickly propose a Jury. This was done and the statutes 28. H. 8. 11. & 12. W. 3. and 4. G. 1. were read and then the Commission &c. and then the Govr. proposed, to adjourn the Court to Thursday,[55]

[50] That is, of JA's Admiralty Book. At the present point in the MS appears the material separately set out as Doc. VI.

[51] Presumably during the May 1769 sitting of the Superior Court at Plymouth.

[52] 4 Geo. 1, c. 11 (1717), "An Act for the Further Preventing Robbery, Burglary, and Other Felonies, and for the More Effectual Transportations of Felons, and Unlawful Exporters of Wool; and for Declaring the Law upon Some Points Relating to Pirates."

[53] JA omits: "and shall and ought to be utterly debarred and excluded from the benefit of clergy for the said offenses; any law or statute to the contrary thereof in any wise notwithstanding." The statutes referred to are 11 & 12 Will. 3, c. 7 (1700), and 28 Hen. 8, c. 15 (1536).

[54] Rex v. Bonnet et al., 6 State Trials 156 (S.C. Vice Adm., 1718).

[55] See the discussion of the chronology, text at notes 13, 14, above.

and to hear Council [i.e. Counsel] this afternoon in the Council Chamber, upon the subject of a Jury.

In the afternoon We accordingly attended, and a Difficulty was started by the Lt. Governor about the Venire's. Whether they should be directed to the Sherriff, to summon a Jury as in England, or whether the Venires should issue in any manner analogous to the Laws of this Province relative to this subject? In the Afternoon, We had the argument, and the whole Court seemed convinced that a Jury must be had. The Govr. indeed, talked that they might be sent to England for Tryal, &c.

But the next Morning, when Mr. Otis was to have prepared and produced a Venire facias to the Sherriff to return a Jury, We found *all aback*. The whole Court, Advocate Genl. Mr. Sewall, and Mr. Fitch all of opinion that we had been all wrong, and that a Jury could not be had. The Lt. Govr. had in the Course of his Lucubrations, discovered this great secret, that by Law two Ways of Tryal are pointed out and provided, one by 28. H. 8., the other by 11. & 12. of W. 3. and that his Majesty may grant a Commission in Pursuance of Either. That this Commission was expressly limited to 11. & 12. W. 3. and therefore could not proceed, according to 28. H. 8.

III. PLEA TO THE JURISDICTION [56]

Special Court of Admiralty, Boston, May 1769

Province of the	
Massachusetts Bay	

Province of the
Massachusetts Bay
⎱
⎰
To the Honble. the Commissioners ⟨of the⟩ constituting the Special Court of Admiralty for the hearing and determining of Piracies Robberies and Fellonies committed upon the high Seas, begun and held at Boston in the County of Suffolk, and Province of the Massachusetts Bay in New England in America on the twenty third day of May in the Ninth Year of the Reign of George the Third by the Grace of God of Great Britain, France and Ireland, King Defender of the Faith &c.

[56] In JA's hand. Adams Papers, Microfilms, Reel No. 184. Docketed in another hand: "Michael Corbett & the 4 sailors who kill'd Panton in defence of th[eir] liberty." There were of course only four sailors involved. Similar pleas in JA's hand in behalf of John Ryan and Pierce Fenning are in MBAt:Ezekiel Price Papers. See notes 61, 62, below. Quotation marks supplied.

Humbly shews Michael Corbit of Marblehead in the County of Essex, Mariner that this Hon'ble Court ought not to take Cognizance of the Matters and Things sett forth and alledged in the said Articles exhibited against him by Ezekiel Price Gentleman, because the said Michael says, that by an Act of Parliament made in the Twenty Eighth Year of the Reign of King Henry the Eighth, it is among other Things enacted, "That all Treasons, Felonies, Robberies, Murthers, and Confederacies, hereafter to be committed in or upon the Sea, or in any other Haven, River, Creek or Place where the Admiral or Admirals, have or pretend to have Power, Authority or Jurisdiction shall be inquired, tried, heard, determined, and judged, in such Shires and Places in the Realm as shall be limited by the Kings Commission or Commissions to be directed for the same, in like Form and Condition, as if any such offence or offences had been committed or done in or upon the Land; and such Commissions shall be had under the Kings Great Seal, directed to the Admiral or Admirals, or to his or their Lieutenant, Deputy, and Deputies, and to three or four such other substantial Persons, as shall be named or appointed, by the Lord Chancellor of England for the Time being, from Time to Time, and as oft as need shall require, to hear and determine such offences after the common Course of the Laws of this Realm, used for Treasons, Felonies, Murthers, and Confederacies of the same, done and committed upon the Land within this Realm," And "that such Persons to whom such Commission or Commissions, shall be directed, or four of them at the least, shall have full Power and Authority to enquire of such offences, and of every of them, by the oaths of Twelve good and lawfull Inhabitants in the shire limited in their Commission, in such like manner and Form, as if such offences had been committed upon the Land within the same shire, and that every Indictment found and presented before such Commissioners, of any Treasons, Felonies, Robberies Murthers, Manslaughters, or such other offences, being committed or done, in or upon the Seas, or in or upon any other Haven, River or Creek, shall be good and effectual in the Law and if any Person or Persons happen to be indicted for any such offence, done or hereafter to be done upon the seas, or in any other Place above limited, that then such order, Proscess, Judgment and Execution shall be used, had, done and made, to and against every such Person and Persons, so being indicted, as against Traytors, Felons and Murtherers, for Treason, Felony, Robbery, Murther or other such offences done upon the Land, as by the Laws of this Realm is accustomed; and that the Tryal of such offence or offences, if it be denied by the offender or offenders, shall be had by twelve lawfull Men, inhabited in the shire limited within such Commission, which shall be directed as is aforesaid, and no Challenge or Challenges to be had for the Hundred; and such as shall be convict of any such offence or offences, by Verdict, Confession or Proscess, by authority of any such Commission, shall have and suffer, such Pains of Death, Losses of Lands, Goods and Chattells, as if they had been attainted and convicted of any Treasons, Felonies, Robberies, or other the said offences done upon the Lands." [57]

And the said Michael further shews, that by another Act of Parliament made and passed in the Parliament holden in the Eleventh and Twelfth Years of the Reign of King William the third, it is, among other Things declared and enacted "That all Piracies, Felonies, and Robberies committed in or upon the sea, or in any Haven, River, Creek or Place, where the Admiral or Admirals have Power, Authority or Jurisdiction, may be examind, enquired of, tried, heard and determined and adjudged, according to the Directions of this Act, in any Place at Sea, or upon the Land, in any of his Majestys Islands, Plantations, Colonies, Dominions, Forts or Factories, to be appointed for that Purpose by the Kings Commission or Commissions under the Great Seal of England, or the Seal of the Admiralty of England, directed to all or any of the Admirals, Vice Admirals, Reer Admirals, Judges of Vice Admiralties, or Commanders of any of his Majestys Ships of War, and also to all or any such Person or Persons, officer or officers, by Name, or for the Time being, as his Majesty shall think fit to appoint, which said Commissioners shall have full Power jointly or severally, by Warrant under the Hand and Seal of them, or any one of them, to commit to safe Custody any Person or Persons against whom Information of Piracy, Robbery, or Felony upon the sea, shall be given upon oath which oath they or any one of them, shall have full Power, and are hereby required to administer and to call and assemble a Court of Admiralty on ship board, or upon the Land, when and as often as occasion shall require; which Court shall consist of seven Persons at the least" and "that such Persons called and assembled," as in said Act is particularly described, "shall have full Power and Authority, according to the Course of the Admiralty, to issue Warrants for bringing any Persons accused of Pyracy or Robbery before them to be tried, heard and adjudged and to summon Witnesses, and to take Informations and Examinations of Witnesses upon their oath; and to do all Things necessary for the Hearing and final Determination of any Case of Pyracy, Robbery and Felony; and to give sentence

[57] 28 Hen. 8, c. 15, §§1, 2 (1536).

and Judgment of Death and to award Execution of the offenders convicted and attainted as aforesaid, according to the civil Law, and the Methods and Rules of the Admiralty; and that all and every Person and Persons so convicted and attainted of Pyracy or Robbery, shall have and suffer such Losses of Lands, Goods and Chattells, as if they had been attainted and convicted of any Piracies, Felonies and Robberies, according to the aforementioned statute, made in the Reign of King Henry the Eighth." [58]

And the said Michael further saith that by another Act of Parliament made and passed in the fourth Year of the Reign of King George the first it is among other Things declared, "that all and every Person and Persons who have committed or shall commit any offence or offences, for which they ought to be adjudged, deemed, and taken to be Pirates, Fellons, or Robbers, by an Act made in the Parliament holden in the Eleventh and Twelfth Years of the Reign of his late Majesty King William the Third, intituled, 'an Act for the more effectual suppression of Pyracy,' may be tried and judged for every such offence in such manner and Form as in and by an Act made in the twenty Eighth Year of the Reign of King Henry the Eighth is directed and appointed for the Tryal of Pyrates, and shall and ought to be utterly debarred and excluded from the Benefit of Clergy, for the said offences; any Law or statute to the Contrary thereof in any wise notwithstanding," and "that this Act shall extend to all his Majestys Dominions in America, and shall be taken as a public Act." [59]

Now the said Michael says that the Commission whereby this Honourable Court is constituted authorises it, to proceed only according to the Directions in the said Act made in the Reign of King William the third, according to the Course of the Admiralty, According to the civil Law, and the Methods and Rules of the Admiralty; [60] and that the Matters and Things contained in the Articles aforesaid against the said Michael, ought now by Law to be heard and tryed, by a Court constituted according to the said Act made in the Reign of King Henry the Eighth, and ought to be tryed and judged in such manner and Form as in and by the same Act is directed and appointed, that is to say by a grand Jury and a petit Jury of the said County of Suffolk and as by the Laws of the Realm of Great Britain is accustomed.

Wherefore the said Michael ⟨says⟩ prays Judgment if this Court

[58] 11 & 12 Will. 3, c. 7, §§1, 4 (1700).

[59] 4 Geo. 1, c. 11, §§7, 9 (1717).

[60] The commission recited all three statutes, but in constituting the court it gave it only powers provided by the Act of William III. See p. 276, note 8 above. Compare JA's report, text following note 55 above.

will take any further Cognizance of the Matters and Things charged upon said Michael in said Articles.[61]

IV. ADDITIONAL PLEADINGS [62]

Special Court of Admiralty, Boston, May 1769

And the said Ezekiel Price says, that he to the said plea of the said John Ryan above pleaded to the Jurisdiction of this honorable Court, has no necessity nor is he oblidged by the Law of the Land in any manner to answer, because he says that the same plea is not sufficient in Law to put this honorable Court from taking further Cognizance of the Matters and Things contained in the Articles aforesaid and this the said Ezekiel is ready to verify; wherefore for want of a sufficient plea in this behalf, he prays this honorable Court would take further Cognizance of the Matters and Things charged upon the said John Ryan in the Articles aforesaid; and that the said John Ryan may be put to answer to the Same.   Ez. Price

And the said John Ryan says, his said Plea is Sufficient to put this Honorable Court from taking further Cognizance of the Matters and Things contained in the Articles aforesaid, and thereof prays Judgment.   J. Adams

[61] The plea of John Ryan (and, *mutatis mutandis*, that of Pierce Fenning) concludes as follows: "Now the said John says that the Commission whereby this Honourable Court is constituted, authorizes it to proceed only according to the Directions in the said Act made in the Reign of King William the third, that is to say according to the Course of the Admiralty, according to the civil Law, and the Methods and Rules of the Admiralty: And ⟨that the Matters⟩ according to the other particular Rules and Methods, therein ⟨partic⟩ described and explained: And the said John further says that the Matters and Things contained in the Articles aforesaid, exhibited against him, by Ezekiel Price Gentleman, ought now by Law to be heard and tryed, by a Court constituted according to the said Act of Parliament made in the Reign of King Henry the Eighth, and ought to be enquired of heard, tryed, determined, and adjudged, ⟨accor⟩ by the oaths of twelve good and lawfull Men, in such manner and Form as in and by the same Act of King Henry the Eighth, is directed and appointed, and as by the Laws of the Realm of Great Britain is accustomed.

"Wherefore the said John prays Judgment if this Court will take any further Cognizance of the Matters and Things charged upon ⟨said Michael⟩ him in said Articles." In JA's hand. MBAt:Ezekiel Price Papers.

[62] In Jonathan Sewall's hand, signed by Ezekiel Price, and in JA's hand, signed by him, appended to pleas of Ryan and Fenning, notes 56, 61, above, MBAt:Ezekiel Price Papers.

9. ROBERT TRAILL, BY BENJAMIN BLYTH

10. ROBERT "KING" HOOPER, BY JOHN SINGLETON COPLEY

A MONUMENTAL INSCRIPTION

ON THE

Fifth of March.

Together with a few LINES

On the Enlargement of

EBENEZER RICHARDSON,

Convicted of MURDER.

AMERICANS!
BEAR IN REMEMBRANCE
The HORRID MASSACRE!
Perpetrated in King-ftreet, BOSTON,
New-England,
On the Evening of March the Fifth, 1770.
When FIVE of your fellow countrymen,
GRAY, MAVERICK, CALDWELL, ATTUCKS,
and CARR,
Lay wallowing in their Gore!
Being *bafely*, and moft *inhumanly*
MURDERED!
And SIX others badly WOUNDED!
By a Party of the XXIXth Regiment,
Under the command of Capt. Tho. Preston.
REMEMBER!
That Two of the Murderers
Were convicted of MANSLAUGHTER!
By a Jury, of whom I fhall fay
NOTHING,
Branded in the hand!
And *difmiffed*,
The others were ACQUITTED,
And their Captain PENSIONED!
Also,
BEAR IN REMEMBRANCE
That on the 22d Day of February, 1770.
The infamous
EBENEZER RICHARDSON, Informer,
And tool to Minifterial hirelings,
Moft *barbaroufly*
MURDERED
CHRISTOPHER SEIDER,
An innocent youth!
Of which crime he was found guilty
By his Country
On Friday April 20th, 1770;
But remained *Unfentenced*
On Saturday the 22d Day of February, 1772.
When the GRAND INQUEST
For Suffolk county,
Were informed, at requeft,
By the Judges of the Superior Court,
That EBENEZER RICHARDSON's *Cafe*
Then lay before his MAJESTY.
Therefore faid *Richardfon*
This day, MARCH FIFTH! 1772,
Remains UNHANGED!!!
Let THESE things be told to Pofterity!
And handed down
From Generation to Generation,
'Till Time fhall be no more!
Forever may AMERICA be preferved,
From weak and wicked monarchs,
Tyrannical Minifters,
Abandoned Governors,
Their Underlings and Hirelings!
And may the
Machinations of artful, *defigning* wretches,
Who would ENSLAVE THIS People,
Come to an end,
Let their NAMES and MEMORIES
Be buried in eternal oblivion,
And the PRESS,
For a *SCOURGE* to Tyrannical Rulers,
Remain FREE.

AWAKE my drowfy Thoughts! Awake my mufe!
　　Awake O earth, and tremble at the news!
　　In grand defiance to the laws of God,
The Guilty, Guilty murd'rer walks abroad.
That city mourns, (the cry comes from the ground,)
Where law and juftice never can be found:
Oh! fword of vengeance, fall thou on the race
Of thofe who hinder juftice from its place.
O MURD'RER! RICHARDSON! with their lateft breath
Millions will curfe you when you fleep in death!
Infernal horrors fure will fhake your foul
When o'er your head the awful thunders roll.
Earth cannot hide you, always will the cry
Of Murder! Murder! haunt you 'till you die!
To yonder grave! with trembling joints repair,
Remember, SEIDER's corps lies mould'ring there;
There drop a tear, and think what you have done!
Then judge how you can live beneath the Sun.
A PARDON may arrive! You laws defy,
But Heaven's laws will ftand when KINGS fhall die.
Oh! Wretched man! the monfter of the times,
You were not hung " by reafon of *old* Lines,"
Old Lines thrown by, 'twas then we were in hopes,
That you would foon be hung with *new made* Ropes;
But neither *Ropes nor Lines*, will fatisfiy
For SEIDER's blood! But GOD is ever nigh,
And guilty fouls will not unpunifh'd go
Tho' they're excus'd by judges here below!
You are enlarg'd but curfed is your fate
Tho' *Cufhing's* eas'd you from the prifon gate
The --*Bridge* of *Tories, it* has borne you o'er
Yet you e'er long may meet with HELL's dark fhore.

II.　BROADSIDE CONCERNING EBENEZER RICHARDSON

No. 56. Rex v. Corbet

V. ADAMS' MINUTES OF THE TRIAL [63]

Special Court of Admiralty, Boston, June 1769

Mr. Fitch.
About the Time of the Blow—the 2d Pistol was fired.
Commission from Commissioners.
Instructions.

Witnesses.

Peter Bowen. I have seen all the Prisoners on Board the Brigg Pit Packet on the 22d. April last. In the Fore Peek. I knew Lt. Henry Gibson Panton, lately deceased. He was Lt. of the Rose Man of War. He was on Board the Brigg Pit Packet when I saw those Men.

Mr. Panton went on Board, and I with him. We enquird for the Master, who proved to be the Person we spoke to. Master, Mr. Panton and I went down in the Cabin. When below Mr. Panton enquired from where the Brig came? Master made answer from Calais [*Cadiz?*] bound to Marblehead. Mr. Panton then asked him *for his Bills of Lading, clearance, and other Papers.* Master answerd he had no Papers except *a Bill of Health which he produced. Next Mr. Panton asked how many Men he had on Board?* Master answerd 6 before the Mast besides himself and Mate. *He then asked for his Log Book?* Master *produced it. Mr. Panton desired the Hatchways and scuttles* [64] *might be opend, and he would send his People down to search for uncustomd Goods or to that Purpose.* Master said it should be done. Mr. Panton and I went upon Deck leaving the Master in the Cabin. *Mr. Panton desired the Mate to send all his Hands aft. At the same time orderd the Roses People to go below to search.* The Mate said he would send what Hands there was aft. *Mr. Panton said he must send 'em all.* Mate said he could not send 'em all aft but he would go and call them. Mate went forward. Mr. Panton orderd me to go with him. *Mate called the People, but none of them answerd,* of which the Mate went aft and informed Mr. Panton.[65] *Mr. Panton said We must search for them.* Lights were got. *Mr. Panton orderd me with 2 of the Boats Crew to search in the main hold for the Men. We searched. We found nor heard none.* I came out of the main Hold and went forward. *Gibson, one of the Boats Crew said to me theres a Scuttle, pointing to one be-*

[63] In JA's hand. Adams Papers, Microfilms, Reel No. 184.
[64] In margin: "Mem. Motion by Advocate General that he might have a written Account prepared before." A scuttle is a small opening in the deck with a moveable lid. See *OED.*
[65] In margin: "Note."

fore him. We orderd him and Churchill another of the Boats Crew, to unlay. Churchill taking up the Scuttle, called out *"Here they are,"* and *desired the Men he saw to come up.* Briggs People swore they would not, meaning those in the fore Peek, and that the first Man that dared to approach em, they would cut his Limbs off. Which of em said this I cant tell. They all spoke to that Purpose—at the same Time shewing a Hatched [Hatchet,] Harpoon, a Musquet and a Fish Gigg. *I then said, the Lt. wanted to see them and desired em the Prisoners to come upon deck.* They swore they would not. I informed Mr. Panton of what happend. Mr. Panton, hearing it, went forward. I went with him. *Mr. Panton mildly desird the Briggs People the Prisoners to come out—* which they refused to do, swearing they would die in the Hold before they would suffer themselves to be impressed. *Mr. Panton then said he wanted to search the Hold, and asked them to let him come down where they were.* They repeated to him what they had threatened to me and shew him their Weapons. *Mr. Panton desired a 2d. Time that they would come out, adding if they persisted in refusing he must oblige them. One and all of them said to Mr. Panton if he brought any Arms against them, he should be their Mark and they would put his Lamp out first. Mr. Panton ordered the Roses Boat to be manned and sent Mr. Stanhope aboard the Rose for Assistance,* which I did. I returned to Mr. Panton, and found him talking with the Prisoners, *endeavoring to perswade them to come out, explaining the folly of being obstinate.* The Prisoners said several Times in my hearing, *if there were 50 men armd they would not be taken, and told Mr. Panton if he had any Regard for his own Life, he would let them pass. He said it was his Duty and he could not do it.* They said they knew he was Lt. and knew his orders, and desird them again to let them pass, swearing and repeating their Threats against him particularly. Mr. Panton had a Candle in his Hand, the Place being very dark, *which he gave to one of the Prisoners. Desird they would let him see what sort of a Place they were in. One of em took the Candle and lighted it about where they stood.* Mr. Panton said *He could not see what sort of a Place it was, and wanted to go down. They said he should not go down,* and if he attempted it they would shoot him, and Pierce Fenning presented the Musquet and said it was loaded with sluggs and primed. Then returned the Candle. Mr. Panton Aye! will you shoot me? In a joking, chearfull Manner, added, I will take a Pinch of Snuff first, *and ordered me to go and see if the Boat was come back.* I informd him the Boat was just returnd. Mr. Peacock, Mr. Stanhope, Forbes the Master at Arms, and the Boats Crew. *They all came below.*

Mr. Panton *asked the Prisoners if they would surrender.* They said they would not. Mr. Panton *orderd* Mr. Peacock and *the Boats Crew to go below in the main hold, and open the Bulkhed where the Prisoners were. As soon as the Crew began to work upon the Bulk head, the Prisoners all of em at different Times said they would shoot the first Man that made a Hole.* One of em, which I cant say, *advised the others to shoot the Lt. first* and *divide themselves, 2 to defend* the Scuttle *and one the Bulk head.* One of those at the Scuttle *presented a Musquet,* the other a *Fish gig.* One from within called out *fire. Mr. Panton and I having our swords drawn, I with my sword struck the Musquet out of its Direction at Mr. Panton.* Mr. Panton came over towards me and orderd the Scuttle to be laid down, which Woodgate one of the Boats Crew did and stood upon it, to prevent their Doing any Mischief that Way. Mr. Panton and I went below to see what Mr. Peacock and the Crew had done there. *The Master att Arms had made an opening with an Iron Crow in the Bulkhead,* and having made a small one, *one from within presented a Musquet thro it, at him, ⟨threatening⟩ to the Master at Arms, threatning to shoot him.* When we went below the Roses People had seperated themselves, at each End of the Bulk head. Mr. Panton went to the starboard side, where Mr. Peacock, and some of the Crew were. I went to the Larbord side where Forbes, Silley and Sinclair were. The Man who presented his Musquet at Forbes, went over to the other side, upon which Forbes *took up his Crow and broke off a large Plank, and then gave the Iron Crow to Sinclair and took up his ⟨gun⟩ Pistol. One within presented a Musquet at Sinclair, which he snapped 3 times, the others calling out to fire damning the Peice for not going off.* Silley got hold of the Musquet, but by himself could not keep it—those within drawing it from him. *Then Silley went to Mr. Pantons side. Almost immediately after I heard the Report of a Pistol which Silley at that time said was fired by him, without Ball at the Man who threatned the Lt. so hard,* who the Man was I cant tell, being on the other side. Mr. Panton, all this time, frequently *begging of them to surrender or he must clear his Way to them. Some of them again said they would shoot Mr. Panton first. And Forbes the Master at Arms ⟨afterwards⟩ next, before they would be taken. Upon Hearing the Report of a 2d Pistoll* I turned about and saw Mr. Panton had been wounded in the Throat. I did not see the Harpoon. I saw the shape of the Harpoon upon the Throat—and [he] had fird a Pistol as I then thot, at the receiving of that Wound. Mr. Peacock was with him, and Ransford one of the Boats Crew endeavouring to stop the Effusion of Blood with their Hankerchiefs. Then went on deck. With Help of 2

Men of the Boats Crew, I carried Mr. Panton to the Briggs Cabbin, where he expird in less than 2 ⟨*Minutes*⟩ Hours. I believe the Wound I saw was the Occasion of his Death.

Qu. by ⟨*Mr. Fitch*⟩ Mr. Trail.[66] Did Mr. Panton declare he wanted to search for uncustomd Goods, when the Candle was handed down.—He did not at that Time.

Q. by me. Do you know what orders Mr. Panton had before he left the Rose, and by whom given.—No.

Q. Did Mr. Panton ask the Master if he had any favour[67] for any of his Crew and if he had he would not take him.—No.

Q. Did you hear Mr. Panton say he did not intend to have taken more than 2, but as they had hid he would take all 4.—He did not tell the Master so, *but he told the Prisoners so while the Boat was gone aboard the Rose.*

Q. Did Mr. Panton perswade the Men to go on board the Man of War.—*He told em they should have good Usage if they would go.*

Q. Did he say, after the Candle was moved about did [*he*] not say he was satisfyd there was no uncustomd Goods there. No.

Q. What arms had Mr. Panton and his Party, when they went first on board.—No Body but Mr. Panton had any when they first went on board, and he only a sword.

Q. What Arms were brot on bord the Brigg by the Boat, when she came the 2d. time?—Cutlasses, Pistolls and Musquets—how many I cant say.

Q. Any of Mr. Pantons Party used any threatning Expressions to the Prisoners, and what. *They said if they hurt any of em with their Weapons they would fire upon them. This was before the first Pistol.*

Q. Any of Mr. Pantons Party presented their Pistolls at the Prisoners, or made any Rushes at them with their swords or Hangers before the fatal Blow was given.—*They kept their Pistals in their Hands,* but the Men had no swords, and none made any Pushes.

Q. *Had all the Boats Crew Pistols.*—I cant say that. The Lt., 2 Midshipmen, the first Time, there were more than the Boats Crew [the] second Time. Boats Crew 7. 2 Midshipmen. 4 more might come the 2d. Time. ⟨*About*⟩ 10 the first Time.

Q. Were all the Persons from the Man of War below.—Not all the Time I believe. They were about the ship.

Q. *Did not the Prisoners often say they did not want to hurt him or*

[66] Robert Trail or Traill (d. 1785), Comptroller of the Customs at Portsmouth, later to be proscribed as a loyalist. Jones, *Loyalists of Mass.* 278–279; 2 Sabine, *Loyalists* 361.

[67] BA's reading. MS (apparently): "favr."

his Men, they only wanted their own Liberty?—Yes. *I dont know that I heard 'em more than once.*

Q. Whether they beggd and pleaded that the Lt. would let 'em alone.—Yes.

Q. When the Prisoners said they would die before they would be pressed, did the Lt. tell 'em *he did not want to impress 'em, but only wanted to look for uncustomed Goods.*—No.

Q. *Did the Lt. ever tell em he did not want to impress them?*—No *never in my Hearing.*

Q. Was the Opening in the Bulkhead such, that the Lt. might see into the Forepeak, whether there was uncustomed Goods there or not.—I dont know.

Q. Did you hear the Prisoners say to Lt. Panton they had nothing against his searching if he would let them alone.—No.

Q. Did they take the Candle in order to shew him there was none goods.[68]

Q. Whether the Prisoners took the Candle from the Lt. and moved it about, that he might see there was no Goods there?—Lt. desird them to take it that he might see what sort of Place they were in.

Q. Lt. said he could not see and wanted to come down.

Q. by Mr. Fitch, whether the Hold was not so full of Cargo that they could not stand upright.—In the main hold we were obligd to set down on the Salt. I was never in the forepeak.

Q. by ⟨*Mr. Auch*⟩ Judge Auchmuty. How long between the two Pistols.—I cant tell it might be a Quarter of Hour more or less. I cant tell.

Q. by Gov. Bernard. Do you know which Prisoner gave the Wound? —No.[69]

[68] Thus in MS.

[69] JA's supplementary notes (see text at note 25 above and note 95 below): "Mr. Bowen, Midshipman. Was with Mr. Panton, when he went on Board the Brigg. The Mate threw out a wharp [i.e. a line] for the Boat. Panton enquired for the Master and went down to the Cabin with him as did Mr. Bowen and Mr. Stanhope, another Midshipman. Panton enquired where the Brig came from. Master said from Cadiz loaden with Salt, for Marblehead. Mr. Panton demanded his *Bill of Lading, Clearance* and *other Papers*. Master replyed he had *no Bill of Lading* or *Clearance,* only a *Bill of Health which was all the Papers he had,* and produced it, having it in his Hand ready. Mr. Panton next enquired *how many Men he had on Board?* Master answered 6 before the Mast, besides himself and Mate. Mr. Panton asked *for his Log Book*; and *said He would order the Roses People to go down into the Hold, to search for unaccustomed Goods, or to that Purpose*; and *desired the Hatchways and Scuttles to be opened, which the Master said should be done.* Mr. Panton, Mr. Bowen and Mr. Stanhope, went upon Deck leaving the Master in the Cabin and *there desired the Mate to send all his Hands aft,* at the same Time *ordered the Roses Boats Crew to go down below and search.* The Mate said he would send what Hands

Mr. Henry Stanhope. Midshipman cozn. [cousin] of E[arl of] Chesterfield.[70]

there was aft. Panton made answer, *he must send them all.* Mate said he could not send them all aft, but he would go and call them: Mate went, and *Mr. Panton ordered Mr. Bowen to go with him. The Mate called the People, but none answered.* Mate went aft and informed Mr. Panton. *Mr. Panton then said We must search for them. Lights were got. Mr. Panton ordered Mr. Bowen with two of the Boats Crew, to go into the Hold and search for the Men,* but found nor heard none. Mr. Bowen came out of the main hold and went forward. Gibson, one of the Boats Crew said to Mr. Bowen There is a Scuttle, pointing to one before him, which Mr. Bowen ordered him and Churchill, another of the Boats Crew, to take up. Churchill taking up the Scuttle, called out, "here they are!" and desired the Men he saw to come up; they, the Brigs People, *swore bitterly,* that *the first man, who dared to approach them,* they would *cutt his Limbs off,* at the same Time shewing a *Hatchet,* a *Harpoon,* a *Musquet* and *fish Gig.* Mr. Bowen then said *his Lieutenant wanted to see them,* and *desired* they would *come upon Deck.* They swore they would not. Mr. Bowen informed Mr. Panton of what had happened. Mr. Panton, hearing it, went forward himself with Mr. Bowen and *mildly desired the People to come up, which they refused to do, swearing they would die in the Hold, before they would suffer themselves to be impressed.* Mr. Panton then said *he wanted to search the Hold, and asked them to let him come down where they were for that Purpose. They repeated to him, what they had threatned to Mr. Bowen, and shewed Mr. Panton their Weapons.* Mr. Panton desired them a second Time, to come out, adding, if they persisted in refusing he must *oblige them.* One and all of them said to Mr. Panton, if *he brought any Arms against them, he should be their Mark, and they would put his Lamp out first.* Mr. Panton ordered Mr. Bowen to *man the Roses Boat,* and send Mr. Stanhope *on Board for assistance.* Mr. Bowen returned to Mr. Panton and found him talking to the People endeavouring to *perswade 'em to come* out, *explaining the Folly* of being obstinate. They said several Times in Mr. Bowens Hearing, if *there was 50 men armed, they would not be taken,* and told Mr. Panton, *if he had any Regard for his own Life, he would let 'em pass.* He answerd it was his Duty, and he could not do it. They said they knew he was a Lt. and his orders, and desired him again to let them pass, swearing and repeating their Threats against him particularly. *Mr. Panton had a Candle in his Hand (the Place being very dark) which he gave to one of them, desiring they would let him see, thro the scuttle, what Sort of a Place it was they were in. One of 'em, took the Candle, and lighted it about the Place where they stood,* Mr. Panton said he could not see it and wanted to go down; They said he should not go down, and if he attempted it, they would that Moment shoot him; presenting their Musquet, which they said was loaded with Sluggs, and primed. Then they returned the Candle. Mr. Panton said, Aye? will you shoot me? And in a joking manner added I will take a Pinch of snuff first; and ordered Mr. Bowen to go and see if the Boat was returned. The Boat was just then come back with Mr. Peacock a Midshipman, Mr. Stanhope, Forbes the Master at arms, and Boats Crew. They all went below. Soon after, Mr. Panton orderd Mr. Peacock and Boats Crew to *open the Bulkhead of the Place, where the Briggs People were.* As soon as the Boats Crew began to work upon the Bulkhead, the Briggs People said they would shoot the first Man that made a Hole. One of them *advised the others to shoot the Lt. first* and divide themselves. 2 to defend the scuttle and 2 the Bulkhead. One of those at the scuttle, presented a Musquet, another a Fish gig and one from within *called out Fire. Mr. Panton and Mr. Bowen having their Swords drawn, Mr. Bowen with his, struck the Musquet downwards,* out of its Direction at Mr. Panton, Mr. Panton then went towards Mr. Bowen and ordered the Scuttle to be put down, which Woodgate (one of the Boats Crew) did and stood upon it, to prevent their *Doing Mischief that Way, or coming out.* Then Mr. Panton and Bowen left the scuttle and went to the Bulkhead to see what Mr. Peacock and the Boats Crew had done there. The Master

No. 56. Rex v. Corbet

Mr. Panton was Lt. of the Rose Man of War. Knows the Prisoners, saw em 22d. April last on board the Pit Packett. I went on Board the Brigg, with Mr. Panton. The Mate threw a Rope to the Boat. Lt. enquird for Master who was the Person he spoke to. We went down into the Cabin with him. Panton, Bowen and I. When below, Lt. demanded of the Master the Bills of Lading and Clearance. He informd he had none but Bills of Health. *Mr. Panton then asked for his Log Book which he produced. He then askd how many Hands he had on Board.* He anserd 6 before the Mast, besides himself and Mate. Lt. went upon Deck, the Master came up a little after. *Lt. told the Master he must let his Men search for prohibited Goods, which the Master readily comply'd with replying "very well." Lt. sent Mr. Bowen with two of the Boats Crew to search the Hold.*[71] Mr. Bowen came up and related what had happend. Lt. orderd me to stay upon deck and look after the Roses Boat. Presently Mr. Bowen came up and told me it was *Mr. Pantons orders, that I should go on board for assistance.* I went with 4 of the Boats Crew, and acquainted the Captn. with what had happend. Returnd with Mr. Peacock, and Forbes the Master at Arms and others I cant recollect *who, with Arms, Cutlasses, Pistolls, and Musketts.* On my Return I know but little of what happd after. When Mr. Bowen came up, he said there were Men aboard *who swore the first Man approached them, they would kill.*

---

at arms had begun to make an opening, with a Crow, and having made a small one, one from within presented a Musquet thro it, threatning to shoot him. When Mr. Panton and Mr. Bowen went to the Bulk head, the Roses Men were seperated at each End of it. Mr. Panton went to the starboard side, where Mr. Peacock was, with some of the Boats Crew; Mr. Bowen to the Larboard side, where Forbes, Silley and Sinclair were. The Man who presented the Musquet at Forbes, removed to the other Side upon which Forbes with the Crow broke off a Piece of Plank, then gave the Crow to Sinclair *and took up his Pistol*; again one within presented a Musquet at Sinclair which he snapt, 3 times; all the others calling out to Fire, damning the Musquet for not going off. Silley got hold of the Musquet, but by himself could not keep it, those within, drawing it from him: *Then Silley went to Mr. Pantons side* and almost immediately Mr. Bowen *heard the Report of a Pistal, which Silley says was fired by him, without Ball at the Man, that threatned the Lt. so hard, and had several Times snapt his Musquet at him; in order to frighten them and make them submit.* Mr. Panton during all this Time, frequently *begged of them to surrender or he must clear his Way to come to them.* But *all of 'em said they would shoot Mr. Panton first and Forbes after before they would be taken.*

"*Upon hearing the Report of a Second Pistol, Mr. Bowen turned about, and saw Mr. Panton had been wounded in the Throat with a Harpoon, and a Pistol had been fired at the Person who did it*, and Mr. Peacock endeavouring to stop the Effusion of Blood with his Hankerchief. P[anton] expired in less than 2 Hours."

[70] In margin: "[Learnt?] it perfectly before I came into Court." Philip Dormer Stanhope (1694–1773), fourth Earl of Chesterfield, and author of the famous *Letters*, was Midshipman Stanhope's cousin.

[71] In margin: "Q. for what."

Q. by me. *Was the Lts. order to Mr. Bowen and 2 of the Boats Crew to search the Hold for Men or for prohibited Goods.—I cant say. He told em to search the Hold for what Purpose I know not.*

Q. by Mr. Fitch. Was the orders to search presently after he told the Master he must search for Goods.—*In a short time after, but the orders were given on deck. What was said to the Master was in the Cabin.*[72]

Mr. William Peacock.

Mr. Panton was Lt. of the Rose. I knew all the Prisoners aboard the Pitt Packet 22 last April. At my first Arrival on board the Brigg, I enquird of the Mate where Mr. Panton was. He said down in the fore hatchway. I went down directly followd by the Boats Crew. I enquird the Cause of the Disturbance. *He told me that [despite] all the Arguments he could make use of, the Briggs People, 4 in Number, were down the fore Peak, and said they were resolved to die, sooner than be pressed on Board a Man of War. Mr. Panton then orderd me down the Main hold, with the Boats Crew, to force down a bulk head, which Parted the main from the forehold.*

I went down directly, *and orderd the People to break down the bulk head, which they began.* The Brigs People the Prisoners from within threatned to kill the first Person they saw. *Upon a Holes being made by our People in the Bulkhead, they presented a Piece thro that hole and snapped it 3 different times.* The People in the mean time breaking the Bulk head down. *So that in a little time I could discern 4 Persons differently armed, with Gun, fish Gig, Ax and Harpoon, still struggling to hurt our People as much as lay in their Power.* Mr. Panton then came down, and orderd the People to desist from breaking the Bulkhead down, till he had spoke to those within, the Prisoners. *He represented to em the folly of persisting vs. a superiour Number, acquainting em with the Impossibility of their Escape and promising*

---

[72] JA's supplementary notes: "Mr. Stanhope, Midshipman, says he went on board with Mr. Panton, that the Mate threw a Rope to the Boat. Panton went down to the Cabbin, Bowen and Stanhope followed. Panton demanded Bills of Lading and Clearance. Master answerd he had only Bills of Health, which Mr. Panton desired to see. Mr. Panton then [asked] for his Log Book, which he produced. Mr. Panton enquired how many Men there were on board. Master said 6 besides himself and Mate. Mr. Panton then said he must *open his Fore and After Peak, and let his Men search for prohibited Goods*, or to that Purpose. Master answerd very well. They went upon deck and the Master came up after. Mr. Panton then ordered *Mr. Bowen and 2 of the Boats Crew to go down into the Hold*, and *Mr. Stanhope upon deck to look after the Roses Boat.* Mr. Bowen came upon the Quarter Deck and acquainted Mr. Panton, that there were Men below, who swore, *the first Man who came near 'em was a dead Man.* Soon after he was sent on board the Rose for Assistance, and knows but little more."

them good Usage if they would come out voluntarily. They told him they would not, and *that they knew him to be a Lt., that the Men acted by his orders, and that the first Man that offerd to touch the Bulkhead they would do for him* (meaning Mr. Panton). *One of our Men, then hearing this threat,* ⟨snapped⟩ *fired a Pistol at the Man who told Mr. Panton so, loaden with Powder only, which must be true, as it only scorchd his Upper Lip* and made it bleed, in order to intimidate him as the Man declard. James Silley the Man. The Man Corbit said to Mr. Panton, *see what one of your Men has done pointing to his Lip.* Lt. made answer, *it was not done by his Order,* when ⟨you⟩ He meaning Corbit, *came on board the Rose he would shew him the Man that did it. In order as I suppose to get satisfaction. Lt. then askd them if they would come out and promisd them good Usage again.* They said they would not, and that the first Person that offerd to approach them they would kill him. Michael Corbit was the chief Speaker, and said this in Particular. What he said the rest generally joind in, and assented to. Lt. then gave new orders, to break down the Bulk head, which our People did as well as they could being interrupted by the Prisoners. Immediately after, Mr. Panton gave orders to stop a second time, and askd them if they would come out again. They said No. Lt. then askd one of 'em, to lend him his Ax that he might beat the Bulk head down the sooner, in a Joking manner. He within [answered] he'd lend it to scalp him. Lt. then orderd [*us*] to break down the Bulkhead. Which we were just going about, when Corbit the Prisoner at the Bar, *struck at Mr. Panton with his Harpoon.* Mr. Panton immediately said after the stroke, Peacock *"the Rascall has stabbed me, thro the Jugular Vein." I immediately fired my Pistol at the Person who wounded him, who was Corbit.* I saw his Blood spout out amazingly before I fired my Pistol.

Q. by the Govr. In what Posture was Mr. Panton?—He was sitting on the salt opposite to Corbit and was not any Ways attempting to force an Entry.

Q. by Commodore Hood.[73] I distinguishd Corbett, by the Blood on his Face.

When Silley fired the Pistol, Lt. took the Pistol from him and gave orders that no one should fire, without his orders.

Q. by Lt. Govr. Did the Prisoners discover that they heard these orders.—I did not see any Difference in their Behaviour. I cant tell whether they heard. There was a Noise, I was quite close to him.

[73] Here, as on some other occasions in JA's minutes, the answer appears without a question.

Q. by J[udge] Auch[muty]. How long between the 2 Pist[ols]—1/2 an hour I am sure it was.

Q. by Gov. B[ernard]. Did Mr. Panton ever give orders that his Men should fire at the Prisoners?—No sir. Never.

Q. by me. What Number of Men and what Arms.—A. 8 came with me and Mr. Stanhope. We brought 2 Musquetts, 4 Pistolls, and 4 Cutlaces.

Q. by me. What Threats were used by any of the Lts. Party, to the Prisoners?—The firing of the Pistol, and damning one another, but no other Threats that I heard. Mr. Panton might say they had better come out by [fair?] Means.

Q. Did you draw up your first Deposition Yourself?

Q. by J[udge] Auch[muty]. Have you any Doubt upon your Mind but that he intended to impress the People, or not?—No sir.

Q. by Lt. Govr. Whether the other 2 Men were impressd.—They were carried on board the Rose, but immediately dischargd.

Q. Did you hear the Prisoners say to Lt. they did not want to hurt him or his Men?—I heard Corbit say to Mr. Panton see here what is done? What Right has your Men to do this.

Q. Did you hear the Prisoners or any of 'em say to Lt. or any of his Party, I can fly from you no further, I must defend myself.—They said they were resolved to defend themselves.

Q. Did any of the Prisoners say they were no Deserters, and Lt. could have no orders to impress them in time of Peace.—No. Not as I heard.[74]

[74] JA's supplementary notes: "Mr. Peacock, Midshipman, says, at his Arrival on board the Brigg he enquired at the Mate, where Mr. Panton was who informed him, he was down the Fore hatchway; Mr. Peacock went down immediately followed by the Boats Crew, and asked Mr. Panton what was the Reason of the Disturbance, who told him, *the People were so obstinate, that all the arguments he could make Use of, were to no Effect,* that they had told him *they were resolved to die, sooner than be pressed on board a Man of War. Mr. Panton then ordered Mr. Peacock down the main Hold to force down a Bulkhead, which parted the main Hold from the fore hold where the men were.* He went down and ordered the Boats Crew to knock down the Bulkhead as fast as possible. When they began the Briggs People within threatned immediate Death, to the first Person they saw, and presented a Gun thro one of the Holes, which they snapp'd 3 Times. By this Time. the Bulkhead was so much down as to give an *imperfect Light of the Place.* We could observe there were 4 men in it, differently armed, with a fish Gig, Harpoon, Musquet, and ax, still threatning to kill whoever durst approach them. Mr. Panton then came down, and orderd the Men to withhold from breaking the Bulkhead till he had spoke to them within. He then represented to them the folly of persisting, against such a superiour Number, the *Impossibility of their Escape, promising them good Usage,* if they would ⟨surrender⟩ voluntarily come out. But they were deaf to all he said, told him, *they knew him to be a Lt. and the Men acted by his orders: that the first Man they saw offer to break the Bulkhead, they would do for him* (meaning Mr. Panton). One of our Men then fired a Pistol at the Man who told Mr. Panton so, loaden with Powder only, as the

Forbes Master at Arms.

I knew Lt. Panton very well. I know all the Prisoners very well, saw 'em first on Board the Pitt Packet belonging to Marblehead.

I was called and orderd to go aboard the Brigg to Mr. Pantons Assistance, which I did. I walked forward to the starboard side of the forecastle. I heard one of the Briggs Crew, call out from below, "come on you Dogs, here we are." I took off my Coat and threw it upon the forecastle, then went down below, one of the Boats Crew with me with a Light to shew me the Bulkhead, which I saw by the Light. I laid my Hand upon it. I said there was nothing to be done [without] an Iron Crow. I went up the main Hatchway to look [*for*] one. I met the Lt. He askd me where I was going. I told him I was going to look for an Iron Crow. I turnd aft and found one, and carried it down to break open the Bulkhead by Mr. Pantons orders. Lt. at the same time told me, they were well stowed forward. I gave 2 Strokes at the Bulk head with the Crow. One of the Crew, which the rest calld Corbit, by his Voice I judge, said that was all they wanted. 5 or 6 Blows made a Hole in the Bulk head so as We could see them and they us. Lt. crawld along forward. As soon as the Prisoners see him, they in general threatned him with death. And one of em whom the rest calld Corbit said Mr. Lt. I will kill you first. *And you may be sure of death if you dont go about your Business.* And at the same Time presented a Musquet at Mr. Panton. Others of the Prisoners within presentd fish Gig, Harpoon and Ax at the Lt., without the least Abuse from that Gent. the Lt. I seeing em present their Weapons, towards the Lt., I was afraid they would kill him. I call'd out to 'em, and desird em not to point their Weapons to kill so good a Gentleman as what that was for he

---

Man afterwards declared (who fird), in order to intimidate them, which must be true as it had no other Effect, than scorching the face of the Person fired at. Upon which the Man whose face was scorched asked *Mr. Panton why his Men fired at him, and desird him to look what was done.* Mr. Panton then replyed it was not done by his order, and that he would shew him the Man, when he came on board (meaning as Mr. Peacock understood) he should get Satisfaction and immediately took the Pistol from the Man, and gave strict orders *no one should fire without his Directions.* Mr. Panton then desired the Men to proceed with knocking down the Bulkhead, which they did as well as possible, being interrupted by those within, who kept presenting their Piece, and striving to hurt our Men with their other Weapons. Mr. Panton gave orders to stop, and asked those within, whether they would come out, they answerd they would not; Mr. Panton then asked one of them, *if he would lend him his ax,* to knock down the Bulkhead a little faster? who answerd he'd lend it to scalp him. *Mr. Panton then gave orders to knock down the Bulk head directly,* which we were going about, when one of those within made a *Lunge* at Mr. Panton with a Harpoon *and Mr. Peacock immediately fired his Pistol.* He stood in his former Position, for a few seconds, and then said, Peacock, the *Rascal has stabbed me in the Jugular Vein.* Mr. Peacock ran, and bound his Neck with his Hankerchief. He died in less than 2 Hours."

meant them no harm. And if you *do not leave off pointing your Weapons at him I will fire among you*, which by a Rally I made upon them I drew them to my side and I frequently presented my Pistoll to 'em ⟨to⟩ [as] it is proper a Man should preserve his own Life. One of the Prisoners, the rest called Ryan, was in the Larbord Wing with a fish Gig in his Hand. He hove it at me. The length of his Arms, not doing the Ex[ecutio]n they would have him, Corbit cryd out kill the Buger, and accused him of Cowardice for not doing it. Corbit ran to the Larboard side where he Ryan was and catchd the staff in his Hand. And he took hold of the staff and the Grain came off.[75] Upon Corbits return to the other side, he took a Musquet from another, and snapped it at one of the Boats Crew 3 times, then went to his own Quarter again. The Opening I made was so big that the wounded Man came out. It was all down to a Piece of a Plank, which Corbit made several Attempts to pull down, swearing at the same time he wanted room to kill the Lt. One of the Boats Crew with me, made 2 or 3 attempts to hall this Plank down. But a Musquet being presented at him by one of the Prisoners he catched hold of it, but not being able to keep his Grip, he flew over, to the side where the Lt. and the rest of the Gentlemen were, took up a Pistal. Corbit seeing that dard him to fire. He told him he would if he did not put his face back from the Bulk head. Fire if you dare, I will kill the first of ye. Then I heard the Pistall go off. Silly who fird it, came over to my side. Lt. call'd out, but cant say what he said. He seemd to speak hot. Silly came over to my side, with a loaded Pistall in his Hand, I know there was priming in it, there[fore] I conclude was loaded. The Prisoners after this were very hot, pushing their Weapons at Us. I called out to the Lt. and said *I must be obliged to fire to save my own Life*. He called me by my Name, and forbid me to fire more than *once, or else I'd have shot every Man of them*. At the same time, the Lt. demanded Silleys Pistal from him, Lt. thinking Silly as hot as I was. Blew out the priming and gave it to one of the Boats Crew. The next thing I observd, 2 or 3 Minutes after, was Corbit darting out a Harpoon thro the Bulk head, where the Lt. used to sit [i.e. had been sitting]. I did not see the Lt. at that Time. In a Moment as quick as possible, I heard a Pistall go off. I dont know who fird it. The Pistall was followd by a groaning in the Hold among the Prisoners. Corbit said he was shot thro the shoulder, and lost the Use of one of his Arms. Ryan said the same afterwards. I advised em to come out and get our Doctor that they might not bleed to death. Corbit said he would not. That he would die there, and bleed to death. I

[75] Grains are prongs of a fish gig. *OED.*

advised Ryan to come out, and helped him out, with a Pistal in my Hand, cockd and [primed?], they with their Weapons [threatening] to kill me if it [i.e. I] came in. They admitted me to come to the Bulkhead. One of the Boats Crew came down and said that Mr. Panton was dead. The first I heard or thot of it. I said to Corbit you are the Rascall that has killd the Gentleman and youl be hangd for it. He said he would kill me next for he believed I was an officer of Marines. I told him let me be what I would, I would have the satisfaction of putting him in Irons by and by both Leggs, which I had and if there had been 25 I would have put 'em all in. Ay says he you are Master at Arms, if I had known that I would have killd you long ago.

Q. by Govr. Was the ⟨hold⟩ Hole where the Lt. was wide eno for the Lt. to get thro.—I cant think it was. The largest Breach was at the larbord side. A Man might have got his Head thro. I saw Corbit make a Push with the Harpoon, but could not see that Lt. by Reason of a Trunk.

Q. by Prisoner Corbet. How could you see when there was no Light, the scuttles being down.—There was no Light among 'em, but we had Lights and the Planks were all clear where we were. The Light shone full upon them.

Q. by Mr. Otis. Had Lt. a sword or Pistal at the Time he fell?—To my Knowledge I never saw any Weapon in his Hand but a snuff Box.

Q. Do you remember Corbits requesting intreating the Lt. to go about your Business, and stand off?—They said go about your Business and stand off. Their constant Cry was, if we would not go about our Business they would kill.

Q. ⟨Do you⟩ Did Corbit and the rest frequently say, he did not desire to hurt him if he would go about his Business.—Not to my Knowledge.

Q. Did you consider yourself as searching for Goods, or as one of a Press Gang?—When the Lt. said they were well stowd forward, I thought there were goods. I am not to be a judge of my officers Business. I imagine it was for seizing Smugglers as well as any thing else. I am not a judge whether Lt. would have pressed them. The latter End they behavd so rough and turbulent that the Lt. I believe would take some of 'em on board the Rose.

Q. Did you hear Lt. say he would press em?—I did not that I remember.

Q. Did you frequently hear the Prisoners declare they would die before they would be impressed on board a Man of War.—I heard Corbit say, he would not go on board a Man of War. At the time when he said he was wounded, he said he would die, before he would go aboard a

Man of War. They said that all they had in the World was there and they were defending it.

Q. Did you hear em say they were in defence of their Liberty.— They might say so, I cant say I heard it. There was many Words said that I dont remember.

Q. Was you in the forepeak?—I never was there.

Q. Do you know of any uncustomable Goods that were found in this forepeak by any of this Party, or any other Part of the Vessell.—Not that ever were found to my Knowledge.

Q. Did Corbit express great Grief and Concern when he was assurd that the Lt. was killed?—No.

Q. by the Govr. B. Was it after Corbit knew of Lts. death that he said he would kill you.—Yes.

Q. by Govr. Do you believe the Prisoners heard the Lt., forbid Silly and me [76] to fire.—I do.

Q. by Govr. Did you hear Corbet complain of the first Pistall, and the Answer?—Yes. The Ball missed Corbit if there was one in it. Corbit said to Lt., see what your Men have done. Well says the Lt., come out, and you shall have what Satisfaction you please.

Q. by Mr. Otis. Are you sure there was but one Pistol dischargd before the Lt. fell.—But one.[77]

---

[76] Thus clearly in MS, although BA reads "em."

[77] JA's supplementary notes: "John Forbes, Master at Arms. Says, he heard the People after he came on Board, ⟨say⟩ call out from below, 'come on Ye Dogs, Here we are.' Forbes threw off his Coat, and went down the Main Hatchway to the Bulkhead of the Forehold, where the Briggs People were. One of the Boats Crew followed him with a Light by the Help of which, he saw the Bulkhead, and said it could not be broke down without an Iron Crow. Went on deck and found one; at which Time he saw Mr. Panton who ordered him to *go down and force open the Bulkhead.* He accordingly went, and began to work on the starboard side; the first or 2d. stroke he gave, the People within called out, 'Come on Ye Dogs, thats all we want,' to which Forbes answerd *he expected to get 4 or 5 dollars, for the Vessell yet.* With 5 or 6 Blows he made an opening in the Bulkhead, so as to see the People within. Mr. Panton then came down from the scuttle; Forbes continued to knock down the Bulk head towards the Larboard Side; *The Briggs People all the Time threatning to murder the Lt.,* when one of them called Corbit by the others, saw the Lt., thro the opening that was made, said '*Mr. Lt. I will kill you first and you may be certain of Death, if you do not go about your Business,*' at the same Time presenting a Musquet at Mr. Panton, others with a Fish Gig, Harpoon and Ax, *swearing and repeating Corbetts Threats without Intermission.* Mr. Panton all the Time gave them not the least Provocation or abuse, on the Contrary, very fair Words, Forbes desird 'em to point their Weapons at him, and not hurt a Gentleman who meant them no harm, *and told them if they continued to point their Weapons at Mr. Panton, he would fire at em,* then they made *several Pushes at Forbes, and one called Ryan, striking a Fish Gig at Forbes and not throwing it out far eno to do Execution, the others within called him a Coward and struggling to take the Fish Gigg from him, the Grain dropped from the Pole. The Person called Corbet then took up a Musquet and snapt it 3 Times at Sinclair, one of the Boats Crew, and*

Q. by Prisoner to Mr. Bowen. Did the Lt. draw his sword and thrust it down several Times into the Place where the Prisoners were? —No.

Q. by Otis to Bowen. Did you consider yourself with Mr. Panton as searching for Goods, or as a press Gang?—Ans. as searching for Goods. First I searchd for Men and then for goods.

Q. Whether any of the Party searchd the forepeak for Goods after the Men were out?—I dont know that they did. Peacock and Stanhope no. We went on board the Rose before the Men were out.

Q. to Bowen, Peacock, and Stanhope. Did you hear em frequently say they did not want to hurt em if they'd leave em.—Bowen did. The other 2 did not.

Q. Mr. Bowen. I believe at different Times I might hear em all say, that [*they*] would kill &c. Corbit said he would put his Lamp out first. And the others might say to the same Purpose. I believe some of the others did. It was not always said with the same Voice. I cant tell which took the Candle from the Lt. I am certain Corbit said he would shoot with Gun loaden with sluggs and primed, and they all joind in it. Pierce Fenning presented the Musquet, but who the fish Gig or who cryd fire I cant say. I saw no body have the Musquet but him. The same Man presented it at Sinclair, and snapped it 3 times. *Corbit said he knew him to be a Lt.* Cant say that any other did. There was a Noise.

Q. by Mr. Fitch. Whether Mr. Panton had found a Pistol or any Arms while in the Hold—main hold?—He came down unarmed without his sword. He took the Pistall from Silley [some?] time after, as mentioned before. Silly had loaded it, ⟨for⟩ the or it [*may*] have been another for the Lt. blew the priming out, and gave it to one of the Crew. He had Time to go from side to side between, for Mr. Panton called him to him.

---

afterwards at Forbes damning it for not going off. Forbes by *this Time had cleared away the Bulk head, as far as the Larboard Wing, except a Piece of Plank about Midships which Corbet tryed to pul down himself, saying he wanted Room to kill the Lt.* Mr. Panton, hearing that, said Aye my Lads? Silley who was on the Larboard side with Forbes, made several Attempts to bring down the Board. One of them within pointed a Musquet at him, which he got hold of. But not being able to keep his Hold, went to the starboard side, where Panton was, and took up a Pistall, which the Person called Corbett, seeing in his Hand *dared him to fire.* Silley made answer if he did not go back from the opening he would fire at ⟨Cor⟩ him. Corbet then said, 'Fire if you dare: *I will not go back, I will kill the first of you.*' Immediately after Forbes heard a Pistol go off, and a Person call to the Lt. and those from within, push their Weapons so hard at them that Forbes called out to *Mr. Panton he must be obliged to fire, to save his Life*; which Mr. Panton *strictly forbid him to do upon his Peril, and took a Pistoll from Silley and blew the priming out*; then Forbes saw the Person called Corbet dart a Harpoon at Mr. Panton and immediately after a Pistol go off, followed by a groaning in the Hold."

Bowen see him take the Pistal from Silley, ⟨*and blow the prim*⟩ but did not see him blow the priming out. Stanhope saw him with a sword at the scuttle, but not in the Hold, I did not see him.

Wm. Petty-grew. Physician. I saw the Body before it was buried. Soon after the Vessell came up to the Wharf. He came by his Death I suppose by the Wound he received in his Neck. About 3 Inches long, and of a triangular Figure, cut the Carotid Artery and Jugular Vein. I suppose 3 Inches in depth. There are two Jugular Veins on each side of the Neck.

Q. by me. Are the Artery and vein 3 Inches deep?—I suppose it must have penetrated 3 Inches, for the natural Elasticity of the Artery and vein would have given Way.

Robert Brice. Surgeons Mate. Knew the Lt. I saw him about 1/2 Hour before he died. His death I apprehend occasioned by a try-angular Wound in the left side of his Neck. It must have been the immediate occasion of his Neck [i.e. death]. The 2 Jugulars on the left side and the Carotid Artery were cutt thro. The Wound went down in an oblique Direction. There is an external and internal Jugular Vein. One could have known the Wound by the Instrument that gave it.

There must have been force used in drawing it back, as the surface of the Wound was lacerated.

James Silley. A private Marine. I went on board the Brigg, in the Boat—the 2d Boat. I was one that rowed. I went immediately down in the Hold with Mr. Peacock and the Master at Arms. Mr. Panton orderd Us to open the ⟨*Hold*⟩ Bulkhead.

Q. by Govr. Bernard. Did you fire a Pistall?—Yes I fired a Pistall. The Prisoners orderd us upon our Peril not to approach the appart-ment. If We did they'd kill Us. They'd be the death of the 1st Man that should attempt to break in there. The Pistall I fired, was loaded with Powder only. It was given to me, I dont know by whom, for a Pistall only with Powder. I did not load it and dont know. He dont know by whom it was given to me but believe it was the Master at Arms. I fired it at the Time when I was taking hold of the Musquet that was presented thro the Bulkhead. I dont know that I presented at one any more than another. I had no Reason for firing it, but in Confusion, with no Intention at all. I catched at the Musquet and fird at the same time with the other Hand.

Q. How near was the Mouth of your Pistoll to Corbetts face?—I dont know. It must be very nigh him, I believe, by the Explosion.

Corbit said this is not good Usage.

Mr. Panton said he would shew him the Man when he came on bord. Then a Cartridge was given me by Sinclair and I loaded the Pistall again. The Musquet was pointed thro the Bulkhead again. I seized it and kept it in my Hand for above 2 Minutes. But the Prisoners got it from me, 2 of em. I soon went over to the Larboard side where the Master at Arms were. The Lt. demanded me to give him the Pistol. Accordingly I did. I then assisted the Master at Arms in breaking down more of the Bulkhead with Pretence of getting in. The Prisoners then desired us to keep off upon their Peril for they would not be pressed. I remember Corbit very well. The others said keep clear Gentlemen at your peril for We will not be pressed. Corbit then said ⟨Mr.⟩ you Lt. stand clear if you dont I'le be the death of you. The Lt. made answer you may depend upon it if you kill any one you'l be hanged for it. They Corbit then often attempted shoving thro with the Harpoon, the whole of em desiring Us to stand clear. Soon upon it I heard another Pistall go off and the Cry of a Man. Looking about I saw the People all going out of the Hold and no one there but I and the Master at Arms. Sometime after Gibson came out and said the Lt. was dead. The Prisoners said it was no such thing.

Q. Mr. Panton said he gave no orders to fire.

Q. by Pris[oner]. Did We not tell em We wanted nothing but our Liberty, and not to hurt any of their People?—I heard some of them say they wanted nothing but their Liberty and would hurt nobody if they did not hurt them.

Q. Whether some of the Boats Crew did not say, if We did not come out they would blow our Brains out or shoot us.—I believe there was Words of the Kind passed of both sides. A great deal of that.

Q. Did not I give the Prisoner, a Piece of Bread and say that I wanted not to hurt him or any Man.[78]—Yes.

Q. by me. The Lt. said he had a Deputation to search and would search there. That [...].[79] The Prisoners said there was no prohibited Goods there.

Q. Did the Lt. or any of his Party search in any Part of the main Hold for prohibited Goods.—I did not see em.

[78] The word "Prisoner" is an apparent inadvertence. See testimony of the Marine, Wilks, text following note 100 below, which indicates that it was the prisoners who made the offer of food.

[79] The MS apparently reads "alls," which makes no sense. BA's text reads "also." Presumably, the following sentence is an answer by the witness, but even this is uncertain.

Q. Did you apprehend your Business was to search for prohibited Goods or to impress Men.—I understood that I came on Board in order to [help] Mr. Panton to search for prohibited Goods or to impress Men as he gave orders.

John Bembridge.

Mr. Fitch's Application of the Evidence.

Of the Utmost Importance to society that Murder should be punished.

Shall only state the Evidence summarily.

Mr. Panton an Officer of the Customs, duly authorized to make Searches and Seizures. The Commissioners here authorized by Act of Parliament, to issue commissions. This Commission issued to the officers of the Navy.[80]

As a Custom House Officer he had Authority to go on board any Vessell to search. He went on board, and demanded Papers and Leave to search. The Master readily consented.

Masters explicit consent to search a material Circumstance.

He found the Men, and insisted that they should come out and said he wanted to search that Place for prohibited Goods.

No threatnings on the Part of Mr. Panton. On the contrary he spoke in the mildest and most persuasive manner.

No arms when he went down the hold. Threatning Language from Prisoners. A Pistoll. Mr. Pantons Disapprobation. The Pistoll 1/2 hour before the fatal accident.

Corbit one of the Persons that threw the Harpoon that killed the Lt. They were all active, stimulating one another, and all equally concerned, tho Corbit gave the mortal blow.

Lt. was in the lawfull Discharge of his Duty, and the explicit consent of the Master for this Purpose. Any opposition to him therefore was illegal. The opposition being illegal he was not obliged to give back. No threatnings on the Part of Mr. Panton, by which the Prisoners could apprehend Danger to their Lives—tho they had apprehensions of being impressed.

The Pistolls not fired by him, but vs. his express orders.

The last Pistol after the Wound was given, Peacock saw the Blood.

---

[80] Panton's commission has not been found. As to the powers of naval officers generally, see No. 51, note 1. The Act of Parliament referred to is 7 & 8 Will. 3, c. 22, §6 (1696).

Lt. Governor says he did not see the Blood, till after he fird. The Register has taken it otherwise.[81]

The Threatnings of Prisoners levelled at Mr. Panton himself. We will put your Lamp out first. This shews Malice vs. himself in particular. Why should they single out this Person any more than others.

If any Person is singled out, it is Malice, tho in an Affray.

I will consider the apprehensions the Prisoners were under and the Effect of this upon the Evidence. They were under Apprehension of being impressed. But Mr. Panton did not say he would impress 'em. Ans. Mr. Bowen said, the Lt. told Prisoners he would take em all.[82]

How far this can excuse? Justify I apprehend it cannot.

I am considering, how far the Prisoners Apprehensions could affect the Crime. I think it could not affect the Crime att all, as he was acting under a legal Authority to search for Goods.

What Effect the Firing the 1st Pistol, can have upon the Crime? I apprehend it can have very little weight, as it was done without order, and the Lt. expressly disapproved it.

Lt. unarmed, in such a Position and attitude that he could not be in a Condition of Offence.

Q. Whether these Circumstances can soften the Crime down from Murder to Manslaughter, or whether they are not Proof of Malice forethought.

Law. A Question whether the Court are to proceed by the civil Laws or by the Rules of the Common Law. I apprehend the Crime is the same by both Laws. The same essential Distinctions in both. The voluntarily taking away Life, Dolo malo, with Malice forethought. Manslaughter is not by Name in the civil Law, but the civil Law makes the same Allowances to the Infirmities of human Nature.

Discretionary in civil Law, what Punishment to give to sudden Killing. By 27. H. 8. and 11. & 12. W. 3. compard, taking em together I apprehend no safer Rule can be proceeded by than to proceed by the common Law and this has been the Practice.

I shall confine myself to the Rules of common Law.

[2] H.H.P.C. 16. 17. Q. Whether the statute does not restore Clergy.[83] The offender is to have his Clergy. Lt. Governor said some

[81] These two sentences are apparently a colloquy between Hutchinson and Fitch over Peacock's testimony, Fitch referring to the testimony taken by the Register of the Court of Vice Admiralty. See text at note 17 above. For Peacock's testimony, see text following note 72 above.

[82] Apparently JA's comment. See text following note 67 above; see also note 91 below.

[83] 2 Hale, *Pleas of the Crown* 16–17, discusses 28 Hen. 8, c. 15 (1536): "The

Cases that would be Manslaughter at common Law would be punishd with death by civil Law.

1. H.H.P.C. 455. 457. Implied Malice. Kills without Provocation.[84]

A Bailiff, Constable or Watchman. No lawful Warrant. Capias Distringas.[85] 9. Co. 68.[86] Same Book 458. A Bailiff Jurus and Conus. Pew said stand off. Bailiff laid hold. Pew killd. Murder.[87] A similarity in these Cases. If Lt. had a Right to enter any Part of the Vessell, he is equally under Protection of Law as any other officer, and opposing him is at the opposers Peril.

458. Bailiff, Cook. Cook bid him depart. It was Manslaughter in defence of his House no felony.[88] Tho Lt. might pursue his Authority in an illegal Manner, yet it would be manslaughter. No greater Effect than that, it must be left to the Court whether so great. Should the

offender excluded from clergy; but quære, whether the statute of 1 Edw. 6 c. 12 (1547) does not restore it even in this case." The statute Hale mentions, "An Act for the Repeal of Certain Statutes Concerning Treasons and Felonies," abolished clergy for certain offenses (not including killing on the high seas) and in the same section (§10) specifically allowed clergy "in all other cases of felony other than such as are before mentioned."

[84] 1 Hale, *Pleas of the Crown* 455: "Concerning Murder by Malice Implied Presumptive, or Malice in Law." "When one voluntarily kills another without any provocation, it is murder, for the law presumes it to be malicious." *Id.* at 457: "The second kind of malice implied is, when a minister of justice, as a bailiff, constable, or watchman, etc. is kild in the execution of his office, in such a case it is murder. If the sheriff's bailiff comes to execute a process, but hath not a lawful warrant . . . if such bailiff be kild, it is but manslaughter, and not murder."

[85] *Capias* is a writ ordering the sheriff to take the body of the defendant; a *distringas* orders the sheriff to take goods of the defendant to compel his appearance. Black, *Law Dictionary*. "[I]f a process issuing out of a court of record to a sergeant at mace, sheriff, or other minister, be erroneous, as if a *Capias* issue, when a *Distringas* should issue, yet the killing of such a minister in the execution of that process is murder." 1 Hale, *Pleas of the Crown* 457.

[86] Mackalley's Case, 9 Co. Rep. 65b, 68a, 77 Eng. Rep. 828, 833–834 (1612). This supports the point in note 85 above.

[87] 1 Hale, *Pleas of the Crown* 458: "A bailiff *jurus & conus* had a warrant to arrest *Pew* upon a *Capias*, and came to arrest him, not using any words of arrest, *Pew* said, *Stand off, I know you well enough, come at your peril*, the bailiff takes hold of him, *Pew* thrusts him through; it was ruled murder, tho he used no words of arrest, nor shewed his warrant, for possibly he had not time." Rex v. Pew, Cro. Car. 183, 79 Eng. Rep. 760 (K.B. 1631).

[88] 1 Hale, *Pleas of the Crown* 458: "A bailiff having a warrant to arrest *Cook* upon a *Capias ad satisfaciendum* came to *Cook*'s house, and gave him notice, *Cook* menaceth to shoot him if he depart not, yet the bailiff departs not, but breaks open the window to make the arrest, *Cook* shoots him, and kills him; it was ruled, 1. That it is not murder, because he cannot break the house, otherwise it had been, if it had been upon a *Habere facias possessionem*. 2. But it was manslaughter, because he knew him to be a bailiff. But 3. Had he not known him to be a bailiff, or one that came upon that business, it had been no felony, because done in defense of his house." Rex v. Cook, Cro. Car. 537, W. Jones 429, 79 Eng. Rep. 1063, 82 Eng. Rep. 225 (K.B. 1639). A *Habere facias possessionem* is a writ directing the sheriff to put the plaintiff in possession of a given piece of realty. Black, *Law Dictionary*.

Court think, that am[ount]s to Manslaughter, I see no reason vs. punishing by the civil Law.

Our Witnesses.

Thomas Power. Master of the Brigg.

⟨*. . . Panton said to me The Man of War.*⟩

Q. Did the Man of War hail you before the Lt. came on board.— The Rose fired 2 Guns and hailed us by a Trumpet and order[ed] us to lie to after which Lt. Panton came on board. He enquired for the Master. I told him I was Master of the Vessell. Then he asked me for my Clearance. I told him I had none. He replyed you must certainly have some Papers. I told him I had no other Clearance but a Bill of Health and a Bill of Lading as it was a foreign Port, from whence I came, and we took no Clearance therefrom. He asked me for the Bill of Health which I produced. *He then asked me for a List of my Men.* I produced him my shipping Book. He asked me, if I would walk down into the Cabin. When he came down *He asked me where my People were.* I told him I did not know. Then he called for *Pen and Ink*, and for the Logg Book, and took down the Peoples Names, and he then ordered some of his Party to go and *seek for my People, ⟨then he⟩* and *turn em up* from below. Then he asked me to open my Lazaretto [89] scuttle for em. I told him I would. After he had taken my Peoples Names, he asked me if I had any particular Person, that I wanted a favour done him, let him know his Name, *he would put a Mark against it and when he came upon deck, he would not take him.* I told him I had one Man that was married, and I tho't it was very hard to take him. He said by no means he would not take ⟨*any*⟩ no married Man, for he had orders to take None that was married.[90] *He asked me if I had any more Hands aboard, but what was in the List.* I answered no. Then he desird me again to tell him if I had any more, for if he *found more aboard it should be worse for me.* While he and I were talking, some of his Men came and told him, that they found out the Men, that they were hid in the forepeak, and would not come out. Then he left me in the Cabin, and went upon deck, and I never saw no more of him, till he was brought up, by some of his Men out of the Hold.

---

[89] A place parted off at the fore part of the 'tween decks in some merchantmen, for storing provisions and stores. *OED.*

[90] "The two men belonging to the brig not mentioned in the above account [i.e. the men not in the forepeak], were Americans, they remained on deck the whole time the Rose's people were on board her; the Commodore, out of his great goodness, having given orders, that no American or person married in America, should be pressed." *Boston Chronicle*, 1 May 1769, p. 139, col. 2.

Q. What Condition was he then in?—He was wounded in the Neck on the left side. I perceived an Effusion of Blood. He might live an Hour or an Hour and half. Speechless when he came up.

Q. Was you present when orders were given for the Boat to go on Board the Rose for more Men and arms? Declare all you know.—I was upon Deck when orders came up, to send the Cutter on *Board and bring the Cutter, properly manned and armed*. When the Cutter returned the Roses Men jumped in, upon the Briggs Deck. Some with their Pistolls cocked and some with their Cutlasses drawn. Some of 'em enquird, particularly the Master at Arms, enquired *where the Dogs were, and said they would soon have 'em out*? They then went down between decks to the Lt. All of them, but one Man, left to take Care of the Boat. In a little time afterwards, one of their Men came up upon deck to me, said he was sent by the Lt., (Charles Rainsford now present in Court) for some Tools, to cutt the Bulk head thro, and if *I refused sending them, that he the Lt., would confine me.* I told him I had none. If they could find any, about the Vessell, *they may make Use of them.*

Q. by Mr. Otis. Did Lt. Panton demand a search of your Vessell as a Custom House officer?—No.

Q. Did he demand a search for the Men?—He did not demand a search for them of me, but orderd his People to go and search for them.

Q. For what Purpose did he search. Declare all you know.—I imagined it was to impress em. He said his orders were to take but 2 but as they had hid, he would take the whole four.

Q. Did he say any thing to you about his being a Customs House Officer, or his Having a Right to search for Goods from first to last.—No sir.

Q. Did you ever hear him give orders to any of his People to search the Vessell for prohibited or uncustomd Goods.—No.

Q. What did the Prisoner Corbit say, when he first saw the dead Body of the deceased in the Cabin door?—When he came to the Cabin Door and saw the Lt. dead he shed Tears, turned about to the Marine and said to him, you Rascall, you are the Instigation of this Gentlemans death, and said you are the Person that fird at me.

Q. by the Govr. Did Lt. behave civilly or uncivilly, to your observation?—He behaved civilly to me.

Q. by me. What Country men were your two foremast Men who were not in the forepeak?

Q. Were they Inhabitants of Marblehead, and had they families.—

One had a family in Marblehead, the other was an Inhabitant there.

Q. Were them 2 Men both pressed and carried aboard the Man of War afterwards the same day.—Yes. They were taken away. They were returned before night. I was not requird to settle their Wages, which I take to be the common Practice.

Q. Did one of those 2 Men, deliver you the Key of his Chest and desire you to deliver his Chest to his Wife at Marblehead before he went on Board the Rose?—Yes.

Q. by Com[modo]r[e]. When the Lt. desird you to unlay the Lazaretto scuttle, did he give any Reason for the Request.—No.

Q. by Mr. Trail. Did he ask you what Goods you had aboard?—Yes. I told him Salt.

Q. Did the Lt. say he should take no Americans?—Yes.[91]

Hugh Hill Mate of the Pitt Packett.

On the 22d April we met a ship standing out of the Bay. ⟨*as to the firing before, confirms the*⟩ Bet. 6. and 7 o clock they fired the Gun, and soon after, fird another. We bore down Under the Lee. They hailed Us, told us to bring too, and with our Head the same Way that they were, untill they would send there Boat aboard. Their Boat came on Board, with the Lt., 2 Midshipmen, and seven Men. The Lt. asked for the Master of the Vessell, who was then present. He asked him for his Papers. He told him he was from a foreign Port, he had only a Bill of Health, in Case of being put into another Port, and his Bill of Lading. Lt. asked him for his shipping Book, and asked him to go down into the Cabin with him. They remaind in the Cabin 7 or 8 Minutes, and the Lt. came upon deck again, with the shipping Book in his Hand, asked me if I was Mate of the Vessell. I told him I was. He told me to call our Men to answer to their Names. I ⟨*told*⟩ called to em to come

[91] JA's supplementary notes: "Thos. Power, Master. 22nd. April. 4 leagues from Cape Ann. The Rose fired 2 Guns, and bro't us to. Lt. and two Midshipmen came on board, in the Cutter. Asked me for my Papers and my Clearance. I said I had none, coming from a foreign Port, except a Bill of Health and a Bill of Lading. Then he asked for *a List of my Men*. I brought up my Shipping Book and shewed him. He then desired I would *go down* in *the Cabbin* with him. I did. He there *took an Account of the Peoples Names*, and asked *where they were*? I answerd I know not. He then asked me to order my People to *open the Lazaretto*. I told him it should be done. *While he and I were talking together he ordered* his People to *go and search* and *get my Men*. He then asked me if I had any *particular favour* for any Man. He *would not take him*, but he would *set a Mark* against his Name. He then said He would have taken only 2, but as they had hid themselves, *he would take them all four*. Then a Midshipman or Man came down, and told him, he had *found the People out* and that they had *hid, in the forepeak* and *would not come out for them*. Then the Lt. went upon Dick, and I saw him no more alive."

aft and answer to their Names. The 2 that were upon deck came aft. The Lt. looking upon the Men, seeing no more come but them 2, looked steadfast upon me, and said Go sirrah and turn your People up, *or I shall take you.* I said sir you may use your Pleasure. At that Instant he took up his Sword from our Companion [92] where he had laid it, ⟨*and went forward*⟩ drew the sword, and left the Scabbard and belt and went forward, and went down into the Forecastle, where the Prisoners were. He said My Lads, you had better come up. *I shall take but 2 of you. You shall have an equall Chance.* They replyed they would not. I heard a Number of Voices. Cant say they all spoke. They told him, they would not be impressed, that they would defend themselves, and they told him to keep off from them, *they did not want to hurt him, nor any of His People.* He called to Mr. Stanhope, one of the Midshipmen, to take 4 Hands in the Cutter, and go on board for more Men and Arms, and to have the Cutter properly armed. He then replyed to the Prisoners, that he had often known as stought [93] fellows as you [94] but by God I will have *you all.* He was down below the Upper deck, I was on the Upper deck, the scuttle open, between us, I leaning with my Head over the scuttle. I then went aft. Soon afterwards, he sent up to know if the lower deck Hat[ch]ways was open? I told him that came up, that *all the Hatches and Scuttles in the Vessell were open*, excepting that where the Boat stood. Soon after, he sent for Lights. I orderd the Cook to light Candles for him. Soon after they got the Light the 2d. Boat came aboard, with a Number of Men Armd. The Master at Arms, and Mr. Peacock, came out of the Boat first. The Master at Arms, ⟨*swearing*,⟩ saying "damn the Rascalls where are they? *I'le have them out Immediately.*" The Master at Arms went down forward, Mr. Peacock following, who orderd his Men to follow him. They went down. Soon after there came a Man up, asked for the Master, told him he wanted the Tools belonging to the Vessell, if he did not deliver em the Lt. would confine him. He told him, he did not know where they were, if they could find 'em they might take 'em. They found an Adz, and a Crow Bar, and went down into the Hold again with the Tools. In a short space of Time, I heard a Pistol go off. About 7 or 8 Minutes after, one of the People who came from below, told me that one of our Men was wounded. In 8 or 10 Minutes after, I heard a 2d. Pistall go off, and in 4 or 5 Minutes after, Mr. Peacock came up and hailed the Rose, and told em for Gods sake to send the

[92] That is, the wooden hood placed over the entrance or staircase to the master's cabin. *OED.*

[93] BA reads this as "tough."

[94] Apparently written over "they."

Dr. on board the Lt was wounded. They bro't the Lt. to the forescuttle, and I lent a hand to carry him down into the Cabin. The Dr. came to him. After the Dr. had been with the Lt., He came out of the Cabin, some of the People, asked him to dress the wounded Man, (meaning John Ryan). He answerd let the Rascall bleed and be damn'd. He ought to have a Brace of Balls drove thro his Head. The Man remaining in his Gore, till he was carried on board the Man of War. After they had placed sentries over Corbit James Silley a Marine, told Mr. Newcomb and me, that he fired a Pistol in Corbits face, thinking to make him retreat. Some of the People then after the Lt. was dead made mention that the Lt. was a Customhouse Officer. Our Master asked me if I had seen his shipping Book. I told him No. I went and asked the Midshipmen if they had seen the shipping Book. They told me No. They said they would search the Lts. Pocketts for it. They went down into the Cabbin and took his Papers all out of his Pocketts in my Presence. The shipping Book was not in his Pockett. When the Master of the Rose came on board to search, ⟨he brought a Deputation⟩ The Monday following, viz. the 24th., He brought a Deputation ⟨to search⟩ as a Custom House officer and shew it to Captn. Power. Captn. Power said He need not read it. The Vessell was all open he might search. There was no Parchment in his Lts. Pocketts, when his Papers were taken out. I examind all his Papers particularly, to find the shipping Book.—The Commission being shown him [i.e. Hill] he says it was not there.

Q. Did Lt. Panton deceased from the time of his coming on board the Pit Packett to the Time he fell, make any Demand on Captn. Power, in your hearing, or of any other belonging to the Pit Packett, to suffer him to search the Vessell as a Custom House Officer for uncustomed Goods?—No.

Q. Did the Lt. with his Party, from the Time of his coming on board the Pit packett to the time he fell, conduct him and themselves, in all Respects, merely as a press Gang?—Yes. I understood it so, and had very good Reason, when he told me, he would take me on board the Man of War, if I would not turn the men up!

Q. How long was the Lt. on board the Brigg, before he fell.—It might be 2 Hours, as near as I can judge.

Q. What Part of those 2 Hours was taken up in the forceable Attack upon the forepeak, where the Prisoners had retreated?—The whole Time, excepting what was spent with the Captn. and him, in the Cabbin and on deck, which might be 10 minutes in the whole.

Q. With What Weapons was this Attack made, and what Methods

used by the Lt. and his Party to break into the forepeak. Declare all you know.[95]

Answer. Crow, Adz, Pistolls and Cutlaces, I suppose, that were carried down.

Q. What was said by the Officers, or People of the Man of War, to the two of your Men, when they were orderd into the Boat, ⟨after the Lts. fall,⟩ in order to be carried aboard the Rose.—I dont know I want upon deck.

Q. What did the Officer find on the 24th.—He found our stores, some Bottles of Wine, and some loose Lemons, 5 or 600, in a Barrell, nothing else. He seized the Vessell, put the Broad Ar[row] on the Mast.[96]

Q. by Corbet. What did Corbit say when he first came up and saw the Lt., and what did he say and how behave?—Thro my Perswasion he came up. I told him it would be much better for him. He asked me if I would advise him for [what?] I thought was best for him. I told him I would not give him advice to his Prejudice. He came up and went into the Cabin, seeing the Corps, Tears came from his eyes, He turnd round and saw the Soldier that fird the Pistol upon him. Said you are the Rascall that is the occasion of this Gentleman loosing his Life. He said in the forepeak he did not believe the Lt. was dead.[97]

[95] At this point in the MS are stitched in the eight leaves of rough notes in JA's hand, headed "Witnesses for the Prisoners. Thos. Power, Master. Hugh Hill Mate, John Ronay and James McGlocklin Mariners, on board the Pitt Packett." The second part of the notes is headed "Witnesses against the Prisoners." In the present arrangement the text of these notes has been divided up and each witness' remarks appended as footnotes to the full record of his testimony. See note 25 above.

[96] The "broad arrow" (↑) was, in this connection, the sign that a vessel had been seized for violation of the Customs Acts. See note 8 above. The letter of the Commissioners of Customs ordering the *Pitt Packet* admitted to entry at Marblehead listed her cargo, including three small kegs, two cases, one-quarter barrel, and twenty-seven bottles of wine; sixteen bottles of champagne; three kegs of gin; and three-quarters of a barrel of "lemmons." Commissioners to Salem Customs Officers, 27 April 1769, Salem Custom House Record Book, 1763–1772, fols. 280–281, MSaE.

[97] JA's supplementary notes: "Hugh Hill Mate. Like the Masters [*testimony or, more likely, deposition*] till—I heard the Commander of the Rose, order Captn. Power to heave too, and lay his Head as theirs was, which he did. Then like the Master untill He went down into the Cabin, with the Master. In 5 minutes he came upon deck, and asked me, *if I was Mate? I told him I was.* He told me to *call the People* to *answer* to *their Names.* 2, who were upon deck came aft. He asked me *where the rest of* the People were? I told him, I did not know. He then told me to go, and *turn the People up* from below, or *he would take me.* Use your Pleasure. Then *his People came and told him, the Briggs People* was down in the *Forecastle in the Peak.* He then went down into the *Forecastle,* and said to the Men in the Peak, *my Lads, you had better come up.* They ⟨said⟩ told him *no,* and *to stand off,* and that they did *not want to hurt him or his Men.* He told them, that he had seen as *stought Fellows* as they, and *by God he would have them out,* and called his Midshipman, to take *4 Hands in the Boat,* and go on board the ship for *more Men* and *Arms,* and

John Roney. Mariner on Board the Brigg.

The Cutter came aboard and Lt. and two Midshipmen, and 7 Men. Lt. enquird for the Master. Lt. went below with the Master. He came up with the shipping Book in his Hand, and told the Mate to call the People. The Mate said there was 2 forward and call[ed] 'em accordingly. Lt., looking upon the shipping Book calls Michael Corbet, then he calls John Roney. I answerd to my Name. One of the Roses People came and told the Lt. the Men were down in the Fore peak. Lt. went forward, immediately. Took his sword drawn along with him. Lt. ⟨told⟩ asked the Prisoners to come up. The Prisoners answerd they would not. Lt. made Answer He would have them up. They said they did not want to hurt him or his People they wanted nothing but their Liberty.

Some Time after the Lt. bid one, go aboard the Boat and fetch more Men, and bring the Boat armed and the Master at Arms.

When the Cutter returnd again I hove her a Rope. They had a great many Arms and there was Mr. Peacock and the Master at Arms. The Master at Arms, ⟨*hove off*⟩ took a Pistall in one hand cockd as I thought and a Cutlass in the other. He jumped aboard the Brigg and says, "By Jesus I'le have these Dogs out." Immediately speaking again "where is these Bugers." He went down the forecastle with his Pistoll and Cutlace, I did not hear any more of him for about 30 Minutes. First Thing I heard was the Report of a Pistoll. Mr. Stanhope, standing Centry over the Forecastle scuttle, told me, one of our People was wounded. About 5 or 6 minutes afterwards I heard another Pistol go off. About 4 or 5 minutes afterwards I heard the Lt. had got a deadly wound.[98]

---

to *bring the Cutter, properly armed.* They came on board, and they called for *Lights,* which were given them. Lt. sent a Midshipman up and *demanded Tools, to break down the Bulk Head,* and if they did not deliver Tools *he would confine the Master.* Master said he had no Tools, if they could find any, they might take them. They found an *Adz* and a *Crow bar.* In a short Space of Time after, I heard *a Pistall go off,* and our People told me, *one of our People was wounded.* In 6 minutes after, I heard *another Pistal go off.* Immediately after they said the *Lt. was dead.* Midshipman hailed the ship, and called for the Dr., who came &c. and was asked to dress the wounded Man. He said let the Dog die and be damned. One of their Marines said, he *fired a Pistol in Corbetts face by order of the Lt.,* thinking to make him retreat, which he would not."

[98] JA's supplementary notes: "John Ronay, Mariner. As the Master. After the Lt. came up from the Cabin, I saw him have the *Shipping Book* in his Hand, and he asked the Mate, *where the People were?* Mate replyed, 2 of 'em were forward, and *looking over the* Shipping Book, Lt. called for *Michael Corbit,* and then for *John Ronay.* I answered to my Name. *A Man of Wars man came up and said, one of our People had drove a Pair of Grains thro his Trowsers.* Upon that the Lt. went forward, and talked to em, and said '*My Lads come up,*' and they said they would not come up from where they were. He said then *he would force them up.* They replyed *they did*

James McGlocklin. Cook on board the Brigg.

I was down in the steerage, and the Lt. desird me to get him a Light. I did. Desird me to shew him the Way twixt Decks forward. I shewd him the Way and car[rie]d the Light in my Hand. Lt. asked the Prisoners if they would come up. They replyd they would not. He said it would be better for 'em. *If they would not he would make them.* They said they would not, they were Freemen born free, and would not go aboard a Man of War. *He said He would have em. For Men he came for and Men he would have.* Lt. said if they would come up he would not hurt any of them. *They said say [99] would not, they would stand in their own Defence they did not want to hurt no Body.*

I went aft into the steerage again untill the Boat came on Board 2d. time with more Men and more Arms. Lt. called for another Light. I got it, and carried it forward to him. Heard him say that he had seen as stout Men as them come out very easy before now. They replyed to him they were none of them sort of Men. He said to them I'm *the Man that will bring you out.* Then I went aft. Lt. calld after me to shew him the Hatchways, which I did. Then the Master at Arms came directly with his Cutlace and Pistoll, and askd me for a Crow bar. I told him I did not know where to find one. He ⟨takes⟩ lookd and found a Crow bar. Then says he where's these Buggers, I'le have them out. Lt. and He and the rest of their People went down in the Hold and I went away into the steerage. Presently after I heard a Pistoll go off. One of the Men of Wars men came up and told me one of our People was wounded. Soon after, 4 or 5 Minutes I believe, I heard another Pistoll go off. Presently I see the Wounded Man, John Ryan come out crawling over the Water Casks. Askd me to help him. Beggd of me to get him Water he was faint, &c. Soon after I heard the Lt. was killed.

Q. Did you ever hear Lt. or any of his Party demand leave to search for Goods or say any Thing about it.—No.

Q. Did they behave merely as a press Gang?—Yes, and I never suspected they had any other Design. I saw Lt. have his sword.[100]

---

not want to hurt him, or any of his Men. Then he orderd a Man to hail the ship, and a midshipman did hail her and I got him the Trumpet to hail her. Lt. told one of the Midshipmen to go on board and fetch Men and Arms, and the Master of Arms, who came, and jumped over the Ruff trees and *swore by his Saviour,* that he *would have 'em up,* asking *where are the Dogs?* One of their People made answer they are *down here in the forepeak.* He went down in the forecastle scuttle into the Hold, and in about 20 minutes *I heard a Pistal go off.* A Midshipman told me one of our People was wounded. *About 5 minutes after,* I heard *another Pistall go off,* and about *6 minutes* afterwards I heard the Lt. *was killed.*"

[99] "they"?

[100] JA's supplementary notes: "James McGlocklin. Lt. ordered me to give him a

No. 56. Rex v. Corbet

Edward Wilks. A private Marine on board the Rose.

Q. Did you place the Sentries over Corbit, on board the Brigg after the Lt. was killd?—Yes.

Q. How did he behave and what Conversation had you with him about the unhappy Accident.—The Centrys were planted and I went down to see if every Thing was quiet. I found Disturbances on both sides. I beggd of the Prisoners at the Barr, Ryan excepted to behave in a better manner, for the Lt. was kil'd. They made me answer, that they could not believe it. For they did not mean any Harm to any one without it was them that came armed against them, and further told me, that if I would lay down my Arms, they would lay down theirs, and I might be welcome to eat or drink with them. I made em answer, that I did not choose any Thing of the sort. Corbit desird me, to go to Mr. Hill the Mate, and ask him, as to send em something to stop the Wound, for he was shot. Accordingly I went up. He went down.

Charles Raynsford. A Seaman, on board the Rose. Came [*in*] the first Boat, with the Lt., and was down in the Briggs Hold with him. In going down the Hold, ⟨*I heard Mr. the Master at*⟩ Mr. Peacock was the Head officer, and the Master at Arms. There was orders given to break open the Bulk head. The Prisoners said the first Man that made a Hole they would be the death of him. Presently after a Hole was made. The Prisoners never hurt any of em that made it, tho the Hole was large eno, to have hurt em with their Weapons. Some time after, the Lt. came down, when he came down I did not really see him. The Lt. took my Pistall from me. Mr. Peacock was close by. I made answer I cant stand here with a naked Cutlace only. With that I drew back. Lt. orderd somebody, to go upon deck and fetch an Ax. I went up to the Captain, Power and I asked him for an Ax. I saw the first Pistal that

---

Light, which I did, and to go forward with it to the Forecastle. The Lt. was there, *talking to the People in the forepeak.* He told them to *come out,* for it would be better for them. They said they would not. He said he would *have 'em out.* They told him to stand off, for they did not want to hurt him, or his Men. Then I went aft. Heard Lt. order a Man to hail the ship and to take the Cutter, and *go on board to get more Men and Arms.* Upon the Mens coming on board he ordered me to get another Light and go down into the Hold, and showed him the main Hatchway. *The Master of Arms asked me to look for a Crow bar, to break down the Bulk head,* where the People were. He looked himself and found one, by the Water cask, and carried it down in the Hold. After that I went into the Steerage, and sat there some time and heard a Pistoll fired. Presently after that a Man of Wars man came up and told me, that one of our People, was wounded. Soon after that I heard another Pistoll and saw Jno. Ryan coming in the Steerage, and helpd him over the Water Casks. Then he asked for Water and Cloths, and said he was faint. A few minutes after that, a Report came up that the Lt. was dead, &c."

was fird run close to his face and fird. Corbit said Gentlemen you have wounded me. Corbit askd the Lt. by what Authority he fird at him.

Q. Did you hear Mr. Panton say he wanted to search for uncustomd Goods?—No. I did not.

Capt. Robert Calef. 30th of April, Mr. Bowen came to my House. I said to him an unhappy Accident happd on board the Brigg. How did it happen?—I was as nigh the Man that kill'd the Lt. as the Lt. was when he was killed. I askd him how the affair was. He told me the Man had given him all the fair Warning imaginable and it was Lts. own fault, and they had talked together, the Lt. and Prisoners, while the Boat was gone for.

VI. ADAMS' ARGUMENT AND REPORT[101]

Special Court of Admiralty, Boston, June 1769

But, the first Question that is to be made, according to my Opinion, is, whether Impresses in any Cases, are legal? For if Impresses are always illegal, and Lt. Panton acted as an Impress Officer, Michael Corbitt and his Associates had a Right to resist him, and if they could not otherwise preserve their Liberty, to take away his Life. His Blood must lye at his own Door, and they be held guiltless. Nay I think that Impresses may be allowed to be legal, and yet Corbit might have a Right to resist. To be more particular, when I say Impresses may be legal, I mean that the Lieutenant or other officer who Impresses, may not be liable to any Action of false Imprisonment at the suit of the Party, or to any Indictment at the suit of the Crown, for an Assault, or Riot. The Custom may be admitted to extend so far, and yet it will not follow, that the Seaman has not a Right to resist, and keep himself out of the officers Power, if he can. And whatever may be said of the Antiquity of the Custom, &c. it is very remarkable, that no statute has ever been made to establish or even to approve it, and no single Judgment of any Court of Law can be found in favour of it.[102] It is

[101] In JA's hand, in his Admiralty Book, Adams Papers, Microfilms, Reel No. 184, continuing Doc. II. Printed in 2 JA, *Works* 528–534. It is impossible to say accurately how much of this document is JA's notes for actual trial use and how much is his subsequent embryonic report. See text at note 24 above. See also note 50 above.

[102] This contention is subject to qualification: "It is quite certain that the Crown had the power to impress mariners for the navy. The statutes of the Long Parliament which provided for their impressment practically assume this. There is no recital in them that impressment is contrary to the liberty of the subject; and ... they would have contained such a recital, if Parliament had thought the practice illegal."

found in the Commissions of the Admiralty, and in Warrants from the Admiralty, but no where else.

However the General Question concerning the Legality of Impresses may be determined I humbly conceive it clear, that in America, they are illegal. And that by a particular statute. I mean 6. Ann, c. 37, §9.[103] "No Mariner, or other Person who shall serve on Board, or be retained to serve on Board any Privateer, or *trading Ship or Vessell*, that shall be *imployed* in *any Part of America*, nor any Mariner or other Person, being on Shore in any Part thereof, shall be *liable* to be *impressed or taken away*, or shall be impressed or taken away, by any *officer* or *officers*, of or belonging to any of *her* Majestys Ships of War, impowered by the *Lord high Admiral*, or any other Person whatsoever, unless such Mariner shall have deserted &c.[104] upon Pain that any *officer* or *officers* so impressing or taking away or causing to be impressed or taken away, any Mariner or other Person, contrary to the Tenor and true Meaning of this Act, shall forfeit to the Master, or owner or owners, of any such Ship or Vessell, twenty Pounds, for every Man he or they shall so impress or take, to be recovered with full Costs of Suit, in any Court within any Part of her Majestys Dominions."

This Statute is clear, and decisive, and if it is now in Force, it places the Illegality of all Impresses in America, beyond Controversy. *No Mariner on board any trading Vessell, in any Part of America, shall be liable to be impressed, or shall be impressed, by any officer, impowered by the Ld. Admiral, or any other Person.* If therefore this Statute is now in Force, all that Lt. Panton did on board the Vessell was tortious and illegal, he was a Trespasser from the Beginning, a Trespasser, in coming on board, and in every Act that he did, untill

---

4 Holdsworth, *History of English Law* 329. "[T]he compulsion of men to go beyond or upon the sea, or otherwise imprisoning them, or compelling men to take *prest* money, or otherwise imprison them hath been, I Confess, a practice long in use." 1 Hale, *Pleas of the Crown* 678. And, for a thorough contemporary review of the law, see Rex v. Broadfoot, Foster, *Crown Cases* 154 (Recorder's Court, Bristol 1743). Mr. Recorder (later Mr. Justice) Foster admitted that he knew "of no Statute now in force, which directly and in express Terms impowereth the Crown to press Mariners into the Service. And admitting that the Prerogative is grounded on immemorial Usage, I know of no Necessity for any such Statute." *Id.* at 168. Authority to impress was usually conveyed by Admiralty warrant issued pursuant to Orders in Council. *Id.* at 154–155. No warrant in the name of Panton, or Captain Caldwell of the *Rose* has been found. Since the Crown did not urge the warrant as a basis for Panton's actions, there may have been none.

[103] "An act for the encouragement of the trade to America" (1707). The emphasis is JA's. Quotation marks supplied.

[104] JA omits: "from such ship of war belonging to her Majesty at any time after the fourteenth day of *February*, one thousand seven hundred and seven."

he received the mortal, fatal Wound. He was a Trespasser in going down below, but especially in firing a Pistall among the Men in the Forepeak. It is said that the Lt. with his own Hand discharged this Pistall directly att Michael Corbitt but the Ball missed him and wounded the Man who was next him in the Arm. This therefore was a direct Commencement of Hostilities, it was an open Act of Pyracy, and Corbit and his associates had a Right and it was their Duty to defend themselves. It was a direct Attempt upon their Lives. And surely these unhappy Persons had a Right to defend their Lives. No Custom House officer, no Impress officer has a Right to attempt Life. But it seems that a second Pistall was discharged and wounded Corbit in his Cheek, with Powder before the fatal Blow was struck. What could Corbit expect? Should he stand still and be shot? Or should he have surrendered, to a Pyrate? Should he have surrendered to the Impress?

But it has been made a Question whether this Statute of 6. of Ann is now in Force? It has been reported as the Opinion of Sir Dudley Rider, and Sir John Strange, that this Statute expired with the War of Queen Ann.[105] These are venerable Names, but their Opinions are Opinions only of private Men. And there has been no judicial Decision to this Purpose, in any Court of Law, and I trust never will. Their Opinions were expressed so very concisely, that there is great Room to question whether they were given upon the whole Act, or only on some particular Clause in it. Supposing these Opinions to extend to the whole Act, I have taken Pains, to discover what Reasons can be produced in Support of them. And I confess I can think of none. There is not the least Colour, for such an Opinion. On the Contrary, there is every Argument, for supposing the Act perpetual.

1. It is a good Rule, to consider the Title of an Act, in order to ascertain its Construction and operation in all Respects. The Title of this is "An Act for the Encouragement of the Trade to America." Encouragement of the Trade to America, is [the] professed Object, End and Design of this Law. Is this Trade, only valuable in Time of War? If the Trade to America existed and was carried on only in Time of War,

---

[105] Dudley Ryder (1691–1756) was attorney general of England, 1737–1754; John Strange (1691–1754) was solicitor general, 1737–1742. *DNB.* In 1740, they signed a joint opinion: "We have perused the several clauses in the American Act, and by comparing the several clauses together, it seems to us, that the Act is not now in force, but expired at the end of the war." Chalmers, *Opinions* 232. See also Clark, "The Impressment of Seamen in the American Colonies," in *Essays in Colonial History Presented to Charles McLean Andrews* 198, 212 (New Haven, 1931). In 1716, Sir Edward Northey, the attorney general, had given an identical opinion. Chalmers, *Opinions* 232.

the Act made for the Encouragement of it must expire when the Trade expired, at the End of the War. But the Trade did not expire with the War, but continued after it, and therefore, the Encouragement given it, by this Act, continued and survived too. This is of equal Importance in Peace as in War, and there is stronger Reason why it should be incoured by exempting Seamen from Impresses, in Peace than in War, because there is not the same Necessity for impressing seamen in Peace, as there is in War.

2. The Preamble furnishes another Argument to prove the Act perpetual. "For *Advancement* of the Trade of her Majestys Kingdom of Great Britain, to and in the several Parts of America."[106] This is one End of this Law. Is not this End as beneficial and Important in Peace as in War? Has there been a Year, a Day, an Hour since 1707 when this Act was made when the Trade of Great Britain, to and in the several Parts of America, was of less Consequence to the Nation, than it was at that Time? Surely the Advancement of the British American Trade, is a perpetual object. It is no temporary object or Expedient, it has lasted these 60 Years, and I hope will last 1000 longer.

3. For the Encrease of Shipping and of Seamen, for the Purposes mentioned before in the Preamble, is another End of this Law. Now shipping and seamen are usefull and necessary to a commercial Nation, in Times of Peace as well as War.

4. Some Clauses in this statute are in their Nature temporary, and limited to the Duration of the War. §2. 3. 4. 5. 6. 7. 8. &c.[107] Others are expressly limited to the Continuance of War as §14. "during the Continuance of the present War"[108] and §19. during the Continuance thereof[109] and §21.[110] But §9. and §20,[111] are not by the Nature of them limited to War. They are not expressly and in Terms limited to Years, or to War.

5. If it is not now in force why is it bound up in the statute Book? And why was not the whole Act limited to Years, or to War.

---

[106] JA omits: "for the further encouragement of her Majesty's ships, and private ships of war, the annoying and diminishing the wealth and power of her Majesty's enemies in those parts, and for the encrease of shipping and of seamen for these and other services."

[107] These sections concern prize procedure.

[108] §14 concerns privateers.

[109] §19 relaxes "during the continuance of this present war, and no longer," the requirement of the Navigation Act, 12 Charles 2, c. 18, §1 (1660), that privateers and trading ships must have a British master and a crew three-fourths British.

[110] §21 relaxes "during the continuance of the present war" the requirement of the Navigation Act, 12 Car. 2, c. 18, §1 (1660), that all British ships be British-built.

[111] §20 concerns naturalization of foreign seamen serving in British ships.

If it is once established as a Fact that Lt. Panton acted in the Character of an impress officer, not in that of an officer of the Customs; and if it is also established as Law that no officer has a legal Right to impress a seaman; our next Enquiry must be what the Rules of the civil Law are, relative to Homicide in Cases of Self Defence. Self Preservation is first Law of Nature. Self Love is the strongest Principle in our Breasts, and Self Preservation ⟨*the most important Duty,*⟩ not only our unalienable Right but our clearest Duty, by the Law of Nature. This Right and Duty, are both confirmed by the municipal Laws of every civilized Society.

2. Domat. 638. §6. "He who is attacked by *Robbers*, or by *other Persons*, that are *armed in such a manner*, as to put him in *Danger of his Life*, in Case he does not defend himself, may kill the Robber or the aggressor, without any fear, of being punished as a Murderer." [112]

Woods Inst. civ. Law. 270. "Necessary Homicide is when one for the Defence of his own *Life* kills the Aggressor. This may be done without expecting the first Blow, for that may make him incapable to defend himself att all. But this ought not to exceed the Bounds of self defence.[113] The manner of self Defence, directs that you should not kill, if you can by any means escape," &c.[114]

Cod. Lib. 9. Tit. 16. 2. "De eo, qui salutem suam defendit." "Is qui *aggressorem* vel quemcunque alium, in dubio vitæ discrimine constitutus occiderit, nullam ob id factum, calumniam metuere debet." "3. Si quis *Percussorem*, ad se venientem *gladio repulerit*, non ut homicida tenetur: quia *defensor propriæ salutis in nullo peccasse videtur.*" "4. Si, (ut allegas) latrocinantem peremisti: dubium non est, cum qui inferendæ cædis voluntate præcesserat jure cæsum videri." "Liceat 46 cuilibet aggressorem, nocturnum in Agris, vel obsidentem vias, atque insidiantem prætereuntibus, impune occidere, etiamsi miles sit: melius numque est bis occurrere, et mederi, quam injuria accepta vindictam perquirere."

"Note 46. Homicida non est, qui aggressorem, in vitæ discrimine constitutus, interficit nec primum ictum, quis expectare debet, quia irreparabilis esse potest." [115]

[112] 2 Domat, *Civil Law* 638. Quotation marks supplied in this and following citations by JA.
[113] JA omits: "Now those bounds may be observ'd with respect to the *manner*, the *time* and the *cause*."
[114] Wood, *New Institute of the Civil Law* 270. JA omits: "for you are bound to fly if it may be without danger. Neither is such flight ignominious even in a *Soldier*."
[115] Justinian, *Codex*, bk. 9, tit. 16, "§2. Of those who defend their own safety. He who, when in danger of his life, kills his aggressor or anyone else, should have

Gail. Page 503. Pœna homicidii corporalis, nunquam habet locum, nisi in Homicidio voluntario, quando homicidium, ex proposito, destinata voluntate, et quidem *dolo malo* commissum est. Debet enim verus et expressus intervenire dolus, &c. Et hoc usque adeo verum est, ut etiam lata culpa, non æquiparetur dolo, &c. Dolus non præsumitur regulariter, &c. Quapropter dolum allegans, eum probare debet, &c. Natura enim bona est, a suis Principiis. Ex hac principali Regula, quod videlicit Pœna ordinaria, in Homicidio requirat dolum, multa singularia, et quotidie usu venientia inferri possunt. Et primo, quod Homicidium, cum moderamine inculpatæ tutælæ commissum non sit punibile puta, si quis provocatus se cum moderamine inculpatæ tutælæ defendat, et aggressorem occidat: talis enim Homicida non puniri, sed plene absolvi debet, idque triplici ratione confirmatur. Primo quod Defensio sit Juris naturalis, et omni Jure permissa. Deinde quod Aggressor, sive provocans, non ab alio, sed a seipso occidi videatur. Et per consequens, quod provocatus non censeatur esse in Dolo. Tertio, quia occidens ad sui defensionem, non committit maleficium, cum vim vi repellere liceat, et ubi non est Delictum, ibi Pœna abesse debet.

Et regulariter ex communi opinione, Aggressus, præsumitur omnia facere ad sui defensionem, non autem ad Vindictam Necessitas, Doli Præsumptionem excludit, &c. &c. Ratio, quia *necessaria Defensio*, omni Jure, etiam divino permissa et sine peccato est. Defensio autem moderata, sive cum moderamine inculpatæ tutelæ dicitur, quando quis non potuit aliter se ab offensione tueri &c.

Præsumitur autem in Discrimine Vitæ quis constitutus, eo ipso, quod ab alio, armata manu, et Gladio evaginato aggreditur, *terror ille armorum* aliquem in Vitæ Discrimen adducit, &c.

Sed quid si provocatus *modum inculpatæ tutelæ excedat, et Aggressorem in fuga occidat*, an Pœna ordinaria legis Corneliæ &c. plectendus sit? Minime, sed extra ordinem, Judicis arbitrio, ratione excessus puniri debet, &c. Ratio, quia ut paulo ante dictum, in provocato non

---

no fear of prosecution on this account." "§3. When anyone kills another who attacks him with a sword, he should not be considered a homicide, for the reason that the defender of his own life is not held to have committed an offense." "§4. If (as you state) you have killed a robber, there is no doubt that it will be decided that you have lawfully killed him who had the intention of depriving you of life." See 15 Scott, *Civil Law* 29–30.

The editors have translated the material following "Liceat" as follows:

"It is lawful (46) to kill with impunity one who attacks by night in the fields, or blockades the highways, and lies in ambush for passersby, even if he be a soldier. For indeed it is doubly better to attack, than for an injury suffered to be healed, and to seek vengeance.

"Note 46. He is not a murderer who, in peril of his life, kills an attacker, nor ought anyone to wait for the first blow, because it might be irreparable."

præsumitur Dolus, et animus occidendi, aut Vindictæ studium, sed potius Defensionis Necessitas. Nec etiam fugere tenetur, si fuga ei Periculum Vitæ adferret. Provocatus enim tanquam intenso dolore commotus, non est in plenitudine Intellectus: metus improvisus, instantis Periculi tollit Rectum Iudicium, et consilium deliberandi, et ideo dicunt DD. quod provocatus non habeat Stateram in manu, ut possit dare ictus, et Vulnera ad Mensuram &c. Puniendus igitur provocatus pro isto excessu, non ut dolosus, quia provocatio præcedens a dolo excusat, sed ut culpabilis, &c.

Adeo autem defensio favorabilis est, ut etiam tertius, puta, Amicus, provocati, si intercedendo, aggressorem occidat, excusetur a Pœna ordinaria.[116]

[116] Andreas Gail, *Practicarum observationum tam ad processum judiciarum præsertim imperialis cameræ quam causarum decisiones pertinentium* 503–506 (Cologne, 1721). The editors' translation follows; passages omitted by JA, except omitted citations, appear in brackets:

Corporal punishment of homicide never takes place except in the case of voluntary homicide, when the homicide is perpetrated by design, deliberately, and also with malicious intent. A genuine and express evil intent ought to appear [in such a case, for the punishment of the Lex Corneliae on murder to apply]. And this is always true—to such an extent that even gross fault is not equated to evil intent. [And this is the first extension of this original rule. Secondly, it is extended so that it may apply to statutes imposing capital punishment for homicide, which statutes receive an interpretation at common law. Therefore, they are to be understood to concern homicide committed with evil intent. Hence it is considered the rule in offenses requiring evil intent, that in the absence of evil intent an offense is not committed, at least for purposes of corporal or ordinary punishment.] Evil intent, [moreover,] is not regularly presumed. Therefore he who alleges evil intent ought to prove it [since one is clearly presumed to be lacking in evil intent until the contrary be proved]. For nature lacks evil intent from its origins, [and as its origins are, so its later development is presumed to be. Moreover, evil intent is proved by various circumstances—by place, time, type of weapons, violence itself. And evil intent is regularly presumed from an illegal act—when someone does an illicit thing by that fact alone he is judged to be of evil intent.] From this first rule, that plainly an ordinary penalty in homicide demands evil intent, many unique things which are becoming matters of practice can be inferred. And the first of these is that homicide which has been committed with the excuse of guiltless self-defense is not punishable: for consider the case where a person is provoked and defends himself with the excuse of guiltless self-defense and kills the aggressor—such a murderer ought not to be punished but fully absolved, and this is confirmed on three grounds: First, because defense belongs to natural law and is permitted by every legal system, [which we share with dumb animals.] Secondly, because if the aggressor is the provoker, he is considered slain by his own hand and not by another [and consequently the provoked party is not judged to be of evil intent]; thirdly, because the person killing does not perpetrate an evil deed in defense of himself, since it is lawful to meet force with force, and where there is no offense, then there should be no punishment.

And the rule of common opinion is that a person who has been attacked is presumed to do everything in his own defense and not for revenge: necessity rules out the presumption of evil intent. The reason is that necessary defense is allowed by all law—even the divine—and is without sin. Moreover, defense is considered reasonable if with the excuse of guiltless self-defense, when a person could not defend

No. 56. Rex v. Corbet

Page 509. Sexto infertur, quod Homicidium Calore Iracundiæ per-
petratum, non puniatur Pœna ordinaria, quod est intelligendum de
Iracundia lacessita, quando quis ab alio verbis injuriosis, ad Iram
provocatur, nam eo casu ita excusat Pœna ordinaria &c. quo pertinet,
quod supra dictum est, hominem intenso dolore permotum, non esse
in Plenitudine Intellectus, &c.[117]

Maranta Page 49. Pars. 4 Dist[inctio] 1. 77. Hoc patet, quia Homi-

himself from mishap in any way other [than in the manner by which he defends
himself, as, for example, if, having been placed in peril of his life, he defends himself in the best way that he can, the one who challenged him is not slain unjustly].
Moreover, someone is presumed to have been placed in a position of peril when he
is attacked by another man who has arms in hand and his sword unsheathed by this
very fact, that fear of weapons puts anyone in such a position.

[Therefore, in order to obtain absolution or withdrawal of the accusation of the
homicide committed, the person provoked ought to plead clearly the two most
important items, namely the provocation and the necessary defense, and prove them
by way of purgation and innocence.]

But what if once provoked he goes beyond the manner of guiltless self-defense
and slays the attacker who is in flight? Would he then have to be punished by the
ordinary punishment of the Lex Corneliæ [concerning murderers]? Certainly not—
rather, he who has exceeded reason ought to be punished by the decision of a judge
in a manner other than that laid down by the law. The reason is that, as stated a
while ago, evil intent and the intent to kill are not presumed to exist in the person
provoked, nor is an eagerness for revenge presumed, but rather the need for defense.
Nor is he even bound to flee, if flight would bring him in danger of his life: for a
person provoked, just as one moved by intense vexation, does not have complete
possession of his faculty of understanding: unexpected dread of impending danger
removes correct judgment and prudent deliberation: and therefore the commenta-
tors say that the man provoked does not have scales in his hand to measure blows and
wounds.

[Wherefore it is relevant, that when it is a matter of excusing wrongs, a principle
—and not a conclusion—is sought.] Therefore the provoked person ought to be
punished for that excess, not as a person of evil intent (since the previous provocation excuses him from evil intent) but as one guilty through fault [(since he exceeded the reasonable limits of guiltless self-defense)].

Moreover, defense is likewise favored, as even where a third party, for example, a
friend to the provoked man, is excused from the usual punishment if he intercedes
and slays the attacker.

[117] Gail, *Practicarum observationum* 509. The editors' translation follows;
passages omitted by JA, except omitted citations, appear in brackets:

Sixthly, it is inferred that homicide committed in the heat of anger is not to be
punished in the ordinary way because inquiry must be made as to wrath which has
been provoked, when someone is provoked to anger by another man because of
damaging language: for in that case he is thus excused from the ordinary punishment. [And it is necessary to investigate what was the nature of this proneness to
anger which has deprived the wrongdoer of reason: for angry men are wholly upset
in the mind and lack the use of reason and know not how to speak and cannot use
their senses, and have so much trouble speaking that they are consequently presumed to lack evil intent, and the will to inflict harm arises from an excessive
proneness to anger, which an armed wrath, so to speak, feeds.] Wherefore it is
relevant, as stated above, that a man who has been spurred by intense vexation is
not in full possession of his understanding. [Further, it is most difficult to control
righteous vexation of the mind.]

cidium commissum per culpam, dicitur crimen extraordinariam, et punitur pœna arbitraria, &c. Ubi si maritus occidit uxorem deprehensam in Adulterio, non punitur pœna mortis, sed alia pœna corporali mitiori; et ratio est, quia tale Homicidium dicitur culposum, et non dolosum, ex quo difficile fuit temperare justum dolorem cum ergo ex prædictis appareat, quod homicidium culpa commissum puniatur pœna arbitraria et extraordinaria; sequitur de necessitate quod non potest Judex imponere Pœnam mortis, quæ est pœna ordinaria; &c.[118] Sed vid. Ld. Ray. 1496[119] and Barringtons Observations on the Statutes page 54, bottom, Note.[120]

So much for the Distinction between Homicide with Deliberation and without Deliberation, according to the civil Law, which [is] analogous to that of the common Law between Murder and Manslaughter.[121] But, the Case of these Prisoners does not require this Distinction. I am not contending for the Sentence of Manslaughter, against my Clients. I think they are intituled to an honourable Acquittal. They have committed no Crime whatever, but they have behaved with all that Prudence And Moderation, and at the same Time with that Fortitude and Firmness that the Law requires and approves.

Mr. Panton and his Associates and Attendants, had no Authority for what they did. They were Trespassers, and Rioters. The Evidence must be carefully recapitulated, their Arms, Swords, Pistals, &c. their Threats and Menaces. Pantons orders for more Men, his orders to

[118] Robertus Maranta, *Praxis, sive de ordine judiciorum ... vulgo speculum aureum et lumen advocatorum* 51 (Cologne, 1614). The editors' translation follows; passages omitted by JA, except omitted citations, appear in brackets:

This is evident, because homicide perpetrated by fault is said to be an offense which the law does not cover and is punished with discretionary penalties. Whenever a married man slays the wife he has caught in an act of adultery, he is not given the death penalty but another milder corporal punishment; and this is because this sort of homicide is said to have been committed through fault, but not with evil intent, since it occurred in a situation in which it was difficult to control righteous indignation. [For in his guilty frame of mind there was an element missing due to the justification, and so he is punished more mildly than the man with a guilty frame of mind.] Therefore, since it appears from the aforesaid that a homicide perpetrated through fault is to be punished by a penalty that is discretionary and out of the ordinary course, it necessarily follows that a judge cannot impose the death penalty, which is the ordinary punishment [for in his discretionary judgments a judge can never impose a punishment like an ordinary punishment for a similar wrong].

[119] Rex v. Oneby, 2 Ld. Raym. 1485, 1496, 92 Eng. Rep. 465, 472 (K.B. 1727). *Held*: Killing after aroused passions have had reasonable time to cool is murder.

[120] See text at note 140 below.

[121] JA made this point at somewhat greater length, citing the authorities in notes 115–120 above, in a footnote to the published version of his argument in the trial of the British soldiers. See No. 64, note 218. He also used this argument again before a Special Court of Admiralty in Rex v. Nickerson, No. 57.

break down the bulk Head. Their Execution of these orders, their fetching the Adz and the Crow, but above all their Discharge of a Pistal, right in the face of Corbit, which tho loaded only with Powder, wounded him so badly in his Lip, these Circumstances are abundantly sufficient to shew who was the first Aggressor, and to shew that the Lives of the present Prisoners were in danger. What could Corbit think? when a Pistol had been presented at his Mouth and discharged, loaded he knew not with what. It had wounded him, he knew not how badly. ⟨*He had reason to suppose*⟩ He saw a desperate Gang of armed Sailors, before him, other Pistals, cocked and presented at him, and his Companions, their Heads and Breasts, drawn swords in the Hands of some, continual Threats to blow their Brains out, could he expect any Thing but Death? In these Circumstances what could he do? but defend himself, as he did? In these Circumstances what was his Duty? He had an undoubted Right, not merely to make a push at Lt. Panton, but to have darted an Harpoon, a dagger thro the Heart of every Man in the whole Gang.

If Mr. Panton came as a Custom house Officer, and it may be true that he came in Part, to search the Ship for uncustomed Goods, he had a fair Opportunity to do it. He ⟨*ordered*⟩ asked and was told, that the Hatchways were open. He ordered the Lazaretto open and it was done, and after this instead of searching for uncustomed Goods he proceeds directly to search for Seamen.

The Killing of Lt. Panton was justifiable Homicide. Homicide se defendendo.

1. Hawkins 71. §[14], middle. "The Killing of dangerous Rioters, by any private Persons, who cannot otherwise suppress them, or defend themselves from them, inasmuch as every private Person seems to be authorised by the Law to arm himself for the Purposes aforesaid." [122]

Same page §21. "A Woman [*who*] kills one who attempts to ravish her, may be justified." [123]

Page 72. §23, towards the End, "It seems that a Private Person, and a fortiori an officer of Justice, who happens unavoidably to kill another in endeavouring to defend himself from, or suppress dangerous Rioters, may justify the fact, inasmuch as he only does his Duty in Aid of the public Justice." [124]

§24. "I can see no Reason why a Person, who without Provocation is assaulted by another in any Place whatever, in such manner as

---

[122] 1 Hawkins, *Pleas of the Crown* 71.
[123] 1 Hawkins, *Pleas of the Crown* 71.
[124] 1 Hawkins, *Pleas of the Crown* 72.

plainly shews an Intent to murder him, as by discharging a Pistall or pushing at him with a drawn sword, may not justify killing such an Assailant."[125]

Page 75. §14. "Not only he who on an assault retreats to a Wall, or some such Streight beyond which he can go no further, before he kills the other, is judged by the Law to act upon unavoidable Necessity: But also he who being assaulted in such a manner and such a Place, that he cannot go back without manifestly ind[ang]ering his Life, kills the other without retreating at all."[126]

Keyling. Page 128. Bottom. "It is not reasonable for any Man that is dangerously assaulted, and when he perceives his Life in danger from his Adversary, but to have Liberty for the Security of his own Life, to pursue him that maliciously assaulted him; for he that hath manifested that he hath Malice against another is not fit to be trusted with a dangerous Weapon in his Hand."[127]

Keyling. Page. 136. Top. Buckners Case. Imprisond injuriously without Proscess of Law, &c.[128]

Page 136. 3. Bottom. "3dly. If a Man perceives another by force to be injuriously treated, pressed and restraind of his Liberty, tho the Person abused, doth not complain,[129] &c. and others out of Compassion shall come to his Rescue, and kill any of those that shall so restrain him, [*that is*] Manslaughter."[130]

Keyling. 59. Hopkin Huggetts Case, who killed a Man in attempting to Rescue a Seaman impressed without Warrant.[131]

2. Ld. Raym. Queen vs. Tooley & als. The Case of the reforming Constables. Holt. 485.[132]

[125] 1 Hawkins, *Pleas of the Crown* 72.
[126] 1 Hawkins, *Pleas of the Crown* 75.
[127] Reg. v. Mawgridge, Kelyng 119, 128, 84 Eng. Rep. 1107, 1111 (Q.B. 1706).
[128] The Protector v. Buckner, Style 467, 82 Eng. Rep. 867 (U.B. 1655), cited in Reg. v. Mawgridge, Kelyng 136, 84 Eng. Rep. at 1114. *Held*: Stabbing upon provocation of false imprisonment is not within the Statute of Stabbings, 1 Jac. 1, c. 8 (1603), and hence the prisoner is entitled to clergy.
[129] JA omits: "or call for Aid or Assistance."
[130] Reg. v. Mawgridge, Kelyng 119, 136, 84 Eng. Rep. 1107, 1114 (Q.B. 1706).
[131] Rex v. Hugget, Kelyng 59, 84 Eng. Rep. 1082 (Newgate Gaol Delivery 1666). *Held*: Killing while attempting to rescue man impressed without a warrant is manslaughter.
[132] Reg. v. Tooley et al., 2 Ld. Raym. 1296, 92 Eng. Rep. 349; *sub nom.* The Case of the Reforming Constables, Holt K.B. 485, 90 Eng. Rep. 1167 (Q.B. 1709). Constable arrests a woman without a warrant; prisoners attempt to rescue her; constable calls deceased to aid him; one of the prisoners kills deceased. *Held*: Manslaughter, because constable was not acting within his authority, and the prisoners had sufficient provocation to attack him. "[I]f one be imprisoned upon an unlawful authority it is a sufficient provocation to all people out of compassion; much more where it is done under a colour of justice, and where the liberty of the subject is

No. 56. Rex v. Corbet

Holt. 484. Maugridges Case.[133]

Foster. 312. 316. Vid. Foster 292 the smart &c. for Manslaughter. Also 296.[134]

A Question has been started by Sir Francis Bernard, whether, (as there is no Distinction between Murder and Manslaughter, in the civil Law,) the Court can allow Clergy, if they find the Prisoners guilty of Manslaughter? i.e. whether the Court can do any Thing but pass sentence of Death and Respite Execution, and recommend them to Mercy? He said he had formerly attended at the Admiralty sessions in England, and had heard it said by the Court, that Clergy was expressly taken away by these statutes from Manslaughter, and the Court could not grant it.

But see a Paragraph in Foster to the Contrary. 288.[135]

In this Case, I shall not make a Question whether Corbit and others are guilty of Murder, or of Manslaughter. I am clear they are guilty of Neither. All that they did was justifiable Self Defence, or to use the Expressions of most Writers upon Crown Law, it was justifiable and necessary Homicide, se defendendo. This will be fully shewn, by a particular Examination of the Law, and of the Evidence.

But it may not be amiss to consider, the observation of Sir Francis, in order to remove the Clouds from his Brain. 1. It is total Ignorance to say there is no Distinction between Murder and Manslaughter, in the civil Law, as appears abundantly, already.† [136] 2. I say that Clergy is not expressly taken away by the statutes, from Manslaughter. By the 28. H. 8. all Felonies are to be tryed according to the Common Course of the Laws of this Land. What is the common Course of the Laws of the Land, relative to Manslaughter, which is a Felony? It has its Clergy. It is true the Word Manslaughter is once mentioned in the statute of H. 8. Every Indictment found, &c. of Treasons, Felonies Robberies, Murthers, *Manslaughters*, or such other offences, &c. then such, order, &c. Judgment and Execution, shall be had, as

invaded it is a provocation to all the subjects of England." 2 Ld. Raym. at 1301, 92 Eng. Rep. at 352; see also Holt K.B. at 489, 90 Eng. Rep. at 1169.

[133] Reg. v. Mawgridge, Holt K.B. 484, 90 Eng. Rep. 1167 (Q.B. 1706).

[134] Foster, *Crown Cases*, discusses, at 312 and 315–316, Reg. v. Tooley, note 132 above; at 292, Reg. v. Stedman (unreported) (Old Bailey 1704), in which one who killed a woman after she struck his face with an iron patten was *held* guilty of manslaughter only, because of the "smart" of his wound; at 296, Reg. v. Mawgridge, note 127 above. At this point in the MS appears the narrative set out in text following note 50 above.

[135] Foster, *Crown Cases* 288–289; JA sets out the text at note 142 below.

[136] See text at notes 115–121 above. The dagger appears in the MS, and refers to the text at notes 139–144 below.

against such offences upon Land.[137] What is the Judgment vs. Manslaughter upon Land? They have their Clergy. §3. For Treasons, Robberies, Felonies, Murthers, and Confederacies done at sea, the offenders shall not have Clergy. Here Manslaughter is dropped. So that Clergy is not taken from Manslaughter by this Act.

By 11. and 12. W. 3. Piracies, Felonies and Robberies, are mentioned, but Manslaughter is not. The Word is not in the whole statute. It was needfull to mention it in that of H. 8. because the Tryal was to be by the Law of the Land, and it clearly has its Clergy. But by this statute the Tryal, and Judgment and Sentence were to be all by the civil Law, where the Offence that is called Manslaughter by the common Law, is never punished with death. But it is observable that Clergy is not taken away by this statute from any Crime.

By 4. G. c. 11, §. 7. any Pirate Felon or Robber, within the 11. and 12. W. may be tryd in the manner and Form of 28. H. 8. and shall be excluded Clergy.[138] We see that whenever the Tryal is to be by a Jury and the common Law, Clergy is excluded, from such Crimes as were not intituled to it upon Land, and the Reason was because it is a known Rule of Law, that when the Legislature creates any new felony, it shall be intituled to Clergy if not expressly taken away. Doubts might arise, whether making Crimes at sea Felonies, was not creating new felonies, and so they would be intituled to Clergy. To avoid this the Clause was inserted.

† Sed vid. Ld. Ray. 1496.[139] And especially Barringtons Observations on the Statutes page 54, bottom. Note.[140]

Barrington. 54. "By the Law of Scotland there is no such Thing as Man Slaughter, nor by the civil Law; and therefore a criminal indicted for Murder, under the Statute of Henry the Eighth, where the Judges proceed by the Rules of the civil Law, must either be found guilty of the Murder or acquitted."

Ld. Ray. 1496. "From these Cases it appears, that though the Law of England is so far peculiarly favourable (I use the Word peculiarly, because I know no other Law, that makes such a Distinction between Murder and Manslaughter) as to permit the Excess of Anger and

[137] An accurate condensation of 28 Hen. 8, c. 15, §2 (1536).
[138] 4 Geo. 1, c. 11, §7 (1717). See text at notes 52–53 above.
[139] Rex v. Oneby, note 119 above.
[140] Barrington, *Observations upon the Statutes* 54 note (k). The text appears in JA's next paragraph. JA used this and the passage from Lord Raymond in a footnote to the published text of his argument in the trial of the British soldiers. See No. 64, note 218. Quotation marks have been supplied here and below.

Passion (which a Man ought to keep under and govern) in some Instances to extenuate the greatest of private Injuries, as the taking away a Mans Life is; Yet in these Cases, it must be such a Passion, as for the Time deprives him of his reasoning Faculties;"[141]

Foster 288.[142] If taking general Verdicts of acquittall in plain Cases of Death per Infortunium, &c. "deserveth the Name of a Deviation, it is far short of what is constantly practised at an Admiralty sessions, under 28. H. 8 with Regard to offences not ousted of Clergy by particular Statutes,[143] which had they been committed at Land, would have been intitled to Clergy. In these Cases the Jury is constantly directed to acquit the Prisoner; because the Marine Law doth not allow of Clergy in any Case, and therefore in an Indictment for Murder on the high seas, if the fact cometh out upon Evidence to be no more than Manslaughter, supposing it to have been committed at Land, the Prisoner is constantly acquitted."

Observations on Statute 422. Note (z). "I have before observed, that by the civil Law, as well as the Law of Scotland, there is no such offence as what is with us termed Manslaughter: The Scotts, therefore might have apprehended, that if not convicted of Murder they should have been acquitted."[144]

57. Rex v. Nickerson

1772–1773

EDITORIAL NOTE

On 28 November 1772 Adams wrote in his diary, "The Conversation of the Town and Country has been about the strange Occurrence of last Week, a Piracy said to have been committed on a Vessell bound to Cape Cod, 3 Men killed, a Boy missing, and only one Man escaped to tell the News—a misterious, inexplicable Affair!"[1] The later trial of Ansell Nickerson, the "one Man escaped," for the alleged murder, with Adams and Josiah Quincy Jr. as defense counsel, was only to deepen the mystery.

[141] See note 119 above.
[142] Foster, *Crown Cases* 288–289. JA has paraphrased Foster's opening: "I therefore think those Judges who have taken general Verdicts of Acquittal in plain Cases of Death *per Infortunium* . . . have not been to Blame. They have, to say the worst, deviated from antient Practice in Favour of Innocence."
[143] Foster cites, among other examples, 11 & 12 Will. 3, c. 7 (1700) and 4 Geo. 1, c. 11 (1717).
[144] Barrington, *Observations upon the Statutes* 422 note.

[1] 2 JA, *Diary and Autobiography* 69.

Nickerson had sailed on 14 November from Boston for Chatham as passenger aboard a small fishing schooner under the command of his cousin Thomas Nickerson. In the crew were Sparrow Nickerson, brother to Thomas; their brother-in-law, Elisha Newcomb; and William Kent, a boy of thirteen. About ten o'clock in the morning of Sunday the 15th, Captain Joseph Doane Jr., of Chatham, having sailed from that harbor, sighted the schooner between Chatham and Nantucket, flying a signal of distress. On boarding her, Doane found only Nickerson, "who appeared to be in a great Fright," but who was able to report that about two o'clock that morning those aboard the fishing vessel had seen "a Topsail Schooner, who brought them to, and sent a Boat on board, and after questioning them returned again—Soon after four Boats with armed Men came back from the Schooner." [2]

Nickerson, "fearing he should be Impressed, got over the Stern and held with his hands by the Taffarill,[3] with his Feet on the Moulding, under the Cabin Windows. That whilst he was thus hanging over the Stern he judges by what he heard that the Master, with his own Brother, and a Brother-in-Law, named Newcomb, were murdered and thrown overboard, and a Boy named Kent, carried away alive, as they said, in order to *make Punch for them*—That he heard a Talk of burning the Vessel, but it was finally agreed to leave her to drive out to Sea with her Sails standing. That after perpetrating this inhuman Deed they plundered the Vessel of a considerable Quantity of Cash,[4] knocked out the head of a Barrel of Rum, and after wasting the greatest Part of it, went off with the money and other Booty; tho' they left behind a Quarter of fresh Beef & a number of small Stores.—That when they left the Vessel, he came upon Deck, he found none of the Crew, but saw the Marks of blood, and supposes they were murdered." [5]

[2] *Boston Evening-Post*, 23 Nov. 1772, p. 2, col. 3. See also, *Massachusetts Spy*, 19 Nov. 1772, p. 3, col. 3; 3 Hutchinson, *Massachusetts Bay*, ed. Mayo, 300. The latter adds the details, presumably from Hutchinson's personal knowledge of the case, that the Nickerson schooner was first boarded "by a large boat," rowed with twelve oars, which came from an armed schooner lying to at a distance." Doane also figures in Doane v. Gage, No. 43, and appears briefly in the epic of the *Lusanna*, No. 58. Fitch's account of the evidence (Doc. II) suggests that Nickerson testified that his purpose in going on the voyage was "to get his Cloaths."

[3] That is, the taffrail, the upper part of a ship's stern, sometimes a railing there. The spelling in the text is a corruption of the 18th-century usage, "tafferel" which is derived from the Dutch *taferell*, a panel. *OED*. JA, in a later account, referred to this as "some thing, the technical term for which, in naval architecture, I have forgotten." JA to David Sewall, 29 Jan. 1811, 9 JA, *Works* 627, 628.

[4] Hutchinson described this as "the money which the crew had received at Boston, for the earnings of their vessel the year preceding," assigning robbery as the motive. 3 Hutchinson, *Massachusetts Bay*, ed. Mayo, 301–302. According to one contemporary account, the vessel was returning home after discharging its catch from a fishing voyage at Boston. *Massachusetts Spy*, 19 Nov. 1772, p. 3, col. 3. Compare JA's comment that "A sum of money of no great amount had been shipped on board by one of the other men, which was not found." JA to David Sewall, note 3 above.

[5] *Boston Evening-Post*, 23 Nov. 1772, p. 2, col. 3.

Doane apparently brought the schooner into Chatham, and then sent his account of the episode to Edward Bacon, a justice of the peace in Barnstable. Bacon forwarded Doane's report to Governor Thomas Hutchinson in Boston, and went himself to Chatham on the 16th, where, with another justice, he formally examined Nickerson, who had returned from some unexplained wanderings (Document II). Bacon then dismissed him with the consent of the father of the two deceased Nickersons. In the meanwhile, the *Lively* man-of-war was sent out from Boston to search for the supposed pirate.[6] On the 19th Bacon's examination reached Hutchinson, who, finding "Every part of the passenger's [Nickerson's] account . . . incredible,"[7] consulted with "such of the Commissioners for the trial of Piracies, &c. as were in Town,"[8] and issued a warrant for Nickerson's apprehension. This order reached Barnstable by express at midnight on the 20th. There Nickerson was in jail, the local justices having had second thoughts about his story. He had been taken into custody again, re-examined, and committed, "in order to receive Directions from the Governor." Finally, on the 22d, Nickerson was brought under guard to the Province House at Boston, where Hutchinson, Admiral John Montagu, Lieutenant Governor Andrew Oliver, and Secretary Thomas Flucker, all Commissioners for the Trial of Piracy, examined him from seven until eleven in the evening, and ordered him held for trial.[9]

The *Lively* returned after a fruitless search,[10] and a Special Court of Admiralty for the Trial of Piracies was thereupon convened. There were some, according to Hutchinson's later account, who "were ready enough to charge the piracy and murder to a king's schooner, then expected from Rhode Island," and the Sons of Liberty "professed to make no doubt of its being a man of war schooner; and the governor was charged in the publick prints with too critical and severe an examination of the prisoner, whose innocence, it was said, would appear." The old cry that an Admiralty trial deprived the accused of his right to a jury was also raised,[11] but the Commissioners were not deterred. On 16 December, at a sitting of the Special Court, "an Information was filed and exhibited by Ezekiel Price appointed Register of the said Court, against Ansell Nickerson, a Prisoner in his Majesty's Goal, for the murder of Thomas Nickerson, jun., on the High

---

[6] *Boston Evening-Post,* 23 Nov. 1772, p. 2, col. 3. See also, 3 Hutchinson, *Massachusetts Bay,* ed. Mayo, 300–301; Rowe, *Letters and Diary* 236.

[7] 3 Hutchinson, *Massachusetts Bay,* ed. Mayo, 301.

[8] *Boston Evening-Post,* 23 Nov. 1772, p. 2, col. 3.

[9] *Boston Evening-Post,* 23 Nov. 1772, p. 2, col. 3; Rowe, *Letters and Diary* 236.

[10] In the *Boston Evening-Post,* 23 Nov. 1772, p. 2, col. 3, the *Lively* was reported as having returned "yesterday." Rowe, *Letters and Diary* 236, reports her return "from a Cruize into Nantasket Roads," with "No further account of any Pirate," on 28 November. The discrepancy may be accounted for by the possibility that the vessel made more than one "Cruize."

[11] 3 Hutchinson, *Massachusetts Bay,* ed. Mayo, 300, 302. Hutchinson was attacked in the *Massachusetts Spy,* 17 Dec. 1772, p. 2, cols. 1–2, for his aversion to "fair trials by jury." Nickerson's arraignment (note 12 below) was reported in the same issue, at p. 3, col. 2.

Seas on the 14th of November last." Nickerson pleaded Not Guilty, and, upon motion for time to prepare his defense, he was remanded to jail, and the court adjourned until 2 June 1773.[12]

When the day set for trial arrived, the court did not convene, according to one account, because "some matters of greater importance," presumably the investigation of the burning of the *Gaspee*, "employ at present the time of several members."[13] Nickerson was again examined, however, on the basis of new evidence which was said to militate against him.[14] Finally, in the middle of July trial was set for the 28th of that month.[15]

According to Adams' later recollection, "I was of counsel for Nickerson, but was not engaged till the trial came on, when he requested the court to appoint me." This arrangement seems to have been made sometime after 28 July 1773,[16] when the proceedings actually began. A contemporary account relates that witnesses on both sides were examined from that day until the evening of Friday the 30th. The court then adjourned until Tuesday, 3 August, when Samuel Fitch, Advocate General, after examining several additional witnesses for the Crown, made his opening argument (Document II).[17] Fitch first argued that Nickerson was properly before the Special Court, though charged with murder, since that offense, as well as taking the vessel, constituted piracy. Then, after citing authorities on the nature of circumstantial and presumptive proof, he launched into an extensive review of the evidence. The burden of his argument was that the inherent improbabilities of Nickerson's account were a strong indication of its untruth; that the facts would as well support the Crown's version of the affair; and that the accused had had ample time to bring ashore unobserved the money, theft of which was supposed to have been the motive of his acts.

On the afternoon of 3 August, Adams and Josiah Quincy Jr., began their

---

[12] *Boston Evening-Post*, 21 Dec. 1772, p. 2, col. 3. According to Rowe, the court at this session consisted of "The Governour, Lieut Govr, The Secretary of the Province, The Admirall The Judge of Admiralty, Mr. Fisher the Collector of Salem, Mr. Waldo, The Collector of Falmouth Casco Bay." Rowe, *Letters and Diary* 237. Hutchinson's version is that "the counsel for the prisoner moving for further time, and urging that intelligence might probably be obtained of a pirate schooner having been in the bay, and it appearing that a large armed schooner sailed from Boston, bound to the coast of Guinea, at the same time with the fishing vessel, the court thought proper to adjourn the trial for six months." 3 Hutchinson, *Massachusetts Bay*, ed. Mayo, 301.

[13] *Massachusetts Spy*, 3 June 1773, p. 2, col. 4. As to the *Gaspee*, see p. 104, note 24, above.

[14] *Massachusetts Gazette*, 17 June 1773, p. 3, col. 2; *Massachusetts Spy*, 17 June 1773, p. 3, col. 2. It was later reported that Nickerson had been examined "on the report of money being found, suspected to be hidden by him." *Boston Gazette*, 5 July 1773, p. 3, col. 1.

[15] *Massachusetts Gazette*, 15 July 1773, p. 3, col. 1.

[16] JA to David Sewall, 29 Jan. 1811, 9 JA, *Works* 627, 628; compare 3 JA, *Diary and Autobiography* 297: "He requested my Assistance and it was given." The note which Nickerson gave Adams for his fees was dated 30 July 1773. See text at note 25 below.

[17] *Boston Gazette*, 9 Aug. 1773, p. 1, col. 2.

argument, which was to last through the next day.[18] Quincy apparently opened, probably with a review of the evidence. All that has survived, however, are Adams' fragmentary notes of authorities cited by Quincy, which indicate that the latter concentrated heavily on the quantum of proof needed for conviction where the evidence was wholly circumstantial except for the accused's own statements (Document II). Adams first briefly discussed the information, then made an argument drawn from his experience in *Rex v. Corbet*, No. 56, that since the court sat in Admiralty it should apply the civil-law doctrine that the crime of manslaughter was not punishable by death. He then launched his main attack on Nickerson's several examinations before various officials, treating them as confessions, in which the favorable as well as the unfavorable must be admitted, and attacking their admissibility generally. Next he proceeded to set out authorities, familiar to him both from *Corbet* and *Sewall v. Hancock*, No. 46, requiring that proof be certain and consistent in criminal cases. He closed with observations upon Fitch's treatment of the evidence (Documents I, III).

On Thursday afternoon, 5 August, Fitch "closed the cause," and the Court, after telling the prisoner that if he had more to say in his defense he could say it the next day, adjourned until the morning of the 6th. When the Court reconvened, Nickerson "express'd his Wishes that certain Witnesses (who he apprehended would testify in his Favor) had been present; and concluded with saying that, 'if I lose my Life, I am innocent of the Crime laid to my Charge.' " The court room was then cleared, and the Court undertook to consider the evidence. After two and a half hours the prisoner was called in, and "the President [Hutchinson], after a *solemn Pause*, told the Prisoner, '*The Court have considered of your Offence, and they do not think that the Evidence offered to them is sufficient to support the Charge alledged against you in the Information—and therefore adjudge you* NOT GUILTY.' " On motion by Nickerson's counsel, the Advocate General not objecting, he was discharged. "The Prisoner being informed of it, respectfully bowed to the Court, and said, 'I thank the honorable Court —and GOD—for my deliverance!' " As a contemporary newspaper put it, "Thus ended a Trial, for the most surprizing Event, which has happened in this, and perhaps any other Age of the World." [19]

Later accounts by Hutchinson and Adams differ as to the reasons for the acquittal. The newspapers had reported that, the court being divided four and four on the question, "An Acquittal of the Prisoner followed of Course." [20] Hutchinson, who made no bones about his certainty that Nick-

---

[18] *Boston Gazette*, 9 Aug. 1773, p. 1, col. 2.

[19] The foregoing paragraph is drawn from the account in *Boston Gazette*, 9 Aug. 1773, p. 1, cols. 2–3. A broadside published after the trial related certain further "circumstances" purportedly establishing Nickerson's innocence. Worthington C. Ford, comp., *Broadsides, Ballads &c. Printed in Massachusetts, 1639–1800*, 75 MHS, *Colls.*, No. 1678 (1922). The enduring appeal of Nickerson's adventures is attested by Albert Smelco's play, "The Ansell Nickerson Story," performed at Chatham, Mass., in Aug. 1962. *Boston Globe*, 3 Aug. 1962, p. 8.

[20] *Boston Gazette*, 9 Aug. 1773, p. 1, col. 3.

erson was guilty, confirmed the report of the court's division, but said that the crucial issue was a procedural one. The statute, 11 & 12 Will. 3, c. 7 (1700), under which the court was constituted, gave jurisdiction in piracies and other "felonies," excluding murder, according to the opinion of the Crown law officers in England. The information charged Nickerson with piracy only, but alleged the murder to support it. Four of the Court held that to convict of piracy would be to convict of murder, and thus to exceed their jurisdiction.[21] Adams' notes show that Fitch argued this point (Document II), and suggest that Adams briefly replied (Document III). Adams did not, however, in his subsequent recollections see this as the critical question. He admitted that he did not know the basis of the acquittal, but guessed that the court was moved by lack of direct evidence, and consequent doubt of Nickerson's guilt, a doubt which he shared himself.[22] Either version of the acquittal is supported by the language of the court's decision.

Nickerson himself, who, according to Adams, thereafter "lived many years, and behaved well," [23] did not seem to be overly grateful to his counsel. His comments before and after his discharge at the trial, already quoted, suggest a certain lack of appreciation for their efforts, and a tendency to credit his release to other agencies. Adams later reported that "He had nothing to give me, but his promissory Note, for a very moderate Fee. But I have heard nothing from him, nor received any Thing for his note, which has been lost with many other Notes and Accounts to a large Amount, in the distraction of the times and my Absence from my Business." [24] This note, dated 30 July 1773, for £6 13s. 4d. has been found, too late to enforce payment, and still remains, unreceipted, in the files of the Adams Papers.[25]

I. ADAMS' NOTES OF AUTHORITIES [26]

Special Court of Admiralty, Boston, July 1773

Ansell Nickersons Case.

Woods. Inst. 675, middle. "The Confession of the Defendant to private Persons, or to a Magistrate, out of Court, is allowed to be given in Evidence against the Party confessing; but this Confession cannot

[21] 3 Hutchinson, *Massachusetts Bay*, ed. Mayo, 301. For the opinion of the Advocate, Attorney, and Solicitor General, 5 Nov. 1761, upon which Hutchinson apparently relied, see Chalmers, *Opinions* 525–527.

[22] JA to David Sewall, 29 Jan. 1811, 9 JA, *Works* 627, 628; see also 3 JA, *Diary and Autobiography* 297: "I know not to this day what Judgement to form of his Guilt or Innocence."

[23] JA to David Sewall, 29 Jan. 1811, 9 JA, *Works* 627, 628.

[24] 3 JA, *Diary and Autobiography* 297.

[25] Adams Papers, Microfilms, Reel No. 344.

[26] In JA's hand. Adams Papers, Microfilms, Reel No. 185. Docketed by JA: "Ansell Nickerson's Case. Evidence, Confession, Judication," the three issues with

be made use of against any other. But where a Man's Confession is made use of against him, it ought to be taken alltogether, and with that part which makes for him as well as with that which makes against him." [27]

Vin. Tit. Evidence, page 95. A. b. 23. "3. In an Information for publishing a Libel, the Defendants own Confession was given in Evidence against him, but per Holt C.J. if there was no other Evidence against him but his own Confession, the whole must be taken, and not so much of it as would serve to convict him. 5. Mod. 167. King v. Pain. Hill. 7. W. 3." Note. "So if to prove a Debt it be sworn that Defendant confessed it, but withal said at the same Time, that he had paid it, this Confession shall be valid as to the Payment, as well as to his having owed it. Per Hale Ch. J. and so is the common Practice. Try. per Pais 209." [28]

Vin. Tit. Evid. p. 96. Top. "4. Confession is the Worst Sort of Evidence." i. e. &c.[29] "6. The Examination of the Prisoner himself (if not on oath) may be read as Evidence against him; but the Examination of others (though not on oath) ought not to be read if they can be produced, viva voce." [30]

2. Bac. Abr. 313 "Of the Parties Confession." "But wherever a Mans Confession is made use of against him, it must be taken alltogether and not by Parcells." 2. Hawk. 429.[31]

---

which these notes deal. Intervals of space indicate space breaks in the MS. JA's outline of his own argument is appended to these notes in the MS, but it is here printed separately (Doc. III), so that the arguments can be presented in the order in which they were presumably given. See note 87 below.

[27] The passage appears in Wood, *Institute of the Laws of England* 671 (London, 9th edn., 1763). JA seems to have cited the wrong page inadvertently. This is the only edition in which there are more than 663 pages. 1 Sweet and Maxwell, *Legal Bibliography* 38. Quotation marks have been supplied.

[28] 12 Viner, *Abridgment* 95, tit. Evidence, plea A. b. 23, no. 3. Quotation marks supplied. For King v. Pain, see note 33 below. The "note" in the text appears in the margin in Viner; it is a quotation, with very minor discrepancies, from Duncombe, *Tryals per Pais* 209 (London, 3d edn., 1700). The same passage appears at p. 363 in Volume 2 of the 1766 edition of the latter work, cited below by JA, note 32.

[29] 12 Viner, *Abridgment* 96, tit. Evidence, plea A. b. 23, no. 4. Quotation marks supplied. The passage reads in full, "Confession is the worst sort of Evidence that is, if there be *no Proof of a Transaction* or Dealing, or at least *a Probability* of Dealing, between them as in the Principal Case there was, the one being a Sailor, the other a Master of a Ship. Per Holt. 7 Mod. 42. Mich. 1 Ann. B.R. Anon."

[30] 12 Viner, *Abridgment* 96, tit. Evidence, plea A. b. 23, no. 6. Quotation marks supplied. JA has omitted the citation: "St. Tr. 1 Vol. 169. 780.—2 Vol. 575."

[31] 2 Bacon, *Abridgment* 313, tit. Evidence, L. Quotation marks supplied. JA has omitted the preceding paragraph, which states that the defendant's confession, whether taken according to law by a justice of the peace or magistrate, "or spoken in private Discourse," may be used against him. Both this passage and the sentence quoted in the text appear in substantially similar form in 2 Hawkins, *Pleas of the Crown* 429, which is cited in the margin in Bacon. See notes 34, 90, below.

2. Try. Pr. Pais 427. Same as Viner.[32]

5. Mod. Rex vs. Paine. 165. "If Confession shall be taken as Evidence to convict him it is but justice and Reason, and so allowed in the Civil Law, that his whole Confession shall be Evidence as well for as against him." Page 167, middle, "if there was no other Evidence against him but his own Confession, the whole must be taken ⟨together⟩, and not so much of it as would serve to convict him." [33]

2. Hawk. P.C. 429. "§5. It seems an established Rule, that wherever a Mans Confession is made use of against him, it must all be taken together and not by Parcells." [34]

2. Hale. H.P.C. 290. "Never convict of Murder or Manslaughter unless the Fact be proved to be done or at least the Body found dead." [35]

4 Black. 352. Fourthly.[36]

Dig. Lib. 29. Tit. 5. §24. "Nisi constet aliquem esse occisum, non habui de familia quæstionem." [37]

2 Domat. 667.[38]

---

[32] 2 Duncombe, *Trials per Pais* 427 (8th edn., 1766). The passage contains several more or less accurate quotations from 12 Viner, *Abridgment* 95–96, including those cited in notes 28 and 29 above.

[33] Rex v. Paine, 5 Mod. 163, 165, 167, 87 Eng. Rep. 584, 585, 586 (K.B. 1695). Quotation marks supplied. See note 28 above. In an information for publishing a criminal libel the defendant had confessed that he had written the libel at another's dictation and then had delivered it to one Brereton by mistake. There was also the evidence of the defendant's servant that the libel had been repeated in a room in the presence of a Dr. Hoyle after the defendant had brought in a writing. The jury gave a special verdict raising the question of the defendant's guilt as composer of the libel, but finding him not guilty of publication. The passage quoted from p. 165 is apparently part of the argument of counsel to the jury that that portion of the confession which indicated delivery by mistake must also be taken into account and read to show that there was no publication. The passage from p. 167 is part of the opinion of the court, conceding that if the confession were the only evidence on the question of publication, the defendant was not guilty. The court went on to state, however, that the servant's testimony was also evidence of publication, if it could be established that the paper brought into the room was the libel. The court adjourned without giving judgment.

[34] 2 Hawkins, *Pleas of the Crown* 429, §5. Quotation marks supplied. The passage is cited by Bacon, note 31 above.

[35] 2 Hale, *Pleas of the Crown* 290. Quotation marks supplied.

[36] That is, 4 Blackstone, *Commentaries* *352: "Fourthly, all presumptive evidence of felony should be admitted cautiously: for the law holds, that it is better that ten guilty persons escape, than that one innocent suffer." Blackstone then recites the passage quoted from Hale, note 35 above.

[37] That is, Justinian, *Digest*, bk. 29, tit. 5, law 1, §24, cited by Hale, note 35 above, a passage construing a senatorial decree which inflicted torture upon slaves of a master who met a violent death. Quotation marks have been supplied. See 6 Scott, *Civil Law* 320: "Unless it is established that a man has been killed, his slaves ought not to be tortured."

[38] 2 Domat, *Civil Law* 667, a passage stating the general rule that a confession is to be taken as proof of the fact confessed unless the contrary be established affirmatively. "And this Rule has only one Exception in Accusations of Capital Crimes,

Civil Law.

Woods Inst. 310 "In Criminal Cases, the Proofs ought to be as clear *as the sun at Noon day.*" [39]

Cod. Lib. 4. Tit 19. §25. De Judiciis criminalibus. "Sciant cuncti accusatores eam se rem deferre in publicam notionem debere, quæ munita sit idoneis Testibus, vel instructa apertissimis documentis, vel indiciis, ad probationem indubitatis, et luce clarioribus expedita." Vid. notes also.[40]

Maranta. page 49. pars 4. dist. 1. 77.[41]

Gail. Page 503. "debet venis et expressus intervenire Dolus," &c. "Lata culpa, non æquiparatur dolo." &c. "Dolus non præsumitur," &c. "Quapropter dolum allegans, eum probare debet." [42]

Page 509.[43]

Examen Juris canonici 335. 343. Quid est confessio et quid operatior extra judicialis Confession in criminalibus.[44]

Maranta. Sp. Aur. 313. 114. especially.[45] See Calvins Lexicon Tit. confiteri. Capitulum.[46]

2. Cor. Jur. Can. 118 page of the Inst. De probationibus.[47]

---

where it is not enough that the Party who is accused confesses a Crime which is not proved; but other Proofs are necessary for putting him to Death besides his own Confession, which might be an Effect of Melancholy or Despair, or proceed from some other Cause than the Force of Truth."

[39] Wood, *New Institute of the Civil Law* 310. Quotation marks supplied. Compare No. 46, note 119.

[40] Justinian, *Codex*, bk. 4, tit. 19, §25. Quotation marks supplied. See No. 46, notes 124–125.

[41] Maranta, *Speculum Aureum*, pars IV, Distinctio I, §77. Quoted, No. 56, note 118.

[42] Gail, *Practicarum Observationum* 503, quoted in No. 56, note 116, from which the passage here was probably extracted. Quotation marks have been supplied.

[43] Gail, *Practicarum Observationum* 509. See No. 56, note 117.

[44] Presumably a reference to Gregor Kolb, *Examen Juris Canonici, juxta V. libros decretalium* (Vienna, 1728), a work which JA owned. See *Catalogue of JA's Library* 136.

[45] Maranta, *Speculum Aureum* 313. "114" is presumably an inadvertence for p. 314. See text preceding note 90 below. In JA's copy at the Boston Public Library two passages on these pages are marked. The first states that, even though the defendant's confession contains matter favorable to himself, this must be proved, as in a confession that he killed in self-defense. The second adds the important qualification that on the basis of such a confession the defendant cannot be condemned to death, as for a homicide, but must be given the lesser penalty of banishment.

[46] Johannes Calvinus, *Lexicon Juridicum Juris Cæsarei Simul, et Canonici,* tits., Confiteri, Capitulum (Geneva, 1622). It has not been possible to determine exactly the passages under these heads to which JA referred. The title "Capitulum" seems to contain nothing relevant. Under "Confiteri" there are several general statements concerning confessions which JA may have intended. The citation is omitted in the notes from which he argued (Doc. III).

[47] Apparently a reference to *Institutiones Juris Canonici* 118 (Basel, ed. J. P. Lancelottus, 1695), bound with separate paging as part of *Corpus Juris Canonici*

Number of Witnesses.

New Institute of the civil Law page 316. 2.[48] Dig. Lib. 22. Tit. 5 §12.[49]

Cod. Lib. 4. Tit. 20. §9. §1. and Notes.[50]

St. Tryals. V. 8. page 213. Tryal of Captn. John Quelch and others, at Boston.[51]

St. Tryals. V. 6. 156. Tryal of Major Stede Bonnett at So. Carolina, and 33 others.[52]

Statutes. 28. H. 8, c. 15. "For Pirates." 11. & 12. W. 3, c. 7. for the more effectual Supression of Piracy. 4 G, c. 11. For the further preventing of Robbery &c. and for declaring the Law upon some Points relating to Pirates. §7.[53]

Foster 288.[54] Barrington 54, bottom, Note.[55]

II. ADAMS' MINUTES OF THE ARGUMENT [56]

Special Court of Admiralty, Boston, 3–4 August 1773

Fitch. Not charged with Murder. But as the Killing constitutes Pyracy.

(Basel, ed. J. P. Lancelottus, 1696). At the cited page appears bk. 3, tit. 14, "De Probationibus," a title beginning with several sections concerning proof by confession of the parties.

[48] Wood, *New Institute of the Civil Law* 316, §2, set out in No. 46, notes 106–107.

[49] Justinian, *Digest*, bk. 22, tit. 5, §12, set out in No. 46, at note 108.

[50] Justinian, *Codex*, bk. 4, tit. 20, §9, §1, set out in No. 46, at note 109.

[51] Reg. v. Quelch et als., 8 State Trials 205, 213 (Boston, Ct. of Adm., 1704). Quelch and his crew had taken over a privateer when the master died, and had preyed on friendly shipping in the South Atlantic. The cited page contains a series of objections to the evidence by Quelch's counsel. JA's use of the passage in his argument (Doc. III) indicates that he here referred to an argument that the civil-law rules for accrediting witnesses should apply. This contention, like all the others made for Quelch, was rejected by the court. Quelch and several of his accomplices were ultimately condemned and executed on 30 June 1704.

[52] Rex v. Bonnet, 6 State Trials 156 (S.C. Vice Adm., 1718). See No. 56, at note 54.

[53] See 28 Hen. 8, c. 15 (1536), set out in No. 56, at notes 40–43; 11 & 12 Will. 3, c. 7 (1700), set out, *id.*, at notes 44–49 (see also note 57 below); 4 Geo. 1, c. 11, §7 (1717), set out, *id.*, at notes 52–53.

[54] See Foster, *Crown Cases* 288–289, indicating that there is no crime of manslaughter in Admiralty, set out in No. 56, at notes 142–143.

[55] See Barrington, *Observations upon the Statutes* 54, stating that there is no crime of manslaughter under the civil law, set out in No. 56, at note 140.

[56] In JA's hand. Adams Papers, Microfilms, Reel No. 185. The notes have been dated from a contemporary newspaper account. See text at notes 17, 18, above.

11. & 12. W, c. 7, §9.[57]

Petit Treason at common Law. 25. Ed. 3. defined Treason.[58]

Confining the Master, and taking Vessel into Possession and robbing him is Pyracy.

Evidence presumptive. No Witnesses who saw the Transaction.

1. Domat. 413. T. 6. That a Proof which convinces the Mind.[59] 414. Signs, Tokens, Conjectures, and Presumptions.[60]

2. Sorts of Presumptions. 1. Proofs. 2. Only conjectures without Certainty. A necessary Connection.[61]

[57] 11 & 12 Will. 3, c. 7, §9 (1700): "And be it further enacted, That if any commander or master of any ship, or any seaman or mariner, shall, in any place where the admiral hath jurisdiction, betray his trust, and turn pirate, enemy, or rebel, and piratically and feloniously run away with his or their ship or ships, or any barge, boat, ordnance, ammunition, goods, or merchandizes, or yield them up voluntarily to any pirate, or shall bring any seducing messages from any pirate, enemy, or rebel, or consult, combine, or confederate with, or attempt or endeavour to corrupt any commander, master, officer, or mariner, to yield up or run away with any ship, goods, or merchandizes, or turn pirate, or go over to pirates, or if any person shall lay violent hands on his commander, whereby to hinder him from fighting in defense of his ship and goods committed to his trust, or that shall confine his master, or make, or endeavour to make a revolt in the ship, shall be adjudged, deemed, and taken to be a pirate, felon, and robber, and being convicted thereof, according to the directions of this act, shall have and suffer pains of death, loss of lands, goods, and chattels, as pirates, felons, and robbers upon the seas ought to have and suffer."

[58] 25 Edw. 3, stat. 5, c. 2 (1350), defined petit treason as "When a servant slayeth his master, or a wife her husband, or when a man secular or religious slayeth his prelate, to whom he oweth faith and obedience." Fitch may here have been quoting or paraphrasing 1 Hawkins, *Pleas of the Crown* 98, c. 37, Of Piracy, §2: "It is said that before 25 *Ed.* 3. this Offense [Piracy] was punished at Common Law as Petit Treason, if committed by a Subject, and as Felony, if committed by a Foreigner: However it seems agreed, that after that Statute by which all Treason is confined to the Particulars therein set down, it was cognizable only by the Civil Law." Compare 4 Blackstone, *Commentaries* *71.

[59] 1 Domat, *Civil Law* 413, bk. 3, tit. 6, Of Proofs, and Presumptions, and of an Oath: "We call that a Proof which convinces the Mind of a Truth."

[60] 1 Domat, *Civil Law* 414: "But if it [the identity of the murderer of one killed alone on the highway at night] is discovered, it will be only by Proofs that may be drawn from circumstances which shall happen to be linked together with this Crime, and which will depend on Events that have happened by accident, such as the casual rencounter of some Witnesses, and such signs and tokens as there may happen to be, conjectures, and presumptions."

[61] 1 Domat, *Civil Law* 415: "It may be gathered from these Remarks, that there are two sorts of Presumptions: Some of which are drawn by a necessary consequence from a Principle that is certain; and when these sorts of Presumptions are so strong, that one may gather from them the certainty of the Fact that is to be proved, without leaving any room for doubt, we give them the name of Proofs, because they have the same effect, and do establish the truth of the Fact which was in dispute. The other Presumptions are all those which form only Conjectures, without certainty; whether it be that they are drawn only from an uncertain Foundation, or that the consequence which is drawn from a certain Truth is not very sure.

"It is because of the difference between these two sorts of Presumptions, that the Laws have appointed some of them to have the force of Proofs, and have not left

430. §4. Presumptions of 2 Kinds. Conjectures leave doubt.[62]
2. Domat. 666.[63]

Wood civil Law. page 302. Proof—plena, 2 Witnesses. 2 half proofs make one whole one.[64]

305. 6. Confession, not conclusive alone. Ought to admit the whole. —See this by all Means.—Defence must be proved.[65]

Appeal to the human Mind that it is impossible to divide his Confession.[66]

---

the Judges at liberty to consider them only as bare Conjectures, because in effect these sorts of Presumptions are such, that one sees in them a necessary connexion between the truth of the Fact that is to be proved, and the certainty of the Facts from whence it follows."

[62] 1 Domat, *Civil Law* 430, bk. 3, tit. 6, Of Presumptions, §4: "Presumptions are of two kinds, some of them are so strong, that they amount to a certainty, and are held as Proofs, even in Criminal Matters. And others are only conjectures which leave some doubt."

[63] 2 Domat, *Civil Law* 666, presumably a reference to a passage on the cited page describing the four ways of proving facts in court: "The Confession of the Party, the Testimony of Persons who know the Fact, the Evidence which arises from Deeds and Writings, and the Knowledge of certain Facts, which are linked in such a Manner with that whereof we search the Truth, that one may gather the said Truth from the Connection there is between the Fact in question and those of which the Truth is proved." Immediately following in the text is the passage cited by JA, note 38 above, and cited by him in argument, text following note 90 below.

[64] Wood, *New Institute of the Civil Law* 302 (London, 4th edn., 1730): "Proof is either (*plena*) a full proof, as by two Witnesses or a publick Instrument; or (*semiplena*) an half proof, as one Witness or a private Writing; so that two half proofs being joined together (though of a different nature) make one full proof." Note that the edition cited here and in note 65 below by Fitch is that of 1730. JA's citations to this work in this case and elsewhere are to the first edition of 1704.

[65] Wood, *New Institute of the Civil Law* 305 (London, 4th edn., 1730): "But all Confessions are not to be esteemed a discovery of the Truth, if there are no other corroborating Circumstances. For sometimes Fear or a weariness of Life, or some other Reason hath induced Men to make Confessions of those Things which they were never guilty of. . . . But when the Confession is regular, and admitted by the other Party, he ought to admit the whole as it is qualified, and when it is extended to other matters which are done at the same time; unless there is a presumption against that part. As when one confesses that he kill'd *Titius* in his own defense; the killing shall stand by it self as confessed, and the *qualification* must be proved, because the Law presumes design, and throws the proof upon the Criminal." The phrase between dashes in the text is presumably JA's insertion.

[66] This is apparently a reference to the language of Wood, *New Institute of the Civil Law* 305–306, which follows the passage quoted in note 65 above: "But if the Sentences are distinct, where there is no presumption, the qualification afterwards comes too late, and infers that the Acts are done at different Times." Then follows an example in which "The Libel charges that you receive 100 *l.* of me. You answer, That you did receive 100 *l.* of me which I ow'd to you, and no other Sum; this is but one Sentence, and cannot be divided; for with one Breath I do as it were absolutely deny the Charge. But where the Sentences are divided, there the Confession shall be divided, and part accepted and part rejected. As if you had answer'd, That you did borrow the 100 *l.* but that you have since repaid it: Or that I have promised not to demand it 'till seven years were past. The latter part of this answer must be proved,

The 4 Persons were on board and said [67] with Prisoner. Neg[atu]r. All 4 kill'd.

Prisoner's own Account. Blood spilt, where they came up.

All 4 Missing 9 Mo.[68] No Account of them.

What supposition can be made, consistent with common sense.

Prisoner found alone on board. All staind with blood, the decks reeking with blood.

In Possession of Vessell, and evry Thing, disposing as he thought proper.—Mem. signal of distress.[69]

Woman delivered alone.[70]

Goods taken with the Maner.[71]

His Account improbable, incredible. Therefore makes vs. him not for him. Improba[bi]lities.

His Design in going only to get his Cloaths. Cost him much to come back by Land.

No Wind he says.

No Ax. Crowl[72] says there was. They were to [...] [boards?].

Does not know the Boys Name.

None of the other Vessells saw this Schooner.

None heard the Gun but him.

Incredibility that there should have been a Pirate Vessell. Boats could not board.

He said the Box was gone, tho he said he had not been down the Hold.

Rum on the Boards therefore not carried off.

Fresh Meat, Butter, Cyder, Roots, &c. not taken.

The Pirates must have trod in the blood, and left the Marks in Cabin, hold &c.

---

else you will be condemned." JA may have noted the argument for his own later use, since the statement would seem to cut against the Crown.

[67] Thus in MS, but quite possibly an inadvertence for "sailed."

[68] That is, nine months between the date of the incident in Nov. 1772 and the time of the hearing in Aug. 1773.

[69] Probably JA's reminder to himself that Nickerson's signal of distress was not consistent with a criminal intent.

[70] Probably a reference to an example given in 1 Domat, *Civil Law* 415, following the passage quoted, note 61 above, which recounts Henri II's edict of 1556 that if a woman was brought to childbed without witnesses and there was no subsequent christening or public burial, there should be a presumption that she had murdered the child.

[71] That is, "Manor"? The reading and allusion are unclear. This may be a reference to a presumption as to the title to chattels remaining on the land at the time of conveyance.

[72] Probably a witness, but not identified.

Where was the Prisoner for fear of Impress. Hanging on the Stern.

Is it possible he should have hung there a Minute.

Why did not they discover him, when on the deck and when they came under the Stern.

The Paint clean, not bruised nor broke.

Manner of getting in incredible, impossible.

Account of Coll. Doane different.[73]

If the Prisoner guilty would not every appearance have been as they were.

Liquor, Cyder and Rum in the Pail, and the [Cantien?] he gave, shews they were made drunk and then butch[ere]d.

Conduct after he came ashore—wandering God knows where. No Account can be given of him. An opportunity to bring ⟨it⟩ ashore, the Money.

Confident he should be discharged.

Went a little Way, felt poorly, when he came back. The Witnesses say he could not go on board the Vessell then, but he might go where the Money was hid.

All Night absent going to his Grandfathers. He pretended he was lost.

Went to the Hay Yard to the End of the Stack, to get hay for his Horse.

7 Months after, an handkerchief found.

Otis Lorings Account—dont tell me, where[.]

J. Quincy. Altogether presumptive.

Wood civ. Law 276.[74]

Hawk. P.C.[75]

Viner. Ev. p. 95.[76]

Dig. 42. Tit. 2.[77]

[73] Probably a reference to Capt. Joseph Doane, who found the schooner (note 2 above), although the title, "Coll." suggests Col. Elisha Doane, one of JA's wealthy clients. See Nos. 52, 58.

[74] Wood, *New Institute of the Civil Law* 276 (London, 4th edn., 1730): "*Homicide with Deliberation* is when one kills another upon a premeditated design, and in cold Blood. If the design cannot be proved directly, it may be learnt from circumstances, as when there was Enmity between the Parties, providing Arms, lying in wait, &c."

[75] Hawkins, *Pleas of the Crown.* The page reference cannot be determined from the context.

[76] See the materials quoted in JA's notes, notes 28–30 above.

[77] Justinian, *Digest*, bk. 42, tit. 2, De Confessis. A series of eight laws, most of which deal with the confession of civil obligations, stating the general proposition that confession of a debt is the equivalent of a judgment for that amount. Quincy may have been drawing an analogy to the provisions that this rule does not apply

Cod. 7. Tit. 59.[78]

1. Domat. 430. Thus in a criminal Action, &c.[79]

2. Domat. 668. 9. Consequences from certain facts, known and proved. The natural and necessary Connection between the facts proved, and those inferred.[80]

670.[81]

2. Domat. 618.[82]

1. Ld. Bacon. 251.[83]

2. ⟨*Hawk.*⟩ Hale P.C. 289.[84]

---

where the amount of the debt or the nature of property in question is uncertain. *Id.*, L. 6, L. 8.

[78] Justinian, *Codex*, bk. 7, tit. 59, De Confessis, §1: "Confessis in jure pro judicatis haberi placet. Quare sine causa desideras recedi a confessione tua, cum et solvere cogeris." See 14 Scott, *Civil Law* 202: "It has been decided that confessions made in court have the effect of judgments, therefore you have no right to revoke your confession, as you will be compelled to make payment." A better translation of the first clause might be: "confessions in law have the effect of judgments."

[79] 1 Domat, *Civil Law* 430: "Presumptions are consequences drawn from a fact that is known, to serve for the discovery of the truth of a fact that is uncertain, and which one seeks to prove. . . . Thus in a Criminal Affair, if a Man has been killed, and it is not known by whom, and if it be discovered that he had a little while before a quarrel with another person, who had threatened to kill him, one draws from this known fact of the quarrel and threatning, a Presumption that he who had thus threatned him, may have been the Author of the Murder."

[80] 2 Domat, *Civil Law* 668: "There is likewise a fourth Kind of Proofs which are called Presumptions, that is to say, Consequences which are drawn from certain Facts that are known and proved, whereby to guess at or infer the Certainty of the Fact in dispute, and of which the said known Facts are Marks and Signs; and these sorts of Proofs are called Presumptions, because they do not demonstrate the Fact it self which is to be proved, but prove the Truth of other Fact, the knowledge whereof discovers, points out, and gives room to conjecture and presume the Fact in question, because of the natural and necessary Connection between the Facts that are known, and those which we want to know the Truth of."

[81] That is, 2 Domat, *Civil Law* 670. The precise passage intended cannot be determined from context.

[82] 2 Domat, *Civil Law* 618, a passage stating that the three bases for differentiating between crimes are (1) the degree of heinousness; (2) the motive, whether premeditation, passion, or imprudence; and (3) the circumstances in which the crime is committed.

[83] Probably a reference to Francis Bacon, *Works*, 1:251 (London, 1750), a section of the eighth book of his *De Augmentis Scientiarum*, entitled "De exemplis et usu eorum," which deals with "examples, from which justice is to be derived when the law is deficient," that is, examples of human experience not common enough to have been reduced to custom or law. See 5 Bacon, *Works* 92–94 (London, transl. and ed. Spedding, Ellis, Heath, 1877).

[84] 2 Hale, *Pleas of the Crown* 289. Presumably the reference is to this passage: "In some cases presumptive evidences go far to prove a person guilty, tho there be no express proof of the fact to be committed by him, but then it must be very warily pressed, for it is better five guilty persons should escape unpunished, than one innocent person should die." Hale then gives the example of a man executed for theft of a horse, only to have the true thief later confess that he had given the innocent victim the horse to walk just before his apprehension. There follows on p. 290 the

Ayliff 447. 8.[85]
Wood.[86]

III. ADAMS' NOTES FOR HIS ARGUMENT [87]

Special Court of Admiralty, Boston, 4–5 August 1773

Information.[88]

By what Rule is Prisoner to be tryed? Answer by the civil Law.

Statute 28. H. 8, c. 15. 11. & 12. W. 3, c. 7. 4. G, c. 11, §. 7. then Foster 288. Barrington 54, bottom Note—notwithstanding St. Tr. V. 8, page 213.

It has been customary to look into both Laws, here, as it seems they do in London, at the Admiralty sessions.[89]

But the Principal Rule of Law upon which our defence is grounded is common to both Laws, that the Confession shall be taken alltogether.

Woods Inst. 676. Vin. Evid. page 95 A. b. 23. 3. 5. Mod. 165. 2. Hawk. 429.

Examen Juris Canonici. 335. Maranta Sp. Aur. 313. 314 especially.

---

passage quoted by JA, note 35 above, and cited by him in argument, text following note 90 below.

[85] Presumably John Ayliffe, *Parergon Juris Canonici Anglicani* 447, 448 (London, 2d edn., 1734), a long passage on the sufficiency of proof, containing such statements as, "In the Business of Proof, a Judge ought first to have a great Regard to the Probability thereof" (p. 447), and, "As in all Criminal Causes Evidence or Notoriety of Fact is full Proof, so likewise in such Causes all manner of Proofs ought to be clearer than the Light of the Sun at Noon-day." (p. 448). That this work was available in Boston appears from the Harvard Law School's copy, which bears the signatures of Jeremy Gridley, Samuel Sewall, and Christopher Gore. For another use of Ayliffe by JA, see p. 104 above.

[86] Presumably either Wood, *New Institute of the Civil Law,* or Wood, *Institute of the Laws of England.*

[87] In JA's hand, following, after an interval of space, his notes of authorities, printed as Doc. I. See note 26 above. Only authorities not cited by JA in Doc. I have been annotated in Doc. III. The notes have been dated from a contemporary newspaper account. See text at notes 18, 19, above.

[88] That is, the information or libel containing the articles of the charge against Nickerson. No copy of this document has been found.

[89] That is, into both the common law, and the civil law, which was traditionally used in Admiralty. Compare No. 56. In the English practice, the jury and other features of the common law were made applicable by statute, but certain civil-law rules, such as the lack of the death penalty for manslaughter, applied. See No. 56, Doc. VI; p. 275, notes 2, 3, above. The argument seems to be JA's means of getting around the decision of the Boston Special Court of Admiralty in Quelch's Case (1704), that common-law rules controlled the admissibility of evidence. See note 51 above. For his difficulties with the same problem in the Vice Admiralty Court, see No. 46.

2. Corp. Juris canonici 118 of the Institute de probationibus. This is no more than an extrajudicial Confession. Phillip & Mary.[90]

We must therefore throw all his Confessions and Examinations into the fire, and consider the Case without them.

But then by what Rules? Wood Inst. 310. Cod. Lib. 4. Tit. 19. §. 25. Maranta page 49. pars 4, dist. 1 77 Gail 503. 2. H.H.P.C. 290. 4. Blackst. 352. Dig. Lib. 29. Tit. 5. §. 24. "Nisi constet aliquem esse occisum, non habui [*Familia*] quæstionem." 2. Domat 667.

Then consider Mr. Fitches Observations upon the Evidence—his Improbabilities, Incredibilities, Absurdities, Inconsistencies &c.

[90] Presumably a reference to the statutes 1 & 2 Phil. & Mary, c. 13 (1554), and 2 & 3 Phil. & Mary, c. 10 (1555), which provided that justices of the peace should examine persons accused of manslaughter or felony, either when admitting them to bail or upon commitment, and should certify the examination to the next court of general gaol delivery. According to 2 Hawkins, *Pleas of the Crown* 429 (cited by JA to another point, note 34 above), confessions taken on such occasions could be given in evidence, as could those "taken by the Common Law upon an Examination before a Secretary of State, or other Magistrates for Treason, or other Crimes, not within those Statutes, or in Discourse with private Persons." Compare note 31 above. JA's point seems to be that Nickerson's examinations before Edward Bacon and the Admiralty Commissioners (text at notes 6–9 above) met none of these requirements.

Q. *Admiralty—Prize Jurisdiction*

58. Penhallow v. The *Lusanna*

1777–1795

EDITORIAL NOTE

Until comparatively recent times the valor of naval crews was stimulated by the prospect of a share in the proceeds of enemy vessels and goods captured as prize. The complicated questions of property and the law of war which this system of hazard pay produced were adjudicated in every country by special tribunals, administering a more or less common body of international law. From its 14th-century origins the English Court of Admiralty had exercised a jurisdiction in such matters. By the beginning of the 18th century, when Admiralty's powers in other fields were on the wane, the prize side of the court had become virtually a separate institution, with sessions, rules, and records distinct from the ordinary civil, or "instance" side. Although this jurisdiction was called upon only in time of hostilities, the warlike nature of the times meant a steady demand for it, so that a substantial body of prize law developed and the Admiralty was saved from the extinction which might otherwise have been its fate.[1]

In the colonies, the seat of much of the warfare, there was great need for a similar forum, since trial of colonial prizes in England was impracticable. After 1660, captures were tried first in the courts established by the governors under their powers as Vice Admirals, then in the Admiralty courts created in 1697 for enforcement of the Acts of Trade. Confusion over the source of these courts' power to sit in prize was laid to rest by an Act of 1708, which provided for trial in Admiralty under a precise and simple procedure and established fixed formulas for the division of proceeds among the captors.[2] Under this statute the colonial Vice Admiralty judges, empowered by special Admiralty warrant, exercised the jurisdiction through all the wars of the 18th century. One authority suggests that this branch may have amounted to as much as a third of the courts' total business.[3] Although it may be assumed that the Massachusetts Vice Ad-

---

[1] For a concise history of the English prize jurisdiction, see 1 Holdsworth, *History of English Law* 561–568.

[2] 6 Anne, c. 37 (1708).

[3] Andrews, "Introduction," *Records of the Vice Admiralty of Rhode Island* 41 (Washington, ed. D. S. Towle, 1936). For an account of the development of the jurisdiction, see *id.* at 35–42. For a contemporary account, including a copy of the warrant issued for trial of prizes in 1756, see Anthony Stokes, *A View of the Constitution of the British Colonies* 275–281 (London, 1783). Forms used in the West Indies appear in *id.* at 276–357. For some of the jurisdictional and other problems presented by appeals from the Vice Admiralty courts in prize cases, see Smith, *Appeals to the Privy Council* 186–187, 518–520.

miralty Court sat in prize until the cessation of hostilities in the Seven Years' War in 1763, John Adams had no prize cases before it, as far as is known.

At the outbreak of the Revolution the colonists soon found that, whatever their feelings about the Admiralty had been, the prize jurisdiction was a necessary element in naval warfare. Despite the efforts of advocates of seapower, including Adams, a Continental Navy was slow to develop. George Washington put a fleet of four vessels into action off Massachusetts, and the individual colonies established small navies of their own; but privateers, vessels fitted out at private expense and commissioned by Congress or a colony to sail against enemy shipping, were the substitute upon which the colonists chiefly had to rely.[4] Since profits were even more important to the privateers than to regular naval vessels, Massachusetts as early as 1775 established its own maritime court to exercise jurisdiction in prize matters. The other colonies soon followed suit, and the hated royal Admiralty courts were succeeded by a system of state courts, which, however, were usually limited to prize cases and sat with a jury.[5] Congress was also quick to recognize the need for its authority in this field. In November 1775 it adopted the report of a committee of which Adams was a member, establishing regulations for privateers, defining the objects of capture, recommending that the states establish prize courts, and providing that appeals from all cases of prize in those courts would lie to the Congress. Under this measure appeals were referred to special committees, until in January 1777 a Standing Committee on Appeals was created.[6]

[4] For the first years of the Continental Navy, see Howard I. Chapelle, *History of the American Navy* 52–79 (N.Y., 1949). As to Washington's fleet, see William Bell Clark, *George Washington's Navy* 1–98 (Baton Rouge, 1960). For the colonial navies and privateers, see Gardiner W. Allen, *A Naval History of the American Revolution*, 1:42–52, 132–152 (Boston and N.Y., 1913). As to JA's interest, see 2 JA, *Diary and Autobiography* 201–202 note, 221–222 note.

[5] For the Massachusetts court, see Act of 1 Nov. 1775, 5 A&R 436, 438–441, as amended, Act of 13 April 1776, 5 A&R 474. The jurisdiction was later extended to certain traditional maritime causes such as seamen's wages, salvage, and disputes between part-owners, as well as to offenses against a law prohibiting the exportation of naval stores, but the jury was retained. Act of 29 April 1778, 5 A&R 806; Act of 19 Feb. 1779, 5 A&R 930. For a summary of legislation in other states, see Davis, "Federal Courts Prior to the Adoption of the Constitution," 131 U.S., Appendix xx–xxii (1889); Hampton L. Carson, *The Supreme Court of the United States* 44–47 (Phila., 1892). For the work of these courts, which did much to pass on the Admiralty tradition to the courts of the United States, see Wiener, "Notes on the Rhode Island Admiralty, 1727–1790," 46 Harv. L. Rev. 44, 59–62 (1932); Hough, *Reports* 243–254; Ubbelohde, *Vice Admiralty Courts* 195–201. For JA's later comments on the Massachusetts act, see his letter to Elbridge Gerry, 14 April 1813, 10 JA, *Works* 37.

[6] For the Congressional Resolve of 25 Nov. 1775, and a further resolve of 23 March 1776, see note 108 below. For the work of the special committees and the resolve creating the Standing Committee, see Davis, "Federal Courts," 131 U.S., Appendix xxii–xxiii; 7 JCC 75. For the cases which came before special committees, see McAroy v. The *Thistle*, note 146 below; National Archives, *The Revolutionary War Prize Cases* 26–27 (pamphlet accompanying Microcopy No. 162, Washington, 1954). It has been suggested that the idea of trial by committee may have come

Adams was appointed to the Standing Committee in March 1777 and served until November of that year, when he left Congress for good. Despite a busy schedule, he managed to participate in much of the Committee's work.[7] Its surviving file papers reveal that of eleven appeals decided during Adams' tenure, he sat on at least five. In five others the appellate papers are incomplete, so that the members of the Committee who sat cannot be determined. Thus Adams may well have been involved in additional cases.[8] The papers show that the Committee, which on at least one occasion took the style "Court of Commissioners of Appeals for the American States," viewed itself, and was viewed by Congress, as a judicial body. Thus, its procedure included provisions for notice, payment of costs, and the like, reflecting the legal background of its members. Its decisions were based on a full record of the trial below, as well as upon oral argument. These decisions were handed down with oral opinions, were in the form of judicial decrees, and were accorded the legal effect of such decrees.[9]

---

from the example of the British practice under which appeals from the Vice Admiralty courts in cases of prize went to Lords Commissioners for hearing such appeals, a committee of the Privy Council. Jameson, "The Predecessor of the Supreme Court," in J. Franklin Jameson, ed., *Essays in the Constitutional History of the United States* 13–16 (Boston and N.Y., 1889). It should be noted, however, that after 1762 this committee included the judges of the common-law courts. See 1 Holdsworth, *History of English Law* 565 note.

[7] JA was appointed to the Standing Committee on 12 March 1777, when three members were added to the original five. 7 JCC 172. On 8 May 1777, when the old committee was discharged as being "too numerous," he was one of a new committee of five, "they or any three of them to hear and determine upon appeals brought to Congress." *Id.* at 337. In Oct. he was the only one reappointed to a new committee constituted because "a number of the members appointed to hear and determine appeals are absent." Resolve of 13 Oct. 1777, 9 *id.* at 800. For his relief from the Committee, see Resolution of 17 Nov. 1777, 9 *id.* at 936. During this important year, he also presided over the constantly busy Board of War and Ordnance. There is no reference to the work of the Standing Committee in his diary, which is extremely fragmentary for this period, or in his Autobiography. See 2 JA, *Diary and Autobiography* 262 note; 3 *id.* at 447 note.

[8] The papers are preserved in DNA:RG 267. They have been filmed as National Archives Microcopy No. 162, "The Revolutionary War Prize Cases: Records of the Court of Appeals in Cases of Capture, 1776–1787," and will be hereinafter cited as DNA Microcopy 162, Case — (numbered documents within a case file will be cited as No. —). The five cases on which JA definitely sat were Newman v. The *Sherburne*, DNA Microcopy 162, Case 10 (see note 9 below); Alsop v. Ruttenbergh, *id.*, Case 11 (see note 147 below); The *Industry, id.*, Case 14; Palmer v. Hussey, *id.*, Case 17; The *Greenwich, id.*, Case 19. The appeal papers are incomplete for White v. Sloop *Polly* and Cargo, *id.*, Case 12; The *Leghorn, id.*, Case 13; The *Montgomery* v. The *Minerva, id.*, Case 15; Hopkins v. Derby, *id.*, Case 6; and Fowkes v. The *Roseanna, id.*, Case 20 (JA was familiar with the last-named case, decided just before his departure from Congress. See note 179 below). His name does not appear in the file of Pierce v. The *Phoenix*, DNA Microcopy 162, Case 8, but he had judged another phase of this case in The *Greenwich*, cited above.

[9] For the style of the "Court," see the decree in The *Industry*, DNA Microcopy 162, Case 14. The matters of procedure noted in the text appear in all of the cases having appeal papers which are cited in note 8 above. The attitude of Congress toward the court appears in the report of the Marine Committee on a petition

No. 58. *Penhallow v. The* Lusanna

The Court of Commissioners, and Adams' role in it, deserve a full analysis, which cannot be undertaken here. Despite the limitation of the court's jurisdiction to matters of prize, it foreshadowed the United States Supreme Court as the earliest permanent judicial body with a national jurisdiction. Equally important, the court, and its successor, the Court of Appeals in Cases of Capture, provided an opportunity for the development of an appellate procedure and jurisprudence, and a bar experienced in these matters, which permitted the Supreme Court to undertake its duties in 1789 unencumbered by the need for awkward experiment. Adams, who had had to resign from the chief justiceship of Massachusetts before he could enter upon the duties of that office, was thus finally enabled to serve on the bench in a much more significant way.[10] He was, if briefly, a member of what was in effect the first Supreme Court of the United States; as such, he participated in the establishment of an institution capable of handing on the appellate tradition which it began.

In November 1777, when he took leave from Congress for a much needed rest and return to personal affairs,[11] Adams was probably little aware of the long-range importance of his recent judicial activities. But he was soon to discover that they were of immediate value. Shortly after his arrival at Braintree he was plunged into a prize controversy between his old client Col. Elisha Doane, one of the richest men in New England,[12]

---

apparently transmitted through JA by his former client, Timothy Folger (No. 45), in behalf of the crew of a Nantucket whaler condemned as prize. The court in affirming the condemnation had awarded wages to the crew, as provided by resolve of Congress (note 108 below), but Folger sought a share of the profits for them, claiming this to be the custom of whalers. The Marine Committee reported adversely, on the grounds that the petition raised questions of "construction of the promulgated resolutions of Congress, which make part of the code of laws of maritime war, which laws ought to be construed and applied by the courts of admiralty and commissioners of appeals in their judicial capacity, and not by Congress"; and that since the case had already received "a judicial determination before the said courts" in which the issue might have been raised, it was improper for Congress to act upon it. The resolution was concurred in by Congress on 23 May 1777. See Newman v. The *Sherburne,* DNA Microcopy 162, Case 10; 8 JCC 383–384. The states were not so ready to recognize these decrees. See The *Active,* note 78 below.

[10] As to JA as Chief Justice, see vol. 1:xci above. For evaluation of the court's role, see sources cited in notes 5, 6, above. The continuity between the Court of Commissioners and the Supreme Court is perhaps best illustrated by the fact that James Wilson sat as a Commissioner with JA in many of the cases cited in note 8 above, then argued before the Court of Appeals in Cases of Capture (see note 84 below), and finally took his seat as one of the first members of the United States Supreme Court (see note 95 below).

[11] JA was granted leave on 7 Nov. 1777, left York, Penna., on the 11th, and arrived at Braintree on 27 November. See 9 JCC 880; 2 JA, *Diary and Autobiography* 267–269. An account of his reasons, which included the desire to obtain some of the legal business created by the prize courts, appears in 4 *id.* at 1.

[12] For another JA case involving Doane, see No. 52. Doane has been described as the second richest man in the Province. See Samuel E. Morison, *Maritime History of Massachusetts* 25 (Boston, 1921). Compare 2 JA, *Diary and Autobiography* 61.

and certain New Hampshire privateersmen, which brought into play his newly acquired expertise in such matters. The case is of real interest, not only because it marks Adams' last known appearance as an active trial lawyer, but because years later, in the Supreme Court of the United States, it led to an affirmation of the supremacy of the federal courts in a matter in which the states had yielded sovereignty.

The complicated story of the litigation can be pieced together from various contemporary sources, principally the files of the Continental Congress' Court of Appeals.[13] It begins in the summer of 1775, when the Cape Cod whaling fleet returned from the South Atlantic, having "proved to be tolerable successful," and Doane, whose headquarters were at Chatham, found himself with a considerable stock of whale oil on hand. The presence of the British fleet at Boston, and its evident intention to enforce the restrictions which Britain had laid upon New England's commerce,[14] meant that there was no local market for the oil. Moreover, like many a businessman whose country is on the verge of hostilities with a former trading partner, Doane had a considerable balance in his favor on the books of Lane, Son & Fraser, London merchants, as well as an unsold shipment of whalebone in their warehouse. He determined to realize upon these various assets before the worsening political situation led to their confiscation.[15] Accordingly, he loaded his brigantine *Lusanna*, already carrying considerable oil that she had herself brought back from the whaling grounds, with additional oil and other goods and arranged that his son-in-law Shearjashub Bourne, a lawyer and recanting addresser of Hutchinson, whose business had virtually disappeared with the closing of the courts,

[13] See Doane v. Treadwell and Penhallow; the Brig *Susannah*, DNA Microcopy 162, Case 30. The spelling "Lusanna" has been adopted in the present work for reasons stated in note 77 below.

[14] For restrictions on Massachusetts and the Port of Boston passed in 1774, see No. 53, text at notes 1, 2. New England was further restricted by the statute, 15 Geo. 3, c. 10 (1775), which provided that after 1 July 1775 enumerated goods produced in New England could not be exported and that other goods could be shipped only to Great Britain or the British West Indies. No imports were to be permitted except from Great Britain and, in certain cases, Ireland. The trade of New Jersey, Pennsylvania, Maryland, South Carolina, and Virginia was similarly restricted by 15 Geo. 3, c. 18 (1775). It was not until the Act of 16 Geo. 3, c. 5 (1776), note 173 below, that all colonial trade was embargoed. See generally, Arthur M. Schlesinger, *The Colonial Merchants and the American Revolution* 538–540 (N.Y., 1918).

[15] See Doane to Lane, Son & Fraser, 29 Aug. 1775, DNA Microcopy 162, Case 30, No. 107; Deposition of Joseph Doane, undated, 1778, *id.*, No. 133; Deposition of John Greenough, 19 Jan. 1778, *id.*, No. 127; Deposition of David Greenough, 20 Feb. 1778, *id.*, No. 136. An account furnished Doane in April 1781 by Lane, Son & Fraser, showed that, as of 30 April 1775, Doane's balance was £3690 19s. 6d. and that in April 1779, 34 bundles of whale fins in their hands sold for £530 17s. 1d. MHi: David S. Greenough Papers. For this and all other references to the Greenough Papers the editors are indebted to Mrs. Katherine A. Kellock of Washington, D.C., who has been of great assistance in the case of the *Lusanna*, not only by uncovering sources which might otherwise have been overlooked, but by supplying a chronology of the case, which was a valuable aid in the preparation of this editorial note.

should go with this cargo to London and there see to its sale and to the securing of Doane's other interests.[16]

On 4 September 1775, a week before the effective date of the ban laid on exports to Britain by the Continental Association, the *Lusanna*, Matthew Wood master, sailed from Wellfleet, having earlier cleared out at the custom house in Plymouth. Her cargo consisted of 101 casks of spermaceti oil and 37 casks of head matter belonging to Doane and consigned to Lane, Son & Fraser; 208 casks of spermaceti oil and 82 of head matter, belonging in part to Doane and in part to some of his whalemen, consigned to Bourne; and a quantity of staves and cord wood, belonging to Doane and also consigned to Bourne.[17]

The instructions which Doane gave to Bourne and to Lane, Son & Fraser were very broad. To alleviate a shortage of cash in Massachusetts, the *Lusanna*'s outward cargo of oil was to be sold and the proceeds brought directly to Doane by Bourne. If the acts of Parliament restricting New England were repealed, thus leading to the abrogation of the Continental Association, Bourne was to freight the *Lusanna* home with English goods, bought with Doane's London credits. If the Acts were not repealed, Bourne was to use Doane's funds to send the *Lusanna* with a cargo to the West Indies to be exchanged there for goods which did not violate the colonial ban on imports. If this was impossible, he was to carry English goods to Nova Scotia, take on a new, nonrestricted cargo there, clear out for the British West Indies, and come directly to Cape Cod. In any event he was to use his judgment in light of all the circumstances.[18]

Only a week after his departure Bourne met the setback which was to turn his trip from an ordinary if risky commercial venture into an epic voyage of mischance and duplicity. On 11 September, off Sable Island,

[16] Joseph Doane, who figured also in Doane v. Gage, No. 43, and Rex v. Nickerson, No. 57, had been master of the *Lusanna* on her whaling voyage and supervised her loading for the voyage to London. See his deposition, note 15 above. The *Lusanna*, a square-sterned brigantine of seventy tons, originally built as a sloop in 1760, had been purchased by Elisha Doane from his father's heirs and rebuilt in 1773. *Ibid.*; *Lusanna*'s Register, 28 June 1773, DNA Microcopy 162, Case 30, No. 62. For Bourne's recantation on 27 Sept. 1774 of his participation in the address of the bar to Governor Hutchinson at the latter's departure from the Province in June 1774, see Deposition of Nathaniel Freeman, 18 Aug. 1778, DNA Microcopy 162, Case 30, No. 122. Bourne (1746–1806), Harvard 1764, had been admitted an attorney in the Superior Court in 1767, and a barrister in 1772. Min. Bks. 82, 97, SCJ. He suffered no permanent ill effects from his involvement in the affair of the *Lusanna*, since he sat in the General Court in 1782–1785 and 1788–1790, was a member of the Ratification Convention in 1788, served in Congress from 1791 to 1795, and was appointed a Massachusetts Common Pleas judge in 1799. See *Biog. Dir. Cong.*

[17] See "Invoice of the Brigantine Lusanna's Cargo to London," undated, DNA Microcopy 162, Case 30, No. 103. Bills of lading and other shipping documents appear in *id.*, Nos. 90–99. For the certificates of bond which she gave on clearance, see *id.*, Nos. 63, 64, 66. Compare Deposition of Matthew Wood, 28 Jan. 1778, *id.*, No. 118. As to the Continental Association, see note 121 below.

[18] Doane to Bourne, 29 Aug. 1775, DNA Microcopy 162, Case 30, No. 92; Doane to Lane, Son & Fraser, 29 Aug. 1775, *id.*, No. 107.

about 200 miles east and south of Halifax, the *Lusanna* was "met by a violent gale of wind from E, and then shifting to ENE shattered our sails and rigging to a great degree carryd away our foretopmast without any canvas Spread and caused the brig to leak very much." [19] Thus damaged, she was forced to put into Halifax for repairs; on entering the harbor there, she was seized by a boat belonging to the *Somerset* man-of-war. The *Lusanna* was held for three weeks, although, according to Bourne, the attorney general at Halifax had ruled that all her papers were in order and that she was not in violation of any Act of Parliament.[20] Finally she was released by order of Admiral Graves at Boston, and repairs were undertaken.

When the *Lusanna* was almost ready for sea, she was seized again on 28 October, apparently by virtue of new orders received by the Admiral from England, requiring all New England vessels to be detained until further notice.[21] Bourne at once left for Boston, where he procured the vessel's release, reportedly on condition that he take out a new register in Halifax, listing the vessel as of that port.[22] At the time it was rumored that he had also agreed to bring a cargo back to Halifax.[23] It is even possible that in his negotiations with Admiral Graves he had adopted the role of fleeing loyalist which he later played in England to his subsequent embarrassment, but there is no evidence of this. Whatever Bourne's tactics, his success is attested by the fact that the *Lusanna* left Halifax, probably early in January, and arrived in London, "after a tedious passage," sometime in March.[24]

Once in England, Bourne set about his assignment. The oil market was not at a desirable pitch in the spring of 1776, but, by October, Lane, Son & Fraser were able to report to Bourne that they had sold a good portion of the oil at a price near that which Doane had wanted, and that they expected little difficulty in selling the remainder.[25] Bourne could not yet come home, however. He feared that an American vessel of ambiguous loyalties

[19] Bourne to Doane, Halifax, 29 Sept. 1775, DNA Microcopy 162, Case 30, No. 76.
[20] Bourne to Doane, Halifax, 29 Sept. 1775, DNA Microcopy 162, Case 30, No. 76.
[21] Bourne to Lane, Son & Fraser, Halifax, 3 Nov. 1775, note 125 below; Deposition of Richard Baxter, 9 Jan. 1778, DNA Microcopy 162, Case 30, No. 148.
[22] Bourne to Lane, Son & Fraser, Halifax, 31 Dec. 1775, note 126 below. As to the condition, see Deposition of Matthew Wood, 28 Jan. 1778, DNA Microcopy 162, Case 30, No. 118.
[23] Doane to Bourne, 12 Feb. 1776, DNA Microcopy 162, Case 30, No. 113.
[24] Bourne to Doane, London, 6 May 1776, DNA Microcopy 162, Case 30, No. 77. Deposition of Richard Baxter, 9 Jan. 1778, *id.*, No. 148. On 11 April 1776, Samuel Curwen, chronicler of the doings of loyalists in London, reported that he had dined in company with "a Mr. Bourne, lately arrived from Halifax . . . a grave solid man." Curwen, *Journal and Letters* 52–53 (London, 1842). The editors are indebted to Mrs. Kellock for this reference.
[25] Doane wanted £45 per ton for body oil and a proportionate price for head matter. The sale in Oct. was at £43 for body oil. Lane, Son & Fraser to Bourne, 1 Oct. 1776, PCC No. 44, fol. 311. See Doane to Lane, Son & Fraser, 29 Aug. 1775, DNA Microcopy 162, Case 30, No. 107.

in London at that period would excite a certain amount of suspicion, and he deemed it unwise to hazard apprehension by the British until conditions improved.[26] Other affairs kept him busy. Although witnesses later testified that Bourne had refused to charter the *Lusanna* to the military transport service, Lane, Son & Fraser got her a cargo to Gibraltar, which the evidence indicates was at least in part military stores. After having been registered again, this time as belonging to Shearjashub Bourne "of London," she sailed for the Mediterranean at the end of September 1776, returning in February or March of the following year.[27]

Bourne was also charged with establishing correspondence with a London merchant for a new venture in the commission sale of "Oil, Pot and Pearl ashes &c.," in which he, Doane, and Doane's son Isaiah sought to embark. No details of his "plan" for this enterprise have been uncovered, but he was able to report that he had "settled the correspondence come out for with the best house in England for our interest . . . so that nothing prevents a prosecution but the American war." At the same time he took advantage of his enforced stay to travel around England, meeting influential merchants and learning as much as he could about manufacturing, markets, and trade, for future commercial use. [28]

Another matter which concerned Bourne was Doane's claim to a part of the cargo of the brigantine *Industry*, which had sailed from Wellfleet on 12 September 1775 and was seized off Plymouth on the same day by a British naval vessel. Aboard her were an additional 102 casks of whale oil belonging to Doane, consigned to Bourne or to Lane, Son & Fraser in London. A claim had been entered on behalf of the *Industry*'s owner for vessel and cargo, but on 12 October both were condemned in the Massachusetts Vice Admiralty Court for failure to give bond as required by the Restraining Act of 1775.[29] The troubled conditions in Massachusetts had

[26] Bourne to Doane, 12 Oct. 1776, note 128 below; same to same, 18 Sept. 1776, DNA Microcopy 162, Case 30, No. 78.

[27] See Deposition of Matthew Wood, 28 Jan. 1778, DNA Microcopy 162, Case 30, No. 118; Lane, Son & Fraser to Bourne, 1 Oct. 1776, note 114 below; Deposition of Lot Lewis, 4 Dec. 1777, note 117 below; *Lusanna*'s register, 3 Aug. 1776, note 110 below; Deposition of David Smith, 13 July 1778, DNA Microcopy 162, Case 30, No. 135. Doane had suggested the change in register in a letter of 12 Feb. 1776. *Id.*, No. 113. The *Lusanna*'s account with Lane, Son & Fraser, furnished by the latter in 1781, and a letter of Doane's widow to them, 14 Nov. 1783, confirm that government stores were a part of the cargo out, and indicate that on the voyage the vessel called at Barcelona and took on freight at Malaga. MHi:Greenough Papers; see note 114 below.

[28] Doane to Lane, Son & Fraser, 29 Aug. 1775, DNA Microcopy 162, Case 30, No. 107; Bourne to Doane, 18 Sept. 1776, *id.*, No. 78; see also same to same, 12 Oct. 1776, *id.*, No. 29.

[29] Note 14 above. The papers in the action are in DNA Microcopy 162, Case 30, Nos. 37–58. See note 130 below. See also Deposition of Jacob Williams, 31 Aug. 1778, *id.*, No. 140. The claimant had sought an appeal to the Privy Council, but withdrew it upon advice of counsel. Opinion of Daniel Leonard, 4 Aug. 1777, PRO, Treas. 1:528. The *Industry* herself was reported destroyed in March 1776 when the British left Boston. Bourne to Doane, 18 Sept. 1776, DNA Microcopy 162, Case 30, No. 78. For some earlier problems of her new owners, see PRO, Treas. 1:513,

359

prevented Doane from making an appearance in the suit. When Bourne heard of this he procured from Doane a power of attorney to act in the matter, and a certificate of the collector of customs at Plymouth that he had not had the proper forms available when the *Industry* had cleared.[30]

Extracts from Bourne's journal, and a memorial which he submitted to the Treasury in England, show that, for this purpose at least, he had assumed full loyalist coloration. He sought and obtained the favor of Thomas Hutchinson in London as he pressed his cause, and in the memorial told a sad tale of his flight from the colonies and his persecution at the hands of the villains who now were running the country. This document, prepared in January 1777, did at least reach the proper committee, but the claim was apparently rejected on the basis of an adverse opinion by Daniel Leonard, formerly of the Massachusetts bar, now solicitor to the American Customs Commissioners in London. Leonard found that Bourne could have had no interest in the voyage, that the owners had probably intended to bring back military supplies to the rebels, and that the collector had cleared her only under duress.[31] An unintended result, however, was that journal and memorial were offered in evidence on the subsequent trial of the *Lusanna* as prize, doubtless contributing substantially to the jury's determination against Doane.[32] Unfortunately for Doane and Bourne, Leonard's opinion was not available as a counterweight.

While he was pursuing the *Industry* claim, Bourne was apparently also seriously considering means of getting home. According to the later testimony of David Smith, a Cape Cod whaling captain who met him in London in February 1777, Bourne had at that date already developed what was essentially the scheme that he would later unsuccessfully attempt to carry out. When the last of the whale oil was sold, he planned to purchase a partial cargo for the *Lusanna* with £2000–3000 of Doane's funds, then take on other cargo for Halifax to avoid suspicion and clear out for that port. In Halifax he would obtain the remainder of Doane's English funds by negotiating bills of exchange on Lane, Son & Fraser, then clear the *Lusanna* out for the British West Indies with Doane's goods still aboard and the cash in his strongbox. En route to the latter destination it would be a simple matter to put into a port on Cape Cod or other friendly territory.[33]

---

fol. 266, *et seq.* Notes of the contents of the PRO documents were furnished to the editors by Mrs. Kellock.

[30] See Deposition of John McFarland, In the Exchequer, 28 Jan. 1777, DNA Microcopy 162, Case 30, No. 58; Doane to Bourne, 12 Feb. 1776, *id.*, No. 113; Doane's power of attorney to Bourne, 1 Oct. 1775, *id.*, No. 61; Certificate of Edward Winslow, Deputy Collector, Plymouth, 1 Feb. 1776, *id.*, No. 57. It was later suggested that the claim had been made with Doane's assent and that he could have entered Boston to appear. Opinion of Daniel Leonard, 4 Aug. 1777, PRO, Treas. 1:528.

[31] Opinion of Daniel Leonard, 4 Aug. 1777, PRO, Treas. 1:528, with endorsement of Richard Reeve, secretary to the Commissioners, 27 Aug. 1777, indicating that on the basis of the opinion Bourne's memorial would not be acted upon further.

[32] Bourne's Memorial to Lords of Treasury, 30 Jan. 1777, in note 119 below. Extracts from Bourne's journal in note 158 below.

[33] Deposition of Captain David Smith, 13 July 1778, DNA Microcopy 162, Case

Whether this was the plan or not, the *Lusanna* began loading in June 1777 and cleared out at London for Halifax at the end of July. About 20 August, she left London, actually sailing from the Isle of Wight on 13 September.[34] Her cargo included various goods to the value of about £2000, consigned by Lane, Son & Fraser to Bourne at Halifax, and provisions and liquors worth about £200 consigned by Bourne to himself or Messrs. Thomas Cochran & Co., Halifax merchants. Witnesses later said that Bourne claimed the ownership of all of these goods. The *Lusanna* also carried miscellaneous merchandise shipped by eight other English merchants, some of it consigned to Bourne, the rest to specific consignees in Halifax.[35] Several passengers were aboard,[36] as well as goods belonging to Captain James Shepherd, a Bostonian who had left London aboard the *Lusanna* after a fruitless attempt to appeal the seizure of his ship at Halifax a year earlier. Shepherd had been forced to remain at Cowes on the Isle of Wight, when he had been taken sick just before sailing, but his goods stayed aboard, consigned to Bourne.[37]

Bourne carried with him letters of introduction not only to Halifax merchants, but to Captain William Spry, "Commanding Engineer" there, which recommended him highly and spoke of his intention to remain at his destination, chartering the *Lusanna* as a transport until the war should end.[38] He also carried two letters of credit, permitting him to draw up to £7000 against funds in the hands of Lane, Son & Fraser, in London.[39] His own letter of instructions to Messrs. Cochran indicates the somewhat ambiguous nature of his intentions.

He wanted to sell the goods shipped by others for the interest of the shippers. The provisions shipped by Bourne, which he described as "belonging to myself," were to be sold for his own interest, and an accounting

---

30, No. 135. See also Deposition of William Claghorn, 20 Aug. 1778, *id.*, No. 149. Doane had suggested a somewhat similar plan in his instructions to Bourne on 29 Aug. 1775, note 18 above. See Deposition of David S. Greenough, 20 Feb. 1778, DNA Microcopy 162, Case 30, No. 136.

[34] See Invoice and Bill of Lading, Lane, Son & Fraser to Bourne, 10 June 1777, note 111 below; Certificate of bond for enumerated goods, London, 26 July 1777, DNA Microcopy 162, Case 30, No. 32; Deposition of Thomas Casey, 3 Dec. 1777, note 113 below; Deposition of Lot Lewis, note 117 below.

[35] For the first two invoices consigned to Bourne, see notes 111, 112, below (a complete inventory of the £2000 invoice appears in SF 104193). For the others, see DNA Microcopy 162, Case 30, Nos. 16–27. See also notes 116, 139, below.

[36] See Depositions of Thomas and Mary Casey, 3 Dec. 1777, notes 113, 115, below; Deposition of Edmond Coffin, 2 Sept. 1778, DNA Microcopy 162, Case 30, No. 121.

[37] See note 132 below. As to Shepherd's problems, see Deposition of Matthew Wood, 28 Jan. 1778, DNA Microcopy 162, Case 30, No. 146.

[38] Edward Crosby to William Spry, 16 July 1777, note 118 below. See also William Cochran to Thomas Cochran & Co., 23 Aug. 1777, DNA Microcopy 162, Case 30, No. 35.

[39] See note 160 below. The oil had apparently not been sold at this date, since Lane, Son & Fraser's account in 1781 shows that it was not until Sept. 1778 that £3378 10s. 2d. was credited to Doane as proceeds of its sale, giving him a balance, with interest, of £7732 18s. 6d. No drafts against the letters of credit were ever charged to this account. MHi:Greenough Papers.

made with Bourne, Lane, Son & Fraser, or Doane. The goods in the amount of £2000 shipped by Lane, Son & Fraser, which Bourne also claimed as his, were to be stored until further orders from Doane, Lane, Son & Fraser, or Bourne, and the *Lusanna* was to be laid up on the same terms.[40]

The *Lusanna* sailed as part of a fleet in convoy with the British frigate *Venus*, but on the night of 25 October she lost her escort in the fog, and in the morning Wood and Bourne determined to proceed to Halifax as best they could. Four days later on the 30th, they sighted an American privateer, which later proved to be the *McClary* out of Portsmouth. The *Lusanna* fled, but after a chase of about an hour and a half, she was over-hauled. Several broadsides were fired by the *McClary*, and the *Lusanna*, outgunned as well as outsailed, soon struck.[41]

The *McClary* brought the prize into Portsmouth, where on 11 November 1777 she was libeled in the Court Maritime of the State of New Hampshire.[42] The libelants were John Penhallow and Jacob Treadwell, representatives of the fifteen Portsmouth merchants who owned the privateer; and George Wentworth, agent for the crew, who was also a Portsmouth merchant and the brother of one of the owners.[43]

Bourne at once began a desperate search for counsel; not only were there considerable sums at stake, but the circumstances of the capture were such that his loyalty to the American cause might be questioned. Oliver Whipple, a Portsmouth lawyer, was engaged to watch over the preliminaries. On 17 November, Bourne wrote for assistance to Robert Treat Paine, who had not returned to Congress after his reelection in December 1776, and was now a member of the General Court and Attorney General of Massachu-

[40] Bourne to Messrs. Thomas Cochran & Co., undated, note 116 below.

[41] See Deposition of Thomas Casey, 3 Dec. 1777, note 113 below; Deposition of Lot Lewis, 4 Dec. 1777, note 117 below; Libel, New Hampshire Court Maritime, 11 Nov. 1777, note 107 below. The *McClary*, one of New Hampshire's leading privateers, was herself captured and her crew imprisoned at Halifax in 1778. Richard F. Upton, *Revolutionary New-Hampshire* 110, 112 (Hanover, N.H., 1936). See Library of Congress, *Naval Records of the American Revolution* 381 (Washington, 1906). The editors are indebted to Mrs. Kellock for the latter reference.

[42] See note 107 below.

[43] The owners were John Penhallow, Joshua Wentworth, Ammi R. Cutter, Nathaniel Folsom, Samuel Sherburne, Thomas Martin, Moses Woodward, Neil McIntire, George Turner, Richard Champney, Robert Furniss, Jacob Treadwell, Thomas Dalling, Daniel Sherburne, and Keith Spence. See *A Statement of the Cause of the M'Clary Owners, and Doane & Doane's Administrators from its Commencement in 1777, to its Close in the Supreme-Court of the United States, Feb. 1795* 5 (Portsmouth, 1795). Their counsel is noted by JA only as "Sewall," and no other reference to his name has been found. This is either Jonathan M. Sewall (1748–1808), a Portsmouth lawyer who was also register of the Court Maritime, or David Sewall of York, Maine, about to take his seat on the Massachusetts Superior Court, who was present in company with JA at General Whipple's on 18 December. See Bell, *Bench and Bar of New Hampshire* 629–630; 2 Stiles, *Literary Diary* 238. Since "Sewall" appears twice in JA's minutes (see text at note 107, and following note 117, below), it is possible that both Sewalls argued for the libelants. The second appearance, however, could reflect a recess and a resumption of note-taking by JA. See also note 88 below.

setts. Paine apparently could not take the case because he had to attend the General Court which sat at Boston from 4 to 15 December.[44] Luckily, however, Adams reached Braintree on 27 November and some time thereafter was engaged by Doane.[45] Paine seems to have been kept on retainer, for he was supplied with full notes of the trial, made by Whipple (Document III), and he argued the case on appeal to the New Hampshire Superior Court in March and September 1778.[46] John Lowell, another Massachusetts lawyer, who had lived in Newburyport until some time in 1777, was also engaged by Bourne and Doane.

Lowell filed three claims in the Portsmouth court on 1 December 1777. The first, on behalf of Elisha Doane, was for the *Lusanna* herself, her appurtenances and stores, and that portion of the cargo that had been consigned to Bourne by Lane, Son & Fraser. A second claim, in behalf of James Shepherd, was made for the goods which the unfortunate captain had shipped. The third claim was in the name of Isaiah Doane, the Colonel's son and trading partner, and was for the provisions and liquors which Bourne had shipped to himself, as well as for a few other items, apparently also Bourne's.[47] Bourne had conveyed this property to Isaiah Doane on 24 November 1777 in an admitted effort to divest himself of all interest in the outcome, so that under strict 18th-century rules of evidence he could qualify as a witness.[48] The rest of the cargo was unclaimed.

Originally set for 8 December, the trial was postponed until the 16th.[49] Bourne had urged Adams to arrive in Portsmouth on Saturday night the 13th to allow ample time for consultation and preparation beforehand (Document I). Adams endeavored to comply, but on the 13th, his second

[44] Paine had also had experience on prize appeals in Congress. See notes 146, 148, below. He had apparently already told Bourne's emissary that he could not attend the trial when Bourne wrote him requesting "Council in a Cause which nearly affects my interest, (if not Character)," and asking that Paine reconsider. He went on: "If Sir you are previously engaged, I can say no more. If you are under a retaining *fee* I can only say, I am unfortunate; if you are at liberty and so engaged, that you cannot attend me and Mr. Doane at the first tryal, and it so happens, that an appeal is claimed by either party, I must beg your assistance to support Mr. Whipple and Mr. Lowell, the first of which I have engaged, and the last I have this day dispatched an agent to engage." Bourne to Paine, 17 Nov. 1777, MHi:Paine Papers. The editors are indebted to Mrs. Kellock for this reference. Paine did attend the General Court. See Paine Diary, 4–15 Dec. 1777, and his "Draft of an Address of the General Court to the People—on the Act to restrain the Circulation of the State Currency," 12–15 Dec. 1777, Paine Papers. Whipple (1743–1813), Harvard 1766, came to Portsmouth from his native Rhode Island and was not related to William Whipple, the New Hampshire delegate to Congress. See Whipple to JA, 26 April 1790, Adams Papers. Bell, *Bench and Bar of New Hampshire* 739–741. In the weeks before the trial he was present at the taking of several depositions in Portsmouth. See notes 113, 115, 117, below.

[45] See Doc. I, below; note 11 above.

[46] See note 67 below.

[47] The three claims appear in DNA Microcopy 162, Case 30, Nos. 3, 4, 5.

[48] See Doc. I. As to the rules on interested witnesses, see Gilbert, *Evidence* 122–134; No. 2.

[49] See published notice of monition, dated 14 Nov. 1777, in Portsmouth *Freeman's Journal*, 29 Nov. 1777, p. 2, cols. 2–3.

day of travel, "a horrid cold Rain" that wet him through caused him to halt at Newburyport, while "Coll. Doane who was in a stage Coach and his son who was in a close sulky proceeded on." [50] Adams finally caught up with his seemingly inconsiderate clients at Portsmouth the next evening. After spending a night at "the Tavern, Tiltons," headquarters of Doane's party, he moved to the house of General William Whipple, his friend and colleague in Congress, where his conversation seems to have made more of an impression upon the Reverend Ezra Stiles than his arguments later did upon the jury.[51]

On the eve of the trial Adams wrote most prophetically to Abigail: "The Cause comes on Tomorrow, before my old Friend Dr. Joshua Brackett, as Judge of Admiralty. How it will go I know not. The Captors are a numerous Company, and are said to be very tenacious, and have many Connections; so that We have Prejudice, and Influence to fear: Justice, Policy and Law, are, I am very sure, on our Side." [52] Adams was certainly not the first lawyer to discover that the latter three elements, however valuable, are not enough to outweigh a judge, who, despite old acquaintance, rules the "wrong" way on points of law, and a jury, whether prejudiced or stubborn, which refuses to accept a subtle interpretation of an ambiguous factual situation.

The evidence at the trial consisted primarily of papers found aboard the *Lusanna,* or submitted by Doane from his records, and the depositions of absent witnesses.[53] Probably prior to trial, counsel for Doane had offered a set of interrogatories raising questions as to Bourne's role and the ownership of vessel and cargo, which were to be administered to Bourne, Matthew

[50] JA to AA, 13 Dec. 1777, 2 *Adams Family Correspondence* 369.

[51] JA to AA, 15 Dec. 1777, 2 *Adams Family Correspondence* 374. For JA's conversation on the evenings of 17 and 18 Dec., ranging from politics to law and history, see 2 Stiles, *Literary Diary* 237–238.

[52] JA to AA, 15 Dec. 1777, 2 *Adams Family Correspondence* 374. Brackett (1733–1802), Harvard 1752, A.M. 1755, M.D. (Hon.) 1792, after first studying theology, took up medicine and became a successful practitioner at Portsmouth. After the Revolution he was an officer of the Massachusetts and New Hampshire Medical Societies and donated $1500 toward a Harvard professorship in natural history and botany. He was appointed Judge of Admiralty at the beginning of the Revolution and held the post until the creation of the United States District Court in 1789. The sources consulted do not reveal the basis upon which he was given this position. He was active in the patriot cause, serving on the Committee of Safety, but perhaps his education and intellectual attainments were the qualifications which recommended him for the appointment. See Nathaniel Adams, *Annals of Portsmouth* 321–324 (Portsmouth, 1825); J. Farmer and J. B. Moore, eds., *Collections, Historical and Miscellaneous: and Monthly Literary Journal,* 2:17–21 (Concord, N.H., 1823); MH:Archives. Brackett may have been JA's old friend, but he was undoubtedly a current acquaintance of at least 10 of the *McClary* owners, who, with him, were members of Ezra Stiles' congregation. See 2 Stiles, *Literary Diary* 171–173; see also note 43 above.

[53] There were also apparently at least two witnesses actually present at the trial. See note 123 below. The New Hampshire statute establishing the court required that all papers found aboard ship be filed with the court and permitted witnesses to testify either by deposition or in person. Act of 3 July 1776, 4 *Laws of New Hampshire* 25, 28, 31 (Bristol, N.H., ed. H. H. Metcalf, 1916).

Wood, and "other witnesses." On the libelants' motion Bourne and Wood were rejected by the court as interested in the outcome, thus defeating Bourne's stratagem of conveying away his interest.[54] No other witnesses were called by the claimants to testify to the issues which the interrogatories covered, although many of the same questions were asked of the libelants' witnesses on cross-examination during the taking of depositions.

As Adams' minutes (Document II) and those of Whipple (Document III) show, the libelants asserted two principal grounds of condemnation, based on Resolves of Congress and New Hampshire statutes: (1) That the vessel and goods were forfeited as being the property of inhabitants or subjects of Great Britain. (2) That vessel and goods were forfeited because the *Lusanna* was carrying supplies to the "Fleet or Army" of the enemy.[55] To the first point counsel for the captors argued that the evidence of the register and invoices, as well as several depositions, showed that the property in both vessel and goods was Bourne's, not Doane's, and that Bourne by his statements and actions, including insuring the vessel against loss to American privateers, had revealed himself as a loyal subject of the Crown. They also apparently argued that since English insurers would actually bear the loss, the goods were in effect British property. On the second point the libelants urged both the voyage of the *Lusanna* to Gibraltar in 1776 and her clearance with cargo for Halifax on her last voyage. Adams and Lowell sought to have evidence of the Gibraltar trip rejected as being outside the allegations of the libel, but the court once more ruled against the claimants. As to the Halifax point, the libelants could not offer direct evidence that the cargo was being shipped to the British forces, but pointed again to their evidence of Bourne's loyalist sympathies.

Adams and Lowell argued in opposition that on the facts the property was still Doane's, since Bourne had no authority as his agent to effect a conveyance; in any event, all of Bourne's representations of ownership were a "cover" designed to avert British suspicions. As to Bourne's alleged loyalty to George III, it was part of the "cover," but even if it had been fact, it could not be imputed to Doane. In his argument as reported by Whipple (Document III), Adams contended that the insurance against privateers was also part of the "cover," and that merely because it threw the loss on British insurers, it could not be deemed to pass the property to inhabitants of Great Britain. Having previously lost the argument on the relevance of the Gibraltar voyage, Adams and Lowell were forced to take the position that royal forces there were not "the enemy" within the meaning of the applicable statutes, and that the evidence was inadequate

---

[54] See Interrogatories, with minute of court's ruling, undated, DNA Microcopy 162, Case 30, No. 84. The "Instructions to Privateers," contained in a resolve of Congress, dated 3 April 1776, followed Admiralty practice in requiring the submission to the court of interrogatories taken from the master and principal persons aboard the captured vessel. 4 JCC 253–254. There was no comparable provision in the New Hampshire act, note 53 above.

[55] They asserted a third ground, that the goods were forfeit as being of British manufacture, but it was not seriously pressed and seems to have had little weight. See note 107 below.

to show that supplies had actually been transported to the fleet or army. As for Halifax, they argued that the necessities of the situation, rather than loyalist sympathies, explained Bourne's clearing for that port, and that the evidence was to the effect that none of the cargo had been intended for the fleet and army.

Despite these arguments the jury brought in a general verdict for the libelants, and the court decreed the *Lusanna* and her cargo forfeit.[56] The basis of the verdict of course cannot be known, but it can be justified on the facts. The first ground of condemnation urged in the libel, that vessel and cargo were the property of British subjects, should not properly have been the basis of forfeiture. The general situation and the letters and other papers of Bourne and Doane, which the libelants did not impeach, suggest most strongly that the property remained in Doane throughout, and that all actions and representations on Bourne's part tending to the contrary were only a ruse intended to prevent seizure by the British. The libelants offered no evidence that Bourne had used his own funds for goods or credit. Since the vessel and goods belonged to Doane, and his loyalty was unchallenged, the property could not be that of an inhabitant or subject of Great Britain; further, even if Bourne were a loyalist, to the extent that he acted as a British subject or inhabitant, he would seem to have acted outside the scope of the very broad authority given him by Doane, so that the latter could not be charged with such conduct.

The libelants were on stronger ground with the contention that the *Lusanna* had been carrying supplies to the enemy. The court's decision that evidence of the Gibraltar run was within the libel seems strained, because the analogy to a continuing trespass apparently relied on is dubious. Here two distinct events are in question; moreover, 18th-century practice generally favored an identity of pleading and proof.[57] Once admitted, however, the evidence, if believed, provided an arguable basis for forfeiture. Adams urged that the applicable statutes covered only enemy forces actually arrayed against the colonies (Document III), a reasonable construction of the Resolve of Congress. The New Hampshire statute also relied upon by the libelants could be read to include activities in other parts of the world, however.[58] If Adams argued that the latter statute did not apply in the face of resolves of Congress which occupied the field, Whipple did not record the fact.

As to the Halifax voyage, once again the New Hampshire act was broad enough to include carrying supplies to the inhabitants of enemy territory, as well as to enemy forces. Even if such a construction were not adopted, the evidence of Bourne's loyalist position, which was damning if the explanation of it was not believed, gave rise to an inference that he was dealing with consignees who would sell to the armed forces, thus indirectly supplying the enemy even in the narrower sense. No troublesome ques-

[56] See Decree, New Hampshire Court Maritime, 16 Dec. 1777, PCC No. 44, fols. 263–264.

[57] See note 122, text following note 169, below.

[58] See note 109 below.

tions of Doane's liability for these acts of his agent had to be met, because, under the New Hampshire act at least, condemnation turned on the employment of the vessel, rather than on its ownership.[59]

In fairness to Bourne it should be noted that he had to go to Halifax; he could not leave Britain without clearing for a loyal port, and he could not draw the bulk of Doane's funds except through bills negotiated there, unless he wanted to carry them in specie, subject to both the natural perils of the sea and the danger of British or American naval action. In fairness to the jury, Bourne was in fact headed for Halifax with a history of loyalist sympathy and a cargo consigned there; whatever his intentions, he was still in a position at Halifax to trade with the enemy; and at the trial it was explanations by his counsel rather than hard evidence of his character or motives which were balanced against his prior conduct. Bourne in all probability intended to make for Cape Cod with whatever assets he could salvage as soon as he safely could, but he had sufficiently compromised himself through the exigencies of his situation that he had to bear the risk of being misunderstood. The Portsmouth jury was not only of local origin, but may well have been subject to influence by the *McClary* owners.[60] On the evidence before it, however, the verdict of condemnation was not clearly the result of prejudice and bias.

After the decree the claimants sought an appeal to Congress. This the court denied, on the ground that the applicable New Hampshire statutes provided an appeal only to the state Superior Court.[61] Here was the issue which was to keep the case in the courts until 1795—the question of federal against state power. Adams did not participate in the later phases of the litigation, but his argument at Portsmouth reveals that the problems of overlapping jurisdiction were present even on the lower level. He seemed to assume that the resolves of Congress would control, since, as has been noted, he apparently did not argue the point. Thus, not only did he base his argument entirely on those resolves, ignoring the conflicting language of the New Hampshire act, but he, and Lowell also, cited prior decisions from their experience with the Congressional Commissioners of Appeals as precedents for the construction of the resolves.[62] In addition, Adams supplied a kind of "horse's mouth" legislative history, both of these statutes and of other Congressional measures, such as the Continental Association

[59] The New Hampshire act, note 109 below, makes liable to forfeiture vessels "carrying supplies . . . or whose Masters or Supercargoes shall have design of carrying such supplies." The resolve of Congress in question, note 108 below, deals with "all vessels to whomsoever belonging employed," in carrying supplies, which might be construed to include only voyages to which the owner was privy.

[60] The jury was Perkin Ayers, David Page, Ebenezer Neal, Benjamin Marston, James Neal, Samuel Rand, Joseph Philbrook, Richard Brown, David Lock, Thomas Johnston, Joshua Brackett, and William Simpson. Ayers was appointed foreman by the Court. DNA:RG 267, National Archives Microcopy No. 214, "Appellate Case Files of the Supreme Court of the United States" [hereinafter DNA Microcopy 214], Case 6, fols. 50–51. The relationship of the Joshua Brackett on the jury and Judge Brackett is not known.

[61] See Decree, New Hampshire Court Maritime, 16 Dec. 1777, note 56 above.

[62] See text and notes 146–148, 179, below.

and Declaration of Independence.[63] The jury seems to have ignored these authorities, as well as the implication that they alone were decisive of the case.

The trial of the *Lusanna* marked the end of Adams' active legal career in a very definite way. According to his Autobiography, it was while he was actually attending in court that "Mr. Langdon came in from Phyladelphia and leaning over the Bar whispered to me, that Mr. Deane was recalled, and I was appointed to go to France." [64] The date of this dramatic episode cannot be determined exactly, since the duration of the trial is not known, but it must have been between 16 December and the 20th, when Ezra Stiles reported in his diary that the news was known in Portsmouth.[65] It was almost certainly on the latter date that Adams left for Boston, because he arrived at Braintree on 22 December. On the following day he accepted appointment as a Joint Commissioner to France in a letter to Henry Laurens, President of Congress. He can have had little time or inclination for further involvement in practice during the few short weeks of preparation before his departure from Braintree on 13 February 1778 aboard the Continental frigate *Boston*.[66]

The subsequent history of the *Lusanna* is of great complexity, and can be only sketched here. In March 1778 the case was entered at the Superior Court with Paine now joining Lowell as counsel for the claimants. There the jury disagreed and was discharged. At the September 1778 term of the court at Exeter, the case came on again for a lengthy trial.[67] At least 38 new depositions were produced, nearly all of them for the claimants. The areas in which they sought to bolster their case are an interesting reflection of the weaknesses which appeared at the trial in the Maritime Court. Bourne was again rejected as an interested witness,[68] but Matthew Wood's testimony as to the voyage out and Shepherd's predicament was

[63] See text at notes 176–178 below. The rejection of the interrogatories, note 54 above, is another example of state refusal to accept federal directives.

[64] 4 JA, *Diary and Autobiography* 2–3.

[65] 2 Stiles, *Literary Diary* 239.

[66] As to JA's return to Braintree and acceptance of the appointment, see 2 *Adams Family Correspondence* 375 note. For his departure for France, see 2 JA, *Diary and Autobiography* 269–271. He was retained in at least one other prize case after his return, giving advice to the privateer's agent, probably during his stay in Newburyport en route to Portsmouth in December (note 50 above). The trial at the Feb. 1778 Superior Court went on without him. See Samuel Tufts to JA, 6 Jan. 1778, 2 *Adams Family Correspondence* 377–378. JA was also forced to forgo an appearance in one of the Kennebec Company's numerous land cases set for the Feb. term. See John Lowell to AA, 22 Feb. 1778, *id at* 393–394; ——— to AA, 23 Feb. 1778, *id.* at 394–395. The Company on 14 Jan. 1778 voted to give him a fee of $100 in this cause. 3 Kennebec Purchase Records 132, MeHi.

[67] See Decree of New Hampshire Superior Court, Sept. Term. 1778, DNA Microcopy 162, Case 30, No. 165. See also Paine's notes of both trials in the Paine Law Notes. Paine's diary shows that the March trial lasted from 11 to 13 March; on the 14th "the jury came in and informed the Court they could not agree. The papers taken from them and the Cause Continued." The second trial lasted from 2 to 4 September. Paine Diary.

[68] Interrogatories to Bourne, Sept. 1778, DNA Microcopy 162, Case 30, No. 158.

this time accepted.[69] Other witnesses testified to the extent of Doane's credits in the hands of Lane, Son & Fraser; to Bourne's character as a patriot and his occupation as a lawyer with no trading interests, who went to London merely as Doane's agent; to Doane's ownership of a share of the *Industry*'s cargo; to the common practice among American captains of taking out false registers and clearances in British ports to avoid seizure; [70] and to Bourne's plans in February 1777 to clear out with false papers and make for home.[71]

The chief source of contention seemed to be the status of Halifax, a matter which both sides had left to assumption in the earlier trial. The claimants produced at least twelve depositions to the effect that the British garrison there was small and unwarlike, that the inhabitants were friendly toward America, and that the consignees of the *Lusanna*'s cargo were not army or navy supply contractors.[72] Here the libelants interposed the only new evidence which they offered, two depositions stating that there was a sizable garrison at Halifax with a real military role, and that a substantial number of naval vessels berthed there.[73] Finally, several depositions were offered in behalf of James Shepherd, testifying to his patriotism and to his ownership of the goods which he claimed.[74] Despite this mass of evidence, the jury found for the libelants once more. The claimants' appeal to Congress was again refused,[75] and on 18 September the *Lusanna* and her cargo were sold at auction under the court's decree. After court costs of £59 15s. and costs of sale were deducted, the "neat proceeds," amounting to £33,957 10s. 3 1/2d., lawful money, were divided equally between the owners' representatives, Penhallow and Treadwell, and Wentworth, agent for the crew.[76]

Undismayed by the denial of his appeal, Doane proceeded at once to petition Congress for review, asserting as major defects in the New Hampshire proceedings the prejudice of the local jury in favor of the local owners, and the rejection of Bourne's testimony, which he claimed was vital to his case. On 9 October 1778, his petition was read in Congress and referred to the Commissioners of Appeal.[77] In the meantime Congress was occupied

[69] Depositions of Matthew Wood, 28 Jan. 1778, DNA Microcopy 162, Case 30, Nos. 118, 146.

[70] See note 167 below.

[71] Depositions covering all of the foregoing points are to be found in DNA Microcopy 162, Case 30, *passim.*

[72] DNA Microcopy 162, Case 30, Nos. 120, 124, 126, 130, 131, 132, 142, 143, 144, 147, 150, 152.

[73] DNA Microcopy 162, Case 30, Nos. 125, 154.

[74] DNA Microcopy 162, Case 30, Nos. 121, 123, 134, 146, 151, 162.

[75] Decree of New Hampshire Superior Court, Sept. Term 1778, note 67 above. See Bourne to Paine, 10 Sept. 1778, Paine Papers.

[76] Precept and return, 8 Oct. 1778, PCC No. 44, fol. 273. Costs were to be paid out of the proceeds by virtue of the New Hampshire act of 3 July 1776, 4 *Laws of New Hampshire* 25, 29.

[77] Petition of 14 Sept. 1778, DNA Microcopy, 162, Case 30, No. 166; 12 JCC 992. See also Claim of Appeal to Congress, New Hampshire Superior Court, Sept. Term 1778, PCC No. 44, fol. 317. According to the June 1780 docket of the Court

with the momentous case of the sloop *Active*, an appeal from the Pennsylvania Admiralty Court, in which the Commissioners had reversed a decree based on a jury verdict in matters of fact. When the Judge and Marshal of the Philadelphia court refused to obey the Commissioners' decree, they suspended activities, and the matter was turned over to a special committee of Congress for study. On 6 March 1779, with the delegates of New Hampshire voting Aye, Congress adopted the committee's findings that Congress by virtue of the war power could try questions of law as well as fact in prize appeals; that no state law could interfere with the right to appeal to Congress in such cases; and that the Commissioners were competent to make a final decree in the case. Although the case of the *Active* remained unresolved for another thirty years, the Commissioners went back to work.[78]

The *Lusanna* was set for trial on 21 June 1779. The *McClary* party appeared, attacking the jurisdiction of the Commissioners on the basis of the New Hampshire statutes, as well as on procedural grounds, and perhaps also suggesting that the case was moot, the insurance having been paid to the claimants.[79] The Commissioners held on 26 June that they had jurisdiction of the case, both by virtue of the original resolves of 1775 and under the resolution adopted in *The Active*. They declined to proceed, however, until New Hampshire should have time to react to the latter, which had been transmitted to the state legislature.[80] Before the Commis-

---

of Appeals, the case was "lodged" on 28 Nov. 1778. DNA Microcopy 162, Reel 15. Doane's vessel was called the "Susannah" in the contemporary printed congressional Journal for 9 Oct. 1778. 4 *Journals of Congress* 586 (Phila., 1779). This seems to have been the first appearance of an understandable copyist's or printer's error for "Lusanna." The spelling "Susannah" was adopted elsewhere in the *Journals* and in Alexander Dallas' reports of two later cases involving the vessel (notes 89, 90, below), but "Lusanna" is the form used in virtually all other printed and manuscript sources and is undoubtedly correct. See 4 JA, *Diary and Autobiography* 2.

[78] The matter was settled in favor of the jurisdiction in United States v. Peters, 5 Cranch (9 U.S.) 115 (1809). This decision, which in effect asserted the power of the United States courts over the legislatures of the states, met initial violent resistance in Pennsylvania, but was ultimately accepted. See Charles Warren, *The Supreme Court in United States History*, 1:374–388 (Boston, 1922). For details of the case, see Davis, "Federal Courts Prior to the Adoption of the Constitution," 131 U.S. Appendix xxix–xxxiv (1889); Jameson, "Predecessor of the Supreme Court," 17–23; *The Case of the Sloop Active* (Phila., 1809); Richard Peters, *The Whole Proceedings in the Case of Olmstead and others v. Rittenhouse's Executrices* (Phila., 1809). For the proceedings in Congress, see DNA Microcopy 162, Case 39.

[79] See Commissioners' order of 5 May 1779, that appellants give appellees notice of hearing on 21 June, DNA Microcopy 162, Case 30; Plea, 21 June 1779, and Replication, *Ibid.*; Memorial of Penhallow et al., 20 Oct. 1783, 6 Jefferson, *Papers*, ed. Boyd, 448, 449. That the insurance payment was a ground of attack may be deduced from the presence in the file of the deposition of Thomas Casey, taken at the request of Penhallow on 24 May 1779 for use in the hearing on 21 June. Casey, who had already given evidence as one of the *Lusanna*'s passengers (note 113 below), testified that William Cochran, Halifax merchant just returned from London, had told him on 10 Jan. 1779 that the insurance had been paid, and that this was the general opinion in Halifax. DNA Microcopy 162, Case 30.

[80] See copy of Commissioners' order, 26 June 1779, DNA Microcopy 162, Case

sioners could take further action, Congress on 15 January 1780 established the Court of Appeals in Cases of Capture, to try all prize appeals from the state courts "according to the usage of nations, and not by jury." [81] The roster of three judges was completed on 4 May, and on the 24th of that month Congress ordered all appeals now pending before it or the Commissioners to be referred to the new court.[82]

On 1 March 1781, the Articles of Confederation became effective when they were ratified by Maryland, the last state to do so. Although the Articles contained a grant of exclusive federal jurisdiction in prize appeals, which served to confirm the establishment of the Court of Appeal,[83] it was not until September 1783 that the Court called the case of the *Lusanna* for trial. The owners later complained that they had had no time to prepare, but at the argument held at Philadelphia on 11–13 September, both parties were represented by an array of distinguished counsel. After the jurisdictional objection was once more overruled, the case was reargued on the merits, apparently solely on the record and files of the New Hampshire proceedings. Minutes of the hearing preserved in the files of the Court of Appeals indicate that it was in the form of an appellate argument familiar to lawyers today, with considerably more emphasis on legal questions and authority than had been the case at Portsmouth in 1777.[84] The arguments

---

30. New Hampshire on 18 Nov. 1779 passed an act in response to the *Active* resolution which allowed appeals in cases where the property of friendly foreign nationals was involved. 4 *Laws of New Hampshire* 238. A copy of this statute was duly filed with the Commissioners on 27 Dec. 1779. DNA Microcopy 162, Case 30. According to the certificate of the Clerk of the Court of Appeals, dated 24 Jan. 1784, however, in the minutes of the Commissioners (and presumably in those of the Court of Appeals), "there do not appear to have been any further proceedings in the said Cause untill the Eleventh Day of September 1783." PCC No. 44, fol. 230.

[81] 16 JCC 61–64. See sources cited in note 6 above, and Hogan, "The Court of Appeals in Cases of Capture," 33 *Oregon L. Rev.* 95 (1954). Ubbelohde, *Vice Admiralty Courts* 201, states that establishment of the court without a jury was a recognition of the failure of that institution in the state courts of Admiralty. However, the Court of Appeals was a continuation of the old Commissioners, who had sat without a jury. Most of the state courts continued to employ a jury, so that creation of the Court of Appeals was merely a phase in the conflict between federal Admiralty courts and state civil juries which continued into the 19th century.

[82] 17 JCC 459. As to the judges, see Davis, "Federal Courts Prior to the Constitution," 131 U.S. Appendix xxvi.

[83] Articles of Confederation, Article IX: "The united States in Congress assembled shall have the sole and exclusive right and power of . . . establishing courts for receiving and determining finally appeals in all cases of capture." The form of the Articles had been agreed on in Congress on 15 Nov. 1777, and on 9 July 1778 they were ratified by eight states, including New Hampshire. By 5 May 1779 they had been ratified by four more states, leaving only Maryland, which could not be persuaded to join until 1 March 1781. See Davis, "Federal Courts Prior to the Constitution," 131 U.S. Appendix xii–xiii.

[84] As to the owners' objections, see Memorial of Penhallow et al., 20 Oct. 1783, 6 Jefferson, *Papers*, ed. Boyd, 448, 450. They claimed that they had sought to obtain from England more evidence on the question of the insurance being paid, but the short notice had prevented them. *Ibid.* Counsel at the hearing included "Mr. Rush" (doubtless Jacob, brother of Benjamin) and William Lewis for the appellants, and Jonathan D. Sergeant and Jared Ingersoll for the appellees. James Wilson argued

presented for the *Lusanna* prevailed, and on 17 September, the court gave its decree, reversing the sentence of the New Hampshire court and ordering the restoration of their property to the claimants. John Lowell, Adams' assistant at Portsmouth and now a judge of the Court of Appeals, did not take part in the hearing or decision.[85]

The *McClary* party now turned to legislative channels for redress. With the support of the New Hampshire legislature and General John Sullivan, who acted as their agent, they sought relief in Congress, complaining of the decision in "a cause so essentially affecting the Sovereignty and Independence of this State, as well as the rights and property of your memorialists," by an authority "assumed and arbitrary to an extreme, by no means justified by the confederation, even if that had been completed at the time of the trials in this State, infinitely less so, as it was not until long after the sentence of our Supreme judicial Court within the State." The question was referred to a committee which submitted a report, in Thomas Jefferson's hand, holding that, since the case had arisen and been submitted to the jurisdiction before the ratification of the Articles of Confederation, Congress was ousted of appellate jurisdiction by the New Hampshire statute. In Congress, 30 March 1784, on the question of agreement with the report, the affirmative could not sustain a majority of the states, and the question was lost.[86]

Confirmed in their victory, the administrators of Elisha Doane (who had died in January 1783) [87] and the other claimants set about obtaining satisfaction. Since the Court of Appeals had no power to enforce its own decrees they were forced to turn to the state courts. No record of an attempt to recover in New Hampshire has been found; the steadfast position of

---

also, presumably for the appellants, since he appeared last, following Ingersoll. It is difficult to determine his position from the very brief minutes, however. Principal reliance seems to have been placed on two authorities which indicate a specialized approach to the questions of prize: R. Lee, *Treatise of Captures in War* (London, 1759); Emmerich de Vattel, *Law of Nations* (London, 1760). See Minutes, 13 Sept. 1783, DNA Microcopy 162, Case 30. No authorities appear in Paine's notes of the proceedings before the New Hampshire Superior Court, note 67 above. The jurisdictional argument was held on 11 Sept. 1783 and the case "put off," apparently until the 13th, after the decision. See Minutes, 11 Sept. 1783, DNA Microcopy 162, Reel 15.

[85] Record and Decree, Court of Appeals in Cases of Capture, 17 Sept. 1783, DNA Microcopy 162, Case 30. Lowell had been appointed to the court on 5 Dec. 1782. 23 JCC 862; Davis, "Federal Courts Prior to the Constitution," 131 U.S. Appendix xxvi.

[86] Most of the papers submitted on the petition are in PCC No. 44, fols. 186–324. The selection, being *ex parte*, is rather one-sided on the merits, including none of the depositions favorable to the claimants. For the Penhallow memorial of 20 Oct. 1783, Sullivan's letter of 6 Jan. 1784, Jefferson's report of 8 Jan. 1784, and an account of the proceedings in Congress, see 6 Jefferson, *Papers,* ed. Boyd, 447–455. See also Bourne's memorial, 6 May 1784, supporting his position, which was apparently unneeded. PCC No. 44, fols. 234–235.

[87] Alfred A. Doane, *The Doane Family* 137 (Boston, 1902). Letters of Administration granted to his widow Anna and son Isaiah at Barnstable, 26 Feb. 1783, are in DNA Microcopy 214, Case 6, fols. 95–96.

the state legislature in upholding the earlier decisions of its courts suggests that the effort was not deemed worth making. In June 1784 at the Suffolk County, Massachusetts, Inferior Court, the administrators began an action founded on the Court of Appeals decree. At the February 1786 term, on appeal to the Supreme Judicial Court, the decree was offered in evidence. According to later accounts, it was rejected by Justices William Cushing, Nathaniel Peaslee Sargeant, and David Sewall, on the grounds that the Court of Appeals had lacked jurisdiction and the New Hampshire decree was final. The plaintiffs discontinued their action.[88] Again in March 1786 the administrators, as well as Isaiah Doane in his own right and Shepherd, brought suit in the Court of Common Pleas of Philadelphia County, proceeding by way of foreign attachment against a vessel belonging to one of the *McClary* owners found in Philadelphia. On motion to quash the attachments, the court at the September term, 1787, found it unnecessary to decide the questions of the Court of Appeals' jurisdiction, or whether the discontinuance in Massachusetts was conclusive upon the plaintiffs; it ordered the attachments dissolved, however, holding that a common-law court lacked jurisdiction to enforce the decree of an Admiralty court in a prize case, at least where to do so would raise the question of prize or no prize, which is exclusively of Admiralty jurisdiction.[89]

The case lay dormant until the new system of federal courts decreed in the Judiciary Act of 1789 was firmly established. Finally in March 1792 the administrators libeled the *McClary* owners in the United States District Court for the District of New Hampshire, setting forth the decree of the Court of Appeals and asking that it be carried into execution.[90] Since John Sullivan, Judge of the District Court, had once acted as counsel for the owners, the action was removed to the Circuit Court for the District of

[88] See *Statement of the M'Clary Owners* 29–30; Charles Storer to JA, Boston, 7 April 1786, Adams Papers. See Doane's Administrators v. Penhallow, et al., 1 Dall. (1 U.S.) 218, 219 (Penna. C.P., 1787). The Massachusetts suit is undoubtedly Isaiah Doane et al. v. Thomas Martin et al., SJC Rec. 1785, fol. 22; Docket Bk. 4, SJC Suffolk, Feb. 1786, C–78, an action of trover brought by the Doane Administrators against George Wentworth and the *McClary* owners at the Suffolk Inferior Court in June 1784. In April 1785, seven of the owners appeared, and on a plea of not guilty entered by Christopher Gore, obtained a verdict. In the Supreme Judicial Court the appellants discontinued. The disputed decree does not appear in the file. SF 104193. If it was in fact David Sewall who was of counsel for the libelants at Portsmouth in 1777 (note 43 above), it is curious that he did not disqualify himself in the Supreme Judicial Court as did John Lowell in the Court of Appeal (note 85 above), and James Wilson later in the Supreme Court (note 95 below).

[89] Doane's Administrators v. Penhallow et al., 1 Dall. (1 U.S.) 218 (Pa. C.P., 1787). Although they did not press the point on this occasion, the *McClary* owners had finally succeeded in getting convincing evidence of the payment of the insurance. On 17 Feb. 1787 at Portsmouth, John Lane, the "Son" of Lane, Son & Fraser, had given his deposition *in perpetuam rei memoriam*, testifying that insurance for a loss to an American privateer had been paid to his firm and credited to Doane. *Statement of the M'Clary Owners* 12–13.

[90] See Penhallow et al. v. Doane's Administrators, 3 Dall. (3 U.S.) 54, 62–63. A copy of the libel appears in DNA Microcopy 214, Case 6.

373

New Hampshire under an Act of 1792 providing this procedure for such a situation.[91] In October 1793 the case came on for trial in the Circuit Court before Justice John Blair, the only issues being jurisdictional. Blair found for the administrators and directed commissioners to ascertain the damages. A year later, with Justice William Cushing on the bench, the commissioners reported that at the time of the sale under the 1778 decree the *Lusanna* and her cargo had been worth £5895 14s. 10d. Interest from the date of the sale until the date of the report was £5659 17s. 4d. On 24 October 1794 Cushing handed down a final decree, awarding the administrators the equivalent sum of $38,518.69, with $154.30 costs, to be recovered in full against any one of the respondents separately.[92]

The case came up to the Supreme Court on writ of error and was argued and decided at the February term 1795.[93] Eight errors were assigned, of which the following were the principal ones: (1) That the decree was void because the Court of Appeals lacked jurisdiction; (2) that it was matter of record that Elisha Doane was dead when the decree issued in his name; (3) that the libel sought performance of the Court of Appeals' decree of restitution, rather than damages for nonperformance; (4) that the decree of the Circuit Court held the owners' agents and the captors' agents each in full damages, although the proceeds had originally been divided equally between them; (5) that there was no jurisdiction in Admiralty of the libel filed in the District Court.[94]

The seriatim opinions of Justices Paterson, Iredell, Blair, and Cushing, which take up forty-one pages in the printed report, were primarily concerned with the jurisdictional issue.[95] All four agreed that the Court of

[91] Act of 8 May 1792, c. 36, §11, 1 Stat. 275, 278–279. The same statute also provided for the deposit of the records of the Court of Appeals in Cases of Capture in the office of the clerk of the Supreme Court of the United States, who was authorized to give copies of the records, which were to "have like faith and credit as all other proceedings of the said court." *Id.*, §11, at 279. See also Act of 2 March 1793, c. 22, §1, 1 Stat. 333, providing that where the Judge of a District Court was disqualified, the Supreme Court Justice assigned to the Circuit Court for that District was to sit alone. The *McClary* partisans later intimated that the first of these statutes, at least, had been passed especially for the Penhallow case. *Statement of the M'Clary Owners* 31. Their suspicion is perhaps justified by the fact that Shearjashub Bourne, now acting as agent for the Doane interests, was a member of Congress from 1791 to 1795. See note 16 above. The *McClary* party was also able to effect a statutory change when, on the appeal to the Supreme Court, Justice Cushing demanded a bond in the amount of the full damages. *Statement of the M'Clary Owners* 56. By the Act of 12 Dec. 1794, c. 3, 1 Stat. 404, it was provided that security in appeals need be taken only in the amount of costs.

[92] See 3 Dall. (3 U.S.) 63–64, 108–113. The trial court record as certified to the Supreme Court appears in DNA Microcopy 214, Case 6.

[93] See writ of error and return, DNA Microcopy 214, Case 6. The minutes of the Court for the argument of this case from 9 to 16 Feb. 1795 are printed in Surrency, ed., "The Minutes of the Supreme Court of the United States, 1789–1806," 5 *Am. Jour. Legal Hist.* 375–378 (1961).

[94] 3 Dall. (3 U.S.) 64–66. See Surrency, ed., "Minutes of the Supreme Court," 5 *Am. Jour. Legal Hist.* 381, 384.

[95] 3 Dall. (3 U.S.) 79–120. The opinions are also printed as Dallas reported them in *A Report of the Opinions of the Judges in the Important Cause of Pen-*

Appeals, sitting after the ratification of the Articles of Confederation, was validly constituted and had jurisdiction of the subject matter by the authority of that instrument; thus its ruling that it had jurisdiction in the premises (which could not be overturned by collateral attack) also cured any defects arising from the fact that the case had been filed before the ratification of the Articles. Since the jurisdiction was exclusive, it ousted all claims of the states to create courts of last resort. Only Paterson and Blair clearly held that the inherent war power of Congress was sufficient to validate the jurisdiction in the period before the Confederation. It thus cannot be said that there was a decision of the court on this point.[96] Doane's death was held not material, primarily because the action had been *in rem*, but it was agreed that the question was, in any event, foreclosed by the failure to raise it below. The four justices likewise agreed that the failure to pray for damages was cured by the libel's prayer for general relief; and that the District and Circuit courts had had jurisdiction of the matter in Admiralty, as the only courts competent, and by analogy to the jurisdiction to enforce the decrees of foreign Admiralty courts.

The only disagreement affecting the outcome was in the matter of damages. All concurred that interest should be allowed only from September 1783, the date of the Court of Appeals decree, and that the damages should have been levied severally in proportion to the original award in favor of the *McClary*. Iredell and Blair held that George Wentworth, the agent for the crew, should not be liable, since he had in good faith paid over the entire sum awarded under a decree binding under state law, without actual notice that the appeal was going forward. Since the court was evenly divided on this point, the prior judgment that Wentworth was liable stood, but the Circuit Court decree was modified so that the smaller interest figure was reflected. The total award was divided into two halves of $16,360.68, one half to be recovered against the agents of the owners, and the other against Wentworth.[97]

So eighteen years after Adams had argued their case in Portsmouth, the persevering Doanes prevailed. The decision brought a flurry of news-

---

hallow et al. against Doane's Administrators (Phila., 1795). James Wilson did not participate, presumably because he had been of counsel in the argument before the Court of Appeals, note 84 above. See Surrency, ed., "Minutes of the Supreme Court," 5 *Am. Jour. Legal Hist.* 375–378, 381. Cushing, who had had the same issue before him as a state judge, did not exhibit a similar delicacy, but showed that he was unbiased, by reversing his earlier stand. See note 88 above.

[96] Iredell strongly intimated that he would have held that Congress had the power, but he found it unnecessary to reach the question. See 3 Dall. (3 U.S.) 92–97. Cushing also did not reach the issue, but his feelings on it are less clear. *Id.* at 117. At least in later Supreme Court practice, the rule was clear that although the judgment of a divided court affirmed the result in the court below and was binding on the parties, it did not constitute a decision of the legal questions involved. See Etting v. Bank of the United States, 11 Wheat. (24 U.S.) 59, 78 (1826); The *Independence*, 20 How. (61 U.S.) 255 (1857). Blair's Circuit Court opinion upholding the power of Congress (3 Dall. 108–113) was thus presumably authoritative on this point, although of doubtful weight.

[97] 3 Dall. (3 U.S.) 89, 120.

paper and pamphlet criticism of the court for this blow to the sovereignty of the states, but the court withstood the attack as it has in similar circumstances since.[98] Despite the intensity of the appellees' resistance, the Doanes were apparently able to recover about 80 percent of the sum awarded against Penhallow and Treadwell; Wentworth's liability was discharged on his submission of 10,000 acres of land valued at about $3300.[99] The Doanes' troubles were not yet over, however. The English insurers of the *Lusanna* and her cargo, as patient as their erstwhile clients, now proceeded to sue the administrators in the Federal Circuit Court for Massachusetts to recover the sums paid out under the policy. From the beginning the *McClary* party had pointed to the insurance as defeating Doane, first as a transfer of property, then by making his claim moot through payment. These attacks had been resisted successfully, but now the reckoning must be paid.

Three actions were brought—one against Bourne, one against David S. Greenough (who had married Elisha Doane's widow) "et al.," and one against Greenough's executors. The last-named suit was dropped in October 1801 as a "misentry." In April 1802 a jury found a verdict for Bourne, and the suit against Greenough et al. was continued. At the October term 1802 in the latter action it was "suggested that the Plaintiff is dead," and the case further continued. Finally, in June 1803 neither party appeared. Greenough and Doane now attempted to negotiate a settlement with the insurers. In February 1804 John Lane reported that at least some of the underwriters were ready to settle for their costs, and, in a reply dated 18 May, Greenough and Doane agreed to these terms, "upon condition, that we be secured from any farther suits, &c." In July, however, Lane wrote that a settlement was not yet forthcoming due to the expense and difficulty of obtaining the consent of the individual underwriters involved. Since no further correspondence has been found, the conclusion of the *Lusanna*'s voyage remains unknown.[100]

I. SHEARJASHUB BOURNE TO JOHN ADAMS [101]

Sir   Boston 6th. Decr. 1777

Coll. Doane informs me, that he hath engaged you, in the Cause of

[98] For example, *Statement of the M'Clary Owners*, note 43 above. See also, 1 Warren, *Supreme Court* 123.

[99] See "Invoice of Goods from London taken in Brigg Lusanna in Oct. 1777" [Nov. 1795], MHi:Greenough Papers. This account shows a net loss to the Doanes of $1691.71.

[100] See Greenough and Doane to John Lane, 18 May 1804, and Lane to Greenough and Doane, 23 July 1804. MHi:Greenough Papers. Missing documents prevent a complete reconstruction of the litigation. For final disposition of the three suits, see Shoolbred v. Greenough Exrs., U.S.C.C.D. Mass. Docket Bk., Oct. 1801, C–16; Shoolbred v. Bourne, *id.*, April 1802, C–7; Shoolbred v. Greenough et al., *id.*, Oct. 1802, C–5; *id.*, June 1803, C–5.

[101] RC, Adams Papers, addressed: "Honble. John Adams Esqr. Braintree." Dock-

his Brig[antin]e, and his property found in her, at the time of her Capture;

And as Mr. Paine was not fully engaged at the time you was, he does not attend the Tryal (which is to be on the 16th. of this Month at Portsmouth). I herewith *Inclose* you a *Brief* of *facts* (without many perticular circumstances) which may give you a General Idea of the Question, Wishing it may suffice untill your arrival at Portsmouth; to which place I shall proceed on Tuesday next, not doubting of Seeing you there, the next Saturday night, which (if so) will give me an opportunity of instructing you in every perticular circumstance.

Mr. John Lowell is your assistant. There are three Claims, one in behalf of Coll. Doane for the Brig[antin]e and goods, one other in the Name of Mr. Isaiah Doane, and the third in the Name of Wm. Shepherd.[102] The goods Claimed by Isaiah Doane were sold him by me, for which I have given him a Release, (the Sale is Bona fide) to inable me to be a Witness for Coll. Doane.[103]

Coll. Doane is taking Depositions to his Character as well as Isaiah Doane.[104] Mr. Lowell directs us how to proceed, and if any perticular plan be thot of by you, please to write me by the *Bearer* (Capt. Avory) who will wait your pleasure. By the time you Reach Portsmouth, hope to have it in my power to acquaint you with Every paper filed against us. I think Sir there is an absolute necessity of your beeing at Portsmo. next Saturday night, and wou'd Recommend Mrs. Tiltons House to you, to Lodge at, as I shall provide for the Company there.[105] I am with due Respect *Sir* Your Most Obedt. Hmble Sevt.,   Shearja. Bourne

I think Sir if you Sett Off for Portsmo. next week a friday, you may reach there on Saturday [night], and if you Come to Boston next Week Call on Coll. Doane at his sons house, and he'll be Ready to proceed with you.

---

eted in an unidentified hand: "S. Bourne Dec. 6th 1777." The enclosure mentioned in the text has not been found.

[102] An inadvertence for James Shepherd, the third claimant. As to the claims, see text at note 47 above.

[103] See copy of a bill of sale, 24 Nov. 1777, in which Bourne on receipt of £122 14s. 5d. declared that he did "hereby release to him the said Doane all right title and Interest to" various goods "and all right and title thereto and to all other interest I have on board the brig *Lusanna*." PCC No. 44, fol. 315; DNA Microcopy 162, Case 30, No. 85. The goods were identical to those subsequently claimed by Doane. *Id.*, No. 4. The tactic was unsuccessful. See sources in notes 54, 68, 77, above.

[104] See note 131 below.

[105] See text at notes 50–51 above.

II. ADAMS' MINUTES OF THE TRIAL[106]

New Hampshire Court Maritime, Portsmouth, 16 December 1777

Penhallow and Treadwell vs. Brig. Lusanna and Cargo.
Mr. Sewall. 3 Causes sett forth.[107] Resolve of Congress, 25 Novr.
1775. March 23d. 1776.[108]

[106] In JA's hand. Adams Papers, Microfilms, Reel No. 185.

[107] The libel of John and Jacob Penhallow, agents for the owners of the *McClary*, and George Wentworth, agent for the crew ("the captors"), against the *Lusanna* in the New Hampshire Maritime Court, dated 11 Nov. 1777, alleged that the *McClary* "did on or about the 30th day of October last on the high seas within the Jurisdiction of said Court seize and take the said Brigantine Lusanna and bring [her] into Piscataqua harbor, which said Brigantine the Libellants aver was together with the Cargo on board her the property of some Inhabitant or Inhabitants of Great Britain or some subject or subjects of the king of Great Britain other than the Inhabitants of Bermudas and Providence or the Bahama Islands and said Vessel so captured was at the time of her Capture carrying Supplies to the Enemies of the United States of America by means of all which and by virtue of the resolutions of Congress and the acts and resolves of the state of New Hampshire said Vessel Cargo and appurtenances are forfeited." The libel prayed process and condemnation and distribution "as the said laws resolves and resolutions direct." DNA Microcopy 162, Case 30, No. 2. For the Congressional and state laws involved, see notes 108, 109, below. None of the copies of the libel used in later phases of the case contains the third "cause sett forth." See PCC No. 44, fols. 265–266; DNA Microcopy 214, Case 6. Whipple's notes (at note 152 below) show that it was "That the property on Board was British Manufacture." This basis for the forfeiture either may have been stricken from the libel on the basis of JA's arguments against it, text at notes 176–180 below, or Sewall may have tried to argue that the libel as quoted here should be construed to include it. As to the identity of "Mr. Sewall," see note 43 above.

[108] The Resolve of 25 Nov. 1775, a response to George Washington's complaints about the lack of machinery for dealing with captures, was drafted by a committee of which JA was a member. See 3 JCC 357–358; 3 JA, *Diary and Autobiography* 346–349. It provided for the condemnation as prize of enemy military and transport vessels and cargo; set up a requirement that no privateer cruise without a commission from Congress; recommended that the states establish prize courts sitting with juries, and subject to certain venue provisions; provided for an appeal from such courts "in all cases;" and provided for the distribution of proceeds, confirming prior awards by General Washington. 3 JCC 373–375. The provision relied on here, as modified by a Resolution of 19 Dec. 1775, was, "That all transport vessels in the same [i.e. British] service, having on board any troops, arms, ammunition, cloathing, provisions, or military or naval stores of what kind soever, and all vessels to whomsoever belonging that shall be employed in carrying provisions or other necessaries to the British Army or armies, or navy, that now are or shall hereafter be within any of the United Colonies, or any goods, wares, or merchandizes, for the use of such fleet and army, shall be liable to seizure, and, with their cargoes, shall be confiscated." *Id.* at 437. See Jameson, "The Predecessor of the Supreme Court," in J. Franklin Jameson, ed., *Essays in the Constitutional History of the United States* 6–8 (Boston and N.Y., 1889). The Resolution of 23 March 1776, which authorized the fitting out of armed vessels, provided in pertinent part, "That all ships and other vessels, their tackle, apparel, and furniture, and all goods, wares, and merchandizes, belonging to any inhabitant or inhabitants of Great Britain, taken on the high seas, or between high and low water mark, by any armed vessel fitted out by any private person or persons, and to whom commissions shall be granted,

No. 58. *Penhallow v. The* Lusanna

Law of N. Hampshire, principally relyd on. In June 1776. ⟨1777 *April 19.*⟩ Septr. 5, 1776.[109]

Vessell and Cargo the Property of Sherja. Bourne, who thought it safest to go to E[ngland] and take shelter under the Wing of his Majesty K. George.

Register, in the Name of S. Bourne, 3 Aug. 1776.[110]
Invoices from Lane Son & Frasier, consignd to S.B.[111]

---

and being libelled and prosecuted in any court erected for the trial of maritime affairs, in any of these colonies, shall be deemed and adjudged to be lawful prize; and [*after deducting the wages of the crew of captured merchantmen*] shall be condemned to and for the use of the owner or owners, and the officers, marines, and mariners of such armed vessel, according to such rules and proportions as they shall agree on: Provided always, that this resolution shall not extend to any vessel bringing settlers arms, ammunition or warlike stores to and for the use of these colonies, or any of the inhabitants thereof, who are friends to the American cause, or to such warlike stores, or to the effects of such settlers." 4 JCC 230–231. Other resolutions provided for the distribution of proceeds of captures made by vessels of the United Colonies, or a single colony, or by land forces. *Id.* at 231–232. For JA's role in the passage of this resolve, see 2 JA, *Diary and Autobiography* 233 note 10; 3 *id.* at 371–375.

[109] No "June" act or resolve of the New Hampshire legislature has been found which deals with this question. The first reference is thus in all probability to the Act of 3 July 1776, which expressly incorporated the resolve of Congress dated 23 March 1776, note 108 above, and, perhaps to avoid incorporating the Resolve of 25 Nov. 1775, note 108 above, with its provision for appeal to Congress, further provided that vessels "used in supplying the Fleet, or Army, which have been, or shall at any time be employed, against the United Colonies or Employed by the Enemy in any respect, whatsoever; and those Vessels, which have been carrying supplies of any kind to the Enemy, or whose Masters or Super Cargoes, shall have designs of carrying supplies of any kind to the Enemy, or that shall be returning from the Enemy after having carried such Supplies, and shall be found hereafter on the high Seas, and shall be brought into the harbour of Piscataqua, or any place within this Colony, or found within the same," should be subject to condemnation, with their appurtenances and cargo. Actions under both provisions were to be brought in a specially created "Court Maritime," which was to be held in Portsmouth or elsewhere in the county of Rockingham and was to sit with a jury under elaborate provisions made by the act. Appeals lay only to the Superior Court, except where a Continental vessel was involved. Act of 3 July 1776, 4 *Laws of New Hampshire* 25–32. The New Hampshire Resolve of 5 Sept. 1776 extended the jurisdiction of the Court Maritime to the new definition of belligerent contained in a Congressional resolution of 24 July 1776: "All ships and other vessels, their tackle, apparel and furniture, and all goods, wares and merchandises, belonging to any subject or subjects of the King of Great Britain, except the inhabitants of the Bermudas, and Providence or Bahama island." 5 JCC 606; see N.H. Resolve of 5 Sept. 1776, PCC No. 44, fol. 258.

[110] See a copy of the *Lusanna's* register, taken out at the Custom House, London, 3 Aug. 1776, on the oath of "Shearjashub Bourne of London Merchant," that he "of London in Great Britain is at present Owner thereof." Endorsements dated 27 March and 14 July 1777 show changes of master. PCC No. 44, fols. 275–276; DNA Microcopy 162, Case 30, No. 8.

[111] See Invoice, and bill of lading, 10 June 1777, for £2124 worth of assorted

Provisions consignd to Cockran in the Absence of Doane.[112]

Deposition of Thos. Casey, a Passenger, with his Wife. Understood from Bourne that the Brig. was made over to Bourne. Understood B. was in Conjunction with his Father and Brother Doane. Knows the sewing silk was Shepards. He would store the Goods 3 Year if he could not get a good Price.[113]

Letter from Lane Son & Frasier. Gibraltar.

Employd in carrying Ordnance stores to Gibralter.

Letter speaks of the Brig, as Bournes Property.[114]

---

merchandize, to be shipped aboard the *Lusanna* by Lane, Son & Fraser, consigned to Bourne at Halifax. DNA Microcopy 162, Case 30, Nos. 13, 14.

[112] The MS reads "Doane," but this is probably a reference to "Invoice of sundry goods shipped on board the Lusanna for Halifax in Nova Scotia by Shearjashub Bourne, Esqr. marked and numbered as per margin and consigned to Messrs. Thomas Cochran and Co. Merchants there in the absence of said Bourne." DNA Microcopy 162, Case 30, No. 15. The goods, valued at £208 2s., were food and liquor, in casks marked SB.

[113] See Deposition of Thomas Casey, Portsmouth, 3 Dec. 1777, DNA Microcopy 162, Case 30, No. 9, in which he testified "That on the 21st day of August he embarked as a passenger on board the Brigantine Lusanna bound from London to Halifax. That Mr. Shearjashub Bourne was also a passenger in the same brigantine, from whom this deponent understood that she was formerly ownd by Mr. Elisha Doane of Wellfleet, *but that afterwards She was made over to him the said Bourne.* That this deponent knows that the said brigantine was publickly advertized as a vessel to carry freight from London to Halifax having seen advertizements put up for that purpose about a fortnight before she saild. This deponent understood from conversation with Mr. Bourne that he the said Bourne had some goods on board the said brigantine." After describing the voyage and capture of the *Lusanna* (text at note 41 above), Casey testified that he had "heard Mr. Bourne say that he should be a considerable loser thereby [i.e. by the capture]. Previous thereto said Bourne told the deponent that if the goods on board would fetch a good price at Halifax he intended to sell them there, if they would not, he determined to store them there and keep them two years rather than not sell them to advantage. This deponent says that he understood from Mr. Bourne that his father in law Mr. Doane together with his (Bourne's) brother were connected in trade together. That after the capture Mr. Bourne expressed a desire and his hopes of being retaken by some british vessel. That this deponent, Mr. Bourne, and all the other prisoners told the prize master who was fearful of being retaken that in case that event should happen they would do everything in their power to prevent his being a Sufferer." He further testified that he paid for his passage, 8 guineas in London and £27 in Portsmouth. On cross-examination by Oliver Whipple, attorney for the Doanes, Casey admitted that he did not "know" that the *Lusanna* was Bourne's property, but added that he understood from Bourne that there had been some kind of conveyance of the vessel. He further testified that Bourne had never said that he was Doane's factor, and that he, Casey, knew nothing of any such arrangement. Under Whipple's questioning, Casey testified that he had taken the helm during the chase by the *McClary* in an effort to aid the *Lusanna* in escaping. The deposition closed with his affirmative answer to Whipple's question, "Do you know that 29 lb. of Sewing Silk shipped by Mr. James Shepherd was his property?" PCC No. 49, fols. 272–279.

[114] Lane, Son & Fraser to Bourne, London, 1 Oct. 1776. DNA Microcopy 162, Case 30, No. 12: "We have your favors of the 3d and 27th inst. In respect to your Brig Lusanna, she is but just clear of the Channel. When she was upon the point of clearing out at the Custom House it was discoverd that the person who supplyd the Office of Ordnance with the Timber had made a mistake in the Entry, in consequence

No. 58. *Penhallow v. The* Lusanna

Deposition of Mary Casey.[115]

Mr. Lewis.

Letter Bourne to Cockran, Wait orders from Me, L. Son and Fr., E. or Is. Doane.[116]

Lot Lewis. Deposition. Went in her to Gibralter. Saild 1. Octr. 1776. Timber and Bricks the Cargo.

Ordnance Colours. Understood, the Property was C[olonel] Doanes. Carryd Pitch, Tar, Timber and Bricks to Gibralter. Understood they

of which all the Fir was taken out and relanded, the Commissioners of the Customs insisting it should not go in the Vessel. Many applications were made to fill up with other Timber but refused. At length we had a meeting with the Shipper, who after much altercation agreed to pay full freight for the Goods taken out and also 66 £ for Demurrage. The Board of Ordnance insisted the Vessell should go forward with what was left on board, and finding we could not make the Board or the Shippers of the Wood answerable for any Loss or disappointment in regard to her homeward bound freight, we thought it for your Interest that we should accept the offer made us and let Capt. Wood go about his Business. Indeed, we think it luckey for the concern'd that he did not go sooner, as Six Vessells have been taken by a Provincial Privateer, and as we find our Men of War are now cruizing, apprehend there will not be so much risque by the Time your Vessell gets to Gibraltar as there was a month or six weeks ago. We have supplied Capt. Wood with Letters to our Friends at Malaga and Barcelona, at one of which places hope she will get a freight." PCC No. 44, fol. 311. See note 27 above.

[115] See Deposition of Mary Casey, wife of Captain Thomas Casey (note 113 above), Portsmouth, 3 Dec. 1777, DNA Microcopy 162, Case 30, No. 10: "That she heard Mr. Bourne say in conversation that the reason he did not insure the brigantine Lusanna was that she belonged to his father Doane and in case of her being taken he would claim her. That she also heard said Bourne say that he expected to buy Prize Vessels at Halifax and that by that and his other trade there he expected in the course of the ensuing winter to clear five thousand pounds. That after the capture she also heard him say that he should loose all the profits on his goods. She also heard him say after the Capture that he hoped the brigantine Lusanna would be retaken by some of the Kings ships. That the said Bourne in England shewed this deponent some invoices of goods and offered to entrust her with some of them to sell at Halifax on Commissions." On cross-examination by Oliver Whipple for the claimants, Mrs. Casey testified that she had never heard Bourne say that he acted for Doane, but understood that the two were in partnership with Doane's brother; that she did not know who owned the *Lusanna's* cargo, but that she had known that the silk was Captain Shepherd's. PCC No. 44, fol. 281.

[116] See Bourne to Messrs. Thomas Cochran & Co., undated, DNA Microcopy 162, Case 30, No. 31. The letter advised the recipients, Halifax merchants, of the forthcoming arrival aboard the *Lusanna* of several consignments of provisions which they were to dispose of "to the Best Advantage for the Owners and Adventurers," accounting with them or Bourne; of consignments of provisions belonging to Bourne, which they were to dispose of "to the best Advantage for my Interest," accounting with him, Lane, Son & Fraser, or the Doanes; and of goods on bill of lading which they were to see delivered to the consignees, except that the goods "in *one* other *Bill of Lading* herewith Inclos'd and *marked SB* belonging to me you will store and wait the further order of Myself, Messrs. Lane Son & Fraser, Elisha or Isaiah Doane." Bourne also ordered his correspondents to discharge master and crew and lay up the *Lusanna* until further orders from himself, Lane, Son & Fraser, or the Doanes. By way of postscript he added, "I Order those Goods to You, lest some Accident should befall me on my Passage there as I do not go out in my own Ship." PCC No. 44, fols. 303–304.

were Ordnance Stores because they wore Ordnance Colours, received of a Government Contractor as I took the Gentleman to be.[117]

Sewall. Swearing is a serious Matter. An honest Man must pause. Oath to the Register.

Invoices and Bills of Lading. Marked S.B.

Letter. E. Crosby, to Captn. W. Spry, Engineer at Hallifax. He will have a Vessell or two which he would be glad to get into Governments service.[118] This to shew that Bourne was an Enemy to these States.

Bournes Memorial to the Lords of Trade &c. Always a loial subject.[119] Where Conduct is uniform, I dont blame.

[117] See Deposition of Lot Lewis, mate of the *Lusanna*, Portsmouth, 4 Dec. 1777, DNA Microcopy 162, Case 30, No. 11. Lewis testified that "he understood by the Register that the said brigantine Lusanna was owned by Mr. Shearjashub Bourne tho' he understood the property was in fact Mr. Elisha Doane's of Wellfleet and covered by Mr. Bourne in order to secure the property in that manner." After describing the *Lusanna*'s departure from St. Helen's, Isle of Wight, on 13 Sept., and her voyage and capture, he continued, "That before this voyage the brig Lusanna beforementioned was employed to carry Pitch tar timber and bricks which he understood were ordnance Stores from London to Gibralter and he supposes on account of the Government of Great Britain as the flag they wore had in it the figure of three blue balls and three gun-carriages. That they sailed on the voyage last mentioned on the first day of October 1776. The colours above described were received of a Gentleman who I suppose to be a Government Contractor who used to ask why the Brig did not wear ordnance colours as she had ordnance stores on board; and on being answered that they had no ordnance colours on board the said Contractor supplyd them and afterward made Capt. Wood pay for them." On cross-examination by Oliver Whipple for the claimants, Lewis admitted that he did not "know" that the Gibraltar cargo was King's stores and stated that he had not known the vessel to be Doane's on the original departure from America, but that Captain Wood had told him that Bourne was acting as owner to protect Doane's property. Further questioning on behalf of the libelants brought out that Bourne had said to Lewis that part of the cargo, marked SB, was his. To Whipple's question Lewis answered that he did not "know of" any King's stores aboard the *Lusanna* when she was taken. Further questioning brought out that the *Lusanna* had had aboard two swivels, to be used "to answer signals" only, and some small arms and ammunition at the time of capture, and that the *McClary* had fired at her "eight or ten times" during the chase.

[118] See Edward Crosby to "Capt. William Spry Commanding Engineer at Halifax," 16 July 1777, DNA Microcopy 162, Case 30, No. 36: "This is chiefly to beg leave to recommend to your notice my friend Mr. Bourne, who you may recollect din'd with us at Melatiah Bourne's in Boston. Soon after the present Contest in America he made his Escape to this country. He now proposes going out to Halifax in the first arm'd vessel that is sent out with Stores, and with the flattering hope of the Rebellion in America being finally settled this Season, and to be thereby enabled to join his family in New-England. If not, to remain at Halifax till that event takes place. He has loaded a Brigantine of his with the different kinds of Goods suitable for the Halifax market, which sails with the first convoy. He will likewise have a vessel or two, which he would gladly get into Government Service. If you can be of service to him of yourself in recommending to your Acquaintance shall esteem it a favor. Part of his cargo consists of *Ben Keiston's best*. By the way, I am become as great a Porter drinker as any Jack Roastbeef I meet with." PCC No. 44, fol. 305.

[119] Bourne's Memorial to the Lords of the Treasury, 30 Jan. 1777, DNA Microcopy 162, Case 30, No. 59. Bourne sought recompense for a portion of the cargo of the brigantine *Industry*, consigned to him at London, which had been condemned

No. 58. *Penhallow v. The* Lusanna

If the Goods are Doanes, all Bournes Acts as his Agent are his Acts. Bournes sending the Brig to Gibr[alta]r was Ds. Act.

Goods all insured in London. Why should he guard vs. Privateers. He would wish to be taken. Premium 10. Guins. Pr. Ct. 4 to be returnd.[120]

Continental Association: We will not import.[121] Breach of this, Proof of Disaffection to our Cause.

Indictment for running a Man thro with a sword. Evidence may be given that he cut off his Head with an Ax,—not that he poisoned him.[122]

---

in the Court of Vice Admiralty at Boston in Sept. 1775. See note 130 below; text at notes 29–32 above. In support of his application he urged "That your Memorialist hath ever been and still is one of his Majesty's loyal Subjects and by every Act in his power he hath maintain'd a firm Attachment to Government and his Loyalty to his most Sacred Majestys Person Government and Laws and while in America publicly and privately disavow'd all actions that might have a Tendency to subvert his Majestys Government and the Constitution, and by a steady perseverance had renderd his Person and Property unsafe. That he was obliged to convey himself with a very small part of his property away from his Native Land to this Kingdom and brought with him a very considerable quantity of Oyl, which he apprehended was very much wanted in this Kingdom; Directly contrary to the Resolves of a body of Men who took upon themselves the Stile or Title of the Continental Congress. And your Memorialist from the time of his departure from thence, left orders for the afore-said One hundred and two Casks of Oyl [the cargo of the *Industry*] to be forward[ed] him at the Port of London aforesaid." PCC No. 44, fol. 308. For even more damn-ing evidence, apparently used to bolster the memorial, see the extracts from Bourne's journal, note 158 below.

[120] The invoice of Lane, Son & Fraser, 10 June 1777, note 111 above, shows that the goods there covered were insured to the value of 10 guineas per 100, "to return £4 pr. cent if sails with convoy and arrives." PCC No. 44, fol. 292.

[121] The so-called Continental Association was "a non-importation, non-consumption, and non-exportation agreement" bridging the gap between the earlier colonial non-importation agreements and the Declaration of Independence, and seeking to force British redress of colonial grievances through economic sanctions. See Miller, *Origins of the American Revolution* 385–392. It was signed in Congress on 20 Oct. 1774. After a recital of grievances reminiscent of the Declaration, the Association stated the pledge of its signers "That from and after the first day of December next, we will not import into British America, from Great-Britain or Ireland, any goods, wares, or merchandise whatsoever, or from any other place, any such goods, wares, or merchandise as shall have been exported from Great-Britain or Ireland." 1 JCC 76. Also banned were the importation of duties articles and slaves, the consump-tion of all banned articles, and the exportation of all goods to Great Britain, Ireland and the West Indies after 10 Sept. 1775. Id. at 77. Goods imported before 1 Feb. 1775 were to be reshipped, stored for the duration, or sold with the profits going to relieve Boston; goods received thereafter were to be reshipped. Id. at 78–79. Viola-tions were to be checked by locally chosen committees, "whose business it shall be attentively to observe the conduct of all persons touching this association; and when it shall be made to appear, to the satisfaction of a majority of any such committee, that any person within the limits of their appointment has violated this association, that such majority do forthwith cause the truth of the case to be published in the gazette; to the end, that all such foes to the rights of British-America may be publicly known, and universally contemned as the enemies of American liberty; and thence-forth we respectively will break off all dealings with him or her." Id. at 79. See also an annotated text of the Association in 1 Jefferson, *Papers*, ed. Boyd, 149–150.

[122] The position of this statement in the MS on the page facing and directly op-

Mr. McKay. Bourne said, if I loose her she is well insurd in London.

Mr. Baker. I dont want it insurd again for she is once insurd in England.[123]

C[olonel] Doane wont loose it, nor Mr. Bourne, but the Insurers.

Mr. Doanes Letter, respecting Sheppards Goods.[124]

Mr. Lowell. ⟨. . . Copy of⟩

3 Nov. 1775. Letter to Lane Son and Frasier, from Bourne at Halifax seized. Inferring that Lusanna *belonging to Doane* was seized.[125]

Ditto. 3d. Decr. 1775.[126] 1. Oct. 1776. Letter from L.S. & Fraser, write to Bourne about *his* Brigantine and his Int[erest].[127]

---

posite the notes of Lot Lewis' testimony, note 117 above, as well as its substance, suggest that it is a note by JA of the basis of his objection to admission of evidence on the *Lusanna*'s Gibraltar trip. See text at note 169 below. JA may refer to 2 Hawkins, *Pleas of the Crown* 437: "And therefore it is agreed, That if one be indicted or appealed for killing another with a Sword, and upon evidence it appear that he killed him with a Staff, Hatchet, Bill or Hook, or any other Weapon with which a Wound may be given, he ought to be found guilty, for the Substance of the Matter is, whether he gave the Party a Wound of which he died; and it is not material with what Weapon he gave it, tho' for Form's sake it be necessary to set forth a particular Weapon.... Yet it seems clear, That Evidence of poisoning, burning, or famishing, or any other Kind of killing wherein no Weapon is used, will not maintain an Indictment or Appeal of Death by killing with a Weapon."

[123] Depositions of Baker and McKay have not been found. They were probably passengers or crew members aboard the *Lusanna* who may have testified orally at the trial. It is also possible that they were Portsmouth insurance underwriters who had tried and failed to sell Bourne insurance on his arrival there.

[124] No such letter of Doane's has been located. JA may have meant Bourne's letter to an unidentified correspondent "done in a hurry at Sailing" for Halifax in Sept. 1777. DNA Microcopy 162, Case 30, No. 79. Bourne asked that if the expenses of Shepherd's illness could not be met from resources in the latter's hands, an account should be sent to Lane, Son & Fraser, "for this reason only, as Captain Shepherd has goods on board my Brigantine the Lusanna to the amount of £100 which are insured." If the goods should be taken by privateers, Lane, Son & Fraser would discharge the account from the insurance proceeds; if the vessel should arrive safely Bourne would pay the account from proceeds of sale of the goods which were consigned to him. See note 132 below.

[125] Bourne to Lane, Son & Fraser, Halifax, 3 Nov. 1775, DNA Microcopy 162, Case 30, No. 6, informing them that "on the 4th of September last the Brigantine Lusannah belonging to *Coll. Elisha Doane* of Eastham laded with Oyl 2 Ct. bbl. of which were consigned to your good selves the remainder of the cargo was consigned to me (who married his eldest daughter) sailed from New England for London, and proceeding on our voyage," was forced into Halifax, "and upon entering the port the brigantine was taken in custody by a King's ship." The *Lusanna* was released, then taken again, requiring that Bourne travel to Boston to obtain her release. The letter dealt with other matters including the problems of the *Industry*, notes 29–32 above, and reported the draft of a bill of exchange on Lane, Son & Fraser for the *Lusanna*'s repairs.

[126] Bourne to Lane, Son & Fraser, Halifax, 31 Dec. 1775, DNA Microcopy 162, Case 30, No. 7, repeating the information about the bill of exchange in his letter of 3 Nov., note 125 above, and adding: "You will further note that the *Brigantine*

12. Octr. 76. Letter from Bourne to Doane. His situation very un-happy seperated from Family and Friends. Impossible to alter it, with-out exposing my Person and your Property. Am determind to make an Effort to see you and all Friends.[128]

Letter from B. to his Wife. Expectation of speedily returning.[129]

Libell vs. Brig. Industry at Boston 18 Sep. 1775. Condemnd. Brom-field claimd an Appeal to England. The Oil was consigned to Mr. Bourne, in London for Sale. Bourne applies to Smith Council who drew the Memorial for him to the Lords of Trade.[130]

Depositions of Mr. Hancock. Jno. Bradford, Jno. Emmery. Chas. Miller. Laz. Goodwin. Saml. Emmery.[131]

[*Lusanna*] *was seized as the property of Elisha Doane Esqr.* of Eastham who belongs to New England by virtue of a general order from Lord Dartmouth." He then re-ported that he had obtained the vessel's release at Boston and was about to sail for London, having drawn a second bill of exchange for necessaries. The letter bears the apparently incorrect date of 3 Dec. at the head. The date 31 Dec. which appears at the end is more likely, because Bourne was reported to have been in Boston as late as the 13th. *Id.*, Nos. 112, 113.

[127] See note 114 above.

[128] Bourne to Doane, London, 12 Oct. 1776, DNA Microcopy 162, Case 30, No. 29: "My situation here is very unhappy as you may well think being seperated from my Family and friends; But it is neither in my power to change it nor in the least degree prudent to attempt it this winter without exposing my person and *leaving your property unguarded.* Therefore [I] must for the present remain here until I can return with more Safety to myself and friends." After reporting that his presence in England was working to Doane's great advantage, Bourne concluded, "I am de-termined to make one Effort ere *be*long to see you and all friends when I find the gathering of the Storm to abate. When the Brigantine returns [*from Gibraltar*] I may sell her but that depends on Circumstances and price. Be assured that I have nothing more at heart than the welfare and interest of my friends and if it be in my power to add to their happiness and Interest I shall ever be ready to do it, tho' at the expence of my own small private fortune."

[129] Bourne to his wife, 12 Oct. 1776, DNA Microcopy 162, Case 30, No. 30: "The anxiety under which I labour for your and my children's welfare and peace greatly disturbs me, but my expectations of speedily returning affords me some consolation."

[130] As to the role of the *Industry* in this case, see text at notes 29–32 above. DNA Microcopy 162, Case 30, contains the record of the proceedings in the Court of Vice Admiralty at Boston, including the libel filed against her by Samuel Fitch on behalf of John DeLaTouche, Commander of H.M.S. *Halifax*, dated 18 Sept. 1775 (No. 37); the claim of Henry Bromfield, agent for the owners of the *Industry* for vessel and most of the cargo (No. 38); decrees of Nathaniel Hatch, Deputy Judge, dated 10 and 12 Oct. 1775, condemning the unclaimed portions of the cargo, as well as the vessel and claimed portions (Nos. 39, 42); Bromfield's claim of an appeal to the Privy Council, dated 19 Oct. 1775 (No. 45); and an invoice, dated 7 Sept. 1775 (No. 89), and bill of lading, dated 17 July 1775 (No. 56), under which 102 casks of oil and head matter belonging to Doane were shipped aboard the *Industry,* consigned to Bourne or Lane, Son & Fraser in London. Bourne's journal, note 158 below, and his Memorial, note 119 above, document his petition to the Lords of Trade.

[131] For the depositions of John Hancock, John Bradford, John Emery, Charles Miller, Lazarus Goodwin, and Samuel Emery as to Doane's good character as a

Bills of Lading of two Trunks and 29 lb. silks of Shepards.[132]
Capt. Woods hand Writing to the sailing orders.[133] In the Book. On the Risque of Elisha Doane.[134]

Agreed between Elisha Doane and Mathew Wood.[135]
Letter to Lane Son & Fraser, from C[olonel] Doane.[136]
Letter to Bourne from Doane, consigning Oil &c. by the Industry.[137]
July 17. 1777. Letter, from D. to Bourne.[138]

---

patriot, all taken early in Dec. 1777, see DNA Microcopy 162, Case 30, Nos. 72, 70, 73, 71, 69, and 67. Hancock stated in part that Doane was "a friend to his country an advocate for liberty and an asserter of the rights and liberties of mankind." *Id.*, No. 72. He and the others testified to Doane's services as a member of the General Assembly, selectman, provisioner of the Continental Army, and general supporter of the patriot cause. *Ibid.* Doane was also given a clean bill of health by the Wellfleet Committee of Correspondence. Certificate of 27 Nov. 1777, *id.*, No. 75.

[132] See bill of lading, 10 July 1777, Lane, Son & Fraser, consigning two trunks of merchandize to James Shepherd at Halifax; receipt of Matthew Wood, 10 July 1777 to James Shepherd for 29 pounds of silk to be delivered to him at Halifax; acknowledgment apparently by Bourne, Cowes, 4 Sept. 1777, of indorsement to him by Shepherd of the bill of lading and receipt. DNA Microcopy 162, Case 30, No. 19. See note 124 above.

[133] The orders, signed by Doane and countersigned by Wood, provided that Wood was to proceed directly to London and on arrival there to "deliver your Cargo to Messrs. Lane Son & Fraser and Mr. Shearjashub Bourne agreeable to Bills of Lading and when you have delivered your Cargo apply to them for further directions about a Freight back &c." DNA Microcopy 162, Case 30, No. 104. Dated 21 Aug. 1775 and produced from Doane's copy book, according to Wood's deposition of 28 Jan. 1778. *Id.*, No. 118.

[134] Probably a reference to the invoice of Doane's goods shipped aboard the *Lusanna* "on the proper account and Riske of Elisha Doane," which was apparently also produced at the trial from Doane's copy book. See the invoice, DNA Microcopy, 162, Case 30, No. 103. A similar notation appears on a gauge of the oil obtained by Joseph Doane and consigned to Lane, Son & Fraser. *Id.*, No. 93. Depositions of David Stoddard Greenough, 20 Feb. 1778, and Matthew Wood, 28 Jan. 1778. *Id.*, Nos. 136, 118.

[135] See agreement between Wood and Doane, 29 Aug. 1775, providing that Wood was to have "Ten barrels Priviledge" on the voyage to London and the like en route to New England from the West Indies, if the return trip was made that way. Certain arrangements were made for the division of commissions with Bourne, and Wood was granted living expenses of 2s. 6d. while in London in addition to his wages of £30 per month. DNA Microcopy 162, Case 30, No. 105. This document was produced on the trial from Doane's copy book. See Wood's deposition, 28 Jan. 1778, *id.*, No. 118.

[136] Presumably Doane's letter of 29 Aug. 1775, reporting the departure of the *Lusanna*, commending Bourne to the firm's care, asking them to send him £1500 cash with Bourne, and giving instructions for the return cargo, depending on the political situation. See text at note 18 above. There are in the file, however, other letters, dated 12 Feb. 1776 and 17 July 1777 from Doane to Lane, Son & Fraser, giving further instructions. DNA Microcopy 162, Case 30, Nos. 112, 115.

[137] See Doane to Bourne, 7 Sept. 1775, inclosing invoice and bill of lading for Doane's share of the *Industry*'s cargo. DNA Microcopy 162, Case 30, No. 109. See also Doane's letter to Lane, Son & Fraser of the same date. *Id.*, No. 108.

[138] Doane to Bourne, 17 July 1777, DNA Microcopy 162, Case 30, No. 116: "By your letter of Septr. last which came to hand we had great expectations of

No. 58. *Penhallow v. The* Lusanna

Bills of Lading S.B. Invoice from Edenson & Co. Invoice of ⟨...⟩.[139]
Shepards Property admitted.

Isaiah Doanes, purchased of Mr. Bourne.[140]

Laws of the State of N.H.[141] Resolve of Congress 25 Nov. 75. 23. March. 76. 24. July 76. extended to all the subjects of G.B.[142]

Association.[143]

The Voyage to Gibralter. French, Spaniards, Portuguese, Sweeds &c.[144]

Onus Probandi on the Libellant.

Deposition of T. Casey and Wife.[145]

Maccays Case.[146] Mrs. Alsops Case.[147]

---

seeing you in America before now, but I suppose the difficulty of the times has occasiond your further stay, doubtless by *this time you have settled all my affairs to my advantage and your satisfaction.* When prudence should direct should be very glad to see you here."

[139] As to the various bills of lading in Bourne's charge, see Bourne to Cochran, note 116 above. For Lane, Son & Fraser's, and his own consignments, see notes 111, 112, above. See also invoice and bill of lading of Wm. Edenson & Co., 23 July 1777, consigning goods to the value of £1057 12s. 6d. (including £66 8s. 6d. insurance), to Bourne. DNA Microcopy 162, Case 30, Nos. 27, 17.

[140] See bill of sale, note 103 above.

[141] See note 109 above.

[142] The Resolves of 25 Nov. 1775 and 23 March 1776 are set out in note 108 above. That of 24 July 1776 appears in note 109 above.

[143] That is, the Continental Association, note 121 above.

[144] Probably a comment that trade would be had in the Mediterranean with people of all of these nationalities as well as with British subjects. The *Lusanna* did in fact call at Barcelona and bring home cargo from Malaga. See note 27 above.

[145] See notes 113, 115, above.

[146] Spelling uncertain. Perhaps Roberts v. Schooner *Thistle,* DNA Microcopy 162, Case 1 (Sp. Com. 1776), an appeal from the Pennsylvania Court of Admiralty. The *Thistle* had been taken by the privateer *Congress* while en route from Florida to the West Indies with a cargo of flour, pitch pine, and oak to be sold there. The libel alleged that she was the property of inhabitants of Great Britain (amended to read enemies of the United Colonies), and that she was carrying supplies to the "ministerial army" of Great Britain. The vessel was condemned after a verdict that she was the property in part of inhabitants of Great Britain and in part of enemies of the United Colonies. A special committee of Congress, with Robert Treat Paine a member, reversed on 16 Sept. 1776. The reasons for reversal do not appear in the record.

[147] Presumably Alsop v. Ruttenbergh, DNA Microcopy 162, Case 11 (Commrs. of App. 1777), an appeal from the Admiralty Court of Rhode Island. The *Frank,* originally out of New London, and claimed by Mrs. Alsop, a widow, of Middletown, Connecticut, had been captured by the privateer *Montgomery,* of Providence. The libel alleged that the *Frank* was en route from Newfoundland to Jamaica in one of a series of voyages she had made between those ports after obtaining a change of name and register at the latter. She had allegedly carried supplies to the fleet and army at Newfoundland. In an earlier proceeding based on a libel alleging only that she was the property of inhabitants of Great Britain the *Frank* had been acquitted by a jury. On the second libel, after the court overruled a motion to dismiss based on the earlier acquittal, the jury found that the voyages had been made as alleged and that the *Frank* was carrying supplies to the enemy. On appeal

Bill Jacksons Case.[148] Butlers Letter.[149]
Insured.

1. Q. Is the Property Doanes? Yes.[150]
2d. Does the Voyage to Gibralter, forfeit the Property?
3. Does the Voyage to Hallifax forfeit.
4. Does the Goods being British Manufactures forfeit em and Brig.
5. Does the Insurance forfeit the Goods?

---

before JA, James Wilson, and Thomas Burke, the appellants were heard, but the appellees did not appear. On 20 May 1777, the Commissioners reversed the decree and ordered redelivery.

[148] Presumably Wentworth v. The *Elizabeth*, William Jackson et al., claimants, DNA Microcopy 162, Case 2 (Sp. Com. 1776), a case in which Lowell himself was both a claimant and of counsel. The *Elizabeth* had been seized by three Continental privateers on 3 April 1776, en route from Boston to Halifax carrying loyalists evacuating the former city, their belongings, and goods looted during the evacuation. She and her cargo were libeled as having been recaptured after being in enemy hands for more than 96 hours, and for carrying supplies to the enemy. Under New Hampshire law, which adopted the language of a resolve of Congress, the recaptors of a vessel that had been in the possession of the enemy for more than 96 hours were entitled to one half the proceeds of sale, even if the enemy had not condemned her as prize. Act of 3 July 1776, 4 *Laws of New Hampshire* 30; Resolve of 5 Dec. 1775, 3 JCC 407. For the provision on supplying the enemy, see note 109 above. Jackson, a notorious tory, later tried for his participation, was one of 29 claimants; most of the remainder were citizens of Boston, like Lowell and John Rowe, whose effects had been taken by the departing loyalists. See Rowe, *Letters and Diary* 316–317. The vessel's owner, a Portsmouth merchant, also filed a claim. Jackson himself had gone as a passenger aboard the *Elizabeth*, ostensibly to protect his goods. See generally 1 *Adams Family Correspondence* 373–374. In Aug. 1776, a jury in the New Hampshire Court Maritime found that the vessel had not been captured as prize by the enemy, and was not carrying supplies to the British fleet and army, and that she and her cargo ought to be restored to the claimants. On the captors' appeal by their agent, Joshua Wentworth (also an owner of the *McClary*; see note 43 above), the special committee of Congress, which again included Paine, held that vessel and cargo were not forfeit as prize under the resolve of Congress dated 25 Nov. 1775, note 108 above, and that the Congressional resolve allowing a portion of the proceeds to recaptors was intended only for vessels which might be condemned as prize by the Law of Nations. The Committee ruled that the owners ought to make reasonable satisfaction for the return of their goods, however. The New Hampshire decree was reversed, and vessel and cargo ordered to be restored on condition that the claimants pay one-twelfth of its value to the recaptors. The report was accepted in Congress on 14 Oct. 1776. See 6 JCC 870–873. See also Clark, *George Washingon's Navy* 130–132, 136–138, 185–187.

[149] Probably a reference to the letter of credit on John Butler of Halifax, which Bourne carried. Compare Whipple's notes of Lowell's argument, text following note 165 below. See also note 160 below.

[150] These five questions are JA's notes of the heads of his own argument, repeated in slightly different form in Whipple's notes. See note 166 below.

III. OLIVER WHIPPLE'S MINUTES OF THE ARGUMENT[151]

New Hampshire Court Maritime, Portsmouth, 16 December 1777

John Penhallow and others,
agents for the Privateer McClary vs. Brig Lusannar

The Libel sets forth three Facts as Causes of Condemnation viz.

1st. That the Property of Brig and Cargo belonged to some Inhabitant or Inhabitants of great Britain.

2d. That at the Time of the Capture She was Carrying Supplies to the Enemy.

3d. That the Property on Board was British Manufacture.[152]

NB They then indeavour to introduce a fourth Cause of Condemnation viz. that the Brig made a Voyage to Gibralter with King's Stores in the Year 1776, tho' this Cause is not set forth in the Libel.[153]

There are two Resolves of Congress principally insisted on viz. the one that makes british property confiscate, the other, that makes all Vessels, their Cargoes &c. forfeited carrying Supplies to the Fleets and Armies acting against America, which said Resolves are adopted in our maritime Law.[154]

The Agents Council open the Cause in such manner, as to make Mr. Bourne the ostensible Owner of the Brig and Cargo, and as he has not Claimed the Property, They draw a false Consequence, that Coll. Doane has no foundation or Right of Claim to the Property.

The Council for the Agents first proceed to prove the Property in Mr. Bourne, and that he is an Inhabitant of Great Britain. To this end they Produce the Register in his Name.[155] The Goods being marked in his Name.[156] His Departure from the Country at the Commencement of the Despute.

His Memorial to the Lord[s] of the Admiralty[157] to recover Part of the Cargo of the Brig Industry. His Journal to show him an Enemy to the Country.[158]

---

[151] In Whipple's hand. Paine Law Notes. The notes of Whipple, a Portsmouth lawyer retained by Bourne, were apparently prepared for Paine, who entered the case as counsel after JA's departure for France. See note 44 above.

[152] See note 107 above. Compare JA's notes of the libelants' argument, notes 107–109 above.

[153] See text at notes 168, 169, below.

[154] For the resolves of Congress and the New Hampshire laws, see notes 108, 109, above.

[155] See note 110 above.

[156] See note 112 above.

[157] A possible inadvertence for "Treasury." See note 119 above.

[158] See extracts from Bourne's journal, DNA Microcopy 162, Case 30, No. 60:

Mr. Crosby's Letter of Recommendation to the Commanding Ingineer at Hallifax.[159] Two Letters of Credit from Mr. Lane, and Watson and Company to Mr. Butler at Hallifax in Favour of Mr. Bourne for about 7000.[160]

Also the Deposition of one Casey.[161]

The Deposition of Mrs. Casey.[162]

The Deposition of Mr. Lewis the Mate.[163]

And also produce a Letter from Mr. Bourne to Mr. Cockran at Hallifax.[164]

Answered by Mr. J. Lowell.[165]

By giving a general History of the Voyage and the whole transaction thereof, and showing the Property of the Brig and Cargo to be in Coll. Doane and that the altering the Register was to cover the Property from Seizure.

The marking the Goods SB was for the same Purpose.

His Departure from the Country was not criminal at that Time, as he went for the Purposes of Business for his Father as agent and with Intent to git his property out of England. That the Memorial ought not to be considered as Mr. Bourne's Sentiments, but as his Council's who framed it, to answer the Purpose. That there is nothing in the Journal (saving the Memorial) that looks unfriendly, but it shewes his Intentions were to return to his Family and Friends again.

That Crosby's Letter (whatever were Mr. Bourne's Intentions) cou'd not opperate to defeat Coll. Doane of his Property, nor cou'd

---

"Jany. 30th 1777. This day having all the papers compleated from Mr. Smith my Attorney, carried them to the Court of Chancery to be enrolled, they were accordingly enrolled. After which Mr. Lane and I went to the honorable Jona. Sewall Esqr. to sollicit his favor in order to introduce me to Lord Norths Secretary (Mr. Robinson), but as Mr. Sewall had no acquaintance with the Gentleman I was obliged to apply to Governor Hutchinson for his favor on the topick who readily gave me a letter of Introduction to Mr. Robinson and afterwards wrote to Mr. Robinson to assist me with my memorial by presenting it to Lord North the head of the Treasury." The remainder of this entry, and entries dated 11 and 26 Feb. and 1 and 5 March 1777, record Bourne's continuing and apparently unsuccessful attendance on the Treasury during their consideration of his memorial, notes 119, 130, above. PCC No. 44 fol. 309.

[159] See note 118 above.

[160] See Letter of Credit, Lane, Son & Fraser, to Bourne, 21 Aug. 1777, for £3000, and Letter of Credit in Bourne's favor, Watson & Rashleigh to John Butler, 21 Aug. 1777, for £4000. DNA Microcopy 162, Case 30, Nos. 33, 34.

[161] See note 113 above.

[162] See note 115 above.

[163] See note 117 above.

[164] See note 116 above.

[165] Compare JA's notes of Lowell's argument, text at notes 125–149 above.

any Acts of Mr. Bourne as a Factor, defeat him of his Property. That Mr. Lane's and Watson's Letters were disigned that Mr. Bourne should draw the Money at Hallifax, as an equivalent for Coll. Doane's Property in England in their hands, which Mr. Bourne did not think proper to risque in Specie or Goods across the Water, and disigned to have sent the Money, when received in some secret Way to Coll. Doane.

The Depositions were mostly favourable to the Defense of the Claimants, and were well observed on.

NB Mr. Adams, after recapitulating the main Points of the Evidence, as stated by Mr. Lowell, divided the Cause into the following Heads viz.[166]

1st. Whether it was not legal for any man to git his Property from an Enemy's Country?

2d. Whether taking the Register at Hallifax and another in London, in Mr. Bourne's Name to secure and cover the Property from Seizure, alterd the Property, and made it liable to Forfeiture?

Answer'd by Mr. Adams.

1st. That a man having property in an Enemy's Country, had an undoubted Right to transport that Property to any Place, where there was an appearant Probability, of geting it, or the Proceeds thereof to his Home, that he had a Right to chuse the Mode or Manner of securing his Property and transporting it Home, unless the States had by Law pointed out the Channel in which it was to be done (which is not the Case) and relyed much on the Justice and Equity of permitting it to be done, and concluded that it was the general Sentiment of the Congress to favour the Design.

2d. He observed, that Registers do not always identify the Property, and that taking out a Register and swearing to it was no Method known in Law to convey Property, if it was, it wou'd be in the Power of every man who had the Care of a Vessel, to deprive the rightful Owner of her by taking out a Register; he relyed on the Necessity of altering apparently the Property of a Vessel &c., where liable to be seized, that it was Justifyable upon the Principles of Commerce, and sanctified by almost universal Custom of Persons intrusted with Property abroad.[167]

[166] Compare JA's own summary of the heads of his argument at note 150 above. Whipple has made two heads out of JA's first point. JA's points 2–4 are herein points 3–5. JA's fifth point is an unheaded final paragraph. See note 181 below.

[167] There was testimony at the trial on appeal in the Superior Court that this was a common practice. See Depositions of Jonathan Mason and Nathaniel Libbee, 3 March 1778; John Parrot, Joseph Pierpoint, and Richard Salter, 31 Aug. 1778.

3d. Whether the Voyage She made from London to Gibralter freighting Kings Stores, in the Year 1776, was a Cause of Forfeiture?

NB The Council for the Agents indeavoured to introduce the Evidence of the Brig's haveing made a Voyage to Gibralter with King's Stores tho' not set forth in the Libel as a Cause of Condemnation;[168] This was objected to by the Councel for the Claimants; That no Evidence cou'd be given of any Matter that was Cause of Condemnation unless set forth in the Libel, that every Cause of Condemnation in the Law, ou[gh]t to be shown to the Court, before Evidence given, and that if they might be allowed to give Evidence of Facts that did not appear in the Libel, it wou'd be unne[ce]ssary to have any Libel at all, and that they cou'd not go out of the Libel for Matter of Condemnation, but must abide by their Allegations.[169] The Councel for the Agents likened it, to an Action of Trespass, where if the Evidence of the Fact was before the Time laid in the Declaration, it was good, if the Evidence related to any Part of the Trespass.

NB This is by no Means a similar Case, for Evidence never was given of any Trespass unless specially set forth in the Declaration, but the Judges gave it in their Favour, but wrong.

Answer'd.

He [*Adams*] observed that from the ninteenth of April 1775 none but general Gage and the Troops under his Command, in Conjunction with the Fleet, were looked on as Enemies, nor did the Congress till some Time in the Year 1776 even look on great Britain, or Ireland or any foreign Garrison as their Enemies in a General Sense,[170] and insisted there was no Law or Resolution of Congress that prohibited a Voyage to Gibralter, the Troops and Fleet not coming within the Meaning of the Law ie, Enemies acting against the united States of America. That the Sense of the Law and the Word Enemy was wholly limitted to the Fleets and Armies at that Time here, and on the Coast of America and that there is Yet no Law forbiding the Supplying a foreign Garrison of the King of Great Britain;[171] for if the word Enemy was to be construed in a general Sense to all the Dominions of the King of great Britain, it wou'd be absurd to say, That this Vessel, or any other, That was transporting Goods, or Provisions from one

---

DNA Microcopy 162, Case 30, Nos. 143, 144, 147, 139, 131, 138. Compare *Statement of the M'Clary Owners* 22. For a JA case under the British customs acts in which Doane seems to have attempted to alter a vessel's papers, see No. 52.

[168] See notes 114, 117, above.

[169] See note 122 above.

[170] Compare the Congressional Resolve of 24 July 1776, note 109 above.

[171] See the applicable resolves and laws, notes 108, 109, above.

Place to another within those Dominions, was carrying Supplies to the Enemy; because the Enemy were supplied with the Goods &c. previous to their Imbarkation; That the Superiour Court of the Massachusetts Bay and all other Courts, which had decided on the Question were of a Similar sentiment.[172]

4th. Whether the Brig being bound from London to Hallifax was a Cause of Forfeiture?

Answer'd

That all Vessels in London must be cleared out for some British Ports,[173] that Hallifax was the nighest Port to these States, that is open, except Garrison'd Towns, that there was every Probability if he got his Goods and Property at Hallifax, he might git them for the Doanes from thence in some secret Way, that there was no Law or Resolve, prohibiting the bringing home british Property, or directing the Mode, (as observed before) it is therefore left to the Choice of the Party; nor is there any Law that makes a Vessel forfeited for carrying Freight or anything else to Hallifax, provided it be for the Inhabitants, and not for the express Use of the Fleet and army; That not a single Article of the Cargo was for the Fleet and army, is express in the Depositions of Casey, Wife and Lewis,[174] and that there was no apparent Intention, Design or Mark of supplying the Fleet or Army, unless the Captors cou'd search out the Hart of Col. Doane and Mr. Bourne; and added that all Vessels or Transports bringing supplies or Stores to the Fleet and Army, did not clear out at the Custom House at London or elsewhere, but only had orders and a Certificate to deliver their Stores to the King's Commissary at the Place of Destination.[175]

5th. Whether the Property Claimed, and consisting of English Goods, and insured was a Cause of forfeiture?

[172] It has not been possible to identify with certainty such a case in the Records of the Massachusetts Superior Court of Judicature or Supreme Judicial Court.

[173] That is, vessels clearing for America. Trade with Europe was not prohibited. See 17 Geo. 3, c. 41, §§4, 5 (1777). JA probably referred to the statute 16 Geo. 3, c. 5, §§1, 3 (1776), which prohibited all trade with the rebellious colonies, and provided, with exceptions not material here, that all vessels "found trading in any port or place of the said colonies, or going to trade, or coming from trading, in any such port or place," should be forfeit to the Crown and liable to be taken as prize.

[174] See notes 113, 115, 117, above. At the trial in Superior Court in Sept. 1778 there were numerous depositions to the effect that Messrs. Cochran, Bourne's principal correspondents at Halifax, not only did not supply the royal forces, but were sympathetic to the American cause, supplying American prisoners whenever possible. See text and note 72 above.

[175] The statute 16 Geo. 3, c. 5. §2 (1776) provided that a vessel in His Majesty's service or carrying supplies to Crown forces or the inhabitants of a garrison town should not be subject to seizure as prize under *id.*, §§1, 3 (note 173 above), if it produced a license from the Admiralty, a military or naval commander, or a loyal governor, specifying the voyage and the cargo.

Answer'd

He observ'd that there is no Law now in being against bringing Home british Manufactures, and that the Goods being made in England was no Cause of Forfeiture. The Act of Association, went no further than to forbid Importation of british Goods, but did not declare them forfeited, but were only to be Stored or reshipped as the Importer chose, and all the Penalty was to stigmatize the Importer, "as an Enemy to Liberty." [176]

That the Declaration of Independancy, repeated all former Resolves of the Association; [177] that Independancy, or the Declaration thereof, did not respect british Manufactures, and there is no Expression therein, that prohibits the Importing british Goods, or that makes them liable to Forfeiture as Such; That it was the general Sentiment of the Congress that ⟨Property⟩ Goods in England, tho' british, belonging to Americans, might be brought here without a Liability of Forfeiture, and that it was for the general good of the Country.[178] Mr. Adams then Instanced a Case at Carolina, where Goods were condemned at a maritime Court, because brought from Statia, and were british Manufactury, but on appeal to Congress, the Decree was reversed, it being no Cause of Forfeiture.[179]

---

[176] See note 121 above. JA was a signer of the Association and was present at the debates on it. See 2 JA, *Diary and Autobiography* 137–140, 147–149, 155.

[177] That is, the grievances upon which the Association was based, which were largely the Acts of Parliament raising a revenue and extending the Admiralty jurisdiction, and the so-called Coercive Acts of 1774. These measures were among the far longer list of grievances contained in the Declaration, with the difference that the blame was shifted from Parliament and the Ministry to George III himself. Compare the Association, 1 Jefferson, *Papers*, ed. Boyd, 149–154, with the Declaration of Independence, *id.* at 429–433.

[178] JA presumably meant that such a sentiment was expressed, or at least assumed, in the debates on the Association in 1774 (note 176 above), although he was also an active participant in the debates on the Declaration of Independence in June and July 1776. See 3 JA, *Diary and Autobiography* 396–398; 1 Jefferson, *Papers*, ed. Boyd, 309–315. No record of discussion of this point has been found in either debate, however. That JA correctly stated the position of Congress at this period is suggested by the fact that on 27 March 1781 that body passed a resolution forbidding the practice of bringing property from Great Britain on safe conduct. 19 JCC 314–316. The editors are indebted to Mrs. Kellock for this reference.

[179] Probably Fowkes v. The *Roseanna*, DNA Microcopy 162, Case 20 (Commrs. of App. 1777), an appeal upon which JA may have sat. See note 8 above. The *Roseanna*, owned by John Brown of Rhode Island through his Nantucket agents, had been seized at Cape Fear, allegedly carrying goods the property of British subjects. The libel further alleged that cargo had been loaded at Nantucket ostensibly for non-British islands, but that this had been deception and that she had imported a cargo into the Bahamas to aid the enemy. Further, she had brought a cargo of British-manufactured goods from the Bahamas into North Carolina, contrary to the resolves of Congress. In a trial of the master's claim without a jury, the *Roseanna* was adjudged forfeit on the latter two grounds. The master appealed to Congress.

No. 58. *Penhallow v. The* Lusanna

Mr. Adams observed that the Court of the Massachusetts, agreed in Sentiment with the Congress on that head; for they had given in many Instances, Licenses to People to go to Hallifax, and to others that were there who were desirous to come into these States, to bring their Property consisting of British Manufactures, into these States, without the least Idea of Forfeiture,[180] which if it was not permitted, wou'd opperate as an inconceivable Injury to many Good Subjects of these States.

He observed,[181] That Insurance was only a Wager, that it did by no Means pass the Property, and that every one wou'd act imprudently who did not insure his Property even against Common Accidents; that this was never known to be a Cause of Forfeiture of a Friends Goods, because insured by an Enemy, perhaps they were not insured to half the Value, and then the assured must loose the Remainder. That this Insurance was made for a Cover, that they might not suspect any ill Designs; had it not been done, they on the other Side the Water, wou'd have suspected a Design that the Brig was destined to some Port in America, and he added that if the rankest Tory existing was bringing his Goods to America with a View to settle here, the same wou'd not be subject to Forfeiture.[182]

Mr. Adams spoke largely to each of the foregoing Questions, added many incidental Observations, and concluded, if the Property in Despute had belonged to a Southern State Instead of the Massachusetts, the Owners wou'd Send forth armed Ships to make Reprisals.

No record of the result appears in the files, but according to other sources the decree of the court below was reversed. Davis, "Federal Courts Prior to the Constitution," 131 U.S., Appendix xxxviii.

[180] For examples of licenses to come from Nova Scotia granted by the General Court, see Resolves of 28 Oct. 1776, 19 A&R 624; 29 Oct. 1776, *id.* at 629. A resolve of 23 April 1777 forbade the departure of persons "to Great Britain or elsewhere" under prior resolves, perhaps to prevent one Ephraim Deane from going to Nova Scotia to get his family under a resolve of 19 April 1777. *Id.* at 896, 905. But subsequent petitions were granted, both permitting Nova Scotians to settle in Massachusetts, and permitting Massachusetts inhabitants to go to Nova Scotia for their effects. Resolves of 1 Oct. 1777, 20 *id.* at 146; 15 Oct. 1777, *id.* at 167–168; 17 Feb. 1778, *id.* at 295; 9 March 1778, *id.* at 322; 3 Oct. 1778, *id.* at 502. At the trial in the New Hampshire Superior Court in Sept. 1778, the deposition of one who had gone for this purpose was offered. See Deposition of Joseph Pierpoint, 31 Aug. 1778, DNA Microcopy 162, Case 30, No. 131.

[181] This paragraph is actually JA's fifth point. See notes 150, 166, above.

[182] See Resolve of 23 March 1776, note 108 above.

R. *Criminal Law*

59. Rex v. Richardson

1770–1772

EDITORIAL NOTE

On 22 February 1770, a man named Ebenezer Richardson fatally shot an eleven-year-old German boy. The circumstances of the shooting and the conditions of Richardson's subsequent trial for murder so emphasize the peculiarly disturbed status of the law in Boston at the time that documents pertaining to the case are included in this collection, even though Adams does not appear to have been actively engaged in the matter. The fact is that defense counsel's notes (Document I) remain among the Adams Papers and were docketed "Rex v. Richardson" in Adams' hand; moreover, the legal points raised in Richardson's trial and its aftermath bore particular relevance at the Massacre trials in 1770 (Nos. 63, 64).

Ebenezer Richardson was born in Woburn in 1718, married a Woburn woman, and some time thereafter came to Boston.[1] There he was at least a reputed member of the customs establishment and commensurately disliked. Although the Customs Commissioners were later to deny that he had ever been a customs officer,[2] Richardson had for "many years" before 1770 "been known by the name of THE INFORMER," according to the *Boston Gazette*.[3] Even John Adams was in later times to fulminate against

[1] Stark, *Loyalists of Mass.* 422; William R. Cutter, *Broadside Regarding Ebenezer Richardson, the Informer, Found in the Library of the Historical Society of Pennsylvania at Philadelphia* 9 (n.d.).

[2] See *Boston Evening-Post*, 5 March 1770, p. 3, col. 1; *Boston Gazette*, 5 March 1770, p. 2, col. 1.

[3] *Boston Gazette*, 5 March 1770, p. 2, col. 1. The *Gazette* claimed that Richardson had sworn before a grand jury "not many years past" that he had acted on a "commission or warrant" from Charles Paxton; this Paxton denied, calling Richardson "a d——d villain." According to the *Gazette*, the grand jurors had complained of Richardson's perjury to a magistrate, with no result. The entire story should probably be treated suspiciously. In the first place, grand jury deliberations were secret, or at least were supposed to be; see form of oath, Act of 25 Nov. 1692, 1 A&R 78, 79. Second, if the grand jury believed Richardson to have perjured himself, it could have presented him; finally, even if the story is true, it establishes only that Richardson did not hold a post requiring a commission. Hutchinson referred to him as "a landwaiter, or inferior custom-house officer, and before that, an informer against illicit traders." 3 Hutchinson, *Massachusetts Bay*, ed. Mayo, 193. And Peter Oliver called him "a Custom House Officer." Oliver, *Origin and Progress* 84. Note, however, that Oliver dates the incident as "the beginning of *March* 1770." *Ibid.* See also Hutchinson to ——, 28 Feb. 1770, 26 Mass. Arch. 450: "Richardson, whose name you must remember as an Informer." Richardson could well have acted

him: "If there was even a color of justice in the public opinion, he was the most abandoned wretch in America. Adultery, incest, perjury were reputed to be his ordinary crimes. His life would exhibit an atrocious volume." [4] Whatever Richardson's other faults may or may not have been, later events demonstrated indubitably that he had a short temper.

All this, added to the rough-and-tumble of the fall and winter of 1769–1770 in Boston,[5] almost insured that Richardson would soon collide with the patriots. The occasion arrived on 22 February 1770, a Thursday, which, like all Thursdays, was by Boston custom a market day and a school holiday; [6] plenty of idle schoolboys as well as numerous up-country farmers stood available to bolster the already powerful Boston mob.

The latter's principal object for some time had been the enforcement of the nonimportation agreement. Temporarily checked by the resourceful stubbornness of John Mein,[7] the "well-disposed" were beginning to move against the few holdouts. One of these, Theophilus Lillie, a near-neighbor of Richardson's and "a very inoffensive man, except in the offense of importation" [8] resisted with language which, for sarcasm, at least, rivaled even Mein's: "I cannot help saying," Lillie had written in January 1770, "although I never entered far into the mysteries of government, having applied myself to my shop and my business, that it always seemed strange to me that People who contend so much for civil and religious Liberty should be so ready to deprive others of their natural liberty—that Men who are guarding against being subject to Laws [*to*] which they never gave their consent in person or by their representative, should at the same time make Laws, and in the most effectual manner execute them upon me and others, to which Laws I am sure I never gave my consent either in person or by my representative. . . . I own I had rather be a slave under one Master; for if I know who he is, I may, perhaps, be able to please him, than a slave to an hundred or more, who I don't know where to find, nor what they will expect from me." [9]

For some time, the technique used against men like Lillie had been the

---

as informer without a commission at first and been commissioned after the grand jury incident.

[4] JA to Dr. J. Morse, 20 Jan. 1816, 10 JA, *Works* 204, 210; Cutter, *Broadside Regarding Richardson*, reprints a broadside containing the following couplets: "Woburn, my native place can tell / My crimes are blacker far than Hell / What great disturbance there I made / Against the people and their Head. / A wretch of wretches prov'd with child / By me I know, at which I smil'd / To think the PARSON he must bare / The guilt of me, and I go clear." Cutter attributes the allusion to a protracted incident of 1752, in which the widow Keziah Henshaw gave birth to a child and "at the time of her travail . . . laid it to" the Reverend Edward Jackson. See the details in Samuel Sewall, *History of Woburn* 319–325 (Boston, 1868). Keziah was a sister of Richardson's wife, Rebecca, which explains JA's "incest" charge. Cutter, *Broadside Regarding Richardson*.

[5] See No. 12.

[6] Anonymous report, 3 Bernard Papers 70, MH.

[7] See No. 12.

[8] Hutchinson to Hood, 23 Feb. 1770, 26 Mass. Arch. 444.

[9] *Massachusetts Gazette*, 11 Jan. 1770, p. 2, col. 3.

"exhibition," a sign or placard planted before the offending shop, carrying language whose general import was "Don't Buy from the Traitor." This was usually coupled with the 18th-century equivalent of a picket line, a crowd of schoolboys.[10] As Gordon was to write a few years later, "Boys, small and great, and undoubtedly men, had been and were encouraged, and well paid by certain leaders . . . and still persevered." [11] But, though boys were the actors, Thomas Hutchinson, at least, did not doubt that they were being "set on by Men." [12]

On the day in question, a gang of boys (the witnesses at the trial varied in their estimates: one said as few as sixty, another said as many as three hundred) paraded to Lillie's and placed before his door a large wooden head bearing caricatures of the four leading importers and a hand pointed toward the house.[13] Richardson, seeing the "hundreds" of boys gathered at Lillie's, tried to persuade first "a countryman," then a charcoal vendor, to run their respective wagons against the sign. In desperation, he even took a cart and horse standing in the street and tried to do the job himself. At this, the crowd began to add more solid missiles to the epithets it was already hurling. As Richardson retreated to his house, he passed several of the patriots, including Edward Proctor and Thomas Knox. Crying "Perjury! Perjury!" in apparent reference to what Richardson considered the false nature of the charges implied by the sign, Richardson paused to exchange insults with these men and two others besides. At the trial, there was testimony that Richardson had sworn to "make it too hot" for Proctor and the others; there was also testimony that they in turn had called him a "damn Son of Bitch" and had threatened to have his heart and liver out.

Lieutenant Governor Hutchinson, meanwhile, hearing of the trouble, "gave express directions to the Sheriff to go and suppress this unlawful assembly before the accident happened, but he did not think it safe to attempt it nor is there a J. of P. in the town who will appear upon such an occasion." [14]

With Richardson back in his house, the battle raged on. A witness at the trial was later to testify that stones shattered the windows, carrying away even the lead and frames. George Wilmot, a sailor employed in the

[10] The Sons of Liberty, Hutchinson said, "thought it best that great numbers of Boys should Meet upon such occasions rather than Men." See text at note 6 above.

[11] 1 Gordon, *History of Independence* 277.

[12] Hutchinson to Gage, 25 Feb. 1770, 26 Mass. Arch. 445. For Mein's correspondence with Hutchinson, see 25 Mass. Arch. 455–459.

[13] The events of 22 Feb. are largely drawn from the report in the *Boston Evening-Post*, 26 Feb. 1770, p. 3, col. 1. Although the published story was "almost entirely made up from the facts detailed by [Richardson's] enemies," see Drake, *History and Antiquities of Boston* 777, even the anonymous and patently anti-patriot author of the Reports in the Bernard Papers referred his reader to the *Evening-Post* account without serious correction. 3 Bernard Papers 70, MH. Lillie's shop was located on Middle (now Hanover) Street near the New Brick Church. Stark, *Loyalists of Mass.* 310; Thwing, *Crooked and Narrow Streets of Boston* 60.

[14] Hutchinson to Gage, 25 Feb. 1770, 26 Mass. Arch. 445, 448. See also Hutchinson to Bernard, 20 Oct. 1770, 27 Mass. Arch. 26, 30.

customs service, was at Richardson's house, the reason for his visit not being clear, although the patriots claimed he had originally been sent to tell Richardson to take down the sign.[15] As the violence increased, and the crowd began to push at the doors, Wilmot told Richardson, one of the witnesses later said, "he would stand by him as Long as he had breath." The pelting continued, and Richardson thrust a gun through a window, "snapping" it at the mob. Finally, he fired a charge of bird shot, eleven of which struck and mortally wounded Christopher Seider (or Snider), some after striking the hand of another boy.

Immediately a bell was set ringing and, according to the *Evening-Post* account, a crowd surrounded the house front and rear. The mob completed the breaking and entering, subdued Wilmot and Richardson, and hustled them outside. "[T]he first thought was to hang him up at once and a halter was brought and a sign post picked upon, but one who is supposed to have stirred up the tumultuous proceedings took great pains and prevented it." [16]

The men were dragged through the town, "cruelly abused by the Mob," [17] and put before Justice of the Peace John Ruddock, who ordered them on to Faneuil Hall, where in the presence of a thousand people, he, along with Justices of the Peace Richard Dana, Samuel Pemberton, and Edmund Quincy, examined them and had them committed to jail.[18] "After the Examination, when the Sheriff was carrying them to Gaol, several attempts were made to get a Rope around Richardson's neck." [19] It should be noted that the boy did not die until that evening,[20] so that at the time of their commitment and near-lynching, Richardson and Wilmot could not, by any reasoning, be guilty of murder.

Of course the "Sons of Liberty took care to Improve this Affair to the utmost advantage." [21] On 26 February 1770 the *Gazette* ran an inflammatory report of the "late barbarous Murder" insinuating that the customs officers were behind it all. "Inhumanly murdered" the *Gazette* said of "the unfortunate boy," "the young lad who last week fell a sacrifice to the Rage

[15] *Boston Gazette*, 26 Feb. 1770, p. 5, col. 2. Wilmot had "lived in Boston since 1736 as a master mariner." Jones, *Loyalists of Mass.* 298. He was employed as a seaman on the sloop *Liberty* when she was a revenue vessel, and was serving aboard her when she was destroyed. Richard Reeves in *Boston Evening-Post*, 3 May 1770, p. 3, col. 1.
[16] Hutchinson to Gage, 25 Feb. 1770, 26 Mass. Arch. 445, 448. See also Hutchinson to Hood, 23 Feb. 1770, 26 Mass. Arch. 444, 445, in which Hutchinson identifies Richardson's benefactor as "M——x [Molineux] who probably was afraid how he might be attacked himself by such an action."
[17] 3 Bernard Papers 70, MH.
[18] *Boston Evening-Post*, 26 Feb. 1770, p. 3, col. 1.
[19] 3 Bernard Papers 70, MH. See also William Palfrey to John Wilkes, 5 March 1770, printed in Elsey, "John Wilkes and William Palfrey," 34 Col. Soc. Mass., *Pubns.* 411, 415–417 (1941).
[20] *Boston Evening-Post*, 26 Feb. 1770, p. 3, col. 1. Dr. Joseph Warren performed the subsequent autopsy and extracted the eleven shot, each the size of a big pea. *Ibid.* See also the coroner's inquest, SF 102009.
[21] 3 Bernard Papers 70, MH.

and Malice of an Old Offender and *his Abettors*." Richardson was called "infamous" three times, no less, once all in capital letters.[22] Even the loyalists had to acknowledge the propaganda triumph of the patriots. "So artful were they in their account that it was almost universally believed that the Commiss[ioners of Customs] were Abettors in this Affair." [23]

The funeral was a somber and effective climax to the press attacks. John Rowe, in whose company John Adams attended the rites, was "very sure two thousand people" were there,[24] and Adams' "Eyes never beheld such a funeral." [25] As the cortege wound its way past the Liberty Tree, the mourners could read on a board tacked thereto these appropriate sentiments: "Thou shalt take no Satisfaction for the Life of a Murderer. He shall surely be put to Death. Though *Hand join in Hand*, the Wicked shall not pass *unpunished*." [26] Adams wrote afterward in his diary: "This Shewes, there are many more Lives to spend if wanted in the Service of their Country. It Shews, too that the Faction is not yet expiring—that the Ardor of the People is not to be quelled by the Slaughter of one Child and the Wounding of another." [27] If the articles and the demonstration could have this effect on Adams, whose ability to distinguish patriotic heroes from "saucy boys" was to receive a public demonstration within the year,[28] how well had the affair fulfilled its designed purpose "to raise the passions of the people, and to strengthen" the cause "in which their leaders had engaged them." [29] It is probably fair to say that if the troops had not fired on the mob less than two weeks after Richardson killed young Seider, the Sons would have celebrated not 5 March, but 22 February, as the anniversary of the first effusion of patriotic blood. As Hutchinson pointed out, the funeral of young Allen, killed in the St. George's Fields riot over John Wilkes in 1768 was a good recent example of the technique.[30]

But the King Street riot did occur, and, though its long-run effect on Richardson was to thrust him from center stage, its immediate result was

[22] *Boston Gazette,* 26 Feb. 1770, p. 5, col. 2.

[23] 3 Bernard Papers 70, MH. One of the latter-day believers is O. M. Dickerson. But his "The Commissioners of Customs and the Boston Massacre," 27 *NEQ* 310 (1954), is only lightly based on the sources.

[24] Rowe, *Letters and Diary* 197.

[25] 1 JA, *Diary and Autobiography* 350.

[26] *Boston Gazette,* 5 March 1770, p. 2, col. 2.

[27] 1 JA, *Diary and Autobiography* 350.

[28] No. 64, text at note 226.

[29] 3 Hutchinson, *Massachusetts Bay,* ed. Mayo, 194. The patriots had moved quickly into print to avert any chance of postponing the trial until passions cooled. "It is whispered that the trial of Richardson and Wilmot will be put off until ———." *Boston Gazette,* 5 March 1770, p. 2, col. 2.

[30] 3 Hutchinson, *Massachusetts Bay,* ed. Mayo, 194. For details of the Allen incident and its aftermath, see R. W. Postgate, *That Devil Wilkes* 134-135 (N.Y., 1929). The Wilkes propagandists, by the way, labeled the doings in St. George's Fields a "massacre," which term may have inspired the patriots later on. Incidentally, Wilkes himself received a highly charged account of the Richardson affair from one of the patriot leaders. See William Palfrey to John Wilkes, 5 March 1770, in Elsey, "John Wilkes and William Palfrey," 34 Col. Soc. Mass., *Pubns.* 411, 416-417 (1941).

to render his chance of a fair trial minimal and of acquittal zero. Two things assured this. First, popular prejudice, already heated by the newspapers and the funeral, burst into passionate flame over the actions of the soldiers; Revenge! was the cry, anything loyalist and powerless the object. Second, the rancor against Captain Preston and the soldiers was so great, and, apparently, the official interest in defending them so much higher than in Richardson's case,[31] that, although the court "chose to postpone the Trials, untill there might be some Chance of Justice being uninterrupted," [32] when Sam Adams and a delegation "waited on the Superior Court and insisted upon their proceeding without any adjournment on the tryal of Preston, &c.," [33] the judges were forced to bargain. At first, it is true, the judges "notwithstanding this demand and the risque they run of being torn to pieces should they counteract the will of this Sovereign Committee . . . continued to try civil Causes only." But "The people being very uneasy that the criminal tryals were not brought on, the Court found it necessary in order to keep them a little quiet to arraign Richardson." [34]

"The existence of a state of public opinion which prevents a fair trial is a danger to which the jury system is always open," Holdsworth has written. "And it is a danger against which there is no remedy except the existence of an impartial, a humane, a courageous, and a learned bench." [35] He might have added "and a strong civil authority." In the opinion of Judge Oliver, "had a Trial been refused, it was rather more than an equal chance that the Prisoners [i.e. Preston and the soldiers as well as Richardson] would have been murdered by the Rabble; and the Judges been exposed to Assassinations." [36]

According to the anonymous reporter whose narrative is in the Bernard Papers, "Richardson was arraign'd on a Monday and directed to prepare for his tryal on the Friday following. Accordingly on the Friday he was brought to the Bar and ask'd by the Court if he was then ready. He observ'd to the Court that he had made application to almost every Lawyer in town to undertake his cause, which no one would do, that the Constables had refused summoning his Witnesses,[37] that the Jailer, had used him in so

---

[31] See editorial note to Nos. 63 and 64.

[32] Oliver, *Origin and Progress* 86.

[33] 3 Bernard Papers 76, MH; see 3 Hutchinson, *Massachusetts Bay,* ed. Mayo, 205; Oliver, *Origin and Progress* 87, also refers to this visit, but seems to place it after Richardson's trial. Compare Lynde, *Diary* 194 (14 March 1770): "Com[mitte]e of Boston with Court after Warren."

[34] 3 Bernard Papers 76, MH.

[35] 9 Holdsworth, *History of English Law* 231–232.

[36] Oliver, *Origin and Progress* 86.

[37] In England, there was "no express provision that the defendant in felony shall have process to bring in his witnesses." 1 Chitty, *Criminal Law* 625 note. Hawkins, however, thought that although in capital cases the defendant had "no Right by the Common Law to any Process against his Witnesses without a special Order of the Court . . . it seems that since the Statute of 1 Annae [c.] 9 . . . which ordains, That the Witnesses for the Prisoner shall be sworn, Process may be taken out against them of Course in any Case whatsoever." 2 Hawkins, *Pleas of the Crown* 435. No Massachusetts statute appears to cover criminal cases, although from early pro-

cruel a manner that he was even frequently debarred the Liberty of conversing with his friends, that every Newspaper was crouded with the most infamous and false libels against him in order to prejudice the minds of his jury; that without Counsel, without the privilege of calling upon his Witnesses to support his innocence he was now to be tried for his life. The Judges moved with compassion at this representation put off the trial to a further day. The Court then made application to the several Lawyers present to appear as his Counsel but this one and all of them declined. The court finding that a requisition had no effect asserted their Authority and order'd Mr. Fitch the advocate General to appear on his behalf on his trial. Fitch made use of a variety of arguments in order to excuse himself which the Court did not judge sufficient. He concluded with saying that since the Court had peremptorily ordered him, he would undertake it, but not otherways." [38]

The right to counsel availed Richardson little, because Fitch was sick on the two occasions the case was called for trial, the last one being 17 April.[39] The court thereupon appointed Josiah Quincy; three days later Richardson and Wilmot went on trial.[40] For the Crown, Solicitor General

---

vincial days, the parties in civil causes were entitled to subpoena witnesses. Preston and the soldiers were afforded process to summon witnesses. See editorial note to Nos. 63 and 64, note 63.

[38] 3 Bernard Papers 76, MH.

[39] 3 Bernard Papers 76, MH; Lynde, *Diary* 195 (17 April 1770). The following tentative chronology is based on (1) 3 Bernard Papers 76; (2) Lynde, *Diary*; (3) Paine Diary; (4) the Minute Books for this and the Charlestown terms:

   13 March (Tuesday), Court convenes; indictment sometime during that week.
   19 March (Monday), Richardson arraigned.
   23 March (Friday), Richardson requests counsel.
   27 March (Tuesday), "Attorney General to Ipswich Court; so we on civil actions all the week." Lynde, *Diary* 194.
   2–7 April (Monday-Saturday), civil and routine criminal cases.
   10 April (Tuesday), Charlestown term commenced.
   13 April (Friday), Charlestown term adjourned.
   17 April (Tuesday), second postponement.
   20 April (Friday), trial.
   21 April (Saturday), verdict; court adjourned to 29 May.
   29 May (Tuesday), court adjourned to 31 May.
   31 May (Thursday), court meets, adjourned to 6 September.
    6 September (Thursday), motion for new trial and jury examined.
    7 September (Friday), motion argued.

[40] 3 Bernard Papers 76, MH. Drake, *History and Antiquities of Boston* 777, says without citation that Sampson Salter Blowers was associated with Quincy. A contemporary account (note 43 below) shows that Quincy had help, and the Paine notes indicate that Blowers participated in the late stages of the affair at least. Quincy's service in Richardson's defense has received almost no attention or even notice. Gordon, for example, did not mention it (see note 11 above); nor did Josiah Quincy in his memoir, *Josiah Quincy, Jr.*, or Samuel M. Quincy in his introduction and notes to Quincy's *Reports*. Yet in many respects Quincy's defense of Richardson was even more significant than his participation in the Massacre trials. It is worth noting that whereas in provincial Massachusetts, the court would apparently appoint counsel for a man accused of murder who had none, in contemporary England (and, for that matter, in New York), defendants in felony

Samuel Quincy and Robert Treat Paine divided the prosecution, establishing the pattern they were to follow later that year in the Massacre trials.[41] According to a later newspaper account, "The cause was opened, and the evidence examined in behalf of the Crown by a Gentleman of superior ability, who was assisted by another Gentleman, employed by the Town of *Boston* [42] perfectly acquainted with the law, who performed his part with such distinguished talents, as did honour to himself, and gave intire satisfaction to his constituents. The evidence in behalf of the Prisoner being examined by a Gentleman who did not speak to the case, gave the other Gentleman who was his Attorney a greater opportunity to enlarge on the law and evidence in his favour; who, actuated solely from the motive of humanity, as he did it without fee or reward, and at the hazard of losing his popular reputation, so ably managed the law and evidence, in bringing such pertinent authorities to support the facts, and making such just remarks on the same, as fully convinced me of his abili-

---

trials could not be represented by counsel at all. The rule, it is true, was gradually being relaxed in England, and in at least one reported case of 1758, counsel was cross-examining the witnesses. But not until the Prisoners' Counsel Act, 6 & 7 Will. 4, c. 114, §1 (1837), was a prisoner accused of felonies given the right to have counsel present his full defense. And, even in the mid-18th-century English trials which conceded counsel the right to cross-examine, the attorney was not permitted to address the jury on the prisoner's behalf. See generally, 9 Holdsworth, *History of English Law* 235; 1 Stephen, *History of Criminal Law* 424–425, which discusses the English case, Rex v. Barnard, 19 State Trials 815 (London Sessions, 1758). On the New York practice, see Julius Goebel and T. Raymond Naughton, *Law Enforcement in Colonial New York* 573–574 (N.Y. 1944). The Massachusetts right to counsel may stem from general legislation on attorneys. The "Act for the Establishing of Judicatories and Courts of Justice Within This Province," after conferring on the Superior Court of Judicature "cognizance . . . in all pleas of the crown, and in all matters relating to the conservation of the peace and punishment of offenders," enacted that "it shall be in the liberty of every plaintiff or defendant . . . to plead and defend his own cause in his proper person, or with the assistance of such other as he shall procure being a person not scandalous or otherwise offensive to the Court." Act of 25 Nov. 1692, 1 A&R 72, 73–74, 75. This act and several successors were disallowed, 1 A&R 72; Act of 19 June 1697, 1 A&R 283; Act of 18 July 1699, 1 A&R 372; but finally, in 1701, after the Superior Court received the jurisdiction of the three English common-law courts ("An Act for The Establishing a Superiour Court of Judicature, Court of Assize and General Goal Delivery Within This Province," 26 June 1699, 1 A&R 370, 371) and the Privy Council approved, the General Court passed "An Act Relating to Attorneys," providing that "the plaintiffe or defendant in any suit may plead or defend his cause by himselfe in his proper person, or with the assistance of such other person as he shall procure." Act of 20 June 1701, 1 A&R 467. Arguably, despite its language, this act applied to criminal as well as civil matters.

[41] Paine Diary, 20 April 1770; Drake, *History and Antiquities of Boston* 777.

[42] This was Paine, who had probably been retained as a result of the following resolution: "Voted, that the Selectmen be desired to employ one or more Council to offer to the Kings Attorney as Assistance to him in the tryal of the Murtherers now committed; and in case the Kings Attorney should refuse such Assistance, and the Relatives of those Persons who were murthered should apply for it, that then the Town will bear the Expence that may accrue thereby." Town Meeting, 13 March 1770. 18 Boston Record Commissioners, *Reports* 14.

ties as an Attorney and of his benevolence as a citizen, in endeavouring to preserve the life of a fellow-subject; although his appointment to this task did not add to his reputation among the people at that time, yet the faithfulness and impartiality he shewed for the Prisoner must certainly more than compensate for any loss he might sustain in this or any other respect." [43]

Paine's notes of the trial appear as Document II, below. They set out the evidence and most of the arguments, but do not describe the atmosphere of the courtroom. Some of the passion and hatred that filled the onlookers and tainted the proceedings filters through the subsequent testimony of the jurors and the keeper. But the contemporary accounts detail the picture even more vividly. To appreciate the legal context, it must be realized that Richardson's principal defense had been that, because the mob had attacked him in his own house and endangered his life, he had been entitled to protect himself in any way possible, including killing one or more of his assailants; the prosecution sought to show and to argue that the crowd was composed of nothing more than rowdy schoolboys, whose insults and stone-throwing had never endangered Richardson's life. Moreover, the Crown contended, whatever anyone else was doing, the boy Seider was not, at the moment Richardson fired, threatening his life. These were also the patriot views, and they have generally prevailed among historians. [44] To this last, the defense argued that, because Seider had been part of the illegal enterprise, his killing, although perhaps not justifiable as self-defense, amounted only to manslaughter. Even if Seider had been a wholly innocent bystander, if Richardson had been justified in firing the gun at all, he would not be guilty of murder.

"Richardson's Trial continued till late on Friday night. After the witnesses were examined and the lawyers had done pleading the Judges gave their charge to the Jury. They said it appeared by the Evidence that the prisoner was attacked in his own house by a number of tumultuous people. That what he had done was in his own defence. That self-defence was a right inherent in every man. That the persons who had encouraged putting up these *hands* were guilty of the murder and not the prisoner and they were convinced the jury could find him guilty of nothing more than manslaughter." [45]

"There was a vast Concourse of Rabble at the Trial." [46]

"The Court upon summing up the Evidence to the Jury were all of

---

[43] *Boston Censor*, 28 March 1772, p. 77.

[44] 1 Gordon, *History of Independence* 276: "Provoked, rather than endangered by the assault, he fired and killed." George Bancroft, *History of the United States of America*, 3:371 (N.Y., 1895): "Provoked but not endangered." Edward Channing, *A History of the United States*, 3:119 (N.Y., 1912): "[A]n informer, being attacked by a mob, fired at his assailants from a window and killed a harmless eleven-year-old boy; but beyond a demonstration at the boy's funeral, nothing happened."

[45] 3 Bernard Papers 76, MH.

[46] Oliver, *Origin and Progress* 86. At least three of the spectators had their pockets picked. See Confession of John Bemis, SF 89524; Min. Bk., Suffolk Sess., Aug. [i.e. July] 1770.

opinion that if what the witnesses on both sides had sworn was believed the fact could amount to no more than Manslaughter. Mr. Just. Oliver doubted whether it could amount to that and with great spirit charged the death of the Boy upon the Promoters of the Effigies and the Exhibitions which had drawn the people together and caused unlawful and tumultuous assemblies and he did not excuse such as had neglected suppressing these Assemblies as the Civil Magistrate had done." [47]

"[W]hilst one of the Judges was delivering his Charge to the Jury, and declaring his Opinion, that the Case was *justifiable Homicide*, one of the Rabble broke out, 'D—n that Judge, if I was nigh him, I would give it to him'; but this was not a Time, to attempt to preserve Decorum; Preservation of Life was as much as a Judge dared to aim at." [48]

"After the Judges had done speaking the mob became very outrageous, called out that they hoped no Jury dare acquit him. 'Remember jury you are upon Oath.' 'Blood requires blood.' " [49]

"[The mob] designed to have hanged the Prisoner as he came out of the Court House, to be returned to Prison untill the Jurors Verdict was settled; and they provided an Halter, ready at the Door of the Court Room, for the Purpose; but the Court had ordered the Sheriff, with the Peace Officers, to lock him into the Court Room untill the Mob had dispersed." [50]

"The judges found it necessary to remain in Court for upwards of an hour, and also to detain the prisoner till the mob were in some measure dispersed least they should destroy him in his way from the Court house to the Jail. It is said they had a rope in Court ready to hang him. The judges were hissed and abused in a most shameful manner in passing from the bench to their carriages." [51]

The jury (none of whose members came from Boston) began its deliberations at 11 P.M.[52] and, without food, drink, or sleep, debated until 8 or 9 o'clock the next morning.[53] The verdict as to Wilmot was Not Guilty;[54]

[47] Hutchinson to Lord ———, 21 April 1770, 26 Mass. Arch. 463.

[48] Oliver, *Origin and Progress* 86.

[49] 3 Bernard Papers 76, MH. This extract has been punctuated for clarity and quotation marks have been inserted.

[50] Oliver, *Origin and Progress* 86.

[51] 3 Bernard Papers 76, MH.

[52] Oliver, *Origin and Progress* 86. Lynde, *Diary* 195, 20 April 1770, says "jury went out after noon," which does not seem correct in view of the trial's length. On the jurors' domiciles, see SF 101646b.

[53] Oliver, *Origin and Progress* 86, says eight; Lynde, *Diary* 195, 21 April 1770, says nine.

[54] Wilmot seems to have been almost ignored by lawyers, witnesses, and court, and, except for some early flurries, by the patriot press, too. *Boston Gazette*, 26 Feb. 1770, p. 5, col. 2; *Boston Gazette*, 5 March 1770, p. 2, col. 1. Paine's notes indicate that some effort was made, consistent with English practice, to prove him a principal in the affair, although he had been indicted for "aiding, helping, abetting, assisting, and maintaining" Richardson. Indictment, SF 102009. See testimony of Robert Hewes and Phil Ridgaway, and the authorities cited on the law of accomplices, Doc. II below. But the evidence against him was so weak that not even the mob could demand his life.

as to Richardson, Guilty of Murder. "An universal clap ensued," [55] and "the Court Room resounded with Expressions of Pleasure; 'till, even one of the Faction, who had some of the Feelings of Humanity not quite erased, cried out, 'for Shame, for shame Gentlemen!' This hushed the clamorous Joy." [56]

At first, the grounds for the verdict were unknown. "I have not yet heard whether the Jury did not believe the W[itnesses] for the Prisoner or whether they thought themselves better J[udges of] the Law than the Court or whether they were intimidated by the [. . .] of the Inhabitants of Boston." [57] Notwithstanding, the defense apparently moved immediately for a new trial. This was a difficult motion to carry in the 18th century under the best of circumstances, and the court did not consider it seriously at that time. As Hutchinson noted, "The court was at first in distress. It was hard to be obliged to give judgment upon a verdict which appeared to them directly against law; and it was difficult, in the state of the town, to order the jury out a second time, or to refuse or delay sentence after the verdict was received." [58] So the court compromised. "The Verdict was received and recorded," [59] but the court adjourned without passing sentence until 29 May 1770. [60]

On that date, two of the judges being ill, the court further continued the matter to 31 May and then to 6 September. [61] At last, on 6 September, at least one judge and all the lawyers having dined together at John Adams', the jurors were called back in and individually examined. [62] Judging from Paine's minutes (Document III), the verdict had rested on at least two of the grounds which Hutchinson had hypothesized. The jury had pretty clearly found the facts the Crown's way and it had certainly been exposed to the rancor of the courtroom mob, although the shouts of the crowd were "not mentioned in the Jury Room." [63] But the jury apparently did not consciously take to itself the decision of the law. Indeed, the willingness of eleven jurors to leave the law to the court was the lever which ultimately moved the last man, Thomas Lothrop, who finally agreed to vote Guilty on the assurance of the others that "if the verdict was not agreeable to Law the Court would not receive it." [64]

[55] 3 Bernard Papers 76, MH.   [56] Oliver, *Origin and Progress* 86.
[57] Hutchinson to Lord ———, 21 April 1770, 26 Mass. Arch. 463.
[58] 3 Hutchinson, *Massachusetts Bay*, ed. Mayo, 206.
[59] Oliver, *Origin and Progress* 86.
[60] Hutchinson to Lord ———, 21 April 1770, 26 Mass. Arch. 463; Paine Diary, 21 April 1770; Lynde, *Diary* 195, 21 April 1770.
[61] Paine Diary, 29 May 1770; see also Lynde, *Diary* 196, 29 May 1770. Min. Bk. 91.
[62] Lynde, *Diary* 198. Regrettably, there are no entries in JA's diary in 1770 after August. Hutchinson is apparently wrong in his implication that the court continued the case for further consideration only after learning what went on in the jury room. See 3 Hutchinson, *Massachusetts Bay*, ed. Mayo, 206. The subpoenas, dated 1 Sept. 1770, summoned the jurors to appear in court at 9 A.M. on 6 Sept. to "be enquired of touching" the trial. SF 101646b.
[63] Testimony of Jonathan Ellis, Doc. III below.
[64] Testimony of Thomas Lothrop, Doc. III below.

The jurors having testified (whether on oath or not is unclear), the court heard defense counsel's argument for a new trial. From Paine's minutes, it appears that Blowers made three alternative points: first, that the jury intended to follow the court's direction and find manslaughter, so the court should effectuate that intention; second, that the shouts as the jurors were retiring amounted to conversations with the jury sufficient to nullify a verdict of Guilty; third, that the verdict was so contrary to law and evidence that the court should order a new trial.

There was some authority for granting a new trial to a defendant whom the court considered to have been improperly convicted, and Blowers (or whoever was arguing that branch of the motion) appears to have brought it all to the court's attention. The trouble was that the opinions cited dealt with noncapital offenses, and the English law did not allow new trials in capital cases.[65]

It is apparent from the notes that counsel was very much aware of the doctrine, soon to be tested anew in the English criminal libel trials,[66] that the jury was the proper finder not only of fact, but of law as well. Everyone agreed, and had for a hundred years, that no matter how blatantly a jury disregarded the court's directions, neither it nor any of its twelve members could be punished for so doing.[67] This was true in civil and criminal cases alike. In the former class of litigation, "if the Jury find against Evidence and the Direction of the Court," the judges could alleviate the problem by granting a new trial.[68] Thus, in capital criminal matters, the most that lay in a court's power was to remind the jury that it was on oath to find according to law, that the court knew the law better than the jury, and that the jury would be risking its conscience by finding contrary to the rules laid down by the court. And as Lord Mansfield himself noted, the jury could always end the question by bringing in a Not Guilty verdict, right or wrong.[69] The court could also advise the jury that, if it had any doubts of the law, its safest course was to bring in a special verdict. If the jury followed the recommendation, its verdict would take the form of a series of recited facts, found from the evidence, concluding with a prayer to the court to decide on the basis of those facts whether the defendant was guilty or not.[70]

But the jury, in the last analysis, did have the "final power" to decide

[65] James B. Thayer, *A Preliminary Treatise on Evidence at the Common Law* 178 (Boston, 1898); 1 Stephen, *History of Criminal Law* 311; 1 Chitty, *Criminal Law* 654. And see Rex v. Marchant, 2 Keble 403, 84 Eng. Rep. 253 (K.B. 1699): trial for perjury; the trial judge certified that the verdict was against evidence (that is, that there was no evidence tending to convict, *not* that the verdict was against the weight of the evidence; see No. 12, text at note 49). *Held*: motion for new trial denied, because "there can be no trial de novo for, or against the King." 21 Viner, *Abridgment* 479, tit. Trial, also cites this holding.

[66] See No. 12, notes 74 and 110.

[67] Bushell's Case, Vaughan 135, 124 Eng. Rep. 1006 (C.P. 1670), discussed in No. 12, text at notes 56–60.

[68] 3 Bacon, *Abridgment* 278.

[69] Rex v. Miller, 20 Howell, *State Trials* 869, 894 (Guildhall 1770).

[70] 5 Bacon, *Abridgment* 286.

according to its own view of the law. "This power," as James Bradley Thayer has noted, "where it was uncontrollable, has been considered by some to be not distinguishable from a right; and it is not at all uncommon to describe it thus—as a right to judge of both fact and law." [71]

Faced with the double problem of apparent jury omnipotence and inability to grant a new trial, the Massachusetts court temporized and followed the advice of the 17th-century criminal-law writer, Sir Matthew Hale, "to reprieve the person convict before judgment, and to aquaint the king, and certify for his pardon." [72] This made better political sense, too, than passing sentence and then having the Lieutenant Governor suspend execution pending receipt of the pardon, at which "the people would have been more enraged, than merely at the court's suspending their own determination." [73]

Hutchinson apparently wrote Lord Hillsborough, at an unspecified time after the verdict, recommending a pardon; the Hutchinson letterbooks in the Massachusetts Archives contain nothing precisely on this point. However, in a letter to Hillsborough dated 15 May 1771, Hutchinson referred to "the Instrument which accompanied" one of Hillsborough's earlier letters; this, Hutchinson said, "I have caused to be communicated to the Judges of the Superior Court. Some of them are struck with the informalities of it for the purpose for which it is intended, and they have thought it advisable to defer their determination until their Court which is to be held on the third Tuesday of June in the County of Essex. Whatever it may be as to the sufficiency of the Instrument in point of form, it carries such evidence with it of His Majesty's most gracious pleasure with respect to the immediate Subject of it that must stop all further proceedings against him." The "Instrument" can only be the copy of the pardon order, dated 12 February 1771.[74] When one recalls that the Court did not examine the jurors until 6 September 1770, the probable chronology appears to be this:

After the examination, the court concluded it could do nothing, and Hutchinson wrote to England, asking for a pardon. As a result of the usual delays attendant upon a North Atlantic passage, coupled with the slowness of official action, the pardon order did not issue until 12 February 1771, and was not received in Boston until the beginning of May 1771.

Throughout the summer the judges and Hutchinson temporized. Their chief concern was the form of the "Instrument," which was really only a copy of an order from the King to the Recorder of London to insert Richardson's name in the next "Newgate" Pardon—so-called because it referred to "our poor convicts in Newgate" Prison. As Hutchinson wrote to former Governor Pownall in August, "Neither the Judges nor the Attorney General

[71] Thayer, *Evidence at Common Law* 253.

[72] 2 Hale, *Pleas of the Crown* 309–310. The entire passage is set out, note 173 below.

[73] 3 Hutchinson, *Massachusetts Bay*, ed. Mayo, 206–207 note.

[74] Hutchinson to Hillsborough, 15 May 1771, 27 Mass. Arch. 167–168; the Instrument itself is in SF 102009.

are clear in the discharge of Richardson without some further evidence of His Majesty's pardon. We have no precedent upon record in this province. They say that if there was no other Exception to the form of the Instrument yet it is no more than a Warrant to insert the name of Richardson in a pardon which it does not appear to them has ever been done. If a Copy could be procured of the pardon attested I hope it may be sufficient. I am not acquainted in what manner pardons are passed for such persons whose sentences are respited in the several Counties in England but if it be usual to insert the names of such persons in the Newgate pardons I wish to be furnished with a Certificate that it is so." Hutchinson even proposed that a Royal Warrant issue, permitting Hutchinson to issue the pardon himself, under the Province seal. This was rejected, but not until 3 March 1772 did Hutchinson receive his final instructions.[75]

Meanwhile, Richardson remained in jail, while the patriot press flayed him and his protectors. The *Massachusetts Spy* and the *Boston Gazette* claimed that the court planned to enlarge the benefit of clergy by admitting him to it.[76] By early 1772, the patriots were becoming impatient over Richardson's fate. The *Massachusetts Spy* published some bitter doggerel referring to the two soldiers' having pleaded clergy as well as Richardson's remaining alive: "The *basest* murderers, full of guilt and crimes / Have gone *unhung* by reason of *old LINES* / So we were disappointed in our hopes / But for the future they'll be *hung* by *Ropes*." [77] The *Boston Gazette* ran a lengthy piece signed "Callisthenes" which urged that Richardson was either innocent, and should be released, or guilty, and should be executed. "Is Richardson kept in goal in order to recommend him to mercy?" "Callisthenes" asked. "The *honour* of magistracy ought openly to avow it:—the wisdom of the recommenders ought to justify it. . . . Let not the infamy of the man give origin to an acquiescence in unjustifiable confinement. . . . What is law for a *Richardson* is law for a *Sidney*. If oppression is warranted by law, the Patriot is much more likely to fall a victim than the pimp and pander. *Hampdens* will stain the scaffold with blood, while a robber or murderer finds a city of refuge.[78] *No tyranny so secure, none so intolerable, none so dangerous, none so remediless, as that of Executive Courts.*" [79]

[75] Hutchinson to Pownall, Aug. 1771, 27 Mass. Arch. 210–211; Hutchinson to Lord ———, 12 March 1772, 26 Mass. Arch. 301. See also 3 Hutchinson, *Massachusetts Bay*, ed. Mayo, 206–207 note; Oliver, *Origin and Progress* 87; Hutchinson to Hillsborough, 8 Sept. 1771, 27 Mass. Arch. 224.

[76] *Boston Gazette*, 1 April 1771, p. 1, col. 1, reprinting a note from the *Massachusetts Spy*, 21 March 1771. Because benefit of clergy (respite from execution by reason of literacy) extended only to those convicted of manslaughter, allowing Richardson, who had been convicted of murder, to plead it, would have enlarged the privilege.

[77] Reprinted, *Boston Gazette*, 27 Feb. 1772, p. 3, col. 2. Nathaniel Ropes had been appointed to the Superior Court on 15 Jan. 1772 upon the resignation of Chief Justice Benjamin Lynde. Whitmore, *Mass. Civil List* 70.

[78] This expression had been used in the course of the trial. See Doc. II, text at note 131.

[79] *Boston Gazette*, 10 Feb. 1772, p. 2, cols. 1, 2.

This remarkable document, although too lengthy to be quoted in full, is well worth examination. On the one hand it seems to be urging Richardson's death, on the other it appears to be vigorously asserting his rights. Its appearance in the *Boston Gazette* suggests that its author was certainly of the patriot party. This suggestion is accurate: "Callisthenes" was none other than Josiah Quincy himself.[80] But his purpose in writing the letter defies explanation. It is possible that he knew of the pardon, inaccurately suspected its arrival in Boston, and hoped to stimulate Richardson's release. Another view might be that "Callisthenes" perhaps purposed to provoke the execution. If this was Quincy's aim, it would seem to contrast sharply not only with his duty as an attorney to his erstwhile client, but also with his stand in the Massacre trials.

Whatever Quincy's motive, shortly after his piece appeared, the Chief Justice told the Suffolk County Grand Jury, in apparent response to "a certain Paper, the Contents whereof have not yet transpired," that the court believed the jurors "were ignorant that the Case of Ebenezer Richardson was then before his Majesty." [81]

The suspense increased, even after the pardon safely arrived, for Hutchinson, despite his belief that "The people have never been in so good a temper to submit to his discharge at any time since he was first committed," [82] thought it best to wait a few days longer, until 10 March 1772, when the inhabitants were engaged at their town meeting. Then Richardson was taken hastily into court and brought to the bar, where on his knees he pleaded his pardon, recognized in the sum of £500 to appear again and plead the pardon whenever the court should require him (an empty formality), and then "fled with precipitation and crossed the ferry before the inhabitants were informed of it." [83] "The Rabble heard of it, and pursued him to execute their own Law upon him, but he happily escaped." [84]

So Richardson left Boston, but his reputation remained as soiled as ever. Apparently he lived "at or near Stoneham" for about a year following his

---

[80] Josiah Quincy, *Josiah Quincy, Jr.* 51–52.

[81] The courtroom colloquy took place 22 Feb. 1772. *Boston Gazette*, 24 Feb. 1772, p. 3, cols. 1, 2.

[82] Hutchinson to "JP Esq.," 18 March 1772, 26 Mass. Arch. 305.

[83] *Boston Gazette*, 16 March 1772, p. 3, col. 2.

[84] Oliver, *Origin and Progress* 87. Min. Bk. 95, SCJ Suffolk; Rec. 1772, fols. 15–16. The doggerel of the previous month was echoed in "A Monumental Inscription on the Fifth of March. Together with a few Lines On the Enlargement of Ebenezer Richardson, Convicted of Murder" (Boston?, 1772), reproduced in Massachusetts Historical Society, *Some Early Massachusetts Broadsides*, No. 26 (Boston, 1964): "Oh! Wretched man! the monster of the times, / You were not hung 'by reason of *old* Lines,' / *Old* Lines thrown by, 'twas then we were in hopes, / That you would soon be hung with *new made* Ropes; / But neither *Ropes nor Lines*, will satisfy / for SEIDER's blood! But GOD is ever nigh, / And guilty souls will not unpunish'd go / Tho' they're excus'd by judges here below! / You are enlarg'd but cursed is your fate / Tho' *Cushing's* eas'd you from the prison gate / The—*Bridge* of *Tories, it* has borne you o'er / Yet you e'er long may meet with HELL's shore." Compare text at note 77 above. The *"Bridge"* was Judge Trowbridge. See Clarence S. Brigham, *Paul Revere's Engravings* Plate 18 (Worcester, 1954).

release, and then received an appointment in the customs service at Philadelphia.[85] But, as late as 1774, the mere rumor of his presence in Boston was enough to raise a mob.[86]

I. DEFENSE COUNSEL'S NOTES[87]

Suffolk Superior Court, Boston, April 1770

Dom: Rex vs. Richardson and Wilmot
Upon an Indictment for Murder

1st.   To open the Defence with a proper Address to the Jury to remove all popular Prejudices and Passions and engage them to make a fair, candid and impartial Enquiry and to give their Verdict agreeable to Law and the Evidence, uninfluenc'd by any other Motive; to mention the manner of my becoming engaged as Council for the Prisoners, explain my Duty and the Part I ought and am determin'd to act.

2d.   The Witnesses for the Crown having been carefully and thoroughly cross-examined, to produce those for the Prisoners, and endeavour to find out what the Nature and Degree of Provocation offered; how far the Attack upon the *house was carried*; Whether and to what Degree the Windows were demolished before the firing, and whether the Door was broke open, and any Attempt made upon it; whether any actual Attempt was made to enter; or any Evidence of such Design from threatning Words; Whether Men as well as Boys were not concerned in that Attack; What Weapons were used or thrown into the house; and whether any One within was wounded; and upon the whole whether this is not to be consider'd as an Attack upon the Persons of the Prisoners.

3d.   To sum up the Evidence and state the Facts as they shall appear upon Evidence.

4thly.   To explain the Nature of the Crime of Murder and the different Kinds of Homicide, as justifiable, excusable (as se defendendo) and felonious: and to shew the Distinction between felonious Homicide of Malice prepense, which is properly Murder, and without

[85] *Boston Gazette*, 3 May 1773, p. 3, col. 1; *id.*, 24 May 1773, p. 2, col. 3.
[86] Hutchinson to Earl of Dartmouth, 28 Jan. 1774, reprinted in Hersey, "Tar and Feathers: The Adventures of Captain John Malcom," 34 Col. Soc. Mass., *Pubns.* 429, 449 (1943).
[87] In an unidentified hand, probably Josiah Quincy's; docketed by JA: "Rex v. Richardson." Adams Papers, Microfilms, Reel No. 185.

such Malice, which is Manslaughter. Foster 273. 4. 7.[88] 1. H.H.P.C. 449.[89] 4 Black. Com: 190.1.2.[90]

The Crime in the present Case cannot at most amount to more than *Manslaughter*, as he was in his house peceably and there assaulted, by breaking his Windows and throwing Stones at him. And if an Intent to enter and commit a Felony appear, whether from threatening Words, or an Attempt to break the Door or the manner and Degree of the Attack, it is excusable Homicide Se defendendo, at least, if not justifiable. A Man's house is his Castle and he may defend it by himself alone or with such as he calls to assist him. 1 H.H.P.C. 445. 487.[91] 5 Coke Repts. 91b. Semane's Case.[92] 11 Coke Repts. 82b. Lewis Bowles Case.[93]

A Man is not obliged to retire from his house. 1 H.H.P.C. 486.[94]

So he may justify killing one that attempts to break open his house in the *Day time* with an attempt to Rob or commit other Felony. 4 Black: Com. 180. 3. 182.[95] 1 H.P.C. Page 71 Chap. 28 Sect. 21 and by Sect. 23 of this and Sect. 13 of the next Chap. it appears that ware

[88] The references are to Foster, *Crown Cases* 273, 274, and 277, all of which are within Chapter III, entitled "Homicide founded in Necessity."

[89] 1 Hale, *Pleas of the Crown* 449: "Chapter XXXVI: Touching *murder*, what it is, and the kinds thereof."

[90] 4 Blackstone, *Commentaries* *190–192 distinguishes murder and manslaughter.

[91] 1 Hale, *Pleas of the Crown* 445: "But if A. comes to enter with force, and in order thereunto shoots at his house, and B. the possessor, having other company in his house, shoots and kills A. this is manslaughter in B." 1 *id.* at 487: "[H]is house is his castle of defense, and therefore he may justify assembling of persons for the safeguard of his house."

[92] Semayne v. Gresham, 5 Co. Rep. 91, 77 Eng. Rep. 194 (K.B. 1605). "[T]he house of every one is to him as his castle and fortress, as well for his defence against injury and violence, as for his repose; and altho' the life of man is a thing precious and favoured in law ... if thieves come to a man's house to rob him, or murder, and the owner or his servants kill any of the thieves in defence of himself and his house, it is not felony, and he shall lose nothing. ... [E]very one may assemble his friends and neighbours to defend his house against violence."

[93] Bowles v. Bury, 11 Co. Rep. 79, 82, 77 Eng. Rep. 1252, 1258 (K.B. 1616): "If a Man is in his House, and hears that others will come to his House to beat him, he may call together his Friends, &c. into his House to aid him in Safety of his Person; for as it has been said, A Man's House is his Castle and his Defense, and where he properly ought to remain."

[94] 1 Hale, *Pleas of the Crown* 486: "[A man] being in his own house need not fly, as far as he can, as in other cases of *se defendendo*, for he hath the protection of his house to excuse him from flying, for that would be to give up the possession of his house to his adversary by his flight."

[95] 4 Blackstone, *Commentaries* *180: "If any person attempts a robbery or murder of another, or attempts to break open a house *in the night time* ... and shall be killed in such attempt, the slayer shall be acquitted and discharged. This reaches not to any crime unaccompanied with force, as picking of pockets; or to the breaking open of any house *in the day time*, unless it carries with it an attempt of robbery also." 4 *id.* at *182–183 discusses "homicide *per infortunium*, or misadventure."

one kills another who assaults him *in his house in the Day Time with* Intent to *beat him* only is guilty of Homicide *Se defendendo* and if he appears to have a Design of killing him it is justifiable Homicide. Vid. Sect. 124.[96] Vide also Hales P.C. 40 the reason why it is not justifiable but excusable only is that "they came not to commit a known Felony," and "it cannot be judged whether he meant to *kill me*." [97] But if a man in *the Daytime* breaks the Windows of the house of another and endeavours to enter in order to execute a *civil Process*, and he within kills him this is *Manslaughter and no more*. Cooks Case in Cro. Car: 537. 8.[98] And it appears by Lord Hales brief State of this Case 1 H.H.P.C. 458 that had Cook not known the other to be a Bailiff, it *had been no Felony because done in Defence of his house*.[99] So if A endeavours to enter a house and shoots an arrow at those within and B shoots another out at those who wou'd enter and kills one of the Company. This is ruled not to be *se defendendo*, but *Manslaughter* because there was no *Danger of their Lives* by the Arrow so shot into the house upon them. Harcourts Case 1 H.H.P.C. 485. 6.[100] Vid. also the Case of Dra[y]ton Basset in 1 H.H.P.C. 440. 1 and also in Page 444. 5 which shews who shall be said to be present, aiding, abetting &c.[101]

[96] 1 Hawkins, *Pleas of the Crown* 71, §21 lists various justifiable killings of wrongdoers. *Id.* at 72, §23: "[H]e who in his own Defence kills another that assaults him in his House in the Day-Time, and plainly appears to intend to beat him only, is guilty of Homicide *se defendendo*, for which he forfeits his Goods, but is pardoned of Course; yet it seems that a private Person ... who happens unavoidably to kill another in endeavouring to defend himself from, or suppress dangerous Rioters, may justify the Fact, inasmuch as he only does his Duty in Aid of the publick Justice." *Id.* at 74–75, §13, defines homicide *se defendendo*: "where one, who has no other possible Means of preserving his Life from one who combats with him on a sudden Quarrel, or of defending his Person from one who attempts to beat him (especially if such Attempt be made upon him in his own House,) kills the Person by whom he is reduced to such an inevitable Necessity." Probably 1 *id.* at 72, §24: "And I can see no Reason why a Person, who without Provocation is assaulted by another in any Place whatsoever, in such a Manner as plainly shews an Intent to murder him, as by discharging a Pistol, or pushing at him with a drawn Sword, &c. may not justify killing such an Assailant, as much as if he had attempted to rob him."

[97] Hale, *Pleas of the Crown (Summary)* 40: "But if the assault in my House were not to rob me, but to beat me, &c. there would be only *se defendendo* and Goods forfeited, and a Pardon of course to be granted," and so as in the text. Quotation marks have been supplied in text.

[98] Rex v. Cook, Cro. Car. 537, 79 Eng. Rep. 1063 (K.B. 1639). The text states the case.

[99] 1 Hale, *Pleas of the Crown* 458. Hale does not mention that the breaking took place in the daytime, which, according to the report, it did. It seems likely, therefore, that whoever wrote the instant note had examined the original report in Croke.

[100] 1 Hale, *Pleas of the Crown* 485–486. The text states the case.

[101] The Drayton Basset Case, 1 Hale, *Pleas of the Crown* 440–441, and the dis-

If upon angry Words one man assault another either by pulling him by the Nose or even filliping him upon the Forehead, and he who is so assaulted immediately runs the other through, it is but *Manslaughter*, for the Peace is broken by him that is killed; and he that receives such Indignity may reasonably apprehend a further Design upon him; Maugridges Case, in Keyling's Repts. 135 adjudged and reported by Lord Holt.[102]

D. Williams on a sudden and slight Provocation only of Words kills Marbury, ruled to be only Manslaughter. 1 H.H.P.C. 469 and in 470,[103] another Case mentioned also by Foster 298. 299 where no [104] given but an Officer had violently entered a Room to make an arrest.[105]

Two Boys fight, one is beat and runs home blody and complains to his Father who goes three quarters of a mile and kills the other Boy ruled to be Manslaughter by Reason of the sudden heat &c. 1 H.H.P.C. 453 Rowley's Case taken from 12 Coke Repts. 87.[106] Vide also a Case in Strange Repts. 499 &c. ruled to be manslaughter only a *strong Case*.[107]

On a sudden Affray or Quarrel if the Party has declined the Combat and retreated as far as he Can with Safety and kills his Adversary thro' Necessity and to avoid immediate Death, it is *Se defendendo*;

---

cussion in *id.* at 444–445, concern liability of each member of an unlawful gathering for death caused by any one of them.

[102] Reg. v. Mawgridge, Kelyng 119, 135, 84 Eng. Rep. 1107, 1114, Holt K.B. 484, 90 Eng. Rep. 1167 (Q.B. 1707). JA had dealt with this case recently when arguing Rex v. Corbet, No. 56. His notes for that argument, together with the footnotes thereto, fairly state the case.

[103] Rex v. Williams, W. Jones 432, 82 Eng. Rep. 227 (K.B. 1640). Williams, a Welshman, on being taunted by R., threw a hammer at him, but missed, striking and killing M. *Held*: Manslaughter and, because not within the Statute of Stabbing, 1 Jac. 1, c. 8 (1604), clergy allowed. 1 Hale, *Pleas of the Crown* 470 note, notes the view of Holt, C.J. in Reg. v. Mawgridge, Kelyng 119, 131–132, 84 Eng. Rep. 1107, 1113 (Q.B. 1707), that if the indictment had been for murder Williams ought to have been found guilty for lack of sufficient provocation.

[104] Blank in MS.

[105] Foster, *Crown Cases* 298–299, in a discussion of the Statute of Stabbing, recites the anonymous case here stated. 1 Hale, *Pleas of the Crown* 470, to which Foster cites, attributes the case to the 1657 Newgate sittings before Glynn, C.J. *Held*: The killing was not within the Statute, and so clergy allowed.

[106] Rex v. Royley, Cro. Jac. 296, 79 Eng. Rep. 254 (K.B. 1612), reported anonymously 12 Co. Rep. 87, 77 Eng. Rep. 1364, and set out substantially as in the text, 1 Hale, *Pleas of the Crown* 453.

[107] Rex v. Reason & Tranter, 1 Str. 499, 93 Eng. Rep. 659 (K.B. 1722), discussed at length, Foster, *Crown Cases* 292–294. *Held*: where two against one, deceased stabbed nine times, then shot as he lay on the floor, defendants guilty only of manslaughter, because the evidence supported a finding that the deceased struck the first blow and threatened the defendants.

but if the Combat on both sides is kept up to the time the mortal Stroke is given, and he who gave it was not at that Time in emminent Danger of Death it is Manslaughter, Foster 277.[108]

A Woman strikes Stedman a Soldier who returns the Blow with the pummel of his Sword. She fled he pursued and stabbed her in the back this ruled to be no more than Manslaughter: by Holt. Foster 292.[109] Vide the general Observation by the same author Page 296 *which Note.*[110]

If A shoots at B misses him and kills C, if it wou'd have been Murder supposing he had killed B; it will amount to the same Offence, tho' C is killed, whom he did not intend to hurt. On the other hand if the Blow intended against B arose from a sudden Transport of Passion which if B had died by it wou'd have reduced the Offence to Manslaughter, the Fact will admit of the same *Alleviation* if C shou'd happen to fall by it. Foster 261. 2.[111] 1 H.H.P.C. 442.[112]

By Foster 295 Sect. 3d. it is apparent that tho' base Words of Reproach or Gestures are not such Provocation as to lessen the Crime to Manslaughter. Yet when there is any assault on the Person arising from thence, it is otherwise: This Distinction appears from Maugridges Case: [113] Whenever the Assault is very slight, as two persons justling against a Wall A kills B who had justled him, or if B had

[108] Foster, *Crown Cases* 277: "He therefore who in the Case of a mutual Conflict would excuse Himself upon the Foot of Self-Defence must shew, that before a Mortal Stroke given He had declined any further Combat and retreated as far as He could with Safety: and also that He Killed his Adversary through meer Necessity, and to avoid immediate Death. If He faileth in Either of these Circumstances He will incur the Penalties of Manslaughter."

[109] Reg. v. Stedman, Foster, *Crown Cases* 292 (Old Bailey, 1704): "*Holt* was at first of Opinion that this was Murder, *a single Box on the Ear from a Woman not being a sufficient Provocation to Kill in this Manner, after He had given Her a Blow in return for the Box on the Ear.* And it was proposed to have the Matter found Special. But it afterwards appearing in the Progress of the Trial, that the Woman struck the Soldier in the Face with an Iron Patten, and drew a great Deal of Blood, it was held clearly to be no more than Manslaughter." JA considered this case in the course of Rex v. Corbet, No. 56.

[110] Foster, *Crown Cases* 296: "To what I have offered with regard to sudden Rencounters let Me add, that the Blood, already too much Heated, kindleth afresh at every Pass or Blow. And in the Tumult of the Passions in which *meer Instinct Self-Preservation*, hath no inconsiderable Share, the Voice of Reason is not heard. And therefore the Law in Condescension to the Infirmities of Flesh and Blood hath extenuated the Offence."

[111] Foster, *Crown Cases* 261–262, sets out substantially the point here summarized.

[112] 1 Hale, *Pleas of the Crown* 442, supports this point.

[113] Foster, *Crown Cases* 295: "A. useth provoking Language or Behaviour towards B. B. striketh Him, upon which a Combat ensueth, in which A. is Killed. This is held to be Manslaughter, for it was a sudden Affray and They fought upon equal Terms. *And in such Combats upon sudden Quarrels it mattereth not Who gave the first Blow.*" For Mawgridge's Case, see note 102 above.

whipt A's horse out of the Path and A had alighted and killed B, it had been only Manslaughter. 1 H.H.P.C. 455. 456.[114] Where it also appears that Words of Menace of *Bodily harm* wou'd reduce the Crime to Manslaughter, though Words of Reproach only, woud not.[115] Vid. these Distinctions 1 Hawkins P.C. Page 82 and 83 Sect. 34. 35. 36. 37.[116]

II. PAINE'S MINUTES OF THE TRIAL[117]

Suffolk. Supr. Ct. April 1770.

Dom. Rex vs. Ebenezer Richardson and George Wilmot

S. Quincy.

Wm. Gray. day before Some mention of Effigies. R said he hoped if these was before Importers Doors there be a Dust beat up, wish'd the 14. Regiment there. They would Cut up the d——d Yankees. Some time before he said he would give the Devil a Supper of them if— He has also said he would not hurt any body unless they hurt him.

Deb. Warner. I was Looking out of my Shop door, I saw R by the Eff[igy]. He came by with the Gentlemen and cry'd out Perjury Perjury, and said not you. Went into his house, and then came out and he came out in a great Rage, doubling his Fists and ⟨called⟩ challenged the Gentlemen to the Door. Said it should be hot enough before night. This brought the Boys from the Eff. The Boys threw light stuff. He came out with a Stick, and threatned and then went in the Step of the Door and went in and a brick Batt came out of the House and struck a Man who took it up and threw it in and that was the first of the Windows being broken.

On saying Perjury, he said it shall be hot enough before night.

Before Window broke he swore if they did not disperse he [*would*] make a Lane thro them.

Front Door open when the Gun fired. No body had attempted to

---

[114] 1 Hale, *Pleas of the Crown* 455–456, sets out these examples.
[115] 1 Hale, *Pleas of the Crown* 456: "[W]ords of menace of bodily harm would come within the reason of such a provocation, as would make the offense to be but manslaughter."
[116] 1 Hawkins, *Pleas of the Crown* 82–83, discusses the various provocations and excuses, and collects the applicable cases.
[117] In Robert Treat Paine's hand. Paine Law Notes. As usual in Paine's legal MSS, the handwriting is hasty, careless, and often cryptic, the punctuation chaotic, and the meaning, therefore, sometimes obscure. Some editorial regularization has had to be imposed to make the notes intelligible; doubtless some misreadings remain.

enter; months ago, I have heard R say Let 'em come on me I'm ready, for I've Guns loaded. I said I am not safe.

Hannah Warner. The first I saw, R. was with Gentlemen called P.P.[118] Challenged em up to Door. Boys came, R in great Rage. He ordered em to go off. They said they would not, Kings high Way. He said *he had a Gun loaded and would* fire. Swore by G— he would make a lane, no Men.

Edwd. Procter. I was coming from No[rth] 1/4 past 10, with Some Gentlemen to see Pagentry before Lilly's Door. R cry'd Perjury, Perjury. I said what do you mean. *He said by the Et[e]r[na]l G–d I'll make it too hot for you before night.* I withdrew. I saw the *brick strike* [Soldier?]. He returned it and broke 20 *Squares.* Soon after the Gun fired. R. *doubled his Fist and said Damn* ye come here I'm ready for you.

When the Boys threw, I don't remember *any Men among* 'em.

Saml. Appleton. I heard Boys huzza. The first I saw by Lilly was R. He spake to Mrs. L——, then spake to Country man with Waggon. R. shoke hand and said Perjury. Knox asked him what he meant. He said *damn your blood come here,* I'll make *it too hot for you before night.* Boys got to the Door, threw things. Woman came out. Egg struke Woman.

R: came out and said if you dont go away I'll *blow a hole thro' you enough* to Drive a Cart and Oxen.

At the back Door, I saw R. and W's. Guns. R said *Dam their Blood I don't care what I have done.* He had a Cutlass drawn, and resisted. He said he would resign himself to proper Officer.

Nathl. Noyes. I saw R. level Gun and snapt it at the Door, and went into the House. *No Glass broke at that time.* Then Boys threw Sticks. At *first Snapping Boys* were playing elswhere.

Saml. Lock. I was in Town to sell milk. I saw Boys bringing Show. I was at Lillys, read it, saw People at the Door. He said begone to the Boys. 3 or 4 of us stood before R. Window. Saw 'em thro',[119] no Windows broke. He said if they did not go off he'd make *it too hot for 'em,* as sure as there was a G— in heaven, he'd blow *a Lane thro 'em.* He *flashed a Gun* in the House pointed to the Street.

Robert Paterson. I went up to R, and *I saw R fire the Gun,* from within the House. The Boy fell. The Shot went thro' my Trowsers.

Charles Atkins. I saw him walking in the Room with the Gun on

---

[118] That is, "Perjury, Perjury."
[119] Either the witness saw the boys *throw* at the window, or saw Richardson and Wilmot *through* the window.

his Arm. *Saw him pull the Tricker.* Syder was stooping to take up a Stone as I thought, and was Shot down. 60 or 70 Boys.

Jona. Kenny. The first I saw was 4 or 5 Stones flung *out of R. Windows.* None had been then flung at the House. I saw R knell down and point the Gun out of the Window, and I saw him shoot.

Syder threw nothing stood looking.

One stone struck me.

I was by Syder 5. minutes. Saw *him throw nothing.*

John Home. Woman run out and whipt the Boys. Then they threw Sticks; I saw *him load, saw him point the Gun and fire.*

When he loaded the Gun *no Window* broke.

R. came out swore by G— if they did not go away he'd make a Lane.

Robert Bricks. Heard R. cry Perj:, your a pack of perjd. Villians. Knox come here. R. presented the Gun out of the Door.

⟨*Robert Hews*⟩

David Bradley. Windows broke when I got there. I saw 3 or 4 Stones come out of the Window. I saw *one or two Men* in the Room with Guns in their hands. R put a Gun on edge of Window. I heard the Gun, and run to the back of the house. *R clapt the Gun at me.*

The Boys ceased throwing till R. threw again.

Wilmot was there. He said it was not I but R.

Robt. Hewes. After Guns fired, I saw R at Window. Boy threw. He presented again. *Wilmot* said he was assisting him. *Wil*: presented his Gun out of Window and said Stand off or I'll fire.

Phil Ridgaway. I saw W. at Rs.

When I first came, no Windows broke. Large Stones thrown from house. Then Saw W and R in Yard with Guns. *R. said I don't care what I've done when they told him he had killd a Boy.* I took from *W. a Gun loaded* with *179 Shots. 17. Swan* Shot. The rest Goose and Duck. *She looked* as if flashed. Wilmot said he could not have fired for the Screw pin was gone.

Some men laughed. 10 or 15 Stones thrown by Men with violence, but remember none in particular.

Thos. Young.[120] Wound mortal.

John Loring. Wound mortal.

Black. Anal. 119. Murder and Manslaughter.[121]

[120] Dr. Thomas Young (1731–1777), one of the patriot leaders. See Edes, "Memoir of Dr. Thomas Young," 11 Col. Soc. Mass., *Pubns.* 2 (1910).

[121] William Blackstone, *Analysis of the Laws of England* 119 (Dublin, 5th edn., 1766): "MANSLAUGHTER is the unlawful Killing of another; without Malice, express or implied. This is Felony, but within Clergy; except in the Case of STABBING."

Hales Pl. Cr. 31: Murder what, if the act unlawful.[122] 44. If a man do an act by which Death must ensue, consider, if intended.[123] 45. An Intention of Evil tho not against a particular Person.[124]

F.C. Law. 255. The fact proved, prisoner must excuse.[125]

F. CL 291. §2. The Weapon. Murder.[126]

HHPC. 451. Def. of Malice in fact.[127]

2 Ray. 1489. Malice express, if a Man do an Act that must do harm.[128]

Pris[o]ner.

Sarah Richardson. Mr. Knox and Capt. Matchet followed Father up to the Door and said come out you *damn Son of Bitch, I'll have your Heart out your* Liver out. Boys came there. Knox, Procter and Machet stood behind the Boys. Dont know how long. They *threatned to kill us all.* I staid till no Lead, no Frame, and then went away.[129] Stones hitt my Father, hitt me, could not tarry without danger of Life. Outer Door shut when they threw Stones. Broke Cieling. *They broke Doors open.* Stones hit Mother. Wilmot said he would stand by

"MURDER is when a Person of sound Memory and Discretion, unlawfully killeth any reasonable Creature, in Being, and under the King's Peace; with Malice aforethought, either express or implied. This is Felony, without Clergy; punished with speedy Death, and Hanging in Chains, or Dissection."

[122] Hale, *Pleas of the Crown (Summary)* 31: "But if the act be unlawful, then death ensuing, Manslaughter or Murder." *Id.* at 32: "So that an unlawful act, without an ill intent, Manslaughter; with an ill intent, Murder."

[123] Hale, *Pleas of the Crown (Summary)* 44: "Malice implied in the manner of doing. . . . If a Man do an act that apparently must introduce harm, and Death ensue. . . . But note, that if it were with an intention to do harm, then Murder; if without such intention, Manslaughter."

[124] Hale, *Pleas of the Crown (Summary)* 45: "For an Intention of Evil, though not against a particular Person, makes a Malice."

[125] Foster, *Crown Cases* 255: "In every Charge of Murder, *the Fact of Killing being first proved,* all the Circumstances of Accident, Necessity, or Infirmity are to be satisfactorily proved by the Prisoner, unless they arise out of the Evidence produced against Him: for the Law presumeth the Fact to have been founded in Malice, until the Contrary appeareth."

[126] Foster, *Crown Cases* 291: "And it ought to be remembered, that in all other Cases of Homicide upon slight Provocation, if it may be reasonably collected from the Weapon made use of, or from any other Circumstance, that the Party intended to Kill, or to do some great bodily Harm, such Homicide will be Murder."

[127] 1 Hale, *Pleas of the Crown* 451: "Malice in fact is a deliberate intention of doing some corporal harm to the person of another. . . . Malice in fact is a deliberate intention of doing any bodily harm to another, whereunto by law he is not authorized."

[128] Rex v. Oneby, 2 Ld. Raym. 1485, 1489, 92 Eng. Rep. 465, 468 (K.B. 1727): "Malice express, is a design formed of taking away another man's life, or of doing some mischief to another, in the execution of which design death ensues."

[129] That is, she remained until the window lead and frame were destroyed. The Knox referred to is Thomas Knox. See indictment, SF 102009, where he is listed as a witness.

him as Long as he had breath. Wilmot asked if he had any Gun. R. said he must get his Gun.

Kezia Richardson. Knox, Matchet and Procter Challenged my Father. Knox challengd him and he said he'd have his Heart and Liver in his Hand. They broke the Door open. It was locked. Mother and father Wounded with a Stone. The Wall broken. Father desired Wilmot to [...].

John Codman. School Boys Surrounded R's House, throwing Dirt and Stones at the House. They said he had Snapt a Gun at us. Not large Stones. A Man said to me you dont know What provo[cation] the Boys had had. Windows broke when I came. Men did not seem to have any Concern. The Doors open. Girls there, unconcerned. A Stone came from the back of Richardsons House. It could not come from Boys.

Mrs. Ann Caldwel. The Boys were assembled and said they were a going to have a Frolick. More than 50 [....] The Side of the House battered.

Katherine Winch. My back Yard and R join. I saw the Boys throw Stones after R apprehended Wall broke.

Lee Esqr. I saw R. Windows broke, Codman reproving the Boys. Man from other side way came and said he did not know the Provocation. Only Boys active. Little or no throwing while there, 15 or 20 men in Sight of R. house. I saw no Body in the house. No Passion in any Body.

Willm. Eustice. I saw Boys thro. Stones. Sailor threw short clubb broke the Lead. The Gun went off. 200 men before firing.

Andrew Tewksbury. The Boys said R was an Informer. They threw Limon Peels then Stones. Some Men looked on Boys and they threw faster. Men shew'd no signs of Approbation but laughing. No Glass broke when I got there. 200 or 300 Boys and Men, 20 or 30 men over the Way. Large Stones. None from the House.

Dr. Hill. I was there before Stones thrown, 1 1/2 minutes before Gun fired. The Windows were demolishd. Not broke when I first went. The affair intirely among the Boys. Men not concern'd.

Dr. Perkins. Some Glass broke when I got there. Some Boys threw Carelessly. Not there more than a minute.

Elias Dupee. The boys carried the Pagentry. I tarried till all Glass broke. I spoke to the Boys. A man said the Town will pay for it tis none of my Business. A brick bat thrown out of the Window and a Soldier threw it back after Stones were thrown. I saw a Gun pointed and fired.

David Pulsifer. R. said if ever a mobb come before my house, call away your Friends. The Girls said Wilmot ask'd R. where his Arms and Ammunition was. Some Men about in the Street. Did not heard any threats, but Matchet, Said they deserved to be hang'd 7 years ago.

⟨*H. Laughton*⟩
Freeman Pulsiver.

Quincy.
A man of universal Bad Character, apt to be prejudiced. @ Danger of its Working tother Way. [130]

Theocracy of Jewes. @ City of Refuge.[131]

4 Blackstone [191]. Manslaughter is killing without malice.[132]

HHPC. 449. Murder and manslaughter. What. A sudden falling out.[133]

FCL. 273. Injured Person may justify when known Felony intended. 277.[134]

Keyling 51: The case of turning out of Tavern Room.[135] 60. The Circumstance to reduce to manslaughter must be some striving.[136] 2

[130] Paine apparently used "@" to denote counterarguments or answers to points made by his opponents.

[131] Numbers 35:14–33: "Ye shall give three cities on this side Jordan, and three cities shall ye give in the land of Canaan, which shall be cities of refuge. These six cities shall be a refuge both for the children of Israel, and for the stranger, and for the sojourner among them: that every one that killeth any person unawares may flee thither. . . . Whoso killeth any person, the murderer shall be put to death by the mouth of witnesses: but one witness shall not testify against any person to cause him to die. Moreover ye shall take no satisfaction for the life of a murderer, which is guilty of death: but he shall be surely put to death. And ye shall take no satisfaction for him that is fled to the city of his refuge, that he should come again to dwell in the land, until the death of the priest. So ye shall not pollute the land wherein ye are: for blood it defileth the land: and the land cannot be cleansed of the blood that is shed therein, but by the blood of him that shed it." A similar reference appears in Rex v. Goodwin (SCJ, Falmouth, 1772), Adams Papers, Microfilms, Reel No. 185. See also No. 63, text at note 165, and No. 64, text at note 135.

[132] See also note 121 above.

[133] 1 Hale, *Pleas of the Crown* 449: "Murder and manslaughter differ not in the kind or nature of the offense, but only in the degree, the former being the killing of a man of malice prepense, the latter upon a sudden provocation and falling out."

[134] Foster, *Crown Cases* 273: "In the Case of Justifiable Self-Defence the injured Party may repel Force with Force in Defence of his Person, Habitation, or Property, against one who manifestly intendeth and endeavoureth with Violence or Surprize to commit a known Felony upon either." At 277, Foster discusses the difference between manslaughter and excusable self-defense.

[135] Ford's Case, Kelyng 51, 84 Eng. Rep. 1078 (K.B. temp. Hyde, C.J.): killing a man while defending one's right to possession of a room in a tavern *held* justifiable.

[136] Lord Morley's Case, Kelyng 60–61, 84 Eng. Rep. 1082 (K.B. temp. Kelyng, C.

Ray. 1301. Where the Liberty of one Subject is invaded the Liberty of the whole is affected.[137]

@. Fost. 312. Tooleys case denied.[138]

2 Inst. 51; Malice must be with a calm deliberate mind.[139] 57. Manslaughter where it happens on Sudden Shuffling.[140]

12 Co. Boy with bloody nose.[141] Mem. Foster Contra. 295. 3.[142]

HHPC 445. A comes to enter, with force.[143] 485. Killing those who come to [do] Injury to the House.[144] 486. Come to Take Goods a Trespasser.[145]

5 Co. 91. Semaines Case, attacking a House.[146]

11. Co. 84. Bowles Case, a man may call other to defend himself in his house.[147]

J.): "[W]e held that such a provocation as must take off the killing of a man from Murder to be but Manslaughter, must be some open Violence, or actual striving with, or striking one another."

[137] Reg. v. Tooley, 2 Ld. Raym. 1296, 1301, 92 Eng. Rep. 349, 352 (Q.B. 1710): "[W]here the liberty of the subject is invaded, it is a provocation to all the subjects of *England.*"

[138] Foster, *Crown Cases* 312: "The Doctrine advanced in the Case of The Queen against *Tooly* and Others hath, I conceive, carried the Law in favour of Private Persons *Officiously* interposing farther than sound Reason founded in the Principles of true Policy will warrant."

[139] Probably 3 Coke, *Institutes* *51: "Malice prepensed is, when one compasseth to kill, wound, or beat another, and doth it *sedato animo.*"

[140] Probably 3 Coke, *Institutes* *57: "Homicide is called chancemedley or chancemelle, for that it is done by chance (without premeditation) upon a sudden brawle, shuffling, or contention." *Id.* at *55: "There is no difference between murder, and manslaughter; but that the one is upon malice forethought, and the other upon a sudden occasion: and therefore is called chancemedley."

[141] Rex v. Royley, Cro. Jac. 296, 79 Eng. Rep. 254, 12 Co. Rep. 87, 77 Eng. Rep. 1364 (K.B. 1612). See note 106 above.

[142] Foster, *Crown Cases* 295: "[T]he Accident happened by a *single Stroke* with a Cudgel *not likely to destroy* and . . . Death did not immediately ensue. . . . I observe that Lord *Raymond* layeth great Stress on this Circumstance, *that the Stroke was with a Cudgel not likely to Kill.*" *Id.* at 293 is a discussion of Rex v. Reason & Tranter, 1 Str. 499, 93 Eng. Rep. 659 (K.B. 1722). See note 107 above.

[143] 1 Hale, *Pleas of the Crown* 445. See note 91 above.

[144] 1 Hale, *Pleas of the Crown* 485, treats "what the offence is in killing him, that takes the goods, or doth injury to the house or possession of another." See also note 100 above.

[145] 1 Hale, *Pleas of the Crown* 486: "If a man come to take my goods as a trespasser, I may justify the beating of him in defence of my goods, as hath been said, but if I kill him, it is manslaughter. But if a man come to rob me, or take my goods as a felon, and in my resistance of his attempt I kill him, it is *me defendendo* at least, and in some cases not so much."

[146] Semayne v. Gresham, 5 Co. Rep. 91, 77 Eng. Rep. 194 (K.B. 1605). See note 92 above.

[147] Bowles v. Bury, 11 Co. Rep. 79, 84, 77 Eng. Rep. 1252, 1260 (K.B. 1605). The reference appears to be an inadvertence for 11 Co. Rep. at 82, 77 Eng. Rep. at 1258. See note 93 above.

Hale PC 40, if a man come to enter.[148]

HAPC. 72.[149]

Cro. Car. 537. Cokes Case, killing Bailiff.[150] Vid. it was ruled Manslaughter because he might have resisted him without killing him. Ergo were it not he was a Bailiff and broke the House it would be Murder.[151]

Kelynge. 131. Pulling nose, and running thro with Sword.[152]

HHPC: 458: had it not known him to be a Bailiff no felony.[153]

Fos. 298. 99. An officer push'd into room to arrest.[154]

HHPC: 442.[155]

Fost. 261. When a Blow aimed at one Person killeth another, but where the first is evil it is murder.[156] 292: Lutteralls Case.[157]

HPC. 81. 27.[158]   83. 39.[159]

---

[148] Hale, *Pleas of the Crown (Summary)* 40: "If one come to enter into my House, claiming Title, and I kill him, Manslaughter. If *A.* enter wrongfully into the House of *B.* riotously and forcibly, *B.* and others endeavour to fire the house, *A* kills, Manslaughter." See also note 97 above.

[149] Apparently 1 Hawkins, *Pleas of the Crown* 72, which discusses justifiable homicide.

[150] Rex v. Cook, Cro. Car. 537, 79 Eng. Rep. 1063 (K.B. 1639). See text at note 98 above.

[151] The two preceding sentences were inserted in the MS in a very small hand, not Paine's. They refer to the court's ruling that the killing was not excusable, but "manslaughter, because he seeing and knowing him, shot at him voluntarily, and slew him." Cro. Car. at 539, 79 Eng. Rep. at 1064. As to the contention that if it were not for the fact of the house-breaking, the killing, being voluntary, would be murder, compare 1 Hale, *Pleas of the Crown* 485. See text at note 100 above.

[152] Reg. v. Mawgridge, Kelyng 119, 84 Eng. Rep. 1107 (Q.B. 1707). See note 102 above. The reference appears to be an inadvertence for Kelyng 135, 84 Eng. Rep. 1114.

[153] 1 Hale, *Pleas of the Crown* 458. See note 99 above.

[154] Foster, *Crown Cases* 298–299. See note 105 above.

[155] 1 Hale, *Pleas of the Crown* 442. See note 112 above.

[156] Foster, *Crown Cases* 261. See note 111 above.

[157] Rex v. Reason & Tranter, 1 Str. 499, 93 Eng. Rep. 659 (K.B. 1722), discussed in Foster, *Crown Cases* 292. See note 107 above.

[158] 1 Hawkins, *Pleas of the Crown* 81, §27: "And it hath been adjudged, That even upon a sudden Quarrel, if a Man be so far provoked by any bare Words or Gestures of another, as to make a push at him with a Sword, or to strike at him with any other such Weapon as manifestly endangers his Life, before the other's Sword is drawn, and thereupon a Fight ensue, and he who made such Assault kill the other, he is guilty of Murder; because that by assaulting the other in such an outrageous Manner, without giving him an Opportunity to defend himself, he shewed that he intended not to fight with him, but to kill him, which violent Revenge is no more excused by such a slight Provocation, than if there had been none at all."

[159] 1 Hawkins, *Pleas of the Crown* 83, §39: "Also it seems, That he, who upon a sudden Provocation executeth his Revenge in such a cruel Manner, as shews a cruel and deliberate Intent to do Mischief, is guilty of Murder, if Death ensue; as where the Keeper of a Park, finding a Boy stealing Wood, tied him to a Horse's Tail and beat him, whereupon the Horse ran away and killed him."

Fos. 350. 5. Accomplice.[160] 391. bottom. D[itt]o Plummer Case.[161] 353.[162]

Haw. P.C.: 193: Libel whats provoking.[163]

A Man's house his Castle a Doc[trine] highly approved.

The Pagantry must not be considered as Lawful.

A Crime of this Sort not to be presumed. @ R. must Excuse.

A man no[t] obliged to fly from his own House. @ When the assaliant is in his House.

Snider was among Trespassers and therefore not murder to kill him. HHPC: 441. Woman killd by throwing a Stone.[164]

439. 440. Accomplice.[165]

New Trials [166]

5 Bac. 244.[167]

[160] Foster, *Crown Cases* 350, 355, treats the law of accomplices and abettors.

[161] Foster, *Crown Cases* 351–352, discusses Rex v. Plummer, Kelyng 109, 84 Eng. Rep. 1103 (K.B. 1701), in which the court *held* that the shooting of A by B, where both were members of the same gang attempting over the physical opposition of a Crown officer to export English wool contrary to law, was not murder in C (another gang member), it not having been found that the shot was discharged against the officer.

[162] Foster, *Crown Cases* 353–354: "A general Resolution against All Opposers, whether such Resolution appeareth upon Evidence to have been Actually and Explicitly entered into by the Confederates, or may be reasonably collected from their Number, Arms, or Behaviour at or before the Scene of Action, such Resolutions so proved have always been considered as strong Ingredients in Cases of this kind. And in Cases of Homicide committed in consequence of them, every Person present in the Sense of the Law when the Homicide hath been Committed, hath been involved in the Guilt of Him that gave the mortal Blow."

[163] 1 Hawkins, *Pleas of the Crown* 193: "[S]ince the plain Meaning of such Scandal as is expressed by Signs or Pictures, is as obvious to common Sense, and as easily understood by every common Capacity, and altogether as provoking, as that which is expressed by Writing or Printing, why should it not be equally criminal?" This citation indicates that the defense argued that the criminal nature of the sign or "show" at Lillie's rendered the whole affair unlawful and that Richardson had been justified in attempting to destroy it.

[164] 1 Hale, *Pleas of the Crown* 441, setting out Mansell and Herbert's Case, Dyer 128, 73 Eng. Rep. 279 (1556–1557), concerning an attempt by a "great multitude of men" to take goods out of a house. A woman who came out of the house unarmed was struck and killed by a rock thrown by one of the multitude at another. *Held:* Murder (according to the headnote—the report itself is less clear).

[165] 1 Hale, *Pleas of the Crown* 439–440, a discussion of accessories to felony.

[166] The MS page on which the immediately preceding citations appear is left three quarters blank. On the next page is set out (with some alterations) Isabella's speech from Shakespeare, *Measure for Measure*, Act II, scene 2, commencing "Could great men thunder." On the page after that, upside down, appears the material on new trials ending Doc. II. The rest of that MS page is blank, and the following page commences with "SC. Augt. 1770." (See Doc. III.) What role, if any, Shakespeare's lines played in the proceedings, the editors cannot presently say.

[167] 5 Bacon, *Abridgment* 244, concerning new trials, which cites the cases in the two footnotes next following. For a discussion of Bacon's authorities, see No. 12, text at notes 50–55.

No. 59. Rex v. Richardson

Str. 1106.[168]   1142. Evidence on both sides.[169] 887.[170]
May be granted when Defendant found guilty.
Str. 104. 968. 1106.[171]

Bla. Com. 354. The Jury have an unquestionable right to determine
on all the Circumstances and to find a general verdict.[172] 2. Hal.
310.[173]

[168] Smith dem. Dormer v. Parkhurst et al., 2 Str. 1105, 1106, 93 Eng. Rep. 1061
(K.B. 1739): "[T]he point upon which the new trial in this case was denied was,
because they said the evidence was doubtful, and in such a case a verdict at bar
ought to stand," even though the finding had been against the weight of the evidence.

[169] Ashley v. Ashley, 2 Str. 1142, 93 Eng. Rep. 1088 (K.B. 1741): "The Judge
who tried this cause (which was upon a promisory note for £5000 which the defendant insisted was forged) certified that the weight of the evidence was with the
plaintiff, and he thought the jury would find for the plaintiff; but they found for
the defendant. *Et per curiam,* As there was evidence on the part of the defendant,
the jury are the proper judges which scale preponderates. It cannot be said to be
a verdict against evidence, and therefore we will grant no new Trial." See also Smith
v. Huggins et al., 2 Str. 1142, 93 Eng. Rep. 1089 (K.B. 1741), decided the day
after Ashley v. Ashley: "[A] new trial denied; though there was but a weak evidence
for the plaintiff, and the Chief Justice summed it up strongly for the defendant."

[170] Rex v. Huggins, 2 Str. 882, 887, 93 Eng. Rep. 915, 918 (K.B. 1731), reported
somewhat more fully, 2 Ld. Raym. 1574, 92 Eng. Rep. 518. This was an indictment
against the warden of the Fleet Prison for the murder of a prisoner by a servant of
the deputy warden, who had confined the deceased "six weeks without fire, chamber-
pot or close-stool, the walls being damp and unwholesome, and the room built over
the common shore." The jury found specially: that the servant had kept the deceased
as alleged, whereof he had died; that Huggins knew the condition of the room at
least fifteen days before the deceased's death, having seen him there and then having
turned away. But Huggins' guilt or innocence they left to the court. *Held*: No finding
of Huggins' consent to the deputy's acts, the circumstances of Huggins' presence
"were they ever so strong an evidence of consent, they will not be sufficient for us
to ground a judgment upon: we are to determine upon facts, and not on evidence
of facts. . . . It would be the most dangerous thing in the world, if we should once
give into the doctrine of inferring facts from evidence; which is the proper business
of a jury, and not of the court." 2 Str. at 886, 93 Eng. Rep. at 917–918, *per* Lord
Raymond, C.J. The Crown lawyers argued that inasmuch as the courts, since Rex
v. Oneby, 2 Ld. Raym. 1485, 92 Eng. Rep. 465 (K.B. 1727), note 128 above, had
not required the jury to *find* malice, the judges could as well adjudge the consent
as a matter of law. This, Lord Raymond rejected, noting that "malice is matter of
law arising from a legal construction of the act, . . . but consent is an act of the
mind." 2 Str. at 886, 93 Eng. Rep. at 918. Finally, the Crown contended that the
verdict was too uncertain to found a judgment upon, and the court should therefore
require a new trial. Noting first that "no instance could be produced where, in a
criminal case, it was ever done for a fault in the verdict itself," Lord Raymond went
on to hold the verdict good. "There is no incertainty as to the facts that are found:
the only fault is, that there are not such facts found as will amount to murder. The
consequence of which is, that the defendant is Not guilty of murder; and it would
be endless to send it back to a jury, till they find facts enough to make it murder;
besides its being contrary to law, in exposing a man to a second hazard of life." *Id.*
at 887, 93 Eng. Rep. at 918.

[171] See notes 193, 194, below, and 168 above.

[172] 4 Blackstone, *Commentaries* *354–355: "But an open verdict may be either
general, guilty, or not guilty; or special, setting forth all the circumstances of the
case, and praying the judgment of the court, whether, for instance, on the facts

III. PAINE'S MINUTES OF THE PROCEEDINGS ON THE MOTION FOR A NEW TRIAL[174]

Suffolk Superior Court, Boston, September 1770

SC. Augt. [*Term*] 1770

Rex v. Richardson

Motion for new Trial.

Deming. Foreman.[175] Mr. Lothrop was satisfied as to Fact, but not Law. Mr. Clap not so fully satisfied as to Law. I told him the Court knew the Law. We all agreed about 1/2 an hour before we came in on Rich[ardson].

Lothrop. I did not fall in so soon as some, for I thought the time might be as well spent in Argument. Jury in Gen[eral] thought if the verdict was not agreeable to Law the Court would not receive it. It was a motive with me.[176]

I heard some Body say as we passed up stairs *Damn him* don't bring it in *Manslaughter.*

Clap. At first going out I was not so clear as afterwards, for the

---

stated, it be murder, manslaughter, or no crime at all. That is where they *doubt* the matter of law, and therefore *chuse* to leave it to the determination of the court; though they have an unquestionable right of determining upon all the circumstances, and finding a general verdict, if they think proper so to hazard a breach of their oaths. . . . Yet in many instances, where contrary to evidence the jury have found the prisoner guilty, their verdict hath been mercifully set aside, and a new trial granted by the court of king's bench. . . . But there hath yet been no instance of granting a new trial, where the prisoner was *acquitted* upon the first."

[173] 2 Hale, *Pleas of the Crown* 309–310: "But what if a jury give a verdict against all reason, convicting or acquitting a person indicted against all evidence, what shall be done? I say, if the jury will convict a man against or without evidence, and against the direction or opinion of the court, the court hath this salve[,] to reprieve the person convict before judgment, and to acquaint the king, and certify for his pardon."

[174] In Paine's hand. Paine Law Notes. See note 166 above.

[175] "[T]he Jurors were inquired of the Foundation of their Verdict. The Foreman, with a sullen Pride of Revenge, replied, 'that he was not obliged to give any Reasons of his Conduct.' " Oliver, *Origin and Progress* 86–87. The jurors, all of whom testified, were Jonathan Deming (foreman), Thomas Lothrop, Seth Clap, Philip Withington, Jeremy Stoddard, Israel Everet, John Smith, Elisha Gardner, Jonathan Ellis, Joseph Hawes, Ephraim Pratt, and Ebenezer Adams. Min. Bk. 91, SCJ Suffolk, Aug. 1770.

[176] "One of the Jurors declared, that he thought him innocent, and had persisted all Night in that Opinion, against the united Sentiment of the other eleven; but in the Morning, after a tedious whole Nights Fatigue, his Bretheren overperswaded him to unite with them, by urging this Argument upon him, vizt. 'that the Court had delivered their Opinion, in Law, that the Prisoner was innocent, and that his Life would be saved; therefore, that it was not worth while to stand out any longer.' These Arguments alone, he said, prevailed with him to join with the others in their Verdict." Oliver, *Origin and Progress* 87.

Reason offered, such as its being in the Day.[177] Something was said that the Court would not receive it if not right, but it did not weigh with me.

Withington. The Rabble as we were going out said *hang the Dog hang him.*[178]

Stoddard. I heard no such thing.

Leveret. A great hiddalo. But I heard northing.

John Smith. As I passed and [turn'd?] the Stairs down the Stairs some said *hang him no Manslaughter,* but no Body minded it.

Elisha Gardner. I heard a tumultuous noise, no *Manslaughter but Murder,* it appeared with no Connections to the Jury.

Jona. Ellis. I heard some Body cry out *damn him hang him Murder no Manslaughter.* It seemed down stairs. Not mentioned in the Jury Room.

Jos. Hawes. As the Jury were going out I heard some Body say *hang him a dog,* but from whom I dont know. There was some such talk that if the Court did not like the Verdict they would not receive it.

Ephm. Pratt. There was a noise but I heard no Words.

Ebe. Adams. I heard a Noise below but heard no Body speak so as to be understood. Something like hang him. I did not take it to [be] directed to the Jury.

Mr. Usher. Keeper of the Jury. Many People below till 12 or 1 oClock. I heard no Cry of hang 'em &c.

Blowers.

Cro. 778. Wats & Braine. Jury sent out again, 2 dissenting on Ex[aminatio]n.[179]

State Tri. 417. Vol. X. Ashley v. Simons the Jew; Jury mistook their Verdict.

5 Bac. 243. SC.[180]

[177] "One of them said, 'that he should have acquitted the Prisoner, had the killing happened in the Night instead of the Day.' " Oliver *Origin and Progress* 87.

[178] "Some of them acknowledged, that, as they past thro' the Mob, from the Court to their Apartment, they were called upon to bring the Prisoner in guilty." Oliver, *Origin and Progress* 87.

[179] Wats v. Brains, Cro. Eliz. 778–779, 78 Eng. Rep. 1009 (Q.B. 1601): On an appeal of murder, "notwithstanding the Evidence was pregnant against the defendant," eight, and then ten of the jurors voted "not guilty." The two others proposed that the jury bring in a "not guilty" verdict on condition that if the court "disliked thereof," the verdict would be changed to "guilty." When, however, the foreman pronounced "not guilty" the court, "much misliking thereof, being contrary to their direction," polled the jury, discovered the scheme, sent the jury out again, received a verdict of guilty, and fined or reprimanded all the jurors.

[180] Rex v. Simonds, 5 Bacon, *Abridgment* 243–244 (Unreported, K.B. 1752): "The Defendant was indicted for having put some Ducats into the Pocket of the

Cr. El. 189. A Witness ex[amine]d again by Jury.[181]

Trial pr. Pais. A paper delivered to the Jury by Stranger. 224.[182]
225. A Breviate delivered.[183]

222. If the Party says to the Jury *'my Case is Clear'* it is new Evidence.[184]

Styles 383. The del[iverin]g a Breviate to the Jury before Tryal, mistryal: Tayler v. Webb.[185]

1 Vent. 124. Duke Richmond v. Wise. If any of Party say I hope youll find for Plaintiff [tis] *mistryal*.[186]

Vin. Tryal 452. §25. One said to a Jury he'd take care what for it was better for the Bishop than Duke.[187]

Prosecutor with an Intent to charge him with Felony. The Jury found the Defendant guilty generally: But upon a Motion for a new Trial Affidavits of all the Jurors were produced, in which they swore that they only intended to find him guilty of the Fact of having put the Ducats into the Prosecutor's Pocket but not of the Intent; and *Foster*, J. before whom the Indictment was tried reported that his Direction to the Jury was, that in Case they did not think the Defendant guilty of the Intent as well as of the Fact of having put the Ducats into the Prosecutor's Pocket they ought to acquit him. A new Trial was granted; and by *Lee* Ch. J. we do not grant a new Trial in this Case on the Account of any after Thought of the Jurors, for the doing of this might be a very bad Precedent; but because the Verdict was contrary to the Direction of the Judge in a Matter of Law. By *Denison* J. if the Verdict had been as the Jury intended it, that the Defendant was guilty of the Fact but not of the Intent there must have been a *Venire facias de Novo*; for it would have been an incompleat Verdict." The case was also reported in 10 State Trials 411, *sub nom.* Ashley v. Simons the Jew. (Ashley was the prosecutor.) The report sets out interesting background information, the indictment, the affidavits of the individual jurors, the judge's additional charge, and the outcome of the second trial (12 July 1752—acquitted).

[181] Probably Metcalfe v. Deane, Cro. Eliz. 189, 78 Eng. Rep. 445 (Q.B. 1590): The jury, having withdrawn, reëxamined one of the defendant's witnesses, and then returned a defendant's verdict. *Held*: verdict not good, *venire facias de novo* issued.

[182] Duncombe, *Trials per Pais* 224, reports Taylor v. Webb [Style 383, 82 Eng. Rep. 797 (K.B. 1653)]: verdict set aside because jury received writings "after Evidence," notwithstanding affidavit by foreman that the jury made no use of the writings in reaching the verdict.

[183] Duncombe, *Trials per Pais* 225, refers to YB 11 Hen. 4, 18: delivery of brief of evidence to jury, even though it contained no more than was proved in court, avoids the verdict.

[184] Duncombe, *Trials per Pais* 222: "If one of the Parties say to the Jury after they are gone from the Bar, *You are weak Men, it is as clear of my Side as the Nose in a Man's Face*; this is new Evidence, for his Affirmation may very much perswade the Jury and therefore shall quash the Verdict." This can refer only to the litigant's forensic skill, and not to the introduction of new evidence, for a party was incompetent to testify.

[185] See note 182 above.

[186] The Duke of Richmond v. Wise, 1 Ventris 124, 125, 86 Eng. Rep. 86, (K.B. 1672): "[I]f any of the Parties, their *Attorneys or Sollicitors* speak any thing to the Jury, before they are agreed relating to the Cause, *(viz.) That it is a clear Cause, or I hope You will find for such an one*, or the like, and they find accordingly, it shall avoid the *Verdict*; but if words of Salutation, or the like pass between them, (as was endeavoured to be proved in this Case) they shall not."

[187] 21 Viner, *Abridgment* 452–453, tit. Trial, §25: Court being held out of

[11] Mod. 118. Lady Herbert vs. Shaw. A Letter wrote to Jury to attend, to consider the Plaintiff was a poor man, mistrial.[188]

Burr. 390. Bright vs. Eynon.[189]

Foster 266. A Breviate d[elivere]d to a Juryman.[190]

T. Jones 163. Rex v. Smith. Verdicts vs. Evidence.[191]

3 Keeble 525. New Tryal, SC.[192]

Str. 104,[193] 968,[194] 1102.[195]

1 L. Ray. 62, 63.[196]

---

doors in a trial between the Bishop of L. and the Earl of Kent, a *"Tempest of Thunder and Lightning"* drove one of the jurors into a house, *"where diverse said to him that he take Care what he did, for the Matter was better for the Earl of Kent than for the Bishop; and pray'd him to drink with them, and so he did."* After verdict for the Bishop the case was argued in the Exchequer Chamber, where *"the best Opinion was that Fine* [of the Juror, for drinking] *shall be made, and the Verdict good,* and not void."

[188] Lady Herbert v. Shaw, 11 Mod. 118, 88 Eng. Rep. 937 (Q.B. 1707): Plaintiff's father, the Duke of Leeds, wrote to each juror requesting his appearance at the trial, saying: "Which I shall take as a great Obligation, particularly from your self, and shall be glad of an Occasion to shew how much I am, Sir, your Humble Servant." On defendant's motion for new trial, *held*, motion denied: defendant had notice of the letter long before trial and should have raised the issue sooner. Powell, J. referred to an unidentified case in the Common Pleas "where a Stranger writ to a Juryman to consider that the Plaintiff was a poor Man; for which a new Trial was granted."

[189] Bright, Executor v. Eynon, 1 Burr. 390, 397, 97 Eng. Rep. 365, 369 (K.B. 1757): New trial granted where jury drew the "wrong conclusion from facts admitted on both sides."

[190] Foster, *Crown Cases* 266, reports a case in which a coroner's jury found that a man run over by a wagon had been killed by the *wheel* only, and not the horses and cart too. *Held*: neither the higher court nor the coroner "can oblige the Jury to conclude otherwise than They have done." The page contains no mention of the breviate; see, however, text at notes 182, 183, 185, above; Paine, therefore, may possibly be recording two separate references.

[191] Rex v. Smith, T. Jones 163, 84 Eng. Rep. 1197 (K.B. 1682): new trial awarded where, on information for perjury, "an obstinate Jury against the Direction of the Judge, found the Defendant guilty." Dolbin, J., cited precedents where verdicts against the evidence were set aside.

[192] Rex v. Cornelius, 3 Keble 525, 84 Eng. Rep. 858 (K.B. 1676): conviction of perjury for swearing that S. "was at a conventicle, who was not; but it appearing the defendant never made any such oath, and that the foreman was owner of the barn [where the conventicle was held], and challenged, and yet sworn on the jury; which per Curiam is a great challenge to the favor; and a new trial was awarded."

[193] Rex v. Bennett, 1 Str. 101, 105, 93 Eng. Rep. 412, 414 (K.B. 1718): Information in nature of *quo warranto*; after verdict for defendant against evidence, *held* (after consulting all the other judges), equal division, therefore no new trial.

[194] Rex v. Gibson, 2 Str. 968, 93 Eng. Rep. 972 (K.B. 1734): Defendant must be in court to move for new trial.

[195] Rex v. Armstrong, 2 Str. 1102, 93 Eng. Rep. 1059 (K.B. 1739): After judgment signed, defendant may not move for new trial.

[196] Smith v. Frampton, 1 Ld. Raym. 62, 63, 91 Eng. Rep. 938 (K.B. 1695): Action for negligent keeping of fire resulting in plaintiff's house being burnt; verdict for defendant; motion for new trial for verdict's being against evidence. *Held*: "This being a case of hardship, and the jurors being judges of the fact, no new trial should be granted, although *Holt* chief justice, before whom it was tried, was dissatisfied with the verdict."

2 HPC.[197]

5 Bac. 292. Ld. Vaghn Law denied.[198]

2 Ld. R. 1494 Onebys Case.[199]

12 Mod. 336. If Judge in his Conscience is satisfied the Cause deserves a new Tryal.[200]

Rex

CL: 228. Jury may give general verdict.[201]

4 Black. 354. Same vid.[202]

2 Hale 310. Same.[203]

Str. 1142.[204]

3 Black. 375.[205]

Fos. 255.[206]

[197] This may be 2 Hawkins, *Pleas of the Crown* 442: "However it is settled, That the Court cannot set aside a Verdict which acquits a Defendant of a Prosecution properly criminal, as it seems that they may a Verdict that convicts him for having been given contrary to Evidence, and the Directions of the Judge, or any Verdict whatever for a Mistrial." The minute may also refer to a page in 2 Hale, *Pleas of the Crown*, although that was generally cited as "HHPC."

[198] 5 Bacon, *Abridgment* 292: "It is indeed said in one Book [citing Bushel's Case, Vaughan 135, 147, 124 Eng. Rep. 1006, 1012 (C.P. 1670)], that the Jurors are not obliged to ground their Verdict upon the Evidence given in Court; for that this may be grounded upon their own personal Knowledge. But no Authority is cited in Support of this Doctrine, and the contrary Opinion to be the better one.... It may moreover be very fairly inferred, from the constant Practice of granting a new Trial because a Verdict is contrary to Evidence, that the Jury ought to ground their Verdict intirely upon the Evidence given in Court; for if they have a Power to ground it upon any other Evidence, how unreasonable would it be for the Judge before whom the Cause was tried, who must always be a Stranger to what did not appear in Court, to report that the Verdict is contrary to Evidence, or for the Court to set it aside as being so."

[199] Rex v. Oneby, 2 Ld. Raym. 1485, 1494, 92 Eng. Rep. 465, 471 (K.B. 1727): "And the jury may, if they think proper, give a general verdict, either that the prisoner is guilty of murder or of manslaughter."

[200] Anon., 12 Mod. 336, 88 Eng. Rep. 1362 (K.B. 1699), per Holt, C.J.: "In granting a new Trial we ought not altogether to rely on the Certificate of the Judge who tried the Cause, but upon the Reason of the Thing; and sometimes I would grant a new Trial against the Certificate of a Judge, if in my Judgment and Conscience the Matter deserves a Re-examination."

[201] 1 Coke, *Institutes* *228b: "Although the Jurie, if they will take upon them (as Littleton here saith) the knowledge of the Law, may give a general verdict, yet it is dangerous for them so to do."

[202] 4 Blackstone, *Commentaries* *354. For text, see note 172 above.

[203] 2 Hale, *Pleas of the Crown* 310. For text, see note 173 above.

[204] Ashley v. Ashley, 2 Str. 1142, 93 Eng. Rep. 1088 (K.B. 1741). For holding, see note 169 above.

[205] 3 Blackstone, *Commentaries* *375, mentions "the grounds, upon which such new trials are every day awarded, *viz.* that the verdict was given *without*, or *contrary to*, evidence."

[206] Foster, *Crown Cases* 255. For text, see note 125 above. Also: "In every Case where the Point turneth upon the Question, Whether the Homicide was committed Wilfully and Malitiously, or under Circumstances Justifying, Excusing, or Alleviat-

60. Rex v. Ross

1769–1770

EDITORIAL NOTE

Friction between the Boston garrison troops and the populace produced considerable heat even before the so-called Massacre of 5 March 1770. The present case grew out of one of the more notable episodes, a scuffle in the Boston market on 13 July 1769 between Private John Riley of the Fourteenth Regiment and Jonathan Winship, a Cambridge victualer.

Mystery surrounds the precise origin of the fight, although a deposition by Corporal Samuel Heale of the Fourteenth Regiment (taken almost a year later, and for purposes other than use in court) states that Riley attempted to rescue a boy who was being beaten by a man in the market. According to Heale, first the man, and then Winship started fights with Riley.[1]

In any event, Winship, the loser, swore out a complaint before Justice of the Peace Edmund Quincy, who promptly issued a warrant on the strength of which Boston constable Peter Barbour brought Riley before the justice. The complaint was read, Riley pleaded guilty, and Quincy, after hearing other testimony, fined him five shillings and costs of eight shillings threepence, sentence being suspended for one day on the undertaking of John Phillips, Riley's sergeant, to be responsible for payment or to see Riley forthcoming on 14 July.[2] Riley duly appeared the next day, accompanied by Sergeant Phillips, Corporal Alexander Findley, and Private Jonathan Stevenson, all of the Fourteenth Regiment.[3] Because Riley was unable or unwilling to pay his fine, Justice Quincy drew up a mittimus, an order directing Barbour to commit Riley to jail.

Now the stories differ. Barbour testified later that Riley balked and that someone sent for Lieutenant Alexander Ross of the Fourteenth Regiment. On Ross' arrival, and in his presence, a group of soldiers took Riley out of

---

ing; the Matter of Fact, viz. *whether the Facts alledged by Way of Justification, Excuse, or Alleviation are True*, is the proper and only Province of the Jury. But whether upon a Supposition of the Truth of Facts such Homicide be Justified, Excused, or Alleviated, must be submitted to the Judgment of the Court."

[1] Deposition of Samuel Heale, 25 Aug. 1770, 12 Gay Transcripts 51, MHi. This deposition, like others referred to below, was taken as part of what was apparently an effort to collect as much evidence as possible of the antimilitary bias of the Bostonians, and to counter the propaganda effect of the Massacre. See generally the editorial note to Nos. 63 and 64. The ex parte nature of the depositions and the attendant lack of cross-examination seriously reduce their evidentiary value.

[2] SF 101575. The recognizance describes Phillips as being of "Capt. Fordice's Company 29th Regt." SF 89147. Charles Fordyce was, however, a captain in the 14th Regiment. *Army List 1769* 68. See also deposition of Charles Fordyce, 25 Aug. 1770, 12 Gay Transcripts 45–47, MHi, and deposition of John Phillips, 25 Aug. 1770, *id.* at 48–50.

[3] Deposition of Jonathan Stevenson, 25 Aug. 1770, 12 Gay Transcripts 53–54, MHi.

the constable's custody [4] and hustled him away. Ross, in his later deposition, gave a conflicting version. According to him, Captain Charles Fordyce, Riley's commanding officer, had asked him to intervene with Justice Quincy, whom Ross knew, in order to "compound" or settle ("fix" is a term with more accurate Massachusetts connotations) Riley's case. When Ross arrived at Quincy's, he found the justice making out the mittimus. After a vain attempt to persuade Quincy to lessen the sentence, Ross began (he said) to leave. When Riley tried to follow, Ross "told him in a very peremptory manner by no means to do so." Riley persisted, was seized by the constable and others, and fought his way free, "notwithstanding my calling to him several times and as long as I could be heard for [i.e. over] the Crowd not to do so." Ross then pushed through the mob and ordered the soldiers to their barracks.[5]

The incident created a furor; William Palfrey even reported it to John Wilkes.[6] And the day after the riot, the House of Representatives, having heard Barbour and Jeremiah Belknap (who had tried to help Barbour retake Riley), appointed "a Committee to make further Enquiry into the Circumstances . . . and report to the House a State of the Facts," the same to be then transmitted to Denys de Berdt, Provincial Agent in London, presumably for propaganda purposes.[7] The depositions which were taken on 24 July 1769 and printed as part of the "Journal of the Times" are the best known account of the fracas.[8]

A week after the rescue (the technical term for the unlawful taking of a prisoner out of the custody of an officer) Ross, Sergeant Phillips, Corporal Findley, Corporals William Dundass, Thomas Thornley, and John Arnold, and Privates John Lane and Francis Jackson were called before Boston Justices of the Peace Richard Dana, John Hill, and John Ruddock. After a tongue lashing from Dana, Phillips and Ross were discharged, and the others bound over for the grand jury.[9]

At the November 1769 adjournment of the August 1769 sitting of the Suffolk Superior Court, Findley, Dundass, Thornley, Arnold, and Jackson were indicted, as was Ross, for assaulting Barbour, for rescuing Riley, for assaulting some of the townspeople who attempted to aid Barbour, and for breach of the peace.[10]

[4] See generally, Adams' Trial Minutes, below. Ross (1742–1827) was to have a distinguished military career, serving as an aide-de-camp to General Lord Cornwallis, representing him in the Yorktown surrender negotiations. He became a general in 1812. *DNB*; Charles Ross, *Correspondence of Charles, First Marquis Cornwallis* 76 note (London, 1859).

[5] Deposition of Alexander Ross, 25 Aug. 1770, 12 Gay Transcripts 40–42, MHi.

[6] Palfrey to Wilkes, 26 July 1769, printed in Ford, "John Wilkes and Boston," 47 MHS, *Procs.* 190, 205–206 (1913–1914).

[7] Mass., *House Jour.* 1769, 83 (session of 15 July 1769).

[8] See Dickerson, *Boston under Military Rule* 119–123.

[9] Deposition of Alexander Ross, 25 Aug. 1770, 12 Gay Transcripts 40, 42, MHi. See also deposition of Charles Fordyce, 25 Aug. 1770, *id.* at 45–47.

[10] Ross says the grand jury brought in its true bill in September. Deposition of Alexander Ross, 25 Aug. 1770, 12 Gay Transcripts 40, 43, MHi. But the indictment, SF 101575, is dated 21 Nov. 1769. It was drafted and signed by Attorney General

No. 60. Rex v. Ross

The trial took place, apparently, in the middle of December 1769. Internal evidence in the Adams Trial Minutes, below, indicates that Robert Auchmuty was Ross' counsel; Adams' role is uncertain. He may have been participating for the Crown, although his full minutes of the prosecution evidence suggest that he may have been acting for the defense.[11]

As reported by Adams, the case against the soldiers seems strong, although that against Ross is not so clear-cut. The central issue seems to have been whether or not Ross had participated in the rescue, either directly, by encouraging Riley and the others, or indirectly, by failing to restrain them. On that, the testimony seems uncertain, much of the confusion apparently stemming from the words "go" and "don't go." Did Ross, when he said "go," mean "make good your escape," or did he mean "go to jail"? From the testimony as Adams recorded it, one cannot tell.

The jury did not doubt: it found all the defendants but Dundass guilty, whereupon the court fined each soldier £7 and ordered him to post bond for good behavior.[12] Ross' "Lawyer Pleaded an Arrest of Judgment, and was in hopes of bringing on a Fresh Tryal; the former was granted, but I was Bound over for my Appearance."[13] But the court did not sit again until mid-March 1770. By then the "winter of discontent" had bubbled into blood. With Richardson, Captain Preston, the soldiers, and the customs employees on their hands, the judges had neither encouragement nor inclination to invoke the unusual remedy of a new trial for a British officer convicted of interfering with the judicial process. Ross' motion was denied, and he was fined £20 and costs.[14]

ADAMS' MINUTES OF THE TRIAL [15]

Suffolk Superior Court, Boston, December 1769

Indictment vs. Lt. Ross and Soldiers

Peter Barber. I had a Warrant from Justice Quincy. Justice fined Riley 5s. I saw 15 or 20 Men all with their drawn swords.

Jonathan Sewall; the foreman of the grand jury was Thomas Brattle, who later on became, briefly, a loyalist. Jones, *Loyalists of Mass.* 53. On all the recognizances, one of the sureties was William Hill, a baker who had offered his free services to the garrison (and in fact served as the 14th Regiment's baker), *id.* at 164. The next year he sat as one of Captain Preston's jurors. See editorial note to Nos. 63 and 64, text at note 60.

[11] The summons for the witnesses was dated 19 Dec. 1769, but Ross' post-trial recognizance was dated 21 Dec. 1769. SF 101575. In a discussion of mobs some years later, JA referred to this case. "Is not an Assault upon a civil officer, and a Rescue of a Prisoner from lawfull Authority, made by Soldiers with Swords or Bayonets, as bad as if made [by] Tradesmen with Staves?" JA to AA, 6 July 1774, 1 *Adams Family Correspondence* 126–127.

[12] SCJ Rec. 1769, fol. 253.

[13] Deposition of Alexander Ross, 25 Aug. 1770, 12 Gay Transcripts 40, 43, MHi.

[14] SCJ Rec. 1770, fol. 22.

[15] In JA's hand. Adams Papers, Microfilms, Reel No. 185.

Lt. Ross came in. Mr. Quincy went on with the Mittimus. Riley said he would not pay nor go to Goal. The Word was go. He attempted to go. I took him by the Collar. He struck me with a broad sword. A whispering and a Messenger sent for Mr. Ross who came. Lt. Ross said Go. And he went. I did not hear such Words as *do not go.*

Corpl. Finley was there at the Door not in the Room. I saw their broad swords drawn. Arnold and Thornly were there. Cant say I saw these Persons swords drawn.

Jeremiah Belknap. 14 July between 2 and 3 passing thro Dock Square. Saw about a 12 soldiers, I think all with their broad swords. And I heard em say d—n him well wait for him. At the Justices Door. I heard em say d—n him. They shant carry him to Goal at the Justices ⟨*the Serjeants Name is*⟩ Door. And I swear by G—d he shan't go to Goal. Ross was then in the Justices. Justice said Sir take care of your Men to Ross. He answerd *I can do nothing.* Riley said *I'le go.* Barber said you shant go. I seizd Riley, and out at the Door we went, half a dozen broad swords, upon us, and I had 3 fingers cutt.

I did not hear Ross say go or not go. I thought Ross connived, because he held the Door open while Riley passed him.

Dr. Jno. Loring. I saw a Number of Soldiers round Winships Cart, insulting him. ⟨*Justice*⟩ went.

I heard one of the Soldiers ⟨*go*⟩ say to another, go fetch Lt. Ross. Ross came. I heard em sware, Riley should not go to Goal. And if the Inhabitants, insulted em they would take their own Satisfaction. I went and told Ross. He said He could not help it.

I cant swear to any one Person. There were about 15 or 20.

Ross gave no orders or Reproof to the Soldiers.

Thos. ⟨*Ross*⟩ *Foster.* 1/2 Way between Perrys and Quincys. A Cart. I saw a Number of Soldiers there with their Swords in their Hands. Not drawn. They swore by G[od] Riley should not go to Goal.

Finly said G[od] d—n your blood, and I think I saw him draw his sword. One Grenadier carried the Prisoner off. The Inhabitants Soldiers said seize the Prisoner if you dare. Jackson I saw there, and Thornley. It is clear in my Mind that I saw em, and clear that I saw Finly with a sword in his Hand, and saw his Hand on it attempting to draw it.

R.

Wm. Mills. Saw the Soldiers at the Door. They said he should not go to Goal. A Dozen with swords. Saw a Number with their swords drawn. *Arnold. Thornly.* They had Bayonetts. They were in the Company with the Soldiers who said he should not go to Goal.

All in a Bunch, and many said he should not go.

Abraham Hunt. They would be damnd if the Prisoner should go to Goal. Q[uincy] told Ross there was like to be a Rescue. Ross said he could do nothing with em. Rily said he would not pay. I went out and heard the Threats a 2d time. Ross said a 2d Time he could do nothing with em. I saw Ross go towards the Door, and then Riley attempted it too. Barber was knockd down. Q[uincy] told Ross a 3d time to disperse the Men. After the Prisoner was rescued, Ross told the serjeant to take the Men to the Barracks which he did immediately. Ross was in sight of the Blows when struck. Ross was at the Door or in the alley, when Barber was struck, near eno[ugh] to see. Some of the Grenadiers went off with Riley. Some stayd. Jackson and Finley I knew.

Saml. Downes. Ross said What can I do? I cant help it. Ross said he would go. Riley said he'd go too. Ross said dont go.

Mr. Wm. Greenleaf. In my Chamber I heard an unusual Screaming. Soldiers with their Cutlaces flourishing, to keep off the Inhabitants. And afterwards ⟨had⟩ came down 2 Pair of stairs and went out in the street and then heard Ross say go to your Barraks.

Stephen Greenleaf Jnr. Soldiers insulting the Butcher, and challenging. Those Soldiers drew towards the Door cursing and swearing that Rily should not go to Goal. The Soldiers opend to right and left and Rily went threw. And he saying take me now if you dare. Afterwards Ross came out and said you Rascalls to your Barracks directly. Knew Finley.

Jno. Hicks. I heard 'em at the Door say Mr. Ross will be hear in a Minute. Riley said, if you go, I'le ⟨go⟩ follow and defend myself. Ross said dont go, or stay. Then Riley said again I'le go, and Ross made no Answer. I think I saw Jackson. Saw two soldiers sticking [16] the Pavements &c.

Mr. Auchmuty. Mr. Ross's Inactivity, no Proof that he was guilty of a Riot. Nor Proof that he aided, incouraged, and abetted.

---

[16] Or "striking"? The meaning of this phrase is not clear, but it conveys the idea of the soldiers' making threatening gestures with their weapons.

61. Rex v. Moyse and Reader

1769

EDITORIAL NOTE

At the May 1769 Suffolk Sessions, Moyse and Reader were the only men tried among six soldiers who had been presented for breaking and entering, on 16 March 1769, the shop of John Carnes of Boston and stealing 40 shillings of silver and copper coin, 22 pairs of men's shoes (value 6s. each), 30 yards of ribbon (value 20s.), 20 watch seals (value 16s.), 25 yards of holland (value £6), unspecified amounts of printed linen (value 17s. 4d.) and calico (value 6s.), one yard of lawn (value 5s. 4d.), one yard of cambric (value 8s.), one piece of silk handkerchief (value 32s.), 3 pairs of black mitts (value 4s. 6d.), 3 dozen woolen stockings (value £6 3s. 4d.). After the defendants pleaded not guilty, the jury acquitted Reader but found Moyse guilty.

Adams' minutes reflect his interest, if not participation in the case. It should be noted that the minutes reflect no direct evidence of theft, only the circumstantial evidence of possession of the stolen goods. Moyse was sentenced "[to] be whipped 20 stripes on the naked back at the publick whipping post, that he pay to the said John Carnes the sum of £78 13s. 6d. being treble damages, the goods returned to be accounted part thereof according to their value, and that he pay costs of prosecution standing committed until the sentence be performed." [1]

On 19 May 1769 Carnes petitioned the Sessions that Moyse was utterly unable to pay the sentence, that he had been found guilty of theft, and that Carnes "be impowered by an order from your Honors to sell him for such a term of time as you shall think reasonable and just." [2] The court responded with an order "that the said John Carnes be and he is hereby fully authorized and impowered to sell and dispose of said John Moyse to any of His Majesty's subjects for the space and term of three years." [3]

[1] Sess. Min. Bk., Suffolk, May 1769.

[2] SF 89002.

[3] Sess. Min. Bk., Suffolk, 1769. The petition and order were presumably pursuant to the Act of 1 Nov. 1692, c. 18, §3, 1 A&R 52, which, after providing that offenders should pay treble damages to the owners of goods stolen, went on: "And if any such offender be unable to make restitution, or pay such threefold damages, such offender shall be enjoined to make satisfaction by service; and the prosecutor shall be, and hereby is impowred to dispose of said offender in service to any of their majesties' subjects, for such term as shall be assigned by the court or justices before whom the prosecution was."

ADAMS' MINUTES OF THE TRIAL[4]

Suffolk Court of General Sessions, Boston, May 1769

Rex vs. John Moyse and George Reader.

Mr. Carnes.

Simpson.

Clark. Of Mrs. Thorntons, I bought them, one Pair.

Wm. Simpson. I bought another Pair of Mrs. Thornton.

Mrs. Hunt. I sold a Pair to William Clark. I had em of Reader. He told me he had em of Thos. Smith.

Mrs. Thornton. I sold a Pair to Simpson. I bo't em of Reader. He told me he had em from his friends in England. I gave 2 Pist[areens, Pistoles?] and half a Pint of Rum.

Wm. Agnue. I saw a Pair of the Pattern sold to Mrs. Thornton by Reader. He said they were sent by Packett from his friends in England.

Another to the same.

Robinson—same.

Jno. Short. I imported em from G[reat] B[ritain] and Mr. Carnes had a Dozen. I cant swear to the Colour. I sold 11 dozen.

Miss Carns. I know em to be the same that were stole out of my fathers shop. By the different shades. I often spoke of em before they were found.

[...] *Carnes.* I knew em when I first saw em. Had seen em often.

Mr. Symms. Found Combs in Moyse's Knapsack. Moyse said he had em from Hallifax. Reader has em from Moyse. Carnes says he heard Moise and Reader say the same.

62. Rex v. Bell

1773

EDITORIAL NOTE

"Last Thursday Afternoon [28 January 1773] died at the North End, after a few Days Illness, Mrs. Christian Bell, Wife of James Bell, of this Town, Cordwainer, who is a Native of Scotland; it being notorious to Numbers of People that this Woman had for several Years past very undeservedly suffered frequent & cruel Abuses from her said Husband; a suspicion immediately arose after her Death, that she had been murdered by him; in Consequence of which, a Warrant was issued on Friday [29 January] by Mr. Justice Gardner, and the said James Bell was apprehended, and after an Examination had before the said Justice, was on the Evening

[4] In JA's hand. Adams Papers, Microfilms, Reel No. 185.

of that Day committed to Goal. On Saturday [30 January] a Coroners Inquest was summoned, who after carefully examining the Witnesses, and critically inspecting the Body, with the assistance of Messers. Danforth, Rand, and Fudger, Physicians of the Town, upon their Oaths declare, that the said Christian Bell came to her Death in consequence of repeated Blows upon her Body, given her by her said Husband, James Bell; more particularly by one Blow or Blows upon her Head, just over the right Eye, which she received on and since the Evening of the 16th ult." [1]

At the February 1773 Suffolk Superior Court, the grand jury, specifying the fatal wound as two inches long, one inch broad, and two inches deep, indicted Bell for murder.[2] We do not know what part, if any, Adams played in the subsequent trial, although the extensive nature of his notes suggests that he was of counsel for the defendant. The jury returned a verdict of not guilty of murder, but guilty of manslaughter, presumably because the evidence showed no malice aforethought. Bell pleaded benefit of clergy, was branded on the brawn of the thumb, and was discharged.[3]

ADAMS' MINUTES OF THE TRIAL[4]

Suffolk Superior Court, Boston, 25 February 1773

D[omi]n[u]s Rex vs. James Bell. Murder

Sewall, Attorney General. One of the highest Crimes, agravated as it was his Wife.

Inquisition.[5]

Nancy Patterson. Lives in another Street, not so far as the Markett. Went to Bells House. He was in a great Passion with his Wife. She was bloody. He had a Child in his Arms, bloody. Cant tell the Time—whether it was *a fortnight or 3 Weeks before she died.* Her Eye was swelled so that she could not see. She said her Husband had struck her. He said she had been drunk 2 days and provoked him.

Same Saturday night. He knocked her down Stairs, and said by God, if you dont leave off getting drunk I'le be the death of you. He pushed her, down Stairs, cant say whether with Hand or Knee.

He said she provok'd him a good deal, but did not say she struck him.

Cant say that Either of 'em in Liquor—dont think they were.

[1] *Boston Gazette*, 1 Feb. 1773, p. 1, col. 1. See note 5 below.
[2] Indictment, SF 102201.
[3] SCJ Rec. 1773–74, fols. 14–15. The branding took place on 27 Feb. 1773. *Boston Gazette*, 1 March 1773, p. 3, col. 2.
[4] In JA's hand. Adams Papers, Microfilms, Reel No. 185. Dated from *Boston Gazette*, 1 March 1773, p. 3, col. 2.
[5] Probably the coroner's inquest. SF 102327b.

He had a Child in his Arms.

James French. Went to Uncles House, Saturday night. Aunt by the Bed side bloody. She said Uncle had been abusing of her. Uncle said she was drunk. I said he should not abuse her so if she was. About 3 Weeks before she died. He knocked me down on the floor.[6] I saw her the Sabbath Week, after. I saw nothing but under her Eye a little blue. She was getting Victuals. Never saw her again, untill she could not speak.

Richd. Bradford. 6 Weeks before she died, heard the Cry of Murder. Ran in and saw that Man and Wife. She said he had been abusing her. He was abed and said she used him with ill Language. I did not see that she was much wounded at that time. She appeard to have been bruisd after she was dead, from her Head to her feet.

Janet Anderson. The Night before she died. Her skin and Body as whole as mine, only blue about her Knees, on one side. Died Thursday afternoon. Inquest Saturday.

I have seen her intoxicated.

Dr. Danforth. The Body very much discoloured in general—the surface livid, purple. Laid it open to the bone and found the Parts diseased quite to the bone. Found the internal Parts sound. Removing the scalp, I found a bruise next the bone, between the Eyes. A quantity of coagulated and fluid Blood, extravasated. Depression of Brain caused the death. The Appearance of a Contusion. Blood upon the right Side. The Skin appeard quite fair.

Eliza. Baker. One Morning she seemd in Liquor. He said she was drunk. She would not go to bed. He said she should. ⟨*Know nothing*⟩ Tuesday night, the Week before she died, I heard her scream Murder. I took it to be her Voice. Bell said she had an aggravating Tongue.

The Saturday night; scream'd Murder, I took it to be her Voice. I cant say whether he struck her.

Knows nothing of the Squabble 3 Weeks before.

Her Eyes were black and blue, and she said she believd it was owing to his frequently striking her. He deny'd the striking of her. She told me her Husband struck her. Next Wednesday she laid upon her Bedd, stupid.

Presently after, I heard her cry Murder, she came down, bloody, and said her Husband had struck her. He came down and bid her go up. He did not deny Striking her.

I heard somebody fall upon the floor, but cant say he struck or pushed her.

[6] The witness is apparently quoting the decedent.

She drank Tea with me a Month or 6 Weeks before her death.

She screamed Murder once when he did not offer any Abuse to her. I was in the Room with her and he was only trying to put her upon the Bed. He did not take hold with Violence nor Anger, he had hold of one Arm and I hold of the other.

Dorothy Smith. Often heard her scream Murder. She seemd in great distress. She said she did not expect any thing but that he would kill her. I once saw him strike at something, cant tell what. She groaned at that Instant. I am sure it was he. It was her Voice. About a fortnight before she died. Mrs. Patterson was in the Room about that time. I charged him with abusing his Wife. He did not deny it, but said it was none of my Business.

Several Times I heard Cries of Murder, and thought I knew her Voice. It Came from her Chamber, as I thought.

Dr. Rand. Saw her the day before she died, in a Paralitick State near the Close of Life. He said he did not call a Physician because he had no Linnen. External Part was contused upon the back Part. Nothing amiss in the Chest. One or two Parts of the scalp, seemd as if there had been some bruise there.

Blow or blows must have occasiond her death, but she might have receivd it by a fall, or from any Body Else, as well as her Husband. Apoplexies generally in the Ventricles of the Brain.

Edward Burt. About 3 years ago, I was a Neighbor to him. She often scrietched, and screamed, murder. He had an Hatchet, objected to.[7]

Manassah Masters. Bell lived back of me. A Scrietch of Murder. I saw thro the Windows, the Boy jump of [i.e. off] the floor and run down stairs. She said See how the Blood runs. He said D—n you I'le give you more of it, and ran, and struck 3 or 4 times. I could not see her. 16. Jany. Died 28th. ⟨the Woman⟩ This Boy the Witness.

I heard a Groaning, as I thought. I heard the Blows perfectly—with the fist.

John Powell. Saturday night, 3 or 4 days before her death, I heard something fall down, very heavy. Saw nothing. Mr. Bell you have done for me. Heard him say nothing. I was in the next Chamber. Heard Blows and judge it to be Bells Wifes.

Gilbert Anderson. 9. Jany. she came to my House. I saw Mrs. Bell, I askd where Mr. Bell was. I askd how her Blow came. She said she had got it. He said she provoked him, by swearing, pulling his Ears and Hair, and provoked him. I saw her run up and run her fist in his

---

[7] It is not clear whether it was the witness who objected to the hatchet, or, more likely, defense counsel who objected to mention of it.

face, and swear. He said he could not work, she interrupted. He said his Wife drank a whole Quart of Rum. She seemd in Liquor then.

I never heard any Man swear so in my Life. She ⟨never denyd⟩ told me, that he had beat her.

I have seen her lately drunk at different times and at different Manners, so as to fall down.

Ed. Lee.

Andrew Drummond. Fryday before she died, she sat by the fire, one Child on her Knee, 3 by her side. I gave her 6 or 7 Coppers. She arose to get an Hankerchief. I saw she had a black Eye. I askd her if Bell and she had been [dancing?] the Neger dance.[8] She said Bell came home, so and so a little. Sam. French got in betwixt em, and she run downstairs and her Heels trippd up and she fell down stairs, and hurt her Eye. 2 or 3 Years given to drink.

Janet Miller. You d——d son of a Bitch, says she, give me my Mary. For G[od's] sake, says he, be easy. And dont provoke me. She came and took him, by the Ear, and he struck her. 9. day Jany. Saturday. She took him twice by the Eye and Ear. She went to the Glass and danced.

[8] Thus in MS; the reference is unclear.